Louis I Kahn
Robert McCarter

Introduction

A poet is in thought of beauty and existence. Yet a poem is only an offering, which to the poet is less.[1] LOUIS KAHN

Critical events in the history of architecture are most often scripted in stylistic or purely formal terms. Yet for Louis Kahn (1901–74), another definition of architecture was foremost in his mind – a definition concerned much less with fashion and form and much more with the tradition of building and the making of places. For Kahn, architecture was not to do with what a building *looks like* but to do with how its spaces are *ordered*, with how it is *built*, and how these affect what is *experienced* by those who inhabit it. This book endeavours to present the architecture of Louis Kahn in just these terms.

Arguably, the works of Louis Kahn have been the single greatest influence on world architecture during the second half of the twentieth century. Yet, since the architect's death in 1974, there have been remarkably few critical studies of his work.[2] While Kahn's work indirectly inspired both the (historicist) post-modernist and (urbanist) neo-rationalist critique of modernism, his work also demonstrated that a critically developed modern architecture is the only viable mode of construction for our time, directly inspiring the contemporary return to modern tectonic and material order in architecture, exemplified by the best architects currently practising around the world. Yet in April 1983, only nine years after Kahn's death, and at the height of historicist post-modernism, the historian and critic Kenneth Frampton noted that 'almost no one now turns to mention [Kahn's] name', going on to say that 'the subtlety, stoicism, and relevance of Kahn's poetic contribution' should serve as 'a kind of sharp reminder of what we have lost'.[3] This was echoed when, at dinner following a lecture in late 1990, at the height of deconstructivist post-modernism, the late architect James Stirling said to me, 'It is appalling what students talk about in American architecture schools today – Derrida, indeed! Why doesn't anyone study Kahn?'[4]

In a description of the difficulty of designing architecture, which could apply equally well to the task of writing about architecture, Kahn often told the story of the poet who, experiencing perfect beauty, attempts to put down in words the wonder before his eyes. But, as Kahn said, 'the first line on paper

1. Louis Kahn teaching in the graduate architectural studio, University of Pennsylvania, c.1967; Kahn's studio was located in what was originally the upper level reading room of the University Library, designed by Frank Furness.

is less',[5] failing to capture either the magnificence or the subtlety of the mind's vision. Yet Kahn also insisted that, even if something of the original is always lost, our work as architects lies in trying to come as close as possible to what inspired us. Translated to the task at hand, if I am successful in this writing, the reader will feel compelled to visit the buildings designed by Kahn, and to experience the perfect beauty of these places.

Kahn engaged this understanding in his architecture through his conception of the *immeasurable*, the inspirational insight into the nature of the institution, and the *measurable*, the means available to the architect to

build in his place and time. Kahn held that a work of architecture must start with the immeasurable, must be realized through the measurable means of construction, and when completed must allow its inhabitants to experience the immeasurable of its beginnings. What allowed Kahn's work to transcend the limitations of his time was his understanding that the immeasurable inspiration is found in the great architecture of the past, while the measurable means are only to be found in the material and methods of construction of our time. By engaging and transforming the immeasurable and the measurable in the process of design, Kahn's buildings are both timeless and of our time, both ancient and modern.

Kahn was one of the few architects of first importance in modern architecture to teach continuously at a university throughout his career, and to endeavour to articulate the mysteries of the design process for students. This study examines the manner in which larger concepts emerged in Kahn's work and teaching, were developed as part of his ever-evolving definition of design, and were given form in his architecture. Kahn was one of a number of architects who emerged in the 1950s to question the ability of International Style modernism to house the social spaces necessary for the latter half of the twentieth century. Yet Kahn was one of the very few major architects to find a way out of this impasse – a way that may be discovered by experiencing and examining his work.

This study of Louis Kahn is focused as much as possible on Kahn's major designs – on the experience of the buildings themselves – as the way to understand his importance to architecture. While Kahn's *ideas* have been claimed by all manner of designers and theorists, his *buildings* are incredibly precise in their construction of places for people – places we return to again and again because by inhabiting them we rediscover something essential about ourselves. Each of Kahn's major projects or built works is examined at length: first, through analysis of the design process and ordering ideas; second, through examination of the methods and materials of construction, and their reinterpretation by Kahn; and third, by way of an experiential 'walk-through' of the spaces themselves, with particular emphasis on the interior spatial experience. It is my contention that Kahn's primary concern throughout his career, as with Frank Lloyd Wright, was *the space within*, the interior space and its experience, as determined by the way in which it is constructed.[6]

Vincent Scully, who had the foresight to author a book on Kahn in 1962, at a time when it was not yet at all apparent to most critics what stature and significance Kahn would ultimately attain, cautioned: 'No one can sum up Louis I. Kahn.'[7] Bearing this in mind, as well as Vico's motto, *verum ipsum factum* – 'truth through making', I believe that the theories arising from Kahn's architecture are best exemplified by the works themselves. To that end I have endeavoured to weave Kahn's discoveries as to the nature of architecture into the descriptions of his designs and our experience of them, as well as introducing and concluding each chapter with the larger themes which connect Kahn's works – all in an effort to stay as close as possible to the things themselves.

1

Development of an architectural philosophy

What was has always been. What is has always been. What will be has always been.[1] LOUIS KAHN

Previous page. 'Study for a mural upon Egyptian motifs', 1951 (detail); drawing by Louis Kahn of the pyramids at Giza. This drawing is related to the mural that Kahn designed and executed at Weiss House, 1947–55.
1. Bishop's Castle at Kuressaare on the island of Saaremaa, Estonia, fourteenth century. This Late Gothic monumental stone construction was the largest structure on the island where Kahn was born.
2. Louis Kahn in his office, Philadelphia, early 1970s. On his desk are drawings for the Wolfson Mechanical Engineering Building, 1968–74.

Louis Isadore Kahn was born on 20 February 1901 on the Baltic island of Saaremaa (formerly called Ösel) in Estonia, on the coastal edge of imperial Russia.[2] His father, Leopold Kahn, was Estonian and a member of the paymaster corps of the Russian army. His mother, Bertha Mendelssohn, was from Riga, the ancient capital of Latvia, to the south, where as a youth she had been educated in Riga's sophisticated Western cultural tradition. After Leopold's military discharge they settled on Saaremaa, an island in the Baltic Sea only 150 miles (250 kilometres) south-west of Helsinki and the same distance east of Stockholm. Situated between mainland Europe and Scandinavia, the island at various times in its history has been part of Finland, Sweden, Denmark, Germany and Russia.

The largest structure on the island of Saaremaa was the fourteenth-century Bishop's Castle at Kuressaare, its massive, beautifully laid stone walls pierced by small windows and topped with crenellated battlements, centred on an interior courtyard, the whole anchored by a tower and surrounded by a moat. While the Kahn family lived on Saaremaa, Leopold worked as a scribe for residents of the castle, so Kahn's childhood world was closely related to this monumental place. Kahn returned to visit Saaremaa when he was twenty-seven, confirming childhood memories of both the castle's monumental urban scale and its intimate protected interior spaces, and it is clear that Kahn's lifelong love of castles had its beginnings in his early experiences of this powerful structure.[3]

Though Kahn described himself as a Finnish Jew in origin, Kahn's first spoken language was German, and he was raised in a household strongly influenced by German Romanticism. Kahn's family tradition holds that his mother Bertha was related to the German Romantic composer Felix Mendelssohn (1809–47), as well as the composer's grandfather Moses Mendelssohn (1729–86), the famous Jewish philosopher of the German Enlightenment. Kahn's mother was a gifted musician, and Kahn credits her with his deep appreciation, considerable talent and sophisticated knowledge of music. In addition, Kahn's mother read extensively in German

and, as he said, 'raised him upon Goethe', who, along with Schiller, was one of her two favourite authors. She had an expert understanding of both writers' works, which she shared with Kahn during their many long conversations in later years.[4]

Kahn's father's talents were also critical to his formation. Leopold's beautiful handwriting secured him work as a scribe, and it was he who encouraged Kahn to draw from an early age. Leopold also worked as a stained-glass craftsman, both with painted and coloured glass, and Kahn would later develop a particularly powerful sensitivity to light in his own work. The fascination for bright colours was also the likely cause of the terrible accident that befell Kahn at the age of three, when he shovelled burning coals onto the apron of his pinafore. The flames severely burned Kahn's face and hands, scarring him for life.

Despite his parents' best efforts, the Kahn family lived in poverty and in 1904 Leopold emigrated to the United States, where he eventually found work in Philadelphia, Pennsylvania. In 1906 Bertha followed, bringing Louis Kahn, aged five, and his younger sister and brother. The family settled in the Northern Liberties district of the city, along with numerous other new immigrants from Germany, Lithuania and Russia, who arrived to work in the dominant garment industry. Unable to find employment that engaged either his graphic or glass craft skills, Leopold was forced to take work as a construction labourer. A back injury and other health problems soon made even that impossible, and the family, which had to move seventeen times in the first two years,[5] was primarily supported by Kahn's mother, who worked as a seamstress knitting garment samples for local factories.[6]

The city of Philadelphia, where Kahn lived his entire life, was to exert great influence on his conception of the beneficial potential of a city and its architecture in the lives of its citizens. His facial scars, combined with the fact that he started school late (due to his contracting scarlet fever shortly after the family's arrival in the United States), made Kahn shy around other students throughout his adolescence. Yet his considerable artistic talents were soon recognized by his teachers, and Kahn began to take courses at the Public Industrial Art School, whose director, J. Liberty Tadd, emphasized large-scale chalk drawing on the blackboard,[7] a technique which Kahn would later employ extensively. This initial shyness and anonymity, followed by notice of his unique talents, was very probably the source of what would become Kahn's acute sensitivity to the experience of being a student, a characteristic both of his own teaching and of his conception of the appropriate architecture of school buildings.

With Tadd's encouragement and guidance, Kahn's artwork soon won a series of Wanamaker prizes, city-wide awards for young people, and after he was admitted to the Philadelphia school system's flagship institution, Central High School, his drawings received prizes from the prestigious Pennsylvania Academy of Fine Arts. Kahn's musical talents also continued to develop, and it was during this time that he helped with the family finances by playing the piano at a silent-movie house. Later, when the movie house replaced the piano with an organ, Kahn learned to play the organ in a single afternoon in order to keep the job.

At the weekends Kahn walked twenty blocks to take free art classes at the Graphic Sketch Club, later renamed the Samuel S. Fleisher Art Memorial. One day he found an open meeting room with a piano, and he went in and began to play. Helen Fleisher, sister of the art club's benefactor, arrived for a meeting and was so impressed by Kahn's playing that she insisted on giving him a grand piano. As Kahn told the story, because there was no room for both a piano and a bed in the family apartment, he slept on the piano.[8] As with all of Kahn's stories, his focus here is on human actions taking place, within both material and spiritual contexts, thereby allowing his story to be grounded in our shared experience of inhabiting space.

Kahn's talents at the piano were so notable that he was offered a music scholarship, but, on the advice of Tadd, he declined in order to concentrate on the visual arts.[9] In his senior year in high school Kahn was offered a scholarship to attend the Pennsylvania Academy of Fine Arts, which had earlier awarded his work. But the city was to offer one more opportunity to the young Kahn when, in his senior year of high school, he took a course on architectural history, consisting of both lectures and drawing assignments, taught by William F. Gray. Kahn vividly recalled Gray's slide-illustrated lectures on 'Gothic, Renaissance, Greek, Roman and Egyptian architecture', saying at the end of his life, 'I can still see those examples after so many years as the most resounding influence … of powerful commonality.' Kahn was particularly struck by the fact that, unlike the other arts, architecture is experienced through inhabitation – architecture is 'an art you can *walk around* and *be in*'.[10] So powerfully was Kahn engaged by architecture that he decided at that late date to decline the art scholarship and instead enrol in the architecture course at the University of Pennsylvania.

3. Frank Furness (designer) and George W. Hewitt, Pennsylvania Academy of Fine Arts, Philadelphia, 1871–6. The main staircase is the central gathering space of the museum.

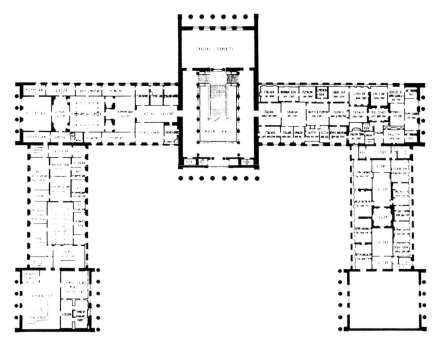

4

Rooms of the city

'A city should be a place where a little boy walking through its streets can sense what he someday would like to be', pronounced Kahn, late in life, recalling his own youth in Philadelphia.[11] 'The city is essentially a meeting place. It is valued by the character of its availabilities',[12] as Kahn also said, and it was in the city of Philadelphia that Kahn's many talents had been recognized, encouraged and supported, and where he discovered his lifelong love of architecture. The opportunities that he had been offered by the city had a profound and long-lasting effect upon Kahn, and he would remain a loyal citizen of Philadelphia for his entire life, endeavouring to pay back the debt he felt he owed the place. While his decision to pursue architecture in college came rather late and rather suddenly, Kahn's experiences while growing up and beginning his professional career took place in a number of the greatest works of architecture in Philadelphia. Such buildings could not have failed to make a deep impression on the sensitive young man.

William Penn's brilliant 1682 urban plan for Philadelphia, with its north–south (Broad) and east–west (Market) boulevards crossing at the City Hall, and its grid of streets and quarters, each centred on a large park, stretching east to west from river to river, would become Kahn's absolute given starting point for the numerous urban design proposals he would offer to his beloved city. Though he would sometimes question its effectiveness as a civic institution in contemporary society, Kahn always had the deepest respect for the historical significance of the Philadelphia City Hall and, as an immigrant, he was almost reverent in his affection for the various structures associated with Independence Mall, which memorialized Philadelphia's critical part in the birth of the United States as a nation.

4. Horace Trumbauer and the firm of Zantzinger, Borie and Medary, upper level floor plan, Philadelphia Museum of Art, 1919–28. The monumental staircase is an independent, freestanding element in the central hall.
5. Graham, Anderson, Probst and White, 30th Street Station, Philadelphia, 1929–34. The train station was always Kahn's preferred place of entry into his beloved city.

Both in his youth and as an adult, Kahn's drawings were exhibited in the Pennsylvania Academy of Fine Arts, built in 1872–6 to the designs of the great Philadelphia architect Frank Furness. This extraordinary series of top-lit galleries, focused on the great top-lit stair hall, are formed with Furness's characteristically expressive structure and richly textured walls. Standing in this space, which was later restored with Kahn's advice, it is clear why the young Louis Sullivan, later mentor to Frank Lloyd Wright, came to Philadelphia in 1873 to work for Furness before establishing his own practice in Chicago.

Sitting on a riverside hilltop, like the Parthenon on the Acropolis, approached by an equally monumental set of stairs, the Philadelphia Museum of Art was designed by Horace Trumbauer and the firm of Zantzinger, Borie and Medary, and constructed from 1919 (Kahn's senior year in high school) to 1928. Yet it is the museum's great entry hall, a cubic masonry space open to the building's full height, surrounded by a colonnaded mezzanine, and centred on the simple but powerful stone stair which rises and parts to form a T-shape in plan, that was to be a particularly important influence on Kahn.

Finally, the 30th Street Station, built in 1929–34 to the designs of Graham, Anderson, Probst and White, would hold special poignancy in the life of Louis Kahn. For Kahn, the part that the spaces of the city played in people's lives

was not an abstract matter but was made concrete in everyday events and the choices they entailed. Kahn believed that one should not enter the city by arriving at the airport and being brought in by automobile on expressways that had been ruthlessly sliced into the city's fabric without any regard for its fundamental historical and spatial order. Throughout his life, Kahn lamented the deleterious effects of automobile use on the historical city. All of his plans for Philadelphia involved various means of protecting the city (often in the literal forms of shielding walls) and integrating the automobile into the city while minimizing its impact on the city's historical fabric and order. In this it is most revealing that Kahn never possessed a driver's licence, and, as a result, was later in life a favourite customer of cab drivers all over the city, whose opinions he solicited on every imaginable matter during his frequent rides.[13]

For Kahn, then, the proper way to enter Philadelphia was by train, arriving at the 30th Street Station, rising up from the tracks beneath into the grand yet severe main hall, its monumental colonnades facing the city to the east and the university to the west. Tall windows open under the high square-coffered ceiling and between the massive piers, with steel walkways placed between the glass layers, through which only the sky is visible. The 30th Street Station is set on the west bank of the Schuylkill River, adjacent to the university, and exit through its main doorway places one on the Market Street axis to the City Hall, into the very heart of Philadelphia.

History as the architect's friend

Kahn entered the architecture course at the University of Pennsylvania, located directly across the Schuylkill River from downtown Philadelphia, in the autumn of 1920. At that time, Kahn's 'home town' university had what was recognized as the highest quality architectural programme in the United States, based (as all were at that time) on the teaching methods of the École des Beaux-Arts in Paris. Paul Philippe Cret, a graduate of the École who taught in Philadelphia from 1903 to 1937, led this academic approach to classical architectural design at the University of Pennsylvania. Cret's teaching (paralleled by that of Cret's former students and architectural office staff who were on the faculty, such as John Harbeson, Kahn's first-year critic) was to exert a fundamental and lasting influence on Kahn. Furthermore, Cret's interpretation of the classical inheritance would be of particular importance to Kahn's own development. While Cret believed that classicism was the only valid mode of architectural design, he also felt that contemporary architectural design should be more concerned with the correct composition of elements for the particular situation than with any predetermined style. This problem-solving approach accepted the idea that new functions and new contexts would lead to new modes of formal expression.[14]

Cret introduced his students to the two opposing theories of architectural design, which had emerged in the nineteenth century from the French Rationalist École des Beaux-Arts. Kenneth Frampton has noted that Cret engaged his students 'in debating the oppositions that existed between on the

6. Eugène-Emmanuel Viollet-le-Duc, 'Perspective view of interior of large hall', plate from *Entretiens sur l'architecture*, 1872. This drawing illustrates Viollet-le-Duc's proposed integration of heavy masonry and lightweight iron.

one hand the Structural Rationalism of Viollet-le-Duc and De Baudot, with their strong affinity for the Gothic, and on the other hand the classicism of Durand's permutative system, with its rather arbitrary method for combining facades with the modular fabric of the building itself.'[15] Cret himself embraced aspects of both theories, employing Durand's somewhat a-material system in his own design process yet stating that the architect 'cannot allow himself to forget … that the "spirit" of a steel form is not the spirit of stone'.[16] This debate proved to be of critical importance to Kahn, whose later architectural work attempts, with remarkable success, to integrate these two apparently contradictory points of view.

Eugène-Emmanuel Viollet-le-Duc's *Entretiens sur l'architecture* (2 vols. 1853–72) and *Dictionnaire raisonné* (1854–68) proposed an interpretation of architectural history and a form-language of design determined and inspired by the necessities of construction, with particular emphasis on structure. Almost fifty years before Kahn began his studies in architecture, Viollet-le-Duc had dedicated the second volume of his *Entretiens* to construction. Viollet-le-Duc not only reviewed current practices but proposed astonishing (yet tectonically logical) hybrid structures of steel and masonry, including the famous perspectives of 'market hall with room above', 'interior of large hall' and 'iron and masonry – vaulting of large spaces', which must have made a deep impression on Kahn.

The Bibliothèque Nationale in Paris of 1854–75 by Viollet-le-Duc's fellow École des Beaux-Arts professor, Henri Labrouste – where masonry perimeter walls enclose a grid of cast-iron columns supporting arched wrought-iron trusses, which in turn carry the nine top-lit domes of the ceiling – clearly inspired Viollet-le-Duc's illustrations and text for his *Entretiens*. Examples of later buildings that were in turn influenced to some degree by Viollet-le-Duc's proposals include Hendrik Petrus Berlage's Stock Exchange in Amsterdam of 1897–1903, with its brick walls and stone abutments carrying the steel-structured roof; and Anatole de Baudot's St Jean de Montmartre Church in Paris of 1894–1904, employing wire-reinforced perforated brickwork filled with concrete, and thin concrete roof shells, resulting in a modern building that comes remarkably close to the Gothic ideal even as it employs the most contemporary materials and methods.

Jean-Nicolas-Louis Durand's *Précis des leçons d'architecture données a l'École Polytechnique* of 1802 and 1805, and *Recueil et parallèle des édifices de tout genre, anciens et modernes* of 1800, were to have far-reaching influence on the teaching and practice of architecture during the nineteenth century. Durand's text and, more importantly, his extensive sets of meticulous illustrations propose that design may be undertaken with an almost scientific precision, by employing his system of composition based on the fundamental spatial elements of architecture. Durand 'posited the grids, enfilades, colonnades, and elevations of his *Précis* as essentially empty elements which, if appropriately chosen and combined, could be arranged to accommodate an infinite variety of programs', as Frampton notes.[17] Durand's system of design tended to de-emphasize the specific function or architectural programme, as

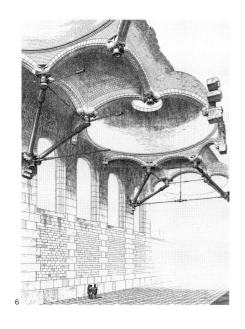

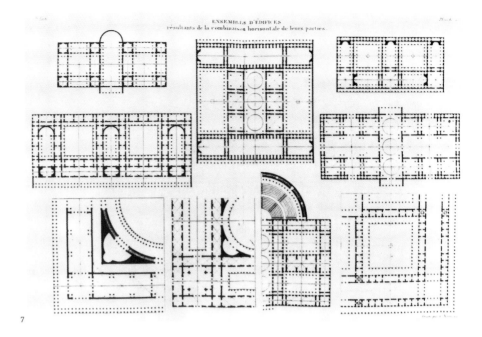

7

Jean-Nicolas-Louis Durand, plate from *Précis des leçons d'architecture données a l'École Polytechnique*, 1802–5. Examples of plan compositions using tartan grids (a-b-a), and ways of combining circular and rectangular forms are shown.
8 & 9. Auguste Choisy, up-view partial plans and axonometric sections of the Pantheon, Rome (left) and of Pontigny Abbey, France (right), from *Histoire de l'architecture*, 1899. The ancient Roman Pantheon was an important precedent for Kahn in the primacy of its interior space enclosed within massive construction, while Romanesque and Gothic architecture, with their articulation of light through structures, served as a principal touchstone for Kahn.

well as any specific material properties, in order to privilege the universal validity of a neutral spatial order composed of pure solid and void. The influence of Durand's compositional method had been further extended through its development by Julien Guadet, Cret's teacher at the École, in his *Éléments et théorie de l'architecture* of 1899, which Cret introduced, along with Durand's *Précis*, to his students. The emphasis on composition of elements would have the greatest influence on Kahn, who would employ an elemental approach to design in his later work.

While almost all the buildings of École graduates from the nineteenth century were to some degree products of Durand's design system, North American examples that Kahn is likely to have known include Charles Atwood's Palace of Fine Arts at the 1893 Chicago World's Columbian Exposition; John Carrère and Thomas Hastings' New York Public Library of 1911; and Charles McKim, William Mead and Stanford White's Pennsylvania Station, New York, of 1910.

Cret and his faculty employed as a text Auguste Choisy's *Histoire de l'architecture* of 1899, a remarkably comprehensive study of architecture and construction from around the world and throughout history. Most of the book's 1,700 figures are cut-away (in both plan and section) upward-view axonometrics which strongly emphasize mass and interior volume. The drawings (which Kahn was later to admit were for him inevitably the most influential part of any book), while depicting an astonishing range of architecture, nevertheless render all into a certain unity through their shared drawing technique, which emphasizes mass but not specific material, and above all the shaped volume of space. Choisy's book (which for Kahn was a kind of architectural equivalent to what would later become his other favourite book, biologist D'Arcy Thompson's *On Growth and Form* of 1917) was of critical importance not only to Kahn's development as an architect –

something he would repeatedly acknowledge – but to the development of many others, including Le Corbusier and Alvar Aalto, making it the most important book of architectural history for the first generation of modern architects.[18]

Kahn later related to Vincent Scully how, as was typical for Beaux-Arts architecture students at the time, he 'traced and adapted forms from the archetypal books',[19] including Paul Letarouilly's extraordinary *Édifices de Rome Moderne* of 1840–57, three volumes of etched plates showing plans, sections and perspectives of all the major buildings of Renaissance Rome, and the three volumes of Hector D'Espouy's *Fragments d'architecture* of 1905, also containing hundreds of examples of classical architecture through to the Renaissance period. Throughout his life Kahn kept copies of all these books in his personal library, and he frequently brought them into his architectural office, indicating their continued importance to his work.[20]

During his four-year course of study at the University of Pennsylvania Kahn was introduced to a variety of other influential architects, including three that we can establish without question as being of particular importance in Kahn's later career: Étienne-Louis Boullée and Claude-Nicolas Ledoux, Durand's great eighteenth-century precursors whose work Kahn would 'rediscover' in 1952; and the peerless archaeologist, historian and designer Giovanni Battista Piranesi, whose eighteenth-century etchings of Rome gave views that were accurate yet charged with the most sublime spatial power – a power that would soon draw Kahn to Rome – and whose fantastic imaginary 'reconstruction' of the Campus Martius district of Rome would hang above Kahn's drawing table for most of his career. Finally, it is not clear to what extent Kahn was introduced while in school to the work of the early nineteenth-century British architect John Soane, whose obsession with layered space and bounced light was inspired by the same Baroque sources that Kahn would later discover in his own obsessive exploration of this theme. While it appears likely that all these precursors, and many others, were introduced to Kahn

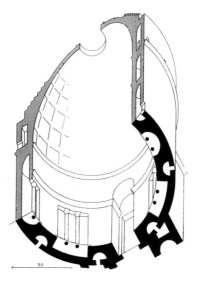

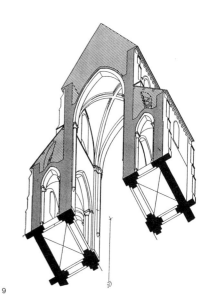

10

at the University of Pennsylvania, these latter examples would lie dormant in Kahn's memory, only emerging to affect his work thirty years later.

Kahn's student work at the University of Pennsylvania was not exceptional, though in his senior year in Cret's studio he won a number of national awards for his designs. While he would later fondly remember the 'yellow light and blue shade' of the section drawings, it was the making of axial floor plans – symmetrical (Parthenon) and asymmetrical (Erechtheum) – which remained the most fundamental aspect of the Beaux-Arts training that Kahn received. The University of Pennsylvania encouraged a somewhat more relaxed axial planning compared with the multiple symmetrical crossed axes typical of the École, and several of Kahn's larger student projects display dynamic balance and local symmetries not unlike what would evolve in early modern architecture.[21]

It is important to remember that this tradition of plan-making, drawn directly from the monuments of antiquity, also underlay the work of modern architects such as Frank Lloyd Wright and Le Corbusier, who could not help but acknowledge the dominance of the Beaux-Arts system of education in their published attacks upon it. The plan was of paramount importance to Wright, and he was explicit in arguing that axes and symmetry belonged to no architectural style, but were a fundamental part of human nature. Likewise, Le Corbusier in his 1923 *Vers une architecture* stated that 'The plan is the generator', and that 'Architecture is based on axes',[22] and that neither the plan nor the axis was exclusive to the methods of the École des Beaux-Arts.

In 1908 Frank Lloyd Wright, whose work would prove to be the most important inspiration for Kahn, wrote of his Prairie Period work in the *Architectural Record*: 'In laying out the ground plans for … these buildings a simple axial law and order and the ordered spacing upon a system of certain structural units definitely established for each structure in accord with its

10. Frank Lloyd Wright, Unity Temple, Oak Park, Illinois, 1905–8. This view shows the sanctuary on the left, the school building on the right and the entry between.
11. Frank Lloyd Wright, entry level plan of Unity Temple (north to right); redrawn under author's supervision.
12. Elevation and plan of 'A Shopping Center', 1924. Louis Kahn designed this while he was a student at the University of Pennsylvania.

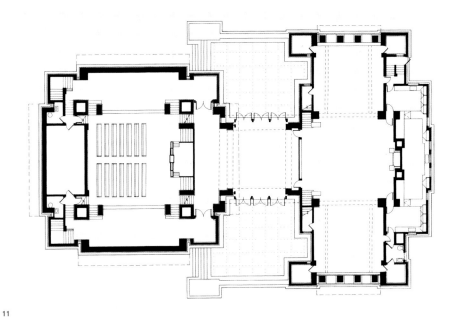

11

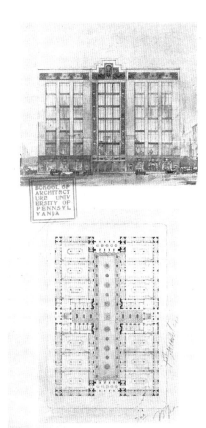

scheme of practical construction and aesthetic proportion, is practiced … and, although the symmetry may not be always obvious the balance is usually maintained.' He went on to state that 'all the forms are complete in themselves … This tendency to greater individuality of the parts emphasized by more and more complete articulation will be seen in the plans of Unity Temple.'[23] While this statement accords in general with the principles of Kahn's Beaux-Arts training, Wright's special emphasis on the spatial and structural independence of elemental units of composition – so clearly demonstrated in Wright's Darwin Martin House in Buffalo, New York of 1903–5; the Larkin Building in Buffalo, New York of 1902–6; and Unity Temple in Oak Park, Illinois of 1905–8 – would have enormous importance for Kahn.

At the end of his life, Kahn acknowledged the importance to his architectural design work of his Beaux-Arts university training under Paul Cret, despite practising all his life as a modern architect. In fact, certain of Kahn's late designs actually recall his student projects. The student design for 'A Shopping Center' of 1924, for example, bears a striking resemblance to the Family Planning Centre in Kathmandu, Nepal, only completed after Kahn's death in 1974. Kahn would also remark on the influence that the Beaux-Arts methods had on his teaching, particularly in terms of the emphasis on intuition, as when a student was required to develop his or her initial idea for a design through 'the sketch [which] depended on our intuitive powers. But the intuitive power is probably our most accurate sense. The sketch depended on our intuitive sense of appropriateness. I teach appropriateness. I don't teach anything else.'[24]

As Scully so insightfully pointed out in his seminal 1962 book on Kahn, the Beaux-Arts education at the University of Pennsylvania 'insisted upon a masonry architecture of palpable mass and weight wherein clearly defined and ordered spaces were to be formed and characterized by the structural solids themselves.' Scully even perceived in Kahn's student work premonitions of his later 'characteristic difficulty with the skin of the building, with, that is, the element which seemed to him neither structure nor space'. Finally, and most importantly, Scully states that the Beaux-Arts education encouraged Kahn 'to regard the buildings of the past as friends'.[25]

Beginning in Europe

In June 1924 Kahn graduated from the University of Pennsylvania with a bachelor's degree in architecture. For his first three years of apprenticeship he worked in the office of the City Architect of Philadelphia, John Molitor, an indication of Kahn's dedication to his beloved Philadelphia and his intention to repay the debt he felt he owed the city. After a year of serving as a draughtsman, Kahn was appointed chief of design for the buildings of the Sesquicentennial International Exposition. This 1926 celebration of the 150th anniversary of the signing of the Declaration of Independence gave Kahn the opportunity to design and build, in less than a year, six enormous buildings totalling 1.5 million square feet (139,355 square metres).[26] Designed in the 'stripped

13

classicism' typical of Paul Cret and other leading designers of the time, with massive square piers and coffered ceilings, the buildings' sublime grandeur was captured by Kahn in his powerful rendered perspectives used to present the project to the public in 1925. While these were temporary constructions, steel frames clad in wood and stucco, they allowed Kahn to make monumental urban-scale spaces far sooner after graduating than would normally be the case.

Kahn next worked for a year in the office of the architect, William Lee, who was engaged in designing buildings for Temple University. Kahn lived at home with his parents during this time, and saved enough money to make a long trip to Europe, the expected culmination of Beaux-Arts architectural training. The importance of similar trips in the development of modern architects such as Le Corbusier, who made four trips through Europe in 1907, 1908, 1910 and 1911 (this last trip documented in the book *Le Voyage d'Orient*), and Frank Lloyd Wright, who travelled to Japan in 1905 and lived in Europe from 1909 to 1911, should also be noted. While the impact on Kahn of his later time in Europe, particularly the period he spent at the American Academy in Rome in 1950–1, is often noted, the arguably greater importance to Kahn's development as an architect of this first trip has been less recognized. Kahn's sensibilities and principles as an architect would be fundamentally reshaped by this initial first-hand experience of the architecture of Europe, and it would lay the foundation for his later re-engagement of history in the discipline of architecture.

In April 1928 Kahn left for England, and he would travel in Europe for almost a full year. His extensive sketches and watercolours from this trip show not only his keen interest in historical architecture, both famous and anonymous, but also the changes, brought about by his experiences during the trip, in his perception and documentation of space, material and light.[27] Kahn spent two weeks in Britain where he made incredibly precise drawings, with particular attention to detail and material. He spent over a month travelling through the Netherlands and Germany, arriving in Denmark in late June. From there he passed fairly quickly through Sweden and Finland before stopping to visit relatives in Riga, Latvia and on the island of Saaremaa, where he had been born. He spent a month rediscovering this place and its castle from his childhood memories, and 'while he was there slept on the floor of his great-aunt's one-room dwelling. He recalled with relish eating the simple fare of little red potatoes and flat fish.'[28] Kahn left for Berlin in mid-August, and after two weeks in Germany he spent most of September along the Danube River in Czechoslovakia, Austria and Hungary.

At the beginning of October Kahn arrived in Italy, and he was to spend the next five months travelling its length and breadth, experiencing its unparalleled integration of architecture, landscape and life. He travelled very slowly, making drawings that were increasingly concentrated on the powerful effects of shade and shadow on stonework, and making watercolours that in a few bold strokes captured both the forms of the landscape and their atmospheric colouring. 'To abstract' means 'to draw from' or 'to draw out of', and Kahn's drawings of this period grew ever more abstract in the

14

13. Sesquicentennial International Exhibition Building, Philadelphia, 1925, drawing by Louis Kahn. Kahn developed this design while employed in the office of John Molitor, City Architect for Philadelphia.
14. Temple of Poseidon, Paestum, Italy; drawing of a Greek temple by Kahn, 1929.

15   16

precision with which they captured the essence of a view, a building, a space, recognizing and documenting the presence given to architecture by the strong Mediterranean sunlight.

At this time Kahn began to use carpenter's pencils and charcoal sticks, whose wide rectangular edges captured the horizontal and vertical strata of stonework raked by the sun in ever bolder strokes; excellent examples are the drawings of the Monastery of St Francis at Assisi, the towers of San Gimignano and the many studies of the hilltowns on the Amalfi Coast. For the hazy, thick atmosphere and multiple reflections of Venice, Kahn tried crayon, both black and coloured, and was able to make rapid yet compelling drawings of this magical place where sky and ground are equally full of light, with architecture floating between. In addition to much time spent in the Italian countryside, Kahn visited and made drawings and paintings in Milan, Florence, the Tuscan hilltowns, Rome, the Roman ruins at Pompeii and the great Greek temples at Paestum,[29] and spent an extended period in Positano, Amalfi, Ravello and Capri, where he executed a remarkable series of drawings and watercolours.

In the spring of 1929 Kahn travelled through Switzerland, where he made numerous landscape drawings and paintings, and then on to France. He spent a month in Paris, visiting his University of Pennsylvania classmate, Norman Rice, whom he had known since he was ten and who was then employed in the office of Le Corbusier – very probably the first American to work there.[30] Yet, during his year in Europe, Kahn made no sketches of, and probably did not visit, any examples of modern architecture. While travelling, Kahn not only met old friends but also made new ones, particularly among fellow US architects such as Edward Durrell Stone and Louis Skidmore (future founding partner of the giant Skidmore, Owings and Merrill, called SOM), whom Kahn met in Italy and with whom he travelled for a brief period. In April 1929, Kahn sailed from England for home.

15 & 16. Drawings by Louis Kahn of a Tudor house, London, 1928, and the Duomo, Assisi, Italy, 1929.

Becoming a modern architect

Immediately upon his return Kahn was employed in the office of Paul Cret, where he worked for the following year as a junior designer. Assisting the senior designers, who included his former professor, John Harbeson, Kahn worked on a variety of projects, including the Folger Library in Washington, DC. During that same year, his drawings from the European trip were exhibited in the Pennsylvania Academy of Fine Arts, Kahn's favourite building by Frank Furness. Cret would remain influential in a variety of ways in Kahn's life, not the least of which was the fact that Kahn proposed to Esther Israeli, a beautiful research assistant in the Neurosurgery Department at the University of Pennsylvania, during a visit to the Rodin Museum, which had been designed by Cret.[31] Louis and Esther were married on 14 August 1930.

During this period, Cret was engaged in designing both his signature 'stripped classical' buildings as well as structures with a more modernist inflection. Cret's cautious exploration of modern architecture came as no surprise, for he had stated in a 1923 meeting of the T-Square Club of Philadelphia that 'Our architecture is modern and cannot be anything else', and at a 1927 club meeting Cret gave a generally favourable review of the English translation of Le Corbusier's *Vers une architecture*,[32] published as *Towards a New Architecture*.[33] As a French native and École des Beaux-Arts graduate, Cret understandably focused on this French (actually Swiss-French) version of modernism. Yet the now canonic readings of this period, asserting that modern architecture was imported to the United States from Europe, have overlooked the fact that the work of the European modernists – Mies van der Rohe and Walter Gropius, in particular – had been inspired by the early work of Frank Lloyd Wright. Kahn was well aware that, while the winds of change then bringing the Modern Movement to America blew from Europe, they had originated in his adopted homeland.

The then sixty-year-old Frank Lloyd Wright's series of essays – five in 1927 and nine in 1928 – published in the monthly *Architectural Record* under the collective title 'In the Cause of Architecture', were of the greatest relevance to this reintroduction of modern architectural ideas. Wright's essay of January 1928, entitled 'The Logic of the Plan', would have reinforced Kahn's growing understanding of the fundamental shared principles underlying all great architecture:

> *A good plan is the beginning and the end ... its development in all directions is inherent – inevitable ... There is more beauty in a fine ground-plan than in almost any of its ultimate consequences ... To judge an architect one need only look at his ground-plan. He is master there, or never. Were all the elevations of the genuine buildings of the world lost and the ground-plan saved, each building would construct itself again. Because before the plan is a plan it is a concept in some creative mind.*

Wright's proposal that 'a concept in some creative mind' is the basis for the architectural plan would be paralleled more than twenty years later by Kahn's emphasis, in his teaching, of the importance of 'the idea' in architectural design.

17

Later in the same essay, Wright would remark, 'Usually you hear music as you work',[34] a comment that would have been particularly provocative to Kahn.

The Depression, triggered by the stock-market crash of 1929, soon had a devastating effect on the US architectural profession. In 1930, when Cret's office ran out of work, Kahn moved to the firm of Zantzinger, Borie and Medary (architects for the Philadelphia Museum of Art), where he worked on one of the first major public-works projects, the enormous Treasury Building in Washington, DC. But when this project finished in February 1932 Kahn was again unemployed, and would remain so for most of the next four years, he and Esther living with his wife's parents (as they had since they were married), and being largely supported by his wife.

Yet Kahn was not idle in this period. As he would do again in other periods of under-employment, he used this (involuntary) free time to engage in an intense re-examination of his discipline and the new demands he perceived being placed upon it. In 1931, before leaving the Zantzinger office, Kahn organized the Architectural Research Group: thirty young architectural designers, many out of work, who together set up what amounted to both a school and a practice for the exploration (in both discussion and design) of modern architecture. As Sarah Goldhagen has pointed out, at the root of this effort, to which Kahn committed full-time after losing his job, was modernism's 'axiomatic conviction, which Kahn shared with his colleagues, that the architect's main responsibility was to change society for the better', as well as Kahn's deeply held personal belief 'that bringing people together in domestic or public collective settings would engender social good'.[35]

Even in the depths of the Depression, Philadelphia once again proved to be the place of opportunities for Kahn. George Howe, American aristocrat, École des Beaux-Arts-trained architect, middle-aged convert to modernism, and Kahn's future partner (who late in life told Kahn that, rather than an architect, 'I should have been a patron'[36]), would play a multi-faceted part in the re-establishment of modern architecture in the United States, and Philadelphia in particular.[37] Howe and William Lescaze's Philadelphia Savings Fund Society (PSFS) Building, built from 1929 to 1932, was the first modernist skyscraper, where, as William Curtis has said, the 'inherited typological thinking about the American skyscraper and the emergent vocabulary of the International Style came together in a way that modified each'.[38] Howe and Lescaze's design resolves a number of dichotomous aspects of the urban high-rise, including the elegant weaving of horizontal floor lines with vertical structure; the tower's clear relationship between office spaces and elevator volume; and the sensitive way in which the lower mass of the banking hall and shops meets and reinforces the existing urban street wall, while simultaneously acting as a base for the thinner, more dynamic volumes of the tower above. It is interesting to note that the PSFS Building was completed only two years after the construction of the last great Beaux-Arts building in Philadelphia: the monumental 30th Street Station, which Kahn would use his entire life. It can be argued that in many important ways Kahn's career would be framed by these two buildings and the architectural ideas that formed them.

17. Esther and Louis Kahn on their honeymoon, 1930.
18. George Howe and William Lescaze, Philadelphia Savings Fund Society (PSFS) Building, Philadelphia, 1929–32. A highly influential design, the PSFS Building involved the adaptation of European International Style elements to American skyscraper typology.

With his characteristic inexhaustible energy, Kahn went about making himself into a modern architect. The transformation was so complete that he could say late in life, 'Every man has a figure in his work who he feels answerable to. I often say to myself, "How'm I doing, Le Corbusier?" You see, Le Corbusier was my teacher. I say Paul Cret was my teacher and Corbusier was my teacher.'[39]

The spirited debate that took place in Philadelphia in this period was both stimulated and documented in the publication *T-Square Club Journal of Philadelphia*, a new magazine funded by Howe starting in late 1930 and based upon the meetings of the architects' social club of the same name, of which Kahn was a member. The Beaux-Arts architects of Philadelphia, such as Paul Cret and his associate John Harbeson, practitioners of Art Deco including Ely Jacques Kahn and Raymond Hood, and modern architects such as Le Corbusier, Richard Neutra and Frank Lloyd Wright, were all published in its pages, as were Kahn's own sketches from Europe and his essay, 'The Value and Aim in Sketching'. It is important to note that during this period 'no other magazine in America offered anything like this range of advanced opinion'.[40]

In February 1932 the Museum of Modern Art in New York held an exhibition entitled 'Modern Architecture – International Exhibition', which opened at the Philadelphia Museum of Art in April of the same year. This exhibition, and perhaps more so the accompanying book authored by Henry-Russell Hitchcock and Philip Johnson, *The International Style: Architecture Since 1922*, published the same year, emphasized the formal aspects of the European interpretation of modern architecture. While the exhibition and book provided US architects with a readily applicable new style, the works were presented without any reference to the commitment to social responsibility and mass housing which in fact underlay the vast majority of European modernism, and the book did not address this deeper reason for the passionate interest of so many US architects, including Kahn and his Architectural Research Group. Thus while the projects that were designed by Kahn's group, including the 1933 multiple-unit housing project for the Philadelphia Housing Corporation, do show the influence of the International Style, they also reveal a knowledge of US developments – particularly in the work of Frank Lloyd Wright, and his pinwheel plans for multi-family housing, which date back to 1901.

Wright, despite arguably being the primary source of the Modern Movement, was not included in the book and was only given a small place in the Museum of Modern Art exhibition, whose 'since 1922' time limit was part of curator Philip Johnson's attempt to edit out Wright from this newly scripted history of modern architecture; an attitude later summarized in Johnson's mean characterization of Wright as 'the greatest architect of the nineteenth century'.[41] Wright's principles of beginning with the singular room, regional identity, local construction methods and the specifics of the site were ignored in the International Style's emphasis on the promulgation of universally applicable and predetermined formal models. It is hardly

19

surprising, then, that Wright, never one to let others control his publicity, was producing during the very same period a series of projects and writings that are in direct opposition to what the International Style represented. In his February 1928 'In the Cause of Architecture' essay in *Architectural Record*, pointedly subtitled 'What "Styles" Mean to the Architect', Wright wrote, 'The room within is the great fact about the building – *the room* to be expressed on the exterior as *space enclosed*. This sense of the room within ... is the advanced thought of the era in architecture.'[42] In 1932 Wright published *An Autobiography*, a book that would prove widely popular during Kahn's career, and in which is a description of the design of Unity Temple in 1905, wherein Wright again stated that the room, as the place of gathering, is the beginning of architecture – an idea that would have the greatest consequences for Kahn.[43]

Over the previous thirty years Wright had designed numerous communities and multi-family housing projects, culminating in his Broadacre City proposal of 1934 and his parallel conception of the affordable 'Usonian House' for the American middle class, and Kahn would certainly have been interested in this great American architect's designs that addressed this once again urgent need. Starting with his two years as a housing architect for the Philadelphia Planning Commission (1933–5), Kahn would be involved in the design of dozens of communities and housing prototypes over the next twenty years, a period of his career that has most often been under-appreciated, if not ignored outright, but during which many of his most fundamental principles were established.

While multi-family housing would form the vast majority of Kahn's work during the following decade, he began to receive commissions for both single-family residences and a few institutional buildings, including the Ahavath Israel Synagogue of 1935, the thirty-four-year-old architect's first major independent built work. Set in a row of two-storey houses in Philadelphia, this remarkably reserved structure presents to the street

19. Ahavath Israel Synagogue, Philadelphia, 1935. The solid, massive street elevation is complemented by glass block and large windows on other facades.
20. Ahavath Israel Synagogue. This interior view looks towards the rear of the sanctuary, with the balcony above and entry below.
21. Oscar Stonorov and Alfred Kastner, Carl Mackley Houses, Philadelphia, 1931–4, view across the courtyard. The Mackley Houses were 400 units built for the hosiery workers' union. Stonorov and Kastner were later Kahn's partners in professional practice.

20

a square, brick-faced facade, relieved only by the subtle asymmetrical composition of the wide doorway at the base and three small windows set one above the other, marking the internal floor heights and lighting the stair. The sanctuary is an elegantly proportioned (double-square in section) double-height space at the second level, lit by a series of large, industrial steel sash windows along the north side and by a high glass-block window running the full width of the front wall. The simple pier-and-beam structure articulates the room's unadorned surfaces and, along with the walls and ceilings, is clad in smooth wood panelling, making the space within a surprising counterpoint to the building's severe industrial exterior.

At the very start of this period, Philadelphia was once again the site of an important architectural 'first' in the United States: the Carl Mackley Houses.[44] These four parallel, three-storey masonry buildings, containing more than 400 apartments and extensive neighbourhood services such as day care, were designed in 1931–3 for the hosiery workers' union by Oscar Stonorov and Alfred Kastner – both of whom would be future partners of Kahn – and completed in 1934. Late in 1935 Kastner brought Kahn to Washington, DC, where he worked with Kastner for more than a year on the Jersey Homesteads, a project to relocate 200 Jewish garment workers and their families from New York to Roosevelt, New Jersey. Kahn developed twelve house types, which were capable of being paired to produce a wide variety of shapes, and which were built of concrete-block walls, with the floors and flat, overhanging roofs employing reinforced concrete slabs. Kahn's designs for the combined school and community centre show the strong influence not only of Le Corbusier's

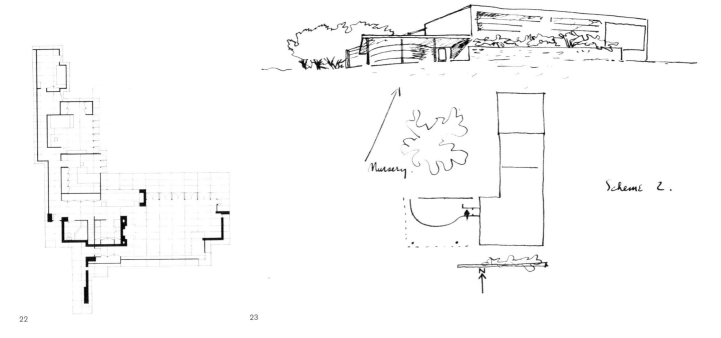

22

23

22. Frank Lloyd Wright, plan of the Herbert Jacobs House, Madison, Wisconsin, 1936–7 (north down); redrawn under author's supervision. Wright's modest middle-class housing prototype provided high quality interior space as well as reduced energy use.
23. Plan and perspective of Jersey Homesteads Community Center and School, Roosevelt, New Jersey, 1935, Louis Kahn and Alfred Kastner. Kahn's sketch was probably influenced by the drawing style of Le Corbusier, whose work Kahn studied when it was published in 1929 and 1934.
24. Plans of Oser House, Elkins Park, Pennsylvania, 1940 (ground floor, left; second floor, right). This house was one of Kahn's first independent single-family residential commissions.
25. Frank Lloyd Wright, section of three types of cantilevered roof and column, Johnson Wax Building, Racine, Wisconsin, 1936–8. The concept of the column supporting an 'umbrella' roof would be used by Kahn repeatedly throughout his professional career.

forms but also, even more strikingly, of his drawing technique, indicating Kahn's careful study of the first (and possibly second) volume of Le Corbusier's *Oeuvre complète*, which had appeared in 1929 and 1934 respectively.

Kahn returned to Philadelphia in early 1937 where, before becoming a consulting architect for the Philadelphia Housing Authority in August, he supervised the construction of Ahavath Israel and developed a series of studies for prefabricated steel housing. These meticulously worked-out plans, employing steel in all aspects of the housing unit, were designed by Kahn and Henry Klumb, who from 1929 to 1934 had been an apprentice of Frank Lloyd Wright. Even without this direct connection to Wright, Kahn could hardly have avoided seeing the *Time* magazine cover story on Wright on 17 January 1938, and much less the January 1938 issue of *Architectural Forum*, completely dedicated to Wright, with its Wright-designed cover and in-depth presentation of Wright's new work. This included the expanded Taliesin complex in Wisconsin of 1932, home of the Taliesin Fellowship school which Klumb had attended; the first examples of Wright's 'Usonian' affordable middle-class houses, including the prototypical L-shaped Jacobs House in Madison, Wisconsin of 1936–7; the astonishing Kaufmann House called Fallingwater in Mill Run, Pennsylvania of 1935–7 (a rendering of which had appeared behind Wright on the *Time* cover), cantilevered out over a waterfall; Wright's 'Ocatilla' temporary desert camp in Chandler, Arizona of 1929, built with standardized materials and a vented canvas roof; and finally the Johnson Wax Building in Racine, Wisconsin of 1936–8, with its thin-shell concrete 'dendriform' columns based on Wright's study of the hollow internal structure of the great saguaro cactus.

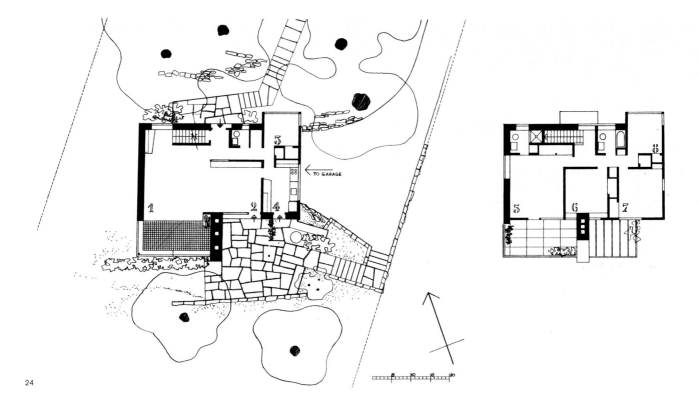

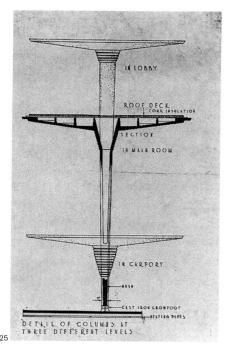

This astonishing re-emergence of the great American modern architect whom most assumed, at age seventy, had long since retired from practice, would have enormous impact on young architects such as Kahn. As will be seen later in this text, Wright's work would be of critical importance to Kahn, and here it will only be noted that on the very last page of the magazine, Wright quoted from the poetry of Walt Whitman: 'Chanting the square deific, out of the One advancing, out of the sides, Out of the old and the new, out of the square entirely divine, Solid – four sided – all sides needed. I am time, old, modern as any.'[45] Wright's work, exemplified in his great Unity Temple, inevitably engaged the square and cube as both its spatial beginning and its underlying proportional regulation, and Wright believed, as did Whitman, that the square was a fundamentally sacred and timeless geometry. Kahn came to share this belief, and on several occasions late in his life he stated emphatically that, in designing a building, 'I always start with a square, no matter what the problem is'.[46]

In 1938 Kahn was teamed with George Howe and Kenneth Day, and they were charged by the Philadelphia Housing Authority with designing several large but ultimately unrealized urban redevelopment projects. In 1939 Kahn was appointed a consulting architect to the United States' Housing Authority, and worked on several publications and the New York Museum of Modern Art exhibition 'Houses and Housing'. The following year, Kahn independently designed the Jesse and Ruth Oser House in Elkins Park, Pennsylvania. A remarkably well-resolved design, the Oser House indicates Kahn's maturity as a designer. A two-storey cubic mass in which a subtle pinwheel is developed, it features a wood-clad volume cantilevered beyond the

26

stone-clad main mass at the front, while a glass-enclosed volume is anchored to the ground and shifted along the massive stone fireplace hearth towards the back. The whole possesses an elegance of proportion and confidence in formal restraint, while also indicating a familiarity on Kahn's part with houses designed by Howe as well as by Walter Gropius and Marcel Breuer,[47] the last two only recently arrived in the United States from Germany.

With the onset of World War II George Howe again approached Kahn, this time to propose a partnership to work on government housing projects. By April 1941 they had secured, from the newly formed Federal Works Agency, the contract to design 500 housing units for Pine Ford Acres, Middletown, Pennsylvania, and 1,000 units at Pennypack Woods in north-east Philadelphia.[48] Kahn's intention from the start was to set the standard for this type of design, and the four-unit buildings at Pennypack Woods are both cleverly organized, providing covered open spaces to all four units, and elegantly proportioned and detailed, using two sizes of wooden siding to give the buildings varying scale and rhythm.

With Howe increasingly being called to Washington, DC, for consulting work, he and Kahn asked Oscar Stonorov to join the firm late in 1941. As noted above, Stonorov had been part of the Mackley Houses team, and prior to that had been one of the editors of the first volume of Le Corbusier's *Oeuvre complète*, providing Kahn with a direct connection to the architect whose work he would later use as a measure for his own efforts. While Stonorov was to have little effect on the design work in the office, his union connections and political activism, and the types of projects these attracted,

26. Four-unit building, Pennypack Woods Housing, Philadelphia, 1941, George Howe and Louis Kahn. Designed by Kahn, the Pennypack project involved the building of 1,000 homes.
27. Two-unit building, Carver Court Housing, Coatesville, Pennsylvania, 1941–3, George Howe, Louis Kahn and Oscar Stonorov. This project involved the construction of 100 homes.

would fundamentally change the practice. In their design for Carver Court, 100 units of housing built near Coatesville, Pennsylvania, the row housing was lifted to the second floor on full-depth walls, freeing the ground floor for a car park, storage and other services. Kahn applied this same approach to the 300-unit Stanton Road Dwellings in Washington, DC, and the 150-unit Lincoln Highway project, also in Coatesville.

Kahn felt that this design addressed a fault in most government-sponsored housing when compared to typical developer 'home-builder' housing stock, which, despite its poorer ventilation and inefficient floor plans, provided basement space for parking, storage and workshops. In Kahn's 1942 article entitled '"Standards" Versus Essential Space', there is a hint of his later 'servant' and 'served' space concept in the critique of the well-ordered 'actual space for living' of typical government housing, which nevertheless 'becomes bedlam' if the storage, laundry and workshop is left out of the plan, as these activities (Kahn's 'servant' functions) must take place in the living room, kitchen and bedroom of the house (Kahn's 'served' spaces).[49] This may also reflect Kahn's own experiences as a new father and family man, coming with the birth of his daughter Sue Ann in 1940.

With the Carver Court project Kahn received significant publicity, particularly with its inclusion in the Museum of Modern Art exhibition, 'Built in USA, 1932–1944'. In February 1942 Howe was appointed the supervising architect of the Public Buildings Administration, and from 1942 to 1948 Kahn and Stonorov continued their partnership. Kahn's responsibilities were increasingly focused on design, with Stonorov almost

exclusively responsible for the political work required to secure government housing commissions, and get them built. The 'Bomber City' project, which began as a proposed community of 20,000 residences at Henry Ford's Willow Run aeroplane factory, was never to be realized, despite Stonorov's best efforts. For the 475-unit Lily Ponds Housing project built in Washington, DC, Kahn designed a remarkable four-unit, one-storey structure where the bathrooms are grouped at the centre, covered by a butterfly-wing roof, with the four chimneys marking out its corners. This roof shape (the opposite of the typical pitched roof), as well as the project's rustic tile exterior and exposed unfinished wood, very probably indicates Kahn's awareness of similar elements in Le Corbusier's recent work, illustrated in the third volume of his *Oeuvre complète,* which had arrived in the United States in 1939.[50]

By 1943 Kahn and Stonorov had begun to focus on projects – many of them imaginative – intended to shape post-war construction. The texts of the two booklets that the firm designed for the Revere Copper and Brass Company, using Philadelphia neighbourhoods as test cases showing what was possible, are largely Stonorov's work, but the illustrated design projects are all Kahn's work. Their first booklet, *Why City Planning is Your Responsibility*, involves

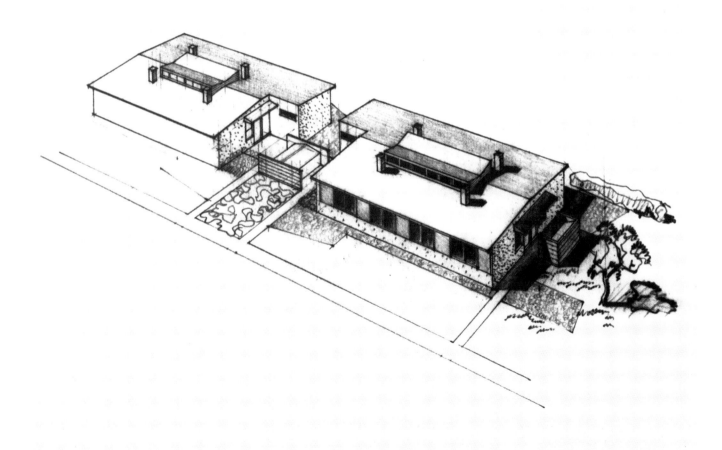

a model neighbourhood rehabilitation project, and in it Kahn makes the case, almost unheard of at the time, for the 'conservation' and rehabilitation of existing housing, while providing new schools and other institutional infrastructure to strengthen the older residential neighbourhood.[51] The second booklet, entitled *You and Your Neighborhood: A Primer for Neighborhood Planning*, includes Kahn's illustration 'The Plan of a City is Like the Plan of a House', relating the individual rooms of the house to urban elements (living room = meeting hall, study = cultural centre, kitchen = industry, pantry = stores, bedrooms = residential areas, and the corridors = roads), reflecting Kahn's lifelong belief in the essentially identical nature of architecture and urban planning.

In 1942, *Architectural Forum* invited Kahn to submit a design for their 'New House 194X' feature, and though he was too busy to meet that deadline he and Stonorov submitted a design for the 1943 issue, entitled 'New Buildings for 194X', which focused on prototypical 'main street' institutions for a mid-sized city. Kahn and Stonorov's assignment was 'A Hotel for 194X'. Their design involved a slab with extensive metal shading elements, housing the hotel rooms, which worked in concert with a low L-shaped building housing community services, to create a public plaza. Indebted to some degree in its form to the PSFS Building, the project is most notable for the manner in which Kahn used large urban masses to frame community space. It is important to note that among the other projects published in the same issue of *Architectural Forum* was Mies van der Rohe's 'Museum for a Small City', in many ways the canonical International Style 'free plan' example against which Kahn would later have such a strong reaction in his own search for the relationship between structure and space.

A project from this period worthy of particular note is the Parasol House construction system and various housing prototypes developed by Kahn for the Knoll Furniture Company in 1944. In yet another attempt to engage prefabrication in housing construction, Kahn proposed a modular component consisting of a 12 foot (3.7 metre) square, steel-framed roof supported by a single central steel-tube column. These umbrella-like units, which are clearly related to Frank Lloyd Wright's 'dendriform' columns in the Johnson Wax Building, were proposed by Kahn to be assembled to produce a wide variety of volumes, including two-storey and one-storey versions.

Without question the most dramatic of these assemblies was the (seemingly endless) linear assembly, which either begins or ends beyond the edges of Kahn's drawing, joining dozens of separate units under one enormous roof, punctuated by irregularly spaced courtyards. Under this great common roof, and within its grid of columns, the non-load-bearing walls of the units engaged in a rather aggressive version of the non-rectilinear 'free plan'. Similar to Mies van der Rohe's courtyard house prototypes, but pre-dating US versions such as Paul Rudolph's 1948 project for six linked houses for Revere Copper (the sponsor of Kahn and Stonorov's booklets), Kahn's design is more powerful in its suggestive extension, reaching a truly urban scale.

28. Lily Ponds Houses, Washington, DC, 1942, Louis Kahn (designer) and Oscar Stonorov. This aerial perspective by Kahn shows a four-unit building; the project involved the construction of 475 homes.

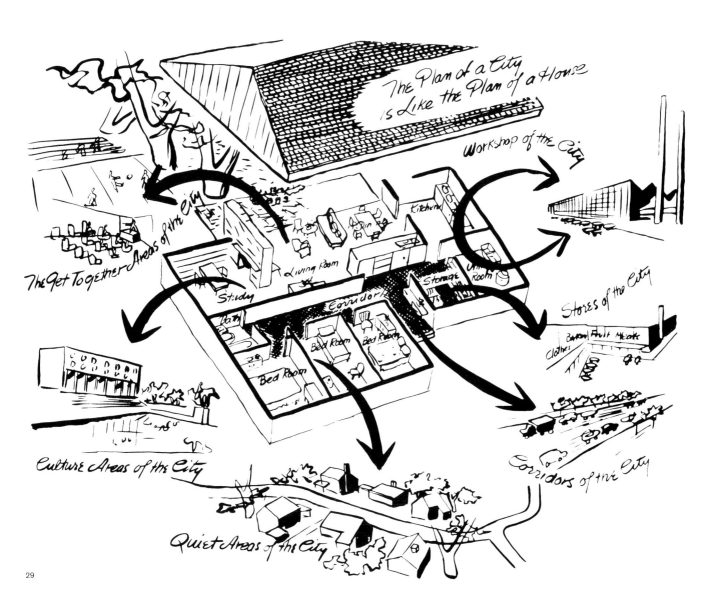

The Plan of a City is Like the Plan of a House

Workshop of the City

The Get Together Areas of the City

Kitchen

Living Room

Study

Corridor

Storage

Utility Room

Bath

Bed Room

Bed Room

Bed Room

Stores of the City

Clothes Bread Fruit Meats

Culture Areas of the City

Corridors of the City

Quiet Areas of the City

30

29. 'The Plan of a City is Like the Plan of a House',
1943, drawn by Louis Kahn for the city-planning
booklet, *You and Your Neighborhood*.
30. 'A Hotel for 194X', 1942, perspective drawing
by Louis Kahn. Kahn's invited design was published
in *Architectural Forum*, May 1943.

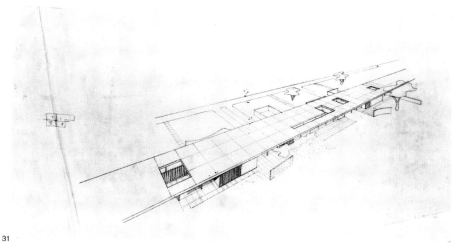

31

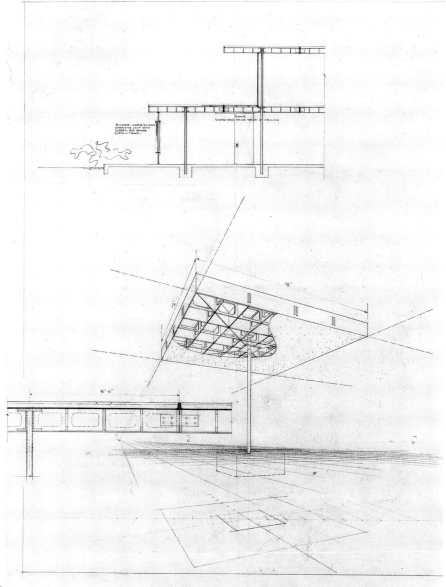

31. Linear housing block to be built with the Parasol
House construction system, 1944, Louis Kahn
(designer) and Oscar Stonorov. Aerial perspective
by Kahn.
32. Sketch study, section and perspective of the
Parasol House construction system, 1944; drawings
by Louis Kahn. Kahn's first use of the 'umbrella' roof
concept was inspired by Frank Lloyd Wright's
Johnson Wax Building, 1936–8.
33. Glass and wood facade, Solar House Prototype,
1946, Louis Kahn and Oscar Stonorov, sponsored
by Libby-Owens-Ford Glass Company. Perspective
drawing by Kahn.

32

33

The prototype Solar House of 1946, commissioned by Libby-Owens-Ford Glass, is the last of these projects designed by the office of Kahn and Stonorov. Again the design is Kahn's, in this case with the assistance of the newest member of the office staff, Anne Griswold Tyng, who had recently graduated from the Graduate School of Design at Harvard, a course directed since 1938 by Walter Gropius.[52] Kahn's design, intended for Pennsylvania, folded three lightweight glass and wood facades with protective overhangs around the east-, south- and west-facing sides of a wedge-shaped plan, and the fourth, north-facing wall was to be made of solid masonry, pierced only by openings for entry and ventilation. The services were clustered along a central interior spine, running north–south and anchored to the north masonry wall so that in the winter the sun could penetrate to the full depth of every room on the three open sides.

This project was to prove important for reasons unrelated to its design, for serious disagreements over attribution of the design revealed that the partnership of Stonorov and Kahn, and their respective commitments to political involvement and design, was no longer tenable. In March 1947 the partnership was dissolved, and Kahn opened his own independent practice. This pivotal moment in Kahn's life coincided with the beginning of his university teaching career in the autumn of the same year.

Monumentality

Kahn had worked almost exclusively on multi-family housing since the mid-1930s, his designs largely employing the vocabulary of European modernism, yet during World War II he had begun to question the capacity of the International Style to embody contemporary cultural meanings and social institutions. In this Kahn was not alone, for the issue of monumentality, and the fact that the Modern Movement was predicated to a large degree on non-monumental or even anti-monumental conceptions of architecture's place and function in society, emerged as common concerns among leading architects, critics and historians during the war. It was a subject of debate among leading writers such as Sigfried Giedion, author of *Space, Time and Architecture*, the 1941 publication which in many ways canonized the International Style based on the work of Le Corbusier, Mies van der Rohe and Walter Gropius;[53] and Lewis Mumford, who had never embraced the International Style, championing instead the North American modern architecture of H. H. Richardson, Louis Sullivan and Frank Lloyd Wright. By the mid-1940s a rare unanimity had emerged, holding that an appropriate modern form of monumentality was needed, and that the housing-based design formulae of the International Style had proved incapable of addressing this need.

It should be noted that the architects were well ahead of the critics in this perception, and it was largely their work that had stimulated this debate. Le Corbusier, in unrealized but widely publicized projects such as the 1927 League of Nations Building – an elegant exposition of functionally articulate volumes – and the 1931 Palace of the Soviets – a powerful spatial composition formed by heroic structural elements – as well as in built works such as the 1929–33 Cité de Refuge in Paris and the 1927–8 Centrosoyus in Moscow, had designed buildings that were at once modern and yet undeniably monumental. A generation earlier – in works such as the Larkin Building and, later, the Midway Gardens in Chicago of 1913 and the Imperial Hotel in Tokyo of 1914–22 – Frank Lloyd Wright had engaged in the development of an appropriately American form of monumentality, addressing both the inability of his inheritance from Sullivan and the Chicago School (the steel frame skyscraper) to impart a sense of monumentality, and the need to equal the monumental potential of the Beaux-Arts version of classicism without employing its exhausted vocabulary. It is important to note that Kahn's partner George Howe singled out Wright's Unity Temple as an exemplary modern monument particularly appropriate to American democracy.[54]

In the 1944 book, *New Architecture and City Planning, A Symposium*, edited by Paul Zucker, Kahn published an extraordinary essay entitled 'Monumentality' (see page 455),[55] wherein he defined monumentality in architecture as a spiritual quality conveying a sense of eternity, of timelessness and of unchanging perfection. Kahn argued that modern society had failed to give full architectural expression to the institutions of human community, and he pointed to the great monuments of the past which, while not possible literally to duplicate, nevertheless embodied the qualities by which all new buildings should be measured. Finally, he indicated the critically important part played by structural perfection and material character in the creation of historical monumental form, calling for a re-examination of contemporary norms of construction. While he had yet to find their appropriate expression in his architectural designs, Kahn here established what would be the key principles and themes of his career.

Kahn starts the essay by defining monumentality in architecture as at once material and social – a structure that attains a sense of timeless, eternal perfection while simultaneously making places for contemporary social and cultural life. He begins, 'Monumentality in architecture may be defined as a quality, a spiritual quality inherent in a structure which conveys the feeling of its eternity, that it cannot be added to or changed.' He immediately follows this by maintaining that if we have not achieved monumentality in the contemporary world, it is because we have not 'given full architectural expression to such social monuments as the school, the community, or culture center'.

For Kahn, the monumental is defined through construction, yet he argues that it is not the quality of the material but the quality of purpose and use of the material – our conception and craft – that achieves monumentality:

> *Monumentality is enigmatic. It cannot be intentionally created. Neither the finest material nor the most advanced technology need enter a work of monumental character for the same reason that the finest ink was not required to draw up the Magna Carta. However, our architectural monuments indicate a striving for structural perfection which has contributed in great part to their impressiveness, clarity of form, and logical scale.*

Yet these exemplary architectural monuments were structures built in the distant past, formed by ancient cultures, and thus presented the problem of what, if any, part they might play in contemporary design:

> *No architect can rebuild a cathedral of another epoch embodying the desires, the aspirations, the love and hate of the people whose heritage it became. Therefore the images we have before us of monumental structures of the past cannot live again with the same intensity and meaning. Their faithful duplication is unreconcilable. But we dare not discard the lessons these buildings teach for they have the common characteristics of greatness upon which the buildings of our future must, in one sense or another, rely.*

Kahn then summarizes 'the lessons these buildings teach', the structural and constructive characteristics of the Greek and Gothic periods, which he describes in the past tense. This contrasts sharply with the way he introduces Roman architecture:

> *The influence of the Roman vault, the dome, the arch, has etched itself in deep furrows across the pages of architectural history. Through Romanesque, Gothic, Renaissance,* and today, *its basic forms and structural ideas have been felt.* They will continue to reappear *but with added powers made possible by our technology and engineering skill* [my emphasis].

In this passage, Kahn speaks of Roman architecture as a living, contemporary tradition, indicating that by this date, well before his return to Rome in 1950, Kahn had come to see the abstracted elements of Roman architecture as potentially generative within his own design process. In this, Kahn was looking at architectural history as an architect, not as a historian, and his view was both selective and operative. In describing Michelangelo's similarly selective attention to the Roman ruins, as reflected in his late Renaissance architectural designs, James Ackerman noted how 'Every great architect discovers his *own* history'.[56]

In the light of the fundamental tectonic lessons to be learned from history, Kahn criticizes contemporary construction practices, emphasizing the way in which the expressive possibilities of the structure – the 'graceful forms which the stress diagrams indicated' – are often lost in the process of selection and application of standardized components. Kahn argued for the inherent beauty and strength of tubular sections and for the structural continuity achieved by welding steel members, and in this may be discerned the beginnings of his later fascination with both the potential uses of the hollow spaces in tubular structures and the structural continuity and 'graceful forms' possible with reinforced concrete. Recalling the collapse of the medieval Beauvais Cathedral, due to its builders' attempting to build spans that exceeded the capacities of stone, Kahn declares that 'Beauvais Cathedral needed the steel we have'. He goes on to describe the construction of a cathedral employing contemporary construction materials and technology. Kahn illustrates this with a drawing of an enormous ribbed structure (complete with modern 'gargoyles' perched at the top of its buttresses), next to which he places a tracing of Choisy's section of Beauvais Cathedral.

Kahn then states that 'the cathedral, the culture center, the legislative palace … the monuments to commemorate the achievements and aspirations of our time' should not only be built with contemporary materials and methods, but

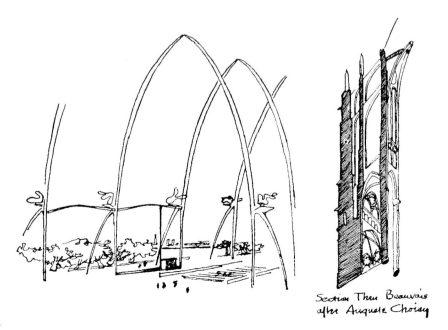

Section Thru Beauvais
after Auguste Choisy

should be designed using modern architectural principles. In this effort, Kahn notes that 'Outstanding masters of building design … have restated the meaning of a wall, a post, a beam, a roof, and a window, and *their interrelation in space*' [my emphasis]. This intriguing reference by Kahn is to those he considers his precursors in modern architectural design: Frank Lloyd Wright and Le Corbusier, both of whom early in their careers 'restated', translated and abstracted the fundamental elements of architecture in order to redefine them in modern terms – Wright in his 1908 'In the Cause of Architecture' (and restated even more clearly in his 1932 *An Autobiography*), and Le Corbusier in his 1926 'Five Points of a New Architecture'.

As a kind of demonstration of this modern monumentality, Kahn then presents his design for a cultural centre, along with the imaginary story of its commissioning and construction. Kahn's elegant drawings show a tubular skeletal structure, its continuous tapering members standing on points and thickening as they rise (similar to the columns in Wright's Johnson Wax Building), braced by being woven together, and supporting a giant roof composed of a grid of translucent domes. The structure itself, exposed with no wall or other infill, is undeniably organic in its constant change of section, and the whole possesses a powerful sculptural beauty. That these drawings were sincere attempts to come to terms with the concepts of construction that Kahn was proposing is evidenced by the fact that he almost immediately employed very similar structural forms in his design for the Jefferson National Expansion Memorial Competition of 1947.

In describing the successful design process for this imaginary cultural centre, Kahn begins by saying, 'Time was not "of the essence"', indicating his belief – which would become more fervent in later years – that contemporary society's demand for ever more rapid production of architecture is fundamentally detrimental to the quality of architecture and the civic spaces of

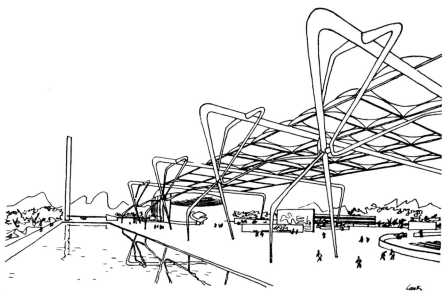

34. Perspective of 'A Cultural Center' and tracing of Auguste Choisy's axonometric section of Beauvais Cathedral, 1944, drawings by Louis Kahn. Both of these appeared in Kahn's 1944 essay 'Monumentality'.
35. Perspective of 'A Cultural Center', 1944, drawing by Louis Kahn. This appeared in the same essay. The tubular skeletal structure, with columns tapering to points at their bases, supports a roof grid of translucent domes.

the city. Kahn goes on to indicate that, though the cultural centre is not as large as many of the city's buildings, these other buildings 'do not impress us with the same feeling of receptiveness' and lack the centre's sense of openness and invitation. Kahn established the three fundamental aspects of the building, all of which would characterize many of his later designs: the 'ground sculpture' of the foundation and earth-work, 'the gigantic sculptural forms' of the building's structure and volumes, and the roof, with its 'surfacing of domes … an integral part of the structural design', giving light to the whole from above.

Kahn ends his imaginary tale of the cultural centre by telling of 'an older sculptor', whose works influence the younger artists, and

> … *who has developed* a theory of scale in relation to space. *He has argued that as the size of the* structural *work is increased the monolithic character of smaller work does not apply. He chose for the large work a small consistent part or module of a definite shape, a cube, a prism, or a sphere which he used to construct block over block, with delicate adjustments to the effect of light and shadow, the overall form. His work seen from great distances retains a texturally vibrant quality produced by these numerous blocks and the action of the sun upon them* [my emphasis].

While this probably describes Frank Lloyd Wright, particularly in the use of a 'module of definite shape' and the resulting 'texturally vibrant quality' of his concrete block houses, and employs terms Kahn would later use in describing Wright's contemporary work,[57] it may also be a witty autobiographical invention of Kahn's, reflecting a new confidence in his potential as an architect.

Teaching architecture

In the autumn of 1947, the year Kahn (at the age of forty-six) established his independent architectural practice, he also began what would be a lifelong parallel career as an architecture teacher. Kahn was invited to teach in Yale University's distinguished visiting critic programme – the traditional focus of the advanced level design studios – by Yale's new dean, Charles Sawyer, and new architecture department chair, Harold D. Hauf. That same autumn Edward Durrell Stone (with whom Kahn had travelled in Italy in 1929) was appointed chief critic in architectural design, a position he would hold until Kahn formally assumed the title in 1950.[58] While Kahn had previously been offered a teaching position at Harvard,[59] the fact that Yale's visiting critic appointment involved only two days teaching each week allowed him to maintain his residence and practice in his beloved Philadelphia. Kahn commuted to New Haven by train, passing twice each week through New York's great Beaux-Arts Pennsylvania Station and its spectacular 120 foot (37 metre) tall, top-lit train concourse, where steel trusses carried the glass-lens-filled mezzanine floors and the full glass roof high overhead.[60]

The experience of teaching at Yale for the next ten years would prove pivotal in Kahn's development as an architect. The architecture course at Yale was evolving dramatically during this period, and by 1950 would form a distinct contrast with what was considered the leading architecture course, that of Harvard under the direction of Walter Gropius, where the discipline of

36

architecture was aligned ever more closely with landscape architecture and urban planning. While equally committed to modernism, Yale developed a course that took advantage of its position in a fine arts school, and the discipline of architecture was seen as related to its sister arts of sculpture and painting.[61] In this way, Yale was moving closer to the methods and spirit of the original Bauhaus in Germany, an ironic development given that the leaders of the Bauhaus were now directing other North American schools of architecture, with Gropius at Harvard and Mies van der Rohe at Illinois Institute of Technology in Chicago.

Kahn had for years been committed to the integration of architecture with landscape and urban design in all his work, and so the new exposure to the ideas of leading modern artists had a far greater effect on him than that which is likely to have resulted from an involvement with Harvard. In Kahn's engagement of concepts of contemporary art, the former Bauhaus teacher Josef Albers would prove to be of the utmost importance. Albers had been a student at the Bauhaus, studying under the painters Paul Klee and Johannes Itten, who taught the foundation design courses required of students from all disciplines,[62] and Albers had himself taught the required *Vorkurs* course, translated as 'beginning design'. In 1933, when the Bauhaus was closed due to Nazi intimidation, Albers and his artist-wife, Anni, were brought to the United States to teach in the newly formed Black Mountain College, outside Asheville, North Carolina, at the recommendation of Philip Johnson, curator of architecture at the Museum of Modern Art. Teaching the required introductory course to students in architecture, painting and sculpture, Albers immediately became the leading figure at Black Mountain College, which was without question the most progressive and modern school of the arts in North America from 1933 to 1949 (the year Albers left the faculty).[63]

In 1948 Albers had been appointed to the council set up to reorganize the Yale department of art,[64] and in autumn 1949 Sawyer and Kahn invited Albers to teach the collaborative studio that Kahn was directing at Yale, involving advanced students from architecture, sculpture and painting. Kahn and Albers immediately became friends, and in 1950, with Kahn's strong backing, Albers was appointed to the permanent faculty as the head of the newly formed department of design, which incorporated the sculpture and painting courses.

At Sawyer's request, Kahn himself had been steadily taking over Stone's administrative duties as chief architecture critic, including inviting Pietro Belluschi and Eero Saarinen as visiting critics during the 1948–9 academic year.[65] In the spring of 1949, chairman Harold D. Hauf resigned to become editor of *Architectural Record*, and Kahn was instrumental in Sawyer offering the chairmanship to Kahn's former partner, George Howe, then architect-in-residence at the American Academy in Rome. As Robert Stern has noted, 'Howe was the first major American architect of the Modern Movement to be offered a position of administrative and philosophical importance in American architectural education',[66] bringing to Yale not only his extensive government-housing leadership experience but also his design experience on the PSFS and other noted buildings. For Kahn, Howe's assumption of leadership of the architecture course at Yale was important, not least for the fact that Howe, like

Kahn, was a Beaux-Arts trained architect who had converted to modernism. Almost immediately upon Howe's arrival in 1950, Kahn was officially appointed chief critic in architecture, a position that gave Kahn effective control over the selection of design critics for the final years of the architecture course.

The experience of teaching at Yale had the immediate effect of stimulating Kahn with many new ideas and possibilities, including the concepts of existentialist philosophy, with its emphasis on questions of being and becoming; abstract expressionist painting, with its focus on revealing the process and materials of making in art;[67] as well as such diverse architectural thinkers as Philip Johnson, who – at the time of his arrival at Yale in 1950 – was introducing classical order into modernism, and Buckminster Fuller, whose geodesic domes were seen as the most organic manifestation of modern industrialized production.

Of all these influences, Kahn's architecture was to be most deeply affected by the art and teaching of Albers. Both Albers' art and his teaching began with the concept that in order to design, one must first *see* – and for him art education was 'the disciplined education of the eye and hand'. Albers noted that, while most people could hold a tune, the visual memory was so poorly trained in contemporary society that few could accurately recall a 'shape or form, the size of things, the extension of space and volume'. For Albers the implications are clear: 'We cannot communicate graphically what we cannot see ... For this reason we learn to test our seeing, and systematically study foreshortening, overlapping, the continuity of tectonic and of movement.'[68]

Albers' own artwork, much of it produced during his time at Yale, exemplified just such a rigorous and precise exploration of space: his 'Homage to the Square' series (1950–76), a set of differently coloured squares set within each other creating an effect of foreshortening in one-point perspective; his 'Variant' series (1947–55), where T- and U-shaped, crisply rectangular elements are layered to create an ambiguous and complex perspective; and his 'Structural Constellation' series (1949–54), with their white lines framing several overlapping cubic volumes which appear to be rotating and folding through space.[69] Virtually all of Albers' paintings actively engage space, and would prove to be immediately influential in the thinking of architects. Sarah Goldhagen has noted the effect Albers' work had upon Kahn's own drawings, which at this time exhibited abstract overlapping volumes, cubic frames and strong perspective effects, often rendered in black ink, not Kahn's typical medium.[70]

Albers stated that in all art, 'precision – as to the effect wanted – and discipline – as to the means used – are decisive', and his emphasis on the experienced qualities of each *material* – texture, colour, depth, hardness – and the way it received and returned sunlight would have particular importance for Kahn. In a 1944 essay featured in the same collection as Kahn's 'Monumentality', Albers had argued that architecture students should be educated in what was, after all, still the 'handmade' craft of building, to experience the qualities of the materials with which they built, and to reveal in the finished building the process of its construction.[71] In his teaching, Albers had his students first draw a wide variety of materials, attempting to capture the subtle differences in texture and colour, and then employ those same materials in collage-like compositions intended to highlight each material's inherent character. According to Albers, the primary intention of these exercises was to 'develop understanding of and respect for material',[72] a direct source for Kahn's concept of honouring the material.

While Albers' extraordinary stained-glass artworks, such as 'Walls and Screens' of 1928, date from his Bauhaus years, he brought most of them with him to the United States, and he exhibited a number of them in New Haven in 1956, when Kahn was still teaching there.[73] That his father had been a stained-glass craftsman would have hardly been the only reason Kahn would have found these extraordinary works inspiring. The lines of colour woven and layered through these glass works are clearly related to the art of modern weaving that reached its peak at the Bauhaus, and in the work of Anni Albers.[74] It was Anni Albers who, in 1946, made the extraordinary characterization of modern art, summarizing Albers' concept of the generative power of the materials themselves: 'Being creative is perhaps not the desire to do something, but listening to that which wants to be done, the dictation of the materials.'[75] This last comes quite close to a number of Kahn's own aphorisms (including his asking the brick 'what it wants to be'), and the effect of the thinking of both Josef and Anni Albers on Kahn would be profound and lasting.

Unlike at Harvard, history was welcomed at Yale University.[76] In this it is important to note that the new chairman, George Howe, came to Yale

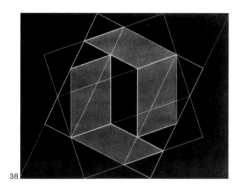

38

37. 'Transparency, No. 2', 1948–50, drawing by Louis Kahn. In subject matter – cubic spaces seen in one-point perspective, floating frames or transparent surfaces and folded planes – and medium – pen and ink – this drawing shows the influence of Josef Albers on Kahn at this time.
38. Josef Albers, 'Structural Constellation: Transformation of a Scheme No. 12', machine-engraved Vinylite mounted on board, 1950.

directly from living in Rome, was himself an expert on the Italian Renaissance and Baroque, and 'stressed the role of history as a reference for all design'.[77] Of the art and architecture history faculty, whose work would have been familiar to Kahn,[78] above all there was George Kubler's unprecedented interpretation of art and architectural history, as recorded in pre-Columbian artworks and architectural spaces, published in the 1962 book entitled *The Shape of Time*. Kubler proposed that works of art and architecture from the past 'are still open to further elaboration by new solutions'. He held that the timeless artistic problem, and its previous solutions, take possession of the artist, who believes he can improve upon it. Kubler also argued for closely attending to the material aspects of a work of art, not just to its symbolic connotations, and that the artist 'was bound to achieve his unconventional aim with conventional means'.[79]

In addition, William MacDonald was studying Roman vaulting techniques and their employment in the Romanesque and Byzantine periods,[80] and Frank Brown was already internationally recognized as an authority on ancient Rome.[81] Brown would guide generations of scholars (including Kahn) as resident archaeologist of the American Academy in Rome. Last but by no means least, the young Vincent Scully began his teaching career at Yale during this period, and his inspiring lectures examining the Greek sites[82] and the Roman spaces re-established these ancient cultures as relevant to the education of modern architects. Scully's teaching also increasingly focused on North American modern architecture, and even more precisely on the work of Frank Lloyd Wright. Scully's intense examination of Wright during the 1950s, and his enthusiastic descriptions of the experience of space in Wright's buildings, had an effect on his friend Kahn.[83] The earlier work of Wright, particularly buildings from the Prairie Period, such as Unity Temple and the Larkin Building, and those from his great resurgence in the 1930s, such as the Johnson Wax Building and the 'Usonian' Houses, would prove to be highly influential in Kahn's designs.

Yet many of Wright's later large-scale works, such as the Huntington Hartford Play Resort of 1947, exhibited a total lack of the simple geometry, formal restraint, ecological balance and constructive order that had been so evident in the earlier work, and which were so important to Kahn.[84] During the early years when Kahn taught at Yale, the work of the architecture students was strongly influenced by these later works of Wright. William Huff recalls that the spirit of Wright hung heavy over the school: 'Those students who were "with it", literally carried Hitchcock's *In the Nature of Materials* under one of their arms and spouted verbatim passages from *Autobiography*, which they carried under the other.'[85]

The student work from the studios taught by Eugene Nalle, the charismatic instructor of the first-year course throughout the time Kahn taught at Yale, was often characterized by direct copying from the recent work of Wright.[86] This mimicking of the late work of Wright is most probably the cause of Kahn's strong aversion to the work of 'imitators of Frank Lloyd Wright'.[87] That this 'Wrightian' influence remained strong at Yale until the mid-1950s is evidenced by the fact that it was a Wright-imitator who was cast as the student-hero of Edwin Gilbert's novel, *Native Stone* (1955), a book based directly upon the Yale school of architecture and its faculty in this period.[88]

Gilbert's novel contains the following description of Louis Kahn (who is given the name Homer Jepson in the novel):

> *... an almost gnome-like figure encased in an oxford-grey suit, all three buttons buttoned. Though he always wore an elegant foulard bow tie, it was always indifferently knotted, so that one end hung down, dangling inelegantly. The faintly bulging blue eyes dominated his small face, the lumpy nose, and always one clump of his grey steel-wool hair hung over his furrowed forehead ...* [Jepson was the chief design critic, and would] *imbue and jab and incite his students with his knowledge, his gifts of erudition and experience.*[89]

Vincent Scully's description of Kahn in this same period confirms the remarkable personal presence that Kahn had developed by this time: 'The impression was of deep warmth and force, compact physical strength, a printless, cat-like walk, glistening Tartar's eyes – only bright blue – a disordered aureole of whitening hair, once red; black suit, loose tie, pencil-sized cigar. It was at this time that he began to unfold into the rather unearthly beauty and command of a Phoenix risen from the fire.'[90]

Independent practice

Over the first two years of his independent practice Kahn designed five houses, of which three were built, and saw the construction of his first major public institution. When he opened his practice in 1947, Anne Tyng and David

39. Genel House, Montgomery County, Pennsylvania, 1948–51. This photograph shows the raised living volume, its roof structure extending to form a trellis projecting out across a stone retaining wall.

39

Wisdom made the move from the former practice with Stonorov to Kahn's new office. Wisdom would remain Kahn's lead associate throughout his career, and Tyng and Kahn had already become involved romantically before the move.[91] At the new office, Tyng began to have an increasingly important effect upon Kahn's designs, her evident brilliance in spatial and structural thinking appealing to Kahn's evolving sense of order. During this same period, from 1946 to 1952, Kahn held the appointment of consulting architect for the Philadelphia City Planning Commission, during which he produced a major urban planning study for the Philadelphia Triangle Area, with new and old buildings woven together and treated with equal attention – unusual for that time of 'urban renewal' and its rampant destruction of older buildings.

The Ehle House project of 1947–8, designed for Haverford, Pennsylvania, is composed of two independent rectangular volumes positioned to make an L-shape in plan, with the stone-floored entry forming the joint between. The plan is quite similar to Wright's prototypical 'Usonian' House in terms of the L-shape itself, the organization of rooms in the two volumes, the entry on the outside corner of the L-shape, and the garden cradled in the inside corner. Kahn raised a butterfly roof over the living room, and both volumes employed Wright's layering of door-top and high roofs, with clerestory windows set between them. The Genel House of 1948–51, built in Montgomery County, Pennsylvania, began as a rigorously ordered T-shaped plan, with the living spaces in the top bar and the bedrooms in the bottom bar, and an open, stone-paved entry court between. As built, the plan is quite close to that of Wright's 1909 Robie House, being composed of two volumes, the bedrooms to the south and the living spaces to the north, which are slid past each other, and anchored where they overlap by the fireplace and stair.

The plan of the Weiss House of 1947–50, also built in Montgomery County, Pennsylvania, is contained in a double square, defined by the continuous roof framing along the south side. Within this precinct Kahn divides the plan into two clear volumes, the living spaces to the west and the bedrooms collected to the east, with the entry a narrow connection between the two volumes. The services are gathered into a central spine that, joining with the entry foyer, connects the two volumes, projecting slightly out of the bedroom block to the east and extending as stone paving to the outdoor fireplace to the west. Low stone walls run along the west side of the entry to the north, and along the east side of the small court and terrace to the south, creating a pinwheel of space at the centre. The whole is covered by an asymmetrical butterfly roof, its frame exposed as a trellis in the small courtyard to the south.

The double-height south facade of the living room of the Weiss House is made of five sections of floor-to-ceiling glass, each 5 feet (1.5 metres) wide, framed in large wooden posts and divided exactly in the middle vertically. Here Kahn invented a system of sliding frames and shutters which allow the window-wall to be opened, closed and shuttered by sliding elements between the upper and lower sections, making possible an extraordinary variety of views, privacy, ventilation and – most importantly – natural lighting. When all the shutters are in the down position, for instance, the room enjoys complete

40

40. Louis Kahn, left, Anne Tyng and Kenneth Welch in Kahn's office at 20th and Walnut Streets, Philadelphia, c.1955. Anne Tyng had just returned to the United States after two years in Rome.
41. Mural on fireplace wall with abstract pyramidal forms, 1955, designed and executed by Louis Kahn in the Weiss House, Montgomery County, Pennsylvania, 1947–50.
42 & 43. Plan and exterior photograph of the Weiss House, 1947–50. The photograph shows the double-height south-facing facade with movable shading panels and operable window sashes. The Weiss House was one of Kahn's first buildings that enabled inhabitants to manipulate natural light.

41

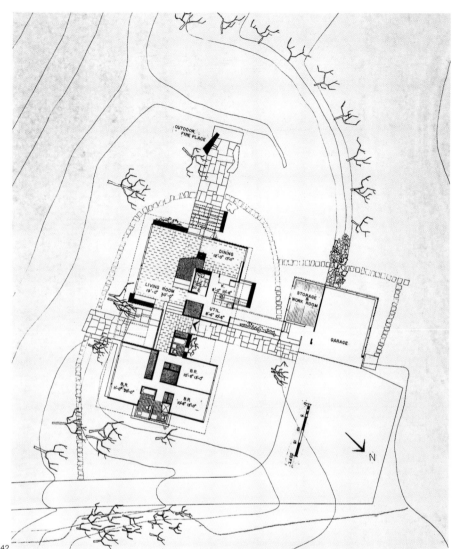

42

43

privacy, with only sky views upward. When the room was being used by the family, however, the five lower and five upper sections would be formed into more random patterns, reflecting the shading and lighting needs of the family's activities at a specific time of the day. This was exactly Kahn's intention.

In a mural designed for the wall next to the Weiss House fireplace, shown on a sketch from this period (though not executed by Kahn until 1955), Kahn employs a square grid to order a series of abstracted pyramidal forms, composed of white (light) and black (shadow) triangles (similar to the mural he had proposed for the Jefferson Expansion Memorial Competition in 1947), and again reflecting the influence of Albers' paintings. Kahn was to employ similar abstracted forms in his 1951 sketches of the Egyptian pyramids, yet it is clear these forms and concepts – at once ancient and modern – were already part of Kahn's definition of contemporary architecture well before his trip to Egypt.

Kahn had been engaged by the Philadelphia Psychiatric Hospital back in 1944, but his earlier designs had not been realized. The Hospital's Radbill Building of 1948–54 and Pincus Occupational Therapy Building of

44

45

1948–51 were built in Philadelphia, and thus were Kahn's first major public buildings. The Radbill Building is three storeys in height and Y-shaped in plan, its three wings differing in length, with a cafeteria and offices on the ground floor and treatment rooms above. In its basic form the design bears some resemblance to Alvar Aalto's famous tuberculosis sanatorium built in Paimio, Finland in 1933. Kahn's focus in the design, as would be typical, was on the issue of sunlight. The south- and east-facing facades received a complex series of sunshades in the form of projecting horizontal slabs which were pierced by square, tubular terracotta sections, producing a rather startling shadow pattern on the building's facade, with constantly changing small trapezoidal shapes of direct sunlight in the larger field of deep shadow. The west-facing wall of the stair hall, in the short wing, has narrow bands of windows set into the wall along the floor and ceiling, providing light but no views. The strong horizontal lines of light wash the floor and ceiling, so that the solid wall mass between appears to float in light.

The Pincus Occupational Therapy Building is a long, narrow, rectangular double-height volume, housing a series of workshops and a large multi-purpose room. The roof is supported on exposed steel trusses which bear on steel columns; these are embedded in the exterior wall along the long east side, and on the long west side are cylindrical in shape and set outside the exterior wall. This west exterior wall, shaded by the cantilevered roof, is composed of continuous full-height windows equipped with large wooden shutter panels, similar to the system that Kahn had developed in the Weiss House living room. But here Kahn has provided added flexibility for the sun and for privacy control, as every other window bay has a shutter that can slide up and down (always leaving one half of the window open to light), while the alternating bays are given a shutter at the bottom that swings open like a door. Thus the lower windows may all be opened, with alternative top windows closed; or all

44 & 45. Exterior and interior photographs of the Radbill Building, Philadelphia Psychiatric Hospital, 1948–54. The interior view shows the narrow horizontal windows set at the ceiling and the floor.

46

47

the lower windows may be closed, leaving all the top windows open; or the occupants may adopt one of the innumerable other possible combinations that might arise from everyday use. As exemplified in these buildings, the introduction of sunlight into inhabited spaces, and the ability of architecture to modulate the quantity and affect the quality of that light, had become Kahn's primary focus in design.

Rome and the power of ruins

By 1950 Kahn had become a leader in his profession, though more through his membership and leadership in organizations such as the T-Square Club of Philadelphia (of which he was president), the American Society of Planners and Architects, and the Architectural Advisory Committee for the Federal Public Housing Agency (of which he was committee chair for the entire east coast region), than for his design work up to that time. He was also considered a leader of the profession for his inspired teaching at Yale, and it was this, and his friendship with George Howe, which led to his appointment in late 1950 as the architect-in-residence at the American Academy in Rome.

Kahn's time at the American Academy was considerably less than the year he spent in Europe in 1928–9, but despite the brevity of this stay the effect on him could hardly have been more profound. To understand the intensity with which he threw himself into this visit, it should be noted that during only three months he made the same number of drawings (ninety) as he had made during the twelve months of his 1928–9 trip. On this occasion Kahn drew with charcoal and pastels, and according to his travel companions from the American Academy took no more than twenty minutes to complete

48

a drawing.[92] Kahn drew ancient Italian, Greek and Egyptian sites, alongside vernacular buildings and landscapes; his drawings from this trip include no examples of modern buildings. Except for a brief visit to the construction site of Le Corbusier's Unité d'Habitation in Marseilles,[93] it appears that Kahn did not attempt to visit any examples of the modern architecture which had so influenced him, and to which he was now so completely committed in his own work. This is a clear indication that Kahn chose his subjects of study on this trip very carefully, focusing intensely on a very few ancient structures.

Starting in December 1950, Kahn was based at the American Academy in Rome, built to the designs of McKim, Mead and White by the American Beaux-Arts establishment to house the Rome Prize Fellows in painting, sculpture, music, architecture, landscape architecture, writing, archaeology, classical studies and art history during their year residency. There Kahn spent time conversing with Frank Brown (Kahn's fellow Yale faculty member), who, as the Academy's resident archaeologist, brought the Roman ruins to life for generations of Fellows. So deep was Brown's understanding of the ancient Roman world and its architecture that he was said to be 'the last living ancient Roman, so at home in the Roman ruins that he seems no longer a part of the modern world'.[94]

As Brown took Kahn through Rome, Ostia and possibly even Pompeii, he pointed out aspects of the Roman architecture that would have been immediately significant for Kahn. Brown begins his book on Roman architecture by stating, 'The architecture of the Romans was, from first to last, an art of shaping space around ritual', and his descriptions of Roman buildings could very well be applied with equal accuracy to Kahn's later work: 'The basilica was ... an augustly luminous volume, doubly wrapped by shadowed galleries', and 'the expertly compact spatial composition, with its running counterpoint of cubical and spherical, dome and cross or barrel vault, gave compelling unity.'[95]

Walking through Rome, Kahn studied its monumental buildings, stripped ages ago of their decoration, their brick relieving arches revealed, their massive brick and concrete structural walls and vaults exposed, showing how they were made. Kahn typically spent only part of his time among the ruins, often sitting in the garden behind the American Academy during the afternoon, saying that what he had already seen was sufficient stimulation to thought for the time being, and that the Roman ruins needed to be contemplated from a distance to be fully understood.[96] Years later, when asked what he did while he was a resident at the Academy, Kahn replied, 'I watched the light.'[97]

Of particular importance to Kahn was Trajan's Market, and its multi-levelled basilica space lit at all levels by natural light: the various methods of constructing openings in its brick walls would have direct parallels in Kahn's later work. The great civic monuments of Rome had an important effect upon Kahn, and he would later speak of the importance to his work of the Pantheon, that great spherical interior space with its central oculus open to the sky. That building became his favourite example of both the need to take each programme back to the very beginning, and the critical part that could be played by institutional architecture if it was fundamentally engaged in civic life.

46 & 47. Exterior and interior photographs of the Pincus Occupational Therapy Building, Philadelphia Psychiatric Hospital, 1948–51. The exterior view shows the steel roof trusses bearing on exterior steel columns; the interior view shows the double-height movable shading panel system, also employed in the Weiss House.
48. A Roman wall, Italy, drawing by Louis Kahn, 1951. Kahn focuses on the masonry mass of the wall, the deep shadows at its openings and the relieving arches seen on its surface.

During that same month Kahn made trips to Siena, Florence, Venice, Pompeii and Paestum. His drawings of the public spaces – the *piazze* – of Italian cities, such as that of Il Campo in Siena, are compelling. Then, early in January 1951, Kahn travelled with a group of Fellows to Egypt and Greece, spending the following two months moving from one ancient site to the next. The group was briefly delayed in Cairo, allowing Kahn a week at the pyramids at Giza, which astonished and overwhelmed him.[98] Kahn's pastel drawings of the pyramids are alive, their pure geometries and earth-tone colours transformed by the sunlight. The drawings reveal that Kahn saw the pyramids not only as enormous masses, timeless and eternal, but also as 'vehicles of light ... reflectors of the sun's rays', as Scully has noted.[99] Kahn's drawings of the temple complexes at Luxor are equally powerful, reflecting both the intensity and movement of the light and the weight and permanence of the stones.

In Greece, Kahn's drawings indicate his understanding of the importance of the landform in ancient Greek sites, and he lavishes as much attention on the buttressed foundations underpinning the Acropolis hill as on the elegant columned monuments standing atop it. He made several drawings of the sunken circular Oracle at Delphi, a site with both spiritual and architectural meaning, typifying the ancient Greek habit of inscribing their sacred spaces into the ground. Kahn has also left multiple sketches of the sacred mountain peak of Arakhova; of the ruined city of Mycenae, the place of origin of the Greek civilization and the temples at Corinth. What all these sites had in common was their massive masonry construction, their precise enclosure of inhabited space and their powerful engagement of the landscape and urban form in the making of monumentally scaled place.

49

50

Though relatively brief, this period of historical rediscovery would prove to be pivotal in Kahn's development as the most important modern architect of his time. It led to his renewed understanding of the importance of history in contemporary design, summarized by his saying that 'what will be has always been'.[100] The eternal quality of heavy construction and the spaces shaped by massive masonry made a lasting impression on Kahn. This is evidenced by the fact that, though the building he had completed just prior to leaving for Rome (the Pincus Occupational Therapy Building) was of steel construction, after his three months abroad Kahn would never again make use of lightweight steel structures, building only with reinforced concrete and masonry.

49 & 50. Egyptian column capitals and Il Campo in Siena, Italy, pastels by Louis Kahn, 1951. When asked what he did on his travels in 1950–51, Kahn replied, 'I watched the light.'

Rediscovering an architecture of mass and structure

From what the space wants to be the unfamiliar may be revealed to the architect. From order he will derive creative force and power of self-criticism to give form to this unfamiliar. Beauty will evolve.[1] LOUIS KAHN

During his time at the American Academy in Rome, Kahn made a startling decision: from that time forward he would not build with light and thin materials but would instead make his architecture out of heavy and thick materials – the structural mass out of which was constructed the great architecture of Rome, Greece and Egypt, which he had recently so movingly experienced. Kahn's refusal to employ the structural construction materials most typical of modern architecture was in effect a rejection of modern architecture's pronounced privileging of lightness, exemplified by Buckminster Fuller's rhetorical question, 'How much does your house weigh?'[2] This fundamental decision would also initiate Kahn's parallel search for a way of making space that would relate structure to inhabited volume, a conception directly opposed to the 'free-plan' disposition of non-load-bearing walls within the universal grid of columns typical of International Style modernism.

Kahn's rediscovery of the architecture of mass and structure was his intuitive response to the call for a return of monumentality in architecture. While in his 1944 essay on monumentality Kahn had used a tubular welded steel structure to demonstrate a modern monumentality, he would now begin to turn more and more to the ancient Roman materials of brick and concrete as his preferred means of achieving monumental space. At the age of fifty, Kahn recognized his own innate sympathy with mass, perhaps dating back to his Beaux-Arts training with its emphasis on mass and void in plan, but more importantly arising from his recognition of his own growing inability to engage light structural materials effectively. As Kahn would eventually say, steel belonged to Mies van der Rohe, who honoured it with his work; Kahn's work would honour concrete and masonry, for with this decision to make space with mass and structure, Kahn found his own way of building, of making architecture.

The fundamental nature of this change in Kahn's conception of architecture, and the entirely different perspective that resulted, is illustrated

Previous page. Louis Kahn at Yale University Art Gallery, 1953. The heavy ceiling structure is the most powerful presence in the space.
1. Louis Kahn in his office, c.1950.
2. Auguste Choisy, up-view axonometric section of San Pietro, Rome by Michelangelo, from *Histoire de l'architecture*, 1899.

by a story told by Vincent Scully. Kahn and he were in Moscow in 1965, and one evening they took a walk together around the Kremlin. As Scully recalls, he said of its domed towers, '"Look how they point", and they do, if you read it that way. But [Kahn] said, "Look, instead, at the way they bring the weight down"'. Scully continues, 'it is true, they are all masonry, and one can really see the compression coming down the wall ... I always thought that was the key to Kahn's architecture. He never went for the gesture ... It was that compression of matter making something, the structure that convinces you of its reality.'[3] While Scully was focusing on what the towers did, on their gesture, pointing towards something absent (as Robert Venturi and the post-modern historicists would also do), Kahn instead focused on what the towers were, on how they were made and structured, on their mass and weight being carried down to the ground, and how this gave the towers such undeniable presence.

Michelangelo, the great Renaissance sculptor and architect whom Kahn later singled out as a significant influence on his thinking, was unusually sensitive to the inner life and nature of his materials, and to the massive weight of stone. One of Michelangelo's favourite sayings, taken from the Tuscan masons as a caution while they worked, but holding deeper meanings for the artist, could also serve as a motto for Kahn's architecture of mass and structure: 'Weight never sleeps.'[4]

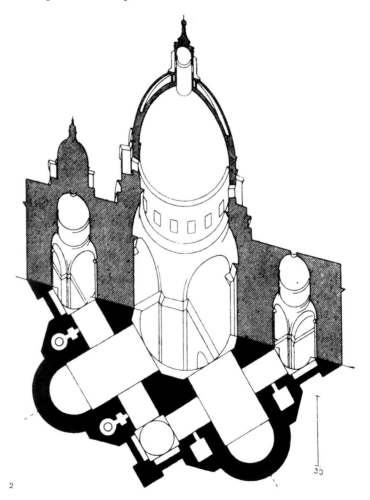

Yale University Art Gallery
New Haven
Connecticut
1951–3

While Kahn was still at the American Academy in Rome, he was commissioned to design the Yale University Art Gallery in New Haven. The brief for the building had been worked out in Kahn's absence by George Howe, who was instrumental in convincing Yale to award the building to Kahn. Philip Goodwin, designer with Edward Durrell Stone of the Museum of Modern Art in New York of 1939, had made designs for the Yale site in 1941 and then again in 1950. When Goodwin withdrew from the project he recommended Philip Johnson, who had begun to teach at Yale while Kahn was in Rome, but both Johnson and Howe insisted that Kahn should receive the commission. Thus while Kahn's building would in fact be the first modern building constructed on Yale's hitherto historicist campus, the precedent had been established by Goodwin's modern design being approved earlier by the university.[5] For a variety of reasons,

including the prospect of construction material rationing for 'non-essential' buildings, due to US involvement in the Korean War, the brief called for the building initially to be both an art gallery and design studios, called the 'Design Laboratories and Exhibition Space'.[6] In fact, the building would function as both the Architecture Department and the Art Gallery extension until the completion of Paul Rudolph's Art and Architecture Building in 1963. Thus while the space would be required to function as studios, offices and art gallery for a number of years, it was ultimately intended to function exclusively as an art gallery. This intention had been given added reinforcement by Katherine Dreier's 1941 donation to Yale of the *Société Anonyme* collection, an unparalleled group of more than 600 modern works of art, given with the understanding that a new art gallery be built to house it.

Kahn's building is sited adjacent to the Yale University Art Gallery of 1928, designed by Edgerton Swartwout, to which it is also connected. Together with that building it formed, at the time of the building's construction, the edge of the Yale campus (p. 78; a). In its overall form, Kahn's Art Gallery is powerful yet understated, its simple rectangular massing alternating between subtly detailed all-brick and all-glass facades. Yet even with its reserved form, Kahn's building addresses the differing characteristics of its site boundaries, with a shallow, stone-paved plaza and solid brick wall fronting Chapel Street to the south, and a carefully designed set of garden terraces opening in front of the building's glass facades looking west and north to the campus. As required in the brief for the interior, Kahn's building provides open, flexible, well-lit spaces on four levels. These are organized in two simple rectangles which together define a double square, the larger volume being a golden-section proportion in plan,[7] and the smaller 40 foot (12 metre) square space recessed on the north and south sides and serving as the link to the existing Art Gallery. The main volume was in turn divided into three primary spaces, with two 40 foot (12 metre) wide column-free galleries flanking a central service zone.

The Art Gallery's primary street facade, on Chapel Street, was from the start of Kahn's design process conceived as a massive wall built of grey-brown-coloured brick, pushed out towards the street and serving as a counterpoint to the more ornate facade of Swartwout's building, with its tall arched windows. This south-facing facade receives sun all day, and its solid surface is relieved only by subtly projecting limestone string-courses which serve to mark the location of the floor-lines within. A smaller section of brick wall is set back at the new building's juncture with the original gallery, creating the small entry court where, up a few steps, one enters through a narrow glass facade between and at right angles to the offset sections of brick wall (p. 78; b). In placing the entry between two sheared planes of the facade, and bringing us into the corner and along the edge of the space – rather than directly into the centre – Kahn employed an entry sequence identical to that often used by Frank Lloyd Wright. It is here at the entry that we can begin to discern the subtle yet insistent manner in which Kahn articulated the building's constituent elements, and the manner in which they are related.

3. Early perspective sketch by Kahn of the Chapel Street elevation, Yale University Art Gallery. Kahn's solid facade for the gallery is in the distance, to the left of the existing 1928 University Gallery.

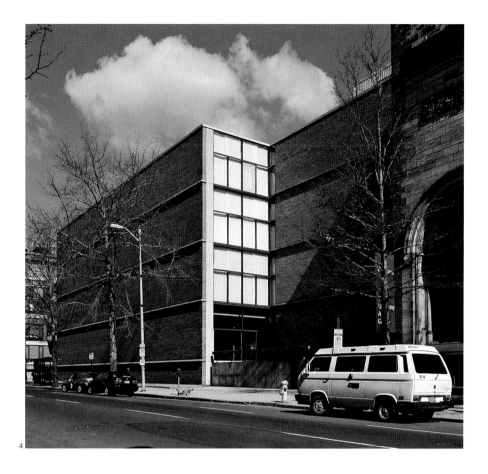

4

At its left edge, the entry facade exposes the depth of the brick wall and the fact that, despite its monolithic character, it is not part of the load-bearing structure. Directly adjacent to the door – so close that we can touch it as we enter – a concrete column stands flush with the glass wall, while the deep concrete edge beams that the column carries can be seen set back behind the glass 'curtain wall' (so called because it is literally 'hung' like a curtain from the primary structure). On the right edge of the glass entry facade the brick wall is pulled away from the corner so that the glass wall turns the corner, creating a small slot of glass peeking out at Chapel Street. Kahn placed a matching vertical slot of glass at the point where the brick wall of the new gallery meets the existing building, and this use of glass – and light – to articulate the joint between masses and planes would become one of Kahn's typical details.

Upon entering, we are brought to a sudden stop by the astonishing ceiling that spreads out over us. A massive triangular grid, spanning galleries measuring 40 by 80 feet (12 by 24 metres) – double squares, literally anchors the interior spaces. In the first example of what would become a common characteristic of Kahn's work, this truly extraordinary ceiling above is far more active than the wood floor below in the making of the room. The most beautiful and meticulously resolved plan of the Yale Art Gallery is the reflected ceiling plan – 'looking up' at the ceiling rather than 'looking down' at the floor – and this was chosen by Kahn as the primary plan with which to represent the gallery in later publications (p. 81; h). As in many works of Wright (such as the

4. Entry court, Chapel Street elevation, Yale University Art Gallery.
5. (Opposite) Chapel Street elevation, Yale University Art Gallery. The solid brick south facade is articulated by stone courses marking floor lines, while the full-height glazing of the west wall reveals the tetrahedral ceiling structure within.

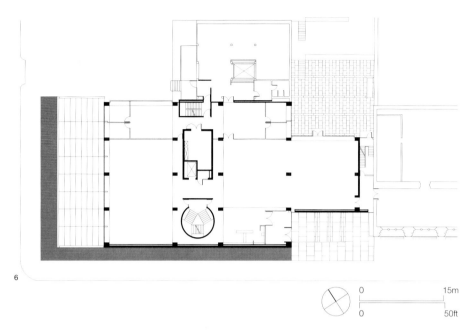

6

0   15m

0   50ft

Darwin Martin House, Unity Temple and the Johnson Wax Building) it is the ceiling overhead that defines the spaces below, and in Kahn's building the articulate heavy mass hovering overhead, as experienced, imparts the paradoxical impression that gravity emanates from above.

As our eyes grow accustomed to the dimmer light of the interior, we perceive that there are spaces opening upwards into the depth of the ceiling, and that, beyond the triangular grid at the bottom, tetrahedral facets (three-sided pyramids, rising from a triangular opening) disappear into the shadowed space contained within the ceiling structure. The openings in the triangular grid alternate between the tetrahedral volumes and interconnected hollow spaces, the latter allowing all mechanical services for the galleries, including ventilation, heating and cooling, electricity and lighting, to be distributed through the spaces within the ceiling structure. Conceived by Kahn as a reinterpretation of the space-frame in concrete, the 3 foot (0.9 metre) thick floor structure comprises a flat concrete slab at the top, structurally bonded to a series of angled concrete beams underneath, which are in turn braced by bent double-triangle elements, together forming the triangular grid and tetrahedral volumes seen within the ceiling space (p. 80; f). Kahn designed the movable exhibition panels used throughout the gallery, which are spaced away from both floor and ceiling by thin tubular supports in order to maintain the continuity and unity of the overall space, dominated by the ceiling.

The exhibition spaces open out diagonally, the bottom surface of the triangular grid of the ceiling lit by the light from the full-height windows to the west and north. Directly ahead of us, across from the entry, is the cylindrical concrete stair enclosure, located in the central service zone, standing out as the only non-rectilinear volume in the space. Typical of Kahn's later designs, this stair is experienced as the central ordering element of the building, the cylindrical form serving to orientate us in the ever-changing exhibition spaces. The stair within the concrete cylinder is triangular in plan, elegantly detailed

6. Ground floor plan of the Yale University Art Gallery; redrawn under author's supervision.
7. North-south section, looking west, through entry court, left, and 40 foot (12 metre) gallery, Yale University Art Gallery; redrawn under author's supervision.

with concrete treads, stainless-steel pipe handrails and wire mesh guards. The concrete cylinder emerges above the roof to terminate in a clerestory light at its top, itself made of three beams forming an equilateral triangle and supporting the circular roof, under which runs a band of glass block the depth of the triangular beams. As the only light in the stair comes from this clerestory at the top, we are compelled to look up, and we again find our space defined by the powerful articulation of the ceiling, an arresting composition of dark triangles floating in a circle of light. Here it is clear that for Kahn, geometry was not an instrumental means but was an end in itself. By employing the circle, triangle and square to structure the Yale Art Gallery plan and give form to its primary elements, Kahn sought to anchor his building in a timeless, cosmic order.

The materials of construction employed in the building form a carefully coordinated group, uniformly exposed by Kahn throughout; both the individual experiential qualities of the materials and the interplay among them are important in our comprehension of the building. The west and north walls of the galleries are full-height curtain walls of glass that run past the tetrahedron floor structure which is folded back at the building edge, with only the 6 inch (15 centimetre) thick floor slab extended to support the metal glazing frames. The inside of the brick exterior walls and the rectangular service block are faced with specially made 5 by 8 inch (13 by 20 centimetre) concrete blocks, better scaled to the smaller interior spatial dimensions than full-size, 8 by 16 inch (20 by 40 centimetre) blocks. The floors of the gallery spaces (under the tetrahedral ceiling) are made of thin oak wood strips (similar to gymnasium floors), while the floor of the service zone is made of polished black terrazzo. This zone has a metal mesh ceiling, covering the mechanical and electrical lines that feed to the galleries from this area. The structural column-piers spaced at 20 by 40 feet

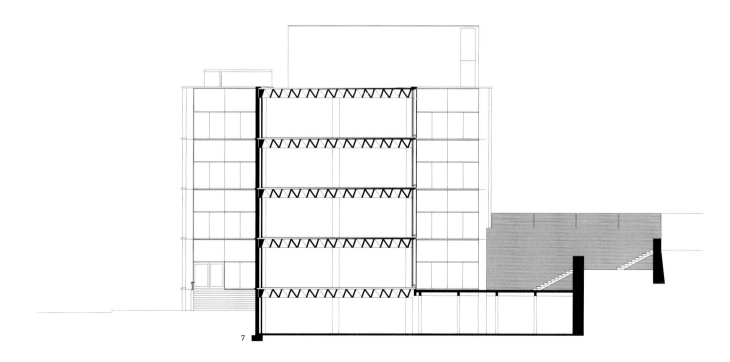

7

(6 by 12 metres) – double squares – and the walls of the cylindrical stair tower are constructed of reinforced concrete, and the pattern of narrow vertical wood boards, used as the formwork into which the concrete was cast, can be clearly seen.

The remarkable floor structure, exposed in the ceiling, is also made of reinforced concrete, but cast into the unique forms of Kahn's design. As can be seen in the construction drawings, the ribs and beams of the tetrahedrons – the bottom or ceiling side – were first cast into metal forms set on temporary plywood supports. After this first concrete pour had set and the metal formwork was removed, the heating and cooling ducts and electrical conduits were threaded through the horizontal passages in the structure. The concrete floor slab was a second pour, structurally anchored to the tetrahedral beams and ribs by reinforcing rods (p. 79; c). Once the concrete had set, the flat slab and the tetrahedral beams and ribs were structurally bonded, acting together to support the 40 foot (12 metre) spans of the gallery spaces. Acoustical boards lined the bottom of the formwork for the floor slab, and became a permanent part of the structure, hidden in the shadowed recesses at the top of the tetrahedral ceiling, and acting to quiet the reverberant structure.

Kahn's first design for the floor structure consisted of a rather mundane series of closely spaced concrete beams cast together with the concrete floor slab; the structure was to be covered by vaulted ceiling panels hung below it (p. 79; d). During the summer of 1951 Kahn conceived of the concrete version of the space-frame, and in this a large measure of credit must be given to the increasing influence of Anne Tyng in Kahn's work of this period. Buckminster Fuller, whom Kahn had known since the 1930s, was at this time the foremost proponent of curved, space-frame constructions called geodesic domes, which Fuller valued for their combination of lightness and strength. In 1951 Fuller, with the assistance of the students, had assembled the first of his paperboard geodesic domes at the Yale School of Architecture (p. 81; g). Following Fuller, Tyng was interested in both the complex geometries and the structural efficiency of space-frames, yet in his designs for the gallery's triangulated floor structure Kahn sought something heavier – hollow spaces buried within mass. It was the hollow spaces within space-frames, not their inherent lightness, that intrigued Kahn, and when Tyng built a model of her design for a lightweight steel space-frame in the office (p. 80; e), Kahn used it to test his idea of feeding service ducts through the openings in the structure.[8]

Thus while Kahn's floor structure was very probably inspired, at least indirectly, by Fuller's geodesic domes and the wide interest in space-frames at the time, Kahn's triangular grid of poured-in-place concrete, exposed in the ceilings below, is a powerful and heavy presence quite the opposite of the lightness obsessively idealized by Fuller. Incorporating the mechanical and lighting services within its dark pyramidal depths, Kahn's floor structure is also the exact opposite of the structurally and spatially neutral flat slab typical of International Style buildings. Again contradictory to International Style planning precepts is the main stair of Kahn's building which, while employing

8. (Opposite) Bottom section of metal formwork for the concrete ceiling structure, Yale University Art Gallery.

9

a curved form typical of the mobile elements in a 'free plan', is in actuality a giant hollow structural column. The concrete cylinder carves its form and volume through the four floors, a vertical spine fusing the layered spaces and anchoring the building. A fourth, and more subtle, manner in which Kahn intentionally contradicted the typical formula of the International Style is in the detailing of the building's glass curtain wall. Multi-storey International Style buildings, following the examples of Mies van der Rohe, invariably were designed so as to emphasize the vertical, most often by fixing I-beams to the exterior face of the wall, running continuously up the building and across the floor lines. By contrast, Kahn's design emphasized the horizontal, present in the heavy massing of the concrete ceiling structure, by

9 & 10. *Société Anonyme* collection and historical collection displayed on Kahn's 'pogo stick' panels, Yale University Art Gallery. The panels do not touch the ceiling or the floor.

12

11. (Opposite) Inside the main stair, Yale University Art Gallery. A triangular stair is set within a cylindrical concrete tower; light fills the tower from a glass-block clerestory band at roof level, which is supported by triangular beams.

12. Interior of Yale University Art Gallery, after renovation by Paul Rudolph; Rudolph's renovations covered Kahn's exposed structure and materials, while the 'pogo stick' display panels were replaced with full-height walls.

13. Interior view at gallery window wall, Yale University Art Gallery. The ceiling structure folds up at the building edge so that the glass wall continues up past the concrete structure to the floor slab above.

14. (Overleaf) North elevation at night, Yale University Art Gallery. Seen from the north court, the glazed curtain wall reveals the concrete ceiling structure within.

13

supporting and stopping the curtain wall at the continuous edge of the slab at each floor, separately framed, with no continuous vertical elements. Thus Kahn's first widely published building may in fact be understood as an intentional and systematic rejection of the then-dominant International Style's characteristic emphasis on lightness, neutral floor slabs, non-bearing free-form walls on the interior, and vertically-continuous curtain walls on the exterior.

Kahn's rediscovery of the architecture of mass, his employment of Euclidian geometric forms and his belief in exposing structure and construction, coming at the beginning of the 1950s, has interesting parallels in the emergence of abstract expressionism in painting. As exemplified in the work of Kahn's Yale faculty colleague Willem de Kooning – as well as his fellow artists Mark Rothko, Robert Motherwell, Barnett Newman, Hans Hofmann, Clyfford Still and Richard Diebenkorn – abstract expressionism involved the employment of solid masses of unmixed colour, fundamental geometries, and the expression of the act of making – such as leaving exposed the underlying construction lines, the layers of over-painting and the movement of the hand recorded in the brush stroke itself. David Anfam, in his study of abstract expressionist painting, notes

> the remarkable affinities between the buildings and thought of the American architect Louis Kahn and the attitudes of ... Newman and Rothko ... [Kahn] pursued as they did over the same years elemental divisions of light and darkness, the structuring of an environment for an individual's spiritual uplift and the sense of 'place', all of which probably articulated ... a reaction against the anonymity of 1950s Establishment culture (encapsulated by the rapid American adoption of Mies's International Style that Still for one loathed).[9]

In the Yale Art Gallery, Kahn had already gone a long way towards demonstrating how these ideas could operate in architectural design, and yet, as would be his habit, he only later articulated them in verbal statements.

Kahn's insistence on what for him was the moral imperative to expose structure, materials and the process of making, was already evident when, at the time the Art Gallery was opened, Kahn said of its unadorned and uncovered construction, 'Its planes speak of Being and Truth.'[10] The terminology is that of existentialist philosophy. In an indication of the effort involved in conceiving architecture that is composed of the most minimal forms and yet, at the same time, is built in such a way that the process of making is powerfully present in our experience of its spaces, Kahn stated, 'I believe in frank architecture. A building is a struggle, not a miracle, and the architect should acknowledge this.'[11] In describing the cylindrical stair of the Art Gallery, Kahn returned to the idea of construction as a 'struggle' that needed to be revealed: 'The through-ties in the formwork ... were left in as holes in the concrete so that in every way, how it was made is apparent. We accentuated the struggle of the building; of building from floor to floor, because the joint is the critical thing in construction ... I believe that these joints are the beginning of ornament.'[12]

Yale University Art Gallery

Concept development

Kahn received the commission for the Yale University Art Gallery when he returned from his appointment at the American Academy in Rome. His time in Italy, Greece and Egypt influenced his choice of materials in that here he built with only heavy materials, masonry and reinforced concrete, rather than the more typical steel. Kahn's structural design was inspired by Buckminster Fuller's contemporary experiments with geodesic domes, space-frames and other lightweight structures (the concept development of the structural system of the ceiling appears overleaf on pages 80–81). Yet he made his gallery's similarly hollow, triangulated floor structure heavy and massive, exactly the opposite of Fuller's search for ever lighter buildings. Kahn was also inspired by ancient interpretations of the triangle, square and circle – forms he used to shape the elements of the gallery, including the stair – originating in the work of the French Enlightenment architects Étienne-Louis Boullée and Claude-Nicolas Ledoux. The facades of Kahn's building, with their masonry walls and horizontal curtain walls of glass were detailed very differently from the facades of the International Style and Mies van der Rohe (early sketches of the building appear along with the site plan and construction documents on these pages).

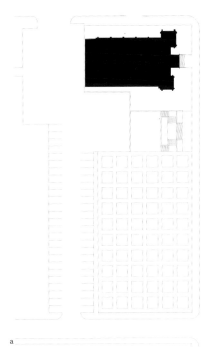
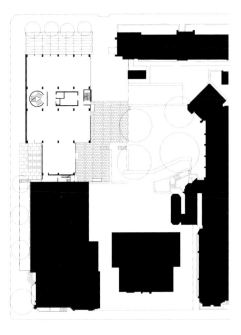

a

a. Site plan of the Yale University Art Gallery and surrounding structures on Chapel Street. The location of the later British Art Center is shown to the south on the left; redrawn under author's supervision.
b. Early perspective drawing of the entry and Chapel Street facade.
c. Section and reflected ceiling detail from construction drawings, showing how the ceiling structure meets the glazed curtain wall.
d. Early perspective of the north, garden facade, showing the vaulted ceiling structure.

b

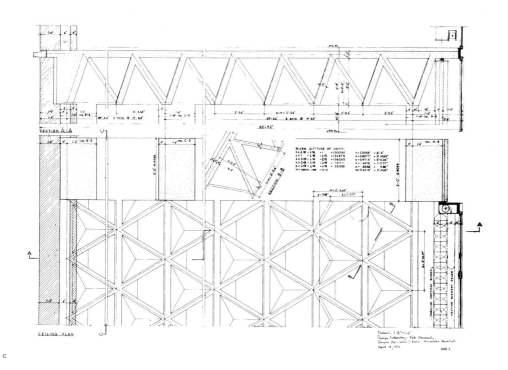

c

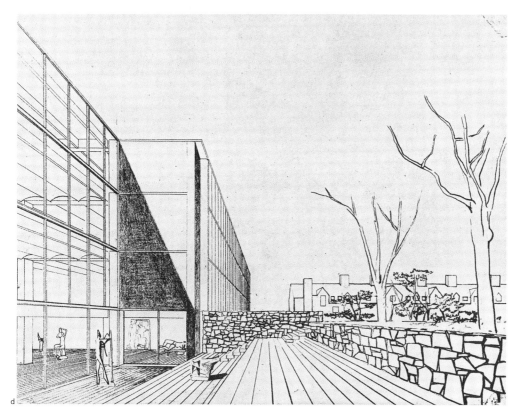

d

e

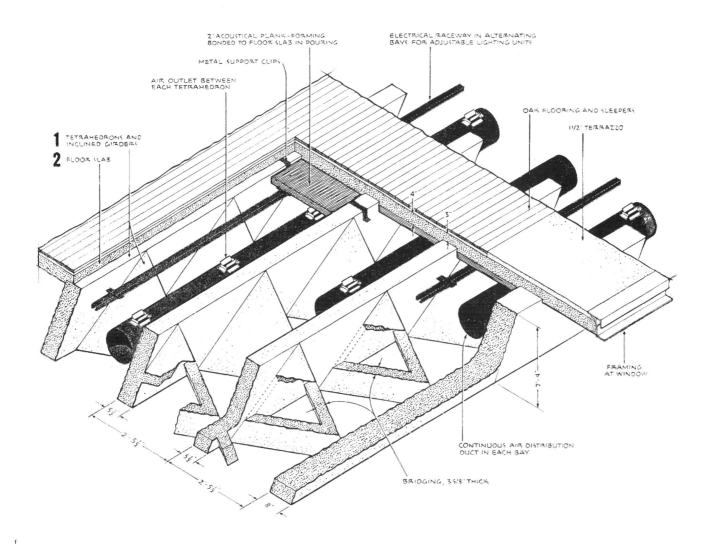

2" ACOUSTICAL PLANK - FORMING
BONDED TO FLOOR SLAB IN POURING

ELECTRICAL RACEWAY IN ALTERNATING
BAYS FOR ADJUSTABLE LIGHTING UNITS

METAL SUPPORT CLIPS

AIR OUTLET BETWEEN
EACH TETRAHEDRON

OAK FLOORING AND SLEEPERS

1 1/2" TERRAZZO

1 TETRAHEDRONS AND
INCLINED GIRDERS

2 FLOOR SLAB

4"

3"

2'-4"

FRAMING
AT WINDOW

5 1/2"

2'-5 1/2"

5 1/2"

2'-5 1/2"

8"

CONTINUOUS AIR DISTRIBUTION
DUCT IN EACH BAY

BRIDGING, 3 5/8" THICK

f

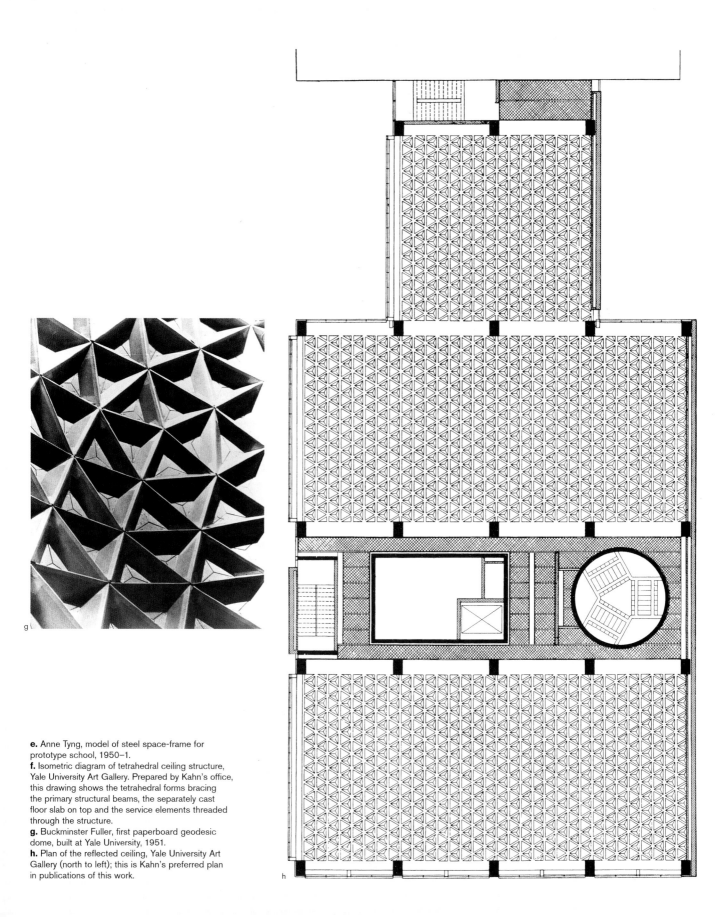

e. Anne Tyng, model of steel space-frame for prototype school, 1950–1.

f. Isometric diagram of tetrahedral ceiling structure, Yale University Art Gallery. Prepared by Kahn's office, this drawing shows the tetrahedral forms bracing the primary structural beams, the separately cast floor slab on top and the service elements threaded through the structure.

g. Buckminster Fuller, first paperboard geodesic dome, built at Yale University, 1951.

h. Plan of the reflected ceiling, Yale University Art Gallery (north to left); this is Kahn's preferred plan in publications of this work.

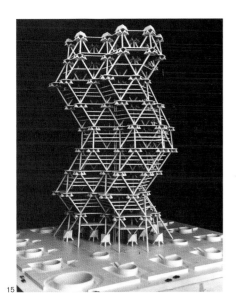

15

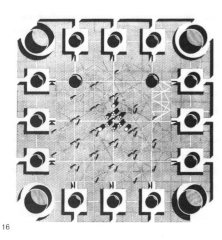

16

15. Model of City Hall Tower, 1956, part of Kahn's 'Plan for Midtown Philadelphia'. This self-bracing tower structure is developed on a triangular grid, producing angled stepping in and out of section.
16. Plan of the plinth at street level, City Hall Tower. A remarkably massive foundation anchors the tetrahedral tower structure to the city street grid, as well as providing parking levels below.

Building with hollow stones

During the period when the Art Gallery was in construction, Kahn, in his capacity as a consulting architect to the Philadelphia Planning Commission, worked on a 'Plan for Midtown Philadelphia', composed of a number of projects from the urban scale to the single building. At the same time Kahn was also commuting each week from Philadelphia to New Haven, and Buckminster Fuller, now also on the faculty at Yale, joined him for the New York to New Haven portion of this trip.[13] Though Kahn and Fuller had widely divergent definitions of architecture (Kahn's massive buildings would surely fail Fuller's weight test), the provocative stimulation Kahn received from these twice-weekly animated discussions with Fuller was immediately evident.

In an extended essay on his midtown Philadelphia plan published in 1953, Kahn introduced, as a general statement of principle, his belief in the essential edification provided by revealing the process of making in the completed building, and how the hollow spaces within modern structure should fundamentally change our conception of architecture. Kahn began this statement by directly connecting these recently evolved concepts to his 1944 definition of monumentality in architecture:

In Gothic times, architects built in solid stones. Now we build with hollow stones. The spaces defined by the members of a structure are as important as the members. The spaces range in scale from the voids of an insulation panel, voids for air, lighting, and heat to circulate, to spaces big enough to walk through or live in. The desire to express voids positively in the design of structure is evidenced by the growing interest and work in the development of space-frames. The forms being experimented with come from a closer knowledge of nature and the outgrowth of the constant search for order. Design habits leading to the concealment of structure have no place in this implied order. Such habits retard the development of an art. I believe that in architecture, as in all art, the artist instinctively keeps the marks which reveal how a thing was done. The feeling that our present-day architecture needs embellishment stems in part from our tendency to fair joints out of sight, to conceal how parts are put together. Structures should be devised which can harbour the mechanical needs of rooms and spaces. Ceilings with structure furred in tend to erase scale. If we were to train ourselves to draw as we build, from the bottom up, when we do, stopping our pencil to make a mark at the joints of pouring or erecting, ornament would grow out of our love for the expression of method. It would follow that the pasting over the construction of lighting and acoustical material, the burying of tortured unwanted ducts, conduits, and pipelines, would become intolerable. The desire to express how it is done would filter through the entire society of building, to architect, engineer, builder, and craftsman.[14]

This statement was written as an introduction to Kahn's design for the City Hall Tower, one of the varied projects Kahn proposed in his 'Plan for Midtown Philadelphia', and developed in various versions from 1952 to 1957.

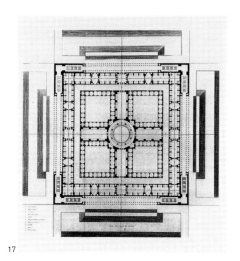

17

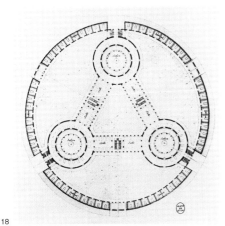

18

All the designs involved Kahn's vision of a modern city hall, one that was able to inspire and accommodate both modern administrative functions and civic activities no longer associated with the town hall, such as the hotel, meeting and performance halls, and cultural centre. Kahn believed that this more comprehensive civic centre was the appropriate modern expression of the sense of community engendered in the early American village green and meeting hall.

Kahn's designs, initially developed with Anne Tyng (credited as 'associated architect'), varied in size from eighteen floors (216 feet/66 metres) to fifty-four floors (616 feet/188 metres) in height, employing various hexagonal plans structured by an equilateral-triangle column assembly. At 66 foot (20 metre) vertical intervals, where three of the concrete columns intersected, the building shifted in section, its exterior glass and metal skin moving in and out to create an astonishingly vibrant and unique urban form. Of equal importance to the angled form of the tower was its powerfully articulated base, a massive sculpted plinth with large cylindrical walls forming open courts that let sunlight into the parking levels below. The tower designs all employed the tetrahedral concrete floor structure, exactly as in the Yale Art Gallery, without any of the modifications that would have brought it closer to being a true space-frame. This is a clear indication that, even five years later, Kahn continued to believe in his design for the floor system of the Art Gallery, despite the considerable criticism of its hybrid nature (neither pure space-frame nor pure slab-and-beam), and that he believed its heavy massive presence overhead was required to impart the necessary gravity to the experience of the City Hall Tower.

While Kahn would employ primary Euclidian geometries throughout his career, this principle only emerged fully formed during the construction of the Yale Art Gallery. In 1952 Kahn's belief in the primacy of the square, circle and triangle was given powerful confirmation by the publication of Emil Kaufmann's study, 'Three Revolutionary Architects, Boullée, Ledoux, and Lequeu', in a Philadelphia journal.[15] The plans of Boullée and Ledoux, to which Kahn had been introduced at architecture school, involve compositions of squares, circles and triangles, and many bear a striking resemblance to designs by Kahn. While some have seen in these formal similarities evidence of direct 'influence' on Kahn,[16] Kahn's design process never involved something so simple as the direct copying of forms. When late in his life Kahn was asked if specific historical forms exerted an 'influence' on his work, he replied, 'No. I would say *influence* is another of those words that can be misinterpreted by everyone. It could mean that you sat down and copied it. I'm not constructed that way. I'm not one who takes things verbatim from some place. I think things out for myself.' When told about publications by critics comparing his building and Hadrian's Villa, as if to show the source of his ideas, Kahn burst out, 'Ridiculous! ... who owns the circle?'[17]

What is certain is that Kaufmann's reintroduction of the great Enlightenment architects Boullée and Ledoux into Kahn's thinking served as both reinforcement and affirmation of his own developing conception. Of the three primary geometric forms, Kahn was particularly interested during

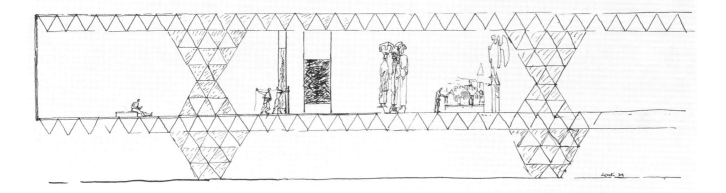

20

this period in the triangle: the basis for space-frame construction, which many leading architectural figures at this time felt to be the major contribution of their generation, a mode of building that would lead to the evolution and rejuvenation of modern architecture. Kahn's continued interest in this structural system is shown by his 1954 sketch for the Yale Art Gallery, drawn after the building was finished, proposing that the columns be constructed of the same triangulated frame as the floor. This post-facto sketch shows the continued influence on Kahn of Anne Tyng, who from autumn 1953 until early 1955 lived in Rome, where she studied with a Fulbright grant and gave birth to Kahn's child, Alexandra.

Kahn's letters to Tyng while she was in Rome describe not only the ongoing projects in the office, including the first version of the 'revised' Yale Art Gallery and City Tower structure sketch, but Kahn's thinking on architecture in general during this critical period in his development. Kahn felt that modern architecture had lost its sense of beginnings, and that 'enumerable architects, some of our best, are still just modifying what has long lost its life'. Echoing Frank Lloyd Wright's concept of the internal room shaping the external form, Kahn stated that 'external shapes must wait until "the nature of the space" unfolds'. Kahn repeatedly expressed frustration at not yet receiving the kinds of commission that would allow him, with his 'classical training and modern ideas', to design buildings that would affect the course of contemporary architecture: 'I must build one of the great buildings of the time.'[18]

In Kahn's design for the Adath Jeshurun Synagogue in Elkins Park, of 1954, he found a third inspiration, after Tyng's interpretation of Fuller's ideas and Kaufmann's presentation of Boullée and Ledoux, for employment of triangular geometry: Frank Lloyd Wright. In giving Kahn the commission in 1954, the building committee of Adath Jeshurun 'clearly felt pressure to produce a landmark that could compete with Wright's recently announced Temple Beth Sholom, to be constructed on a site less than five miles up the

19. Section of alternative design for Yale University Art Gallery, New Haven, Connecticut, 1954, sketch made after construction by Louis Kahn.
20. Frank Lloyd Wright, Beth Sholom Synagogue, Elkins Park, Pennsylvania, 1954 The design is based on a triangular plan with three columns, and an overall tetrahedral form.

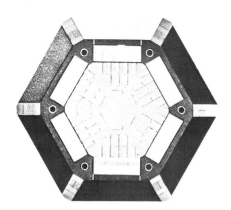

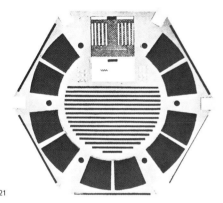

21

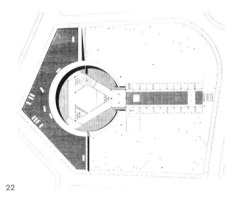

22

21. Two early plans of the sanctuary, Adath Jeshurun Synagogue, Elkins Park, Pennsylvania, 1954. Kahn's initial plans proposed a hexagonal structure with six columns.
22. Final plan of Adath Jeshurun Synagogue, 1954. The sanctuary is now a triangular plan with three column clusters, set within a circular landscape precinct.

road', as Goldhagen has noted.[19] In addition, Kahn was aware that Wright's Beth Sholom Synagogue was proposed to be a modified tetrahedron in overall form, its plan a triangle with its sides folded out slightly (almost exactly the same plan-form as that used by Kahn in his first City Tower design), anchored at its corner by three enormous piers that rose from the concrete base to support the translucent, tent-like pyramidal roof.

While Kahn was keenly interested in Wright's engagement of his own recently favoured geometries of tetrahedron and triangle, he initially proposed a series of hexagonal plans in his designs for Adath Jeshurun. Kahn's first plan employed six large columns, and he set them part-way into the hexagonal plan, creating a smaller, inner sanctuary (to be used for smaller weekly congregations), surrounded by balconies (to accommodate the larger holy day congregations) – in concept quite similar to Wright's Unity Temple.

Kahn's final plan for the synagogue is a triangle, in the corners of which stand three triangular column clusters – each being composed of three triangular groupings of three triangular columns. Each cluster contains a set of triangular stairs (as in the Art Gallery), the mechanical services and skylights. As Kahn described them, 'Each column cluster harbours a stairway as though captured in a great hollow trunk. The columns thus spread grip the floor and roof like outspread fingers. It is what the space wants to be. A place to assemble under a tree.'[20] This fundamental concept of assembly under a tree would remain one of Kahn's most persistent references to the beginnings of architecture and, while he later employed it more often in reference to the origin of the idea of a school, it first emerged in describing the Adath Jeshurun.

Kahn would most probably have arrived at this concept from several sources. These included the passage describing the origins of Jewish religious celebrations taking place 'out-of-doors' in a book entitled *Churches and Temples* given to him by one of the authors, his friend, Henry Kamphoefner, Dean of the School of Design at North Carolina State College;[21] the explicit references to the tree as the *axis mundi* connecting earth to the heavens, forming the beginning point for sacred space, as described in the writings of the theologian and cultural anthropologist, Mircea Eliade;[22] and in *An Autobiography* by Frank Lloyd Wright. In fact, all three metaphors employed by Kahn had earlier been used by Wright in describing his high-rise designs beginning in 1923, with their hollow structural 'trunks' supporting the cantilevered floor 'limbs and branches'; the dendriform columns in the Johnson Wax Building having evolved from Wright's studies of the hollow structure of the saguaro cactus, which he called 'a perfect example of reinforced building construction'; and the Imperial Hotel in Tokyo, where Wright designed the columns to 'carry the floors as a waiter carries his tray on raised fingers'.[23]

On the other hand, as it rose from the plan, the section and elevation of Kahn's Adath Jeshurun was quite unlike Wright's Beth Sholom. Where Wright's building rose in a great pyramidal form to a point high above, Kahn proposed a relatively low, flat-roofed structure, the floor and roof built in a variation of the Art Gallery's triangulated concrete structure, and the whole enclosed by a glass curtain wall with a triangular grid in the early version and

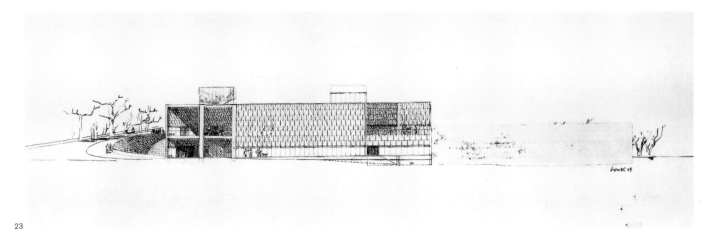

23

24

23. Early elevation study of Adath Jeshurun Synagogue, Elkins Park, Pennsylvania, 1954, drawing by Louis Kahn. A woven triangular curtain wall similar to the City Hall Tower project is employed here.
24. American Federation of Labor (AFL) Medical Services Building, Philadelphia, 1954–6. The cast concrete Vierendeel truss structure, with hexagonal openings, is visible through the glass curtain wall.
25. Elevation of the Weber DeVore House, Springfield, Pennsylvania, 1954. This was Kahn's first use of masonry block-sizing to differentiate structural (smaller) from non-structural (larger) elements. He would repeat this technique many times.
26. Plan of the Weber DeVore House (north to right). Independent pavilions are separated by a wall into public and private zones.
27. Plan of the Adler House, Philadelphia, 1954. Each major room is developed as a separately structured pavilion-like volume.

a rectangular grid in the final scheme. By far the most intriguing aspect of Kahn's design was his proposal to place skylights at the tops of the three column clusters, a reinterpretation of his sky-lit cylindrical stair tower at the Art Gallery. This new use of the hollow space within the structure to bring sunlight into the building would become an important theme in his future designs. Finally, Kahn set the entire triangular plan of the synagogue within a huge landscape circle, half excavated into and half elevated above the sloping site – a feature remarkably similar to the circular agricultural terraces that are a common sight on the hillsides of northern Greece. Unfortunately, Kahn's design for Adath Jeshurun was to remain unrealized.

Perhaps less directly related to the fundamental themes in Kahn's work of this time is his American Federation of Labor (AFL) Medical Services Building, built in Philadelphia in 1954–6, and demolished in 1973 to make way for an expressway. The building was structured using a series of 4 foot (1.2 metre) deep concrete Vierendeel truss-beams (named after their inventor), placed 9 feet (2.7 metres) on centre in both directions to form a square grid, and pierced by large six-sided openings through which the mechanical services ran. Once again, Kahn places a heavy, deep ceiling structure above us, with a relatively quiet, smooth floor below. The powerful grid formed by these truss-beams could be seen clearly from the street through the facade, which was all glass on the lower two floors, and glass alternating with vertical polished granite panels on the upper two floors. In its overall massing, and even more so in the thin horizontal stone line marking the floors and projecting beyond the otherwise flush facade of the building, the AFL Medical Services Building bore an uncanny resemblance to the Art Gallery – a transparent skeletal ghost of a building, marking the last time Kahn would use glass as a skin until after 1970, when it would return in changed form in his final works.

Three unrealized house projects, designed by Kahn during Tyng's time in Rome, indicate a new development in Kahn's concept of the room as the generator of architecture. The Fruchter House project of 1951–4, for Stamford, Connecticut, is composed of three 24 foot (7.3 metre) square pavilions, organized around a triangular central atrium. Each of the square pavilions is divided into four rooms, square in shape, with masonry structural walls

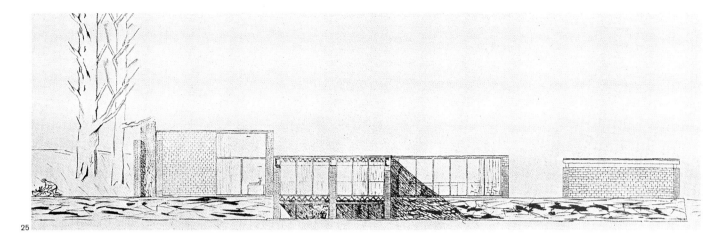

25

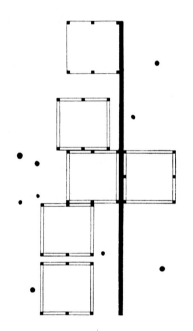

26

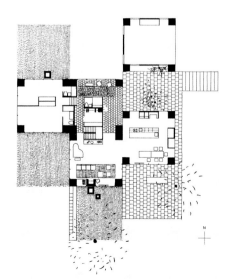

27

forming a pinwheel and anchoring the corners. While Kahn's continued fascination with the triangle during this period gives the Fruchter House its powerful form, it is the remarkable independence of the three square volumes that indicates Kahn's new direction.

In the Adler House project of 1954–7, for Philadelphia, Kahn proposed a series of independent rooms, each housed in its own 26 foot (7.9 metre) square pavilion, framed by four massive 3 1/2 foot (1 metre) square brick piers at the corners, and each initially covered by its own pyramidal roof. In his sketches for this project, Kahn arranged the five square room-pavilions in various configurations, including a cruciform plan as well as the final asymmetrical plan. The final plan, covered by a flat roof, engages square volumes of exterior space, paved on the entry side and grassed on the private side, in dynamic compositions of solids and voids.

The Weber DeVore House project of 1954, proposed for Springfield, Pennsylvania, is a further evolution of this concept, with five 24 foot (7.3 metre) square room-pavilions arranged along a massive retaining wall which divides the house and site into two zones, with the house's public functions set at the top of the rise, to the south, and the bedrooms suspended over the sloping landscape on the other side of the wall, to the north. In plan, the Weber DeVore House is an astonishingly powerful geometric composition, equal in its abstract asymmetry to contemporary works of art,[24] yet at the same time the square aedicule-like pavilions provide an archaic and primitive sense of place and enclosure. Each room is given its own clearly perceivable structure in the form of 18 inch (46 centimetre) square concrete-brick columns set in the four corners, with the four walls between either solid (concrete block) or void (full-height glass). This appears to be Kahn's first proposed use of two scales of concrete block in a masonry wall to distinguish between load-bearing structure (smaller concrete brick) and non-bearing infill (larger concrete block), a technique he would employ for many of his designs over the next two decades.

Jewish Community Center
Trenton, New Jersey
1954–8
Part built

In his designs for the Trenton Jewish Community Center complex Kahn developed the concept of each room as an independent (square) pavilion into a fully articulated method, and in his design and construction of the Bath House, Kahn declared that he found himself as an architect.[25] Kahn's concept of designing with independent spatial units, each with its own integral structure, fused space and its structure in the occupant's experience in a way entirely different from the work of his contemporaries. In his early book on Kahn, Scully noted that 'space, as in the late work of [Frank Lloyd] Wright, the developed International Style, and some contemporary criticism, was no longer to be the whole determinant for Kahn. Nor, as for example in the work of the eminent Beaux-Arts architect, [Auguste] Perret, was structure alone to dominate. Instead, Kahn was to attempt an integral union of space and mass, solid and void.'[26] To which I would add, room and structure.

Kahn's first design for the Trenton Jewish Community Center proposed a separation of the main Community Center structure (with its mix of uses including a gymnasium, locker rooms, a large auditorium and numerous small meeting rooms organized along a linear circulation spine) from the

swimming pool and its Bath House. The main building was positioned parallel to the entry road to the south-east, and the pool and Bath House hidden behind it to the north-west, across a grass lawn. Beyond the Bath House were to be located the playing fields and Day Camp structures (p. 104; a). As the client wished to have the swimming pools functioning on the site as soon as possible, Kahn's designs of the first year were predominantly for the Bath House. Kahn began with two squares, one being the raised earth plinth or terrace into which the pools were to be sunk, and the other a matching square bosquet of trees.

In early February 1955 Kahn placed the Bath House as a rectangular volume, running full-width between the squares of the pool plinth and the trees. In this intriguing scheme, one entered the Bath House by first walking through the square bosquet of trees, and the Bath House was not so much an object-building as a thick infill 'wall' between the pool and the grove. In a design dated a week later, Kahn designed the Bath House as a smaller compact square and positioned it along the north-east side centre of the pool terrace, opposite the square bosquet of trees, with entry now directly into the Bath House from the main lawn. Notes from a meeting with the client were made directly on this drawing, and Kahn also sketched roof concepts, including a rotated square form in plan and a series of pyramids in elevation, both of which would eventually be employed in roofing the Bath House (p. 105; f).

Kahn's next step in the design of the Bath House was to have the greatest implication for his architecture: the plan now assumed its definitive form as a cruciform, with four pavilions comprising the arms and an open court at the centre. The cruciform plan would become, along with the square, a fundamental starting point for Kahn in his later designs, and while this is the first instance where Kahn carried this concept through to construction, he had proposed a cruciform plan in earlier projects, including a sketch for the Adler House of the previous year (p. 105; e).[27] While it is likely that Kahn would have been aware of cruciform plan designs published the previous year, including at least one with pyramidal roof forms,[28] this does not explain the primordial power which Kahn was able to elicit from these simple, universal forms in his design for the Bath House.

The cruciform is such a fundamental and ancient geometric figure, used in building since prehistoric times, and belonging to all as part of our human heritage,[29] that one is amazed it could hold such new inventive power for Kahn at this critical moment in his career. Kahn's highly personal rediscovery and redeployment of primary forms, such as the cruciform, square, circle and triangle (pyramid) that he employed on the Bath House, was a new beginning both in Kahn's architecture and in architecture as a whole. As Scully has noted, 'The impression becomes inescapable 'that in Kahn, as once in Wright, architecture began anew. With Kahn, as with Wright, the germinal project was cross-axial in plan.'[30] We shall see that this small Bath House will play as important a part in Kahn's architectural development as the Prairie House had played in Wright's, and that Kahn would employ a number of design concepts drawn from Wright's work.

The design of the basic concrete-block-walled cruciform plan was set by April 1955, and involves four square rooms, 38 feet (11.5 metres) on a side, with a 22 foot

(6.7 metre) clear space in the centre and four 8 foot (2.4 metre) square, U-shaped 'hollow columns' at their corners (p. 105; c). These four square rooms overlap at the centre, sharing the four hollow columns that define the open court, also 22 feet (6.7 metres) square. This overlapping of the volumes at the hollow columns created a tartan grid plan, with wider primary spaces (22 feet/6.7 metres across) and narrower secondary zones 8 feet (2.4 metres) across, alternating in both directions. All the concrete block walls, including those that make the hollow columns, are 10 feet (3 metres) tall. Above the hollow columns are set 8 foot (2.4 metre) square concrete caps, which roof the spaces housed in these square corner-piers and carry at their centres the edge beams of the larger wood roofs above.

These hollow columns were a major development for Kahn, in that they combined and gave form to two important concepts: first, that modern architects build with 'hollow stones', as he had said earlier; and second, that architectural space consists of spaces which are *served* – the primary uses of the building – and spaces that *serve*, the 'servant' spaces. These contain the various services, including heating and air conditioning, electrical and plumbing, together with structure, storage and other uses without which the primary functions of the building could not take place. Kahn combined these concepts in the Bath House, making hollow columns that housed the service, structure and circulation elements required for the building, thus freeing the 'served' spaces between the hollow columns for inhabitation and use. Rather than disappearing behind coverings, in the Bath House the 'servant' spaces become the most powerful element in the plan, the grid of massive 8 foot (2.4 metre) square hollow columns acting to structure and give order to the primary served rooms, literally forming the space in which they can appear.

The entry room, where there is a desk and where clothing baskets are kept, has its three outer walls set flush with the inner edge of the hollow columns, so that the hollow columns are set forward like corner towers as we approach around them. The major rooms to the left and right, containing the changing rooms, showers and toilets for women and men, have their three outer walls set flush with the outer edge of the hollow columns. The walls separating the women's and men's changing rooms from the central court are set on the centre-line of the 8 foot (2.4 metre) square hollow columns, and extend 2 feet (0.6 metres) into the open space of each U-shape to create a privacy vestibule at both corners. The room leading to the pools, across the court from the entry, has no walls between the hollow columns, and is open in all four directions; the pools are accessed up a 22 foot (6.7 metre) wide flight of stairs between the last set of hollow columns.

The front elevation of the Bath House is solid, showing no opening, and the dual entries, located at the inner corners on either side, are found by moving around this projecting volume – one must choose, left or right. Once inside, access to the changing rooms is also through corner entries, in this case from the four corners of the central court. While this was not Kahn's first use of a closed front facade and corner entry (the Yale Art Gallery had both),[31] here Kahn made systematic his employment of the cross-axial cruciform and cubic volumes while denying (the expected) central axial entry – an ordering

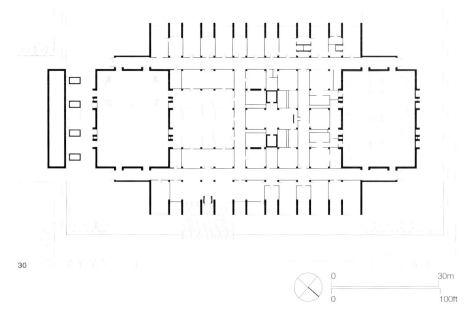

30

0   30m
0   100ft

principle drawn directly from the Prairie Period work of Frank Lloyd Wright. Here, in the unusual dual equal entries, there are direct precedents in Wright's own Studio in Oak Park, Illinois of 1895, the Unity Temple of 1905–8 and the Hardy House in Racine, Wisconsin of 1905.

Three other important aspects of our experience of Kahn's Bath House are typical of Wright's Prairie Period work: first is the employment of the tartan grid of narrow–wide–narrow spatial zones or bays; second, making the square crossing of the narrow bays into service (or 'servant') spaces (as Wright had done most famously in the brick piers housing heaters, lights and bookcases in the Darwin Martin House, Buffalo, New York, 1903–5); and third, the movement along the edges rather than the centres of otherwise axially symmetrical rooms, encouraged by entering at the corners. In the Bath House, Kahn elegantly suggests this peripheral movement to the changing-room corner entries by placing a 22 foot (6.7 metre) diameter circle at the centre of the court, originally intended to be gravel, but realized as grass – the only space without a concrete floor in the building.

This surprisingly primitive circle, with its seemingly unfinished stone edge, establishing a dialogue between earth and sky at the very centre of the building, is one of the most effective aspects of our experience of the Bath House, literally grounding us even as the sky is opened overhead. While the plan of the Bath House and its central court may be clearly related to Roman atrium houses, the earthen circle remains the building's most mysterious element. The slightly swelling circular form reminds us of Michelangelo's piazza at the Capitol in Rome, the floor of the Pantheon, and the circular stone-lined disc at the central focus of ancient Greek theatres – all considered presentations of the 'navel' of the world, the *axis mundi* joining earth and sky.

Plans and sections of the first cruciform plan indicate that from the start Kahn intended to cover the four peripheral, masonry-walled spaces of the Bath

29. (Previous page) Central court, Bath House, Jewish Community Center. The stone circle at the centre of the square court, suggestive of a ruin, was left incomplete on purpose by Kahn.
30 & 31. Plan and elevations of the main building of the Jewish Community Center, June 1958, final design. Low, square pyramid roofs are clustered around higher long-span, precast concrete, folded plate roof structures; redrawn under author's supervision.

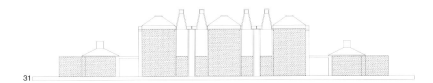

31

House with a lightweight roof structure, consisting of four independent square elements, each 30 feet (9 metres) square, and touching only at their inner corners.[32] Kahn's initial design, developed in May, built as a model in June, and shown on the drawings as late as October, involved a steel pipe structure clad in corrugated metal to form a shallow X-shape in section, with ridges running diagonally from corner to corner, with valleys at the centre of each span (p. 104; b). These valleys would drain into scuppers, which would in turn direct the rainwater runoff into circular basins or splash-pads, set at the centre of each outside wall, as was shown clearly on the plan of 28 April 1955 (p. 105; c).

The ridges of this roof plan and the roof designs for the Bath House which followed run diagonally from corner to corner of each square space, marking the first time that Kahn had employed a rotated square in a built work. The rotated square is an ancient proportioning device employed in architectural design, which was extensively used in medieval times, particularly as a method of determining the appropriate structural and aesthetic proportions for each diminishing stage of Gothic cathedral towers. The rotated square was revived by early modern architects intent upon basing their work on the principles of Gothic rather than classical architecture; examples would include the father of modern Dutch architecture, Hendrik Petrus Berlage, and Frank Lloyd Wright.

Kahn's library included numerous books on medieval architecture, and one book on Gothic buildings was marked at the section entitled, 'Rules for constructing a pinnacle'.[33] On the same page are sequential diagrams illustrating the procedure for rotating the square. A second square is constructed inside the starting square, rotated 45 degrees from the first, and diminished exactly one quarter in dimension and one-half in area. A second, smaller rotated square aligns with the starting outer square, and diminishes to one half the original dimension and one quarter the area – and so on (p. 105; d). In the Bath House, Kahn used rotated squares not only to give form to the roof but also to order and proportion the grid of squares that underlies the plan, and in this the rotated square may be understood as an integral extension of Kahn's habit of always 'starting with a square'.

Kahn's initial roof design, a merging of the triangulated space-frame with traditional pitched roof forms, was replaced by the final four-pyramidal design only in the autumn, several months after the Bath House and pool were officially opened – without roofs – in late July 1955.[34] As built, the Bath House roofs are pyramidal in form, constructed using a wood frame which is exposed and visible from underneath, with a square oculus opened at each of their centres. The base of the wood frame is braced at the centre of each span by a rotated square of wood beams, which are in turn braced to the corners of the main frame by secondary beams, and the whole is tied together by cable stays across the centre. The wood frame at the outer, lower edge of each roof does not sit directly on the four hollow columns, but is lifted off the concrete cap by a bearing block so that the lightweight wood roofs float above the heavy, earth-bound masonry walls that enclose the open-air spaces.

33

This 'floating' of the roof above the masonry walls creates the most astonishing aspect in the experience of this small building, namely the variety of daylight and the precision with which it defines the various rooms within. The edge of the roof aligns with the walls only between the changing rooms and the central court, leaving a gap of only 1 foot (30 centimetres) through which sunlight enters horizontally, giving a glimpse of the sky over the central court to the changing rooms. Everywhere else in the Bath House the roofs either overhang the walls by 4 feet (1.2 metres), as at the entry and basket room, creating deep shadow effects (and protection from rain) on the three entry facades, or are set in 4 feet (1.2 metres) from the outer walls, as at the three outer walls of the changing rooms. This 4 foot (1.2 metre) opening to the sky along the edges of the changing rooms allows sunlight to fall directly into the space, bathing the inside surfaces of the walls, as well as giving a generous view upwards to the sky all around.

The small oculus at the top of each pyramidal roof gives very little light by comparison to these large spaces between wall and roof edge, yet the glimpse of passing clouds seen through the central opening again reminds us of the experience of the Pantheon, just as the strong side-light and wide views of the sky reminds us of Trajan's Market. In Kahn's Bath House we are enclosed securely all around by thick, heavy masonry walls, covered by that most primal of roof forms, the pyramid, our privacy further protected by the dark labyrinthine entries housed in massive corner piers. Yet at the same moment we can look out to the sky in all directions from under the paradoxically lightweight pyramidal roof, floating like a tent or kite above us, feeling connected to the larger landscape in a way perfectly appropriate to our activity of swimming.

For contemporary architects, the Bath House came as a revelation – at once modern, being built of concrete block and wood frame (the most typical and inexpensive of materials), and yet at the same time ancient, a mysterious and

32. Bath House, Jewish Community Center.
Note the mural by Kahn at the entry.
33. Bath House, Jewish Community Center.
This view is from the raised swimming-pool plinth.

strangely moving place where earth and sky meet, signified by the unfinished stone circle in its central court. For Kahn it was an absolutely critical and pivotal design, crystallizing his concepts of 'servant' and 'served' spaces; the tartan grid plan; building with 'hollow stones'; and the cruciform, square and rotated-square planning concepts; and he immediately sought to develop its implications at a larger scale in his designs for the rest of the Community Center.

Kahn succinctly summarized the lessons of the Bath House in his 1957 article in *Perspecta*, subtitled 'Order of Spaces Integrated with Order of Construction':

The Trenton Bath House is derived from a concept of space order in which the hollow columns supporting the pyramid roofs distinguish the spaces that serve from those being served. The thirty-by-thirty-foot spaces under the roofs remain undivided and the eight-by-eight-foot hollow columns provide the needs of smaller spaces ... This Bath House had simple space requirements. The Community Building now being planned ... is a further development of this concept of space order. Spaces of a variety of dimension and character supported by their own space needs lend themselves to the development of meaningful form by space distinctions in a more complex hierarchy of spaces.[35]

From the earliest site plans for the whole Trenton Jewish Community Center complex, Kahn's plans involved extensive landscape design as an integrated part of the architectural planning. Rather than positioning his buildings on the site as objects in an open field, Kahn wove them into a fabric of exterior spaces constructed and shaped by planted rows and gridded block-like masses of trees, sharply defined paved courts and broad circular grass lawns like great outdoor rooms, each given its own 'play' function. While the location of the Bath House and pool plinth was fixed early in the design process, with construction beginning in May 1955, Kahn changed the orientation of the main Community Center building in June, rotating it 90 degrees so that it now framed a long space that opened off the entry road and terminated in the Bath House, which was previously hidden behind the main building.

The second design for the Community Center, which Kahn worked on from early June 1955 until late 1956, was based upon a grid of octagonal spaces, which meet adjacent octagons on four sides and meet smaller square volumes at the other four sides (p. 106; g). Kahn intended these octagonal forms to encompass both plan and section, and the resulting elevations suggest a geodesic structure, leading some to conclude that this plan was developed by Anne Tyng (who would later design a very similar plan during the early stages of the Bryn Mawr Dormitory project), but it is clear that this design was of Kahn's making. In a site plan of early June, Kahn renders the hollow columns of the Bath House in the same manner that he renders the small square spaces of the Community Center, clearly indicating his intention that the smaller squares should act as the hollow columns for the Community Center, serving the octagon spaces between them. Thus, despite their radically differing geometries, the underlying structure of the Bath House was the source of the Community Center plan.

Kahn presented this design for the Bath House and this second design for the Community Center, and discussed them both at length with the British historian and theorist, Colin Rowe, and the US painter, Robert Slutzky, when they visited Kahn's office in late 1955.[36] It was doubtless this visit, and the gift to Kahn from Rowe of Rudolf Wittkower's book *Architectural Principles in the Age of Humanism*[37] – an extensive analysis of the tartan planning grids and interior proportioning systems of Renaissance buildings – that stimulated Kahn's interest in precisely defining what he had found in designing the Bath House, what he called in his notebooks 'the bay system' of room-making (p 106; h & i). In his notes, Kahn began by criticizing the separation of structure and space in International Style architecture: 'Space made by a dome then divided by walls is not the same space ... A room should be a constructed entity or an ordered segment of a construction system.' Reflecting his discussions with Rowe, and the diagrams of Rowe's teacher Wittkower, Kahn went on to write, under the heading 'The Palladian Plan': 'I have discovered what probably everyone else has found, that a bay system is a room system. A room is a defined space – defined by the way it is made.'[38] Kahn sought an integration of inhabited space – in both plan and section – with

34. (Previous page) Changing room, Bath House, Jewish Community Center. Here a hollow column is employed as the entry from the central court, left.
35. Wooden roof structure with central oculus, Bath House, Jewish Community Center.

structure and construction, where the making of structure was also at the same time the making of space.

Sometime in late 1956 Kahn abandoned the octagonal-unit scheme and developed a scheme based upon a tartan grid and square spatial units similar to the Bath House. This third Community Center plan may be considered the first of Kahn's monastic plan-types, its grid of small cellular spaces – each covered with its own dome-like pyramidal roof – surrounding larger rooms and courts at the centre, being clearly related to the plan configurations of medieval and Renaissance monastery buildings. This third plan was composed of a rectangular tartan grid of 20 foot (6 metre) square, pyramid-roofed primary spaces (each with a cubic glass skylight lantern at its peak), with 10 foot (3 metre) wide secondary zones between, creating a grid of 10 foot (3 metre) square structural column clusters at the corners of the primary spaces (p. 107; j & k). While this tartan grid of square column clusters (hollow columns) gave this plan an even stronger resemblance to Wright's Darwin Martin House than the earlier Bath House, Kahn's building would have provided a radically different experience within. As can be seen in Kahn's perspective studies of the interior, his third Community Center design created individual, cellular rooms under each square pyramidal roof which are quite independent, so that space would have been held within them, not flowing and interpenetrating as it did in Wright's buildings (p. 109; p).

This cellular character of the space, each room an identical, independent, self-supported volume, would prove to be both the greatest strength and the greatest weakness of Kahn's square-grid design for the Community Center. In developing this third design, the largest spaces in the building's 'complex hierarchy of spaces', the gymnasium and auditorium, with their requirement for taller ceilings and long spans without columns, proved especially difficult to accommodate in the small-scale cellular order Kahn had conceived. In Kahn's initial version of this third design, documented in a large model, he proposed lifting twelve of the pyramidal roof shells on massive deep Vierendeel trusses to create the double-height gymnasium, as well as lifting four roof shells one half-level to create the auditorium (p. 109; o). In this way the building's 'spaces of a variety of dimension and character' – the main single-storey cellular mass and these two larger spaces – were integrated and given a uniform scale and texture by all sharing this fabric-like covering of identical pyramidal roof shells.

That Kahn was aware that this third design for the Community Center was an important breakthrough is evidenced by his publishing the drawings and model in both the May 1957 *Architectural Review*, a British magazine, and in Volume 4 of Yale's *Perspecta* that same year. While historians have often focused on this scheme, no doubt due to its wide publicity, Kahn was not satisfied with this plan, with its varying scale spaces covered by the uniform roofing grid of 20 foot (6 metre) square pyramids, and felt compelled to redesign in search of an appropriate expression for the Community Center's hierarchy of spaces. Kahn's next design, developed in the summer of 1957, was a variation on this third scheme, and proposed covering the gymnasium with a series of longer-span, precast concrete, folded plate roof beams, covering the auditorium with a large pyramidal form topped by a cruciform light monitor, while leaving the rest of the building covered by the one-storey 20 foot (6 metre) square pyramidal roof forms. Kahn also broke the strict rectilinear massing of the previous scheme by adding two pyramid-roofed entry porches, one at each side of the gymnasium, which create a shallow entry court and reflecting pool facing the 'community green'.

The site plan for this design, dated 1 July 1957, is the most elegant that Kahn proposed for the Jewish Community Center project, and is among the most beautiful landscape designs of his entire career, showing his mastery of landform, landscape walls, paved terraces, trees and plantings in the creation of spaces for inhabitation (p. 107; l). Tightly spaced rows of trees are marshalled to shape exterior spaces rigorously, including the two narrow bosquets framing the 'community green' onto which the Community Center and Bath House fronted; the U-shaped rows of trees that surround the pool plinth on three sides, with the Bath House set between them on the fourth side; the square grouping of trees surrounding the Day Camp in the far western corner of the site; and even the parking, strictly ordered in eight court-like spaces, is divided and framed by rows of trees on all four sides, which, together with the Community Center building, defines the 'community green' (p. 108; m).

Even as Kahn believed he was developing an ever more resolved design for the Jewish Community Center, his clients were at the same time becoming ever less certain as to exactly what functions and spaces they thought should be included in their building.[39] While his clients' demands for repeated revisions to the design were undoubtedly frustrating for Kahn, he always welcomed the opportunity for further design, being convinced of the simple fact that the longer he had to work on a project, the better it would be.

Kahn's next scheme, designed in early 1958, is a transitional one, being mid-way between the previous, third scheme and the final, fourth design. In this intermediate plan, Kahn rotated the gymnasium 90 degrees, consolidated the two interior courts of the previous schemes into one, located the (single) entry on the central axis of this court, and created the beginning of a cruciform massing by projecting small wings out at either narrow end of the building.

The fourth and final design for the Jewish Community Center was completed by June 1958, and this was the only scheme for the main building that Kahn fully developed through preliminary construction drawings, which are dated 11 August 1958. The gymnasium and auditorium are placed at either end of the plan, with two of their three bays projecting out of the building. All the spaces of the building are once again covered by the uniform grid of 20 foot (6 metre) square pyramidal roof shells or domes, now proposed to be of precast concrete, and the nine domes each over the column-less gymnasium and auditorium are supported by long-span, inverted V-shaped, precast concrete, folded plate beams.

36

36. Detail of the wooden roof at the central oculus, Bath House, Jewish Community Center.

Kahn's employment of precast, pre-stressed reinforced concrete structures in this final design doubtlessly reflects his recently initiated association with August Komendant, a structural engineer specializing in this form of construction. Komendant would serve as Kahn's primary consultant on the majority of his commissions for the rest of his career, and though Komendant does not discuss the Jewish Community Center in his book on his involvement with Kahn, the roof designs for this final scheme reflect Kahn's new knowledge of this material and its process of fabrication. Shortly after they first met, in the autumn of 1956, Kahn brought a group of his students with him when he visited a concrete precasting and pre-stressing plant in Lakewood, New Jersey, for which Komendant served as a consultant.[40] For Kahn, this then-emerging construction material was a revelation – a heavy, massive material that could nevertheless be formed into structural elements of infinite variety and exquisite refinement, their shape the precise expression of structural forces they carried. From that

point forward, Kahn would employ precast, pre-stressed and post-tensioned concrete structural elements on virtually all of his commissions.

In Kahn's final design, the somewhat labyrinthine circulation pattern of the earlier schemes is clarified by the provision of two corridors running the length of the building on the outer edges of the gymnasium and auditorium. Between these corridors is placed the court (p. 109; q), with the entry centred upon it, and the various service spaces such as locker rooms. On the outside of these corridors are placed the smaller meeting rooms, with windows to the exterior. The exterior wall is given a syncopated rhythm by the alternating projection of the 20 foot (6 metre) primary spaces and the recession of the 10 foot (3 metre) service zones – producing in plan an effect very similar to what Kahn would later design for the Rochester Unitarian Church. The exterior walls would have clearly distinguished between the load-bearing columns, to be cast-in-place concrete, and the non-load-bearing infill walls, to be built of concrete block. Despite its being virtually ignored by historians studying Kahn, of all his designs for this project this fourth and final design for the Jewish Community Center was clearly both the most elegantly resolved design *and* the easiest to build. It is a great loss for architecture that this final design of Kahn's was not realized.[41]

37. Day Camp, Jewish Community Center. The camp comprises two open pavilions and two closed service structures. This recent photograph shows the overgrown condition of the Day Camp, with the circular plinth no longer visible.

Following completion of the Bath House, the only other element of Kahn's design for the Jewish Community Center to be built was the Day Camp. Located at the far western corner of the site, this modest cluster of four buildings is nevertheless an important counterpoint to the rest of Kahn's overall site design. The final design, dated 8 July 1957 and almost immediately constructed, places the four structures on a circular low plinth, whose dimensions, 56 feet (17 metres) in radius and 112 feet (34 metres) in diameter, would prove to be of particular fascination for Kahn, recurring in building designs throughout his career (p. 108; m). The encircling plinth of the Day Camp recalls the stone circle found in the central atrium of the Bath House. In stark contrast to all the other trees proposed by Kahn in his site plan of the same date, which were ordered in strictly regimented, closely spaced rows, the trees surrounding the Day Camp were to be randomly spaced, and the circle-in-square grouping that they form is highly irregular. The four structures of the Day Camp are also positioned in a way that is radically different from the other buildings – rotated 45 degrees from the grid of the Bath House and Community Center, and then subtly shifted off axis to form a loose grouping around a central court space with open corners and a hearth. Kahn's plan of the Day Camp is clearly related to the planning of ancient Greek sites, in the manner in which buildings are shifted from parallel and perpendicular in order to open up specific views to the larger landscape.[42]

Jewish Community Center

Concept development

In his designs for the Jewish Community Center and Bath House, Kahn first developed the concept of each room as an independent, pavilion-like structure. He began by organizing both the interior and exterior programme volumes as a series of squares, and the landscape plans throughout this project exemplify Kahn's belief in shaping exterior space with the same rigour as interior space. The Bath House, which with the open-air Day Camp was the only realized portion of the design, was Kahn's first full employment of the cruciform plan, the primary plan form of Frank Lloyd Wright. A series of overlapping square volumes, the Bath House also engages the rotated square as an ordering principle (as shown on these pages). While Kahn's early plans for the Community Center were composed of 'organic' octagonal modules, he later rejected this approach in preference for a bay system, the tartan or a-b-a grid of both Wright and the Renaissance architects. In the unrealized main building of the Community Center, Kahn also first proposed a pre-cast, pre-stressed concrete roof structure (drawings related to the development of the Community Center building appear overleaf). The definitive scheme, including the Day Camp, is documented on pages 108–9.

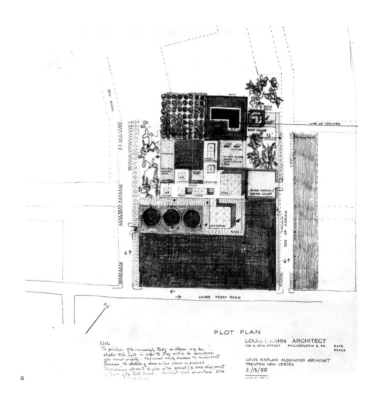

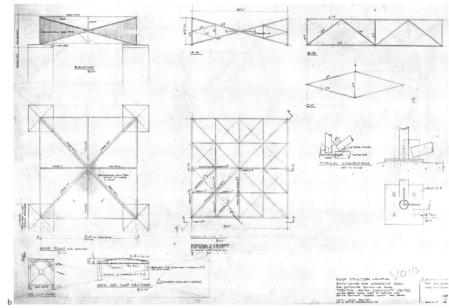

a. Early site plan, Jewish Community Center, Trenton, New Jersey, March 1955. The Bath House and square grouping of trees are at the top, the main building in the centre, and the entry lawn and playing fields at the bottom.
b. Plan, elevation and section of an early steel-structured Bath House roof design, 20–24 May 1955.

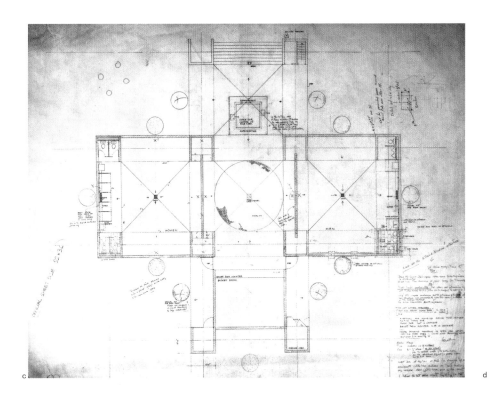

c

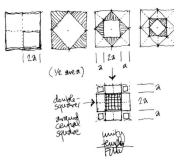

d

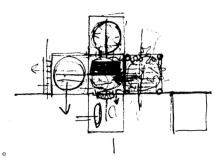

e

f

c. Plan of the Bath House, Jewish Community
Center, 28 April 1955.
d. Diagram of the development of the rotated
square (above), with application to Frank Lloyd
Wright's 1905–8 Unity Temple plan (below);
drawing by author.
e. Sketch plan of the Adler House, Philadelphia,
1954; drawing by Kahn. This is Kahn's first use
of the cruciform in plan.
f. Early sketch plan of the Bath House, Jewish
Community Center, 13 March 1955. Kahn's meeting
notes and his roof sketch studies are visible at the
top edge of the drawing.

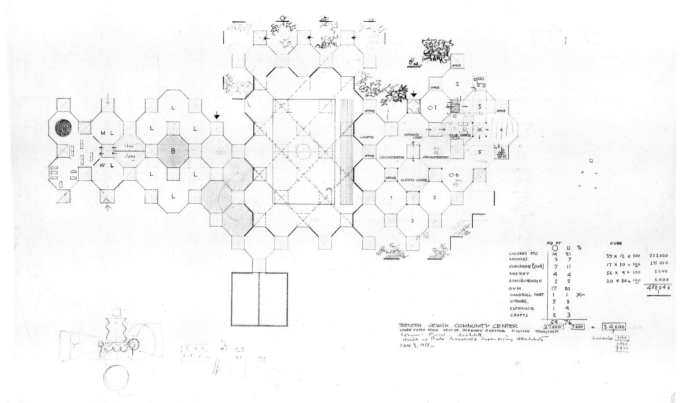

g

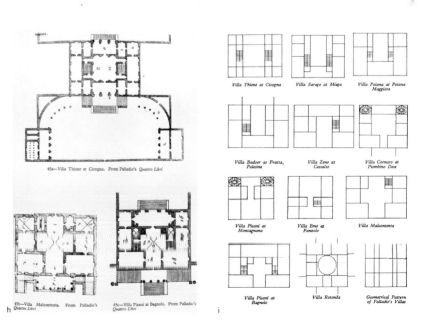

45a—Villa Thiene at Cicogna. From Palladio's *Quattro Libri*

45b—Villa Malcontenta. From Palladio's *Quattro Libri*

45c—Villa Pisani at Bagnolo. From Palladio's *Quattro Libri*

h

Villa Thiene at Cicogna	Villa Sarego at Miega	Villa Poiana at Poiana Maggiore
Villa Badoer at Fratta, Polesine	Villa Zeno at Cessalto	Villa Cornaro at Piombino Dese
Villa Pisani at Montagnana	Villa Emo at Fanzolo	Villa Malcontenta
Villa Pisani at Bagnolo	Villa Rotonda	Geometrical Pattern of Palladio's Villas

i

g. Preliminary plan of the main building, Jewish Community Center, 3 November 1955. The plan has octagonal 'served spaces' and square 'servant spaces'. The site scheme appears as a diagram in the lower left corner.

h. Andrea Palladio, plans of three villas, from Rudolf Wittkower, *Architectural Principles in the Age of Humanism*, 1949.

i. Rudolf Wittkower, analyses of structural subdivision of rectangular volumes using tartan (a-b-a) rhythms or bays in Palladian villa plans, from *Architectural Principles in the Age of Humanism*, 1949.

j. Model of the Jewish Community Center, third scheme, 1956.

k. Plan of the reflected roof, Jewish Community Center, third scheme, late 1956. Kahn's preferred plan shows the tartan grid of narrow 'servant' space bays and square pyramid-roofed 'served' spaces.

l. Site plan of the Jewish Community Center, 1 July 1957. The plan indicates Kahn's proposed extensive use of trees, planted in gridded masses, to enclose and define exterior spaces.

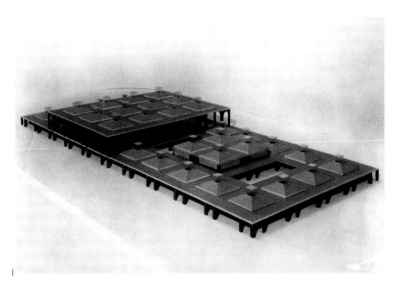

j

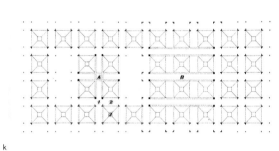

k

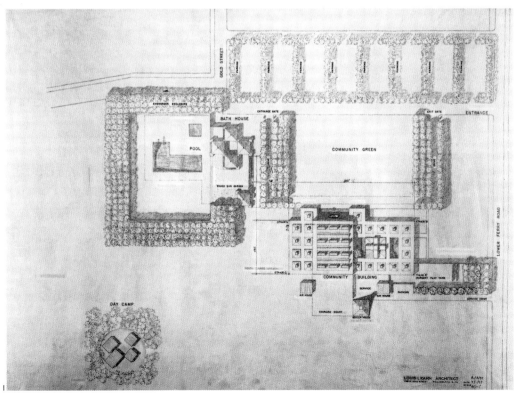

l

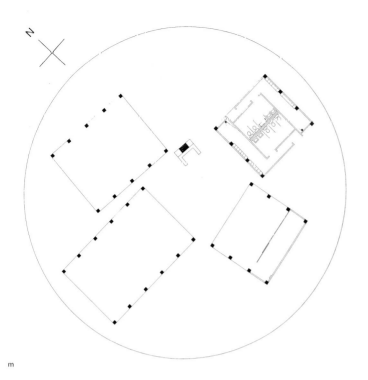

m

n

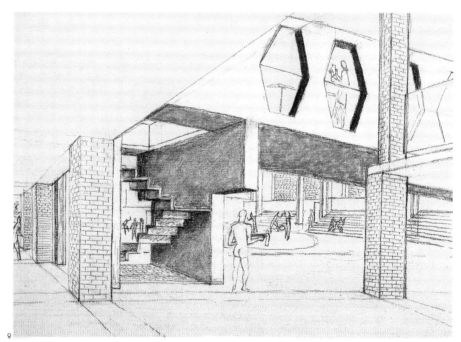

q

m. Plan of the Day Camp, Jewish Community
Center, 1957; four freestanding pavilions are set
upon a cleared, circular plinth in the woods.
n. Model of site plan of the Jewish Community
Center, 1957; built under the author's supervision.
o. Perspective view of the gymnasium, Jewish
Community Center, third scheme, 1956; drawing by
Kahn. Vierendeel trusses support the roof.
p. Perspective sketch of typical interior space,
therapy bath in men's locker rooms, third scheme,
1956; drawing by Kahn.
q. Perspective view of the courtyard, fourth and
final scheme, 1958; drawing by Kahn.

p

q

Building and teaching

From the Yale Art Gallery's completion in 1953 until he left Yale in 1958, Kahn had the rare privilege of teaching his architecture studios within a building of his own design. Students and fellow faculty recall that Kahn's confidence in his teaching, and the clarity with which he expressed his ideas, increased dramatically with the move into his building.[43] In addition to Kahn, Philip Johnson, Buckminster Fuller and Frederick Kiesler were teaching at Yale, and Albers' introductory course was now required of all architecture students. For both Kahn and the students it was a most exciting time to be at Yale, captured in this description by Jacquelin Robertson, then a student:

> You could in a day experience young Vincent Scully, a kind of demonic Irish firefly darting back and forth before huge flickering images of White and Sullivan … and Richardson and Wright – literally, a man on fire; or discover the mystery of seeing for the first time your own hand at work exploring (with eraser-less pencil) the differences between paper and stone, under that hawk-like unrelenting gaze of Albers, always afraid of your own clumsiness yet excited at the magic of self-revelation and the power of the teacher; or wander into one of those paper-strewn late afternoon sessions high above the glowing reddish court and listen to the funny, little, white-haired, pock-marked man, Louis Kahn, sometimes so clear, sometimes opaque, who talked so lovingly with his hands about the 'idea of architecture'; and showed you by the building you were in that he had built, that somehow the idea could survive, at least in part, its translation 'from becoming to being'. Kahn also re-injected into architecture the 'sense of place' – long before we'd heard of Aldo van Eyck – and a profound respect for history. He was a cultured man.[44]

Kahn taught as much by example, through the crystalline clarity of concept exhibited in his Yale Art Gallery building, as through his ceaseless search for the best way to speak of fundamental architectural principles. Late in his life Kahn would confirm the importance of the lessons that can only be drawn from inhabiting a building, and he would conclude that, though he was a teacher of architecture all his life, the only true lesson one architect can give another is in their buildings: 'And so it is, when a work is done, that the work actually teaches tremendously. It teaches by example, or rather I would say by deed, and that, of course, is the powerful force of Le Corbusier, Frank Lloyd Wright, and Michelangelo … They did not teach in a school. They taught by their work.'[45]

Yet even after the completion of his Yale Art Gallery building, Kahn was still recognized more for his teaching of architecture than for his work as an architectural practitioner. Indeed, when Kahn was made a Fellow of the American Institute of Architecture in 1953, it was for his contributions to architectural education, not architectural design.[46] Thus it came as no surprise when in the following year, George Howe, Kahn's friend and former partner, offered Kahn the position of Chair of the Department of Architecture, the post from which Howe was retiring. In urging him to accept

38. Louis Kahn drawing a circle and enclosed flower spray using both hands simultaneously. As Kahn noted, he developed this technique, which emphasizes a balance of tactile sensitivity and motor skills in both hands, from his childhood art classes with J. Liberty Tadd.

the position, Howe told Kahn, 'You are, after all, more of a teacher than an architect.' It was at that moment, Kahn recalled, 'that I realized I was more an architect than a teacher',[47] and he declined the offer. Howe died only a year later, in 1955. In his exemplary practice and self-styled 'patronage' of architects of Kahn's generation, and in his founding of the publications *T-Square Club Journal* in Philadelphia and *Perspecta* at Yale, he had been instrumental in creating the architectural culture in which Kahn came to maturity as an architectural thinker and designer. Kahn was devastated, and, as his wife Esther remembers, rather than attending Howe's funeral he 'went off ... for a day to Atlantic City to walk by himself by the sea and to think'.[48]

Paul Schweikher was appointed to the position of Chair of Architecture in 1954, but his tenure lasted only two years, and in 1956 Vincent Scully was a member of a group that again nominated Kahn for the position.[49] When the president of Yale offered the position to Kahn, he again declined, choosing to dedicate himself to his rapidly developing practice. An interim chair was appointed for a year, and then in late 1957 the Florida architect, Paul Rudolph, accepted the appointment, effective the following spring. Rudolph's arrival, his assumption of leadership in the school's design education, and the inevitable conflicts that almost immediately arose between the two strong-willed architectural thinkers, led to Kahn's increasing disengagement from Yale. Yet even before Rudolph's appointment, Kahn had begun to teach as a visiting professor at a number of other institutions, including MIT and Princeton.

In 1955 Kahn began teaching part-time at the University of Pennsylvania,[50] right up the street from his office, and he was finding it increasingly difficult to rationalize his long commutes to New Haven and Boston. That one of Rudolph's first official acts as chair was the 'renovation' of Kahn's Yale Art Gallery, covering the carefully exposed construction with drywall and replacing the freestanding display walls with fixed full-height partitions, was certainly an indication to Kahn that his ideas were no longer valued at Yale. Perhaps a more personal cause for Kahn's disillusionment with Yale was the forced resignation of his friend, Josef Albers, as Chair of the Department of Design in 1958, a full eight years before reaching Yale's mandatory retirement age, in order to make way for the 'reorganization' of the departments into the School of Art and Architecture, provoked by Rudolph's arrival.[51] In the end, the University of Pennsylvania convinced Kahn to join their faculty full-time by using the same incentive that Yale had used to retain Kahn after his return from Rome in 1951 – a building commission.

University of Pennsylvania Medical Research Towers
Philadelphia Pennsylvania 1957–65

In early 1957, largely due to the efforts of the Dean of the Architecture School, G. Holmes Perkins, Kahn received the commission for the Medical Research Building at the University of Pennsylvania, named upon dedication the Alfred Newton Richards Building. Kahn proposed three individual laboratory towers, each of them square in plan, with their structure, stairs and exhaust stacks grouped at the centre of each side so that the primary working space – the laboratories, which Kahn conceived of as 'studios' – could be placed at the cantilevered corners, and thereby provide generous light and views ('A scientist is like an artist … he likes to work in a kind of studio').[52] The three laboratory towers were gathered in a pinwheel formation around a fourth tower, which would contain the major mechanical machinery, research animal housing and other services. In the summer of 1958, biology research laboratories were added to the brief, and Kahn designed these in two additional towers to the east of the medical research laboratories, which began construction in December of that year.

39 & 40. Model of precast, post-tensioned concrete floor and column structure (left) and brick stair, air supply and exhaust towers, and entry stairs and plinth (right), University of Pennsylvania Medical Research Towers.

39   40

The basic plan of the towers was set relatively early, with the 45 foot (13.5 metre) square floor plates of the laboratory towers, the third-point (15 feet/4.6 metres) locations of the columns, and the mid-point locations of the structurally independent stair and exhaust shafts (p. 125; d), leaving the floors of each tower entirely free of structure or services. The majority of Kahn's early sketches for this project involve varying designs for the stair shafts – at first cylindrical, then square and finally rectangular – and the exhaust shafts. Kahn's drawings indicate his initial intention that the form of the exhaust shafts should directly reflect their varying volumes of exhausted air, smallest at the lowest laboratory floor and increasing incrementally as they rise. As the laboratories, stairs and columns were to remain of constant dimension, these expanding exhaust shafts – their form exactly following their function – would have been the most pronounced feature of the building. This, and the great expense of building such articulated features, led Kahn to abandon this idea, finally designing both the stair shafts and exhaust shafts as rectangular towers (p. 124; a).

The exhaust and stair towers, constructed of cast-in-place concrete and clad in brick, rise high above the top of the laboratories. These unarticulated vertical brick shafts contrast strongly with the horizontal cantilevered precast concrete Vierendeel floor trusses that Kahn developed with Komendant. In the early plans and a model for a typical research tower, Kahn was obsessed with the precise geometric subdivision of each 45 foot (13.5 metre) square floor (the primary square) into the nine 15 foot (4.6 metre) secondary squares by positions of the columns at third points, each of which was in turn divided into nine 5 foot (1.5 metre) tertiary squares. While Kahn was eventually convinced to divide each of the nine secondary squares into four, rather than nine, sub-squares, his original intention to work only with the most 'perfect' subdivision of the square reflects Kahn's continued deep belief in the power of geometry in the making of place.

The construction went rapidly, once the cranes were in place to raise the precast concrete columns and beams, with up to three floors a week rising on the tight campus site. During the building's construction Kahn was fascinated by cranes erecting the 3 foot (0.9 metre) deep precast concrete trusses, at first feeling that the cranes were 'monsters', overwhelming the building and making it seem 'out of scale'. Kahn's initial reaction reflected his belief in the inherently human scale of building as a craft (as Albers had maintained in his 1944 essay on architectural education), yet Kahn also had come to believe that building with precast concrete members was the most appropriate method of construction for him and for his time, and he later held that the crane should be understood as 'the extension of the arm, like a hammer'.[53]

The elegantly proportioned and complexly jointed structural members unquestionably dominate our perception and experience of the completed building, and this, Kahn's first use of precast concrete, is perhaps his most structurally expressive building. Kahn carefully articulated what he called the 'knuckles and joints' of these trusses, allowing us a surprisingly empathetic, anthropomorphic reading of this advanced technological form (p. 125; c).[54] For example, in the stepping change in the depth of the trusses we can clearly

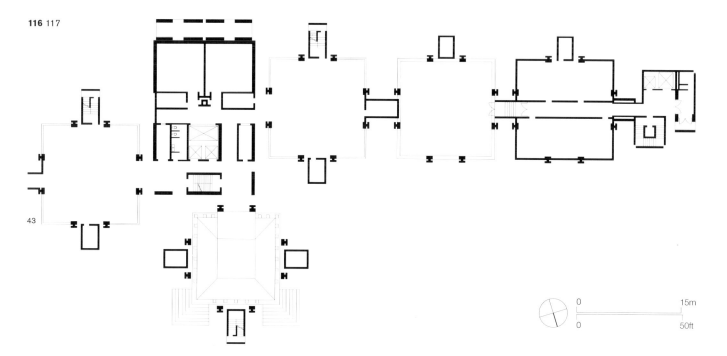

43

0 — 15m
0 — 50ft

read the diminishing structural bending moment as the trusses span from the thick seat at the column to the thin profile at the cantilevered corners. The question of the place of structure in architecture was put to Kahn when his friend, the great Finnish-American architect, Eero Saarinen, visited the construction site and asked, 'Lou, do you consider this building an architectural or a structural success?' Kahn immediately answered, '"structure" and "building" cannot be separated, the one evolves the other!'[55]

Kahn placed the entry under the middle of the three medical research towers, the ground floor of this tower (as well as that of one of the later biology research towers) being left open to the outside. The primacy of the cantilevered corner laboratories above is clearly indicated by the fact that we enter on the diagonal, not at the centre (which is blocked by the stair shaft) of the square floor. As we rise up the corner stairs, the entire system of the building is revealed above us, for again the ceiling overhead is the primary way in which Kahn shapes our spatial experience. With no laboratories for which to provide services on this entry floor, the structure is empty of mechanical piping, revealing the interlocking system of precast members and thus giving us a clear image of the building's skeleton, which is understandably obscured on the laboratory floors above.[56]

On a typical laboratory floor, its ceiling again shows us how the building works, with the hot and cold water and drain piping, the electrical conduits and the critically important supply air ducts running from the main service towers, and return air ducts running into the exhaust shafts, all feeding through the exposed structure overhead. Yet when the first laboratory's piping was installed during construction, Komendant recalled that 'it looked terrible: the pipes criss-crossing at different elevations, some of them running diagonally, no order whatsoever'.[57] Kahn was furious, and ordered it to be dismantled and the piping rearranged to his specifications, so each mechanical

41 & 42. (Previous pages) Exterior views of the University of Pennsylvania Medical Research Towers. The view from the south (left) shows the clustered air supply and exhaust towers behind the entry building, flanked by laboratories on the left and right. The view from the north-east campus approach (right), shows the entry on the right under the cantilevered laboratories.
43. Entry floor plan, with the Medical Research Laboratories on the left and the Biological Research Building on the right, University of Pennsylvania Medical Research Towers; redrawn under author's supervision.
44. Perspective drawing of the concrete structural frames and masonry service towers, University of Pennsylvania Medical Research Towers; drawn under author's supervision.

system could be clearly read, and so all would conform to the rectilinear order of the building structure. Not surprisingly, this was the first and last time Kahn attempted to expose the mechanical services so completely.

When originally occupied, the building provided an unprecedented level of service flexibility combined with spatial freedom, orderly services and an extroverted character – exactly opposite to the typical compartmentalized, chaotically serviced, introverted laboratory. The facade is a complex weave of vertical (brick shafts and concrete columns) and horizontal (concrete truss carrying brick and glass), and the building's massing steps powerfully forward and back, so that the independence of the various volumes and elements is clearly established. At the corner laboratories – cantilevered out into the light, with their extensive glass walls on two sides as well as in the depth of the concrete truss – we can look out of the building across the campus and also to the corner laboratories in the neighbouring towers. Here Kahn's vision of laboratories as 'studios' is perfectly achieved.

2. Rediscovering an architecture of mass and structure

46

47

45. (Opposite) Exhaust towers of the main service building, University of Pennsylvania Medical Research Towers.
46. Entry terrace, under the central laboratory tower, University of Pennsylvania Medical Research Towers.
47. Typical laboratory floor interior, University of Pennsylvania Medical Research Towers.

The Biological Research Building, designed after the Medical Research Building, employs a simplified and visually heavier precast structural system, and does not possess the same elegant character as that of the earlier buildings. The mechanical service requirements were also significantly less, so that only one exhaust tower is provided to each Biology Tower. The top floors house the research library, and at the building's corners are the first built examples of Kahn's conception of the reading carrel as a 'building-within-a-building', an idea he later developed to its full potential in Exeter Library. Here pairs of cubic volumes are cantilevered out from the face of the tower, each having a large window above, providing generous light to the reading room beyond, and a pair of small windows below, opening directly into the carrels. This articulation of the diverse 'functions' of the window – sunlight, views and ventilation – and the manner in which these various methods of admitting sunlight create widely

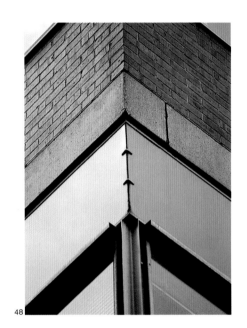

48

49

48. Butt-glazed corner detail of clerestory
windows of a typical laboratory, University
of Pennsylvania Medical Research Towers.
49. Biological Research Building (on right),
University of Pennsylvania Medical Research
Towers. The library carrels project from the
two upper floors.
50. Stair and service tower, Biological
Research Building, University of Pennsylvania
Medical Research Towers.

differing qualities of experience for those within, would evolve to become one of the most important and influential characteristics of Kahn's architecture.

By dividing the programme into five distinct and separate research towers, Kahn created a very urban quality of space, dense and vertical in character. Various historical precedents have been mentioned for this design, and while the windowless masonry towers of the medieval Italian hilltown of San Gimignano are often suggested as the inspiration for the stair and exhaust shafts, it is Wright's Larkin Building, with its vertical brick stair and mechanical shafts and its generous horizontal bands of glazing and brick, that most clearly inspired Kahn's design thinking (p. 124; b). Kahn had never hidden his admiration for Wright's early work,[58] and the Larkin Building, which at the time it was built established a new standard for the quality of space, light and services in office environments, as well as the clear expression of mechanical spaces, served Kahn as an entirely appropriate modern precedent for the Medical Towers.

Even before construction had been completed on the Biological Laboratories, the University of Pennsylvania Medical Research Towers was hailed as a modern masterpiece. In June and July of 1961, Kahn's Richards Medical Towers were the subject of a rare single building exhibition at the Museum of Modern Art in New York, where Philip Johnson was instrumental in obtaining this significant honour for Kahn. While the building has been seen by many architectural historians as a major breakthrough for Kahn, and while it was his first design to receive international acclaim, for Kahn the Medical Towers were more of a transitional project between lesser known and often unbuilt designs, such as the Jewish Community Center, where he felt that his true breakthroughs had been made. Ten years later Kahn would declare, 'If the world discovered me after I designed the Richards towers building, I discovered myself after designing that little concrete-block bath house in Trenton.'[59]

51. Louis Kahn at an exhibition on the University of Pennsylvania Medical Research Towers, Museum of Modern Art, New York, 1961. On Kahn's right is an early model of the building and behind are studies for the exhaust towers.
52. University of Pennsylvania Medical Research Towers under construction, c.1958.
53. (Opposite) A typical glazed corner laboratory looking towards another laboratory in an adjacent tower, University of Pennsylvania Medical Research Towers.

University of Pennsylvania Medical Research Towers

Concept development

A breakthrough building for Kahn, this design saw his first clear articulation of the concept of 'servant' and 'served' spaces, in which the main laboratory spaces occupy the cantilevered glazed corners, or 'studios' as Kahn called them, while the services are housed in independently structured vertical shafts standing outside the laboratory spaces. The resulting series of multiple towers – horizontally glazed (laboratories) and vertical masonry (stairs and services) – assume a distinctly urban character, and the medieval hill towns of Italy, such as San Gimignano, are often suggested as a source. Yet for Kahn, Frank Lloyd Wright's Larkin Building of 1902–6, with its similarly horizontally glazed workspaces and freestanding masonry service and stair towers, was clearly the primary inspiration. In this building Kahn also first employed what would become his preferred structural material: precast, post-tensioned reinforced concrete. The articulated structure, with its exposed joints and interlocking members that become thinner as they cantilever out towards the corners, is perhaps Kahn's most elegant design. Kahn's sources of inspiration for the design, as well as sketches and drawings of various stages of design development for the building, are shown here.

a

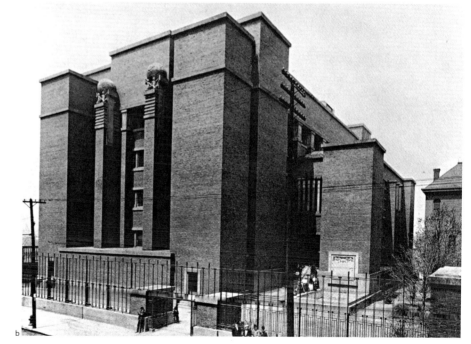

b

a. Early perspective sketch of the University of Pennsylvania Medical Research Towers, 1957, by Louis Kahn. Stair and air supply and exhaust towers are shown.
b. Frank Lloyd Wright, Larkin Building, Buffalo, New York, 1902–6. Note the freestanding stair and air supply towers at the corners.
c. Axonometric diagrams of precast, post-stressed concrete floor and column structure, University of Pennsylvania Medical Laboratories; drawn by Kahn's office.
d. Early plan and elevation sketches, 1957; drawing by Kahn. Each type of service is given a different plan form. The exhaust shafts increase in size as they rise and note the arched floor structure.

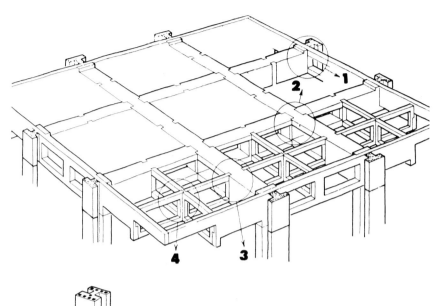

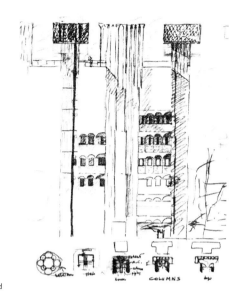

d

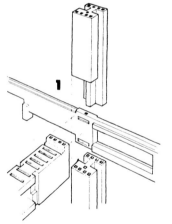

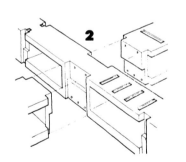

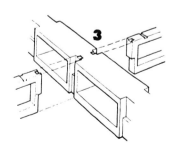

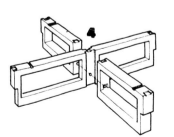

c

The Philadelphia school of architecture

In 1958 Louis Kahn became a full-time architecture faculty member at the University of Pennsylvania, Philadelphia, where he had been teaching for several years. Kahn had been recruited by G. Holmes Perkins, who since assuming the position of dean in 1951 had been building one of the greatest faculties in the country. One of Perkins's first appointments had been Lewis Mumford, the famous architectural historian and social critic whose numerous books, essays and 'Skyline' columns for *The New Yorker* magazine set a standard that has never been matched in architectural journalism.

Under Perkins's leadership, the architecture course at the University of Pennsylvania was profoundly different from the one at Yale where Kahn had spent his previous ten years' teaching. Where Yale emphasized the aspects of the design process shared by all the arts, the course at the University of Pennsylvania emphasized social activism and urban issues, taking the lead in criticizing suburban sprawl, the decline of traditional downtowns and the loss of the sense of place in contemporary cities.[60] The landscape architects, Ian McHarg and Karl Linn, both of whom worked with Kahn on his professional projects, were joined by the urban planners, Herbert Gans and Edmund Bacon, as well as the architects who, along with Kahn, would later be referred to as 'the Philadelphia School': Robert Venturi, Romaldo Giurgola, Tim Vreeland, Robert Geddes and George Qualls, several of whom worked in Kahn's office.[61]

While the thinking of these fellow faculty members had a profound influence on Kahn, and one that registered immediately in his urban design studies for Philadelphia of this period, more important to Kahn's development as an architectural thinker were the two colleagues he engaged in his studio teaching. The first was Kahn's classmate and lifelong friend, Norman Rice, who worked for Le Corbusier in the late 1920s. The second, and perhaps the most decisive, influence on Kahn, was the brilliant structural engineer, Robert

54. Perspective drawing of the Civic Center for Philadelphia, 1957 by Louis Kahn. The cylindrical structures are perimeter parking and shopping buildings, intended to protect the historic city centre from the damaging effects of automobile traffic.
55. Perspective drawing looking west, 'Plan for Midtown Philadelphia', 1952–3; drawing by Kahn. The spiral elements, which Kahn called 'wound-up streets', are parking garages.
56. Plan of proposed automobile traffic, parking and pedestrian travel patterns (north at top), 'Plan for Midtown Philadelphia'; drawing by Kahn.

Le Ricolais, a visionary poet of structure whose early work in stressed skins and triangulated space-frames would be of the utmost importance to Kahn, as well as his extensive experience (more than twenty years) of directing the experimental structures workshop at the University of Pennsylvania, where he searched for structures of 'zero weight and infinite span'.[62] Less regularly, Kahn also involved in his studio the precast concrete expert, Komendant, Kahn's primary consultant in his office, and various visiting faculty, including the Dutch founder of Team 10, Aldo van Eyck, whose work has remarkable parallels to that of Kahn (and about whom we will have more to say later).

In his 'Plan for Midtown Philadelphia' of 1952–3, Kahn had recognized that automobile traffic posed the greatest threat to the historical city, yet had to be accommodated in order for the city to survive. Kahn's initial approach involved the observation that 'the present mixture of staccato, through, and stop and go traffic makes all the streets equally ineffectual'. Kahn proposed instead the separation of traffic of differing sorts in a design not intended to maximize speed – the typical goal of planning – but to provide 'order and convenience'.[63] Kahn's diagrammatic plan for the downtown, still astonishing in its visionary potential fifty years later, indicated proposed movement patterns separated by type: through streets; go streets; stop streets; docks (for loading and access); pedestrian ways (free of automobile traffic); expressways; and parking garages. Perhaps the most powerful concept to emerge from the 1953 plan was Kahn's idea of ramped parking garages as 'wound-up streets', and their positioning around the perimeter of the downtown, where the expressways were terminated, so that elevated high-speed roadways would no longer need to penetrate the centre of the city.

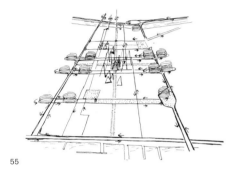

55

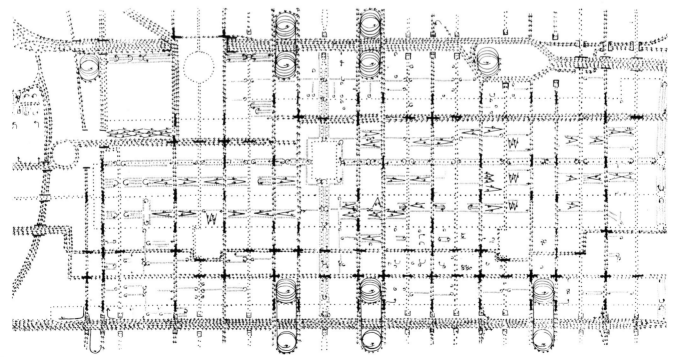

56

57

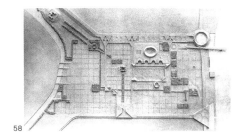

58

In his Civic Center for Philadelphia of 1956–7, Kahn gave powerful form to his earlier suggestion that a modern city centre without protection from the automobile (in the form of perimeter parking garages) was like the medieval city of 'Carcassonne without walls'.[64] In a series of perspectives Kahn positioned a series of cylindrical bastion-like buildings – with circular garages at their core, hotel and office slabs wrapped around the outside, and elevated plazas at their centre – around the existing and new monuments of the city centre. In his later Market Street studies of 1961–2 Kahn went even further, proposing to construct the peripheral elevated expressways as a 'viaduct architecture' – a series of arched walls, strikingly similar to Roman aqueducts, which would not only direct the automobile traffic into the parking 'docks' or bastions but would form literal walls around the city, protecting the city and giving it definition, form, outline and edge at the same time.

Kahn's design for the Martin Research Institute for Advanced Science, proposed for Baltimore, Maryland in 1956–8, involved two distinct types of space – laboratories and common spaces (entrance, library, dining hall, etc.) – which Kahn housed in two connected structures, both strongly influenced by his contemporary design for the Trenton Bath House. In plan the common space building assumed the form of a square, made up of five interlocking cruciform spaces, with the entrance hall at the centre and the four primary functions in the corners. The whole is organized on a tartan grid, with a smaller, square 'servant' space at each corner of the five larger, primary cruciform 'served' spaces. In addition, the columns supporting the intersecting hipped roof forms were set at the inside corners of the five cruciform-shaped primary spaces.

The laboratories were proposed in a stepped diamond-shaped plan, made up of four peripheral cruciform-shaped volumes, connected at the centre to create a fifth cruciform. Four square courts were proposed between the arms of the cruciform laboratory blocks, and the flat roofs of the five square spaces that

59

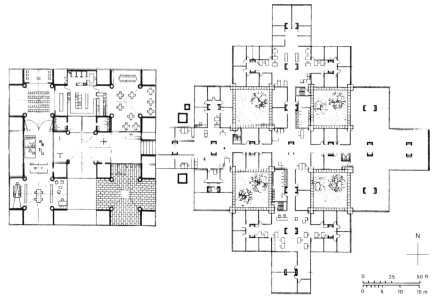

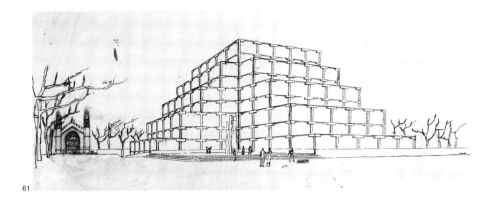

61

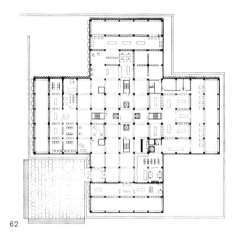

62

formed each cruciform were held up by a central column, very similar to Kahn's Parasol House design of 1944. The roofs over the central spaces of each of the five cruciform-shaped blocks were lifted, and the section through the middle of the building shows how the roofs alternated up and down, creating clerestory windows all around the four sides of the higher roofs.[65] Aside from its geometric elegance, generous natural lighting, and rich interweaving of interior and exterior space, this horizontal, grounded design is an interesting contrast to Kahn's contemporary University of Pennsylvania Laboratories.

The Washington University Library competition design, submitted in May 1956, is another development of the cruciform plan concept, and here Kahn proposed that the massing be stepped in section, creating a massive stepped-pyramid form. While the design does succeed in creating a truly monumental presence on the campus, the structural grid of columns fails entirely to provide for the possibility of either articulate 'servant'-and-'served' spaces, or differing scales and qualities of inhabited space. Kahn would very soon come to believe that the typical applied sunscreens, here placed over the building's otherwise undifferentiated facades, were no longer an acceptably integrated design concept for the all-important interface between interior and exterior (this important evolution in Kahn's work is the subject of the next chapter). Kahn's struggle to discover how to develop the human-scaled yet monumental space of the Trenton Bath House into much larger projects is clearly evident in the Washington University project, and as a whole this design remains one of Kahn's least convincing efforts.

Yet, while the competition's short timeline clearly did not allow sufficient time for 'beauty to evolve', Kahn's thinking on the library programme did not cease with the termination of this project. As is often the case with Kahn's unrealized projects, his concepts for the library, only given convincing form ten years later in Exeter Library, first emerged in his descriptions of what he discovered in working on the competition design. Rejecting the standard brief, calling for a reading room separate from the book stacks, Kahn stated, 'Books and the reader do not relate in a static way.'[66] A year later he declared, 'A man with a book goes to the light. A library begins that way. He will not go fifty feet to the electric light. The carrel is the niche which could be the beginning of the space order and its structure.'[67] Typical of Kahn's slow but unceasing design process, once his thinking was stimulated by a commission, Kahn would

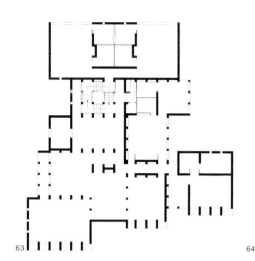

63

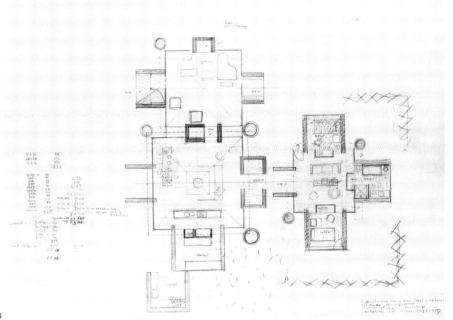

64

65

63. Final plan of the Morris House, Mount Kisco, New York, 1955–8 (north to right). Four foot (1.2 metre) square modules of masonry walls and columns are the basic organizing element of the design; redrawn under author's supervision.
64. Early plan of the Morris House, 1955; sketch by Louis Kahn. This plan may be related to the University of Pennsylvania Medical Research Towers as well as numerous cruciform house plans by Frank Lloyd Wright, such as the Darwin Martin House, Buffalo, New York, 1903–5.
65. Model of the Morris House, 1958.
66. Plan of Mill Creek Community Center, Philadelphia, 1957–63 (north at top). Four square corner rooms, each with a pinwheel beam structure and central skylight, are served by the central cruciform entry and service space.
67. Corner room during construction, Mill Creek Community Center. Note the skylight opening at the centre of the pinwheel ceiling beams.

return to the function again and again, each time with greater poetic insight into its fundamental nature.

The Morris House, proposed for a site in Mount Kisco, New York, and designed in 1955–8, went through two distinct phases, both influenced to a large degree by the designs of Frank Lloyd Wright. Kahn's early schemes of 1955 involved the superimposition of a cruciform on a square plan (the underlying geometry of Wright's Unity Temple) to produce a series of symmetrical pavilions, which were in turn arranged in various cross-axial sequences (similar to Wright's Darwin Martin House). When Kahn returned to this design in 1957 he proposed a dynamic, asymmetrical plan based initially on a 4 foot (1.2 metre) grid of square columns, and developed in the final design as a constantly changing concrete masonry wall composed of columns, piers and panels, the latter with slit windows slicing the wall from top to bottom every 4 feet (1.2 metres). In its pyramidal massing, its incessantly vertical concrete-block pier-walls, and its tall narrow windows recessed into the thick masonry walls, Kahn's final Morris House design was clearly inspired by Wright's Lloyd Jones House of 1929.[68]

Finally, Kahn produced a series of designs for the Mill Creek Public Housing project, begun in 1951 and built from 1953 to 1963, in Philadelphia. These included hundreds of housing units, organized in towers and row-houses, all constructed using brick masonry walls and columns with precast concrete lintels, beams and floors. The Mill Creek Community Center, designed in 1957 and built in 1961–3, is a far more important design in Kahn's development than we might suppose, given that it has largely been ignored in previous studies of Kahn's work. The earliest designs for the Community Center are very similar to those for the 'commons' building of the Martin Research Institute project, with four cruciform-shaped spaces arranged to form a larger

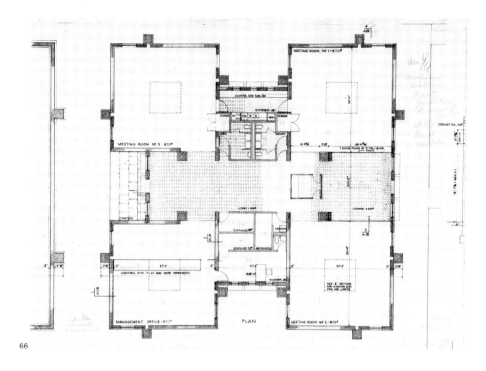

66

67

square plan, and small square courts set at the corners of the larger spaces, so as to interweave interior and exterior space. The geometric subdivision of the larger square into four smaller squares which underlies the Community Center plan was made explicit in Kahn's plan of the immediately adjacent gardens and terraces – four low-walled square spaces, separated by crossing axial walkways.

The plan of the Community Center as built has four square rooms at the corners, with a cruciform-shaped volume at the centre. In these square rooms, housing the primary functions of the Community Center, Kahn achieves a stunning synthesis of structure and space, carrying forward the discovery made in the Trenton Bath House. Each 30 foot (9 metre) square room is supported by four brick columns, one at the third-point of each wall, which in turn support precast concrete beams that form a pinwheel pattern above, with a clerestory light monitor at the centre. In this design Kahn clearly intended that the visitor be able to perceive the supporting structural columns, even when in this case they fall outside the enclosing brick walls, for he designed a slot in each wall through which the inside face of each column could be seen. As Kahn said, 'A beam needs a column, a column needs a beam. There is no such thing as a beam on a wall.'[69] Yet, in a short-sighted attempt at cost-saving, this last detail was not built. The importance of such a seemingly insignificant detail to our experience can be measured by the fact that, in its absence, the large concrete beams pass into what is clearly a non-load-bearing brick wall, leaving us mystified as to how the ceiling is supported – the exact opposite of what Kahn had intended.

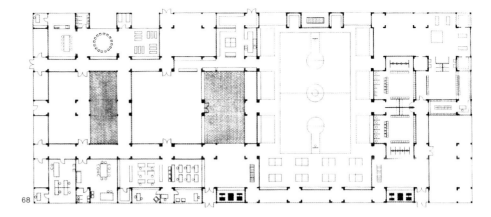

68

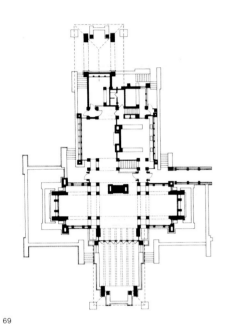

69

Conclusion: structure and space

The visit to Kahn's office by Colin Rowe in 1955, and their later correspondence regarding the evolution of Kahn's designs for the Jewish Community Center, had a significant effect on both men. Rowe's thinking can be seen particularly in his two brilliant essays written in 1956–7 (though not published until some years later), titled 'Neo-"Classicism" and Modern Architecture', I and II.[70] The second essay opens with a precise description of the International Style system of space-making, which 'postulated a skeleton structure whose function of support was to be separately expressed from any non-structural function of enclosure … Detached from the liberated columns, the walls were now to become a series of freely disposed screens … the "free plan".' While Kahn by this time had come to believe that in our experience of a space, it is important that we perceive how the space is made, and how its ceiling or roof is supported, Rowe noted how 'International Style space was a system which tended to prohibit any display of beams … [and required] that the *under* surfaces of the roofs and floors should present uninterrupted planes'. In International Style buildings, 'the column does not promote the spatial expression of the structural bay, nor do a series of columns define individual structural cells'.[71]

Rowe then analysed several designs by Mies van der Rohe, including his 1942 'Museum for a Small Town', published as part of the same 'New Buildings for 194X' issue of *Architectural Forum* in which Kahn and Stonorov had published their 'Hotel for 194X' design. Rowe noted that while Mies and Le Corbusier engaged symmetry in their designs, they avoided its spatial implications: 'Centralization? The repetitive nature of the grid which … remains and is likely to remain the basic component of modern architecture, resists the idea.'[72] But how can the hierarchy of spaces – large and small, tall and short, central and peripheral – typically included in a public programme be accommodated within the uniform grid of modern architecture?

Here Rowe introduces Kahn's third design for the Trenton Jewish Community Center, the design closest to the Bath House, and a design that Kahn evolved in late 1956, after his meeting with Rowe.[73] Rowe began by noting that 'Kahn is able to accept the pressure of structure upon space', that he makes space out of 'individuated spatiostructural cells', and that he 'can augment Mies's columns and equip them with mass so that they articulate rather than probe space; similarly, in place of Mies's flat slab he can engender a whole colony of pyramids'. Rowe then traces what he perceived to be the sources that had inspired the design: 'Kahn lays out a complex grid of maybe Wrightian, maybe Beaux-Arts origin; and this grid gives to his project something of that Scotch plaid quality which is characteristic of ... the Martin House at Buffalo as it is of so many Prix de Rome.'[74]

Rowe concludes that 'the Jewish Community Center is emphatically the most complete development to date of themes [of spatial cells, centrality, hierarchy and structural–spatial order implicit in classicism]; and, compared to the other neo-"Classical" manifestations [in modernism], it seems so far to present the most comprehensive solution to the problems initiated by the anxiety to introduce centralization and/or vertical stressing of space.' While at the end of his essay Rowe would predict that the future belonged not to Kahn but to Mies and Le Corbusier, who 'recognize and accept what is surely the normative condition of twentieth-century building – the flat slab and its point support', he also noted that this normative condition had proven utterly incapable of accommodating and giving form to the growing desire for centrality, hierarchy and vertical spatial development inherent in ancient architectural examples such as the dome.[75]

In a lecture given in 1957, the year Rowe wrote these essays, Kahn articulated what had by this time become his fundamental belief: 'Architecture is the thoughtful making of spaces. Reflect on the great event in architecture when the walls parted and columns became ... The arch, the vault, and the dome mark equally evocative times ... Today these forms and space phenomena are as good as they were yesterday and will always be good because they proved to be true to order and in time revealed their inherent beauty.'[76] Kahn would soon after state that 'civilization is measured by the shape of your ceiling',[77] and it was exactly these fundamental aspects of spatial experience, to which Rowe had called attention, that Kahn was reintegrating into modern architecture through his engagement of mass and structure in the making of space.

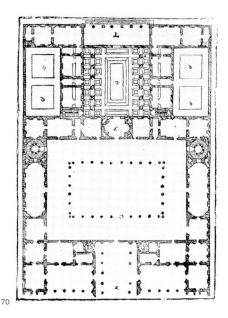

70

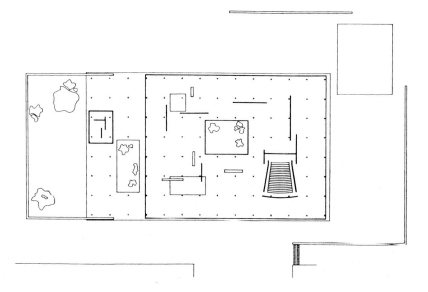

70. Andrea Palladio, plan of 'Reconstruction of the Roman House', Barbaro's edition of Vitruvius, 1556, from Rudolf Wittkower, *Architectural Principles in the Age of Humanism*, 1949.
71. Ludwig Mies van der Rohe, plan of 'Museum for a Small Town', 1942; published in 'New Buildings for 194X' issue of *Architectural Forum*, May 1943.   71

Shaping an architecture of light and shadow

A great American poet once asked the architect, 'What slice of sun does your building have? What light enters your room?' – as if to say the sun never knew how great it is until it struck the side of a building.[1]
LOUIS KAHN

Having found himself as an architect, as he said, in the little Bath House of the Trenton Jewish Community Center, Kahn now entered a period of the most astonishing creative development, producing dozens of important and innovative designs in only a few years. Kahn's methodical, inspired and rigorous search for beginnings in each new project resulted in designs that were immediately recognized as being of the greatest significance for contemporary architecture. Kahn's break with the International Style, just as it had reached the peak of its influence and application in the mid-1950s, would have the most profound implications for the following generations of modern architects throughout the world.

The architecture of mass and structure is a maker of powerful shadows, and at this time Kahn began to see sunlight as the most important characteristic of space in architecture. In the quotation that heads this chapter, Kahn paraphrases a line from a poem by Wallace Stevens to illustrate his belief that natural light was the primary determinant of a room's quality as a space. Kahn's focus on the interior spatial experience of sunlight was a significant difference from his 'teacher' Le Corbusier's famous definition of architecture as 'the masterly, correct and magnificent play of volumes brought together in light'[2] – that is to say, as sculptural forms seen from the exterior. As had Frank Lloyd Wright, Kahn made the focus of his work the space within, and our inhabitation of it: 'The room is so marvellous that its size, its dimension, its walls, its windows, its light – *its* light, not just light – have an effect on what you say and what you do.'[3]

Kahn believed that 'no space is really an architectural space unless it has natural light',[4] and that architectural space could only be made by sunlight. 'Artificial light is only a single, tiny, static moment in light and is the light of night and never can equal the nuances of mood created by the time of day and the wonder of the seasons.'[5] Kahn held that even programmes that did not require natural light, like a cinema, must still have some natural light to become architecture. 'Even a space intended to be dark should have just

Previous page. Salk Institute for Biological Studies, La Jolla, California, 1959–65. Floor paving of the central courtyard at sunset with water flowing towards the Pacific Ocean.
1. Court, Temple of Khons, Karnak, Egypt, drawing by Louis Kahn, 1951. The ancient stone construction is illuminated by sunlight and given depth by shadow.

enough light from some mysterious opening to tell us how dark it really is.'[6] Kahn believed that natural light defines our experience of space: 'I regard natural light as that which makes a room have its nature, its characteristic, its mood.'[7]

The relationship between that which makes space – the structure – and that which gives a space life – its natural light – became Kahn's primary focus. He came to feel that the design of the structure was the design of the light, holding that 'the making of spaces is the making of light at the same time',[8] and that 'a space does show evidence of how it was made within the space itself – not just for enclosure alone, but for light that you want this space to have, the natural light'.[9] Kahn thus declared that, in architecture, 'structure is the giver of light. When you decide on the structure, you're deciding on light',[10] and that 'the vault, the dome, the arch, the column are structures related to the character of light'.[11] Kahn held that 'a plan of a building should read like a harmony of spaces in light ... Each space must be defined by its structure and the character of its natural light.'[12]

Kahn called light 'the giver of all presences', and believed that the mass and structure of architecture 'was made to cast a shadow, and the shadow belongs to the light'.[13] Thus for Kahn, the counterpoint of mass and structure is light and shadow, and Kahn's compositions became increasingly preoccupied with sunlight and its modulation, in terms of how it characterized the experience of the spaces within. It was at this time that Kahn first began to argue against the modern mechanisms of climate control, such as air conditioning and applied sunshades, and to argue for traditional architectural methods of tempering climate, for what he later called 'the order of wind, the order of light. The order of light tells you that the porch belongs to the sun and the place inside the porch belongs to man. It has nothing to do with *brises soleil* devices to make shade. It has nothing to do with air conditioning ... It costs money to fight the sun.'[14] Kahn believed this difference to be fundamental: 'If I had been looking only from the functional standpoint, I would have made a *brise soleil*. But, since I was thinking in terms of architecture, it has to become a porch. And the porch is a room ... I was creating buildings within buildings.'[15]

It was at this time that Kahn began to develop designs with layered walls at their periphery so as to create volumes of light-filled space, at once inside and outside the building, protecting the interior spaces within. He often spoke appreciatively of ruins which, when freed of the limitations of use, stand as hollow masses flooded with light and shadows. As Scully has pointed out, 'Kahn's characteristic difficulty [was] with the skin of his building, with, that is, the element which seemed to him neither structure nor space',[16] and in the layered spatial shells of masonry ruins Kahn found structure and space in its purest form.

Tribune Review Publishing Company Building
Greensburg Pennsylvania 1958–62

The Tribune Review Publishing Company Building, on which design began in the autumn of 1958, was the first of Kahn's projects to demonstrate the architect's emerging articulation of the relationship between structure and light. It was also the first of a series of industrial buildings which, rather than being projects taken on just to pay the office bills, were conceived by Kahn as opportunities to develop construction systems that were at once economical and expressive of the fundamental aspects of their programme of use. In the case of the Tribune Review Building, Kahn was required to house the publishing offices, the typesetting machinery and the printing plant, along with the associated paper storage facilities, two-storey-tall roll machines, photography development equipment, presses, and assembly and delivery operations.

From the start, Kahn conceived of this building as consisting of a large, open, column-free, well-lit workspace, with services initially placed in a series

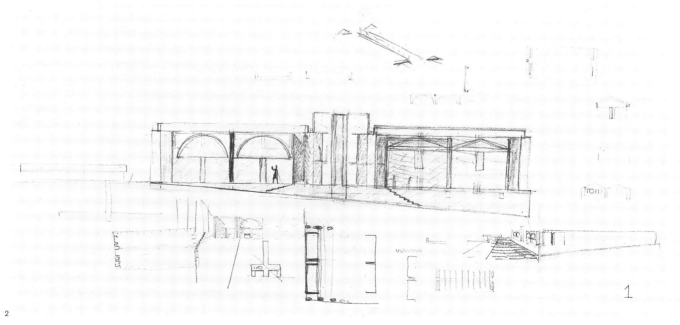

1

of independent elements at the perimeter of the main volume. Kahn's own early sketch studies contain plans of a rectangular volume with service blocks at the corners and a square office annexe, strikingly similar to Wright's Larkin Building of 1902–6 (p. 148; a), as well as plans of two square volumes with service blocks at the mid-points of each side, very similar to Kahn's University of Pennsylvania Medical Research Towers. As can be seen in the other sketches on this same sheet, Kahn soon understood that the services required for this project, distributed in this way, would take up most of the perimeter, and thus bring them into conflict with his primary intention – maximizing the introduction of appropriately distributed natural light into the workspace.

Kahn soon fixed the plan as two rectangular primary volumes, each 50 by 132 feet (15 by 40 metres) – eleven bays of 12 feet (3.7 metres) each – with a 20 foot (6 metre) wide service zone between, leaving three sides of each rectangular workspace free to bring in light. The basement contained the storage and delivery areas as well as the mechanical equipment, and a grid of columns supported the ground floor above (p. 149; c). The main spaces were column-free, being spanned by 50 foot (15 metre) long pre-stressed, precast concrete beams, which are spaced on a barely discernible tartan grid, alternately measuring 12 feet (3.7 metres) to the outside faces and 12 feet to the inside faces. This is the first instance of what would become Kahn's typical manner of imparting a subtle variation to what at first glance appears to be a repetitive rhythm of structural bays. The precast beams bear on concrete brick piers, which frame the service area at the centre and project beyond the enclosing walls on the outside of the building. The non-bearing walls between the load-bearing concrete brick piers are constructed of full-size concrete block, so that the structure is clearly articulated, both inside and outside.

Kahn's primary design efforts now focused on finding the proper articulation for the windows, which he intended should not only indicate the difference between the load-bearing and non-load-bearing walls but also should address the several traditional functions of the window itself, as an architectural element: light, view, communication between interior and exterior, and ventilation. This development of the window marked Kahn's next critical break with the International Style, for its standard 'curtain-wall' window was completely disengaged from structure, and addressed only view and light – combining them in a window that was not appropriately sized or positioned for either function. Perhaps inspired by the multi-opening window compositions in masonry walls that he had seen in Rome and Ostia, Kahn began at this time to experiment with the idea of making a separate window shape and position for each function.

While natural light provides the best light for working, in that it carries the change of season and time of day, Kahn argued that a large window set in the centre of a wall not only produces glare, as the eye must choose between the brilliant glass and the dark surrounds, but also throws light onto the floor, so that it does not penetrate into the space, failing to illuminate the work surfaces within. Kahn proposed that the largest window opening, the full width of the structural bay, should be placed high in the room, against the ceiling, so that

2. Early design sketch of north elevation of the Tribune Review Building; drawing by Louis Kahn. Here Kahn explores various window shapes.

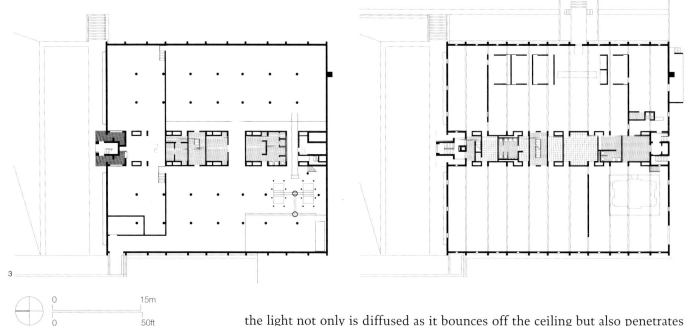

3

0   15m

0   50ft

the light not only is diffused as it bounces off the ceiling but also penetrates deeply and evenly into the space, falling from above onto the work surfaces within. Next Kahn explored the idea of providing a smaller window below, which was scaled not to the building structure but to the standing and seated occupant, set at a height to allow eye-level views out, while its smaller size minimized glare (p. 149; d & e).

One of Kahn's early sketches for the Tribune Review Building is the first instance in his work where the upper portion of the window is a large, full bay wide semicircle in shape, set over a narrow rectangular opening below – recalling the arched openings over smaller square windows or doors that Kahn had seen in the Roman ruins. It was this window design, perhaps more than any other, which gave form to Kahn's poetic concept of a window that quite literally follows the arcing path of the sun across the sky above, while at the same time precisely framing the individual, vertically orientated view for the inhabitant on the earth below.[17] For the Tribune Review Building, Kahn also sketched slot-like windows set against the walls at the corners of the room, which would act to minimize glare further and increase the penetration of light into the room by having the sunlight bounce off, or 'wash' the walls – exactly as in the Dutch paintings of Vermeer. In the margins of one of the office drawings for this project, Kahn sketched the plan of Le Corbusier's Ronchamp Chapel of 1950–54 (which he visited in 1959, during a trip to be discussed later in this chapter), showing how light from tall narrow openings washes the building's massive folded walls.[18] While he did not employ either of these ideas in the final design for the Tribune Review Building, Kahn would return to these reinventions of the window and wall in later projects.

As built, the Tribune Review Building is an exercise in the most economical yet elegant expression of structure and its articulation by light. Entering the building, the precast concrete beams span across the shorter dimension of each major room. On the long east and west elevations, Kahn reveals that the

3. Plans of the Tribune Review Building; printing, storage and loading level (left), and office and layout level (right); redrawn under author's supervision.
4. Section looking east (above) and west elevation (below) of the Tribune Review Building; redrawn under author's supervision.

concrete block walls between the piers are non-load-bearing by placing glazing between the tops of the walls and the roof structure above, within the depth of the beams. Under these upper windows, the infill walls are split at their centres by tall narrow windows that run from these upper windows to the floor. Together, the horizontal and vertical windows produce a T-shaped opening, large at the top to bring in maximum light, narrow at eye-level to allow views but minimize glare. Across the space, at the central service spine, the vertical mechanical shafts are clad in concrete block and placed at the centre of every other, wider structural bay, where they rise to emerge and exhaust at the roof. The roof over the service zone is lowered, housing cooling equipment and allowing windows to be opened, in the depth of the beams, in the alternating, smaller structural bays, bringing high light into the very centre of the space.

On the shorter, south and north elevations, the precast concrete beams span from the concrete brick piers at the outer edge to the pier at the central service zone, so that the entire wall between is non-load-bearing. Kahn expresses this clearly by constructing this wall of full-size concrete blocks, and by detailing these walls with deeply shadowed joints (called 'reveals') to indicate that the walls stop both before they reach the precast beam above and before they reach the concrete brick piers at either end (where Kahn inserted a 4 inch [10 centimetre] wide piece of black slate to accentuate this joint). Kahn also designed a window pattern for this non-bearing wall on the north and south facades that differs from that on the load-bearing east and west facades; here a large square upper window is placed over a small vertical rectangular window. The smaller window is 6 feet (1.8 metres) tall, precisely framing the view when we are seated, and the larger window opens from 6 feet (1.8 metres) to the bottom of the beam above (p. 148; b).

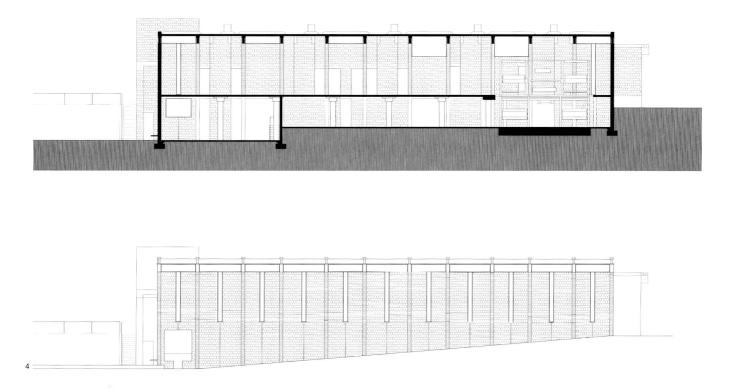

5

6

7

5. East facade and public entrance of the Tribune Review Building.
6. North facade and employee entrance of the Tribune Review Building.
7. South facade of the Tribune Review Building. This view clearly shows Kahn's first use of smaller masonry units for structural piers and larger masonry units for non-structural walls.

8. Ground floor office space of the Tribune Review Building. This view shows the non-load-bearing north wall on the left and load-bearing piers on the east wall at the far end; note also the beam-depth horizontal glazing in the east wall.

8

As we stand within, these two types of windows not only reveal for us the solar orientation of the building, with its ever-changing light, but also profile and highlight the precast structure and its masonry supporting piers. Through the north and south windows we can also see the masonry walls stopping to reveal the span of the precast concrete beams, while the light from the east and west windows precisely reveals the depth of these same beams. Here Kahn has unquestionably achieved his ideal that we should be able to see precisely how the space we inhabit was made and supported.

On the exterior we can perceive Kahn's subtle play with the expected honorific status of the building's two primary facades. The building is terraced into the hillside so that the north facade, with the employee entrance to the printing plant, is two storeys in height, while the east facade, with entry to the management offices, is a single storey in height. The two-storey north facade is symmetrically centred on the tower-like projection of the mechanical zone, exit stairs and employee entrance. A precast concrete bench is cantilevered out of the base of this wall to provide seating for employees on their break – reminding us of the benches built into the bases of the urban palaces of the ruling families of Renaissance Italy, such as the Palazzo Farnese in Rome of 1517–89, designed by Antonio da Sangallo the Younger and Michelangelo. By contrast, the single-storey

9

10

9. View from the north-east, Tribune Review Building. A later addition, not by Kahn, can be seen behind.
10. The roof on the east side (detail), Tribune Review Building. On the right is the precast, post-tensioned concrete beam end, with beam-depth horizontal glazing on either side and non-structural infill masonry below.

public entry facade to the east is provided with an asymmetrical, off-centre, uncovered entry. Taken together, these characteristics indicate that, for Kahn, the facade of the printing plant used for entry by the larger number of workers was of significantly greater importance than the facade used for entry by the management.

The detailing of the building throughout is rigorous, minimal and elegant, indicating that Kahn believed all building programmes deserved equal thought in design and construction, regardless of whether they were constructed in marble or concrete block – a concept he had first articulated in his 1944 essay on monumentality (see pages 455–61). In the Tribune Review Building, which is rarely studied and almost never considered among his greatest works, Kahn achieved his most resolved expression to date of the relation between structure and light. He not only discovered new ways to bring natural light into the space, but also revealed the structure in its light.

Tribune Review Publishing Company Building

Concept development

Kahn's first clear articulation of his emerging understanding of the reciprocal relationship between structure and light, the Tribune Review Building belies its industrial nature in the precision and elegance of its detailing. It is built of the most modest materials – concrete masonry unit walls and precast, post-tensioned roof beams – yet it is nevertheless a tour-de-force in articulate construction. The plan is a development of Kahn's own plan for the Yale Art Gallery: two large open spaces with a narrow service zone between. In this design Kahn was inspired by the window apertures in masonry walls that he had seen in ancient Roman ruins in Rome, Ostia and Pompeii, and he experimented with combining vertical and horizontal rectangular openings to provide smaller, human-scaled windows for viewing below and large, room-scaled openings for general illumination above. Kahn also uses these openings to articulate the load-bearing or non-load-bearing nature of the wall and roof structure with sunlight, so the structure literally becomes the giver of light. These pages document Kahn's early sketch plans, intermediate elevation studies and plans for the final built work.

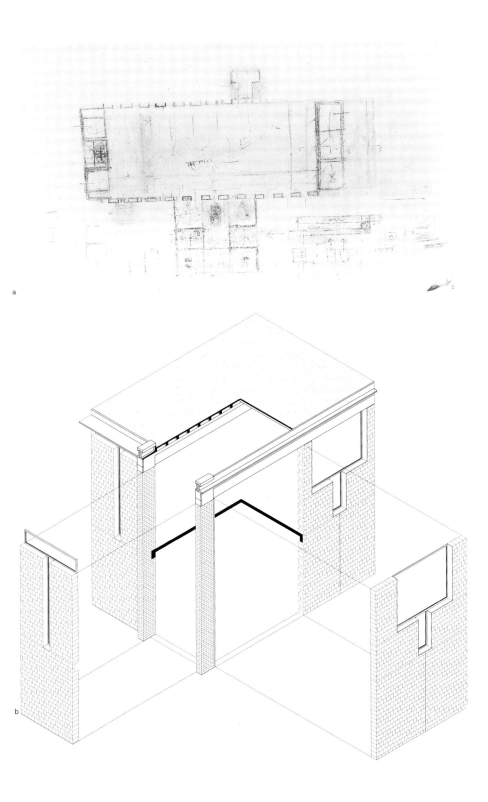

a

b

a. Preliminary plan sketch of the Tribune Review Building; drawing by Kahn. This plan is virtually identical to that of Frank Lloyd Wright's Larkin Building, Buffalo, New York (1902–6), with service blocks at either end, a thickened structure producing hollow walls along both sides, and a square entry annexe.
b. Exploded isometric drawing of the north-east corner of the Tribune Review Building, showing non-load-bearing masonry walls (pulled away) and structural masonry piers; drawn under author's supervision.

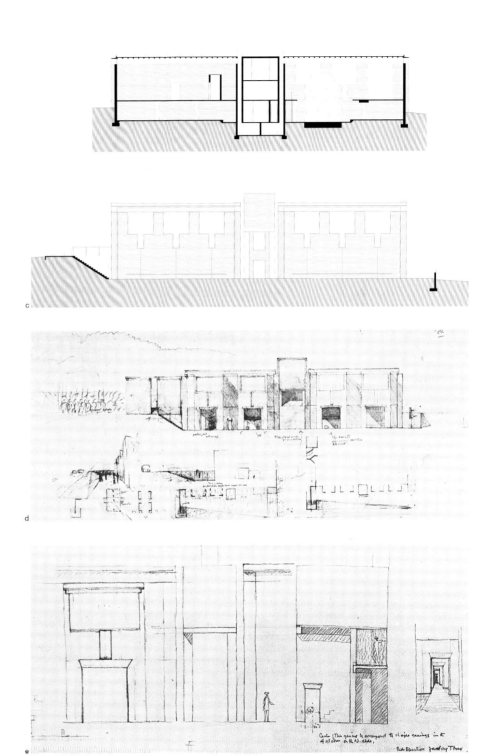

c. East-west section, looking south (above), and north elevation (below), Tribune Review Building; redrawn under author's supervision.
d. North elevation, partial plan and perspective sketches of an intermediate scheme for the Tribune Review Building; drawings by Kahn.
e. North elevation, section and perspective sketches of an intermediate scheme for the Tribune Review Building; drawings by Kahn.

United States Consulate Chancellery and Residence
Luanda, Angola
1959–62
Unbuilt

In the US Consulate project for Angola, commissioned in late 1959, Kahn from the very start focused the design on issues of sunlight, and the way structure articulated it and architecture modulated it. While noting that the design was intended to have 'a reposeful character' as appropriate to an embassy – 'a dignified building for a dignified activity of man' – Kahn believed that this 'sense of appropriateness' with respect to institutions was a learned habit and thus was not 'deeply fundamental'. For Kahn, the real purpose of the building was 'to demonstrate to the man on the street a way of life' derived directly from 'the very characteristics of the air, and the light, very simple everlasting presences that should constantly talk to you in architecture'. Kahn then stated his developing belief in the necessity for regional variations in modern architecture, rather than the universal uniformity of the International Style: 'You cannot forget that light of a certain character has to do with that which distinguishes the architecture of one region from that of another.'[19]

11

When Kahn visited the site in equatorial Africa, he was forcefully struck by the fiercely bright and hot sunshine, and realized that his buildings must respond to this climate by creating a place of shadow where dwelling could take place: 'The glare is killing, everybody looks black against the sunlight. Light is a needed thing, but still an enemy ... I came back with multiple impressions of how clever was the man who solved the problems of sun, rain, and wind.'[20] Kahn noted how, rather than face the direct sunlight coming through the windows, the people of Luanda 'would turn their chair toward the wall and do whatever they were doing by getting light indirectly from the wall to their work', because the sunlight that bounced off the walls was both diffused and carried no heat. Kahn believed that an appropriate design would 'find an architectural expression for the problems of glare without adding devices to a window'. He noted that the indigenous sunscreens of wood or masonry grillwork were unsatisfactory because they produced 'a multiple pattern of glare, little pin-points, little diamond points of glare against the grillwork',[21] a criticism he had earlier levelled at the applied sunscreens of International Style architecture.

Kahn instead proposed using a second set of walls to modulate the sunlight, placing 'a wall a small distance in front of every window' to catch and bounce the light into the space within (p. 159; n). Yet, 'placing a wall in front of a window would cut the view ... so I thought of placing openings in the wall; the wall then becomes part of the window'. This concept of a double set of walls layered around the inhabited rooms within, while developed from observing indigenous conditions, was also tied by Kahn to the beginnings of architecture itself: 'I thought of the beauty of ruins, the absence of frames, of things that nothing lives behind, and so I thought of wrapping ruins around buildings.'[22] Kahn was not interested in ruins as a preconceived image of the beautiful: 'I didn't want anything pretty: I wanted to have a clear statement of a way of life.'[23]

Kahn next addressed the problem of the fierce heat of the sun, and 'the importance of the breeze in carrying away the warm air that accumulated around the building'.[24] While the layered exterior walls would accomplish this on the elevations, which faced the sun at different periods of the day, Kahn recognized that most of the heat from the sun would enter a building through the roof, which faced the sun all day long. Again Kahn noted how the indigenous buildings dealt with this problem: 'Another thing that impressed me: I saw some buildings that were conscious of the heat generated by roofs. They had large ... separations between the ceiling and the roof, small openings which were visible from the outside in which the breeze could come in and ventilate the areas in the ceiling and roof planes.' At this point, as he had done with the facades, Kahn conceives of this indigenous design being reinterpreted as a series of planes layered in space: 'And it came to mind to have a sunroof purely for the sun and another roof purely for the rain'.[25] Kahn placed the roof layers 6 feet (1.8 metres) apart (so that one could walk between), allowing the breezes to pass through and exhaust the heat normally trapped within a single-layered roof (p. 159; o).

11. Model of the Chancellery (left) and the Residence (right), US Consulate.

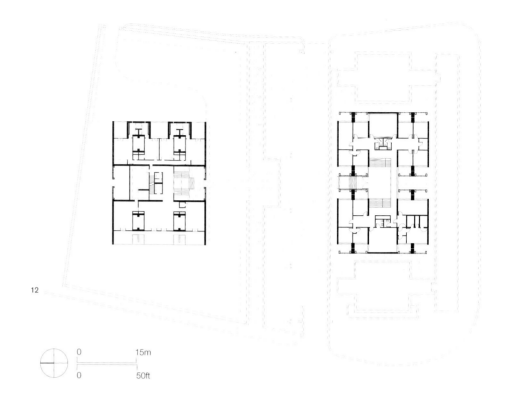

12

0　　　　　　　　　15m

0　　　　　　　　　50ft

Only after describing the developments of the layered surfaces of facades and roof does Kahn introduce the plan and spaces of the Consulate, which involved the design of both a chancellery, with its various diplomatic offices, and a residence for the ambassador, with requirements for official entertaining as well as private areas for the family. Kahn's initial plans started with the square once again, and he explored a variety of options where both the Chancellery and the Residence were square in plan (p. 158; i), each with a square central space, often the result of a cruciform and square interpenetrating, as in Wright's Unity Temple, Oak Park, Illinois. Kahn's final plan proposed two rectangular structures, set across from each other, the Residence to the north and the Chancellery to the south, with a stone-paved entry plaza crossing the site between them. While the Chancellery was to be set on a series of paved terraces framed by shallow pools of water on three sides, and opening directly onto the entry plaza to the north, the Residence was placed in a grass lawn with trees on either side, and was to be separated from the entry plaza by a 6 foot (1.8 metre) wall. The two buildings were to be of the same height, and were to be both covered by layered sun and rain roofs.

In both buildings the north and south facades are closed by solid walls (pp. 157, 159; g & q), while the east and west facades are recessed and deeply shadowed (pp. 157, 159; f & p). Each building is subdivided into two primary volumes, opening on to a central entry court (p. 158; j), which in turn opens to the north and south. In describing these buildings, Kahn first stated his belief that a space must clearly indicate its use, 'One should have a feeling of entrance and reception not by way of sign but by its very character.'[26] We enter into the shaded centre in both buildings, beginning at the ground and rising up

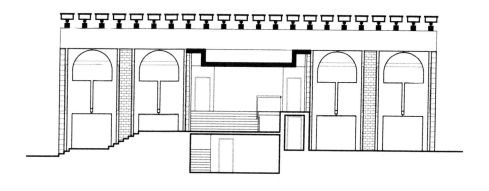

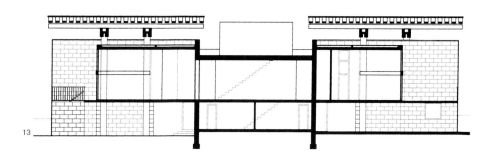

ceremonial stairs to the second floor (pp. 157, 158; d, e, k & l). As in an Italian Renaissance palazzo, the primary functions of both buildings are found on this second floor, with the services being clustered into vertical cores or placed on the ground floor. Within both buildings, the majority of the interior spaces are not air-conditioned; those spaces that are air-conditioned can also be opened to the breeze when the weather allows. While both buildings are symmetrically ordered about the shared central entry axis, they are subtly differentiated by the manner in which the concept of layered sun protection is articulated.

In the Chancellery, Kahn fully developed the shading walls as independent, freestanding, precast concrete elements that surround the two primary volumes of the building, eight facing east and eight facing west, shading both the exterior and the central courtyard facades. The glass-skinned interior rooms open out into the 10 foot (3 metre) deep 'inside-outside' spaces behind these shading walls (p. 156; a, b & c). Kahn developed several designs for the sixteen shading walls, finally settling on a three-part composition, open at the ground (to allow through breezes), with a narrow central slot above, and the whole topped by a large semicircular opening tracing the path of the sun (first developed for the Tribune Review Building). From within the building there are thus two layers of enclosure – the glass wall and the precast concrete shading wall beyond – and two types of view – the play of sunlight and shadow within the space made by the outer walls, and the view to the landscape beyond through the shaped openings in the outer walls.

In the Residence, Kahn recessed the enclosed spaces to the east and west, providing expansive, raised and shaded terraces serving the second floor. The two primary volumes house the main living spaces on the west and the

12. Site plan and second floor plan of the Residence (left) and the Chancellery (right), US Consulate; redrawn under author's supervision.
13. Sections of the Chancellery (above) and the Residence (below), US Consulate; redrawn under author's supervision.

bedrooms on the east, with parking, services and covered outdoor spaces below. Kahn placed into the plan four small courts, two in each of the primary volumes, which both bring shaded light deep into the plan and act as 'chimneys' to create through ventilation. The sunroof of the Residence is divided into two rectangular sections, one over each primary volume, with a roof terrace recessed between (p. 159; q). These two sunroofs are cantilevered on precast concrete girders supported by the four pairs of masonry piers rising up through the small interior courts, floating above the rain roof below, and creating an umbrella-like covering overhead. In contrast, the sunroof of the Chancellery covers the entire building (p. 157; g & h). The roof is supported by eight massive, 10 foot (3 metre) deep masonry piers set at the perimeter of the building (p. 156; a), where they stand between each pair of shading walls, together creating an enveloping sun-shading skin around the entire edge of the structure. In both buildings, the rain-roof is never pierced by the masonry piers that support the sunroof above, a critically important detail.

15

The sunroofs of both buildings were developed as elaborate constructions, conceived as tree-like shade canopies, the upper, outer layer of which Kahn initially proposed to be 'clay tiled leaves which form the sun tree on the sunroof which covers the entire building'.[27] Kahn's intention, clearly shown in the models prepared for the client, was that sunlight would fall directly through the sunroof only at midday, and then only in thin lines (p. 158; m), rather than either the sharp contrast of full shadow or the strong pattern of glare.[28] After exploring the possibility of a wooden lattice-like layer, similar to indigenous constructions, Kahn's final designs for the shading elements called for precast concrete 'sun shields' 3 feet (90 centimetres) wide, 1 foot (30 centimetres) deep, with an 8 inch (20 centimetre) slot between, so that 'when you come into the building here you sense the entire leaf-like structure above … they'd be open enough so that the light can come through', while also allowing heat to be vented through the roof. That this superb design, where Kahn felt he 'was telling the man on the street his way of life [by] explaining the atmospheric conditions of wind, the conditions of light, the conditions of sun and glare', was never realized is indeed tragic – particularly today, forty years later, as we still struggle to learn the fundamental lessons of sustainable construction so fully integrated into Kahn's design.[29]

14. Computer reconstruction of view through precast concrete sun shield walls across entry court, from one second floor office to another, Chancellery, US Consulate.

15. Computer reconstruction of view through sun shields to central court, Chancellery, US Consulate.

United States Consulate Chancellery and Residence

Concept development

Kahn's design for the Chancellery (as shown on these pages) and the Ambassador's Residence (overleaf) was from the start determined by his experience of the fierce sunlight and heat of Africa, and the manner in which the indigenous buildings dealt with the climate. Kahn developed his concept of double-walled structures, the outer walls tempering the climate and the inner walls enclosing the living spaces, with covered but open-air spaces between. For this design, Kahn dealt with the glare of the bright sunlight by making a series of freestanding walls, and he addressed the heat of the sun by placing a second roof – a sunroof – above the lower rain-roof, again with an open-air space between to allow the prevailing winds to exhaust the heat both from under the sunroof and from within the structure itself, through a series of small open-air courts. Thus the architecture, rather than mechanical equipment, would keep the internal spaces cool by casting a protective shadow over and all around them, whilst allowing the breezes to ventilate the structure. Kahn's overall Embassy site plan concept is also shown on pages 158–9.

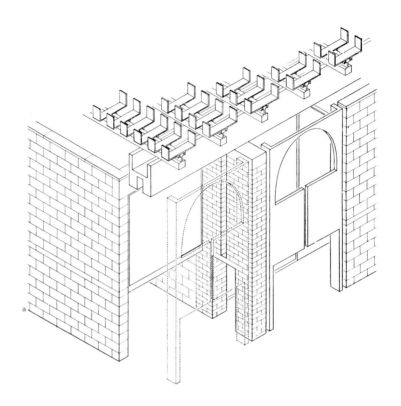

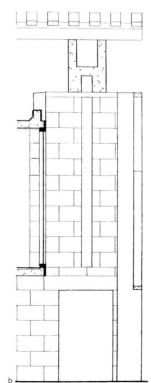

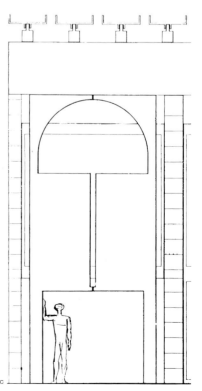

a. Axonometric drawing of corner of the Chancellery, US Consulate. The drawing shows the sun shield walls and shade roof. Note the use of smaller masonry units for the structural pier in the centre and larger masonry units for the non-structural walls on the left and right.
b. Section of the Chancellery with sun shield wall on the right, the light court and glazed interior wall on the left and the sunroof above.
c. Elevation of sun shield wall of the Chancellery, with sunroof above.

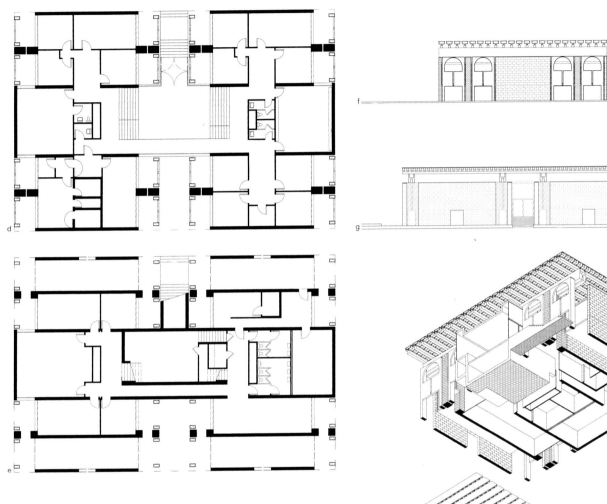

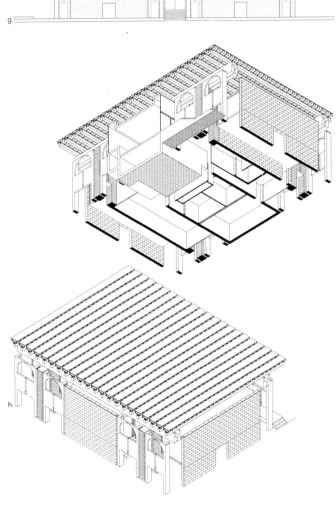

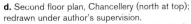

d. Second floor plan, Chancellery (north at top); redrawn under author's supervision.

e. Ground floor plan, Chancellery (north at top); redrawn under author's supervision.

f. East elevation, Chancellery. The west elevation is identical; redrawn under author's supervision.

g. North (entry) elevation, Chancellery; redrawn under author's supervision.

h. Isometric cut-away section drawings of the Chancellery, up-view (above) and down-view (below). The drawings show the relation of the sunshade roof to the inhabited spaces; drawn under author's supervision.

i

j

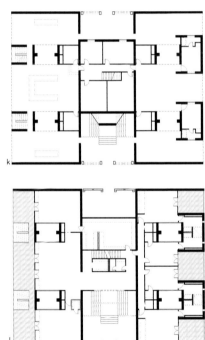

k

l

m

i. Perspective sketch of the Chancellery in front
and the Residence behind, US Consulate, early
design, 1960; drawing by Kahn. Both buildings
have square plans.
j. Perspective sketch of entry court, US Consulate,
with the Chancellery on the right and the Residence
on the left, early design, 1960; drawing by Kahn.
k. Ground floor plan, Residence (north at top);
redrawn under author's supervision.
l. Second floor plan, Residence (north at top);
redrawn under author's supervision.
m. Model of the Chancellery and Residence,
showing sunlight patterns at midday; only thin
lines of light penetrate the shadow of the roof.

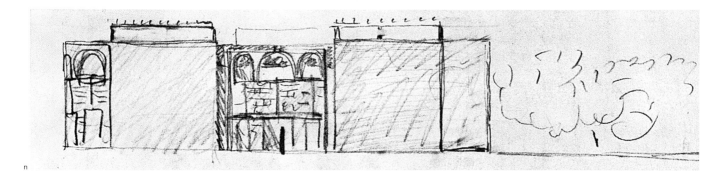

n

o

don construction
solid panel

p

q

n. Early sketch of the south elevation, Residence; drawing by Kahn. The semi-cylindrical sun walls, centre and left, are similar to those proposed for the Salk Institute Meeting House.
o. Early design sketches of the south elevation of the Residence, axonometric drawing of both buildings and details of structural beams supporting the sunroof; drawings by Kahn.
p. East elevation, Residence. The west elevation is identical; redrawn under author's supervision.
q. South (entry) elevation, Residence; redrawn under author's supervision.

Building shadow and space with folded walls

In the Esherick House, built in Chestnut Hill, Philadelphia, Pennsylvania, in 1959–61, Kahn continued his development of the concept of layered exterior walls. Here Kahn wrapped 'thick' exterior walls around the house; these served not only to accommodate service elements for the interior rooms but also to modulate the sunlight and breezes within their densely folded depth. The initial sketch plans for the Esherick House began with the square, and the final plan is composed of two half-squares (each a double square), divided by the recessed entry (from street and to garden) and stair, with a service zone added to the south-west side. To the left of the entry is the dining room, while the two-storey living room opens to the right. Beyond the dining room are the kitchen and laundry, and the bedrooms and bathroom are above on the second floor. The front (north-west) and back (south-east) walls of the main rooms are folded to provide more than 2 feet (60 centimetres) of thickness, into which are set bookcases, storage and wooden shutters. Beyond the otherwise solid south-west wall of the living room is projected the fireplace, with a window opening above it to reveal the chimney rising outside.

16. Esherick House, Chestnut Hill, Philadelphia, Pennsylvania, 1959–61. View from the garden into the double-height living room.
17. Plans of the Esherick House (ground floor, below; second floor, above).
18. Sections of the Esherick House, part of construction drawings.

16

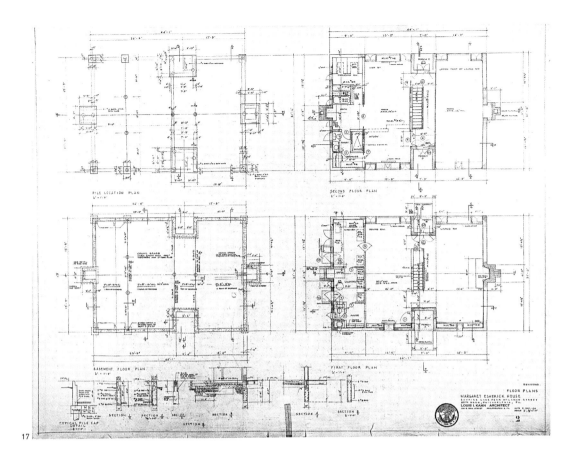

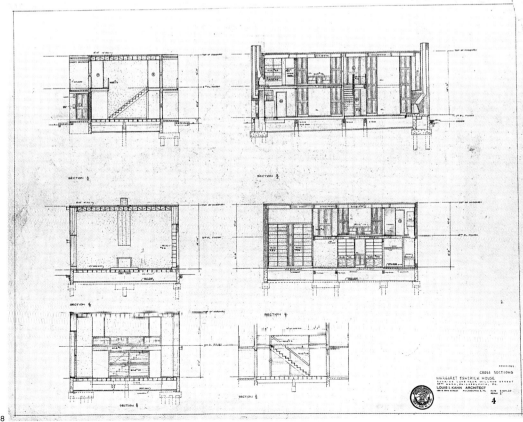

17

18

Our experience of these simple geometric volumes is powerfully shaped by Kahn's design of the thick walls and their openings. The front facade, to the north-west, is largely closed at the ground floor to provide privacy, with only two narrow openings and the recessed entry porch breaking the smooth, solid stucco-faced concrete-block wall. At the second floor each primary volume is given a large fixed-glass window, which in the living room forms – with the narrow ventilation slot below – a T-shape, reaching the full height and width of the double-height space. The south-east garden facade reveals the underlying tartan grid that structures the main volumes of the house: here the living and dining rooms both open their full width, with a large, full-height fixed glass window set flush to the outside face of the wall at the centre, and two narrow screened ventilation openings set flush to the inside face of the wall on either side, each with full-height wooden shutters. In warm weather, the ventilation apertures may be opened to admit light and air, while in the colder weather they are shuttered, dramatically modifying the amount of sunlight entering the rooms – in this way our experience within the house is characterized by the climate and its change through the seasons.[30]

19

20

21

19. South-west facade of the Esherick House,
with freestanding living-room fireplace chimney.
20. Street facade of the Esherick House, with
recessed entry on the right and main bedroom
on the left above.
21. Service facade of the Esherick House facing
left, with street facade to right.
22. Dining room, Esherick House; view towards
the garden.

22

First Unitarian
Church and School
Rochester, New York
1959–69

Perhaps more than any other project, Kahn's designs for the First Unitarian Church are indicative of the importance of Frank Lloyd Wright's early work as a starting point for Kahn. From the very first concept to the final built work, Kahn's First Unitarian Church is strikingly similar to Wright's Unity Temple, Illinois, 1905–8. In both, the sanctuary is a tall, central, top-lit space enclosed by solid walls offering no eye-level views out, which is entered through a low, dark narthex and surrounding ambulatory. This parallel is hardly surprising, given that both the congregation and Kahn were well aware that Wright's Unity Temple was considered the fundamental precedent for Unitarianism's modern architectural form.[31] In his initial designs for the First Unitarian Church and School, Kahn again started with the ancient tradition of square-and-cruciform plan and top-lit central space (of which Wright's Unity Temple is the leading modern example), but in Kahn's design, the encircling outer layers of space took on new meaning.

23

In discussing the Unitarian faith with various ministers, Kahn came to the conclusion that, at a fundamental level, Unitarianism involved putting things into question and seeking the foundation of shared beliefs. Kahn's first sketches explore the possibility of organizing the school around the common central space of the sanctuary, so that it is both formed and protected by the school. Drawing a diagram of his design, Kahn began with the square central sanctuary, into which he put a question mark – what he called the place of questioning. Around this he made an ambulatory, for those who were not yet ready to enter the central place of questioning, but who wished to remain near. Around the ambulatory, Kahn then drew a corridor that served the outermost layer of spaces, the school. In this way the school, which Kahn believed raised the question, became the walls that enclosed the sanctuary, the place of questioning.

Kahn's early designs for the plan of the building (and, even more strikingly, for the site plan) are virtually identical to Wright's Unity Temple, with their square central space surrounded by an ambulatory, with four axial projections forming a cruciform while four larger spaces anchor the outer corners (p. 176; a). In Kahn's first section sketches, he proposed a grid of skylights at the roof of the sanctuary, initially twenty-five squares (5 by 5, exactly as in Wright's Unity Temple); then nine squares (3 by 3); and finally four large squares (2 by 2) at the corners, joined at the centre by a cruciform-shaped folded-plate beam and skylight, similar to those Kahn had designed for the final Trenton Jewish Community Center scheme. Yet, as we have seen in the relation of the school to the sanctuary, Kahn initially took a different approach to that of Wright's Unity Temple, where the school and sanctuary are housed in separate volumes, joined by their common entry. Instead, Kahn began by ringing the sanctuary with the classrooms so that they formed the outer wall defining the central space.

In this design, Kahn could be said to be true to Wright in another way. It is clear that Kahn was engaging the same tradition as that which had been on Wright's mind in designing Unity Temple – the tradition of centralized plans, particularly strong in late Roman structures and in the centralized church plans of the Renaissance.[32] Examples of drawings for centralized churches by Leonardo da Vinci, among others, were to be found not only in Wittkower's *Architectural Principles in the Age of Humanism* (a copy of which Colin Rowe had given Kahn in 1956), but also in several other books in Kahn's library (p. 177; f & g).[33] One of Kahn's early section drawings has two small sketches in the corner that are strikingly similar to these Renaissance plans and, with their cellular chapels ringing the central domed space, these plans are close to Kahn's idea of wrapping the classrooms around the sanctuary (p. 177; e).[34] A common, transhistorical geometric space-making tradition unquestionably unites the Renaissance centralized churches, Wright's Unity Temple and Kahn's initial designs for this project.

Kahn's visit to Le Corbusier's Ronchamp Chapel, which he sketched during his 1959 trip to Europe (p. 178; i), also had a strong effect on his designs for the First Unitarian Church. In one of his early drawings for the church

23. Model of First Unitarian Church and School, intermediate scheme. This model shows the modular concrete roof shells and cross-shaped light monitors.

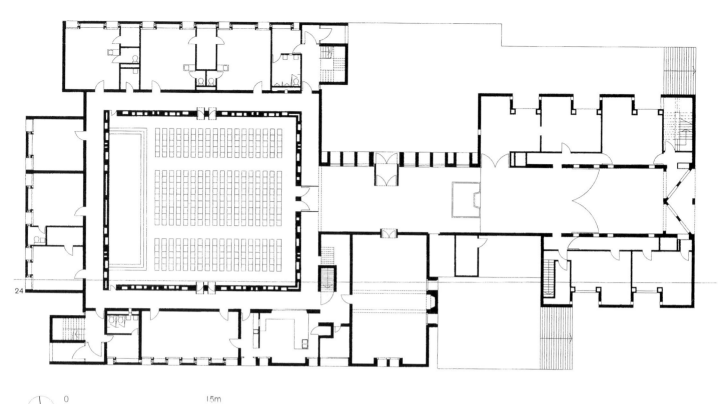

0   15m

0   50ft

24 & 25. Final plan and section of First Unitarian Church and School; redrawn under author's supervision.

(mentioned above), Kahn proposed that the roof of the sanctuary be elliptical in section, swelling at the centre both above and below, so that the ceiling would curve down into the space, lower at the centre than at the edge (p. 177; e). In its shape, its structure (an internal lightweight steel truss supporting the cast concrete outer shell) and the manner in which sunlight is introduced around the perimeter – between the roof and the enclosing walls – so as to wash the underside of the ceiling, Kahn's design is strikingly similar to Le Corbusier's Ronchamp Chapel. While Kahn would soon abandon the structural idea for the roof of this project (it would return in his early studies for Dhaka), the introduction of light at the perimeter would return in later schemes, and the downward slope of the roof (the opposite of the dome's upward thrust) would remain in Kahn's final design.

Kahn's first formally presented scheme was remarkably close to his idealized diagram for the project: a square sanctuary surrounded by an almost circular (twelve-sided) ambulatory and corridor, with the classrooms – solid-walled at the centre and glass-walled at the corners – forming the outer, square form of the building (p. 176; b & c). The clients strongly disapproved of this plan, however, saying that their 'greatest concern was the inherent "squareness" of the building',[35] and insisting, as Kahn recalled, 'that the sanctuary must be separated from the school – that was a terrible blow to me'. Kahn reluctantly presented the sanctuary and school as separate, 'but I did this only in diagram, not in actual plan. I never could be forced to make a plan which satisfied this', indicating that he could not bring himself to draw a plan in which he did not believe. He then asked the congregation questions about the nature of the school and the sanctuary, and the activities that would take place and, after examining the use of each room, it soon became clear that, in fact, all the elements of the school programme needed to be near the sanctuary. As Kahn said, 'we were back where I had started. It had to be that way because of the very nature of the activities, and I sensed right from the beginning that these things had to be close.'[36]

However, this revised plan was by no means exactly the same as before, and in fact was quite different from the first design. To begin, it was no longer bi-axially symmetrical, either in its overall form or in the central sanctuary, which had gone from a square to a rectangle in plan. As Kahn said, the programmatic requirements for rooms of varying sizes not only eliminated the four glass volumes at the outside corners but also 'prevented the development of a clear geometric form on the exterior of the building'.[37] This challenge of finding a non-symmetrical order made of fragmented geometric figures gave rise to what would later become one of Kahn's most typical design concepts: the clustering of independent, self-supporting spaces of varying sizes and geometric shapes around a primary and powerful central space.

The plan Kahn now developed was in some ways even closer to Wright's Unity Temple. Square stairs were now placed at the exterior corners to the north-east and south-west; and entry was not directly into the main sanctuary volume, but into a separate narthex placed on the east side. The sanctuary's interior dimensions also bore striking similarities to Wright's building, being in plan 58 by 66 feet (17.5 by 20 metres) (this last the exact exterior measurement of Unity Temple), and in height to the light monitors 30 feet (9 metres) (the exact height of the sanctuary of Unity Temple). These dimensional parallels are hardly coincidences, and they remind us that Kahn, like all the great architects, knew the dimensions of important architectural precedents and used them as a means of scaling his own work, ensuring achievement of the intended spatial experience. A final parallel was to come with the addition to the First Unitarian building, designed in 1965, where Kahn placed the new school and community spaces, including

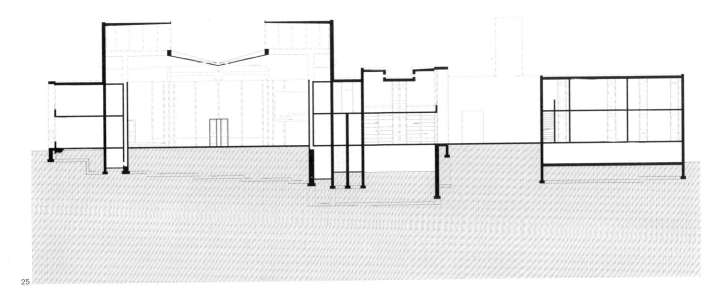

a fireplace, in an 'annexe' volume attached to the east side of the narthex, their entry now across a court and into a recessed foyer between the two primary masses – all exactly as in Wright's Unity Temple and its school, Unity House.

This plan changed very little as the project went through the six fully developed schemes that followed, wherein Kahn's focus was on evolving the roof forms for the top-lit sanctuary, with its ceiling plan of four large square dome-like light monitors, pushed to the corners, and a cruciform-shaped set of beams at the centre. In exploring his designs for these roof forms, Kahn made a series of cut-away, upward-view axonometric drawings (p. 179; k & l), the same type of drawing as that used to illustrate Choisy's *Histoire de l'architecture*, a copy of which was in Kahn's library. These drawings show the roof and ceiling as seen from below; that is to say, from the inhabitant's point of view. The sanctuary below was enclosed by a lower inner wall, while the ceiling above reached over to a higher outer wall; the two walls together formed the encircling corridor, off which opened the classrooms at the outer perimeter. The majority of these designs proposed that the roof be supported both by columns in the inner wall (and thus visible to the occupant) and by the outer wall – as it would be in the final built work.

Yet Kahn also designed a remarkable scheme involving four columns, standing within the sanctuary, which supported the four large 'light towers',

26. First Unitarian Church and School. This view from the south-west shows the light towers at the corners of the sanctuary rising above the classrooms.

as Kahn called them, at their centres. This 'umbrella-like' structural system, a recurring theme in Kahn's work, allowed the entire concrete roof to be lifted free of the surrounding walls, and Kahn created a horizontal slot of clerestory light all around to articulate this structural separation for the occupants within. On the section (p. 178; h), Kahn drew an eye at standing eye-level, with a line pointing to the horizontal light slot, and at the bottom of the same drawing he wrote, 'the light strips under the light towers [are] to be visible as a dash of light when [the] eye is far enough back – the purpose is to show the lightness of the structure'.[38] While the columns standing within the space were not carried forward in later designs, Kahn would return to this concept in the design of the Hurva Synagogue. The idea of the light slot between roof and walls, however, was included in three of Kahn's six proposed schemes for the church, and here we can again perceive the influence on Kahn of his recent visit to Le Corbusier's Ronchamp Chapel, where the ceiling appears to 'float' above the wall all around, separated from it by a thin horizontal line of light.

While one scheme, dated late March 1960, proposed employing identical roof forms for both sanctuary and school, to create 'a structural system with some inherent unity' (p. 179; m)[39] in a way quite similar to the third scheme for the Trenton Jewish Community Center, Kahn's final design returned to the concept that the sanctuary and the surrounding school spaces should differ from each other in massing, exterior elevation and roof form. As was to be typical of Kahn's work, the exterior forms of the building were first evolved from the spaces within (another parallel with the work of Wright), beginning in this case with the character of the sanctuary and its relation to the surrounding classrooms.

Kahn then developed the building's primary volumes to both introduce and modulate sunlight through layered exterior walls, and in his search for a historical beginning for such an architecture of thick walls, Kahn returned to his beloved medieval castles.[40] Kahn was fascinated by the way in which castles such as Comlongon in Dumfries and Galloway, Scotland,[41] begin with a primary central hall, around which is wrapped a masonry wall 20 feet (6 metres) thick (p. 176; d). The wall houses within its thickness a variety of smaller rooms of every conceivable shape, alongside circular stairs and battered window openings which give only a small opening to the exterior and splay open to become room-like spaces on the interior.

When we approach the First Unitarian Church and School today, it is the powerfully folded brick outer walls of the school rooms, creating an alternating rhythm of deeply shadowed vertical recesses, that first capture our attention. Beyond and above rise the four great 'light towers' that mark the corners of the sanctuary at the centre, their cast concrete walls clad in brick to match the rest of the building. While the overall massing of the building is in fact rather low, the school being only two storeys in height, the projecting and recessing outer brick wall and the light towers rising up behind combine to give the building a surprisingly strong vertical articulation. This articulation becomes more effective the closer we approach. The entry court is flanked on the left (east) by the wall of the classroom addition and to the right (west) by the

sanctuary's solid outer wall – the only place on the exterior where we can see this wall come to the ground, without the protective layer of the original classrooms. Entering through the vertical brick piers (first proposed for the Morris House of 1955–8), we find ourselves in the low foyer or narthex, with the community room opening to our left and the solid wall of the sanctuary to our right – all exactly as in the entrance to Wright's Unity Temple.

The doors to the sanctuary are housed in a small wooden vestibule, the walls of which project forward from the concrete-block wall of the sanctuary, the surrounding ambulatory corridor opening to either side. We first enter the sanctuary under the low ceiling – and in the deep shadow – of the choir balcony above, which cantilevers out into the room. Stepping out from under the balcony onto the simple, smooth cast concrete floor, we look up and first perceive the full extent of the sanctuary space. We can now see that the sanctuary rises above the two floors of classrooms, and that its ceiling reaches over the concrete block inner wall to the cast-concrete outer wall of the corridor so that, from within, the sanctuary appears to have a double boundary, nearer below and farther above.

The roof of the sanctuary is a gently folded plane of cast concrete, lifting to large clerestory lights at the corners so as to form a huge cross-shape overhead.

27. Entry facade of the First Unitarian Church and School. This view shows the entry court and door on the right, the later school addition on the left and the fireplace chimney above.
28. East facade of the later school addition, First Unitarian Church and School.

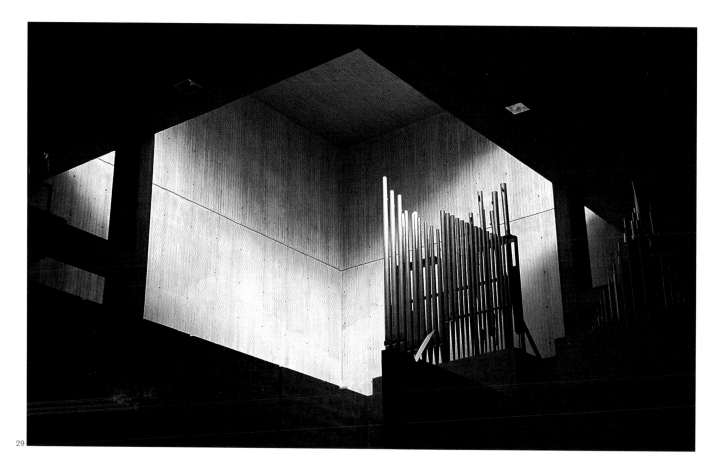

For Kahn, the rectangular geometry of the space required that light enter the room from all four corners, to 'give expression to the form, the shape, of the room chosen'.[42] While the square crossing acts to centre the space strongly, the light towers opening upwards at the corners and the manner in which the sunlight they admit bounces off the outer wall as it enters, together create a sense of multiple boundaries and layered edges to the space. The inward-folding, downward-sloping form of the ceiling is lowest and darkest at the centre of the room, with light coming into the space at the corners. In this way, Kahn's ceiling is the exact opposite of classical church domes, as well as his beloved Pantheon, which are highest and brightest at their centres. Along with the room's layered outer edges, the ceiling and its light-filled corners impart an expansive, boundless character to the sanctuary space, creating a powerful sense of place, of a world within, distant from the outside world.

The roof of the sanctuary is made of cast concrete, and on the surface of the ceiling we can clearly discern the imprints of the wood-board forms into which the concrete was cast. The roof spans as a folded-plate slab across the room. It is supported at three points on each side by thin concrete columns that stand within the thickness of the sanctuary's inner concrete block wall, exposed to the corridor and revealed in the sanctuary through 4 inch (10 centimetre) vertical slots in the wall. Three of the four central columns also stand in the doorways of the sanctuary, so that we perceive and touch the

29. Sanctuary, First Unitarian Church and School; this corner view shows one of the four roof clerestory light monitors, this one is adjacent to the organ loft.
30. View at the corner of the sanctuary, looking straight up, First Unitarian Church and School. This view shows the clerestory, light monitor, cast concrete roof and concrete masonry inner wall.

structure that supports the room at the very moment of entry. The four central
columns expand to form a square bracket at their top, which not only is split
at its centre to allow the fold of the ceiling to pass through but is also braced
to the columns to either side by narrow free-spanning beams. By taking
a substantial part of the load of the roof into the solid, cast concrete outer
corridor wall, Kahn could make the columns – the only means of support for
the roof visible to those in the sanctuary – remarkably thin, 'to show the
lightness of the structure'. Describing the experience of the space, with its
folded roof, corner light towers, columns and 'flying' beams, Kahn remarked,
'It's very Gothic, isn't it? Does that bother you? I like it myself.'[43]

The inner wall surrounding the sanctuary is constructed of concrete block
and is 2 feet (60 centimetres) thick, the hollow spaces within it housing the
ventilation supply and return ducts. The return air enters through the 2 inch
(5 centimetre) vertical slots placed at regular intervals on the inside (sanctuary)
and outside (classroom corridor) faces of this wall, while the supply air is
fed into the sanctuary out of the top of the wall, which stops well short of
the ceiling. Kahn designed tapestries, to be hung on the inner wall of the
sanctuary, which presented the spectrum of colours within natural light in a
series of vertical, overlapping bands. Kahn called upon his old friend, Anni
Albers, to execute these weavings, which were installed in 1964.[44]

Throughout the building, Kahn employed wood extensively in the
construction of doors, walls (as at the entry vestibules), furniture, shelving and
storage, perhaps inspired by his visits to wood-panelled English manor houses

31

32

33

with Alison and Peter Smithson in 1959.[45] The construction drawings for the church are the first examples of what would become Kahn's signature flush-finish, square-cornered woodworking details, and this is the first building in which Kahn employed wood and concrete together, the warmer, softer wood and the colder, harder concrete complementing each other perfectly. It is important to note in this regard that Kahn intended the floor of the sanctuary also to be wood (it was changed to concrete by the client to reduce costs). As Kahn designed it, the wood floor and the concrete ceiling, cast into wood board forms, would have engaged the sanctuary space itself in this dialogue of materials.

The classrooms, entered from the ambulatory, form a thick protective layer around the sanctuary, their brick exterior walls folded, projected out to house window seats, and recessed in to produce a deeply shadowed space into which large windows are set. The window seats are each given two small windows, opening to the recesses on either side, so that a little light is let into the dark spaces between the large, bright windows, further modulating the glare. These window seats also had a functional purpose. Kahn felt that, as a result of the often 'multi-purpose' nature of many of the spaces, and the uncertainty of activity, 'there's a great feeling that a window seat should be present because there is no telling how the room will be used'.[46] As an inhabited edge, literally built into the light, the window seat is a place where one can retreat and be by oneself. These window seats are effective both as sun modulators, in the way the light bounces off the side walls of the recesses before entering the interior spaces, and as independent 'rooms' built into the thick walls – their small and narrow side windows reminding us that Kahn discovered this concept in the castle.

In designing the First Unitarian Church and School, Kahn carefully developed the four elevations of the building, rendering them to indicate the strong effects of the sun and shadow. Kahn deployed the same shading wall on all four elevations, in all orientations, and in his drawings he shows the sun's effects on the four elevations – facing, in this case, the four cardinal directions – as being exactly the same (p. 178; j). The sunlight appears to come from the same direction and angle on all four drawings. This, of course, is impossible, for the sun has a precise path through the sky, and the shadows on the four elevations can never be the same. In his designing the walls as if sunlight comes from all directions equally, rather than developing different shading 'devices' for each orientation, we perceive that Kahn's conception of sunlight and its effect on buildings was in no way 'scientific', or even realistic – quite the opposite, in fact. Kahn conceived of light as an idealized material, coming towards us from all directions (either directly or bounced). In illustrating a later lecture, Kahn drew light as a pattern of straight and wavy lines completely surrounding and filling space. He believed that by designing buildings as centred places, where the ever-changing and varied effects of the sun through the day and the seasons plays across the unchanging and pure geometric volumes of the interior spaces, he was honouring the true nature of light.

31. Sanctuary, First Unitarian Church and School. This view looks towards the entry, balcony and organ at the rear, with the pulpit in the centre; acoustic weavings designed by Kahn and executed by Anni Albers hang along the right wall.
32. Folded concrete roof, support column and organ, First Unitarian Church and School.
33. Side entry doors to the sanctuary with projecting oak wood vestibules, First Unitarian Church and School.
34. Window seat between full-height glazing in the folded brick exterior wall of the classroom, First Unitarian Church and School.

34

First Unitarian Church and School

More than any other of Kahn's designs, the First Unitarian Church and School was inspired directly by Wright's Unity Temple and Unity House of 1905–8 (Kahn's early designs and inspirations are shown on these pages). He began with an almost exact replica of Wright's cruciform-in-square sanctuary plan, and his final design for the sanctuary, in both its form and dimensions, remains close to this precedent. Yet in his design process, Kahn discovered a different relationship between the sanctuary and the school. Separated into two buildings in Wright's Unity Temple and Unity House, Kahn instead wrapped the brick-clad classrooms around the central concrete sanctuary, creating a multi-layered, thick, protective wall. This last element indicates that Kahn was aware of the similarly thick, inhabited walls of Scottish castles. In addition, he was inspired by the line of light around the edge of the downward-curving roof at Le Corbusier's Ronchamp Chapel (1950–54), as well as by the umbrella-like roof structures of Wright's 1936–8 Johnson Wax Building. In his early schemes for the design of the sanctuary roof, shown overleaf, Kahn attempted to combine these two precedents.

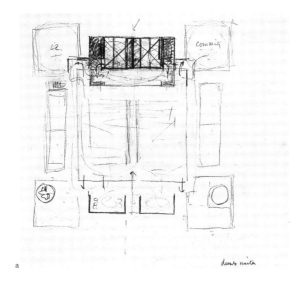
a

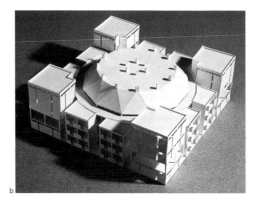
b

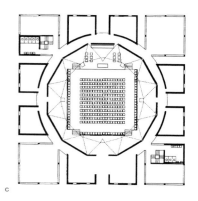
c

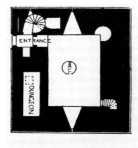
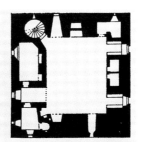
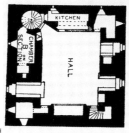

d

a. Sketch plan of First Unitarian Church and School, drawing by Louis Kahn. The plan is directly related to Frank Lloyd Wright's Unity Temple, Oak Park, Illinois, 1905–8.
b. Model of First Unitarian Church and School, first scheme.
c. Plan of First Unitarian Church and School, first scheme. The square sanctuary, centre, is surrounded by a twelve-sided wall and circular ambulatory, with the classrooms forming an outer square.
d. Plans, Comlongon Castle, Dumfries and Galloway, Scotland. These plans showing thick, inhabited walls are from a book in Kahn's library.

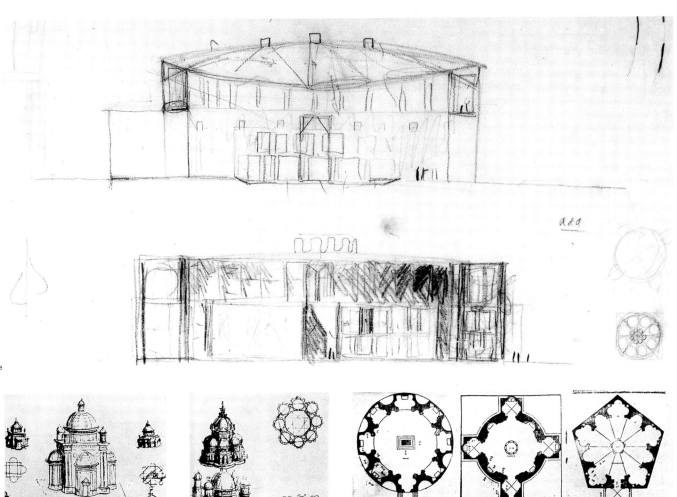

e

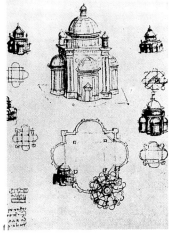

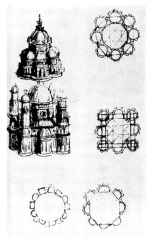

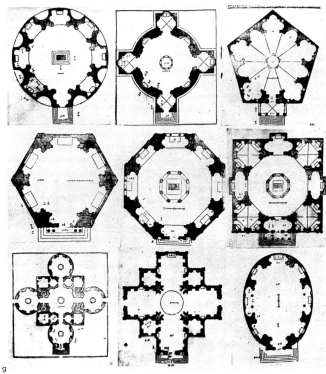

g

e. Sketch of section and elevation, First Unitarian
Church and School, first scheme; drawings by Louis
Kahn. Kahn relates the centralized church plan to
Renaissance plans drawn in the lower right corner.
f. Leonardo da Vinci, plans and axonometric drawings
of centralized Renaissance churches, plates from
Rudolf Wittkower, *Architectural Principles in the
Age of Humanism*, 1949.
g. Sebastiano Serlio, plans of centralized
Renaissance churches, 1547; plate from Rudolf
Wittkower, *Architectural Principles in the Age
of Humanism*, 1949.

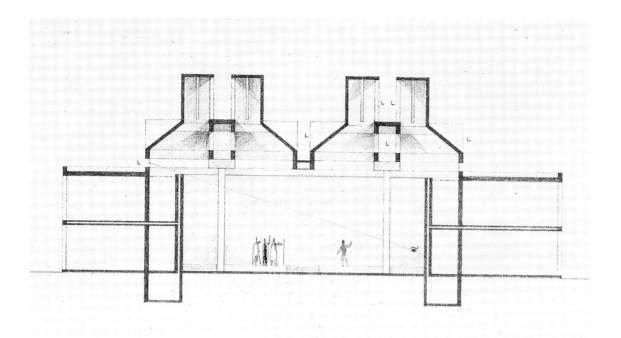

h

i

j

h. Section of four-column and 'umbrella'-roof design, intermediate scheme, First Unitarian Church and School, August 1960. Note the eye drawn in the lower right corner of the sanctuary with a line of view towards the upper left, indicating that the slot of light running below the roof is visible from the ground.
i. Interior of Le Corbusier's Ronchamp Chapel, 1950–4; sketch by Kahn made during his 1959 trip to the CIAM Conference, Otterlo, the Netherlands.
j. South elevation (top), with west, east and north elevations in descending order, First Unitarian Church and School. These drawings show the same sun angle and shadows on all four elevations as if the sun shone equally from all four cardinal directions.

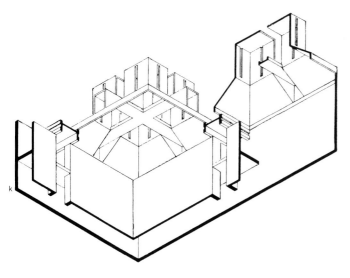

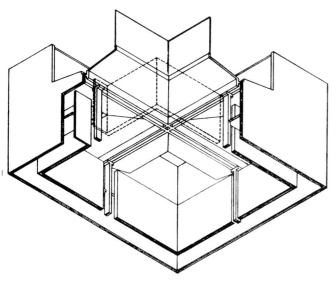

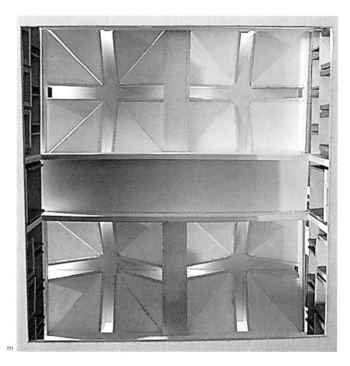

k & l. Up-view, cut-away axonometric sections of early (above) and later (below) designs for the sanctuary roof, First Unitarian Church and School. The drawings, which show the folded cast concrete shells and light monitors, and the enclosing double wall, are similar in style to the drawings of Auguste Choisy in *Histoire de l'architecture*, 1899.
m. Study model of the sanctuary roof and its light, viewed looking up, intermediate scheme.

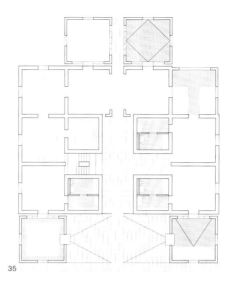

35

Wrapping ruins around buildings

In the Fleisher House, an unbuilt project for Elkins Park, Pennsylvania of 1959, Kahn took the next step in his exploration of the relationship between sunlight and space. Precisely at the time when he was being required to design an asymmetrical institutional building (the First Unitarian Church and School), Kahn produced for the Fleisher House his first completely symmetrical house design. Kahn proposed that each cubic room-bay of the house be given a large semicircular sun-window set above a smaller slot-like view-window (as in the studies for the Tribune Review Building). Finally, Kahn made four of the cubic room-bays, the two flanking the entry court and the two projected to the rear, into roofless 'rooms', gardens open to the sky. These may be considered Kahn's first attempt at 'built ruins', walled exterior spaces whose purpose was to receive and modulate the sunlight for the interior spaces behind.

In his unrealized design for the Bristol Township Offices, Bucks County, Pennsylvania, of 1960–61, Kahn formed the various units of local government as independent buildings, all gathered into a long narrow rectangle, with public entry off a plaza and amphitheatre, and entry to the police station at the opposite end from an enclosed courtyard. Both entrances were accomplished with projecting vestibules, as in the First Unitarian Church. The police station is a square mass organized around a square central courtyard and surrounded by a perimeter corridor. The city offices are organized along an interior hall, in alternating large and small bays. The large bays project into the court as half-cylinders and project out of the building as solid walls, with the smaller recessed bays between providing entry from the hall and opening sideways as light courts on the exterior. The meeting room, a solid rectangular volume, is set at the end of the main hall, terminating the entry axis. Entry is through a porch flanked by 'light courts', similar to those at the front of the Fleisher House – an idea that would return in the entry porticos of the Kimbell Art Museum, Fort Worth, Texas.

36

37

35. Plans of the ground floor (left) and second floor
(right), Fleisher House, Elkins Park, Pennsylvania,
1959 (north down). The project was never built;
plans redrawn under author's supervision.
36. Model of the Fleisher House.
37. Plan of the Bristol Township Offices, Bucks
County, Pennsylvania, 1960–61 (north at top);
entry (left) and police station (right).

Salk Institute for Biological Studies
La Jolla, California
1959–65
Part built

The Salk Institute is unquestionably Kahn's greatest and most seminal design. Here he first fully developed the concept of surrounding primary spaces with shadow-giving walls, which he described as 'wrapping ruins around buildings'; the concept of the plan as a 'society of spaces', a series of independent room-buildings, each with their own geometry and structure, gathered around a top-lit central space; and the concept of shaping 'served' and 'servant' spaces, in both plan and section, within the precisely constructed volumes of a folding structure. That none of these three concepts was in the end realized on this project does not detract from its significance for Kahn's career; indeed, the case can be made that all of Kahn's later buildings are directly developed from concepts first presented in his designs for the Salk Institute.

Dr Jonas Salk, inventor of the polio vaccine (p. 210; a & b), first became aware of Kahn through a friend who had heard Kahn speak on the Richards Medical Research Laboratories in Pittsburgh in autumn 1959.[47]

Initially visiting Kahn's office only to ask for recommendations on architects for his own research laboratories, Salk went on a tour of the Richards Building with Kahn, and was so taken with Kahn's description of the thinking behind the design that he decided to hire him. In Salk, Kahn had found a kindred spirit, exemplified by Salk's statement during their initial talk that he desired the Institute to be a place where the modern rift between the arts and the sciences could be bridged. This understanding that research breakthroughs in the sciences could be inspired by interactions with those in other disciplines was reflected in Salk's selection of mathematician and humanist, Dr Jacob Bronowski, to be one of the nine original faculty members of the Institute. In what was without question the greatest challenge ever given to Kahn, Salk asked him to design the Institute to be the kind of place where Picasso could be invited to meet the scientists.[48] Thus, from the very beginning, Kahn's designs for the Salk Institute focused both on the places of work – the biological laboratories – and the equally important places of meeting, discussion and contemplation.

Kahn visited the spectacular site, set high on the cliffs facing the ocean, in early 1960, and he presented his first scheme for the Salk Institute in March. Salk had provided very little in the way of brief for the Institute, so Kahn's designs reflected his own interpretation. From the very start, Kahn organized the Institute into three distinct clusters of buildings. The place of work, the laboratories, he placed near the main road to the east. The place of repose, the residential buildings, he positioned along the edges of the canyon, which opened through the centre of the site. The place of meeting, Kahn situated on the bluff closest to the ocean to the west. The three building clusters were positioned so as to share the view of the ocean, and to ring the canyon at the centre of the site.

Kahn's interpretation of the programme closely paralleled that of the medieval monastery, one of his most beloved historical building types, and one which Salk had specifically suggested as a model for the kind of place he had in mind for the Institute. Salk's reference was to the monastery of San Francesco at Assisi (p. 215; q), with which Kahn was very familiar, having extensively sketched it in 1929. Set at the end of the ridge of a rugged hilltown, with its arcaded plaza leading up from the town below and its stone-paved central cloister, this monastery has parallels not only with the programme of the Salk Institute, but also with its overall site design and the character of its spaces. In the summer of 1960, Kahn wrote of his desire to visit Europe, 'specifically northern Italy, to see again the wonderful monasteries which have a bearing on what I am doing for Dr Salk in San Diego'.[49]

Kahn's initial designs involved the laboratories being proposed in towers, arranged as square or cruciform clusters (similar to the Richards Medical Research Building), which were in turn set onto four circular plinths (similar to that of the Jewish Community Center Day Camp). From the parking area provided directly off Torrey Pines Road, a road and walkway were proposed to run in a straight line along the top of the northern ridge, with the residential buildings set along it. The Meeting House was placed at its far end, across a bridge, on a bluff directly above the ocean (p. 211; c). By early 1961 Kahn had

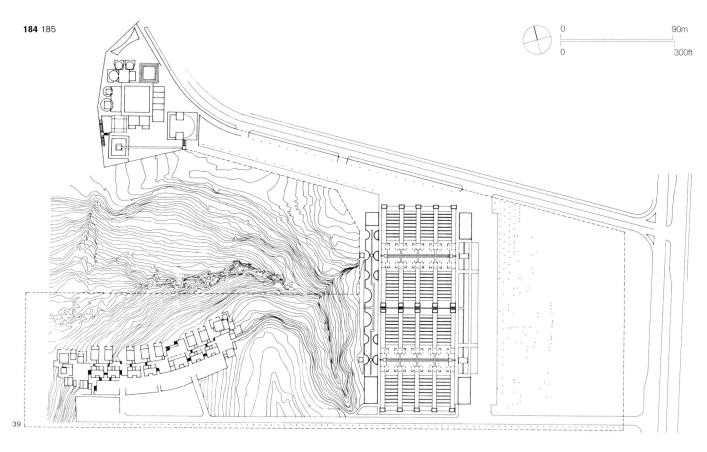

39

39. Site plan of the Salk Institute, first four-laboratory block scheme, 1960–2 (north at top). The plan shows the Meeting House (top), laboratories (right) and residences (left).
40. Entry level plan of the Meeting House, Salk Institute; shaded areas indicate roofed interior spaces; redrawn under author's supervision.
41. Section of the Meeting House, with open court at centre, Salk Institute; redrawn under author's supervision.

developed what would substantially remain the final site plan. The laboratories lined up along the road to the east, the residences nestled along the south edge of the canyon, and, at the end of the tree-lined plaza along the northern ridge, the Meeting House overlooked the ocean.

From the earliest designs, it is clear that Kahn intended the Meeting House to be the dominant element of the Institute, and it was invariably given the purest geometries and most massive form, as well as the prime position on the site. Kahn's initial designs, for the bluff closest to the ocean, involved a rectangular plan, the long side of which was parallel to the beach below, with the primary rooms formed as independent square buildings (very similar to the Bristol Township Building). These rooms were set towards the west and entered from a great hall running the length of the building, and accessed by a bridge. The final site for the Meeting House was set back from the ocean, at the end of the northern ridge of the canyon, and all of Kahn's later designs propose that the building be placed on an irregular, five-sided plinth. Throughout the design process for the Salk Institute, the unusual shape of this plinth never changed, and, while it is usually held to have been derived from the contours of the landform,[50] in fact these curving lines do not correspond very closely to the faceted plan – which does, however, bear an uncanny resemblance to the plinth of the Acropolis in Athens (p. 211; d).[51]

Like the Acropolis's irregular plinth and perfectly regular buildings, Kahn's early designs for the Meeting House involved the juxtaposition of symmetrical, centralized square and rectangular plans upon the irregularly angled plinth.

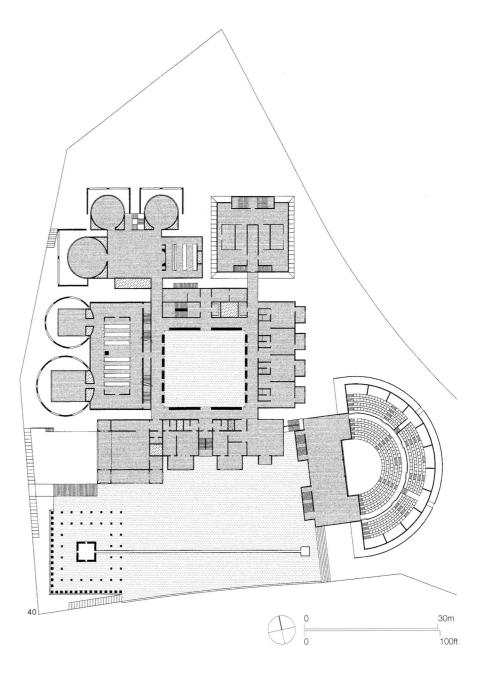

40

0   30m

0   100ft

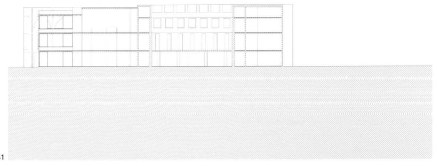

41

43

His first sketches explore a series of plans based upon Wright's Unity Temple,
with a square and a rectangular volume separated and joined by the entry hall
between. Kahn next proposed a series of plans where four primary spaces are set
within a larger square structure, producing a cruciform space at the centre, into
which is placed a central hall leading from the entry to the auditorium. He then
joined the four primary square spaces into two rectangular volumes, which
together framed the central colonnaded hall, the whole square plan surrounded
by a wall, with small square masses anchoring the four corners. This plan,
of which there are multiple variations among Kahn's designs, is quite close to

the plan of the Roman Emperor Diocletian's Palace at Split, Croatia, which is in fact sketched in the margins of one of Kahn's drawings (p. 211; e).

Though it has been overlooked in other studies of this project, Kahn also developed a parallel series of designs for the Meeting House that involved asymmetrical compositions of independent, geometrically pure elements arranged to accommodate the irregular form of the plinth. These schemes may also have been inspired by a Roman villa, Hadrian's Villa at Tivoli, as has often been suggested,[52] but another source lay closer at hand. It was during this period that Kahn first hung a copy of Piranesi's imaginary plan of a

45

‘reconstruction’ of the Campus Martius section of ancient Rome (p. 212; h), published in 1762, in front of his desk in his office.[53] Piranesi’s map is largely composed of his own powerful geometric designs, carefully woven into the few fragments of ancient Roman buildings that were known at that time.[54] Piranesi’s plan of the Campus Martius contains countless independent, geometrically pure structures, composed of every imaginable combination of circles and squares, endlessly and inventively subdivided and multiplied, filling the large panel which Kahn chose to place in his view as he worked.

In designing the Meeting House, Kahn explored as precedents both a Roman urban villa, with a clearly defined rectangular outer form and a square planning grid (Diocletian’s Palace), and a Roman rural villa, with an irregularly defined outer form and a multi-angled planning grid (Hadrian’s Villa). But most important for Kahn was the manner in which these forms were combined in Piranesi’s Campus Martius plan, which is ordered as a set of independent, freestanding room-buildings, each with its own geometry and structure. Rather than this being a discovery made late in the design process, as it is usually described, Kahn explored this type of plan from the start, and what

44. Entry approach, looking west through bosquet of trees towards the central courtyard, Salk Institute. This image was taken before recent additions that have destroyed Kahn's original entry sequence.
45. Service towers at outer edges of laboratory blocks, south side, Salk Institute.

would be his final solution for the Meeting House in fact already exists in several of his earliest sketches.[55] In these plans, a square central room is surrounded by a larger square volume and outer wall, with spaces of various shapes and sizes joined to the central square along its axes of symmetry (p. 212; g).

Kahn's final plan for the Meeting House combines a square central court-building, which gives order to the plan from within, with an irregular outer edge, formed by clusters of independent room-buildings. With attributes of the Roman villa, the castle, the centralized Renaissance church and the monastery, yet emphatically modern in its articulation, this plan was perhaps Kahn's greatest invention. It allowed him to achieve geometric purity in the independent room-buildings, and find asymmetry and dynamic balance in the overall form and massing. The independence of the various room-buildings within the larger Meeting House was so complete that Kahn was able to design each room as a separate building, only later returning them to their place within the larger assembly. Unity of the whole is achieved by the absolutely uniform roof height of all the assembled room-buildings.

Though not typically a responsibility of the architect, Kahn took the lead in developing the brief for the Meeting House.[56] Salk's desire to bring Picasso to the Institute, as Kahn said, changed the project from a 'plain building ... to one which demanded a place of meeting which was every bit as big as a laboratory. It was ... the place of arts and letters. It was a place where one had his meal, because I don't know of any greater seminar than the dining room.'[57] Kahn proposed apartments for visiting scholars to be arranged along the east side facing the city and an apartment for the director on the south side, overlooking the forecourt. The House also included a gymnasium, kitchen and dining rooms on the north side, looking up the rugged coastline; and the

47

library and its reading rooms on the west side, directly facing the ocean.
A 500-seat, freestanding amphitheatre was placed to the south-east, at the end
of the tree-lined access road. Finally, forming the centre of the building was
the main court, measuring 60 feet (18 metres) square, which had no formal
programme and 'no name. It was the biggest room, but it was not designated
in any way',[58] acting as entry hall, central court, occasional banquet room
and place of unplanned meetings. The whole, in its programme and plan, and
in its splendid isolation at the end of the ridge overlooking the ocean, could
hardly have been more monastic in character.

One would have approached the Meeting House along the tree-lined plaza
on the northern ridge of the canyon (p. 214; m), moving around the curved
back wall of the theatre and entering a stone-paved forecourt (p. 212; f) – here
we should note the similarities to the paved piazza fronting San Francesco in
Assisi. This 'garden', as Kahn called it, was framed by the wall of the Meeting
House to the north and open to the canyon to the south, with the view of the
ocean directly ahead. A 'noisy fountain' was the source for the water than ran
down a narrow slot in the pavement to the 'quiet fountain' at the other end,
at the centre of the square space formed by a series of standing columns
without beams. The idea for this line of water slicing through the stone floor,
which Kahn would employ in the final laboratory design as well, originates
in the medieval Alhambra in Granada, Spain, where, as in the Meeting House,
the line of water terminates in a pool set within a columned space (p. 213; k).
At once like trees in a bosquet, and yet forming an almost solid wall on the
west and south sides, these columns would be experienced as both a garden of
stone ruins and as a displaced arcade, being the exact dimension of the
building's central court. Given the prime site, overlooking both canyon and
ocean, these columns rising above the plinth would have clearly recalled the
columns of the Parthenon rising above the plinth of the Acropolis (p. 214; o).

46. Laboratory before occupation, Salk Institute.
47. Service floor and laboratory ceiling under
construction, looking east, 27 April 1964; note
slots for services to feed down into laboratory.

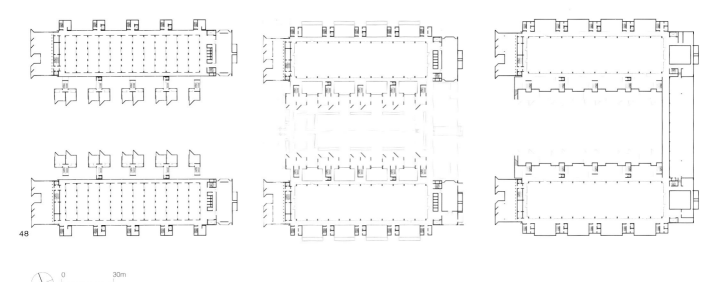

0   30m

0   100ft

As in most of Kahn's buildings, the entrance would not have been readily apparent. After finding it in the south-east corner and passing through a small low foyer, one would emerge in the large top-lit central court, three floors in height, encircled by hallways off which open all the spaces of the building (p. 213; k). This is the first of Kahn's great entry halls, a place where one could not only perceive the fundamental purpose of the building, and access its various rooms, but also one could have 'unplanned meetings', encouraging the kind of informal discussions that lead to new discoveries.[59] The four walls of the central court, with smaller openings below and larger openings above, do not meet in the corners, appearing as freestanding facades. Here Kahn engages the classic 'corner problem', a timeless architectural challenge brought to its highest level during the Renaissance. The solution of removing the column from the corner, opening what is normally the most solid point in the wall and giving a diagonal emphasis to the square room, was most memorably presented in the courtyard design for the Palazzo Ducale in Urbino, by Francesco di Giorgio and Luciano Laurana in the mid-fifteenth century.[60] While office drawings exist that indicate a roof over this central court, all the models Kahn had made, as well as all of his own aerial perspective drawings of the project, show that Kahn intended this space, ideally, to be an open court, exactly like the courtyard of a Renaissance palazzo.[61] In the temperate southern California climate, with rain coming only during one winter month and temperatures in the mid-70 degrees Fahrenheit (23 degrees celsius) year-round, this courtyard plan is even more appropriate than in its Roman place of origin.

Immediately off the corridors surrounding and overlooking the central court is a layer of service spaces, providing a transitional zone to the primary rooms beyond. Directly across from the entry is the gymnasium, a solid, cubic mass bevelled in at the outer edge of each ceiling to provide horizontal ventilation and lighting slots.[62] To the left, the rectangular double-height book-stack room of the library leads to the reading rooms, which are projected out into the sunlight. Diagonally across the central court, the dining rooms are similarly projected out so as to turn the corner from north to west. These

49

dining and reading rooms, which also functioned as seminar rooms, gave Kahn's concept of 'wrapping ruins around rooms' its most articulate and poetic form. Employing the primary geometries of circle-in-square and square-in-circle, the cubic concrete 'sun shields' house the three levels of cylindrical glass-walled dining rooms, while cylindrical concrete 'sun shields' house the three levels of cubic glass-walled reading rooms (p. 213; j). 'A glass wall needs protection from glare', Kahn said in explaining this design.[63] Yet the experience we would have is one of both protection – afforded by the enormous 50 foot (15 metre) tall, hollow concrete towers – and exposure to spectacular views and powerful moving shapes of sunlight and shadow, as we sit in an all-glass room.

This outer range of rooms facing the ocean, with their massive, hollow, cylindrical and cubic concrete shells wrapped around and shading glazed rooms within, all set upon the great faceted plinth, would have given the whole Meeting House an unparalleled monumentality (p. 213; i).[64] Appropriately, the Meeting House would have been perceived as the centre and focus of the Salk Institute, for it is here that Kahn sought to create spaces that would encourage and support discovery and invention. As Kahn said of the Salk Institute, 'Essentially it is a laboratory building, but you must not forget that the place of meeting is of utmost importance.'[65] It is therefore indeed unfortunate that the Meeting House, this most important component of Kahn's design for the Salk Institute, and one in which he first discovered so many concepts that would become fundamental in his process of architectural design, was never to be built.

Kahn's designs for the laboratories, while part of his overall vision for the Salk Institute, which included the Meeting House and the residential components, quite naturally focused on the scientists' work of biological research. Kahn's very first proposals had placed the laboratories in vertical towers, yet in all subsequent designs he was to organize them as large horizontal volumes, with service towers along their long sides. During the first two years of design, Kahn proposed four rectangular laboratory blocks, placed at the east end of the site near the main road, and ordered perpendicular to the

48. Plans of the Salk Institute showing service floor and study level (left), ground or court level laboratory (centre) and basement laboratory level (right), redrawn under author's supervision.
49. Section showing alternating laboratory and service floors (left and right), and central court flanked by scientists' studies; redrawn under author's supervision.

50

coastline (p. 214; m). Early schemes show these four rectangular blocks each being composed of three square laboratory clusters, each cluster symmetrically organized around a central court, yet developed in twelve different plans – giving overall order yet providing individual identity for the scientists. Between the pairs of rectangular laboratory blocks were two gardens, and at the centre and outer edges were service towers. While the four laboratory blocks are shown parallel to each other in most schemes, there are intriguing proposals among the office drawings for splaying the outer blocks to create gardens that opened towards the ocean.[66]

In the final version of this design, the four laboratory buildings were to be two storeys in height, providing a full-floor laboratory, 100 by 250 feet (30 by 76 metres), for each of the eight Nobel biologists. Kahn proposed studies for the scientists, at first semicircular and later square, to be placed as freestanding buildings in the two gardens. The gardens were to have a fountain at the east end feeding a thin channel of water slicing through the centre of the garden and spilling into a catch-basin at its west end.[67] Along the east end of the laboratories, the animal area and delivery area were to be recessed into the ground. At the west end of the laboratories, the administration, technical library and other

51

support functions were to be similarly recessed into the ground, serving as a
terrace overlooking the ocean at the end of the gardens, and taking advantage
of the fall of the land to open fenestration towards the west.

This scheme was fully developed, with a complete set of preliminary
construction drawings showing the laboratories as column-free spaces, with
deep folded-plate beams spanning 50 feet (15 metres) east–west to floor-deep
box girders spanning 100 feet (30 metres) north–south, all to be fabricated of
precast, pre-stressed reinforced concrete (p. 214; l).[68] The extensive mechanical
requirements for the laboratories were to be generated from the service towers
at the outer ends of the square box girders, through which they would feed to
the triangular folded-plate beams, and from there directly into the laboratory
spaces. While early versions of this scheme proposed curved vaulted forms,
split down the middle, for the folded-plate beams, the final version employed
an elegant triangular form, with openings at both the top and bottom where
the angled beams met. Kahn had a series of elaborate large models built (p. 214;
n), showing how these floor-deep beams created alternating triangular bays,
folding down into the laboratory to house the mechanical piping and ducts,
and folding up to create a 14 foot (4.3 metre) high vaulted space – the peak

52

52. Details of the Salk Institute. Cast-in-place concrete with projecting joints and lead tie-hole plugs (top left); travertine paving stones in central courtyard (top right); concrete structure and oak wood interior door (below left); concrete wall with rainwater scupper at walkway floor along outer edge of laboratories (below right).

opened with a continuous thin skylight at the second floor. Our experience of this powerfully folding ceiling structure would have been the perfect presentation of Kahn's belief that a space must reveal how it was made.

Yet by 1962 Salk had begun to question the four-building, two-garden scheme, saying that it would tend to divide, rather than join the scientists. As Kahn said, 'I realized that the two gardens did not combine in the intended meaning. One garden is greater than two because it becomes a place in relation to the laboratories and their studies. Two gardens were just a convenience. But one is really a place; you put meaning into it; you feel loyalty to it.'[69] Kahn consolidated the four buildings into two larger buildings, with service towers along their outer edges and a single garden at the centre (p. 215; p). In order to accommodate in two buildings what had previously been housed in four, each building now had three levels of laboratories, and three service levels. This required that two levels be placed underground, and the buildings be built of cast-in-place concrete (p. 215; s).[70] Kahn decided to give up the folded-plate precast concrete structure, even though both his structural and mechanical engineers strongly supported it. This was, as Kahn said, a 'drastic change. I felt the loss of the folded-plate construction'.[71] That this decision haunted Kahn for the rest of his career is evidenced by the fact that the folded-plate concrete structure would reappear in a number of his later projects, most notably the Kimbell Art Museum, Fort Worth, Texas.

It is not entirely clear why, late in the project, Kahn felt so strongly the necessity to change the design drastically, such that he was willing to bear the concomitant loss of the folded-plate structure that would have so powerfully shaped the experience of the scientists. Yet, it is hardly coincidental that at this same time doubts had begun to arise as to whether the Meeting House would in fact ever be built. Without the Meeting House, Kahn and Salk's initial concept for the Institute, their vision – of a monastic life of work, discussion and contemplation for the scientists – would be severely compromised. It is very probably this, more than anything else, that led to Kahn's revised, two-building laboratory scheme – for, with its single, central garden flanked by individual studies, the final design is far more monastic in character than its predecessor.

As built, the Salk Institute Laboratories must be recognized as one of Kahn's greatest works,[72] not least because of the unprecedented and unmatched quality of its concrete construction. Not wanting the usual cold grey colour for the concrete, Kahn added a small amount of pozzuolana (used by the ancient Romans) to the concrete mixes, producing a warmer tone. Kahn intended to control the quality of the concrete precisely, 'Every bit of formwork was designed; nothing left to the contractor.'[73] His office produced hundreds of construction drawings, many full-size, indicating the exact manner in which the wooden formwork, into which the concrete was cast, should be fabricated, and how the concrete pours should be staged (what height each pour should reach) in order to leave the desired markings and joints in the finished concrete.[74] The plywood forms were coated with polyurethane to ensure the smoothest concrete finish, the circular tie-holes were filled with lead plugs, and the joints between plywood panels were carefully

detailed as V-shaped protrusions, which today cast delicate shadows across the faces of the shining concrete walls. At the Salk Institute, Kahn raised concrete to a new level, virtually reinventing the material. As he later said, 'You must know the nature of concrete, what concrete really strives to be. Concrete really wants to be granite but can't quite manage. Reinforcing rods are the play of a marvellous secret worker that makes this so-called molten stone appear wonderfully capable – a product of the mind.'[75]

The laboratories are structured by 9 foot (2.7 metre) deep Vierendeel cast-in-place, post-stressed concrete trusses, set 20 feet (6 metres) on centre and spanning 65 feet (20 metres). The trusses have large openings so that mechanical ducts and piping can be placed and changed as needed with the greatest possible flexibility. The Vierendeel trusses have 10 inch (25 centimetre) thick integrally cast concrete floors above and 8 inch (20 centimetre) cast-in-place concrete floors suspended below, producing a flat ceiling in each laboratory. These act to conceal the structure, ducts and piping – a dramatic difference from both the shaped spaces under the folded plate beams of the previous scheme, and the exposed structure and mechanical piping of the Richards Laboratory Building. Each laboratory floor is 65 feet (20 metres) wide and 245 feet (75 metres) long, with an 11 foot (3.4 metre) ceiling. The ceilings are provided with openings every 5 feet (1.5 metres) through which the services are fed down into the laboratories, and the lighting fixtures are mounted between these openings. Concrete piers at 20 foot (6 metre) spacing march down the long sides of the laboratories, which are otherwise entirely surrounded by full-height glazing, outside of which run continuous covered open-air walkways.

At the outer perimeter of the laboratories to the north and south, five service towers march down the length of each building, with courts opened between to let light into the basement laboratory level. Severe and solid, these towers house the fire stairs (lit by a thin vertical slot in the west wall), lifts, lavatories and the exhaust for the laboratories. At the eastern end of the laboratories are mechanical buildings, where the heating, cooling and ventilation supply air (100 per cent fresh air, with air change required every five minutes), as well as the extensive hot water, steam and distilled water requirements of the laboratories, are generated and fed through the trusses in the service floors. At the western end of the laboratories, a five-storey office block faces the ocean, housing the administration offices, technical library and other support services, and opening on to the basement level terrace that Kahn created at the western end of the court.

Along the inner edge of each laboratory, on either side of the court, five towers containing the scientists' studies march down the length of the court. Four storeys in height, these concrete towers contain studies only on two floors (the second and fourth), opposite the mechanical service floor spaces, and are left open as covered 'porticos' on the floors aligning with the laboratories (the ground and third), so that the scientists can see both between and through the towers to the court beyond. As Kahn said, 'Dr Salk thought of the idea that there should be no study opposite

55

53. (Previous page) South side of the central court, Salk Institute. The towers house the scientists' studies, identifiable by their teak wood walls and operable windows, with the laboratories just visible behind on the left.
54. (Opposite) Interior of a scientist's study, with concrete structure and ceiling, oak floor, oak wood cabinetry and blackboard, Salk Institute.
55. Interior of a scientist's study, with full-height vertical slot windows on the right and behind the desk, and view window with shutter, Salk Institute.
56. Library wall under the west arcade at basement level, below the court, with teak wood doors, window frames and louvred shutters, Salk Institute.

a laboratory, but there should be a garden opposite a laboratory so that the study is not visible to the scientist.'[76] Likened by Salk to the cells in a monastery,[77] these studies were separated from the workplace of the laboratories, both in plan, by the space containing the stairs, and in section, by requiring one to climb either up or down a flight of stairs from the laboratories to the studies. This space between the laboratories and the studies, into which the stairs are set, reaches 20 feet (6 metres) below the level of the court, and has an urban quality in its vertical density and labyrinthine layering of concrete and glass planes – an unexpected change both from the calm, cool, horizontal spaces of the laboratories and the open, sun-drenched court.

Kahn believed that the scientists needed both the laboratories of 'stainless steel and glass' and the studies of 'the oak table and rug'.[78] The thirty-six studies are enclosed by teak wood walls set into the openings between cast concrete walls, and the teak is spaced away from the concrete at either edge by a 6 inch (15 centimetre) vertical slot of glass, washing the concrete walls with light. Each study has one window facing the court and one facing the ocean – behind a wall turned 45 degrees out from the face of the tower to capture the view – and each large opening contains three layers: glass window, screen panel and wooden shutter, any or all of which can be opened by sliding into a pocket within the wall. On the third floor between the studies the concrete walls are left open, so that there are views through the building and across the court. The furniture that has come to occupy these portico spaces suggests their usefulness as a place of informal 'unplanned meetings' with others, between the collective workspace of laboratories and the privacy of the individual studies. At ground level, these portico spaces create a shaded arcade along the two sides of the court, open to the east but intriguingly closed by a wall at the west end, so that in order to again have the view of the ocean, we must re-enter the central court.

The importance of the central court in the final design of the Salk Institute cannot be overestimated. The plan of the laboratories is based upon a square, which Kahn then subdivides into a series of triple groupings: the whole has three parts – laboratory, court, laboratory; the central space – studies, court, studies; each laboratory – walkway, laboratory, walkway; the court itself is divided into three square spaces (leading towards the ocean); and finally, the buildings have three laboratory floors – one below ground, one at ground (the level of the court), one above ground – each topped by a service level. In this way, and in many others, Kahn constantly reinforces our perception and understanding of the court as the true centre and focus of the design.

Yet, until construction of the laboratories was almost complete, Kahn continued to show the central space as a garden, planted with grass and poplar trees, and split down its middle by the water course (p. 215; p & r). While this design conformed to the traditional monastery courtyard it remained unresolved for Kahn, and his drawings for the garden lack the conviction evident in other parts of the design.[79] In December 1965, as the laboratories were nearing completion, Kahn visited the Mexican architect Luis Barragán, who had trained as a landscape architect, at his home in Mexico City. Kahn

67. (Opposite) Library, Salk Institute. Originally planned as part of the Meeting House, the library was sited on the lower basement level, below the court, after the decision was made not to build the Meeting House; its teak wood doors and louvred windows open onto the west arcade.

was struck by the simple, severe yet powerful character of Barragán's garden, saying, 'His gardens have nothing but a trickle of water, and still are so immense that all the landscaping in the world couldn't equal it.'[80] Kahn immediately invited Barragán to the Salk Institute to consult with him on the final design for the garden of the laboratories. As Kahn recalled:

> *When* [Barragán] *entered the space he went to the concrete walls and touched them and expressed his love for them, and then said as he looked across the space and towards the sea, 'I would not put a tree or a blade of grass in this space. This should be a plaza of stone, not a garden.' I looked at Dr Salk and he at me and we both felt this was deeply right. Feeling our approval,* [Barragán] *added joyously, 'If you make this a plaza, you will gain a facade – a facade to the sky.'*[81]

59

60

61

58. View of the court and scientists' studies, Salk Institute; the laboratories are just visible behind on the left. The view is seen from the arcade beneath more scientists' studies.
59. View along the arcade beneath the scientists' studies on the south side of the court, Salk Institute.
00. View of the administrative block from the north, with the library at basement level, Salk Institute.
61. View of sunken courts along the edge of the central courtyard, Salk Institute; the laboratories are on the left, with stairs in the centre and retaining wall on the right.

And so, in a curious twist of fate, Kahn and Salk were brought back, at the very last moment, to the source of their original inspiration. For it may be remembered that the central courtyard at the monastery of San Francesco at Assisi, surrounded by the monks' cells, is in fact neither a grass court nor a garden but a piazza paved with stone, with a kerb running all around, and a well at its centre. With this decision, Kahn's uncertainty vanished, and he rapidly developed the final design for this central court.

Originally one entered the Salk Institute by walking through a seemingly random but nevertheless carefully positioned grove of trees to the east, coming suddenly upon the symmetrical, axial court as if from out of the woods, the path ahead blocked by a long low bench of stone, so that one had to move off-axis to enter – exactly what Kahn intended.[82] The court is paved with travertine, a stone used by the Romans, warm in colour with a naturally pocked surface, and this was Kahn's first use of this material, which he immediately recognized as perfectly complementing both the cast concrete and the teak wood. Water emerges from under the lip of the cubic fountain near the east end, pouring into the thin stone waterway that runs down the centre of the court, slicing the stone paving in two. At the west end, the line of water pours into a large pool stretching across the west end of the court, from which it cascades down a series of falls into a basin on the lower terrace level which overlooks the ocean.

THEODORE GILDRED COURT

64

The court is breathtaking in its sublime power, and is perhaps Kahn's greatest 'entry hall' and 'room with no name'. As Barragán said, simply and unforgettably, it becomes a facade to the sky. The angled concrete walls of the study towers march down either side, together creating a solid folding wall, framing the view of the ocean ahead when first seen from the entry. The court changes throughout the day and throughout the season, the airy walls of studies and porticos to the north (never in sun) and south (always in sun) producing a constant play of light and shadow. If you are there at sunset, as the scientists are every day, you see the most magical of transformations. The golden glow that fills the sky to the west is first reflected in the water of the ocean, and then shoots like a line of fire, up through the gathering darkness of the plaza's stone floor, to reach its source in the cubic fountain. The perfect example of Kahn's understanding that great architecture is truly timeless, this court is at once both ancient and modern. Today this plaza, without any formal programme of use, remains one of the most powerful and deeply moving spaces ever built

62. (Previous page) View across the court, looking east towards the entry, Salk Institute.
63. (Opposite) View across the court, looking west to the Pacific Ocean, Salk Institute.
64. The lower terrace at the western end of the court, with south study towers above, Salk Institute.

Salk Institute for Biological Studies

Concept development

Kahn's designs for the Salk Institute mark his first full deployment of three design concepts: surrounding spaces with shadow-giving walls, or 'wrapping ruins around buildings'; the plan as a 'society of spaces', a series of independent room-buildings, each with their own geometry and structure; and shaping 'served' and 'servant' spaces, in both plan and section, within a folding structure. In this design, Kahn was inspired by a number of precedents, including the monastic courtyard of San Francesco at Assisi, which was transformed into the central court between the laboratory buildings, the Acropolis plinth, the Palazzo Ducale in Urbino, Piranesi's Campus Martius plan reconstruction and the Roman ruins on the Palatine Hill, which were transformed into the base, courtyard, plan and 'wrapped ruins' respectively for the unrealized Meeting House (designs for which are shown on pages 211–13). Kahn's initial design for the folded-plate concrete laboratory structure (the laboratory schemes are detailed on pages 214–15), housing the services and providing an articulated ceiling with natural light introduced through thin slits running down the centre, would later be realized in the Kimbell Museum.

a

b

a. Louis Kahn, centre, and Dr Jonas Salk, on Kahn's right, with three of the original resident fellows of the Salk Institute.
b. Dr Jonas Salk, inventor of the polio vaccine, at the Salk Institute.

c

d

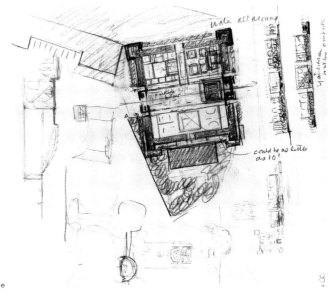

e

c. Early site plan of the Salk Institute, 1960; drawing
by Kahn. It shows the Meeting House (left), the
promenade with residences (centre) and four circular
laboratories (right); the perspective sketch (far right)
shows the view from the Meeting House back
towards the laboratories.
d. The Acropolis, Athens, pastel by Kahn, 1951. The
drawing emphasizes the plinth rising from the cliff.
e. Early sketch plan of the Meeting House, 1961;
drawing by Kahn. The design is reminiscent of
Roman emperor Diocletian's Palace at Split,
modern day Croatia.

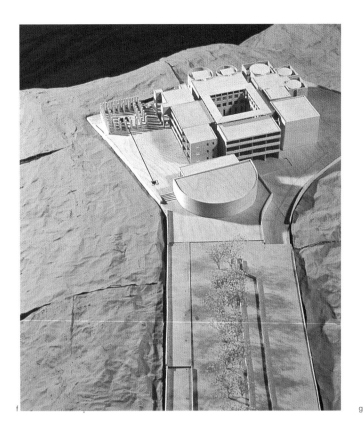

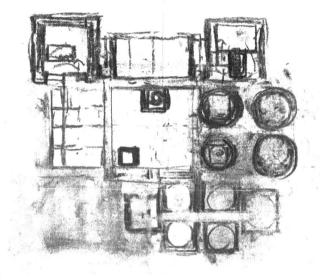

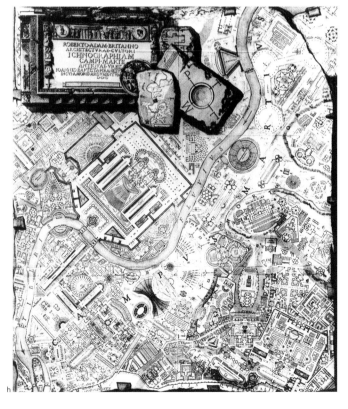

f. Model of the Meeting House, Salk Institute, looking west; built under author's supervision. This model shows the approach plaza with its line of trees.

g. Early sketch plan of the Meeting House, 1960–2; drawing by Kahn.

h. Giovanni Battista Piranesi, imaginary reconstructed plan of the Campus Martius district, ancient Rome, 1762. Kahn had a copy of this etching on the wall of his private office.

i. Perspective sketch of the reading rooms (right), and the dining rooms (centre), Meeting House, Salk Institute; drawing by Kahn.

j. Model of the reading room and sun shield, Meeting House.

k. Model of the Meeting House, looking north; built under author's supervision.

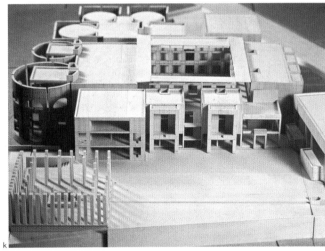

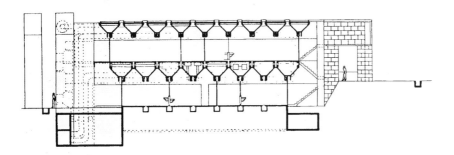

l

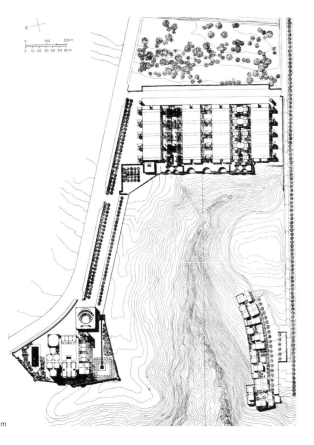

m

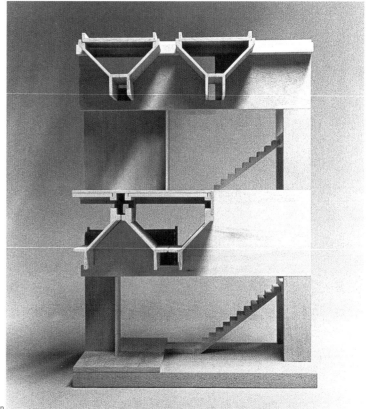

n

l. Section through laboratory block, Salk Institute, four-laboratory scheme, 1960–2. Note that the watercourse (right) is already shown at the centre of the court.
m. Site plan of the Salk Institute, four-laboratory block scheme, 1960–2 (north to left, Pacific Ocean below).
n. Model of the laboratory building, Salk Institute, four-laboratory scheme, 1960–2; a folded-plate precast concrete long-span structure carries the services.
o. Model of the Salk Institute, first scheme, 1960–2, with four laboratory blocks (top), the Meeting House (left) and residences (right).

o

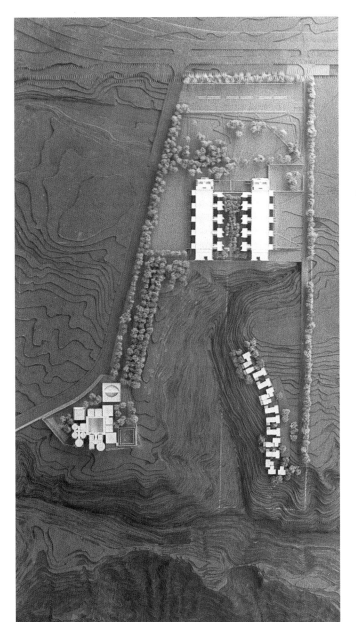

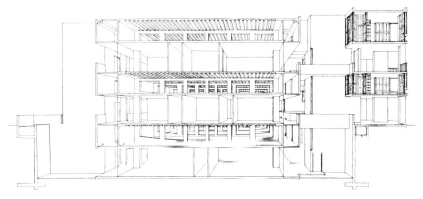

p. Site model of the Salk Institute, final two-laboratory block scheme (north to left, Pacific Ocean below), 1962–5. Note the trees in the courtyard between the two laboratory blocks.
q. Monastery of San Francesco, Assisi, 1253; view looking down into the central courtyard.
r. Perspective sketch of the central court planted with poplar trees, by Louis Kahn.
s. Perspective section of one side of the Salk Institute, 1962–5; the laboratories and service floors are in the centre and the studies are on the right, facing the central plaza.

65

Conclusion: the hypostyle hall, the kasbah and the cosmic garden

Three experiences during this period would prove to have a profound effect upon Kahn. The first was Kahn's renewed admiration for the work of Frank Lloyd Wright, whose works of the 1950s had drifted far from the ordering concepts underlying such early works as Unity Temple, leading Kahn to characterize Wright's work of this late period as 'arbitrary, personal, experimental or disdainful of tradition'.[83] Yet in 1959, shortly after Wright's death, Kahn first visited Wright's Johnson Wax Building of 1936 in Racine, Wisconsin, and as Scully recalls, he 'to the depths of his soul, was overwhelmed'.[84] This great room – with its light-giving ceiling supported by the first thin-shell concrete column and roof structures ever built, which stand in a 20 foot (6 metre) grid like a modern hypostyle hall, and the space enclosed with brick walls which are sliced open by light at the cornices to indicate their non-structural role – was, quite simply, the most astounding revelation for Kahn. Shortly thereafter, Kahn, in discussions with his students, said that when you are 'in an inspiring place, like the Johnson Wax Building, you feel … honoured'.[85]

The depth of Kahn's debt to Wright has rarely been acknowledged, and has in fact most often been underestimated if not entirely ignored.[86] Yet a brief review of the ordering principles that Kahn shares with Wright reveals the true measure of this inspiration: the room as the generator of all architecture, and the expression of interior volume in exterior form; the central, introverted, top-lit, noble room as the focus of all institutional buildings; emphasis of the plan and section over the elevation; the ceiling or roof as the primary shaper of spatial experience; tartan grid planning, and 'served' and 'servant' spaces; hidden entry followed by entry sequence of dark, low, compressed space leading to light, tall, expansive central space; closed centres and opened corners, often requiring

65. Walls of Carcassonne, France, sketch by Louis Kahn made during his trip to the CIAM conference, Otterlo, the Netherlands, 1959.
66. Frank Lloyd Wright, Johnson Wax Building, Racine, Wisconsin, 1936–8, view of the main room. Kahn visited the Johnson Wax Building for the first time in 1959.

circulation along edges rather than through centres; design beginning with the square and cube, the cruciform, the double square, and the rotated square; symmetry and axial planning, yet with solid centres and open corners; each room having its own structure; spaces of unplanned meetings; interlocked and communicating rooms, or the plan as a society of rooms; seeking 'the nature of materials', and the use of materials and construction to characterize spatial experience; the use of light to delineate structure and separate materials; thin 'slot' windows set at corners or rooms with a view window at the centre; the challenging of the instrumental aspects of industrialization and modernization; history as a source of principles, not forms; the resolving of paradoxes within design; and the profound commitment to architecture as the creation of an ethical framework for daily life.

The only significant difference of principles between Kahn and Wright centres on the issue of exposing or concealing structure. As we have seen, for Kahn, the exposure of structure – how the room was made and supported – was nothing short of an ethical imperative, and concealing structure was absolutely wrong. Yet Wright believed that the 'nature of materials' was profoundly inflected by the spatial and experiential intention of the design, and should not be determined by any rationale arising from outside the work itself. In responding to criticism of the hidden steel structure in many of his Prairie Houses, Wright stated, 'Why should you always expose structure? I call it indecent exposure.'[87]

The second experience also occurred in 1959, when Kahn was invited by Alison and Peter Smithson to attend the CIAM (Congrès Internationaux d'Architecture Moderne) meeting in Otterlo, the Netherlands.[88] We have already noted that it was on this trip that Kahn visited Le Corbusier's Ronchamp Chapel, which was to have considerable influence on his designs for the First Unitarian Church, but it is interesting to note that Kahn also visited the medieval towns of Albi and Carcassonne in France. While he made only two sketches of Ronchamp, he drew thirty-three sketches of the walled town of Carcassonne, and completed twelve sketches of the Ste Cécile Cathedral in Albi. This attention to historical urban form was most appropriate to this trip, for Kahn was witnessing one of the most important events in post-war modern architecture in Europe: the formation of Team 10.

CIAM had been founded in 1928 by twenty-four early modern architects from throughout Europe, headed by Le Corbusier, and focused on issues of urbanism and mass housing. By the eighth meeting in 1951, CIAM's initial emphasis on 'minimum existence' standards for housing and 'tabula rasa' plans for new cities had been superseded by concerns for monumentality and the historical city, devastated by bombing in World War II. A group of younger architects, led by Alison and Peter Smithson and Aldo van Eyck, began to question the precepts of CIAM, particularly the so-called 'Athens Charter' of 1933, and its neglect both of the historical development of cities, and that which lies between the house and the city – the neighbourhood. The decisive break occurred at CIAM 10, the 1956 meeting held in Dubrovnik, where this group, hereafter called Team 10, assumed control of the agenda, paralleled by Le Corbusier's decision to call for the passing of leadership for developing modern urbanism to the next generation.[89]

Kahn gave a lecture at the end of this, the first Team 10 meeting, where he stated that 'modern space is really not different from Renaissance space … We still want domes, we still want walls, we still want arches, vaults, arcades and loggias.' Kahn held that 'in the beginning, in the first form, lies more power than in anything that follows', and argued that these beginnings belong to all; 'a man who discovers things that belong to the nature of things does not own these things. The designs belong to him but the realizations do not … It belongs to the realm of architecture.'[90] Kahn presented his Trenton Jewish Community Center, his University of Pennsylvania Medical Research Building and his urban design studies for Philadelphia – the latter of which were extensively published in the group's later summary manifesto, *Team 10 Primer*.[91]

Yet what Kahn received in inspiration from this meeting was very probably far more than what he gave, for here he met Aldo van Eyck, the Dutch founder of Team 10 whose design process and buildings so amazingly paralleled Kahn's own. From Van Eyck's ingenious public housing projects and playgrounds of the 1940s to the great Orphanage in Amsterdam of 1955–60, its modular domed spaces so remarkably similar to Kahn's Trenton Jewish Community Center of roughly the same date; to the Roman Catholic Church in The Hague of 1964–9, with its massive concrete-block walls, precast concrete Vierendeel trusses, and enormous cylindrical skylights; and finally to the little Sonsbeek Sculpture Pavilion in Arnhem of 1965, with its square plan of parallel concrete-block walls under a translucent roof – the parallels are indeed striking.[92]

During the Team 10 meeting Kahn visited Van Eyck's recently completed Orphanage in Amsterdam, and heard Van Eyck speak about his search for architectural beginnings outside traditional western classical culture, looking instead to primitive African tribal structures, medieval cities, and the kasbah and mosque of the Islamic world for inspiration. Arguing against modernity's 'deterministic' pattern of thinking, Van Eyck said: 'Architecture implies a constant rediscovery of constant human qualities translated into space. Man is always and everywhere essentially the same. He has the same mental equipment … Modern architects have been harping continually on what is different in our time to such an extent that even they have lost touch with what is not different, what is always essentially the same.' Van Eyck argued for the concept of history as a living, timeless tradition, perceived through human experience: 'We meet ourselves everywhere in all places and ages.'[93]

While the effect on Kahn of his meeting Van Eyck was immediate, it would be years before Kahn could express what it meant to him. Late in life, Kahn would paraphrase Van Eyck's concept of the fundamental unchanging quality of man: 'The man of old had the same brilliance of mind as we assume we only have now.'[94] Around the same time, Kahn began an interview by stating, 'Van Eyck to me is a significant architect. He's more than significant, he's a great architectural mind who has had little opportunity.' Kahn followed this with a story inspired by Van Eyck's conception of architecture as being formed by the daily rituals of life: a grandfather and grandson are climbing the stairs, and the architect has thought to make a large landing at the mid-point of the climb, with a window seat and bookcase, so that the grandfather can suggest they stop and read a book, rather than reveal to his energetic grandson that he is tired from the short climb.[95] Kahn went on to describe how, at the Team 10 meeting in 1959, Van Eyck 'made a speech about the meaning of a threshold just before you enter a room. It was magnificent, because through this he could build a whole architecture.' Later in the same interview, Kahn first gave poetic voice to his profound belief: 'History is that which reveals the nature of man. What is has always been. What was has always been. What will be has always been.'[96]

The third experience took place in 1961, when the great modern sculptor Isamu Noguchi was commissioned to design the Levy Memorial Playground in Riverside Park, New York, and he asked Kahn to collaborate with him on this project. As Dore Ashton has noted, 'Kahn was perhaps the sole living American architect whose way of thinking about his art was profoundly akin to Noguchi's own', and they shared belief in the sanctity of nature, the reverence for sunlight, the significance of history and the oldest things, a 'deep respect for the Greek vision expressed on the Acropolis', and the idea that the fundamental order of the cosmos was to be found in geometric form.[97] 'I do not believe that beauty can be created overnight. It must start with the archaic first', Kahn maintained,[98] a statement that could just as easily have been made by Noguchi. In turn, Kahn had no doubt taken note of Noguchi's 1960 publication in *Perspecta* of photographs of the astronomical observatory built in Jaipur, India around 1734, an astonishingly abstracted landscape, consisting of a series of building-sized instruments incised into and raised out of a vast stone-paved plaza, structured so as to allow the inhabitant to recognize the annual solar events of solstice and equinox, as well as the path of the celestial constellations.[99]

While the Levy Playground project, after five often-exasperating years of effort, was doomed to become yet another of both Kahn and Noguchi's growing list of unbuilt works, the collaborative design process was, as Noguchi said, 'an enrichment and education'[100] for them both, and Kahn's own designs soon showed its effect. Only after first seeing Noguchi's example did Kahn begin to use plasticine modelling clay for his own site models, an office standard for the rest of his career. The ability to work the clay as one might work the earth itself, making both the gentlest curves and the sharpest incisions, would change Kahn's approach to the building site and foundation, and all his later projects show a dramatically increased emphasis on the initial marking of the ground, the making of the anchoring base or plinth of the building, that is the first act in the construction of architecture. As Kahn said at the end of the project: 'I did not speak in terms of architecture. He did not speak in terms of sculpture. Both of us felt the building as a contour; not one contour but an interplay of contours so folding and so harbouring as to make, by such a desire, no claim to architecture no claim to sculpture.'[101] It would be Noguchi who offered the last tribute to their collaboration when, after Kahn's death, Noguchi installed four stone sculptures in the lawn adjacent to the Kimbell Art Museum.

67

68

67. Aldo van Eyck, Municipal Orphanage or Children's Home, Amsterdam 1955–60, aerial view. Kahn toured this building with Van Eyck during the Otterlo CIAM conference in 1959.
68. Model of Levy Memorial Playground, Riverside Park, New York, 1961–5, Louis Kahn and Isamu Noguchi.

Inspired compositions
in the poetics
of action

I think the most inspirational point from which we might try to under-stand architecture is to regard the room, the simple room, as the beginning of architecture ... I think the plan is a society of rooms[1]
LOUIS KAHN

1

Previous page. Detail of assembly hall ceiling, Assembly Building, Bangladesh National Capital, Dhaka, 1962–74. This ceiling structure is made of concrete roof shells with marble strips, over clerestory windows.
1. Louis Kahn teaching during a studio project review, University of Pennsylvania, 1969; the structural engineering professor Robert Le Ricolais is on the right.

With the design of the Salk Institute Meeting House, Kahn arrived at his fundamental redefinition of architecture as being ordered not by predetermined programmes of functions but rather by the poetic interpretation of human action, rediscovered in the inspired beginnings of ritual. In direct opposition to both the modernist prescription that 'form follows function'[2] and the International Style free plan of space-in-extension, Kahn conceived of architecture as beginning with the room, with each human activity requiring its own room-as-place and the building plan to be understood as 'a society of rooms', their spatial relationship articulating their collective institutional purpose. This was not merely a change in professional procedure, for Kahn believed that the way in which a society defined its spaces was directly related to that society's own nature, and that, throughout history, 'the continual renewal of architecture comes from changing concepts of space'.[3]

Beyond the particular architectural discoveries Kahn made in designing the Salk Institute, it was the lack of a formally written brief and prescribed programme of functions that instigated his questioning of the habitual understanding that architectural form should follow a predetermined functional formula: 'Without the restriction of a dictatorial program, it became a rewarding experience to participate in the projection of an evolving program of spaces without precedence.'[4] For Kahn, this insight changed the nature of the architect's task: 'I believe it is the duty of every architect ... not to accept programs but to think in terms of spaces.'[5] Elsewhere he stated that 'architecture ... is not the filling of areas prescribed by the client. It is the creating of spaces that evoke a feeling of appropriate use.'[6]

Kahn found that functionalism, even though a fundamental part of modern architecture, had become instrumental and 'dictatorial' in the way it was employed – a literally thoughtless beginning for architectural design, directly opposed to Kahn's belief that 'architecture is the thoughtful making of spaces'.[7] Kahn believed that form should not follow function,[8] and that architecture was not really about function, at least as it was commonly defined: 'I think you can talk about machines being functional, bicycles being functional, beer plants being functional. But not all buildings are functional. Now, they must function, but they function psychologically.'[9] For inspiration, Kahn once again looked to history, and to Rome: 'If you look at the Baths of Caracalla – the ceiling swells a hundred and fifty feet high. It was a marvellous realization on the part of the Romans to build such a space. It goes beyond function.'[10] Kahn called for 'spaces which have as much of a sense of nobility as you can give them. If you look at the Baths of Caracalla … we know that we can bathe just as well under an eight-foot ceiling as we can under a hundred-and-fifty-foot ceiling, but I believe there's something about a hundred-and-fifty-foot ceiling that makes a man a different kind of man.'[11]

Kahn believed that this 'psychological function' of ennobling mankind had nothing to do with the typical brief handed to an architect at the beginning of a project, but was more concerned with the underlying meaning of the institution: 'There are few clients who can understand philosophically the institution they are creating … Few clients have it or even sense the lack of it. Usually a written program [brief] is handed to you and you must assume the role of philosopher for the client.'[12] Kahn took the brief given to him by his clients as a starting point for quantity, never for quality, testing it against the realities of human occupation, interpreting and expanding the programme of uses in ways both culturally resonant and socially suggestive, and evolving a plan that reflected his acute observations of human interaction and understanding of spiritual desire. 'Now I think the first act of the architect is … to change the program for what is good for the institution … change the clients' program – which reads in the form of areas – into spaces. He must change corridors into galleries; he must change lobbies into places of entrance; he must change budgets into economy.'[13] In this way, Kahn dramatically broadened the range of what should be considered a legitimate programmed function, holding that the full palette of human experience must be re-engaged.

Kahn had tremendous faith in the initiating ideas of human institutions, and in his development of plans he sought to understand the beginning – in discovering an institution for the first time, its inherent nature is revealed. For Kahn, 'the beginning of any established activity of man is its most wonderful moment. For in it lies all its spirit and resourcefulness, from which we must constantly draw our inspirations of present needs. We can make our institutions great by giving them our sense of this inspiration in the architecture we offer them.'[14] Thinking about the beginning of an institutional activity, we discover the fundamental nature of human action, and 'the nature of space reflects what it wants to be'.[15] The return to beginnings, to the foundational inspiration of a type of spatial occupation, had the paradoxical effect of allowing Kahn to rediscover both the most ancient historical precedents and unprecedented spaces not yet known. Simultaneously grounded and freed by this understanding of the place of disciplinary history in the design process, Kahn now interpreted each new project as a chance to begin again, exemplified in the astonishing statement: 'You plan the library as though no library ever existed.'[16]

Tempio di Venere appresso il Circo Apollinare negl' Orti di Salustio vicino all'antica Porta Salaria.   *Piranesi inc.*

2

Kahn's conception of architecture began with the room, the simple room, designed with a poetic understanding of human actions as inspired, not prescribed: 'I make a space as an offering, and do not designate what it is to be used for. The use should be inspired.'[17] This concept of inspired use soon led Kahn to the conclusion that all preconceived notions of programme and function must be abandoned in design, that labelling rooms must be avoided, for 'one of the most devastating faults today that destroys the ultimate creative instinct is to give something a name before it earns one'.[18] To be truly the beginning of architecture, 'rooms must suggest their use without name',[19] spaces must be conceived with an understanding of the human actions they inspire, without relying on assigned function. The room, thus understood, may then take its place within a plan: 'I think that a plan is a society of rooms. A real plan is one in which rooms have talked to each other',[20] engaging the poetics of human action, of inspired ritual, so that 'the society of rooms is a place where it is good to learn, good to work, good to live'.[21] Echoing Frank Lloyd Wright's belief that architects should start with the conception of an interior room and work outwards toward exterior building form, Kahn wrote in 1953 that 'external shapes must wait until the "nature of the space" unfolds ...'[22]

In developing his concept of 'the plan' as 'a society of rooms' Kahn reordered the hierarchy of spaces within a building. He made the secondary spaces of circulation between primary rooms, such as hallways, arcades, stair landings, porches, vestibules and thresholds, into 'the events of the building',[23] as important to the overall experience of the building as the primary spaces given in the brief: 'You must spend as much time designing the staircase as you will designing the whole house.'[24] In 1959, Kahn wrote,

> *The places of entrance, the galleries that radiate from them, the intimate entrances to the spaces of the institution form an independent architecture of connection. This architecture is of equal importance to the major spaces though these spaces are designed only for movement and must therefore be designed to be bathed in natural light. This Architecture of Connection cannot appear in the program of areas – it is what the architect offers the client in his search for architectural balance and direction.*[25]

In 1961, Kahn would argue that the architecture of connections determined the quality of both the institution and its architect: 'The institution is truly an inspired place by reason of the entrance, the galleries of movement, and the harbours leading to the various spaces. This is the measure of the architect.'[26]

Kahn believed that his generation of architects was responsible for redefining the institutions of public life in their time, and that this could only be accomplished by questioning the utilitarianism underlying modernist functional planning. In this, Kahn was remarkably close to the great philosopher of human action and the public realm, Hannah Arendt, who, in her 1958 book *The Human Condition*, stated that architecture, like all human artifacts, 'becomes a home for mortal men, whose stability will endure and outlast the ever-changing movement of their lives and actions,

2. Giovanni Battista Piranesi, etching of Temple of Venus at Circus Apollinarius, Rome, 1748, from *Varie vedute di Roma antica e moderna.*
3. 'Architecture comes from The Making of a Room', sketch and statement by Louis Kahn, 1971.

only in as much as it transcends both the sheer functionalism of things produced for consumption and the sheer utility of objects produced for use'. Architecture and its rooms are of critical importance in human history, Arendt argued, for 'no activity can become excellent if the world does not provide a proper space for its exercise. Neither education nor ingenuity nor talent can replace the constituent elements of the public realm, which make it the proper place for human excellence.'[27]

Architecture comes from The Making of a Room
The Plan A society of rooms is a place good to live work learn

A great American Poet once asked The Architect 'What slice of the sun does your building have, what light enters your Room' as if to say the sun never knew how great it is until it struck the side of a building.

The Room

is The place of the mind. In a small room one does not say what one would in a large room. In a room with only one other person could be generative The vectors of each meet. A room is not a room without natural light. natural light gives the time of day and the mood of The seasons to enter.

Erdman Hall Dormitory Bryn Mawr College

Bryn Mawr
Pennsylvania
1960–5

In the design for Erdman Hall Dormitory, requiring 130 small private rooms and several large public halls, Kahn once again started with the square-and-cruciform plan. The earliest scheme bears a striking resemblance to Frank Lloyd Wright's Unity Temple of 1905–8, with a cruciform-in-square central public space, wrapped by a layer of bedrooms, with three smaller cruciform-in-square public spaces arrayed in an adjacent rectangle ringed by bedrooms, and the two masses linked by the main stair hall (p. 234; b). Other early studies explored various arrangements of larger public rooms ringed by bedrooms to produce cylindrical and cubic masses, organized into various tripartite grid-and linear forms, and related on either parallel or diagonal axes (p. 235; d). Though during the design of the dormitory Kahn moved away from his initial concept of the public rooms being wrapped in a protective 'thick wall' of bedrooms, he would return to it in his final proposal.

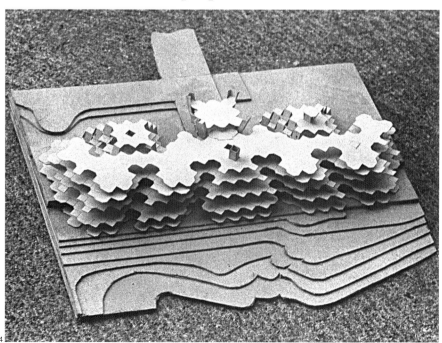

4

The design process for Erdman Hall was unusual even by Kahn's standards in that, after the initial schemes outlined above, Kahn and Anne Tyng developed two quite different schemes, both of which were presented to the client, Bryn Mawr president, Katharine McBride Tyng's design, which retained the initial concept of wrapping the bedrooms around the public spaces, was based upon complex, cellular, octagonal geometries, in both plan and section – quite aptly named the 'molecular' scheme by McBride.[28] Meanwhile, Kahn organized the bedrooms and the public rooms in two separate buildings, linked by a main stair hall (p. 234; b) – similar to his early house plans, where the bedrooms had been separated from the living rooms. This process of 'competing schemes' was further complicated by the fact that it took place in the same period in which Kahn and Tyng's romantic relationship came to an end, precipitated by Kahn's involvement with Harriet Pattison, who later became a landscape architect, and with whom Kahn had a son, Nathaniel, in 1962.[29]

While Tyng's 'organic' designs, being a fabric woven from the small structural cells of the bedrooms, failed to express adequately the large public volumes, they did maintain the concept of the bedrooms wrapping the public rooms. In arriving at his final, unified design, Kahn recognized that this initial insight had been correct, that his intermediate notion of placing the bedrooms and living rooms into separate buildings had been a mistake, and that the 'sense of hospitality, or reception, of getting together' in the public rooms 'must be part of the fabric of the house itself', close to the bedrooms.[30] In his final design, with the individual bedrooms wrapped around the cubic central common rooms like a thick wall, Kahn combined the attributes of his favourite historical building types, the monastery and the castle (p. 234; a):

> The walls of the castle cannot be thick enough to satisfy the seriousness of defense. The hall – the space within – has faith in the eventual freedom from such security. The needs of light to the interior, the needs of a service room, of a kitchen, of a place away from the central hall, act with courage to justify the making of spaces within the walls … This is the pragmatism and the humanity of the castle. Its life in architecture is inspiring because its statement is clear in spirit and in bondage of use.[31]

Kahn's final designs combined the cellular fabric of the bedrooms, which retained Tyng's octagonal geometry until the very end, with large-scale central halls lit from above, which were proposed as circular (p. 235; c), cruciform and square before assuming their final octagonal form. The final tripartite arrangement, with three large public rooms, has the attributes of both the continuous, thick wall of the bedrooms and the episodic, communal places of the public rooms, with the entry hall (the room with no programmed function and 'no name') given the central position. 'I have made not simply an entrance, but a meeting place. I considered it not a dimensional problem, but an environmental one. What I did was make an entrance room equally as important as a dining room, a living room, that central entity in the ground plan became the entrance meeting place.'[32]

As built, Erdman Hall has three 100 foot (30 metre) square clusters of dormitory rooms, linked diagonally at their corners. They respectively house at their centres a top-lit dining room, an entry hall and a living room, each

4. Study model of Erdman Hall Dormitory, Bryn Mawr College. Louis Kahn's office developed two preliminary schemes for this project; shown here is the design by Anne Tyng, which was based on an octagonal and square grid.

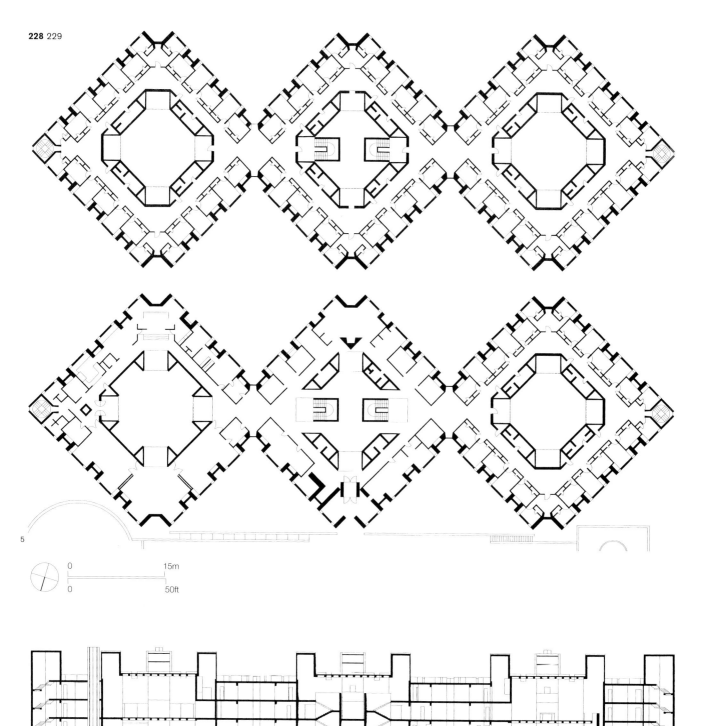

5. Plans of the second floor (above) and the ground floor (below), Erdman Hall Dormitory; redrawn under author's supervision.
6. Longitudinal section of Erdman Hall Dormitory, taken through three central rooms with stair towers at either end; redrawn under author's supervision.
7. (Opposite) Erdman Hall Dormitory from the street to the south.

8

a 33 foot (10 metre) square – the exact interior dimension of the sanctuary of Wright's Unity Temple. We enter into the central of the three square clusters from a covered portico directly into the entry hall, an octagonal volume 20 feet (6 metres) in height, set at the second of three floor levels, its walls constructed of cast-in-place concrete, left exposed on the interior, with a heavy precast concrete square-coffered ceiling and a dark stone floor. The massive concrete stairs project into this room from the left and right as freestanding rooms-within-a-room, combining entry hall and stair hall to produce a meeting place, landings and balconies at various levels giving the whole an almost urban feeling. The stairs establish the primary east–west diagonal axis that runs through the centres of the three square buildings, joining them at their overlapped corners, where square foyer-like spaces open to the living room to the west and the dining room to the east, both of which have wood floors.

Forming the thick, protective outer wall defining the shared spaces at their centre, the individual bedrooms have interlocked rectangular and T-shaped plans that are set forward and back on the exterior, as Kahn said, to 'distinguish each space, each room as a single entity, not just a series of partitions'.[33] The tectonic hierarchy of the building is made evident in the contrast between the exposed cast-in-place concrete walls of the central rooms and the concrete masonry walls of the bedrooms, which are clad on the exterior with light stone and dark slate panels. On the elevation, wide projecting planes alternate with narrower recessed planes; each wider plane has a solid panel of slate in the centre and is framed at its outer edges by vertical bands of light stone, against which the windows are set, while each narrower plane has windows filling its width. Within this alternating elevation pattern – wide, projected, in sunlight and narrow, recessed, in shadow – Kahn also develops a regular

8. East corner of the Erdman Hall Dormitory. Slate and stone cladding cover the cast concrete and masonry structure.
9. Living room, Erdman Hall Dormitory. The room is illuminated by four light towers providing clerestory at the corners.

rhythm of both repeating and overlapping dimensions. Thus the elevation of Erdman Hall, which is often interpreted only as an archaic, heavy, thick, crenellated wall, is also articulated as modern, light, thin, overlapping layers, producing what Colin Rowe and Robert Slutzky described as 'phenomenal transparency'.[34]

While they are orientated outwards, the 'extroverted' bedrooms also have direct connection across the cloister-like hallway to the central rooms within, which are 'served' and framed by service zones on four sides. The entry hall, living room and dining room are 'introverted' rooms, lit from above by four clerestory monitors that rise from the recessed corner volumes of each room. Opening out (rather than in, as those of the First Unitarian Church), these light towers allow direct sunlight to fall into the central rooms, as well as providing views of the sky for those within. In these truly monumentally scaled and constructed rooms, Kahn places us within the protective folds of a heavy, ancient, castle-like thickness. Yet where ancient architecture is most solid, at its corners, here the walls open and sunlight floods in – a modern conception originating with Frank Lloyd Wright. In Erdman Hall – at once castle, monastery and modern monument – Kahn achieved his poetic interpretation of the great central room as 'a world within a world'.[35]

Kahn's concept of the order of the castle, where a geometrically pure, central shared space is surrounded and protected by irregularly-shaped individual spaces, exemplified by the Salk Meeting House and the Erdman Hall dormitory, continued to evolve in his designs. In the design for the Goldenberg House, an unbuilt project for Rydal, Pennsylvania, of 1959, Kahn again began with a cruciform-in-square plan, but in this case he analysed it

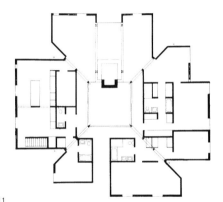

11

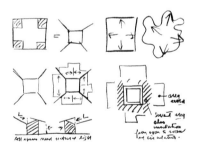

12

10 & 13. Central stair hall of Erdman Hall
Dormitory, seen from the top floor (left) and
the ground floor (right).
11. Final plan of the Goldenberg House, Rydal,
Pennsylvania, 1959 (north is 45 degrees down
and to left). Entry is directly into a central square
courtyard, around which the rooms of the house
are clustered; the plan is related to the Meeting
House, Salk Institute.
12. Plan sketches of the Goldenberg House.
These diagrams by Kahn show the design
developing from a cruciform-in-square plan
to a central courtyard with diagonal walled
rooms around.

critically, noting that the four corner spaces can only be accessed by circulating through the primary rooms in the arms of the cruciform. Kahn proposed instead a square courtyard at the centre of the house, from the corners of which diagonal walls would run to an undefined outer edge, thus inverting the original diagram. In developing the plan Kahn placed a covered arcade around three sides of the courtyard, with a layer of service spaces beyond and the primary rooms of the house around the outside. Only the living room opens to both the courtyard and the exterior edge. As each room assumed its required size and shape, the outer wall of the house became fractured, setting in and out, so that in the final plan the square central court is the only geometrically pure element, with the other spaces clustered around it. Rather than holding the rooms as partitioned spaces within the larger preconceived plan shape, Kahn proposed to let the individual rooms 'exfoliate' outwards so as to assume their varying scale, lighting and relationships – sacrificing the geometric purity of the plan to achieve the appropriate design for each room.

Erdman Hall Dormitory Bryn Mawr College

Concept development

In the early designs for the Erdman Hall Dormitory, Kahn came to a fundamental watershed in his manner of initially conceiving a building. Kahn developed two parallel schemes, the first employing the 'organic' octagonal geometry derived from D'Arcy Thompson's *On Growth and Form* (1917), while in the second Kahn started from the square and cruciform derived from Wright's Unity Temple of 1905–8. Kahn eventually chose the square-and-cruciform plan type, first aligning a series of these volumes into a long wall, then shifting them diagonally so they only touched at the corners, and finally rotating the square volumes 45 degrees, again only connected at the corners, allowing all the dormitory rooms unobstructed views outwards. All of the Erdman Hall Dormitory schemes engaged one of Kahn's favourite inspirations, the castle and its thick, protective walls, as shown here. In his final design, the individual dormitory rooms act as a layered wall, wrapping around the top-lit shared spaces at the centre of each of the three square clusters.

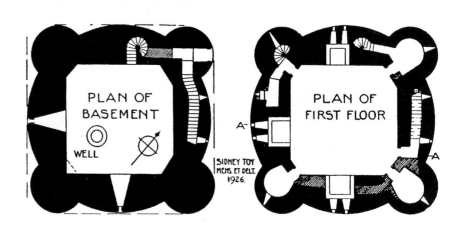

a

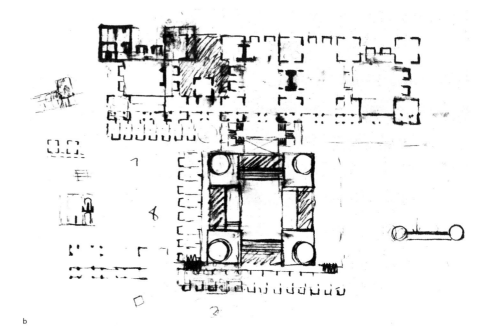

b

a. Plans of Houdan Castle, France, c.1130. Kahn was inspired by the thick wall containing smaller spaces, which surrounds and defines the central, primary room.
b. Early plan of Erdman Hall Dormitory; sketch by Kahn. The composition of a central cruciform and corner square rooms relates to Frank Lloyd Wright's Unity Temple of 1905–8.
c. Second floor plan, intermediate scheme, 5 March 1962, showing cylindrical central common rooms and octagonal dormitory rooms.
d. Early sketch plan which shows the connection of five primary square volumes at the corners; drawing by Kahn.

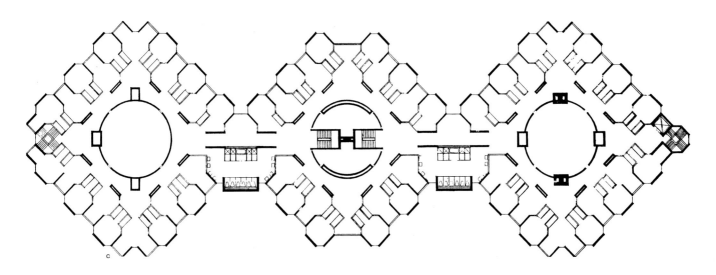

c

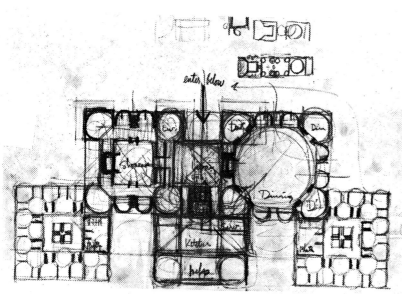

d

Indian Institute
of Management
Ahmedabad, India
1962–74

The Indian Institute of Management was intended
as a centre for training the next generation of Indian
business leaders, and its methods were to be based
on those of the Harvard School of Business
Administration. The project was sponsored by the
Sarabhai family of Ahmedabad, who had previously
commissioned Le Corbusier to design their own
house, the Mill Owners' Association Building and
the municipal museum. The Sarabhais initially offered
the commission for the Institute of Management to
Balkrishna Doshi, who had worked with Le Corbusier,
but Doshi recommended Kahn for the project, and
arranged the commission so that the architecture
students at the Indian National Institute of Design
would have the opportunity to work with this great
architect. Doshi became Kahn's associate architect
and close collaborator on this project, which would
engage Kahn for the rest of his life.

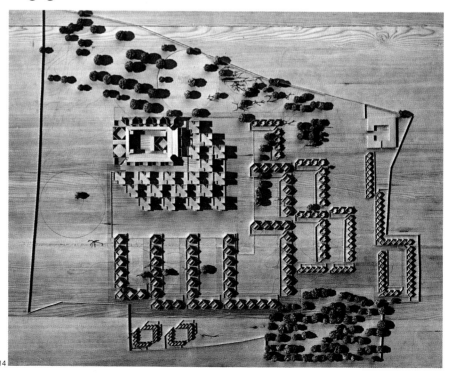

14

Throughout his career Kahn was fascinated with the school as an institution, employing it more than any other example in lectures to illustrate the need to redefine programmes and reform institutions in our time. Yet Kahn was only rarely commissioned to design a school, and the Indian Institute of Management is without question his greatest educational design. The Institute was conceived by its founders as a residential institution where business management was to be taught using the case-study method, based less upon formal lectures and more upon informal seminar discussions. Kahn believed that this educational model was similar to the manner in which he had long taught his own design-studio classes, and the fact that students and faculty were both to live and to work on the campus reinforced Kahn's consistent preference for the monastic enclave as a starting point for institutional design.

Kahn began his description of his initial concepts for the Institute: *The plan comes from my feelings of monastery ... The unity of the teaching building, dormitories and teachers' houses – each its own nature, yet each near the other – was the problem I gave myself ... Orientation to wind and shade from the sun has given architectural elements to the composition ... The fullness of light, protected, the fullness of air, so welcome, are always present as the basis for architectural shapes.*[36]

Kahn's first overall plan, remarkably maintained through the course of design, addressed both the monastery precedent and the local climate by placing the classrooms, library, dining hall and faculty offices in the main building – with the dormitories arrayed in diagonal linear structures set along two sides of the main building – and the faculty housing forming an L-shape edge across a lake from the dormitories – all shaded from the sun and ventilated by the prevailing breezes (p. 254; b).

Kahn's first design for the main building was square in plan, with a cruciform inscribed to produce a central, square courtyard and square masses at the four corners. In describing this project, Kahn said, 'I use the square to begin my solutions because the square is a non-choice, really. In the course of development, I search for the forces that would disprove the square.'[37] As he had in the Salk Meeting House, Kahn soon moved away from the square as defining the overall exterior form of the building, but he invariably returned to it as the plan-form for virtually all of the room-buildings or 'architectural elements' making up the final composition. As he had done in the Goldenberg House, Kahn's early schemes for the Institute of Management proposed a central court space, initially occupied by the library, with diagonal walls running out from its corners. Here, the diagonal walls were paired to produce open corners, with narrow passages running from the outer walls to the central court, so as to allow the court to be ventilated by the breezes (p. 254; b). While this idea was not carried through to the final design, the great diagonal entry stair now stands in its place.

In the summer of 1963, Kahn made two major changes in the design, the first being to remove the library from the middle of the main building, creating instead a large central court ringed by the classrooms, the dining hall, the faculty offices and the library (p. 254; a). In this scheme, Kahn proposed that

14. Site model of the Indian Institute of Management, intermediate scheme, late 1963; the school is surrounded by the dormitories, top left, with the faculty and staff housing below and on the right. The original design was reorientated to capture the prevailing winds around Ahmedabad.

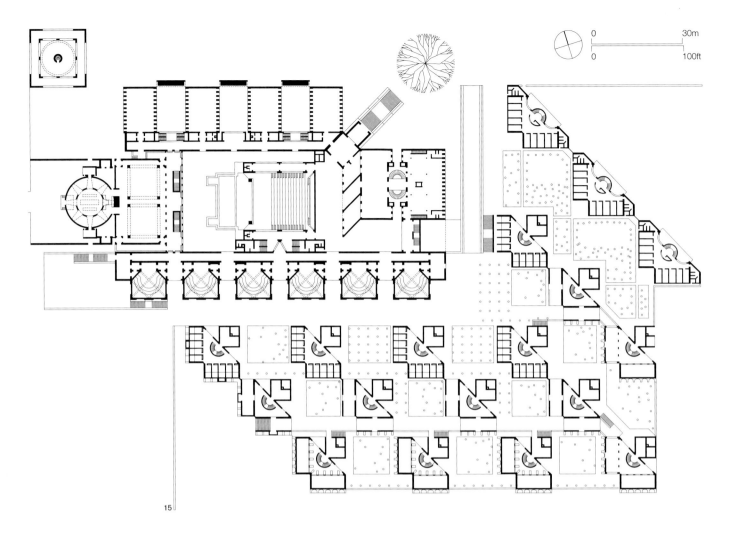

15

the library be housed in a large square block rotated 45 degrees and set into the courtyard at its east end; and that the dining hall be housed in two rotated square volumes, set within larger hollow square 'sun shields', together forming the west wall of the courtyard. The second change came when Doshi, during his first visit to Kahn's office, 'found it best to flip the whole complex over in the opposite orientation',[38] in order to take better advantage of the prevailing wind patterns. Further modifications that occurred in early 1964 were refinements of this scheme, the most important being when the student dormitories were changed from linked linear buildings to a series of independent square blocks, set in stepped diagonal sequence so as to produce a 'chequerboard' grid pattern of alternating square open courts and solid buildings.

Each of these changes in the overall plan for the Indian Institute of Management resulted in the greater geometric purity of the constituent 'room-buildings' making up the programme, and their increasing independence through simultaneously being separated and joined by exterior courts and open-air covered passages. While this development is entirely consistent with Kahn's concept of the plan as a society of spaces, as first evolved in his designs for the Salk Institute, it very probably also reflects

15. Final entry level plan of the Indian Institute of Management at the time of Kahn's death, 1974; redrawn under author's supervision.
16. East-west section of the Indian Institute of Management looking south, 1974; redrawn under author's supervision. The library is on the left, the amphitheatre in the centre, and the kitchen is on the right.

Kahn's increasing knowledge of ancient Indian architecture and the importance of the open-air spaces woven into their plans. During the dozen years Kahn worked on the Institute of Management he made more than twenty trips to Ahmedabad, giving him the opportunity to visit not only modern works, such as Le Corbusier's buildings in Ahmedabad and Chandigarh and Edwin Lutyens's capital at New Delhi, but also the eighteenth-century astronomical observatory at Jaipur (described in a 1960 essay by his friend, Noguchi) and – perhaps most important – the great medieval palace and temple buildings of the Mughal period, including the Royal Fort and Palace at Lahore, the Red Fort at Delhi and the palaces at Fatehpur Sikri (p. 255; c). In describing his designs for the Institute of Management, Kahn often referred to his experiences of these old buildings and the way their court spaces promoted ventilation by the breezes.[39]

Having started as a symmetrical, closed block, the main building of the Institute of Management became progressively more asymmetrical and open as the design was developed, and this was paralleled by its constituent 'room-buildings' becoming more geometrically pure and independent. Kahn began by making the central court, which can be considered the principal room of the building, a double square in plan,[40] and surrounding it with a broad hallway: 'The court is the meeting place of the mind, as well as the physical meeting place.'[41] Kahn conceived of the central court as being the true centre of the institution, where important events would take place:

> The inner court will be shielded during certain ceremonies by a large canopy spanning eighty feet. What gave me the courage to do this were the architectural provisions made in the courtyards of the Akbar Palace at Lahore for the same purpose … This court is different from things I have conceived before. It gives such joy to be the one to discover a beautiful way of life that belonged to another civilization.[42]

Kahn's design for the seminar rooms was also fixed quite early in the process: a semicircle of seating set within a square block-like mass,[43] the walls of the interior half-square of which were folded in at 45 degrees to create an entry foyer, shared with the neighbouring classroom. These open-air entry foyers, which overlapped the wide arcaded hall running around the inside edge of the central court, were clearly not conceived of as being 'servant' spaces, for they are equal in size to the classrooms they serve, and are better illuminated and ventilated. Kahn held that in designing a 'school as a realm

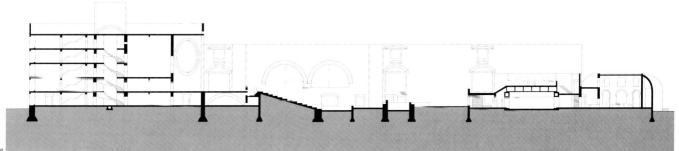

18

17. (Previous page) View up the entry stair of the Indian Institute of Management; the shadow of the large mango tree at the bottom of the stairs can be seen in the foreground, and the faculty office block is on the right.

18. East end of the main building, Indian Institute of Management. The library and classroom hallway vestibule is on the left, the dormitory on the right and the raised plaza in the foreground.

19. (Opposite) A court between the faculty office blocks, Indian Institute of Management. The central courtyard can be seen through the open walkways.

of spaces where it is good to learn … the corridors would be transferred into classrooms belonging to the students themselves by making them much wider and provided with alcoves overlooking the gardens … it would become a meeting connection and not merely a corridor, which means a place of possibilities in self-learning.'[44] Kahn believed that learning takes place not only or even primarily in the classroom and lecture hall, but rather in the informal discussions occurring in shadowed foyers, breezeways, arcaded halls, stair landings, tearooms and courtyards.

Kahn initially conceived of the faculty offices as also being ordered in cubic blocks, each with solid outer walls and opening only to a central glass-walled light court, which Kahn called 'a reverse bay window'.[45] Each of these light courts, which appear to have been carved out of the office blocks, was proposed to be cylindrical, touching the northern edge so as to create a single narrow opening from the light court to the exterior of the building (p. 255; d). In the final design Kahn shaped the faculty offices as four rectangular blocks, each four floors in height, which alternated with rectangular light courts of the same dimensions, opening to the north, with four levels of arched walkways spanning across the south side. The office windows were placed on the east and west, facing the light courts, with solid walls to the north and south, and a barrel-vaulted roof was proposed over each light court to protect the office windows from direct sunlight, and to protect the light court itself from both the torrid sun and torrential rain (p. 256; f). These roofs over the light courts,

20

and the tent-like fabric roof over the main courtyard, remain unrealized, substantially reducing the use of these important spaces. The small courts between the classroom blocks to the south (on to which the shared entry foyers open, and through which the students enter from their dormitories), and the light courts between the faculty office blocks to the north, are opened to the central court through large unglazed apertures, allowing the cooling breezes to ventilate the main building.

The majestic entry stair, a freestanding structure set diagonally to the main building mass, starts at the large existing mango tree to the north-east and gradually rises to the main floor level. The arched portal at the top of the stairs gives access to a square open-air entry hall: to our left opens the arcaded porch of the library; to our right is the hallway leading to the faculty office blocks; and directly ahead the central court opens. The library is separated from the court, and shielded from the hot western sunlight, by a porch four storeys high composed of massive brick walls turned 45 degrees to the courtyard wall, and pierced by enormous circular openings which are aligned to create a 'tubular volume'[46] above our heads. On the north side of the courtyard, the four levels of hallways of the faculty offices overlook the court. To the south, the three levels of hallways of the classrooms converge upon a massive stair block set out into the courtyard. At the level of the primary seminar rooms, we move into the monumental stair hall from the syncopating rhythm of the hallway through a powerful yet elegant series of layered arches, entering through a single opening, with arches pivoting 45 degrees to form a triangular opening above, the courtyard seen ahead through a double set of arched openings. This stair hall and the library porch are without question among the most astonishing and moving spaces Kahn ever realized, and it is important to note that they are part of the 'architecture of connections' and are not part of the original brief.

The central court, named in Kahn's honour after his death, does not contain its most important element, the amphitheatre, which was to have been covered

20. View of the central courtyard, looking towards the library, Indian Institute of Management.
21. View of a typical classroom, Indian Institute of Management.
22. Main stair hall of a classroom building, Indian Institute of Management.

by a fabric roof during ceremonial occasions and in everyday use would have formed the spatial connection between the library terrace and the floor of the court. Also not realized was Kahn's design for the critical fourth wall of the central court, to have been made by the single-storey dining hall – a double square in plan – crossing the court and providing a covered connection between the west ends of the classroom and faculty office wings. Kahn designed the kitchen as a cylindrical domed structure to be placed beyond the western edge of the main building mass, on the central axis of the court, which runs between the two square dining halls (p. 257; i). As built to Doshi's later designs, the dining hall and kitchen no longer enclose the main courtyard, and dining is not part of the daily rituals taking place in the courtyard, thus seriously compromising Kahn's monastic ideal for the whole.[47] The water tower, which was built to Kahn's designs, rises above the entire complex to the north-west, its verticality balancing the horizontal lines of dormitories running diagonally to the south-east.

21

22

24

The dormitory buildings are among Kahn's most masterly compositions of pure geometric forms. Each dormitory is a cubic block, four storeys in height, and has two wings of individual rooms set at right angles to one another, separated by a vertical slot, forming an L-shape on the west and south that creates shadowed common spaces for informal meeting (p. 257; j). A square, tower-like service block is placed on the north-east corner of each dormitory, its corners opened with narrow slots, so that the facades appear to stand free of one another. A diagonal wall, pierced by large circular openings and joined at its mid-point to the service tower, forms the outer edge of the triangular common room, with the semicircular stair at its centre. In Kahn's words:

> The dormitory rooms, in groups of ten, are arranged around a stairway and tearoom hall. In this way, corridors are avoided, favouring the making of rooms which contribute to the central idea, calling for plan and residual spaces for casual and seminar study. The tearoom entrance and positioning of the stair and washroom serve to protect the rooms from sun and glare without obstructing the essential through breeze.[48]

Each dormitory is a cubic block, sliced into from top to bottom, square in plan, with equal-sized square courts opening off all four sides. Each court space is formed on the north and east sides by the open, grid-like walls of the bedrooms, and on the west and south by the solid walls of the bedrooms and service towers, relieved by the recessed diagonal walls of the tearooms. At the north-west and south-east corners of each courtyard, the re-entrant corner at the back of each dormitory block creates a square connecting space

23. (Opposite) View along the edge of the north-east dormitories, Indian Institute of Management. These buildings were designed to be seen across the lake by visitors entering the main building.
24. North-east dormitory, Indian Institute of Management.

to the adjacent courtyards (p. 256; g). The three floors of bedrooms are placed over an open ground floor, formed by the massive semicircular arches and battered buttresses supporting the bedroom walls above. These arched passages form a grid of connecting walkways that pass through the courtyards and under the dormitories, from bright sunlight to deep shadow, connecting to the main building by way of the arched openings between each classroom block – the whole making for a truly urban experience. As Doshi said, 'When one walks around the complex silently ... one gets the vibrations of conversations, dialogues, meetings and activities. The spaces that are created for these activities link the entire complex.'[49]

The three dormitory buildings located along the north-eastern edge, which were to be seen across the lake by those entering the main building at the grand stair, are of a different design. The services are placed at the end of the two bedroom bars, the central stair is rotated 180 degrees so that its solid semi-cylindrical wall faces outwards, and the outer walls of the shared tearooms are curved inwards to meet the ends of the stair wall, only returning to the straight line of the diagonal at the top of the building. The lake, which Kahn proposed to provide 'distance with little dimension'[50] between the dormitories and the faculty residences to the south and east, was never realized; and today we can only imagine the beautiful reflections it would have given (p. 256; e), as well as the manner in which it would have marked the seasonal cycle of monsoon rainfall (through retention) and the

25. Dormitories, Indian Institute of Management. Individual student rooms can be seen at the top, with shared living spaces below. Solid vertical blocks house bathrooms and other service spaces, and the semi-cylindrical stair towers rise above the main building.
26. (Opposite) View of the library stair (detail), Indian Institute of Management.

SECOND FLOOR STACKS
371 - 999

27

important part water plays in the local ecology and economy. The faculty residences are set in lines running north–south and east–west, between a series of solid, two-storey, diagonal, staggered party walls, which allow the houses both to open to the prevailing breezes and to maintain privacy. Developed from ideas that Kahn first realized at the Esherick House, each house is divided into three equal spaces, the central space containing the services and stair, while the outer two rooms are open at both sides to allow through ventilation, with windows placed in all four corners of each room, recessed behind thick U-shaped storage walls.

All the buildings of the Institute of Management were built from brick masonry bearing walls and piers, with concrete floor slabs. While this was not Kahn's first use of load-bearing masonry (he had used load-bearing concrete bricks in the early Tribune Review Building),[51] it did represent an important shift from his typical use of brick as a non-bearing veneer (as in the Yale Art Gallery and the First Unitarian Church), the prevalent pattern of construction in the United States at the time. For Kahn, the systematic employment of brick load-bearing construction integrated the varyingly scaled buildings of the Institute: 'You notice I made all these buildings answerable to each other, even though the scale of the house and the dormitory and the school is so different. The material of brick bearing walls and piers with concrete floors is retained throughout, the larger spans giving rise to arches and buttresses, the more modest spaces simple slabs on walls.'[52] While the semicircular arches, such as those in the ground-level arcades under the dormitories, created minimal lateral thrust, the so-called 'flat' arches (where the arch is less than a semicircle) used throughout the Institute of Management required lateral bracing, and Kahn employed either the ends of the concrete floor slabs or free-spanning concrete beams to create tension ties for the masonry arches. As he said, 'This is a brick and concrete order. It is a composite order in which the brick and the concrete are acting together.'[53]

27. View through the arcade which connects the courtyards at the base of the dormitory blocks, Indian Institute of Management; the space is made by semicircular brick arches.
28. (Opposite) View from the foyer between two classrooms, through the hallway, and into the landing of the main stair, with the central court beyond, Indian Institute of Management.

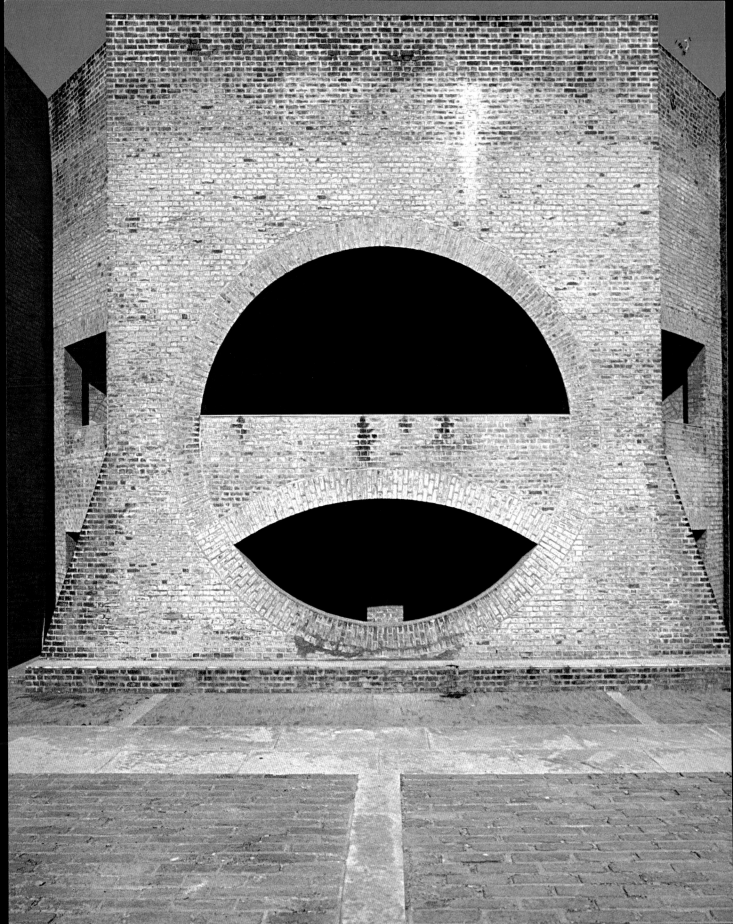

Kahn employed this ingenious device to give appropriate scale and expression to each of the elements of the Institute of Management. The faculty housing employs solid brick party walls with the concrete floor slabs spanning between, and at the outer balcony edges low walls bear upon flat arches, cradled by the ends of the floor slabs, which are separated by a thin slot. The narrow horizontal slot created by the arch at the floor both allows rain to run off the balcony and provides another passage for breezes. At the dormitories, a wider range of scales is created by the various types of arch: from the expression of the individual bedroom, each with its balcony, arched end wall and concrete slab tension tie (similar to the faculty housing) to the solid sidewalls where the floor slabs are again exposed, revealing the relieving arches (originating in ancient Roman construction) carrying the load to the outer buttressed walls; to the monumental scale of the unbraced semicircular arches at the ground and circular arches at the tearooms.

Finally, in the main building, Kahn creates the widest possible range of scales with the brick arches and concrete tie beams, beginning with the simple, repetitive, rectangular grid pattern making up the east and west walls of the faculty office blocks – the true flat (or 'jack') arches forming recessed window openings which decrease in width at each floor from the top to the bottom, in proportion to the increase in width of the brick piers between, directly reflecting the progressive increase in structural load as the weight is brought down. In contrast, the classroom blocks clearly express their tripartite sectional organization, with an outward-stepping, battered wall housing a workroom at ground level; at the middle three projecting pilasters carry two arches, creating thinner, recessed, non-bearing walls between, housing the double-height main classroom; and at the top a large arch leaps the full width of the block, framing the roofless terrace. In the courtyard, the rectangular openings in the surrounding hall clearly express the four similar office floors and the three dramatically differing classroom floors, while the angled porch of the library is opened with a series of full-circle brick arches, without concrete ties. In explaining these circular arches, first realized in the Institute, Kahn said:

> I made these large openings because there are earthquake conditions, and actually the arch below is just as important as the arch above. You have a gravity force, but you also have a [seismic force the opposite way, requiring] the reversed arch. Because Leonardo in his sketchbook says, 'In the remedy for earthquakes you reverse the arches.' I found this book, I must say, after I thought of this, but nevertheless it was very heartwarming to see this wonderful page.[54]

As was typical of Kahn's design process, there was another inspiration for this full-circle arch, one far closer to his beloved ancient Romans, the original employers of relieving arches in massive brick walls (the Pantheon), flat stone lintels across rectangular openings with brick arches above (Pompeii, Ostia and Trajan's Market), and composite wall construction of brick and concrete. Among the more famous of Piranesi's etchings of the ruins of ancient Rome is the section of the Ponte Fabrizio (p. 257; h), cutting through the bridge and its foundations, and revealing that the semicircular arch exposed above the water was completed below ground, forming a full circle masonry arch.

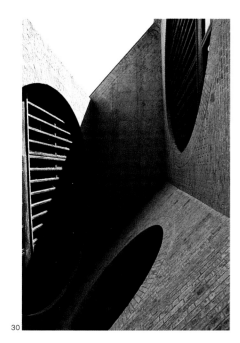

30

29. (Opposite) Management Development Centre, Indian Institute of Management; in his works on the Indian subcontinent, Kahn fully evolved his mature language of masonry structural order, engaging the circle through its division, intersection and completion.
30. View looking up in a loggia connecting the west side of the library to the central court, with circular openings into the library, Indian Institute of Management.

Indian Institute of Management

Concept development

In Kahn's design for the Indian Institute of Management, a residential educational complex, he was able to join two of his most fundamental sources of inspiration: the school and the monastery. Stages in the overall design of the Institute and the main classroom building are shown here, and Kahn's designs for the dormitories appear overleaf on pages 256–7. Kahn typically began with a square plan for the central classroom building, setting the dormitories and faculty housing in long diagonal rows so as to allow ventilation by the prevailing breezes. The orientation of these last elements were shifted 90 degrees on the recommendation of Kahn's associate architect Balkrishna Doshi and as a result of Kahn's personal research into Indian precedents, such as the palaces at Fatehpur Sikri. While the initial schemes for the classroom building were monolithic, only opening at the corners for ventilation, Kahn later evolved the individual room-buildings – classrooms, faculty offices, library, dining hall – as independent, geometrically pure volumes, separated and joined by covered breezeways. In the final design, the dormitories make a series of urban spaces and the entire complex is experienced as a city in miniature.

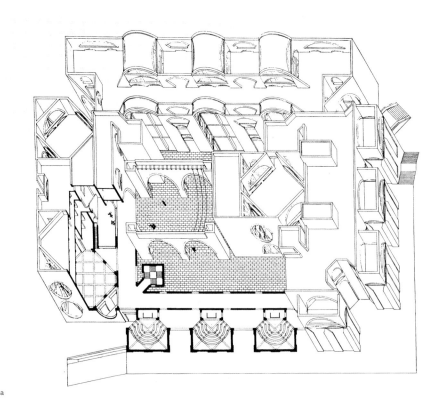

a

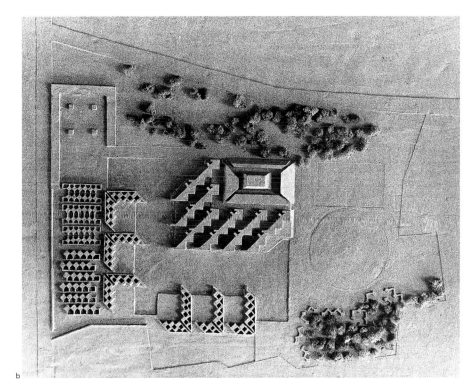

b

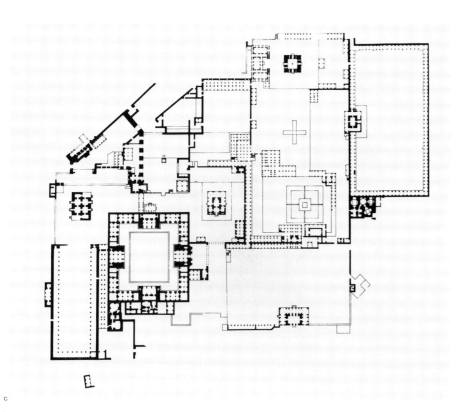

c

d

a. Axonometric cut-away drawing of the main
building, Indian Institute of Management, early
study, summer 1963.
b. Preliminary site model, March 1963; the school
is in the centre with dormitories flanking on two
sides, and the faculty and staff housing is below
and left. Kahn later reoriented the plan to better
engage prevailing breezes.
c. Plan of a palace at Fatehpur Sikri, India, c.1580.
d. Study model of the main building, intermediate
scheme, early 1963, with faculty offices lit by
cylindrical courtyards.

e

f

e. Perspective sketch of the dormitories seen
across the lake, Indian Institute of Management;
drawing by Kahn.
f & i. Models of the main building and adjacent
dormitories, looking towards the entry (f), and the
dining space and kitchen (i).
g. Perspective sketch of the dormitory courtyards;
drawing by Kahn.
h. Giovanni Battista Piranesi, section of Ponte
Fabrizio, Rome, 1756, from his *Antichità Romane IV*.
j. Plan of dormitories (north at top); redrawn under
author's supervision.

g

Spaccato del Ponte Fabricio, detto del quattro Capi. A. Circoli che formano gli archi maggiori del Ponte, composti di un doppio ordine di cunei, di travertini e peperini. B. Gran base su di cui posano i suddi circoli, composta di quattro ordini di cunei di peperini. C. Divota l'estensione della detta gran base oltre l'una e l'altra riva del fiume. D. Speroni semicircolari composti di cinque ordini di peperini, i quali posando sulla gran base oltre l'una, e l'altra riva si estendono a raffrenare i fianchi de'circoli A. E. Semicircoli di cunei, i quali confermano coll'ultimo degli operosi semicircolari D, per maggiore consistenza d'fianchi de'circoli A. F. Altri semicircoli opposti parimenti per corroborazioni degli altri fianchi de'circoli A, dopo l'incrociazioni de'quali cunei, combinano insieme, e s'appoggiano sul gran cuneo tosto al cinnre del semicircolo G, che sostiene insieme la gran pila H. I. Semisvi di cunei incrociati sulla gran base per comento all'opera sopraproseguagli. L. Silizzate sotti quati posa la gran base. M. Terreni ove son piantate le polizzate. N. Suoli di opera incerta. O. Ripari fatti dai Consoli. V. Letto del Fiume lastricato. Cosicchè questo Ponte corroborato da una composizione, così mirabile delle sue parti, si mantiene da tanti secoli nel suo essere primiero, senz'aver dato il menomo segno di debolezza, la quale altrimenti sarebbe apparsa nei cunei, Qvalla sussistenza de'quali sono stati principalmente istituiti tanti rinforzi.

Piranesi Architetto dis. inc.

h

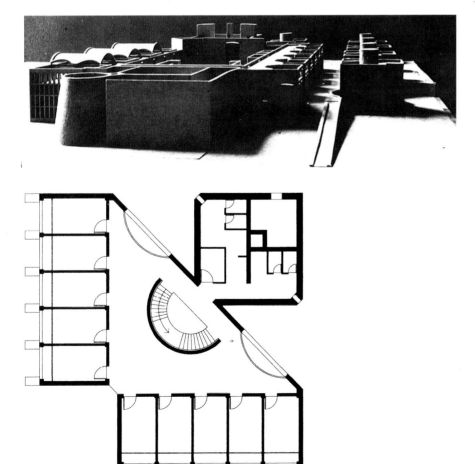

i

j

Bangladesh
National Capital
Dhaka, Bangladesh
1962–74

Sher-e-Bangla Nagar, as it is called today, or the National Capital of Bangladesh at Dhaka is one of the twentieth century's greatest architectural monuments, and is without question Kahn's magnum opus.[55] In a career marked by the bitter disappointments of numerous unrealized masterworks, that the Capital at Dhaka was ever built to Kahn's designs is all the more astonishing when we learn first, that Kahn received the commission only after it had been declined by both Le Corbusier and Alvar Aalto, and second, that the original commission, on which Kahn worked from 1962 until 1971, was not for the nation of Bangladesh at all, but for East Pakistan. Pakistan, a Muslim country, had separated from India in 1947, and consisted of eastern and western sections 1,000 miles (1,600 kilometres) apart.

In an effort to address the difficulties posed to the government by this distance, the president, Ayub Khan, decided in 1962 to build two national capital complexes, one in West Pakistan, at Islamabad, and the other in East Pakistan, at the former capital of East Bengal, Dhaka.[56] Ayub initially selected a local Bengali architect, Mazharul Islam, to oversee the project in Dhaka, but it was Islam who recommended first Le Corbusier, then Aalto, and finally Kahn, whom Islam had met while attending Yale University in 1960–1.[57]

Kahn first visited Dhaka in January 1963, and was given an extensive building programme which included the National Assembly Building, the Supreme Court building, hostels and offices for the representatives and government ministers, a hospital, schools, a library, a diplomatic enclave and residential developments with a market, 'all to be placed on a thousand acres of flat land subject to flood', according to Kahn. He recalled:

> I kept thinking of how these buildings may be grouped and what would cause them to take their place on the land. On the night of the third day, I fell out of bed with a thought which is still the prevailing idea of the plan. This came simply from the realization that assembly is of a transcendent nature. Men came to assemble to touch the spirit of community, and I felt that this must be expressible. Observing the way of religion in the life of the Pakistani, I thought that a mosque woven into the space fabric of the assembly would reflect this feeling . . .
> Also, the program required the design of a hotel for ministers, their secretaries, and the members of the assembly . . . I thought immediately that this should be transformed from the connotations of a hotel to that of studies in a garden on a lake. In my mind the Supreme Court was the test of the acts of legislation against the philosophic view of the nature of man. The three became inseparable in the thinking of the transcendent nature of assembly.[58]

The next day Kahn presented this first idea for the organization of the capital complex to Kafiluddin Ahmad, the engineer in charge of the project for the Pakistan Public Works Department, who approved it while cautioning that the Supreme Court Chief Justice did not want the court located near the assembly. Kahn then presented his design to the Chief Justice:

> I made my first sketch on paper of the assembly with the mosque on the lake. I added the hostels framing this lake. I told him how I felt about the transcendent meaning of assembly. After a moment's thought he took the pencil out of my hand and placed a mark representing the supreme court in a position where I would have placed it myself, on the other side of the mosque, and he said, 'The mosque is sufficient insulation from the men of the assembly.'[59]

In the overall plan, Kahn placed the assembly and the mosque as islands within a lake – which terminated to the south in a large crescent and was framed to east and west by the diagonally positioned hostels – with the Supreme Court on the lake shore to the north. Though developed during Kahn's first trip to Dhaka, this initial conception of the plan of the capital complex remained remarkably unchanged over the next decade of development on the project.

31. Early perspective sketch of the Assembly Building seen from across the lake, Bangladesh National Capital, early 1963; drawing by Louis Kahn.

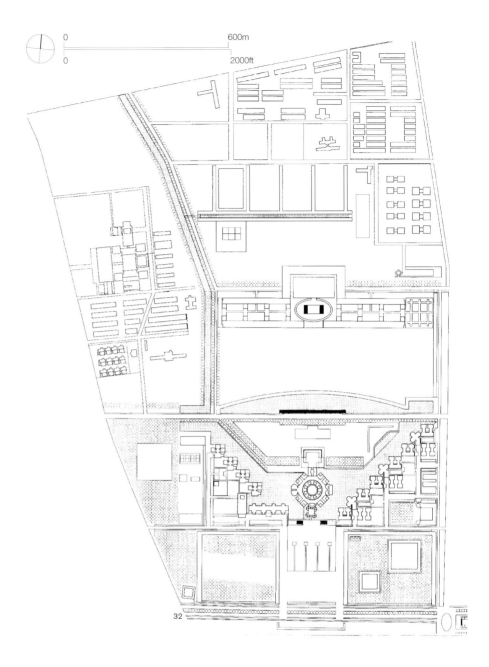

0

600m

0

2000ft

32

32. Final site plan of the Bangladesh National Capital; redrawn under author's supervision. The plan shows the Assembly Building (lower centre), the secretariat (centre), and the Ayub Hospital (upper left).

33. Final second floor plan of the Assembly Building with the prayer hall to the south (left) and the public entry from the Presidential Square through the stair hall to the north (right).

34. Section of the Assembly Building, showing the assembly hall with its final roof design (centre), the prayer hall (left), and the stair hall (right).

During the early years, Kahn focused on the design of the National Assembly Building and the associated mosque, which were the first elements of the project scheduled for construction. Kahn's initial plans and sections also clearly indicate his conception of the Assembly complex as a castle or 'citadel of assembly', as he called it, a diamond (rotated square) in overall form, with the office blocks shaped as four solid battered walls, open at the corners to give access to the assembly spaces within. In this design, the mosque was a square in plan, and the Supreme Court adjacent to it was wrapped around a square courtyard of the same dimensions as the plinth of the mosque. The first sketches of the mosque indicate four tall minarets at the outer edges of the island plinth, and the mosque itself is composed of a square wall surrounding nine enormous columns (p. 282; a), each of which

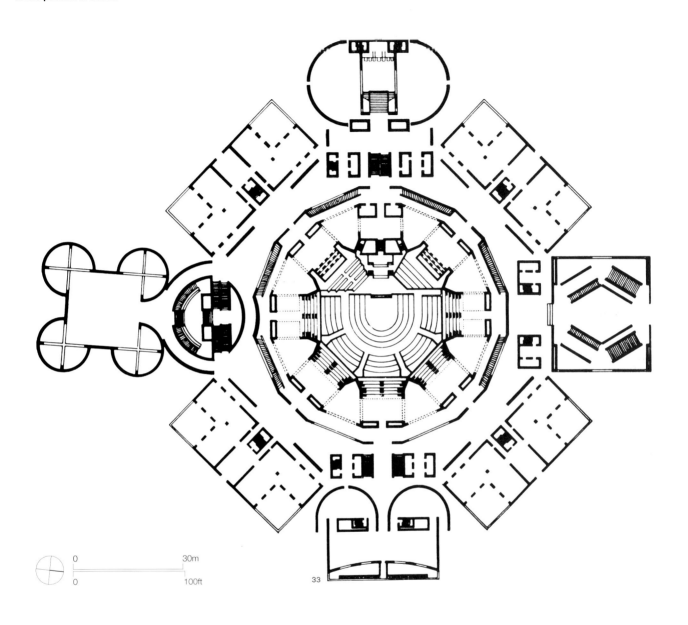

0   30m

0   100ft

33

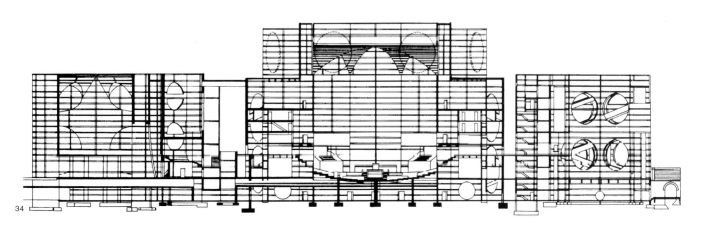

34

supports a cantilevered, umbrella-like roof shell, which rise above the surrounding wall – exactly as in Wright's Johnson Wax Building.

In these early sections, the Assembly Building is composed of double-battered office blocks at either edge, with the assembly hall roof proposed as an elliptical, convex disc-shape, swelling down into the space at the centre and coming to a point at the edges, its structure a truss hidden within a concrete skin – very similar to Kahn's early roof design for the First Unitarian Church and its source, Le Corbusier's Ronchamp Chapel. An office drawing from a meeting in July of 1963 (p. 285; m), which his engineer, Komendant, attended, indicates that Kahn proposed to support the assembly-hall dome with a triangular truss. This is very similar to the type of circular-plan elliptical-section cable-truss, composed of two convex triangulated cable networks, with compression posts between, and a single outer compression ring, which his colleague, Robert Le Ricolais, was developing with his students in his experimental structures course at the University of Pennsylvania from 1960 on – a model of which (p. 284; h) has been displayed in the school ever since.[60] While Kahn's design for the assembly hall would change repeatedly during the first year of the project, this elliptical, cable-truss-supported dome concept for the assembly roof remained a constant element.

In May 1963 Kahn made the only major change in the overall plan, reversing the entire Assembly Building group, so that the Supreme Court was now to the south and the crescent-shaped lake was to the north, facing the 'citadel of institutions' that Kahn proposed to house the schools, museum, market and sports facilities (p. 283; g). The client also requested that the mosque be changed to a smaller prayer hall, which Kahn was then able to incorporate into the main assembly complex. At this stage, the plan of the Assembly Building showed four office blocks forming an inner square space, with diagonal walls running to the outer corners, creating narrow passages to the east and west, and larger openings to the north and south into which were set the entry hall and the prayer hall, respectively. It was at this time that Kahn also first rotated the prayer hall (which he often continued to call 'the mosque') a few degrees to align with the cardinal directions, so it would face east, as required, and giving it a certain independence from the rest of the Assembly Building. A north–south section through the Assembly Building indicates that the square entry hall, circular assembly chamber and square mosque were all to have pyramidal ceiling forms with an arched sunshade roof, allowing only thin slits of sunlight to pass within (quite like the early designs for the Angolan Consulate), covering the spaces of connection between.

In late 1963 Kahn made what would prove to be an important change in the Assembly Building plan, breaking the wall-like office blocks into smaller volumes, and proposing meeting and dining spaces for the assembly members to the east and west (p. 282; b).[61] At the same time, Kahn significantly increased the size, complexity and geometric precision of the central assembly chamber, which now took on the form of an octagon, composed of rotated squares which interlocked with and were braced by a cruciform, housing the

35. (Opposite) View of the Assembly Building, Bangladesh National Capital, looking south to the entry and stair hall from the Presidential Square.

36

36. View from the entry stair of the Assembly
Building, Bangladesh National Capital, with the
prayer hall in the centre and the office block
on the right.

service components. The plans that resulted were no longer defined by a geometrically pure outer boundary, but instead comprised a series of independent buildings, each an element complete in its own geometry, which was bound to the octagonal centre — and the whole composition held together – by the gravity of the assembly chamber. The plan of the Assembly Building now assumed its final character as a true 'society of rooms', each building-element independent and self-defined within its own pure geometry, to be composed within the larger order of the plan as though each element was a piece on a chessboard (p. 283; f). In a telegram to his clients in early 1964, Kahn said, 'Buildings must be like a good position on the chessboard. For its symbolic value no building must be in the wrong place.'[62]

Kahn now set about developing these independent room-buildings (p. 283; d), beginning with the entry hall, proposed as a rotated square void within the larger square stair block to the north, balancing the initial design for the prayer hall as a rotated square solid set on the south side. A central passage runs from north to south through the entry hall, and a second layer of walls is wrapped around the east and west sides of the diamond-shaped interior space, with the stairs placed between. The prayer hall began as a hollow pyramid with stairs climbing up the outer walls; then evolved into a rotated square with four semicircular apse-like spaces opening off it; then became a square with three-quarter circular spaces at each corner; then was briefly proposed as two intersecting circular spaces (forming a *vesica piscis*) housing a double square within; and finally returned to the form of a cubic volume (measuring 66 feet [20 metres] across – the exterior dimension of Wright's Unity Temple), with four cylindrical light towers centred on the corners. While the stairs that serve this south side of the Assembly Building were originally integrated into the prayer hall, running around the outside of the inner cylindrical towers, they were later removed into a separate circular hall located between the prayer hall and the assembly chamber.

The ministers' lounge to the west, while initially proposed to be an oval-shaped, glass-walled space surrounded by a rectangular sun-shield wall (derived from the Salk Institute Meeting House), was finally composed of two semicircles, separated by a rectangular hall and stair at the centre. The ministers' dining hall to the east – which was initially proposed to be a semicircular, glass-walled space, the curved sides of which were to be surrounded by a double-square sun-shield wall – was ultimately composed of two cubic blocks within a shallow light court (a common stair running down the interior of the outside wall), and connected to the assembly hall within by two semicircular walls.

The four office blocks were composed as double squares, each pair separated by a shared hall and a stair placed between, with a smaller square light court opened in the outer quarter of each square. The office floors thus are L-shaped in plan, overlooking and receiving light from the square light courts at their outer corners, which are open at the top and have large openings cut in their two exterior walls, while the central shared hall and stair receive sunlight from the narrow slot aperture running from the ground to the roof, and separating the square volumes on their exterior facade. Kahn had

37

intended the square light courts at the outer edges of the office blocks to be left open at the top to promote natural ventilation (acting like a chimney to draw hot air up out of the building), to allow the rain and the experience of the local climate to enter these interior gardens, and to provide a view of the sky above – as in his beloved Pantheon.[63]

The design of the central assembly hall itself was Kahn's great challenge and, while the section of the entire Assembly Building (from early on similar to that of the Erdman Hall Dormitory) remained relatively constant throughout the process, Kahn struggled with how to roof the assembly hall for almost a decade. Following the initial design for an elliptical-section, cable truss supported dome, Kahn proposed a conical roof and ceiling for the assembly hall (p. 285; l), with a single large light monitor at its centre, and a large scale model was made of this design. Later Kahn explored the possibility of making the assembly hall roof a series of deep beams or Vierendeel trusses, meeting at the centre and opened with large circular apertures to allow the light to enter from the monitors set around the edge. Kahn also developed a rather extended series of folded concrete planes, producing various faceted dome-like forms within (p. 284; i), while opening to the outside to admit baffled sunlight. As late as 1969, Kahn had his associates develop a design for the ceiling and roof made of steel struts and cables, suspending a wood lattice sunscreen (p. 284; j), and this wholly uncharacteristic attempt at a lightweight structure clearly indicates Kahn's frustration with finding the appropriate design for the assembly hall roof.

While among Kahn's office drawings there are numerous studies for the assembly chamber roof that employ multiple overlapping rotated squares, similar to the geometries underlying traditional Islamic domes, in his own sketches of the assembly hall Kahn kept returning to juxtapositions of pure, massive geometries that are of ancient Roman origin. 'My design at Dhaka is inspired, actually, by the Baths of Caracalla', Kahn stated in 1964,[64] and even earlier in the design process Kahn referred to both the assembly hall at Dhaka and the Pantheon in Rome as 'a world within the world'.[65] In fact, the only aspect of the assembly hall design that remained constant throughout this decade of design originates with the Pantheon: a sphere created by doubling the Pantheon's hemispherical, 142 foot (43 metre) diameter dome may be inscribed in its interior space, and would hover less than one foot (0.3 metres) above its flat floor. Right from the very start, Kahn intended the assembly hall at Dhaka to be ordered in the same way, and the 56 foot (17 metre) radius, 112 foot (34 metre) diameter of the central octagon was duplicated in the section of the assembly hall, and a sphere inscribed in the interior space would hover less than 3 feet (0.9 metres) above its sloping floor.

Kahn's final design for the roof of the assembly hall was composed of a series of parabolic concrete shells that create eight enormous clerestory openings above the surrounding lower roof of the Assembly Building, and under which a 112 foot (34 metre) diameter sphere may be inscribed in the assembly hall space. Rather than originating in the Pantheon, with its single

39

oculus in the centre, this roof design is more closely related to the roof structures of other ancient Roman buildings, most especially the vestibule of the Piazza d'Oro at Hadrian's Villa (p. 285; n), and the Renaissance domes developed from it, such as the dome in Bramante's S. Maria delle Grazie of c.1492 in Milan (which Kahn had visited in 1967).[66] As is typical with Kahn, however, there were equally compelling contemporary sources of inspiration for this thin shell, cast-in-place reinforced concrete structure, particularly in the work of the Mexican structural engineer, Félix Candela. Among Candela's designs which are closest to Kahn's final design for the Dhaka assembly hall roof are the octagonal-plan, parabolic-section roof shells of both the 'Los Manantiales' restaurant and the St Vincent Chapel (in Xochimilco, Mexico and Mexico City respectively) – designs published in 1960 and very probably shown to Kahn by Candela during Kahn's visit to the School of Design at North Carolina State College, Raleigh, in 1964, when Kahn lectured on his early designs for Dhaka.[67]

There are numerous striking similarities between Kahn's final plan for the Assembly Building and the plans of Renaissance centralized churches, particularly those plans available to Kahn in his personal copies of books by Wittkower and Richter, mentioned in conjunction with the early designs for the First Unitarian Church.[68] In particular, the interior light courts ringing the assembly hall, which Kahn had introduced as early as 1963, may be related to the small chapels which circle the main central sanctuary in Leonardo da Vinci's ideal church plans. Initially proposed to be circular in plan, like the Renaissance chapels, Kahn conceived of these light courts as hollow columns: 'The columns are hollow and much bigger and ... their walls themselves give light, then the voids are rooms, and the column is the maker of light and can take on complex shapes and be the supporter of spaces and give light to spaces.'[69]

39. View across the lake to the Bangladesh National Capital; the cylindrical, double-shell brick dining halls are in the centre and the hostels are on the right.
40. View of the central entry stair, giving access to the individual dwelling units in a minister's hostel, Bangladesh National Capital.

Once again, we find a modern inspiration for these light-giving columns in Kahn's design. The final, folded V-shapes of these buttress-and-light courts may also be related to Kahn's critique of Le Corbusier's Ronchamp Chapel, presented to his class in February 1961, where, rather than finding fault with the hidden steel truss in the ceiling (which Kahn himself considered for Dhaka), Kahn criticized the thin steel posts holding up the roof, and the fact that they were hidden within what appeared to be solid, massive walls. Kahn proposed instead that the wall become hollow, appearing as a solid, closed mass from the interior and as an open hollow space on the exterior, where the spaces could become small chapels.[70] The relationship of Kahn's reinterpretation of Ronchamp to his design for the assembly hall at Dhaka is direct, for at Dhaka the walls are made to appear solid and massive from within, only to be revealed as hollow – both structural support and light court – from the ambulatory beyond.

In 1971, when Bangladesh declared independence from Pakistan, Kahn's contract was terminated, but he continued work, finalizing the design of the assembly hall roof so that when peace came, the project could be completed (p. 285; k). In 1972 the new government contracted with Kahn to complete what was now to be the National Capital of Bangladesh, and the following year Kahn presented a new masterplan (p. 283; e), calling now for an enormous nine-storey, 2,000 foot (610 metre) long secretariat, rather than the 'citadel of institutions', to be built across the lake to the north of the Capital complex.[71] That this potentially disastrous transition was accomplished so smoothly, and that Kahn's design for an overthrown political structure was immediately accepted by the government of the newly independent state, is truly a remarkable verification of Kahn's sense of the essential nature of the institution he had been asked to design. From the day of its opening, the Bengalis have enthusiastically and proudly embraced this building as their own, and it has become the symbol by which they feel they are known to the world.[72]

The Assembly Building is constructed inside and out of reinforced concrete, cast in 5 foot (1.5 metre) high sections in formwork made from narrow vertical wood boards, giving the walls a subtle vertical texture when seen up close. On the three lowest floor levels, these wood boards were cut away at the edges to produce a thin, V-shaped vertical rib which projects from the surface of the wall to cast a delicate pattern of shadows.[73] The horizontal pour lines, where the daily concrete casting stops, were kept 'as the marks of making' by casting a recess in the concrete into which 6 inch (15 centimetre) bands of white marble were set. These horizontal marble bands occur at 5 foot (1.5 metre) intervals, two per 10 foot (3 metre) floor, the mid-point marked by a band set flush to the concrete surface, and the floor line itself marked by a projecting marble drip which casts a shadow and allows the scale of the floors within to be read – as Kahn had done on his Yale Art Gallery. Here Kahn also employs 12 inch (30 centimetre) bands of vertical flush marble to articulate the joints and rhythms in the massive geometric volumes making up the building. The exterior of the 110 foot (33.5 metre) tall cylindrical and

cubic concrete forms of the Assembly Building is opened up with enormous apertures several floors in height, giving light to the courts within; these square, triangular and circular openings give the building a truly monumental scale even as they simultaneously reveal the human scale through the wooden windows seen on the inner surfaces of the light courts.

The large elevated plazas to the north and south, the hostels and dining halls flanking left and right along the edge of the lake, the extensive retaining walls, connecting arcades, walkways and viaducts; all are constructed in local red brick, so that the light grey concrete and white marble Assembly Building stands out like a jewel in its setting. The hostels, for the secretaries and ministers to the east and for the members of the assembly to the west, are cubic volumes, three floors (30 feet/9 metres) in height, clustered into groups of four around shared stair halls, which step along the diagonal edge of the lake to the east and west, forming a dense urban edge for the large open space into which the Assembly Building is set. The hostels are bearing-wall buildings, opened only with enormous circular arched apertures and full-height rectangular openings topped by flat arches and concrete tie beams, the windows of the interior spaces set within their deep protective shadows. The dining halls for members of the assembly are comprised of sets of three massive brick cylinders, the floors recessed behind semicircular sun courts framed by double-layered walls facing the lake, and a spectacular stair climbing between the double walls and carving its way through the circular arched opening. Kahn designed the hostels and dining halls using the cut-away, up-view axonometrics he had first seen in Choisy's *Histoire* (p. 282; c) and, with their simple pure geometric forms and their glazing hidden deep in the shadows of monumentally scaled arched brick openings, these buildings are the closest to Roman ruins that Kahn ever realized.

To the north of the Assembly Building is the enormous raised plaza, today called the Presidential Square and reserved for ceremonial events, a brick surface lined with marble strips and flanked by banks of marble stepped seating, all of which rests on a massive structure of low brick arches. The deeply shaded space underneath the plaza, formed by a seemingly endless series of wide brick arches, was not part of the original brief; in a similar way, throughout the building we find that Kahn has framed almost every formally programmed function with a parallel 'room with no name'. Opening on to this plaza is the cubic entry and stair block, within which we find a hexagonal central atrium; behind the four sides to the east and west of this are placed the stairs, which are seen through the eight circular openings, two in each faceted wall. The interior walls of the Assembly Building are made of the same banded concrete as the exterior, except that all the marble bands are flush with the concrete, so that the floor lines are not as legible.

In everyday use, we approach the Assembly Building from the south plaza, crossing the lake on a brick-arched bridge, and then entering into the lower level of the prayer hall building. This entry hall comprises a square room with cylindrical light towers at each corner, and four fragments of a cylindrical wall at the centre. Beyond, we move around the large cylindrical stair chamber

41. (Opposite) View of the assembly hall ambulatory and office block, Assembly Building, Bangladesh National Capital.

43

and into the ambulatory that runs around the sixteen-sided assembly hall at the centre, and on to which open the eight individual component buildings making up the outer shell of the assembly complex. This ambulatory is an astonishing 85 foot (26 metre) tall space of ever-changing form, opening first through monumental circular and triangular apertures in layered walls to the rooms along the outer edge, and then through circular openings in the double-shell wall, crossed by the diagonals of stairs, to the light courts that surround the assembly hall at the centre. The ambulatory is covered by a flat roof supported by concrete beams, which have clerestory windows set in their outer ends, so that morning and afternoon sunlight washes the ceiling, and narrow glass-block skylights set parallel to and between them, so that throughout the day thin lines of sunlight fall into the space and move across the walls. The ambulatory roof beams and skylights are set in the cardinal directions, orientated towards the four primary building elements – prayer hall, stair hall, ministers' lounge and ministers' dining hall – the shift of direction occurring at the centre of each office block, providing a means of orientation.

The prayer hall is entered from the hallway ringing the assembly chamber, at the same level as the top of the assembly hall's sloped seating, 20 feet (6 metres) above the floor of the ambulatory. A perfect cube of 66 feet (20 metres) in plan and section, the prayer hall opens at its corners to four 48 foot (14.5

42. (Previous page) View across the stair hall, Assembly Building, Bangladesh National Capital.
43. Interior of the Assembly Building, Bangladesh National Capital. This view looks up towards the ambulatory roof, with the assembly hall on the left and the prayer hall centre right, as seen through a circular aperture. The lines of sunlight are made by glass set between the roof beams.
44. The assembly hall, looking towards the podium, Assembly Building, Bangladesh National Capital.

metre) diameter cylindrical light towers that rise above the ceiling and descend below the floor. Each of these cylindrical towers is crossed at its midpoint by a pair of concrete walls, which are aligned with the walls of the prayer hall. At the eight corners of the cubic interior space, circular openings have been made, cutting through the walls of the prayer hall and the walls within the cylindrical towers to outline spherical volumes which appear to float half above and half below the floor, and at the ceiling. At the upper corners, four walls are folded in at 45 degree angles, meeting at their corners to form a rotated square on the ceiling. These four walls at the corners above are each opened with a circular form, and appear to trace the outlines of the spherical volumes as they project into the inner cubic space of the prayer hall. Sunlight falls in through the open tops of the cylinders and washes down the concrete walls, entering the prayer hall through the circular and semicircular openings in the walls at the corners, and creating a complex layering of spaces and degrees of illumination – a truly boundless place for spiritual experience.[74]

45

The assembly hall itself is truly 'a world within a world' – in both its powerful monumentality and stark simplicity, it is a glorious central, top-lit space as close to his idealized Pantheon as any Kahn would ever realize. The octagonal upper drum-like walls defining the central members' chamber rest upon the inner corners of the eight triangular-shaped 'hollow column' light courts ringing the assembly hall, which from within appear as massive angled buttresses. Recessed between these triangular folded concrete walls are the balcony seating spaces for visitors, with wood-panelled rear walls illuminated by the glazed side walls opening into the light courts to either side, revealing the layered shell-like nature of the structure. Only the west wall, behind the speaker's podium, forms a solid concrete surface reaching from floor to roof. All the concrete walls of the assembly hall are inscribed with the horizontal marble bands at 5 foot (1.5 metre) intervals, with the centre of each octagonal segment marked by a vertical marble band. A flat network of wires holding electrical lights is suspended across the mid-point of the room and, high above, the vaulted roof opens.

The assembly hall's concrete roof shells, each striated by closely spaced inlaid marble strips running from the centre outwards, bear only on their eight narrow points, and appear to be entirely surrounded by light. The crown of monumental light monitors above the assembly hall, rising 50 feet (15 metres) higher than any other building element of the entire complex, ring

45. Prayer hall, Assembly Building, Bangladesh National Capital; the glazing screens were added after Kahn's death.
46. View from a stair landing towards the centre of the stair hall, Assembly Building, Bangladesh National Capital.

this vaulted roof and act to bounce the light indirectly to the spaces within. The large circular apertures at the outer edge of the building's crown open above the triangular light courts surrounding the assembly hall. The eight parabolic openings at the end of the vaults of the assembly hall roof look out on to the inside edge of the inner walls of the building's crown. The sunlight we see from within the assembly hall first enters from above the roof shell, bouncing off the crown's inner wall before entering the assembly hall itself, and direct sunlight enters only through the sixteen thin vertical slots cut in the crown's inner wall. The assembly hall is thus provided with a combination of broad washes of bounced light and little slivers of direct

sunlight, each giving different hues and brightness as they strike the surfaces of the concrete vaults and walls, reflecting from the smooth white marble and absorbing into the rough grey concrete – a wholly modern redeployment of the mix of bounced and direct sunlight played upon light-coloured walls that characterized the great works of the Baroque era.[75]

While construction of the Capital of Bangladesh was not completed until 1983, almost ten years after Kahn's death, the design of the assembly hall roof was the last major design decision to be made on the building, and Kahn presented the final solution following the establishment of the nation of Bangladesh in 1971. As it stands completed today, the Bangladesh National Capital at Dhaka possesses a monumentality unlike anything to come before in the history of architecture – at once ancient and modern, literally hand-built largely of modest, locally produced materials, yet engaging the most modern spatial and structural thinking; at once a monumental symbol of a new nation and an ennobling of the individual citizen, its spaces are scaled to the highest aspirations of humanity.

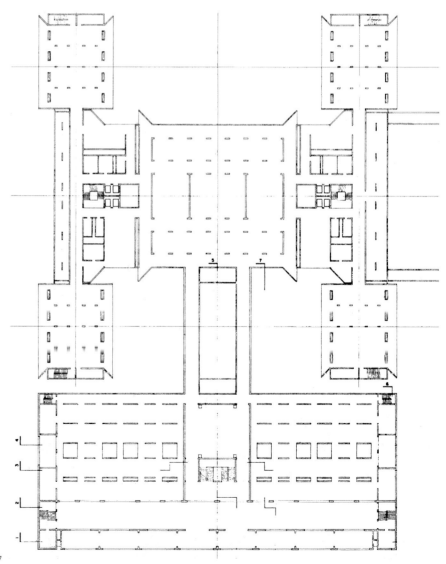

47. Plan of the Suhrawardhy National Hospital, Bangladesh National Capital (north to left); only the lower portion was constructed.
48. North-south section and west-facing elevations of the Suhrawardhy National Hospital. In descending order from top: section through western hospital wards, elevations of the third (interior), second (interior), and first (exterior) brick wall layers.
49. (Overleaf) View of a shaded waiting area between the second and third masonry walls, Suhrawardhy National Hospital. The clinics are on the right.

47

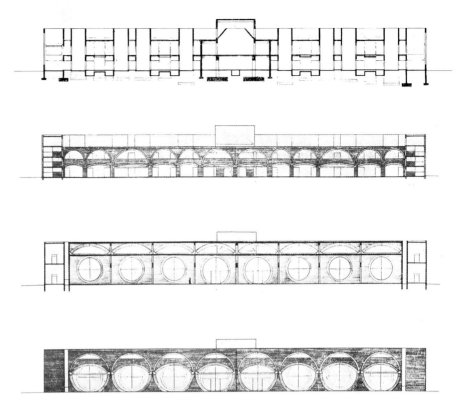

48

Designed as part of the National Capital of Bangladesh, the Suhrawardhy National Hospital was sited to the north-west of the Assembly Building complex, and consisted of a large H-shape general hospital connected by a central bridge to the outpatient clinic to the west. Only this last element of the larger plan was realized, a three-storey rectangular block with service spaces on the north and south edges, a central, top-lit stair hall at the centre, and a long double layer of brick arcades facing the hot western sun. The outermost layer is composed of eight giant three-storey circular arches, tangent to the ground plane to form the entryways, with inset arches leaping across at mid-point, the upper third floor portion originally designed as a roof terrace, but later glazed and enclosed. Behind these outer arches, and running perpendicular to them, are bracing walls, formed by pairs of brick arches – upward-opening above downward-opening. The second west-facing brick wall is composed of eight two-storey circular arches, the centre two intersecting the ground to form the entry. The third brick layer frames the waiting room, its single-storey flat arches and concrete tie beams forming the outer wall of the various clinics. The play of sunlight and shadows across the three layers of monumental arches is wondrous to experience, creating a sense of eternal, timeless place unparalleled in modern architecture.

Bangladesh National Capital

Concept development

Kahn's design for the Bangladesh National Capital complex initially involved buildings for the National Assembly and the Supreme Court, which he separated and joined with a mosque, placing the hostels for the ministers into gardens set along the edge of a lake. Kahn's initial studies for the Assembly Building and mosque attempted to join two of his favoured precedents from modern architecture: the umbrella columns of Wright's 1936–8 Johnson Wax Building and the elliptical roof of Le Corbusier's Ronchamp Chapel of 1950–4. All were to be housed within what Kahn called a 'citadel' or castle, formed as a rotated square with four thick walls of office space surrounding the assembly hall. In composing this enormous plan, Kahn first stated his conception of plan-making as analogous to placing pieces on a chessboard, clearly indicating the relative independence of each room-building. In conceiving the roof of the central assembly hall (detailed overleaf on pages 284–5), Kahn drew on both ancient and modern precedents: Hadrian's Villa from ancient Rome and contemporary thin-shell concrete construction.

a

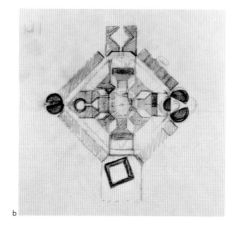

b

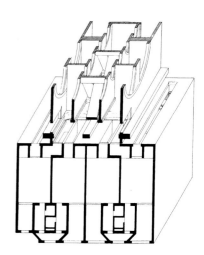

c

a. Early section and plan sketches, Bangladesh National Capital, early 1963. These show the Assembly Building with its elliptical roof, and the Mosque with its hypostyle hall of umbrella columns; drawings by Kahn.
b. Plan sketch of the Assembly Building, late 1963, by Kahn. This shows the assembly hall (centre), offices in four rectangular blocks on the diagonals, the stair hall (top) and the prayer hall (below).
c. Up-view axonometric drawing of a typical hostel, Bangladesh National Capital. This drawing is similar in style to those of Auguste Choisy in his *Histoire de l'architecture*, 1899.

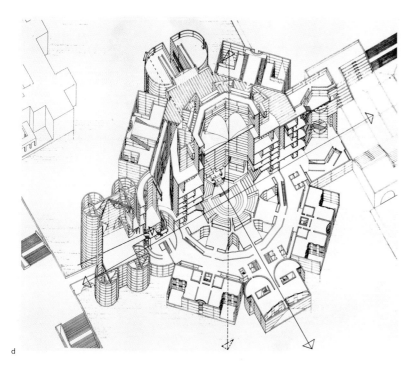

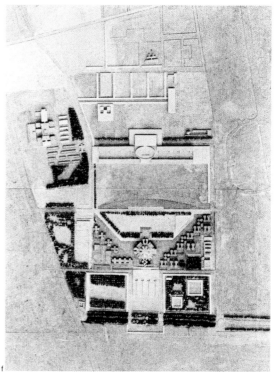

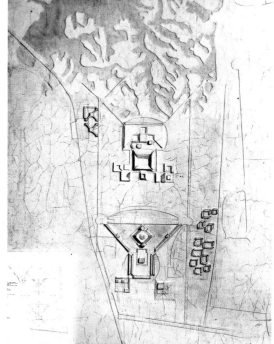

d. Axonometric drawing with plan and section of
the Assembly Building, Bangladesh National Capital;
drawing by Florindo Fusaro.

e. Louis Kahn (left) and his assistants working on the
site model of the Bangladesh National Capital; it was
at this time that Kahn made the analogy between site
design and moving chess pieces on a board.

f. Final site model, 1973; the Assembly Building and
hostels are to the south (below), the secretariat is to
the north (above), and the hospital is to the west (left).

g. Site model, May 1963, with the Assembly Building
and Supreme Court to the south (below), and the 'citadel
of institutions' to the north (above), with a crescent-
shaped lake between.

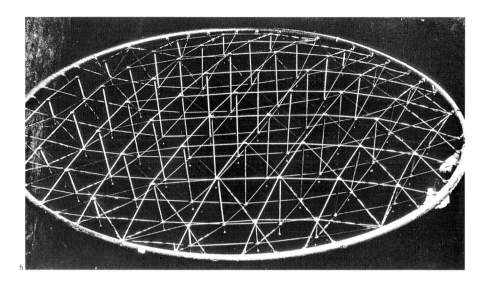

h. Model of elliptical structure, c.1960; built under the supervision of Robert Le Ricolais, structural engineering professor at the University of Pennsylvania.
i. Study models of the assembly hall roof, 1964.
j. Study model of the assembly hall roof, steel frame and cables, with suspended wooden sunscreen, 1969.

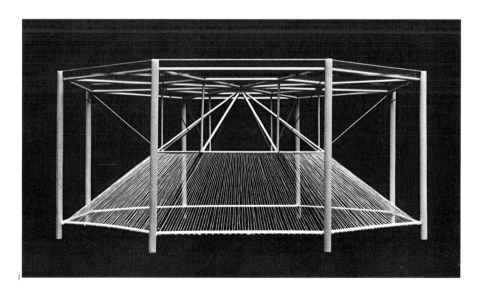

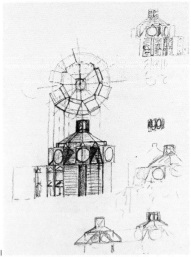

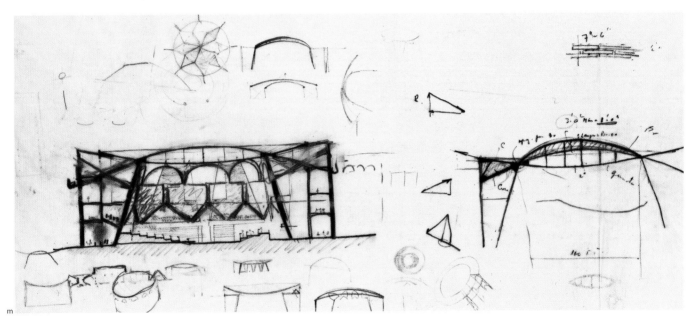

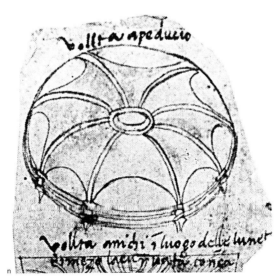

k. Aerial photograph of Bangladesh National Capital, Dhaka at the time of Bangladesh's independence from Pakistan in 1971; the assembly hall is still unroofed.

l. Plan and elevation sketches for the assembly hall roof; drawing by Kahn.

m. Early section sketches with elliptical roof section, July 1963; drawing by Kahn.

n. Francesco di Giorgio Martini, perspective drawing of the vestibule ceiling of Piazza d'Oro, Hadrian's Villa, Tivoli; from a book in Kahn's library, c.1480.

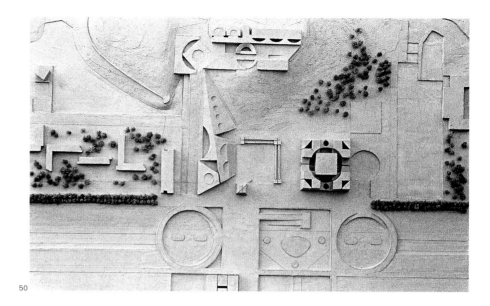

50

51

Carving earth, mass and space

During the period in which the Bangladesh National Capital was being designed, Kahn explored similar concepts of shaping the ground, forming light and assembling independent volumes in plan, in several parallel projects. Kahn's design for the President's Estate and Capital, Islamabad, West Pakistan, 1963–6, intended to complement his work on the East Pakistan Capital at Dhaka, was part of the masterplan by Constantine Doxiadis,[76] which involved a number of other architects. Though in the end nothing would be realized, Kahn's designs are important for at least three reasons. The first is the strong presence in Kahn's design process of Piranesi's Campus Martius plan – given the place of honour on the wall directly in front of Kahn's drawing table – from which several plans for the President's Estate seem to have been almost directly drawn.[77] The second is Kahn's powerful folding of the landforms, and the triangular flattened planes of earth in his plasticine clay models, all showing the inspiration of Kahn's work with Isamu Noguchi. Third is the design of the Assembly Building, which at its centre proposed a cubic or cylindrical chamber, to be set within a square enclosure with diagonally opened corners and massive, battered outer walls – which in several iterations closely presages the later Hurva Synagogue.[78]

Kahn's unrealized design for the 'Interama' Inter-American Community in Miami, Florida, of 1963–9, was commissioned as part of a group of buildings designed by well-known modern architects, a significant recognition for Kahn at the time. Kahn's design for a series of 'Houses of Nations' and exhibition spaces, to be set on a treeless bayfront site looking to the skyline of the city of Miami to the south, drew upon his work in Dhaka, where he had to contend with similar hot tropical sunshine. Kahn proposed the individual residential and exhibition buildings for the seven nations to be composed as a single long building framing the large triangular elevated plaza to the east, and opened with courtyards facing the bay to the west. On the bay front, the projecting and receding masonry walls were to be opened with circular arched apertures similar to those of the hostels at Dhaka, and on the plaza front, the single long wall

50. Clay site model of the President's Estate and Capital, Islamabad, West Pakistan, 1963–6.
51. Ground floor plan of the Assembly Building, Capital, Islamabad, West Pakistan, 1963–6.
52. Plan of the main exhibition building (left) and 'Houses of Nations' for the 'Interama' project, Inter-American Community, Miami, Florida, 1963–9 (north to right); redrawn under author's supervision. The project was never built.
53. Section of the main exhibition building, 'Interama' project.
54. Clay site model of the 'Interama' project, Louis Kahn and others; Kahn's section is on the triangular site.

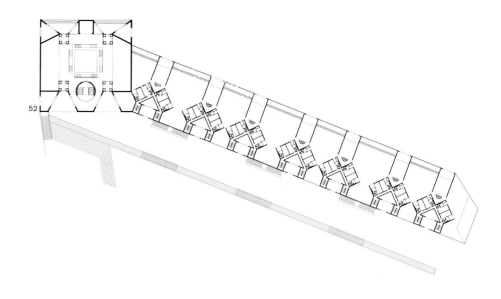

52

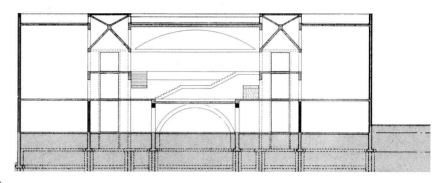

53

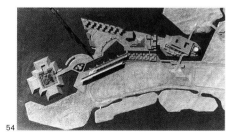

54

was to be opened with a series of large circular arched apertures almost identical to those of the Dhaka hospital. While early plans for each national house took the shape of a cruciform, set at 45 degrees to the shoreline, with a square atrium at its centre, the final plans proposed a triangular atrium formed by three rectangular volumes, with the exhibition space set to the west on the water.

The main exhibition building of Kahn's 'Interama' project was placed at the southern edge of the site, with the view of the city skyline, and comprised a square mass with a cubic central space (33 feet [10 metres] on a side – the same dimension as the sanctuary of Wright's Unity Temple), framed by four stairs forming a pinwheel, its four corners anchored by square clusters of four hollow columns, both structure and service (as in Wright's Darwin Martin House). Mezzanine floors, overlooking triple-height exhibition spaces on either side, spanned between these four square column clusters. At the roof these columns supported an ingenious concrete folded-plate structure which ringed the central space: X-shaped in cross section so as to form four V-shaped spaces within, the upper space housing mechanical ducts, the side spaces bouncing sunlight from clerestory windows above the roof into the exhibition spaces on both sides, and the lower space forming the peaked ceiling over the mezzanines.

Dominican Motherhouse
Media, Pennsylvania
1965–9
Unbuilt

While the Dominican Motherhouse of St Catherine de Ricci was Kahn's first opportunity to design a true monastic structure, the monastery as a traditional building type had in fact served as his starting point for all his previous institutional projects. In March 1965 Kahn was commissioned to design the new Motherhouse, including dormitories, a chapel, a refectory, schoolrooms, and a library and administrative offices, but he did not meet with the sisters to begin the design until April 1966, as they required a year to organize funding for the project. At this first meeting Kahn suggested the administrative offices be placed where they could serve as a ceremonial entry gate, a non-traditional interpretation of the usual monastic programme, welcomed by the sisters, who wished to build a progressive modern institution.[79]

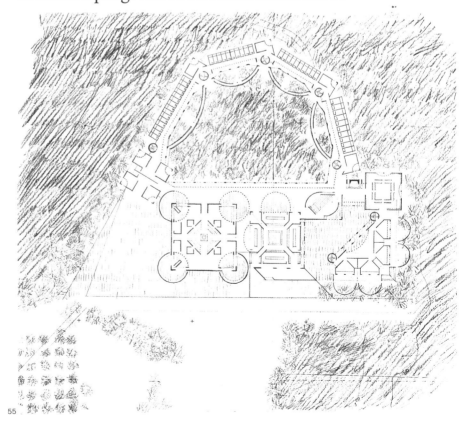

55

Nevertheless, throughout the design process, Kahn would insist upon conceiving of the Motherhouse as being closely related to his beloved medieval monasteries.

Kahn's initial schemes involved four rows of dormitory rooms, sized according to the status of inhabitants – postulants, novices, younger professed sisters and older professed sisters – placed end-to-end in the woods to the south in various arching configurations, so as to create three sides of a traditional monastic cloister-like court, with the institutional elements of the programme forming the fourth, north side of this courtyard. Each of these public elements of the Motherhouse, chapel, refectory, school rooms and entry tower (p. 294; b) again started as a square in plan, with rotated squares and cruciform set within, producing diagonal emphasis on the four corners – those of the refectory were opened as entry halls, while those of the chapel were engaged with circular pools of water.

At a certain point in the process, the public elements or 'room-buildings' of the institution assumed such a degree of independence in Kahn's mind that, rather than endlessly redraw them in different overall plan configurations, he had their square plans cut out, so they became elements in a compositional collage, to be moved around freely to form various alternative plans (p. 295; f).[80] While this was one of the first instances where Kahn engaged this particular method of plan-making, the concept of plans composed from independent, geometrically pure elements was initially developed in his designs for the Salk Meeting House. What Kahn evolved in the Motherhouse, however, is quite different, and the plan, dated October 1966, that emerged from this change in design method maintained the broken form of the courtyard proposed for the earlier schemes, and added the irregularly positioned public elements along the south side (p. 295; c).

In February 1967 Kahn made the last major change in the plan of the Motherhouse, rotating the entire composition 90 degrees so that the front facade of the chapel now faced west (liturgically correct); organized the dormitory rooms as three walls of a rectangular courtyard, with common rooms projecting at the four corners; and finally placed the public elements of the programme within the courtyard itself (p. 295; d). With this plan, Kahn can be understood to have completely 'inverted' his design for the Salk Meeting House: where the Meeting House had a square, symmetrical, geometrically ordered centre and an irregular, asymmetrical outer edge, the Motherhouse now had an irregular, asymmetrical centre and rectangular, symmetrical, geometrically ordered outer edge.

As is typical in traditional monastic buildings, the individual dormitory rooms or cells were organized around three sides of a rectangular courtyard, which was formed as a double square in proportion. But quite unlike the traditional monastery was Kahn's placement of the common public spaces, each treated as an independent building, into the courtyard, effectively filling it, leaving only irregularly shaped exterior spaces between the symmetrical geometries of the entry hall, refectory, classrooms and library. This collapsing of the traditional typological configuration in

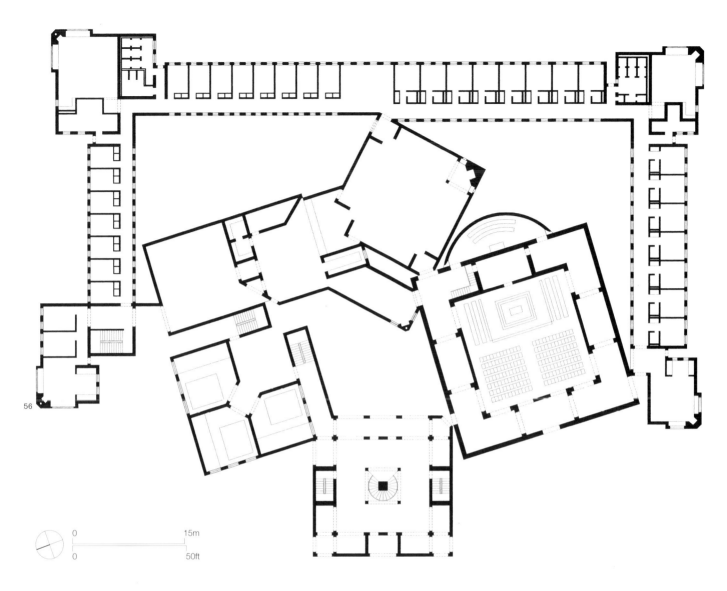

0   15m

0   50ft

56. Ground floor plan of the Dominican
Motherhouse, final scheme, 1967; redrawn
under author's supervision. Private rooms create
a rectangular courtyard into which are placed
the public rooms – school (left), entry tower
(below), refectory (above) and chapel (right).
57. Elevations of the Dominican Motherhouse;
redrawn under author's supervision. From top:
west elevation, with east, south and north
in descending order.

upon itself resulted in a series of 'urban' spaces within the project, a small
'city' that Kahn proposed to stand on its rural hilltop. Reinforcing this
intention is the line of trees that Kahn proposed as the outermost
landscape 'wall' or boundary around three sides of the complex, with
the inner straight wall of a newly created lake framing the fourth, north
side (p. 295; e).

Kahn's final design for the Motherhouse was remarkably nuanced in its
articulation of subtle differences in private, semi-private, semi-public and
public space within the institution. The two-storey courtyard is formed by a
north-facing row of postulant rooms; a longer east-facing wall with a row
of novices on the north end and a row of larger younger professed sisters'
rooms at the south end; and finally a south-facing row of older professed
sisters' rooms. The longer eastern wall is broken at its centre, where it gives
access by intersecting the corner of the refectory, articulating both the
change in dormitory room type and size, and the joint between the two
squares that form the courtyard. At each corner is a service space, with

shared bathing facilities, and a common room with an elegantly designed corner fireplace and seating alcove, lit by narrow slot-like windows between, while on either side of the fireplace alcove two large windows are opened – giving the best views in the whole complex. In the courtyard wall of the dormitories, Kahn opened a window directly across the stone-paved hallway from each bedroom door, whereas the public spaces within the courtyard are given solid walls, receiving their light from above.

When the Motherhouse is approached from the granite-paved drive and parking area to the north, the entry tower, with its bell projecting from the nearest corner, is set farthest forward. At four storeys, the entry tower is the tallest element in the Motherhouse. Here it should be noted that the entry tower is the only public space of the Motherhouse to be aligned with, centred on and placed outside the double-square courtyard formed by the dormitory room walls. To the left, or north, is the sloping roof of the school building, and to the right, or south, beyond the entry tower, is the chapel – at 80 feet (24 metres) square, the largest of the public elements of the Motherhouse. In addition to providing access to the service court and school, the stone paving terminates in a trapezoidal plaza directly in front of the entry tower, indicating its status as the primary place of entry for the public. This primacy

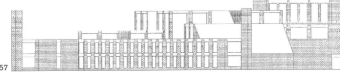

57

of the entry tower is further emphasized by the fact that we must walk across a grass lawn, rather than a paved terrace, to reach the door of the chapel.

Each of the public room-buildings of the Motherhouse is a square in plan, and they intersect at their corners, where doorways are opened. The school building (aligned with the chapel) is divided into four smaller squares, three given to classrooms and the fourth opened to house a double stair to the large lecture room on the second floor, under the sloped ceiling. The refectory (rotated 45 degrees from the chapel) has small squares set in each corner, forming a cruciform-shaped space at the centre, and providing vestibules to the dormitory rooms, chapel and kitchen, with a fireplace set in the fourth corner. The entry tower, ringed by double walls to create a square within a square, houses the entry hall on the ground floor, administrative offices on the second floor, guest rooms on the third floor, and a library and archives on the top floor. Finally the chapel is a cruciform-in-square plan, which is closely related to both Wright's Unity Temple, in its matching internal dimension of 32 feet (9.5 metres) and its square hollow columns at the four corners,[81] and Kahn's own First Unitarian

58

Church, in its double-walled enclosure by an ambulatory and its square light towers rising at the four corners of the sanctuary.

While Kahn was initially requested to design the Motherhouse to be built of stone masonry, budget realities almost immediately led him to select concrete masonry for the project. From the very beginning of the design process Kahn consistently showed the individual dormitory rooms as being built of concrete block construction exposed in the interior and exterior. The first set of construction drawings, dated April 1968, indicate Kahn's intention at that time to employ the flat masonry arches and diminishing masonry piers of his Exeter Library (to be presented in Chapter 5), and a note on a set of prints suggests that Kahn considered using brick in this version of the design.[82] Yet it was also at this time that the steady decline in the number of postulants coming to the Dominican Sisters began to cause severe budget concerns. After a final set of budget cuts, the last set of elevations and plans (p. 294; a), developed between August and December 1968, indicate that Kahn intended to employ brick-sized concrete masonry structural piers, with full-size masonry infill walls between, and precast concrete lintels and beams – an economical system that he had used in the Tribune Review Building. When even these last reductions in dimension and material proved insufficient, Kahn regretfully elected to withdraw from the project. While the sisters and Kahn 'parted friends',[83] it is indeed a great loss to architecture that Kahn's design for the Dominican Motherhouse was never to be built.

58. Model of the Dominican Motherhouse, final scheme; built under author's supervision. A second 'courtyard wall' is made by the trees.

Dominican
Motherhouse

Concept
development

This project was Kahn's first opportunity to design a monastic building, his favourite building type for institutional programmes. Kahn's designs all engaged the traditional monastic plan, with a courtyard formed on three sides by the cells (the individual bedrooms of the sisters and novices) and the fourth side enclosed by the public or shared spaces of the chapel, refectory, library and classrooms. After proposing that the individual cells be freely positioned and the public elements be held in a rectangular bar, Kahn reversed this conception, placing the cells so as to form three sides of a double-square court space, and then moving the public spaces, now conceived as independent buildings, into a variety of interlocking configurations within the court space. This design, in which the outer edge was geometrically ordered and the volumes at the centre were irregularly arranged, inverted that of the Salk Meeting House with its geometrically pure central court and irregular outer edge. These pages show the different aspects of Kahn's design process, including early sketches and the final, unrealized plan.

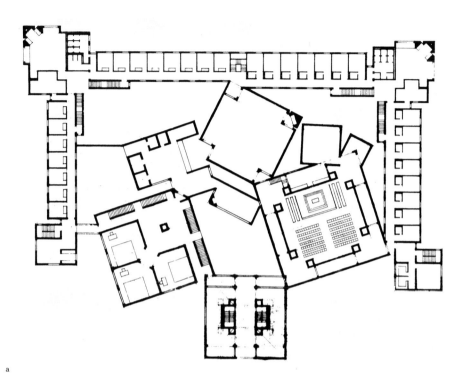

a

b

a. Revised final plan of the Dominican Motherhouse, late 1968, following budget reduction and changes necessitated by the building code. It shows the addition of stairs at the courtyard corners and at the ends and centre of the private room wings. The chapel is oriented on the cardinal directions, with the altar to the east.
b. Early plan sketches for the library and entry tower, c. April 1966, by Louis Kahn. The sketch in the upper right corner is one of the clearest examples of Kahn's design method of assembling independent geometric volumes in an overall cruciform plan.

c

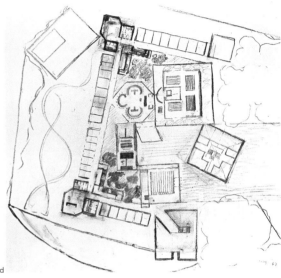

d

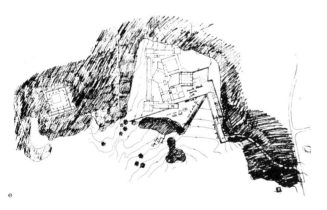

e

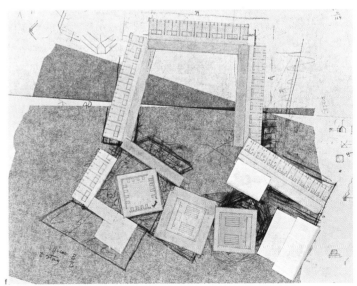

f

c. Site model of the Dominican Motherhouse, early
scheme, October 1966; the public rooms are in the
independent square volumes (right), and the private
rooms are in the staggered bar-like volumes (left).
d. Sketch plan by Kahn, May 1967; here the public
spaces are independent geometric volumes within
a court created by private rooms.
e. Late site plan, 1968; note the trees acting as
a second 'courtyard wall', the artificial lake separating
the building from the open field and the granite
paved entry plaza and parking.
f. Early plan, October 1966; collage by Kahn.

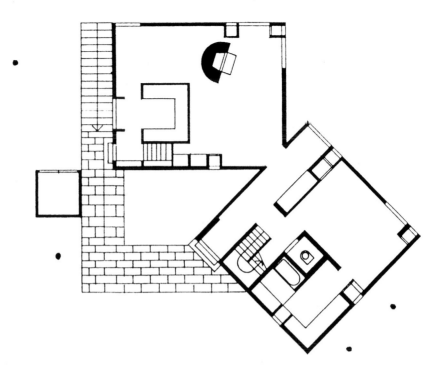

59

60

Composing independent elements

The unrealized project for St Andrew's Priory, a Catholic monastery in Valyermo, California, on which Kahn worked in 1961–7, is closely related to the Dominican Motherhouse. Kahn again organizes the monastery spaces as a series of independent, discrete building elements, which ring the hilltop site; the monastic cells are placed in a long rectangle to the south-east, which steps down the hillside in three terraced levels; the refectory anchors the south-west corner, flanked by the workshops and service court to the north and the chapel to the east; to the north Kahn places the guesthouse and meeting rooms. Together these elements form a trapezoidal-shaped central space, which is in turn divided into three parts: the paved entry court to the west; the monastery court to the east; and the monastic garden to the north – the first separated from the other two by the entry tower near the centre. The entry tower houses a cistern, and from it a system of linear water channels irrigates the gardens and divides the garden and monastery court into a series of triangular, shard-like sections of landscape, similar to Kahn's Islamabad Capital and Levy Playground designs.

Kahn worked on the design for the Fisher House, in Hatboro, Pennsylvania, from 1960, but the plan was not finalized and constructed until 1964–7. The plan clearly indicates that Kahn's dramatic shifting of independent geometric forms in the Dominican Motherhouse was not an isolated incident in his design evolution. The Fisher House is composed as two cubic volumes, a two-storey square plan containing the bedrooms and entry foyer, and a rectangular plan housing the double-height living, dining and kitchen spaces. The square plan bedroom block is aligned exactly with the cardinal directions, while the

59. Ground floor plan of Fisher House, Hatboro, Pennsylvania, 1960–7 (north is 45 degrees up and to left). The plan shows the exterior approach stairs at the side of the living room block.
60. Clay site model of Saint Andrew's Priory, Valyermo, California, 1961–7 (north to left); model built by Kahn.

61

62

rectangular living-room block is rotated 45 degrees to face north-east, with a basement level beneath set into the fall of the hillside down to the creek below. From the approach, the house appears as two simple, solid wooden boxes, set upon a low stone foundation, and as the house steps down the hill, the stone base becomes a full floor in height. The house is clad with thin vertical wood siding relieved only by horizontal drip mouldings at the top, centre and bottom, and the windows are either large fixed glass panels set flush with the wood skin, or narrow vertical slots within which are recessed windows and openable screened panels providing ventilation. The elevations are elegantly minimal yet strikingly abstract compositions, reminding us of Kahn's fascination with the rectilinear structure of contemporary abstract expressionist paintings.

The two blocks composing the Fisher House overlap only at the 4 foot (1.2 metre) wide opening from the foyer into the living room, where Kahn aligns the wood floor with each respective volume to articulate the 45 degree shift between them. When we enter the living room, we find the stone of the foundation rising through the full height of the house in the freestanding, semicircular plan fireplace. The eastern corner of the living room is one of Kahn's most beautiful designs, a sculptural window seat composed of seven different windows (four flush to the outside and three recessed), four wood panels (two of which are openable) and a built-in seat. Perhaps Kahn's most dynamic composition, this window seat is a convincing demonstration of both Kahn's unerring sense of scale and his inspired conception of sunlight in architecture. The detailing throughout the Fisher House is understated yet precise, simple yet elegant, and indicates Kahn's mastery of articulate construction.

61. Exterior of Fisher House, looking west; the bedroom block is on the left and the living room block is on the right, with the basement level below.
62. Double-height living room with window seat, glazed corner and semi-cylindrical fireplace, Fisher House.

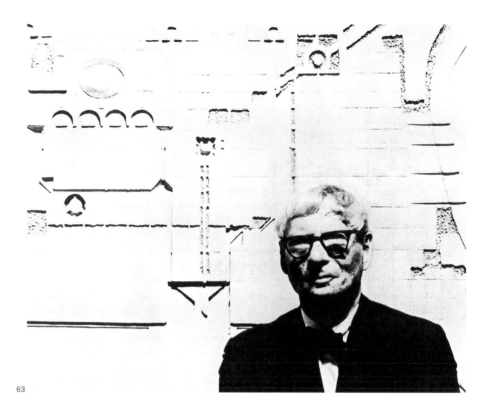

63

Conclusion: starting with space

Kahn's process of designing began with the space of inhabitation: 'You have a society of rooms in which each one has its character, allowing delicate differences to express themselves. In a way, people meeting in them are different people from those who live in division-less space.'[84] The idea that space could be 'division-less', continuous, an undifferentiated free-plan space-in-extension typical of International Style modernism, where space flowed undefined and unrestricted through column grids, was in fact anathema to Kahn: 'I could no more place one column in one space and another in a separate space than I could sleep with my head in one room and my body in another.'[85] For Kahn, structure is 'the beginning of containment',[86] and each room deserved its own clearly articulated and perceivable spatial definition: 'You might say that the nature of a room is that it always has the character of completeness.'[87]

For Kahn, this 'completeness' of each room required that it be developed as a self-defined, self-centred and self-supported element in the larger composition that was the plan. In what was a significant change from his earlier belief in design as an organic process of 'growing a building',[88] he now distinguished 'between design and composition. I think architects should be composers and not designers. They should be composers of elements. The elements are things that are entities in themselves.'[89] These elements were the spatial and experiential 'events of the building',[90] and Kahn's plans now evolved as axial compositions of these independent, symmetrical entities, quite close to those found in Piranesi's Campus Martius plan; geometric, elemental room-buildings that Kahn composed as if they were pieces on a chessboard.

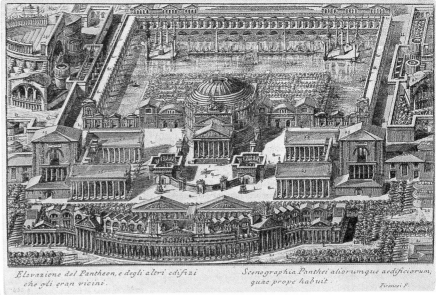

*Elevazione del Pantheon, e degli altri edifizi
che gli eran vicini.*

*Scenographia Panthei aliorumque aedificiorum,
quae prope habuit.*

Piranesi F.

Kahn's profound insight into the relationship between programme and construction, and the essential part played by space in their realization, is unique in modern architectural thinking and practice. Kahn maintained that architecture does not begin with the design programme: 'The space induces the project. If you have a space, something happens, the program then starts. It doesn't start before you make the space.'[91] Kahn also held that architecture does not begin with the construction materials: 'I would never have thought of material first. I'd think of the nature of something, see the emergence of what kind of institution it would be.'[92] It is surprising to find that these propositions of Kahn's have not been more widely noted and discussed in either the architectural profession or in schools of architecture, for they imply a radical reversal of the usual design process, wherein the brief is written and the construction materials selected before the spaces are conceived. Kahn proposes the exact opposite – that one should begin with an idea about the nature of a space as the place of experience and that this spatial conception should then give direction and meaning to the development of both programme and construction.

Precise experiments in the poetics of construction

I dare to think of a building ... a great block of a building, which is cut into from top to bottom in varied places of varied shapes neither forgetting the castle, nor the order of the temple, giving light to spaces and passages on the immediate interior and leading to a glorious central and single space, the walls and their light left in faceted planes, the shapes of the record of their making, intermingled with the serenity of light from above.[1] LOUIS KAHN

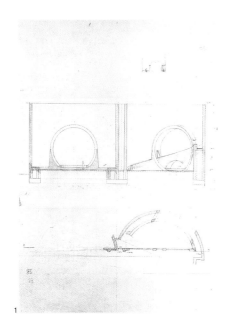

For Kahn, the realization of architecture conceived as the poetics of action required its dichotomous complement, architecture conceived as the poetics of construction: 'Architecture is the thoughtful making of spaces. But these spaces must be clearly defined in their making.'[2] Kahn believed that the way a space is made – its materials and construction – determines how it will be experienced: 'I believe that technology should be inspired. A good plan demands it.'[3] While Kahn sought to engage contemporary materials and methods of construction in an ever more articulate and precise manner, his understanding of the poetics of construction is ancient in origin. As defined by the modern composer Igor Stravinsky in his 1940 *Poetics of Music*:

> The exact meaning of poetics is the study of work to be done. The verb poiein *from which the word is derived means nothing else but* to do *or* make ... For [the classical philosophers] *the single word* techne *embraced both the fine arts and the useful arts and was applied to the knowledge and study of the certain and inevitable rules of craft. That is why Aristotle's* Poetics *constantly suggest ideas regarding personal work, arrangements of materials, and structures.*[4]

Kahn believed that the poetics of construction began with the nature of materials. In this he was inspired by Frank Lloyd Wright, who in 1910 had stated that design is dependent upon 'the nature of materials, the nature of the tools and processes at command, and the nature of the thing they are to be called upon to do'.[5] Kahn engaged in a dialogue with the materials, seeking what they 'desired to be', so that he could use them in the most appropriate manner, honouring their nature. Kahn's famous dialogue with the brick exemplifies his intuitive and empathetic approach: 'You consider the nature of brick. This is a natural thing. You say to brick, "What do you want, brick?" And brick says to you, "I like an arch". And you say to brick, "Look, I want one too, but arches are expensive and I can use a concrete lintel over you, over the opening." And then you say, "What do you think of that, brick?" Brick says, "I like an arch". It is important, you see, that you honor the material that you use.'[6]

Kahn considered this engagement of the nature of materials to be the duty of the architect: 'And it is the beauty of what you create that you honour the material for what it really is. And never say that you use it in a kind of subsidiary way that makes the material itself wonder when the next man will come who will honour its character'.[7] Yet Kahn also believed that it was the duty of the modern architect to engage contemporary methods of construction, and as a result Kahn's buildings often employed both archaic and advanced construction technologies – load-bearing masonry walls with working arches, and precast, pre- and post-tensioned reinforced concrete spanning structures. As Kahn said of his 'composite order' of archaic brick and advanced precast reinforced concrete: 'The brick is always talking to me, saying you're missing an opportunity. The weight of the brick makes it dance like a fairy above and groan below. Arcades crouch. But brick is stingy, concrete is extremely generous. The brick is held by the concrete restraining members. Brick likes this so much, because it becomes modern.'[8]

For Kahn, the poetics of construction required absolute precision and rigorous discipline – 'obstinate rigour', Leonardo da Vinci's motto[9] – in honouring the nature of materials and methods of making: 'I have reached a time where I realize I have my own way of expressing myself, an approach, an attitude toward building that is so tied up with the integrity of the building that I could not disguise a joint, nor could I disguise the material itself.'[10] In this Kahn, like his contemporary, Carlo Scarpa, was engaging what Kenneth Frampton has called 'Giambattista Vico's anti-Cartesian idea of corporeal imagination', exemplified in Vico's motto *verum ipsum factum*, 'truth through making', or, more tellingly, we only know that which we make.[11] For Kahn, like Scarpa, the acts of construction were the only appropriate sources for expressive form in architecture; in a poem honouring Scarpa's work, Kahn wrote: 'The joint inspires ornament, its celebration. The detail is the adoration of Nature.'[12] In what Kahn held to be an ethical imperative, the materials of construction were always to be left exposed, becoming the only ornament appropriate to modern building. Kahn understood that the materials and methods of construction were essential to both the design and the experience of the building, and that the marks of its making should therefore become a record of its creation.

In addition to the requirements placed on a project by the client and society, Kahn imposed limits upon himself, limitations required to honour the nature of the materials he chose to engage. In this, Kahn is close to Wright, who in 1937 wrote: 'The human race built most nobly when limitations were greatest and, therefore, when most was required of imagination in order to build at all. Limitations seem to have always been the best friends of architecture.'[13] It was precisely Kahn's engagement of the materials and methods of construction that made possible his realizations as to the nature of inhabited space itself. In this, Kahn is close to the poet and philosopher Paul Valéry, who in 1894 wrote: 'What we call space is relative to the existence of whatever structures we may choose to conceive. The architectural structure interprets space, and leads to hypotheses on the nature of space, in a quite special manner; for it is an equilibrium of materials with respect to gravity, a visible static whole ... He who designs a monument speculates on the nature of gravity.'[14]

2

Library and Dining Hall, Phillips Exeter Academy
Exeter
New Hampshire
1965–72

The library, like the school, was a place for which Louis Kahn felt the deepest reverence. Books were Kahn's most treasured possessions, for 'the world is put before you through the books',[15] and Kahn felt that books were literally priceless: 'A book is tremendously important. Nobody ever paid for the price of a book, they only paid for the printing.'[16] Therefore, Kahn believed that the library should be a sacred place: 'The book is an offering … The library tells you of this offering.'[17] In 1956, almost ten years before he was commissioned to design the library at the Phillips Exeter Academy in New Hampshire, Kahn had already begun to question the typical programme of the library in his competition entry for Washington University: 'The spaces and their constituent form as a building should originate from broad interpretations of use rather than the satisfaction of a program for a specific system of operation.' Kahn held that the usual library programme led to two quite distinct and separated spaces, 'one for people, one for books', yet he strongly believed that 'books and the reader do not relate in a static way'.[18]

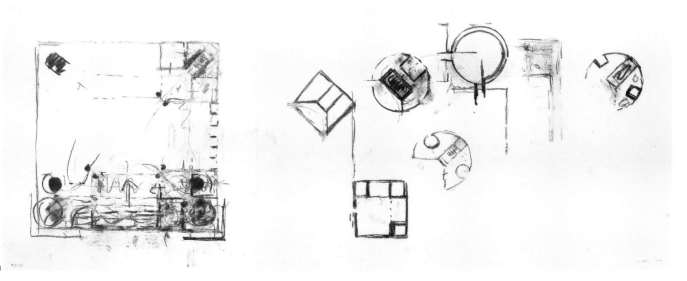

Though not evident in the submitted scheme, it was during the design of the Washington University Library that Kahn first spoke about the pivotal idea of the individual reading carrel, and its generative potential, stating that it was his 'desire to find a space construction system in which the carrels were inherent in the support which harboured them. Reading within a cloistered space with natural light in nearness to the building surfaces seemed good.'[19] Revealing his historical inspiration, Kahn then quoted from a historical description of the medieval monastic library at Durham, England, with its cloister colonnade glazed from floor to ceiling, and carrels equipped with desks set into every window niche, while, on the other side of the cloister, against the wall of the church and away from the sunlight, were placed great wooden cabinets full of books. This source would have been reinforced by Kahn's memories of the 'window' seats, overlooking the central courtyard, built into the upper level of the monastery cloister of Bramante's S. Maria della Pace in Rome (p. 323; e), which Kahn had visited, and which were so beautifully depicted – complete with a monk, shown reading – in one of the plates in Letarouilly's *Édifices de Rome Moderne*, from which Kahn had traced as a student.[20]

For Kahn, the architecture of the library naturally evolved from this inspiring beginning: 'Then from the smallest characteristic space harbored in the construction itself, the larger and still larger spaces would unfold … Wall-bearing masonry construction with its niches and vaults has the appealing structural order to provide naturally such spaces.'[21] While it would be another ten years before Kahn actually designed a building where, as he said, 'the carrel is the niche which could be the beginning of the space order and its structure',[22] the concept was so compelling that Kahn never ceased considering its implications. A year later, in 1957, Kahn arrived at his second pivotal insight into the nature of the library: 'A man with a book goes to the light. A library begins that way. He will not go fifty feet away to an electric light.'[23] Related directly to the concept of reading carrels at the periphery, this empathetic understanding of the nature of the individual act of reading was complemented by Kahn's third pivotal insight – the collective expression of the library as an institution, embodied in the great central room which, upon entry, presents us with the books. Describing a drawing of a 'Library Hall' designed by Boullée, a great barrel-vaulted space, lit from above, with tiered book stacks stepping up the walls (p. 323; d), Kahn noted the manner in which it imparted 'the feeling of what a library should be – you come into a chamber and there are all the books'.[24]

Charged by Richard Day, Phillips Exeter Academy's new principal, with finding an architect capable of giving the school a significant work of modern architecture (as opposed to the neo-Georgian style heretofore characteristic of the campus), the library building committee interviewed a number of the leading architects of the day, including I. M. Pei, Paul Rudolph, Philip Johnson and Edward Barnes.[23] Yet the committee was immediately struck by Kahn's profound and richly nuanced conception of the library as a modern institution, and he was awarded the commission in November 1965.

3. Early sketch of plan and corner stair tower variations, Phillips Exeter Academy Library; drawing by Louis Kahn.

The previous year, Kahn had made the astonishing statement: 'You plan a library as though no library ever existed',[26] indicating his intention to return to the beginnings, to the original inspiration for the library as a place, rather than to accept the prevailing programmatic definition. Kahn's definitive concept for the Exeter Library, developed in 1966, evolved from his three insights into the nature of the library as an institution, and resulted in a literal inversion of the traditional library programme and plan type. The habitual separation of the central reading room from the peripheral book stacks was turned inside out, so that the reading rooms were now at the outer edge, as carrels with natural light; the book stacks were within, protected from the natural light; 'and again the emergence of light in the center',[27] as Kahn said, in the great top-lit central hall where one sees the books upon entry.

From the very beginning of the design process, Kahn conceived of these three types of spaces as if they were three buildings, constructed of different materials and at different scales, buildings-within-buildings – a large-scale interpretation of his concrete 'sunshields' wrapped around glass rooms at the Salk Institute Meeting House – yet here each layer was to be habitable. At Exeter Library, the outermost building layer, housing the double-height reading carrels, was to be load-bearing brick; the inner building layer, housing the single-storey book stacks, was to be reinforced concrete; and the central room, wrapped by the outer two layers, was to reach the full height of the building. In this way, as he had done with his 'composite order' in the Indian Institute of Management, Kahn again engaged both archaic and modern methods of construction in the same building: 'The brick structure was made in an old-fashioned way, and the interior structure was done in today's techniques.'[28] Kahn meant 'old-fashioned' structure quite literally, for in his early studies he indicated that the brick outer building was to have stacked sets of semicircular masonry arches, reminiscent of ancient Roman theatres and arenas, while the central room was to have giant circular and semicircular masonry arches (p. 322; a).

The plan of Exeter Library was from the very beginning heavily indebted to Wright's Unity Temple, not only in its cruciform-in-square plan but also in its location of the stairs in the corners; in its double-square plan mezzanine floors overlooking the central, full-height, top-lit, square space; and – perhaps most telling – in the plan dimensions of the central room: a 32 foot (9.5 metre) square, exactly matching the sanctuary of Unity Temple. Kahn's Exeter Library plan is in fact presaged remarkably closely by Rudolph Schindler's unrealized competition design for the Bergen Public Library of 1920,[29] which was also clearly based upon Wright's Unity Temple plan. That Kahn was very probably entirely unaware of this unpublished library design by Schindler further illustrates the degree to which these ordering principles are part of a shared tradition in modern architecture.

Once this three-layer (reading carrels, book stacks and central hall) cruciform-in-square plan was set, Kahn's early designs for Exeter Library involved an exhaustive exploration of the possibilities of the four outer

4. Second or main floor plan showing the central hall, Phillips Exeter Academy Library; redrawn under author's supervision.
5. Final section of Phillips Exeter Academy Library, with brick, concrete, wood and metal clearly legible; redrawn under author's supervision.

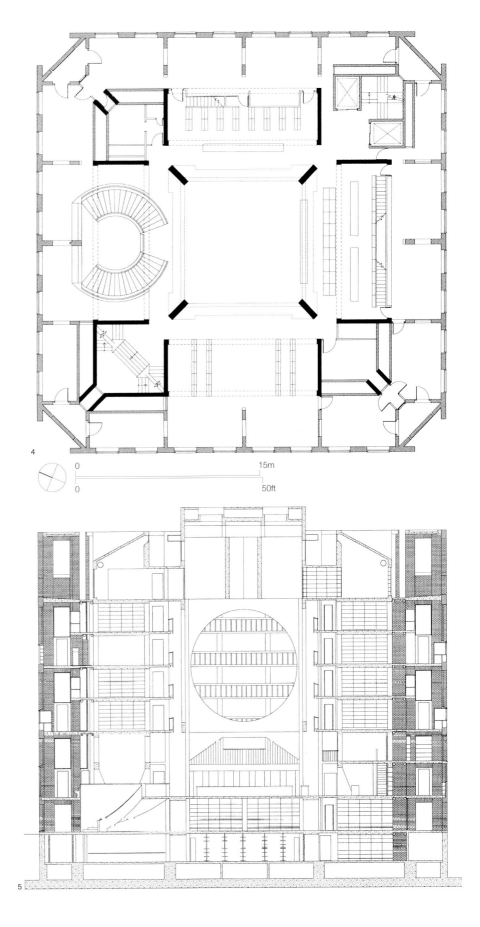

4

0   15m

0   50ft

5

corners, which at various times were proposed as freestanding, projecting towers or retracted, re-entrant corners; as housing the stairs or as seminar rooms; and as trapezoidal, triangular, square, semicircular or circular in form.[30] Of these early designs, the scheme proposing circular corners (pp. 322–3; b & c), housing the stairs set on a 45 degree diagonal to the square main building, is the most monumental, with the grid of windows of the five double-height floors of reading rooms framed by the solid cylindrical corner towers, nearly 100 feet (30 metres) tall, opened only on the diagonal where a vertical slot runs from top to bottom (p. 323; f & g).

The final scheme (pp. 324–5; h) emerged with Kahn's recognition of the primacy of the reading carrels, which he made stand free as 'brick buildings', forming the library's four elevations, and his concomitant removal of the corner towers to create re-entrant corners, which present on the exterior the 16 foot (4.9 metre) depth of the load-bearing brick structure – measured from the outer brick

6

face to the concrete columns of the book stacks within, precisely one-half of the 32 foot (9.5 metre) dimension of the central room. Each structural bay in the 'brick buildings' is 20½ feet (6.2 metres) wide and the brick structure is 12½ feet (3.8 metres) deep, a 'golden section' in proportion. The 'concrete building', housing the book stacks, measures 20 feet (6 metres) deep and 40 feet (12 metres) wide, a double square flanking the square central space – exactly as in Wright's Unity Temple. The height of the four 'middle' floors of the library, which house the book stacks, is 35 feet (10.5 metres), and the width of the central space, measured from outside face to outside face of the concrete wall, is also 35 feet (10.5 metres) – together making a square in elevation, into which Kahn inscribed a circular opening 30 feet (9 metres) in diameter. That these proportions were of significance for Kahn is most clearly indicated by the fact that the height of the central room, measured from the floor to the bottom of the roof structure, which had been set at the beginning of the design in 1966 at 50 feet (15 metres), was changed by Kahn in 1968 to 52 feet (16 metres). This was a seemingly small change, but one of the greatest importance, for, taken together with the 32-foot (9.5 metre) plan dimension, it resulted in the section of the central hall being a perfect 'golden section' proportion (1:1.618), as we see it today.

Seen across the grass lawn of the Phillips Exeter Academy campus, the Library is a massive, cubic brick block, 111 feet (33.4 metres) wide and 80 feet (24 metres) tall, its re-entrant corners stepping back to reveal the four 88 foot (27 metre) wide 'brick buildings' housing the carrels. Each facade extends beyond the last perpendicular brick pier at either end, as well as the recessed 45 degree wall at each corner, thus appearing to be a freestanding plane or screen. In the four facades, which are aligned with the cardinal directions, brick piers are spanned by flat 'jack' arches at the floor lines; a single storey at the ground floor, with four double-height floors above. As the building rises, the brick piers decrease in width; the window openings between the piers increase in width; and the flat arches (the angled masonry of which affects this transition in the piers' width) increase in depth at each floor. The whole forms a 'statically hierarchical' expression of the load-bearing brick walls[31] – the piers thicker at the bottom where the load is greatest, and thinner at the top where the load is least, allowing us to see 'the way they bring the weight down' to the ground.[32] Kahn intended that the inhabitant empathetically read the building's structure, embodied in the brick piers of the facade, perceiving through the changes in their widths the way in which the piers at the top 'are dancing like angels', as compared to 'the bottom, where they are grunting'.[33]

A deeply shadowed arcade runs around the Library at the ground, while the top floor of the 'brick building' is opened as a pergola, through which we can see the sky beyond – dark below, light above. In the three double-height floors between, the openings are glazed, with a large sheet of glass recessed in the depth of the brick wall placed above teak-wood-clad volumes set flush to the outside face of the brick wall, and in which are typically opened small double windows, lighting the pairs of carrels within.[34] At the transition between the recessed upper window and the teak-wood carrel is a bent stainless-steel drip – the only element Kahn allowed to project forward of the brick wall – which

6. Exterior view of Phillips Exeter Academy Library. Independent brick buildings, separated at the corners, house the reading carrels with the entry arcade at the bottom and an open loggia at the top. The large exterior lights are a later addition and were not part of Kahn's original design.

7

makes a sharp shadow line. Red-coloured sandstone coping (cap-beams) are set above the open, 6 foot (1.8 metre) brick balustrades at each corner balcony and at the rooftop pergola. At ground level the brick walls stand upon a band of black stone, expressing the concrete foundation beneath, and the heavy, open arcade anchors the building to the ground; as Kahn stated, 'The arcade is a landscape thing. It belongs to the building, certainly, but it also belongs to the entrance and belongs to the grounds.'[35]

We may enter the Library, as Kahn said, from any direction, through the arcade: 'From all sides there is an entrance. If you are scurrying in the rain to get to the building, you can come in at any point and find your entrance. It's a continuous, campus-type entrance'.[36] Once within the low, brick-floored and brick-walled arcade we make our way to the north side of the building, where a glass-walled entry vestibule is found. Entering, we are in a double-height space, in the centre of which rises a superb double staircase, its tall cylindrical outer walls framing two curved stair sets, left and right, which meet in the middle at the landing above – as in Michelangelo's Laurentian Library (1525) in Florence, we find we have entered at the lower, service level, and must climb this magnificent stair to reach the primary

7. Facade of Phillips Exeter Academy Library (detail). The brick piers decrease in width as they rise, reflecting their diminishing structural load; the light (top left) is a later addition and interrupts the shadow patterns that Kahn intended for the facade.
8. View along the entry arcade, Phillips Exeter Academy Library. This arcade runs around all four sides of the Library at ground level, allowing entry to the building from any direction. It occupies the space directly beneath the double-height spaces housing the reading carrels, at the perimeter of the plan.

8

floor, the *piano nobile*. The outer edge of Kahn's stair forms a 32 foot (9.5 metre) diameter circle – the exact width of the Library's central room – centred precisely midway between the outer edge of the arcade below and the edge of the central room above. The concrete structure of the stair is exposed on its inner curve, but all surfaces that we touch as we climb are clad in travertine marble – the outer walls, the stair risers and treads, and the handrails. Above our heads, a pair of full-floor-deep concrete transfer beams, with triangular buttress-like ends and tension tie beams, span over the stair from left to right, framing large openings through which we see the entry hall.

At the centre of the Exeter Library, Kahn brings us up into the entry hall – a square space that rises the full height of the building, its giant circular concrete openings revealing the books on all four sides, celebrating the purpose of the building; 'So you feel the invitation of the books', as Kahn said.[37] Inevitably, our eyes are first drawn up the lines of the corner piers, over the square concrete walls pierced by the circular openings, to the deep concrete beams which cross at the ceiling overhead, their bottom edges forming an enormous dark X-shape against the brightness above, where the light from clerestory windows opened on all sides strikes the sides of the beams. This great entry hall, composed of the primary geometric forms of squares, circles and triangles, an astonishing space absolutely critical to the experience and function of the building, was in fact absent from the written programme of spaces given to Kahn at the start of the project – a room with 'no name' without which the Library, as it stands today, is simply inconceivable. In this room, Kahn realized his ideal: 'A glorious central and single space, the walls and their light left in faceted planes, the shapes of the record of their making, intermingled with the serenity of light from above.'[38]

A grand piano was placed in the entry hall some time after Exeter Library opened, which would certainly have pleased Kahn, for the sound of music in this great room is truly wonderful. Kahn would also have been pleased by the table which has also been placed in the otherwise empty entry hall, for in 1964 he had imagined such a table in the library, 'upon which the books lie, and these books are open. They are planned very, very cleverly by the librarian to open to pages … with marvellous drawings.' Thus, even before receiving the Exeter commission, Kahn already believed that the library is not only, or even primarily, a place where 'you are thumbing through the files and catalogues' to fulfil assigned homework research, but rather a place that gives each person who enters what was for Kahn the joyful experience of 'discovering a book'.[39]

After taking in this first impression, we begin to examine this room more carefully. The floor of the entry hall is made of light-coloured travertine, as is the stair, and our eye goes first to its corners, where stand four concrete piers, 18 inches (46 centimetres) thick and 6 feet (1.8 metres) deep, which are turned on the diagonal so we see their narrow ends, illuminated in the light from above. Unexpectedly, from the dark corners behind these piers we see thin slices of sunlight, for narrow windows are opened in the outside corner of the two stairs, at the inside of the building's re-entrant corners. This important detail, quite similar to the narrow slit-windows that Wright opened in the

9

shadowed corner stairs of Unity Temple, was arrived at quite late in the design, which had previously shown L-shaped piers at the main floor (with X-shaped piers above), as well as elevators at the centre of the stairs, both of which would have blocked this glimpse of light from the corners.[40] The other two corners also are given narrow windows at their outside corners, but, as these are the lavatories, their inner corners are not opened to the central room.

Across the central hall from the entry stair is the reference desk, to the left and right are the card catalogue and periodicals, all three positioned around the central space, under the book stacks. Each of the 'concrete buildings' housing the books is framed at either end by solid concrete walls, the 16 foot (4.9 metre) depth of the book stacks, with four concrete columns at third-points between, all supporting a thickened concrete slab upon which are carried the metal book cases, illuminated by fluorescent lights (whose light is not deleterious for books, as is sunlight). At the mezzanine level just above the main floor, the full-floor-deep concrete truss-beams receive the load of the pairs of columns supporting the book stacks above, transferring this load to the solid concrete walls at either side. The 40 foot (12 metre) wide space in the depth of the transfer beam is left open at the entry stair, as we have seen, to 'dramatize the support', as Kahn said,[41] and is enclosed with wooden walls on the other three sides of the entry hall. Above these transfer beams at the mezzanine, and reaching to the underside of the diagonal beams at the ceiling, are concrete bracing beams spanning between the four corner piers, each a square opened with a 30 foot (9 metre) diameter circle, through which the four levels of wood-panel-faced book stacks are visible from the floor of the entry hall.

Taking our cue from the glint of light we spotted in the corner, we approach the stairs. Both stairs are set into the space created between the end walls of the 'concrete buildings' that house the book stacks. In the south-east corner, the spiralling square stair is set between the two elevators in front and the vertical

9. Entry stair, Phillips Exeter Academy Library. This stair connects the arcaded entry at ground level to the main, second level and the floor of the central hall.
10. Corner stair from the floor of the central hall, Phillips Exeter Academy Library; note how daylight frames the corner pier at the floor.

10

mechanical shafts behind. The larger stair in the north-west corner has concrete walls on all four sides, with the mechanical shafts beyond the outer pair; the stair comprises a wide set of six risers placed perpendicular to the diagonal approach, and two narrow double-sets of four risers placed in the corners to either side. Both stairs are illuminated by windows opened at the inside of the building's re-entrant corners, giving a view of the campus at every turn. The floor of the stairs is slate, and slate treads are set into the concrete stairs; these project forward to form the toe-space, leaving an edge of concrete on either side into which the stainless-steel posts of the handrail are cast. This sharply contrasts with the light-coloured travertine that covers tread, wall and handrail on the entry stair, making the clearest possible distinction between the single, honorific entry stair and the two 'servant' stairs in the corners.

Emerging from either of the corner stairs, we find ourselves facing one of the diagonal corner piers of the entry room. Hallways run around the inner edge of the four concrete book stack areas, and are edged by low wood-panelled walls, separated from the central room by a 3 foot (0.9 metre) open space between hallway floor slabs and the back of the concrete brace walls. Into this space are projected oak bookshelves topped by an inclined oak surface, on which books can be placed.[42] These wooden table-bookcases around the central edge, by inviting us to lean on the inclined surfaces and peruse an open book, while at the same time overlooking the entry hall and the book stacks opposite, allow readers to be at once in the stacks, separated, and also to be brought together around the central room. For Kahn, the entry hall was 'a connecting architecture',[43] one that brings people together for both planned and unplanned meetings, exemplifying Hannah Arendt's statement: 'To live together in the world means essentially that a world of things is between those who have it in common, as a table is located between those who sit around it; the world, like every in-between, relates and separates men at the same time.'[44]

At the outer edge of the Library are placed the double-height reading rooms, framed by the tall brick piers marching down the 80 foot (24 metre) long space at 20 foot (6 metre) intervals. The reading rooms and the book stacks are connected by the concrete floor slab, which spans between the 'concrete buildings' and the 'brick buildings'. Carpet covers the concrete floor in both the book stacks and the reading rooms, where the carpet is divided by bands of black slate that connect the pairs of brick piers. As Kahn had understood, it is the most natural thing to find a book in the protective darkness of the stacks and carry it the short distance to these sunlit reading rooms. The mezzanine book stack level above is framed at its edge by a low wood-panelled wall, and built into the thickness of the depth of the brick pier are bookcases and places to sit and read, overlooking the reading room below. In the larger upper portion of each opening in the facade, a wooden frame holds a single window, set flush to the inside face of the brick wall, so that the sunlight floods into the reading room from above.

Under each of these large windows, a double study carrel is set into the depth of the brick wall; as Kahn said, 'The name *carrel* implies something which is in the construction itself, which you find as a good place to read.'[45]

11 & 12. (Previous pages) Interior views of the Phillips Exeter Academy Library. The view across the central hall (left) shows the book stacks through circular openings, with crossing roof beams above, lit on all four sides by clerestory windows. The view looking up at the central hall ceiling (right) shows the X-shaped concrete roof beams connecting to corner piers, again lit by clerestory windows.

13. View looking up the centre of the south-east corner stair, a cast-in-place concrete structure with stainless steel railings, Phillips Exeter Academy Library.

13

Each carrel is an elegantly detailed piece of oak furniture, divided at its mid-point by a privacy panel allowing two readers to sit facing without disturbing each other, and providing each reader with an L-shaped desk and return, with book shelves beneath. The inside edge of each carrel is closed by an angled privacy wall, while the outside edge, at the exterior of the building, has a sliding panel with which the small window may be closed and the sunlight modulated to suit the reader: 'The carrel is the room within a room',[46] as Kahn described them. A double set of fluorescent lights provides night-time illumination, the upper one recessed into the concrete slab, lighting the reading room, and the lower one suspended directly over the carrels.

The carefully rendered section of Exeter Library is one of Kahn's most elegant and articulate drawings, clearly revealing not only the concrete and brick 'buildings', but indicating the manner in which the wood cabinetry and metal mechanical services delineate and separate these 'buildings-within-buildings'. The wood panelled 'lining' of shelves and reading tables between

14

15

16

14. The special second floor reading area above the entry stair on the north side of the building, Phillips Exeter Academy Library.
15. Typical double height reading area along the outer edge of the building, viewed from the mezzanine level above, Phillips Exeter Academy Library.
16. View of a typical reading area showing the wooden carrels built into the exterior wall (right) and the mezzanine level with bookstacks (left), Phillips Exeter Academy Library.

the concrete book stacks and the great central hall is perhaps the most obvious. Subtler is the manner in which Kahn created a service zone between the 'brick building' housing the reading carrels and the 'concrete building' housing the books. In the service zone, the heating, cooling and ventilation are fed to the 'served' spaces through cylindrical stainless-steel ducts, which emerge at each floor from the vertical shafts in the four corners of the building and are set in the 3 foot (0.9 metre) wide spaces recessed into the concrete slab ceilings.

At the top floor, the hallway surrounding the central space is closed with floor-to-ceiling wood wall panels, the four small windows allowing us to peek out into the triangular volumes created by the 16 foot (4.9 metre) depth of the crossed concrete beams (p. 324; h). At the top of the 'concrete buildings', housing the book stacks below, are four rare book and seminar rooms, with pitched concrete roofs that angle from high towards the centre – where a continuous band of clerestory windows is opened – to low at the outer edge, where a full-height glass wall opens to the terraces beyond. At the top of the 'brick buildings', housing the reading rooms below, are what Kahn called the 'reading terraces'. These provide a continuous cloister-like brick arcade running around the entire perimeter of the building, covered except at the corners, and enclosed on the outside edge by 6 foot (1.8 metre) high walls, so that our view is only of the sky above. This place to meditate as we walk at roof level, along with the entry arcade at ground level, frames the space of the Library between, and our experience of the building begins and ends within the space defined by Kahn's initial conception: 'Exeter began with the periphery, where the light is', the entry, reading carrels and rooftop terrace each 'a kind of discovered place in the folds of the construction'.[47]

The Exeter Academy Dining Hall was built to the south-east of the Library, which it paralleled in its plan composition as a cruciform-in-square (p. 322; b).

Two T-shaped dining spaces are placed on the east and the west, with entry from the north and the kitchen at the south. Four square-plan rooms are made at the corners, with the room in the north-east corner being larger, and set aside for private dining. At the centre of the Dining Hall, over the serving counters, a square space with a rotated square set within it is recessed into the roof, containing mechanical equipment (p. 323; c). The roof valley beams run diagonally from the corners of this central square to the square dining spaces at the outer corners. The ceilings of the two dining spaces are pitched up to a ridge beam at the centre, and directly in front of each of the four roof peaks, outside the walls of the Dining Hall, stand fireplace chimneys on the east, north and west sides, while the kitchen exhaust chimney stands on the south side.

Analysis of the spatial structure ordering the Library and Dining Hall reveals that they form a dichotomous, reversed pair: high open 'served' space at the centre / low closed 'service' space at the centre; void unoccupied corners / solid occupied corners; rooms on square axes / rooms on diagonal axes; diagonal structure at centre / diagonal structure at periphery; entry all around / entry only at centre of north side; tall cubic mass / horizontal broken mass. In this it is clear that Kahn intended the two buildings he designed for Exeter Academy to be experienced as a pair, for they complement each other in every conceivable manner, sharing only their hybrid construction, brick without and concrete within, and their cruciform-in-square plans. Indicative of the degree to which spatial concepts remained pre-eminent in his design process – even in such an extraordinary exercise in the poetics of construction as Exeter Library – is the way Kahn began his description of the building: 'The space induces the project. If you have a space, something happens, the program then starts. It doesn't start before you make the space.'[48]

Kahn continued this concept of deploying masonry masses to anchor, hold and frame volumes of light in the Korman House, designed and built in Fort Washington, Pennsylvania from 1971 to 1973, which was also Kahn's last realized residence. The plan was bi-nuclear from the start, with the bedrooms to the south-west and the living spaces to the north-east, connected in early designs only by a narrow hall. The final plan is related to several of Wright's Prairie Houses, particularly the Cheney House of 1903 and the Westcott House of 1907, in that the double-height living spaces are placed in a long rectangular volume, with the service and informal areas (ground floor) and bedrooms (second floor) placed in two wing-like volumes – separated by the stair hall at the centre – which are set perpendicular to the living spaces. On three sides of the exterior, Kahn again employs vertical wood siding divided by a drip board at the floor line; on the fourth side, at the living and dining room, Kahn designed an elegant and monumental frame of wood columns holding large windows. This space, closely related to Kahn's early Weiss House of 1947–50, is framed at either end by massive brick fireplaces, the freestanding chimneys of which emphatically mark the boundaries of the public spaces of the house. As Joseph Rykwert has so aptly noted, Kahn was 'the only one of his contemporaries who managed to use such very simple, even commonplace, tectonic means and such straightforward planning to achieve the kind of ceremonious freedom that marks all his houses'.[49]

18

17. Northeast corner of Phillips Exeter Academy Dining Hall, with private dining rooms at the corners and fireplace chimneys at the centre of each elevation.
18. Korman House, Fort Washington, Pennsylvania, 1971–3. Double-height glazing with movable shading panels is used on the north-east facade between the fireplaces and the chimneys which anchor the corners of the living spaces; the living room is on the right.

Library and Dining Hall, Phillips Exeter Academy

Concept development

Kahn's design for the Exeter Academy Library arose from his critique of contemporary library programmes. He literally turned inside-out the received library programme of central reading room and peripheral book stacks, creating instead a concrete building for the books surrounded by a brick building for reading. Yet his design was also inspired by several historical precedents, including the medieval monastic library at Durham and the monastery cloister of Bramante's S. Maria della Pace in Rome. From these Kahn developed his individual wooden carrels built into the glazed outer walls, which allowed reading in natural light. Kahn was also inspired by a drawing of a 'Library Hall' by Étienne-Louis Boullée, and at Exeter Kahn placed a top-lit great room at the very centre of the library, where we arrive and from which we can see all the books. The plan of Exeter is also indebted to Wright's Unity Temple of 1905–8, with its corner stairs, its mezzanine floors overlooking the central top-lit square space, and in the plan dimensions of the central space itself. The early design stages and final site plan for both the Library and Dining Hall appear on these pages, with the final floor plans of the Library overleaf on pages 324–5.

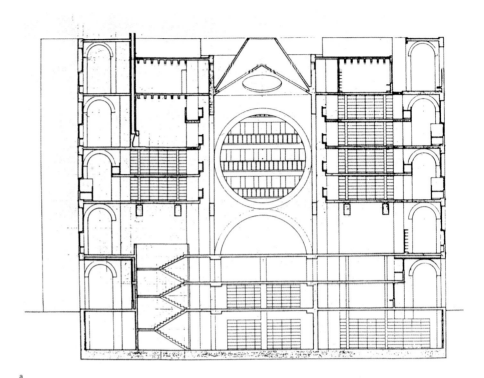

a

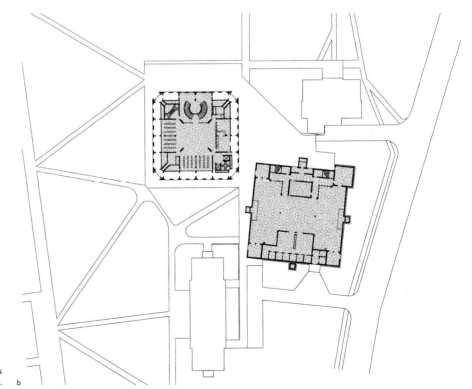

a. Section of Phillips Exeter Academy Library showing brick semicircular arches at outer edges and centre, intermediate design, 10 November 1966.
b. Site plan with the Library on the left and the Dining Hall on the right (north at top); redrawn under author's supervision. The two form a dichotomous, reversed pair.

b

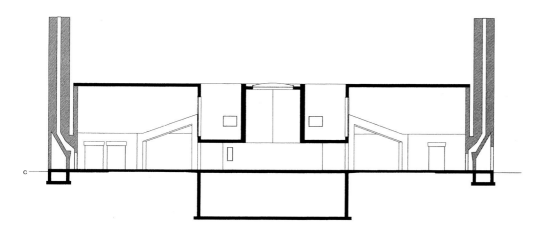

c

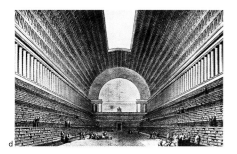

d

e

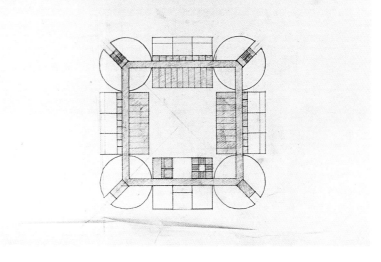

f

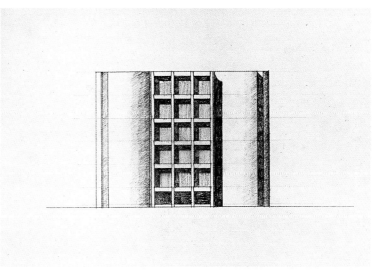

c. East-west section of Dining Hall, Phillips Exeter
Academy, with central serving area, dining rooms,
left and right, and fireplaces at the outer edges;
redrawn under author's supervision.
d. Étienne-Louis Boullée, interior perspective
of proposed 'New Hall for a National Library', 1780.
e. Engraving by Paul Letarouilly showing monk
reading in upper cloister overlooking the central
courtyard of Bramante's S. Maria della Pace
monastery in Rome, from *Édifices de Rome
Moderne*, 1840.
f & g. Plan and elevation of Phillips Exeter Academy
Library with cylindrical corner stair towers and
central hall with open corners, early study, mid-1966;
note the castle-like massing of the elevation.

g

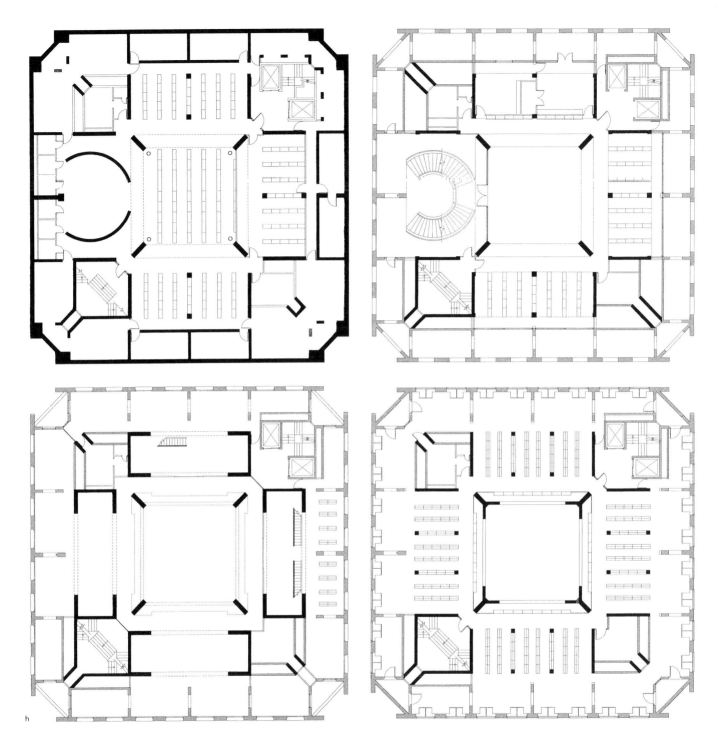

h. Final plans of Phillips Exeter Academy Library (north to left); redrawn under author's supervision. This page, clockwise from top left: basement, ground floor, fourth floor, third floor mezzanine. Opposite page, clockwise from top left: fifth floor mezzanine, sixth floor, eighth floor with special collections and roof-top loggia, seventh floor mezzanine. The second or main floor plan appears on page 307. Concrete is shown in solid black, while brick is shown in cross-hatched grey.

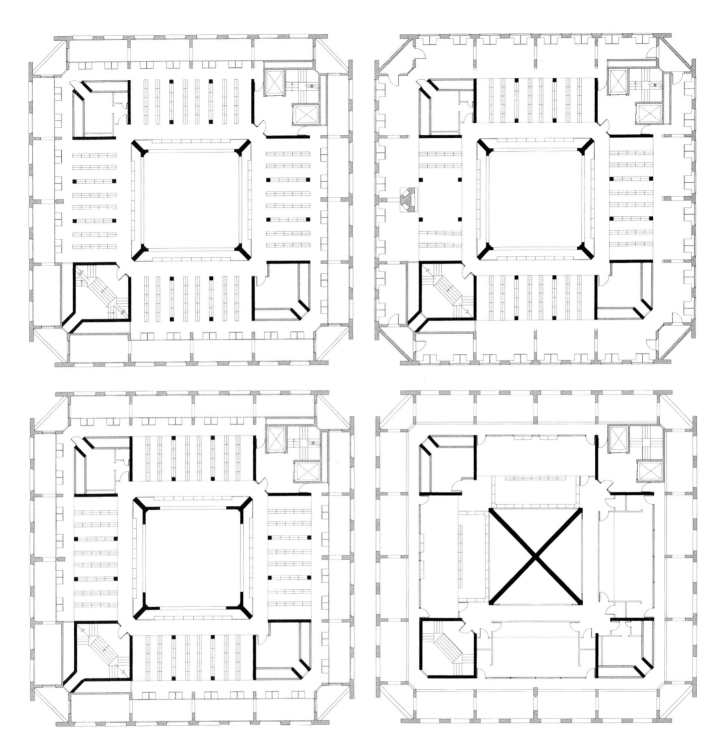

Fort Wayne Performing Arts Theater
Fort Wayne Indiana 1966–73

The Fort Wayne Performing Arts Theater was part of a large fine arts centre that Kahn was commissioned to design from 1959 onwards; the Theater was the only component to be realized. The original proposal, on which Kahn worked for almost ten years, involved buildings for the symphony orchestra, music school, civic theatre, art school and related dormitories, art museum, ballet theatre and dance school, community concert hall, historical society and associated museum, and offices for the Fine Arts Foundation.[50] Kahn began with an ambitious urban plan for all of downtown Fort Wayne, which included, in addition to the buildings of the Fine Arts Center, three massive cylindrical parking structures anchoring a city-block-wide zone of new buildings surrounding the historic city centre like a defensive wall. Kahn's site plans for the Fine Arts Center are perhaps the closest he ever came to the building forms in Piranesi's Campus Martius plan, a series of triangles, circles and squares interlocking along their axes of symmetry, creating equally powerful plaza spaces between (p. 336; b).

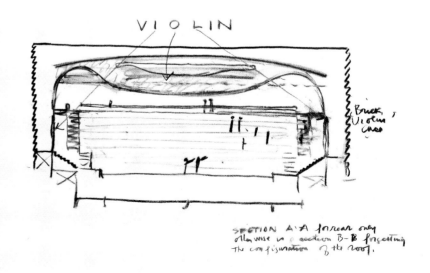

Kahn's early designs for the various components of the Fine Arts Center developed both the geometric purity of the components and the creation of exterior spaces to bring in light and to make the individual buildings interdependent (p. 336; d). The symphony hall involved a square seating area attached to a massive triangular block containing the stage and tower, with square stairs set diagonally at the corners. The music school was to be a square in plan, with cylindrical 'foyers' centred on the corners, the classrooms extended as the arms of an interlocking cruciform, and the central space a lecture hall and rehearsal space. These pure geometric compositions were in turn woven together by exterior spaces, as in the way the historical and art museums were joined by a rotated square-shaped garden, formed by matching triangular spaces carved out of both volumes. The reception centre had eight square light courts cut into its rectangular form, linking its interior spaces with those directly outside; and the symphony hall was anchored by four cylindrical volumes, two triangular stairs and two light courts which interlocked with the entry court. All the buildings were tightly grouped to form a series of interlocking exterior spaces, culminating in the central plaza, which Kahn called the 'Court of Entrances', and a figure-ground study reveals the way in which the light courts and plazas would have formed a series of exterior spaces of truly urban density (p. 337; f).

The Fine Arts Center project was dormant for several years, and in 1966 Kahn was asked to redesign the Performing Arts Theater in such a way that it could initially accommodate dance, orchestra and ballet, as well as its original programme of drama. The new Theater, which was to accommodate 1,000 seats, remained part of Kahn's Fine Arts Center plan, which was anticipated to be built in phases. Over the next two years, Kahn developed a series of plans for the Theater involving tiered seating blocks focusing on the stage (p. 336; a), but it was not until early 1968 that Kahn made his first drawings where the performance hall was placed within a double set of enclosing walls.

In a February 1968 sketch, Kahn labelled the concrete-walled auditorium the 'violin', and the surrounding brick-walled lobby and foyer spaces the 'violin case'.[51] The 'violin', the self-enclosed chamber in which we listen to music or a play, was to be constructed as a building-within-a-building, with the surrounding 'violin case' to house the central lobby and access stair halls to either side, all separated from the resonant auditorium on all sides, above and below. From this insight the final design unfolded through a series of studies, including an elegant plan of interlocking sets of slightly angled walls and integral stairs which bent in and then out along the two sides of the auditorium (p. 336; c),[52] and an equally intriguing section where a continuous clerestory window band is recessed between the brick outer wall and bevelled concrete roof (p. 337; e), appearing from the outside as a kind of massive cornice hovering over the building.[53] Kahn's final design for the Performing Arts Theater placed the tiered theatre seating, stage and 'actor's house', as Kahn called it, with rehearsal and dressing rooms, in a line running from south to north. A service block was attached to the stage on the east side, and the entrance hall, with the lounge above and access stairs to either side,

19. Sketch of the Fort Wayne Performing Arts Theater showing the concept of the 'violin' (concrete interior hall structure) and 'violin case' (brick exterior building structure); drawing by Louis Kahn, February 1968.

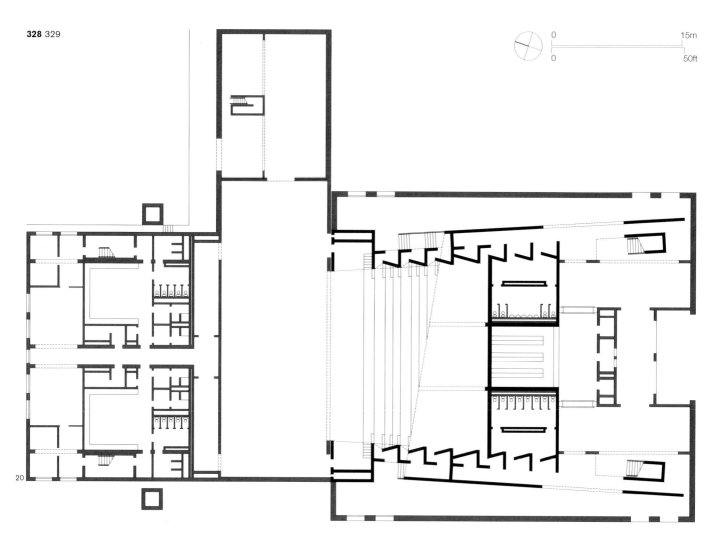

20

20. Final plan of the Fort Wayne Performing Arts Theater; redrawn under author's supervision. The concrete interior 'violin' (rendered in black) in the brick-walled exterior 'violin case' (rendered in cross-hatched grey) is clearly legible.
21. Final north-south section of Fort Wayne Performing Arts Theater; redrawn under author's supervision.

was wrapped around the theatre seating on three sides, cutting back in to mark the edge of the stage.

We first see the Theater not within Kahn's tightly packed urban composition for the Fine Arts Center, which was never built, but alone as a freestanding object – exactly the opposite of Kahn's intention: 'The Theater was conceived to be sympathetic and dependent upon the buildings framing the "court of entrances", and without them the theater alone will look lonely and bare.'[54] The south facade of the Theater (p. 337; h), a solid brick double square with three interlocking, long, low brick arches, joined at the middle by an inverted T-shaped concrete tie beam, has proven controversial, its mask-like form appearing too literal for some critics. Yet it is important to remember that during Kahn's design process, the majority of his elevation studies were not made of this south elevation but of what we today call the 'side' elevations, particularly to the west (p. 337; g) towards the 'Court of Entrances', which, if other buildings in the Fine Arts Center had been realized, would have been the most visible. Kahn had designed the arts centre to be placed directly to the south of the Theater, so that what is today thought of as the 'front' elevation could only have been seen from very close (p. 337; f) –

quite similar in fact to the Roman arched brick facades in the narrow streets of Ostia or in Trajan's Market in Rome.

We enter through the lobby, a narrow, 15 foot (4.6 metre) tall space, which is relatively low and dark in comparison to the brightly lit spaces we see opening at either end. This light draws us either left or right, through the brick arched openings, and into the high, 45 foot (13.5 metre) tall spaces, where the slightly angled concrete stair stands in the bright sunlight of the three stacked sets of large windows reaching to the ceiling. The walls of the lobby, and the lounge above it, are made of brick and concrete masonry; the stair and inner auditorium walls are made of cast-in-place concrete, the tie-holds for the formwork clearly visible; and the outer walls of the building are made of concrete masonry, with brick surrounding the windows. T-shaped precast concrete beams form the roof and ceiling, and the concrete floor is carpeted throughout, except at the transition points under the brick arches and at the bases of the brick walls, where Kahn places bands of polished black granite.

We may either climb up the full flight of stairs that stands in the corner, reaching the spacious lounge above the lobby, lit by the three arched front windows, and from there walk down the gradually declining stair sets towards the north; or we can walk the length of the auditorium to the north end of this side foyer, where the stair sets meet the foyer floor, and from there walk towards the south, climbing slowly up the side of the auditorium. These stairs, the landings of which interlock with the small foyers into the auditorium, reveal the tiered section of the auditorium within. Standing on the stairs, we can also perceive that the walls of the auditorium do not reach the beamed ceiling above, and we are made aware of the contrast between the complex folds of the wall of the auditorium and the simple, massive planes of the building's outer masonry wall.

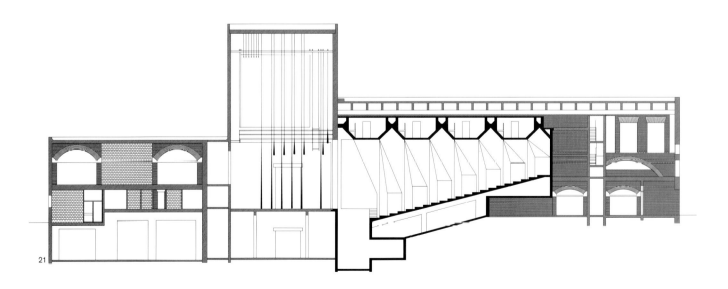

21

22

We enter the auditorium itself through folds made in the cast-in-place concrete wall, Z-shaped forms in plan creating acoustic 'sound-locks' that give access to every third row of seats. Once within, we can see that both the concrete side walls and ceiling are cast as folded planes for optimal sound dissemination, with the concrete floor stepping to produce the tiers of seating. The side walls, complex vertical asymmetries inclined towards the stage, fold to be transformed from the Z-shaped foyers at the floor to a flat surface at the point where they meet the ceiling. The ceiling itself consists of flat lower surfaces alternating with V-shaped folds, the front surfaces of which are provided with openings for theatrical spotlighting. The auditorium is simultaneously massive, geometrically precise and delicate, layered like a sea creature's shell – its walls constructed of reinforced concrete but folded like the thin fabric of a stage curtain.

The folded concrete side walls of the Performing Arts Theater, which must surely be considered among Kahn's most elegant and accomplished architectural designs, are clearly related to Kahn's earlier explorations of the folded-plate concrete floor structure at the laboratories of the Salk Institute, but here they are employed not to support, but to shape and form sound. Kahn was a keen and talented pianist who spoke of music in the same spiritual terms as those he otherwise reserved for his beloved architecture. When told that the great pianist, Rudolf Serkin, after touring the Theater during the final stages of its construction, had been so impressed that he offered to return and perform at the dedication, Kahn was overjoyed: 'Your letter made my day my week my everytime.'[55]

23

22. South-west corner of Fort Wayne Performing Arts Theater, with entry facade on the right. This view shows the isolated condition of the theatre within the incomplete site plan.

23. Entry facade, Fort Wayne Performing Arts Theater. Kahn's unrealized site design intended this close, urban view to be typical.

24 & 25. Details of south facade, Fort Wayne Performing Arts Theater. These details of the double upper arches show the centre concrete abutment (left) and end concrete abutment, tie, floor edge and lintel (right).

24

25

26

26. Entry lobby, Fort Wayne Performing Arts Theater. This view shows the ticket windows, stair hall and brick exterior wall.
27. Second floor lounge above the entry and lobby of the Fort Wayne Performing Arts Theater, with views out over the city and the site of the Fine Art Center's unrealized urban spaces.

27

28

29

30

28. View of second floor lounge from concrete stairs, Fort Wayne Performing Arts Theater.
29. Arched wall separating the lounge from the stair (detail), Fort Wayne Performing Arts Theater; note the polished black granite parapet wall cap.
30. Stair landing between the ground and second floor, with the lounge above and the lobby below, Fort Wayne Performing Arts Theater.

32

33

31, 32 & 33. Views of the Auditorium, Fort Wayne Performing Arts Theater. Entry is through the folded concrete walls which, together with the folded concrete ceiling and the stepped concrete floor, form the acoustic inner shell which Kahn called 'the violin'. Kahn specified a special concrete mixture to impart a warm colour to the surfaces of the room.

Fort Wayne Performing Arts Theater

Concept development

The Performing Arts Theater is the only realized portion of Kahn's large plan for multiple arts structures, and his early designs all place the Theater within a dense urban precinct of his conception, inspired by Piranesi's imaginary reconstruction of the Campus Martius in ancient Rome. For the Theater itself, Kahn's conception for the performance hall was analogous to a violin, while the encasing structure housing the entry, access hallways, services and backstage spaces was analogous to the violin case. These were from the start two separate but interrelated structures, and Kahn's early designs explored the manner in which their independence could be clearly expressed, such as through the introduction of light where they joined. In the final built design, the performance hall was constructed of monolithic cast-in-place concrete, composed of self-supporting, elegantly folded acoustic concrete walls, ceilings and stepped floors, while the surrounding 'servant' spaces were constructed of masonry walls and precast concrete roof beams. These pages present both early designs for the entire Fine Arts Center, as well as intermediate and final designs for the Performing Arts Theater.

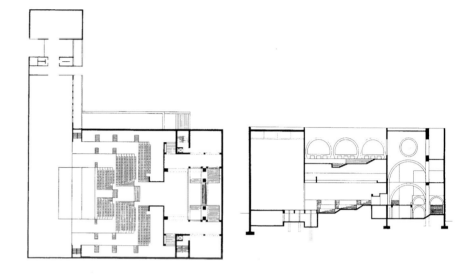

a

b

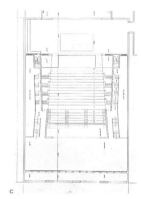

c

a. Plan and section of Fort Wayne Performing Arts Theater, intermediate scheme, 1966 (north to left); this early plan shows the tiered seating focusing on the centre of the stage.
b. Clay study model of site design, Fort Wayne Fine Arts Center, October 1963. Kahn designed the Fine Arts Center as a dense urban enclave.
c. Plan of the Performing Arts Theater, intermediate scheme with folded walls and integral stairs, 29 September 1968.
d. Study model of site design, Fine Arts Center, November 1963. Kahn designed both the voids and the solids, allowing the public exterior spaces to link the various elements of the Fine Arts Center.

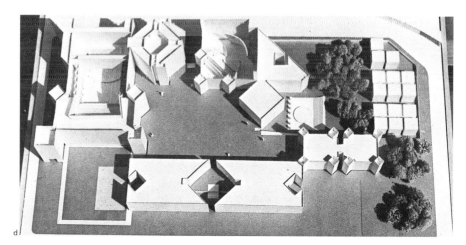

d

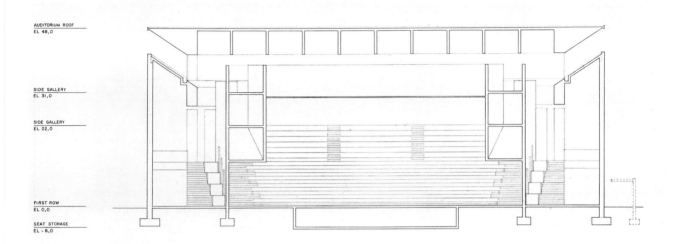

AUDITORIUM ROOF
EL 48,0

SIDE GALLERY
EL 31,0

SIDE GALLERY
EL 22,0

FIRST ROW
EL 0,0

SEAT STORAGE
EL - 6,0

e

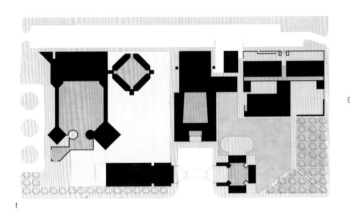

f

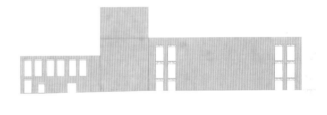

g

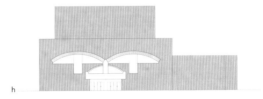

h

e. Section study, Fort Wayne Performing Arts
Theater, intermediate scheme, 5 November 1968;
clerestory windows separate the brick outer walls
from the concrete roof.
f. Final site plan of Fine Arts Center (north at top),
with figure-ground analysis showing exterior and
interior 'served' spaces (greys and white) and
interior 'servant' spaces (black); drawn under
author's supervision. To enter the Performing Arts
Theater, one would have had to pass under the
Arts Building's bridging structure to its south and
into a tight street-like urban space.
g. West 'side' elevation, Performing Arts Theater;
redrawn under author's supervision.
h. South elevation, Performing Arts Theater;
redrawn under author's supervision.

Kimbell Art Museum
Fort Worth, Texas
1966–72

The Kimbell Art Museum is rightly considered Kahn's greatest built work, in that it fully integrates and brings to the highest level of resolution all the elements composing Kahn's conception of architecture: archaic and modern, mass and structure, light and shadow, the poetics of action and construction. Due to its significance among Kahn's works, and the fact that it is thought by many to be the greatest art museum of the twentieth century, the Kimbell Museum has been the most widely published of all Kahn's works, and has been the subject of more scholarly studies than all his other works combined, including several books and numerous essays.[60] The Kimbell Museum was the last building designed by Kahn that he lived to see completed. Intriguingly, rather than evolving from Kahn's contemporary designs, the Kimbell Museum marks a return to the discoveries of his early works, most notably the Trenton Jewish Community Center of ten years earlier, where the space within is formed most powerfully by the ceiling and roof overhead.

The newly appointed director of the Kimbell Art Museum, Richard Brown, considered a distinguished group of architects for the project, including Marcel Breuer, Mies van der Rohe, Pier Luigi Nervi, Gordon Bunshaft (of Skidmore, Owings and Merrill), Edward Barnes and Kahn.

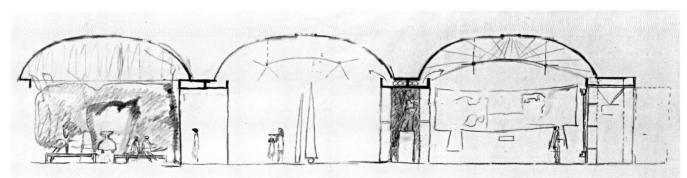

In a wonderfully timed coincidence, Kahn's work was at exactly this time, the spring of 1966, the subject of the only one-man architectural exhibition of the decade at the Museum of Modern Art in New York. When Brown visited Kahn that summer in his unpretentious Philadelphia office, bustling with a young and energetic staff, he was immediately struck by Kahn's creative imagination and his sensitivity to natural light. Brown instinctively knew that he had found his architect, and soon after, in early October 1966, Kahn received the commission for the Kimbell Museum.

While Kahn's only previous art museum, the Yale Art Gallery, designed fifteen years before, had housed an extensive and well-established art collection, the Kimbell collection was both new and undefined. For Kahn, however, this was not an impediment – on the contrary, as Patricia Cummings Loud has noted, Kahn embraced this lack of specificity in terms of the collection's size and content 'as an opportunity to create an ideal setting for works of art'.[61]

Kahn's Yale Art Gallery was compromised by later renovations undertaken by the gallery director, adding new walls that both divided the space and covered the construction Kahn had so carefully exposed (to show how the room was made). In 1959, Kahn stated:

> If I were to build a gallery now, I would really be more concerned about building spaces which are not used freely by the director as he wants. Rather I would give him spaces that were there and had certain inherent characteristics. Then the visitor, because of the nature of the space, would perceive a certain object in quite a different way. The director would be fitted out with such a variety of ways of getting light, from above, from below, from little slits, or from wherever he wanted, so that he felt that here was really a realm of spaces where one could show things in various aspects.[62]

Kahn now believed that the space of an art gallery should not only possess inherent, unchanging characteristics but should also be animated by the ever changing characteristics of natural light. Clearly one of the reasons Brown was drawn to Kahn was the pre-eminent part played by natural light in Kahn's recent works, and the brief Brown wrote for the Kimbell Museum emphasized natural light, which brings the change of the day, the weather and the seasons – and the connection to the natural world without – into the museum.[63] Kahn responded enthusiastically to this direction, arguing that the paintings themselves are made in natural light, and thus are best viewed in the same ever changing light.[64]

The site that had been selected for the Kimbell Museum consisted of 9 acres (3.6 hectares) on the eastern edge of Will Rogers Park, to the north of the Will Rogers Auditorium, Coliseum and Tower, and at the bottom of a gentle tree-covered slope at the top of which stood Philip Johnson's Amon Carter Museum, completed in 1960. Together with the future modern art museum, these buildings would transform the public park into a kind of campus of art museums.[65]

In March 1967, Kahn presented his initial design for the Kimbell Museum. From the start, Kahn intended the museum galleries all to be placed on one

38. Early sketch showing section of the Kimbell Art Museum, with curved thin-shell roof vaults and services at the edges; drawing by Kahn.

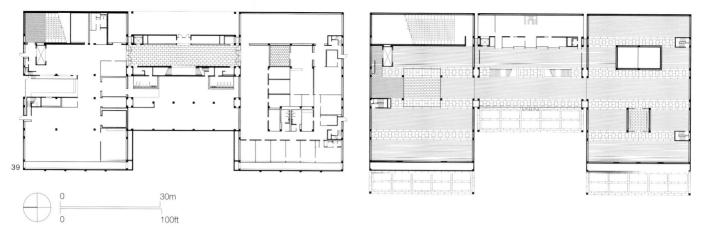

0   30m

0   100ft

level – the top floor, so as to receive light directly from the roof and garden courts – with the extensive service and curatorial spaces located on a lower, basement level. The first scheme again 'started with the square', a 400 foot (120 metre) square plan entirely covered with fourteen vaults running north to south (p. 362; b), each vault 30 feet (9 metres) in height and split open down its centre to admit light. An arcade the depth of one bay of the roof vaults surrounds the building, and the spaces within are organized into two rectangular volumes, the larger to the east and the smaller to the west, which are opened with ten small gardens. These two volumes are separated by a large three-bay-wide garden, and connected at the perimeter by the arcade, and off-centre by the main central hallway, running from the street on the east to the park on the west, where two reflecting pools flank the entry court.[66]

Brown felt this plan was too large, and in November 1967 Kahn presented a reduced and revised scheme, now taking the form of an H-shape in plan (p. 364; f), with the arcade removed on the north and south sides so that the larger gardens open directly to the park. The main hallway was now placed on the symmetrical central axis, joining the larger gallery block to the east and the smaller block to the west, containing the auditorium and the temporary exhibition space, each covered by roof vaults 25 feet (7.6 metres) wide and spanning 150 feet (45.5 metres) in length. Cost estimates were made on this scheme, and during this period Brown came to the realization that the temporary exhibition spaces, often empty, would not make an appropriate first impression at the entry, and asked Kahn to change the design.[67] In September 1968, after a variety of explorations, Kahn arrived at what would be the final scheme for the Kimbell Museum, a double-square overall massing divided into three equal volumes to form a C-shape in plan, the central volume recessed on the west, or park side, to form an entry court (p. 362; a).

The roof vaults remained the constant in Kahn's design for the Kimbell Museum, and their development progressed independently of the evolution of the plan. Kahn's personal sketches and the office drawings contain dozens of studies for the section of a typical vault, the skylight slot at its apex, and the light reflector hung within to diffuse the direct sunlight. Among the studies for the vault section are semi-ellipses; semicircles (true barrel vault); two quarter-circles spaced apart by skylight slots of varying widths; double semicircles

39. Final plans of the Kimbell Art Museum; redrawn under author's supervision. The lower, basement floor plan with entry from the car parking and services is on the left and the upper, ground floor plan with entry from the park and galleries is on the right.
40. East-west sections, Kimbell Art Museum, looking south (above) and south and north elevations (below); redrawn under author's supervision.
41. (Overleaf) Entry portico and garden court, with entry hall through full-height glass wall, Kimbell Art Museum.

with a skylight slot at their meeting point (a variation on Labrouste's vaults at the Bibliothèque Ste Geneviève, Paris, of 1850, which would return in Kahn's early schemes for the British Arts Center); interlocking circular sections with convex vaults above concave reflectors; L-shaped clerestories above concave reflectors; and various V-shaped vaults (combining the First Unitarian Church and the 'lost' Salk Institute folded plate). All of Kahn's designs for the vault involved a spatial bay – the room under the vault itself, spanning from column to column; and a structural bay – the symmetrical bird wing or V-shaped structural beam bearing on the column at its centre, spanning from skylight to skylight; the two types of bay were shifted so as to overlap one another.[68]

The initial designs presented by Kahn to the client in 1967 involved a variation on the V-shaped folded plate structure that Kahn had proposed for both the Salk Institute Laboratories and the University of Virginia Chemistry Building. Here each vault is composed of half of two V-shaped structural roof-shells, with a smaller V-shaped reflector placed at their mid-point and thus integrated perfectly into their folded geometry (p. 363; c). The mechanical services for the galleries were to have been housed in the hollow triangular space within the reflector itself, at the centre of each vault. Among Kahn's

42

personal sketches is a drawing of what is almost certainly the section of Aalto's Museum at Aalborg, Denmark, won in a design competition in 1958. This design is for a light reflector that is embedded within the roof, half-in and half-out of the building, with concave curved sides to reflect light from skylights to either side into the rectangular gallery space below. Aalto's published drawings for this project show people walking through the interior of the reflector, suggesting its use for service space. Careful examination of the drawing reveals that Kahn was also analysing Aalto's gallery space and its light – Kahn drew arrows indicating that the bounced light never reaches the flat ceiling above, which would be dark, as opposed to the curved forms of Kahn's vault designs, across which it was intended that the bounced light would spread evenly.[69]

The final design for the vault returned to one of Kahn's earliest sketches, a semi-elliptical vault which Kahn had consistently employed in all his perspective drawings as the search for the vault's geometric form progressed. In October 1967, Kahn's associate Marshall Meyers located, in a book on shell and surface structures, the geometric form called a cycloid, which Kahn immediately approved for the vault section (p. 363; d).[70] As Frampton has noted, 'The root of vault in the Latin word *volvere* – meaning literally to revolve across – is particularly apt in the case of the cycloid vault.'[71] For the cycloid curve is made by tracing a point on the circumference of a circle as the circle is rolled along a straight line, starting and ending with the point at the bottom – the resulting curve, which changes diameter constantly through its arc, is the height of the generating circle, but its width is much extended. Following Kahn's selection of the cycloid geometry, Komendant developed the structural design for the vaults. Another important decision that was made at around

42. View of Kimbell Art Museum from the south-west, with portico and pool leading to the entry court.
43. South elevation of Kimbell Art Museum, with entry portico and sunken garden. This photograph was taken shortly after the museum's opening in 1972.

this time was to locate the mechanical services in the channels between the vaults, in the narrow zone defined by the supporting columns, rather than in the reflector itself at the vault's centre. This decision also allowed the reflector to return to Kahn's original conception for it – a thin sheet of reflective material, either glass or metal, folded and suspended in the centre of the vault. In describing the Kimbell Museum design, Kahn said in November 1967:

> Here I felt that the light in the rooms structured in concrete will have the luminosity of silver ... The scheme of enclosure of the museum is a succession of cycloid vaults each of a single span 150 feet long and 20 feet wide, each forming the rooms with a narrow slit to the sky, with a mirrored glass shaped to spread natural light on the sides of the vault. This light will give a glow of silver to the room without touching the objects directly, yet give the comforting feeling of knowing the time of the day.[72]

While the cycloid vaults as built are an entirely modern fusion of sophisticated geometric form and advanced engineering, Kahn later described them in more archaic terms: 'My mind was full of Roman greatness. The vault has so etched itself in my mind that although I cannot employ it, it's there always ready. The vault seems to be the best.'[73]

44

Yet, the 'vaults' of the Kimbell Museum do not act structurally as vaults, and are in many ways the opposite of ancient Roman barrel vaults. The cycloid vaults do not bear on their long edges, as traditional barrel vaults, but span from one end to the other, as curved, shell-like beams, only requiring bracing or stiffening at the edges and centre (p. 365; i). Also, the cycloid vaults are not solid at the apex of their arc, as traditional barrel vaults, but are split open to let in light, an idea that Kahn first evolved in his 'lost' folded plate design for the laboratory structure of the Salk Institute. Yet, for Kahn, the manner in which the cycloid vaults created under their arcs such clearly defined and precisely formed rooms, and the way in which light was admitted to these rooms through the open joint running down the centre, made them the perfect structural embodiment of his intentions.

The plan for the upper, gallery level of the Kimbell Museum is perhaps Kahn's most carefully proportioned design, starting with a double square, which is then overlapped at its centre so as to create three golden-section volumes, separated by narrow 3 foot (0.9 metre) wide spaces.[74] The north and south 'wings' have six bays of cycloid vaults, the westernmost bay open as a portico, and the central volume has four bays of cycloid vaults, the westernmost bay open as the entry porch. The exterior walls on the north and south – at the ends of the vaults – are concrete block faced with travertine

44. South elevation of Kimbell Art Museum; the sunken sculpture court houses Isamu Noguchi's sculpture, *Constellation* (for Louis Kahn), of 1983.

inside and out. The exterior walls on the east and west side – at the sides of
the vaults – are cast concrete faced with travertine on the inside and out, except
where openings occur below, at the east entrance and at the west light wells,
where the concrete wall, acting as a deep beam, is exposed. The gallery flooring
is oak wood under the cycloid vaults, measuring 20 by 100 feet (6 by 30
metres), and travertine under the service channels between the columns,
measuring 10 by 100 feet (3 by 30 metres). The structure of the gallery floor is
a lightweight, double-skin, pre-stressed concrete floor system, with sound-
deadening foam fillers in the hollow spaces; these were suggested by
Komendant to reduce the number of columns needed on the lower, service
floor, which has cast concrete walls on all four sides.[75]

Three courtyards are opened in the galleries, the first, a 36 foot (11 metre)
square court in the centre of the north gallery wing, is glazed on all four sides.
A second, smaller, 23 foot (7 metre) square court in the south wing, is glazed
only on the east and west sides. A third court, a double square measuring 46 by
23 feet (14 by 7 metres), also located in the southern wing, is surrounded by
solid walls at the gallery floor, and brings light to the conservator's court and
conservation studio on the lower floor. Two 100 foot (30 metre) long and
7 foot (2.1 metre) wide light wells are located between the entry porticos and
the galleries on the western edge of both wings, and bring light into the offices
and workshop areas on the lower floor. The auditorium, a two-storey space
entered from the gallery floor, is located in the north-east corner of the building,
and has a system of shutters so that its skylight may be closed when needed.

Each post-tensioned, cast-in-place, reinforced concrete cycloid vault spans
100 feet (30 metres), is 23 feet (7 metres) wide inside, 20 feet (6 metres) tall,
and measures $12^{1}/_{2}$ feet (3.8 metres) from the floor to the spring point of
the vault. Each cycloid vault is supported by four 2 foot (0.6 metre) square
concrete columns at its corners, which are spaced 20 feet (6 metres) apart, and
is stiffened by diaphragms at either end and edge beams along its sides, as
well as the flat concrete slab between the vaults (where they are adjacent
in sequence) and at the outer edges of the vaults (where they meet the outer
edge of the building, and at the courtyards and light wells).

The exterior walls of the building on the east and west are cast concrete, but
they do not support the vaults, a fact Kahn revealed by opening 6 inch (15
centimetre) horizontal glazed slots under the edge beams of the vaults, so that
'only a sliver of light separated the cycloid from the wall'.[76] The end walls of
the thirteen interior vaults are also not load-bearing, and Kahn revealed this
by facing these walls with travertine (p. 363; e); Kahn further emphasized
this structural independence by introducing a curved glazed slot between
the concrete vault diaphragm and the travertine wall below. When structural
design necessitated this diaphragm increase in depth from 9 inches (23
centimetres) at the spring points of the vault to 14 inches (36 centimetres) at
the centre apex, Kahn chose to have the lower edge of the slot follow the
profile of the cycloid vault above,[77] so that the glazed band tapers from 9
inches (23 centimetres) at the outer edges to 4 inches (10 centimetres) at the
top, highlighting the difference in profile of the cycloid vault and its end

45

45. Detail of entry portico vault and museum wall, Kimbell Art Museum.
46. (Opposite) Interior detail showing the meeting of the concrete roof vault and travertine-clad end wall, with light slot between and the stainless-steel air diffuser at the bottom edge of the roof vault, Kimbell Art Museum.

diaphragm. Kahn did this, he said, in order 'to give honor to the engineering, and not to disguise it ... It sets up a sense of wonder.'[78]

The beams at the outer edges of each neighbouring pair of cycloid vaults are joined by the flat slab between to form an inverted U-shaped service channel, housing the mechanical ducts, and covered by a stainless-steel soffit below, with stainless-steel linear air diffusers to either side. The soffit panels, loading dock door, handrails and other stainless-steel elements were sandblasted (using pecan shells) to achieve the matt surface texture Kahn specified.

The design of the light reflector under the skylight was developed by Kahn and lighting consultant Richard Kelly, of Edison Price, who had worked with Kahn on the Yale Art Gallery. It was initially proposed as mirror glass and then acrylic, before Kelly suggested that the reflector and its supporting

cradle (which also housed the electrical lighting) be made of perforated aluminium. The final reflector is shaped like a pair of upward-curving wings in section, and its central spine is inserted into the vault's skylight slot to bounce as much light as possible. In the gallery spaces, the centre portion of the reflector, directly under the skylight, is solid, while the sections to either side were perforated. In the entry hall, the bookstore, the library, the cafeteria and the auditorium – those spaces where art is not exhibited – the reflectors are perforated throughout their curves, making it possible to glimpse passing clouds through the skylight. In the famous photograph of Kahn, standing at the front of the auditorium as a thin line of bright sunlight cuts across the wall behind him, his favourite paraphrase of Wallace Stevens is brought to life: 'What slice of sun enters your room?'[79]

In the summer of 1969, construction began on the Kimbell Art Museum. Kahn's office designed the formwork for the concrete walls, which have V-shaped ribs cast in to mark the formwork joints and give order to the surface of the concrete. The formwork tie holes are filled with lead plugs, and Kahn had pozzuolana added to the concrete mix to produce a warmer colour – all as he had done at the Salk Institute Laboratories. In November 1970, Kahn inspected and approved a mock-up of a section of one of the cycloid vaults, and construction on the roof began. After early concerns on the part of the contractor, Thomas Byrne, as to the feasibility of the shell-vault concrete construction of the roof, the process went far more smoothly and rapidly than anyone had expected. The aerial photograph of 18 January 1971 (p. 364; g), with the vaulting of the south wing already half-completed, reveals the process of vault construction in its various stages. As described by Loud:

> The Byrne company developed reusable forms made of three layers of marine plywood (plastic-coated) that could be shifted with relative ease around the site on dollies. On the exterior, slip-forms were raised about one foot at a time during the pouring process. Ribs were placed on the exterior as part of the form, but they were left in place to serve as anchorage for the placement of the insulation and for the plywood decking (which reused the forms) beneath the lead sheathing. Komendant's shell design made possible the skylight in the thirteen interior vaults. On either side of the opening, a raised curb acts as a Vierendeel truss; concrete struts placed across the skylight every ten feet balance any bending moments of the shell. Post-tensioning so strengthened the vaults that they actually carried the flat channels once the reinforcing steel tied vaults and channels together.[80]

The cycloid vaults were covered with lead sheathing, and as the roofs would be visible as one approached the museum, Kahn designed the elegant pattern of layered and seamed lead sheets. Kahn found an unexpected precedent for the roofs of the Kimbell Museum when he travelled to Venice, Italy in January 1969 to present his designs for the Palazzo dei Congressi, and he had the opportunity to visit the roofs of the Doge's Palace and Basilica di San Marco. Kahn later recalled this experience:

47. (Opposite) Louis Kahn in the auditorium, Kimbell Art Museum; as no art is displayed in this space, the light diffuser in the roof vault allows some direct light to enter. This photograph embodies Kahn's paraphrase of Wallace Stevens, 'What slice of sun enters your room?'.

The roofs of Venice are nothing short of fantastic. When you climb there and take a tour of the roofs, it is a sea of lead which you can see in front of you, and the lead is an undeniable material for roofs … What gives me courage in my lack of historical knowledge is that the man who built it did not think of history either, but simply did the job and built it as a roof. The size, the construction rhythm of the lead plates and the making of the joints manifest the truth of the statement that the joint is the beginning of an ornament.[81]

Kahn designed the Kimbell Museum to be entered, on foot, from the park to the west, where one arrives at the main gallery level. This is the result of Kahn's fundamental opposition to the orientation of public buildings to arrival by automobile, rather than any 'flagrant miscalculation of suburban habits', as it has been characterized.[82] In presenting this preference for the pedestrian over the automobile approach, the dramatic difference between the open, fully glazed wall – sheltered under an open vault at the upper (gallery) level, facing the park to the west – and the closed, solid concrete wall, recessed into the lower (service) level facing the parking lot to the east, could hardly be more clear. In addition, it is the park, not the streets and parking lots, that is shared by the cultural institutions making up the campus, and on to which Kahn believed his building should open (p. 163; h).

We approach the Kimbell Museum on long, gently rising walks from the north or south. The north walk rises in stepped levels, each edged by a travertine block, with a low concrete wall to the left, where the service and loading area open below. The south ramp is flat and overlooks a sunken grass-floored sculpture garden to the right, in which Isamu Noguchi placed his group of four basalt monoliths, titled *Constellation*, in 1983. The arched ends of the vaults march towards us as we approach, the columns standing on the solid concrete wall of the lower level, and the curved slot between vault and travertine infill walls giving brief glimpses of light from the skylights within. We mount several stairs and enter the portico, formed by a single complete cycloid vault that opens on all four sides to reveal the structure and spatial module of the museum.

The portico vault leaps gracefully between the pairs of columns at either end, its edge beam lifted 3 feet (0.9 metres) clear of the travertine-clad wall to the inside. Beyond this is the light well, and here we can glimpse the vault and concrete outer wall of the gallery, and the 6 inch (15 centimetre) horizontal slot of shadowed glass between them. The curve of the vault reflects and heightens the sounds made under it, and we become aware of the echoing sounds of our own footsteps. The floor of the portico is made of pebble-faced paving interlaced with travertine banding, and three travertine benches are placed against the inside wall, while two benches spaced between are placed at the outer edge. Towards the park, a two-level pool fronts the porticos, the water pouring in a smooth sheet from the upper to the lower pool, the subtle sound of which merges with that of our footsteps.

Having arrived under the shelter of the portico, we now emerge out into the open again, entering the shade of a T-shaped bosquet of miniature

Yaupon holly trees set in the entry court of the museum. Stepping from the travertine of the portico floor down on to the loose gravel of the forecourt, the loud sound of our own footsteps is reflected off the hard walls on three sides, giving us pause – we have arrived on the central axis of the museum. Making our way through the dense green labyrinth, in the shade of the closely spaced trees, we arrive at the entry portico. At the eastern end of the forecourt, we mount a broad set of travertine stairs and arrive under the third portico vault, also a complete cycloid curve, with a full-height glass wall ahead and travertine end walls of the galleries to left and right. Surrounded by hard surfaces, sounds are now at their most intensely magnified, and we are made aware of any others who inhabit this space with us. At this moment before we enter, the play of sunlight, passing through the 3 foot (0.9 metre) space between the ends of the vaults and falling on the walls and floor of the entry portico, reminds us again of the self-supported independence of each vaulted room.

Passing through the glass doors we arrive in the entry gallery, one of the most beautiful spaces ever built. Without exception, all who enter first lift their eyes to the ceiling above, which, though having the same profile as the porticos outside, is in every other way totally transformed. Where the porticos are continuous curves, the interior vaults are split at their centre by the skylight and reflector; and where the porticos are dark against the bright sky above, the interior vaults glow with the most astonishing, ethereal, silver coloured light. The translucent shimmering surface of the aluminium reflector forms a convex counter-curve to the concave curve of the vaults, and leads the eye to the end of the vault, where the complexly curving slot

48. Kimbell Art Museum, view from the west across the park to the entry court.

admits the brightest line of light, slicing between the concrete diaphragm of the vault above and the travertine wall below. While the gallery spaces flow freely under the ends of the vault, the doubled columns and the arc of sunlight inscribed in the travertine end walls reveal the 3 foot (0.9 metre) wide exterior spaces Kahn placed between the vaults.

In sharp contrast, entering the Kimbell Museum from the parking area to the east we are confronted by the solid two-storey facade – the only openings being the 6 inch (15 centimetre) horizontal slots of glass separating the edge beams of the vaults at the top from the walls beneath – and the entrance at the centre, a low, concrete-walled recess carved out of the lower floor. We move directly from the parking lot, exposed to the hot Texas sun, into the deeply shadowed entry space, and then into the dimly lit lobby beyond. The lower lobby provides access to the toilets at either end, but the public are not allowed to enter the curatorial and service spaces beyond.[83] Directly across from the doors is a travertine-walled double stair, and the stronger light coming from above encourages us to ascend. We arrive not into the centre of the entry gallery but under the low stainless-steel service channel between the entry gallery and the bookshop – a clear indication of the secondary, service status of the automobile-orientated entry, as opposed to the primary, honorific status accorded the ceremonial pedestrian entry from the park.

For the museum visitor, the sensuous range and complementary character of the materials and their colours are astonishing: from the warm, golden, fine-grained sheen of the oak floor; to the tan-white, porous thickness of the travertine floors and walls; to the neutral grey, matt-finish of the stainless-steel service channel soffits, spiral curved handrails and spherical drinking fountain; to the silver, shimmering, textured screens of the aluminium reflectors; and finally to the almost indescribable, cool silvery-grey, smooth curving, massive and floating concrete vaults themselves.

The repetitive pattern created by the cycloid-vault-covered rooms is literally punctuated by the travertine-floored courts which are cut into the museum's south and north wings, where the diaphanous ceilings, through which we can see the blue of the sky, are made by trellises woven of stainless-steel cables supporting climbing vines. These courts emphasize the introverted character of the museum, the exhibition galleries of which are enclosed on all sides by solid stone walls – the only openings the 6 inch (15 centimetre) horizontal slots between the vault and wall, the thin lines of light subtly revealing that we are at the outer edge of the building on the east and west sides. Yet, from anywhere within the museum, we are always aware of the weather outside, for the silver light of the vaults is responsive to the most subtle change in the sunlight – full sunshine imparts a warmer grey hue to the vaults, which a passing cloud suddenly transforms into a colder silver-white, even as the brightness is diminished.[84]

This experience of the museum visitor is complemented by Kahn's careful accommodation of the museum's critical functions, including tracks for electrical lighting both at the lower edges of the vault, along the

49. (Opposite) View up into the roof vault of the entry gallery, with fully perforated aluminium light diffuser, Kimbell Art Museum.

50. (Previous page) Gallery, Kimbell Art Museum, with partially perforated aluminium light diffuser. Materials used in this space include cast-in-place concrete, perforated aluminium, travertine, oak wood and stainless steel.
51. Gallery with one of the light courts on the left, Kimbell Art Museum.
52. Gallery, Kimbell Art Museum.
53. Library reading room, lifted above the book stacks to reside in the space of the vault, Kimbell Art Museum. This is the only place where one can touch the concrete vaults.

service channel, and at the crown of the vault, along the aluminium cradle supporting the skylight reflectors. Also notable is the provision of wall-mounting connections within the soffits of the service channel between the vaults, allowing display surfaces to be organized both parallel and perpendicular to the vaults, and allowing adjacent vaulted rooms to be joined to form any conceivable exhibition arrangement. The small library is accorded a place of honour at the centre of the east elevation, with the reading room elevated into the space of the vault itself. It is lit by the central skylight, the fully glazed vault ends (allowing a close view of the roof detailing and the 3 foot (0.9 metre) space between the vaults) and the 6 inch (15 centimetre) slot running along the bottom of the edge beam of the vault at the floor on the east side. Here in the library is the one opportunity – for most visitors, simply irresistible – to touch the shining surface of the concrete vault.

From the day of its opening in October 1972, the design was hailed as a great functional success, setting a new standard for the quality of museum space. Richard Brown stated that the Kimbell Museum was 'what every museum man has been looking for ever since museums came into existence: a floor uninterrupted by piers, columns, or windows, and perfect lighting, giving total freedom and flexibility to use the space and install art exactly the way you want'.[85] Kahn's design for the Kimbell Museum is a remarkably effective fulfilment of Brown's initial programme requirement for gallery spaces where the experience of viewing the artworks was to be shaped and characterized by the architecture, which Brown hoped could provide 'warmth, mellowness, and even elegance'.[86]

Without question Kahn's most beautiful space, the Kimbell Museum is also his most effective engagement of the poetics of construction, as well as the most rigorously resolved example of his concept of the relation between light, structure and space – the interior spaces receiving natural light in a variety of ways that together precisely outline and articulate the structural elements. Finally, the Kimbell Museum is also Kahn's most elegant demonstration of his considerable skills in landscape design,[87] its entry sequence taking us past sunken sculpture gardens, under a vaulted loggia, past sheets of cascading water, through a gravel-floored courtyard filled with a grid of trees and then, quietly, into the very heart of the gallery itself. As Kenneth Frampton describes this experience: 'In such a setting, perhaps more fitting for a temple than a museum, we find ourselves returned to the tactility of the tectonic in all its aspects; to a meeting between the essence of things and the existence of beings, to that pre-Socratic moment, lying outside time, that is at once both modern and antique.'[88]

Kimbell Art Museum

Concept development

For the Kimbell Art Museum, Kahn envisaged from the start a single-storey series of main galleries, lit from above by sunlight, the roof vault shaping the room below as in ancient Roman architecture. Kahn's initial designs for the vaults themselves drew not on ancient prototypes, however, but on his own experiments in folded concrete construction, resulting in a structural design that allowed each vault to be split down the centre by light. Kahn explored various geometries for the vaults before settling on the constantly changing curve of the cycloid vault, across which sunlight is sprayed by a wing-shaped aluminium diffuser. Each vault was developed as an independent structure, creating an individual gallery below, separated from the adjacent spaces by light slots, with thin arcs of sunlight let in at the ends of the vaults to outline their curving profiles. The concrete vaults and columns, travertine stone walls, aluminium service zones and wood floors clearly articulate the spaces. Early schemes for the building, together with early and final conceptions of the roof vaults are shown here; the evolution of the vaulted spaces of the museum, including their as-built configuration, is documented overleaf.

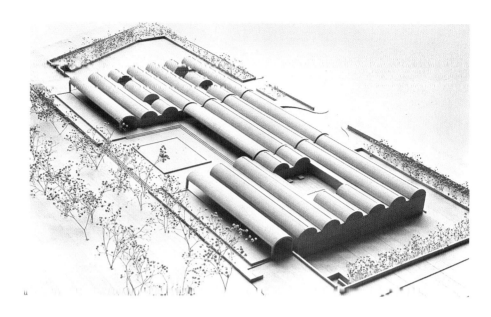

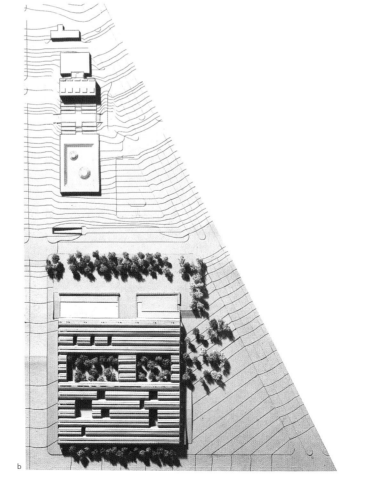

a. Model of Kimbell Art Museum, first C-shaped plan, September 1968.
b. Site model of first scheme, March 1967 (north to right); the Art Museum fills a 400 foot (120 metre) square, with two large garden courts and the existing Amon Carter Museum, top left.

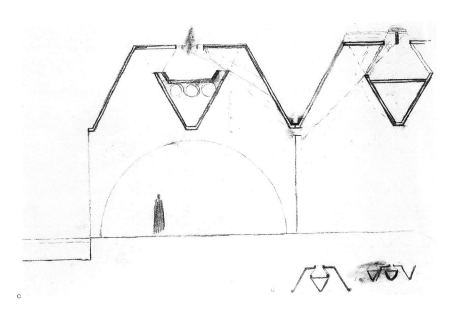

c

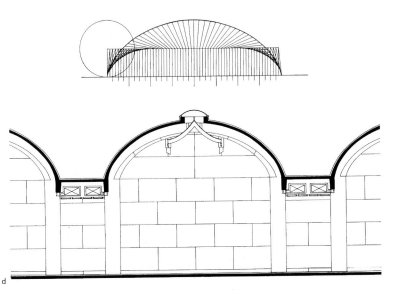

d

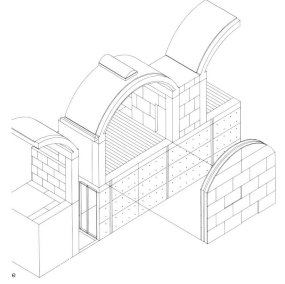

e

c. Early section study of typical roof vault, Kimbell Art Museum, showing V-shaped folded plate construction with services housed in the light diffuser at the centre of the vault; drawing by Kahn.
d. Final section of typical roof vault, below, with diagram of cycloid form, above.
e. Cut-away isometric section, showing two structural bays at the upper gallery floor, with the non-load-bearing end wall pulled away, and the lower service floor beneath; drawn under author's supervision.

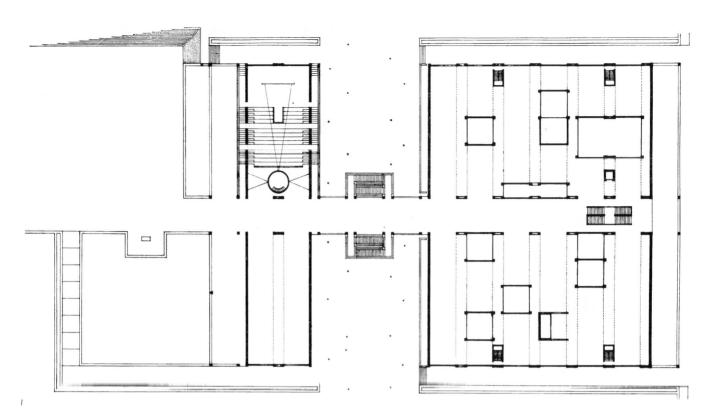

g

JOB # 760
KIMBELL ART MUSEUM
Louis I. Kahn - Architect
Preston M. Geren-Associate Architect
Thos. S. Byrne, Inc.-Genl. Contractors
Photo No.547 Date 18 JAN 71

f. Intermediate plan of Kimbell Art Museum,
H-shaped design, November 1967 (north at top).
g. Kimbell Art Museum under construction,
18 January 1971. The concrete formwork for
the roof vaults is visible on the left in various
states of completion.

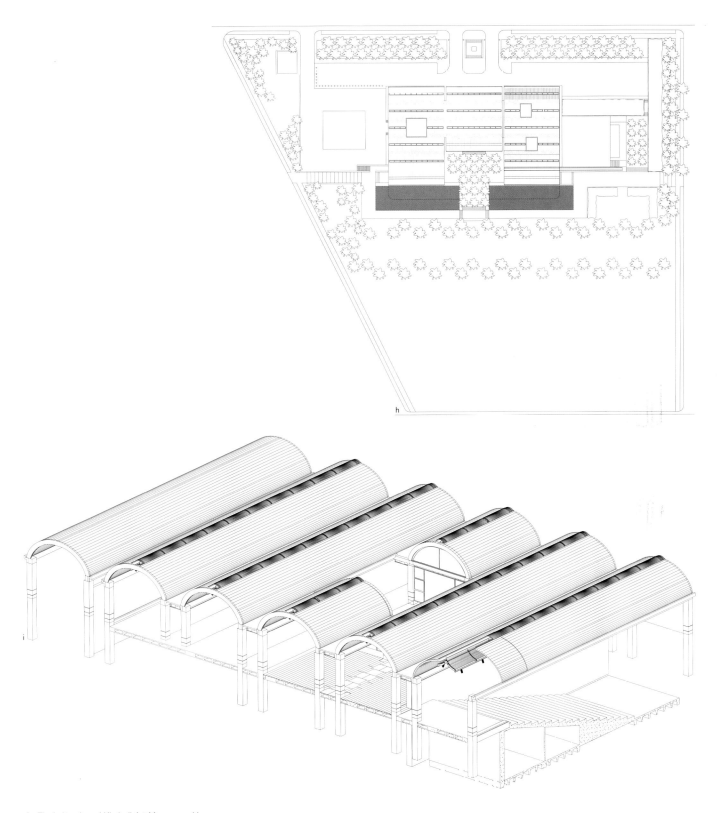

h Final site plan of Kimbell Art Museum, with existing park below and parking lot above (north to left); redrawn under author's supervision.
i. Isometric section showing the entry portico on the left, the central galleries and light court, and the auditorium on the right; drawn under author's supervision.

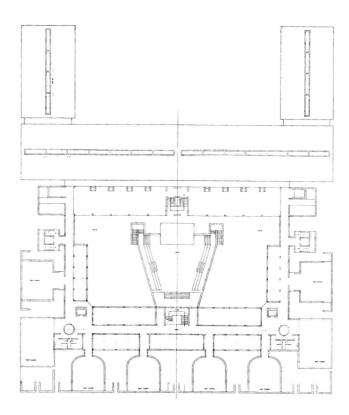

Shaping space under roof shells

The Wolfson Center for Mechanical Engineering, designed between 1968 and 1974 and built at the University of Tel Aviv in 1977, after Kahn's death, was the only building Kahn ever realized in Israel. Kahn once again began his design with a series of square plans, several employing cylindrical light towers at the outer corners. Kahn's plans dating from July 1971 are again based on Wright's Unity Temple, with a rectangular laboratory volume, to the east, on axis with and separated from a square classroom volume, to the west, by the narrower entry space.[89] The final design began to emerge in 1972, with the laboratories proposed as long rectangular spaces, roofed with the concrete cycloid vaults, larger but otherwise identical to those of the Kimbell Museum, complete with skylights at the apex, wing-shaped light reflectors, and curving slot between the diaphragm of the vault and the masonry end wall. The classrooms face massive reflector walls, off which light is bounced to provide diffused, cool illumination.

The Olivetti-Underwood Factory, located in Harrisburg, Pennsylvania, was designed and built between 1966 and 1970. This was a highly prestigious commission for Kahn, as Olivetti was then considered both the leading product design firm and 'the most discerning patrons of industrial buildings' in the world.[90] Not only did Olivetti provide Kahn with materials relating to their other architectural commissions – Kahn's personal sketches include copies of the Olivetti lettering and logo designed by Carlo Scarpa for their showroom on Piazza San Marco in Venice – but they also gave him several books of Italian Renaissance drawings, of which the importance to his

54. Laboratory, Wolfson Center for Mechanical Engineering, University of Tel Aviv, Israel, 1968–74; the laboratories employ a concrete vault and light diffuser detail similar to the Kimbell Art Museum.
55. Plan of the Wolfson Center for Mechanical Engineering, showing vaulted laboratories (top) and classrooms (below; north to left).

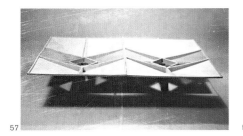

designs has been noted earlier.[91] From the start Kahn intended the Olivetti factory to employ a version of the 'umbrella' structure – a central column group supporting a roof which cantilevers in all four directions – which he had first proposed in the 1944 Parasol House design for the Knoll Company, and which had been revived, but ultimately not employed, in the Martin Research Institute, the First Unitarian Church and the mosque at the Bangladesh National Capital in Dhaka. For Olivetti, Kahn also returned to his conception of this 'tree-like' column being both the structure and the source of daylight – a concept he had first proposed for the Adath Jeshurun Synagogue in 1954.

Kahn initially proposed a large, double-square, single-storey volume for the Olivetti Factory, which was changed to a square plan in the final scheme. As for the roof, after exploring a series of square forms, each with a clerestory monitor raised over the column (or four-column clusters) at the centre, Kahn settled on an octagonal roof form, with skylight monitors set into the square spaces between the octagons, so that light comes through the joints between the 'column-trees' rather than from their centre. This final design of Kahn's involved a grid of columns supporting umbrella-like roofs, which were made of thin-shell concrete, with the rainwater drained down a pipe set in the centre of the column, and with skylights set between the outer edges of the roofs – all exactly as in Wright's Johnson Wax Building, which must be considered the primary precedent for this design.[92] While Komendant developed the structural designs for the 'prismatic shells', Kahn was assisted by the young Italian architect, Renzo Piano, in developing the complex, layered geometric designs for the skylight monitors, which, due to the requirement for glare-free daylight, were fabricated in plastic.[93] As built, the 60 foot (18 metre) grid of columns supporting the 30 foot (9 metre) tall folded roof shells provides a space which is at once totally flexible, able to accommodate extended assembly lines, and yet also strongly syncopated by the rhythm of the columns, the folded ceiling surfaces overhead and the generous pools of daylight.

56. Olivetti-Underwood Factory, Harrisburg, Pennsylvania, 1966–70; under construction.
57. Early study model of 'umbrella'-vault prototype with skylight over column cluster, Olivetti-Underwood Factory.
58. Olivetti-Underwood Factory entrance; the lettering on the sign was designed by Carlo Scarpa.
59. Cafeteria, Olivetti-Underwood Factory.

Yale Center for British Art
New Haven
Connecticut
1969–74

In October 1969 Kahn was commissioned to design the Yale Center for British Art, housing the extensive collection donated by Paul Mellon, which was to be built directly across Chapel Street from Kahn's Yale Art Gallery. Jules Prown, the director of the Center, had visited Kahn's office the previous spring. Describing this meeting, Prown recalled Kahn's acute sensitivity to daylight, such that 'during the conversation [Kahn] wouldn't turn the lights on because he liked the daylight, so that as the day progressed and it became darker and darker and darker, and any other person would flip on the lights, he would just let the day go on in its own way. That created a certain atmosphere that just seemed right: the unpretentiousness of Lou and … his sense of what was important and what wasn't. For me, at least, he inspired a kind of confidence.'[94] The brief Kahn was given in January 1970 was for two institutions in one – a museum and a library and study centre – and from his earliest sketches Kahn conceived each of these two institutions centred on its own square courtyard, with the twofold nature of the Center to be felt in the plans and legible on the facades.

Kahn began with an overlapping double-square plan, the museum and the study centre each forming a C-shape around their respective square courts, with the overlapping zone in the centre a shared entry hall that ran through the building from north to south (p. 381; d). While in the earliest schemes these C-shaped plans opened towards each other and the centre, the museum facing west and the study centre facing east, Kahn soon turned the study centre to also face west, so that its court opened towards the proposed University Art Library (p. 380; a), for which Kahn had also been asked to prepare designs.[95] In this first complete scheme Kahn placed a large stair at the centre, at the edge of the central hall and opening to the eastern court, and four escape stairs together with mechanical shafts in the outer corners, where they were housed in semicircular, stainless-steel-clad towers (pp. 381–2; e & f). Kahn placed the horizontal, vaulted, top-lit exhibition galleries at the roof, along the north, south and east sides of the building. These galleries, which gradually arc down their length (rather than across their narrow width, as at Kimbell), were to be lit by clerestory structures similar to those employed by Aalto in the Aalborg Museum, with flat top and bottom and concave side walls to reflect light back on to the outside walls of the gallery. The Center's primary facade on Church Street was split down its centre by a slot, separating it into two identical buildings, each topped by the gentle curve of a gallery (p. 382; g).

In December 1970, after Prown raised concerns about the long arcing gallery roofs of the first scheme, which he felt were overpowering both in scale and in the sense of compression they would have created as they swept downwards at either end, Kahn developed a second scheme.[96] As usual with Kahn, he did not perceive being asked to start the design over again as in any way a setback – quite the opposite, for Kahn had by now realized full well that the longer he was given to work on a design, the better it became. Kahn's second scheme, while maintaining the two-part massing, the central hall and the stainless-steel mechanical and stair towers, began to integrate the museum and study centre. Kahn raised the western court above the central hall of the library, which was in turn placed above the auditorium. He placed a vaulted roof with skylights over the eastern court, and projected into it a full-height, semicircular, open stair (p. 382; h); and located the library book stacks and window reading carrels in the middle floors of the north and south wings, above which he placed the galleries, their roofs proposed to be double-semicircular vaults running down their length. In what has been called a combination of the Exeter Library and the Kimbell Museum,[97] Kahn's second design began at the ground with a vertical, top-lit, square-plan entry court, and ended at the roof with horizontal, vaulted, top-lit galleries.

Most notable in this second scheme was Kahn's design for the gallery roof vaults, documented in his large-scale working models (p. 380; b). The galleries were double squares in section, divided into thirds at the ceiling, with a triangular structural beam at the centre, carrying mechanical services; and with the outer two bays opening upwards into barrel-vaulted skylights. These barrel-vaulted skylight chambers were each divided at the centre, and the southern half was solid wall while the northern half was glass. In a rather

60. Perspective drawing of the west facade of the Yale Center for British Art, as seen from the sunken court, with access to the auditorium at the far end; drawing by Kahn.

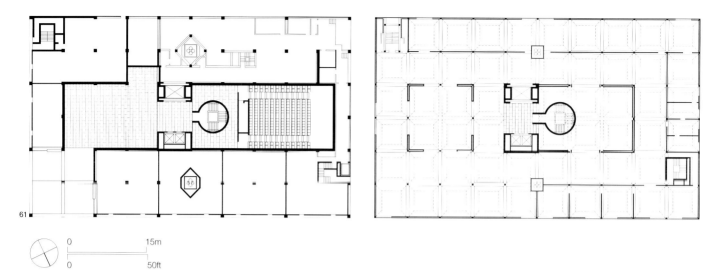

61

0 — 15m
0 — 50ft

startling development and significant change in construction habits, Kahn proposed that the floor structure of the Center be made of concrete Vierendeel trusses, and that the elevation (with the exception of the stainless-steel service towers at the corners) be made of a concrete frame with windows set flush to the outside face of the building. In both ways, far more similar to Kahn's AFL Medical Service Building of 1956 than to any of his more recent buildings.

By March 1971 Kahn had brought this second design to a high level of resolution, and though the estimated cost exceeded the original budget, Prown felt it would make a marvellous museum. Yet Mellon, the primary donor, was also funding the National Gallery of Art in Washington, DC, and when this was combined with the fact that construction costs had increased by a staggering forty-two per cent since the inception of the project, it became apparent that the size of the building, and the complexity of its programme, would have to be substantially reduced. Kahn was paid for the second scheme and given a new brief – Kahn considered this to be the beginning of a new project.[98]

Kahn's third design for the Center for British Art, on which construction began in early 1973, is elegantly simple, a rectangular block set tight on the sidewalk, structured by a square grid of concrete columns, with two light courts penetrating its four public floors. Kahn carried forward from the previous designs only the two courts and the overlapping double-square plan, measuring 120 by 200 feet (36.5 by 60 metres) – two 120 foot (36.5 metre) squares overlapping 40 feet (12 metres) – with the public stairs and elevators located in the overlap at the centre. The escape stairs are placed internally at the north-west and south-east corners, and rotated square mechanical shafts are located on the centreline of the building, flanking the public circulation. The 'breathing' floors are made of concrete with integral return-air chases cast into the slabs (p. 383; j). The main stair, originally a rotated square (p. 383; i), finally a cylinder, was located on the west side, in the library court.[99]

Entry is no longer at the centre but from the north-east corner and into the eastern court, a 40 foot (12 metre) square in plan, ringed by the exhibition galleries above ground level, which rises through the full four-floor height of the building, where it is roofed with skylights. The auditorium,

61. Final ground or entry floor plan (left) and upper, gallery level plan (right), Yale Center for British Art; redrawn under author's supervision.
62. East-west section, looking south, Yale Center for British Art; redrawn under author's supervision. Note that the top of the cylindrical main stair (centre) is here shown flat, exactly as it was built, as opposed to being cut off at a 45 degree angle as it is sometimes shown; the incorrect versions result from tracing Kahn's own final published section, which does not correspond to the stair as built.

entered from the ground floor, steps down to the basement level and opens
to a sunken exterior court to the west (p. 380; c). One level above ground,
and over the auditorium, is the floor of the west court, measuring 40 by 60 feet
(12 by 18 metres), and rising three floors to its roof, a grid of skylights.
The study centre, housing prints, drawings, photographs, rare books and
reference materials, is wrapped around the three outer edges of the west court.
In the most significant change, the plan is composed of a grid of columns
creating 20 foot (6 metre) square rooms, each of which is capped at the
fourth-floor galleries by one of the pyramidal skylights that comprise the roof.

The Center is built across the street from Kahn's first important work, the
Yale Art Gallery. It is difficult to believe that only twenty years separate these
two projects, for where the Art Gallery faces the street with a solid masonry
wall, the Center for British Art presents a fully articulated concrete frame of
columns and beams, infilled with acid-etched stainless-steel panels and flush
glazing. The concrete columns subtly diminish in width at each floor as they
rise, with a deep transfer beam at the second floor line, narrower beams at
third and fourth floor, and the deep, bevelled, precast concrete roof shells at
the top. The double-height spaces within, at the reading rooms of the study
centre on the north, west and south elevations, are clearly legible in the fact that
no floor beam exists at the third floor, and the stainless-steel panels rise two
floors without a break. With the exception of the ground floor on the north
and east sides, where the facade is set back, the infill panels and windows are set
flush to the outside face of concrete columns and beams. The only elements
that project forward, breaking this plane, are the folded stainless-steel drip
mouldings placed at the base of each infill panel, which cast strong shadows
across the surface of the facade. When viewed from the street, both the glass
and the steel panels appear solid and massive, the windows reflecting the sky
and the details of the buildings across the street, while the steel panels have
a lustrous yet matt finish, as Kahn said, similar to lead or pewter: 'On a grey
day it will look like a moth; on a sunny day like a butterfly.'[100]

At the corner we enter the portico, a 40 foot (12 metre) square space
open on two sides, low and dark, paved in brick with bluestone bands

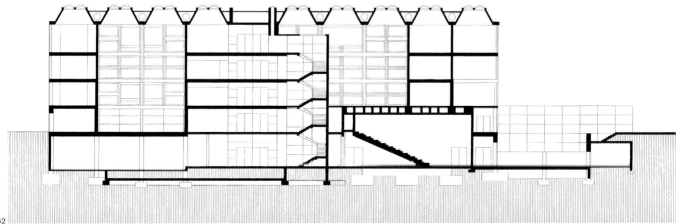

64

65

63. (Opposite) West facade of the Yale Center for
British Art, with sunken court garden. Kahn said that
the steel panels of the facade would look like 'a moth
on a cloudy day and a butterfly on a sunny day'.
64. West elevation, Yale Center for British Art.
65. Aerial view of the Yale Center for British Art; the
corner of Kahn's 1951–3 Yale Art Gallery is visible
on the left.

demarcating the column grid. We then move into the travertine-floored
entry court, a tall, four-storey space, brightly lit by the four pyramidal domes
at its roof, each of which is divided at its centre by a cross-shaped pair of
frames holding four square skylights. The concrete columns, diminishing as
they rise, are recessed, rather than flush, with respect to the concrete beams,
so that the wood panels, which are set flush with the beams, are set slightly
forward of the central columns and conceal the columns at the four corners.
The stainless-steel panels of the exterior are carried inside to clad the lower
floor of the entry court, while white-oak panels infill the upper three floors,
with double openings flanking the central column at the second and fourth
floors. The entry court not only introduces us to the full section of the Center
but, in the change from steel to wood panelling, it alludes to the honorific
museum programme of the upper three floors, as opposed to the commercial,
entry, auditorium and service programme of the ground floor. Our next goal
is now clear – to ascend one floor to the museum, on the *piano nobile*.

Passing through the narrow vestibule on to which the elevators open,
we enter the stair tower, the square-plan stainless-steel treads and handrails
of which are set within cylindrical concrete walls, light from above drawing us
upwards. Arriving at the second floor, the double opening into the entry court
directly ahead invites us into the gallery. Returning to the stair, we now see for
the first time the outer face of the cylindrical concrete stair, around which we
enter the western, library court. In contrast to the vertical entry court, the
library court is horizontally proportioned, with an oak floor, the walls panelled
with wood from floor to ceiling, where the six pyramidal concrete skylight
domes open. At the lower two levels, where the walls of the library court are

solid, large paintings are hung, with double openings only occurring at the top, fourth floor. The elegant yet understated detailing of the wood panelling in the library court gives it an atmosphere remarkably like the main room of a traditional English manor house – exactly what Mellon and Prown had requested. At the same time, the massive, solid, concrete walls of the cylindrical stair tower and pyramidal roof domes give the court what can only be described as an urban character and scale. As a result, we experience

66

67

68

69

66. Entry court, Yale Center for British Art; this view looks towards the entry doors and the street beyond.
67. View from the top floor galleries, looking into the library or gallery court with the cylindrical concrete main stair tower, Yale Center for British Art; note that the stair does not reach the roof vaults.
68. View looking up at the ceiling of the central stair, which is composed of a square stainless-steel-detailed stair housed within a cylindrical concrete volume standing free in the gallery court and lit by a grid of glass blocks, Yale Center for British Art.
69. View into the entry court from the top floor gallery, through unglazed openings, Yale Center for British Art.

the library court as at once intimate and grand, domestic and monumental, room and courtyard, ancient and modern.

Through the large double openings overlooking the library court at the top floor we can see the grid of pyramidal roof domes extending in all four directions, indicating our final goal. Reaching the top of the stair we discover a rotated square skylight composed of a grid of glass blocks cast into the concrete roof of the cylinder, which sits under the pyramidal skylight domes of the library court. As indicated by his extending all north–south section drawings of the Center for British Art to include his Yale Art Gallery across Chapel Street, Kahn clearly intended their cylindrical stairs to be compared.

70

70. Typical top floor gallery, Yale Center for British Art, showing movable display walls of oak and linen, the concrete roof structure with skylights, and the stainless-steel-clad service chase. This service chase is the only instance where Kahn brings the primary exterior skin material into the interior.

71. (Opposite) View looking up from the entry court, Yale Center for British Art; as no paintings are displayed in this space, ultraviolet light filters were not placed on these four skylights.

In fact, with the sole exception of their cylindrical concrete enclosures, the stairs of the British Art Center and the Yale Art Gallery form a perfectly dichotomous, reversed pair: freestanding cylinder / cylinder embedded in floors; stops within building / emerges through roof; embedded at basement / opens at basement; square stair with rotated square skylight / triangular stair with aligned triangular skylight; lighted, void square at centre of ceiling / dark, solid triangle at centre of ceiling.

The top-floor galleries are the culminating experience of the Center for British Art, 20 foot (6 metre) square rooms opening to one another *enfilade*, or in sequence, opening to the two courts on the inside, and opening to views on

72

the outside – each room formed and shaped by the regular rhythm of the roof structure overhead. Fabricated as precast sections lifted into place, these V-shaped folded concrete plates house the mechanical services in the hollow space within, while carrying the skylight grid on their upper edges – the roof structure of the Center for British Art is in many ways a two-directional reinterpretation and final realization of the 'lost' scheme for Salk Institute. This upper floor is also, rather astonishingly, a return to and realization of Kahn's third design, of late 1956, for the Trenton Jewish Community Center, complete with its pyramid-roofed skylights, its four-columned cellular volumes, its square grid structure and its two larger volumes anchoring the symmetrical longer axis of the rectangular mass. The skylights are provided with ultraviolet filters beneath and shade trellises above, allowing the galleries to be suffused with sunlight without causing damage to the art.

The gallery floors are undyed wool carpet, with the column grid marked by bands of travertine, upon which stand the wall panels, unbleached linen framed at all edges with oak trim boards and wood base. The mechanical shafts are clad in the same acid-etched stainless steel used on the exterior, and the ventilation is delivered through diffusers on the bottom of the concrete structure. The exterior windows, equipped with wooden shutters to control direct light, provide animated views of the city and the university

73

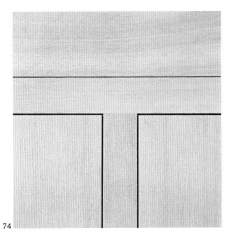

74

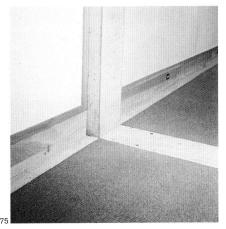

75

76

72. Research library, Yale Center for British Art.
73. Gallery court with the main stair housed in
a cylindrical concrete volume on the right, Yale
Center for British Art; the top-floor galleries are
visible through the openings on the left, above.
74–6. Details of oak panelling (left), gallery floor
at wall and concrete column (centre), and gallery
corner with concrete column and travertine band at
floor, carpet, oak and linen wall panels (right), Yale
Center for British Art.

campus, so that despite the introverted character of the central courts, we
are never far removed from our context. Yet it is the views of the interior,
through the sequences of square rooms and across the gridded courts to the
rooms on the other side, which are without question the most wonderful
aspect of our experience of this superbly resolved building. Here Kahn
has made it possible for us to walk in spaces literally filled with sunlight,
experiencing ever changing compositions of harmoniously coloured,
receding and advancing planes in perspective.

Yale Center for British Art

Concept development

The initial designs for the Yale Center for British Art reflect the programme for two institutions in one – a museum and a library-study centre. Kahn conceived each of these two institutions as being centred on its own square courtyard, with the twofold nature felt in the plans and legible on the facades. In developing the design, he initially proposed long barrel-vaulted galleries at the top of the building, with open outdoor courtyards at ground level. When the programme was re-written to make the institution more singular in nature, he designed the plan on a grid of 20 foot (6 metre) structural squares, with the spaces organized around two interior top-lit courts: an entry court at grade and a gallery court one level above grade. The entire roof of the building is covered with square pyramidal skylights and the top-floor galleries may be understood as a realization of both Kahn's early designs for the pyramidal-roofed Trenton Jewish Community Center and the folded concrete plate roof vaults of the Salk Institute. Both early and late concepts of the overall design are shown here, while pages 382–3 relate to the development of the two programmes into a single unified institution.

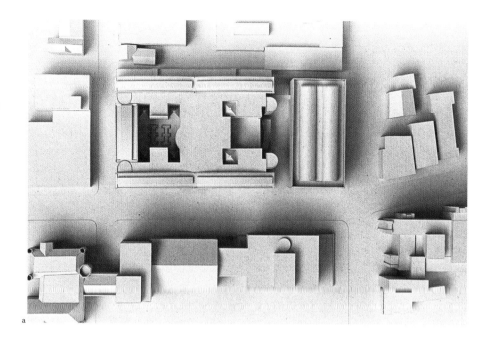

a

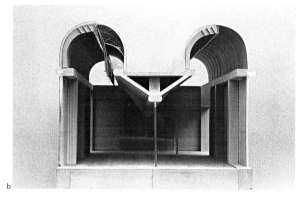

b

a. Model of Yale Center for British Art, first scheme, 1970; the Center for British Art is at the top (centre left), the proposed Art Library is also at the top (right) and Kahn's 1951–3 Yale Art Gallery is below (centre right).
b. Study model of the top-floor galleries, Yale Center for British Art, second scheme, 1971, with double skylights flanking the central service and structural element.
c. Section model showing the entry court (right) and the central cylindrical stair tower and gallery court above the auditorium (centre and left), final scheme, 1972; model built under the supervision of Kenneth Frampton.
d. Early plan study showing two-building concept, 1970; drawing by Kahn.
e. Elevation of Yale Center for British Art, first scheme, 1970 (right) and section through Kahn's 1951–53 Yale Art Gallery (left), proposed to be connected underground.

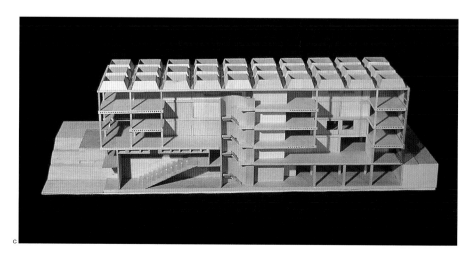

c

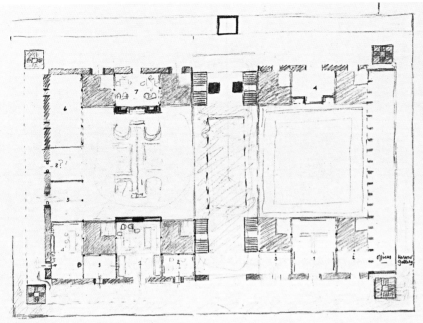

gallery in the way to the greater courts,
facing the court. These rooms are of variety.
Now it appears to be in regular proportions
but it ought to relate the rooms
below by another stairways. LIK

d

2nd Floor Level
Painting Galleries and Rooms
The Paul Mellon Center for British Art and British Studies.
Yale University New Haven Connecticut
Louis I Kahn Architect Philadelphia Pa —

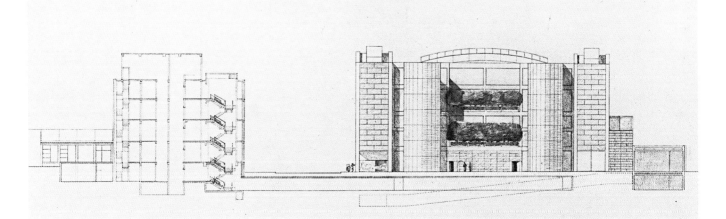

e

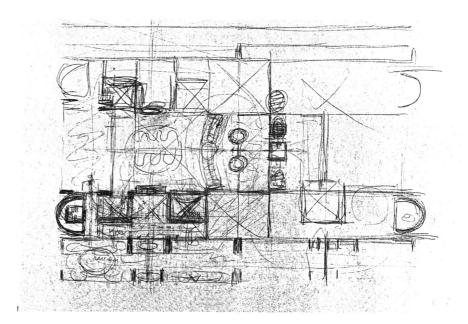

g

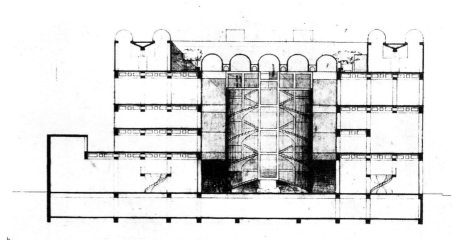

f. Sketch plan of Yale Center for British Art,
first scheme, 1970; drawing by Kahn.
g. North elevation on Chapel Street, first
scheme, 1970; drawing by Kahn.
h. North-south section through the east court,
looking towards the central stair with double
barrel-vaulted galleries, top, left and right,
second scheme, 1971.

h

i. Interior perspective drawing of the library
or gallery court, Yale Center for British Art, third
and final scheme featuring the square stair,
1972; drawing by Kahn.
j. Wall section of construction drawings, third
and final scheme, 1973, showing hollow 'breathing'
floors, stainless-steel-clad exterior walls and folded
plate concrete roof structure, topped by skylights
with light filters.

j

Building with advanced and archaic construction

From 1966 to 1974, Kahn worked on the design for the Kansas City Office Tower, Missouri, one of only two high-rise buildings he ever seriously undertook. Kahn referred to the typical steel frame high-rise as 'tin-can' construction and, along with his engineer Komendant, proposed a slip-form concrete construction system for this twenty-four-storey structure that would be both more rapid in erection time and less expensive than standard steel construction.[101] Kahn's proposal involved first building the four double corner columns (producing an open corner, as at Exeter Library) and a massive truss structure at the roof, and then constructing the floors, from the top down, which would be suspended from the truss at the top of the building.[102] The second notable feature of Kahn's design, after it was relocated to a more prominent site, was the formation of the public spaces at the street, where Kahn developed a dense layering of urban amenities together with a raised plaza, all holding the street wall. This great design was never to be realized, though Kahn continued to work on it until early in 1974 when, without notifying Kahn, the client gave the project to another architect, Skidmore, Owings and Merrill. Kahn was devastated, and stated that this episode exemplified 'what is wrong with our profession, no ethics'.[103]

The partially built Family Planning Centre in Kathmandu, Nepal, 1970 to 1974, was designed as an H-shape in plan, with stairs and services placed at the intersections of the north and south wings with the central spine – four large volumes with fenestration on three sides, and the central volume with fenestration on the east and west sides. Four freestanding open stair towers were to be placed at the ends of the north and south wings, with entry provided symmetrically at the centre of each wing, along the central cross-axis. The double-layered walls of the building are created by U-shaped masonry piers,

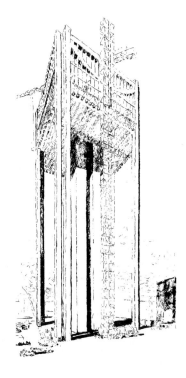

77. Perspective drawing of Kansas City Office Tower, Missouri, 1966–74, under construction being built from the top down; sketch by Louis Kahn.
78. Baltimore Street view of Kansas City Office Tower.

77

78

which form deep, shaded recesses for the windows, within which the wooden shutters may be opened. These masonry piers rise unbroken from floor to roof, and are opened into a rooftop loggia (as at Exeter Library), and the resemblance of both the plan and elevations of this late design to Kahn's 1924 Beaux-Arts student design for a shopping centre is astonishing.[104] In this design, we see the remarkable degree to which Kahn fused the modern and the classical in his own timeless way of building.

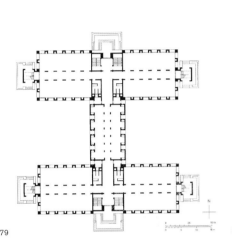

79

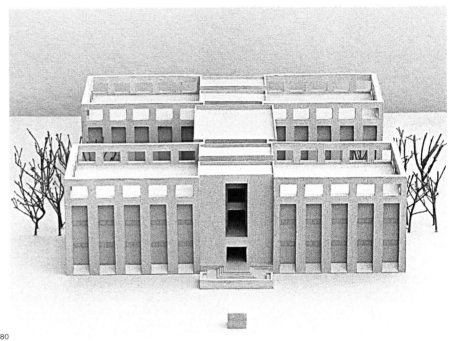

80

81

79. Plan of Family Planning Center, Kathmandu, Nepal, 1970–4.
80. Model of Family Planning Center.
81. Exterior view of partially realized Family Planning Center.

Conclusion: the profession is in the marketplace, architecture is in the university

Kahn was one of the very few architects of first importance in modern architecture to teach in a university continuously throughout his career, and to endeavour to articulate the mysteries of the design process, first for his students, and later, in his lectures, for the architecture profession. Kahn's Monday and Friday afternoon master classes at the University of Pennsylvania, held in the top-lit, triple-height rotunda of the Library designed by Frank Furness, also allowed Kahn to develop his ever evolving definition of design, which was later given form in his architecture. In sharp contrast to what had become the norm in US architecture schools, Kahn brought all his major commissions into the university studio class, often assigning them to his students at the same time as he began to work on them in his professional office. Kahn's students were able to design not only from actual briefs, but often with the client and engineers' involvement in their periodic review sessions as well. In this way, Kahn was also able to contemplate the nature of each new project both at the office and at school. As Kahn noted, 'The work of students is not pointed … to the solution of problems. Primarily, it is to sense the nature of the place.'[105]

Throughout his life, Kahn was deeply sceptical as to the value of received pedagogies in architectural education. In 1953, the year he began to teach in his own Yale Art Gallery building, Kahn made the sobering assessment that 'the nature of space is something we really don't know much about',[106] going on to note that architects tended to copy forms rather than develop their designs from first principles. G. Holmes Perkins, the dean at the University of Pennsylvania, recalled that Kahn always taught from the 'sincere respect for the craft of building [which] underlay all his own work', and that 'in his search for true integration, he relied on two architectural concepts which he categorized as an articulation of "servant and served spaces" and, secondly, the unifying concept of "the central space",'[107] both derived from the work of Frank Lloyd Wright. Jacob Bakema, the Dutch Team 10 member, tells the following story illustrating Kahn's ability to teach directly through the experience of architecture: 'Visiting [Wright's 1909] Robie House in Chicago with some students in 1962, we approached the door just hearing inside a hoarse voice: "This really is a door even making welcome being closed, and giving protection being opened". Then the door opened and Louis I. Kahn stepped out.'[108]

Kahn became increasingly critical of the manner in which universities were adopting the methods and values of business, finding this to be against the very nature of the university: 'The university has nothing to do with the marketplace.'[109] For Kahn, the discipline of architecture belonged in both practical and academic settings, but in a fundamentally different way, which he summarized by saying: 'The profession is in the marketplace; architecture belongs to the university.'[110] Kahn believed that the art of architecture was a fundamentally unchanging ideal, whereas the profession must be constantly changing to address evolving circumstances: 'The profession is certainly going to change; but Architecture isn't going to change.'[111] Kahn believed that architecture's fundamental first principles were being lost even as the profession increased in stature and influence. For Kahn, architecture was a deadly serious matter, and in his later years he became in many ways the conscience of the profession. As Scully noted, 'No one could ever go back to what I refer to as the sullen anti-intellectualism of the American architectural profession after encountering Kahn, and in a funny way nobody ever touched the conscience of the profession as much as Kahn did.'[112]

Kahn's method of working out his concepts was fundamentally oral – he rarely read more than the first few pages of the many books he bought, though he studied the illustrations with an unmatched intensity. In this, Kahn was deeply dependent upon conversations with colleagues and friends, and the spoken word held a special place for him. As described by Abba Tor, his engineer on the Yale Center for British Art, Kahn's 'office was run as a combination of architectural office, artist's studio, and master-class', telling how when Kahn reviewed a project, all his assistants would gather round listening and participating in the discussion.[113] At school and in the office, Kahn's discussions of architecture 'promoted a sense of discovery and wonder',[114] and Kahn's manner of speaking of the experience of architecture, of speaking directly to the matter at hand in describing the design and construction of his works, was also profoundly different from the typical architectural lecture, as noted by Alison and Peter Smithson: 'No architect with a memory of a Kahn lecture can not be aware of another level, another pattern of architectural thinking.'[115]

82

Kahn spoke incessantly in his search for the most fundamental beginnings, talking to get reactions, questions, confirmations and objections. However, in his later years, Kahn increasingly received only reverent silence, and it is indeed ironic that, exactly at the time he was engaged in constructing buildings of unparalleled precision and order, Kahn began to gain the reputation of being a mystic. In this, the most important event was very probably Kahn's discovery of, and discovery by, the deeply spiritual tradition of the Indian subcontinent. As noted by Brownlee and De Long, 'In mystical, timeless India, Kahn discovered that the unchanging essence he sought in all things seemed to lie closer to the surface, and he was in turn discovered by Indian admirers who were immediately receptive to his way of looking at the world. For the rest of his life, Indian students flocked to the University of Pennsylvania to study in his master's studio … Doshi spoke for many of them when he said, "Lou appeared to me a Yogin" [a yogi or guru]'.[116] Yet Kahn was no mystical, detached figure – quite the opposite, Kahn had a five-fingered grasp of reality unmatched by any contemporary architect. As Scully has perceptively noted, 'Certainly it was better at the beginning at Yale when students were questioning him, than later when they took him as a great guru. That is not good for anybody; it was bad for Frank Lloyd Wright, and it was bad for Kahn. Lou was as far from being mystic as you can get … [Kahn's teaching and work] in a fundamental way is very realistic.'[117]

82. Louis Kahn (centre) during a review of his graduate studio at the University of Pennsylvania, c.1972; Robert Le Ricolais is on Kahn's right.

Unbuilt offerings: in the spaces of eternity

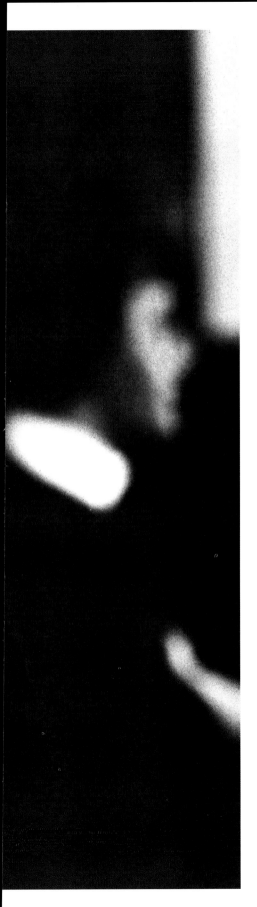

I do not believe that beauty can be deliberately created. Beauty evolves out of a will to be that has its first expression in the archaic. Compare Paestum with the Parthenon. Archaic Paestum is the beginning. It is the time when the walls parted and the columns became and when Music entered architecture. Paestum inspired the Parthenon. The Parthenon is considered more beautiful, but Paestum is still more beautiful to me. It presents a beginning within which is contained all the wonder that may follow in its wake.[1] LOUIS KAHN

Architecture is unquestionably among the most difficult of disciplines, balanced as it is between the incommensurable demands of art and science, and being the most public of acts, requiring the participation of many to realize, yet often originating in a single individual's poetic vision. Even so, the number of unrealized designs among Louis Kahn's total commissions is unusually high, and their quality is simply staggering. In fact, if we evaluate only Kahn's unrealized designs, they constitute one of the most significant contributions to twentieth-century architecture.[2] To name only the more important, beginning with the Trenton Jewish Community Center, the US Consulate in Angola, the Salk Institute Meeting House, the 'Interama' Community, the Dominican Motherhouse, the University of Virginia Chemistry Building, the Kansas City Office Tower; along with the five projects to be examined in this chapter, we have altogether twelve major unbuilt designs of equal importance to the twelve major built works already presented.

Architectural historians and critics have generally tended to ignore unbuilt designs, yet, as we have seen, it was in the unrealized projects that Kahn first evolved the fundamental concepts that would later form the foundations for his famous built works. Kahn's own attitude towards his unrealized works was one of unfailing optimism: 'That which is not built is not really lost. Once its value is established, its demand for presence is undeniable. It is merely waiting for the right circumstances.'[3] By studying these great designs, only by chance and circumstance never realized, we may understand the magnitude of Kahn's vision of architecture as a new beginning in our time.

Previous page Sanctuary, Hurva Synagogue, Jerusalem, Israel, 1967–74, first and definitive scheme. This computer reconstruction shows the view from the top of the stairs through the centre of the sanctuary.
1. Louis Kahn during a lecture and discussion with students, University of Pennsylvania, c.1970.

Mikveh Israel Synagogue
Philadelphia Pennsylvania
1961–72
Unbuilt

In May 1961 Louis Kahn was commissioned to design the Mikveh Israel Synagogue, and he assisted the congregation in selecting the splendid site in the historic city of Philadelphia: on the Christ's Church Walk, and adjacent to Independence Mall on the west, and the Friends Meeting House on the east (p. 401; d). From the very beginning, Kahn felt strongly that the various types of use – the study of scripture, the community social gatherings and the rituals of worship (housing small numbers of worshippers in daily services and large numbers on high holy days) – should be housed in separate spaces of differing character.[1] While there are at least ten complete designs by Kahn for the Mikveh Israel Synagogue, four major schemes may be identified; the fifth scheme, which was completed ten years later, should be considered separately, for it was developed by Kahn in response to a radically changed brief and a new building committee.

2

Kahn's first proposal, dating to before April 1962, again starts with the square (p. 400; a). He locates the square sanctuary on the eastern street, to be entered from a narrow court at the middle of the site through a square entry hall, with the square daily chapel at the exact centre of the site, the square museum on the western edge – on Independence Mall – and the school and social spaces set between. A continuing characteristic of these various elements of the design is the manner in which they exist somewhat independently on the site, which in effect has 'fronts' on all four sides. The second major scheme (p. 400; b), dating from June 1962, joined the square sanctuary and the double-square entry hall – flanked by Kiddush and history rooms – in a rectangular block, with a larger courtyard opened at the centre of the site, framed by the sanctuary entry on the east, the chapel on the west, a permanent sukkah structure to the north and a garden to the south. The school and social spaces were placed on the western end of the site, separated from Independence Mall by a walled garden.

Kahn's third scheme (p. 400; c), dating from August 1962, marks the emergence of his light chamber concept for Mikveh Israel, continuing his contemporary preoccupation with the light-giving and shadow-making layered building facade of the Salk Institute Meeting House. He proposed enclosing the square sanctuary and its adjoining entry hall, Kiddush and history rooms, as well as the separate square chapel, with regularly spaced cylindrical light towers. Kahn conceived of these cylinders as being integral, rather than additive, to the sanctuary space, as indicated by the plan being ordered on a grid of circles, defined by the diameter of the cylinders. The cylinders are centred on the rectangular bounding wall, which splits them exactly in the middle, so that half the cylinder stands outside the sanctuary, and half stands within, and they were to be opened, inside and out, with vertical, rectangular apertures. Sections indicate that Kahn intended the portions of the cylinders that fall outside the square sanctuary walls to stand on the elevated floor of the sanctuary and not to reach the ground. As experienced, from outside one would have clearly seen the square inner form of the sanctuary where the building met the ground, and the cylindrical light towers would have appeared to lift off the earth, rising into the light of the sky.

The fourth major scheme for Mikveh Israel, dating from October 1962 and refined over the following year, has rightly been considered Kahn's final and definitive design. The sanctuary is housed in a double-walled octagonal volume, lengthened along the east–west axis of the site, its corners defined by eight 20 foot (6 metre) diameter cylindrical light towers, or 'window-rooms', as Kahn called them.[5] The spaces of the light towers, together with the outer double walls, are connected to form the ambulatory that rings the sanctuary. The ark is located between the two light towers at the eastern end, with seating stepping up to the north and south, and two cylindrical towers joining with the two at the western end of the sanctuary to define the square entry hall.[6] The square chapel, also defined by four cylindrical light towers, forms the entry court with the sanctuary. The school and multi-purpose social space are housed in an L-shaped block at the western end of the site, into the solid-walled volumes of which four cylindrical light courts, which Kahn

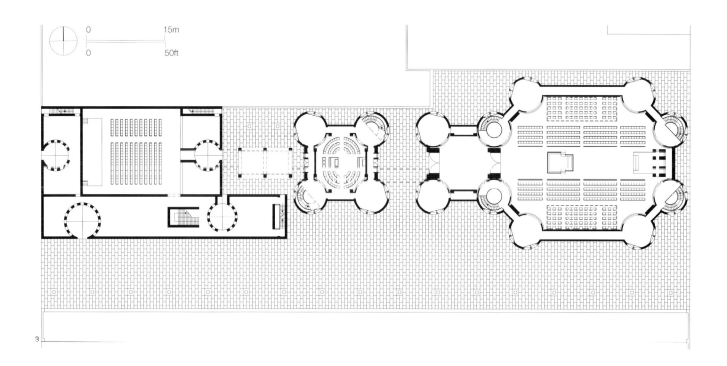

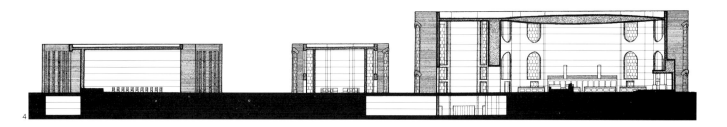

3. Plan of the Mikveh Israel Synagogue, fourth and definitive scheme, 1962–3; redrawn under author's supervision.

4. East-west section of the Mikveh Israel Synagogue, looking north, fourth and definitive scheme, 1962–3; redrawn under author's supervision.

5. (Opposite) Computer reconstruction of the sanctuary, Mikveh Israel Synagogue, fourth and definitive scheme, 1962–3.

called 'exterior roofless rooms', have been carved.[7] The entire site is paved in stone, initially set in a simple running bond pattern, and later proposed by Harriet Pattison to be set in concentric arcs around the cylindrical light towers.[8]

Seen from the exterior, the Mikveh Israel would have appeared remarkably like a castle in overall mass and form, its cylindrical light chambers built of cast-in-place reinforced concrete and clad on their exterior surfaces with brick (p. 402; f & g). The influence in this design of Kahn's 1959 trip to the cathedral of Albi and the town of Carcassonne, and his many sketches of their cylindrical outer masonry towers, may be recognized.[9] Kahn intended that we would first move into the entry hall, defined by four close-set cylindrical light chambers, beyond which the space of the sanctuary expanded both horizontally and vertically. The concrete-walled sanctuary was to be surrounded by the cylindrical concrete light chambers, into which sunlight would fall, and which would in turn be the sole source of light for the space within. The inner wall of the ambulatory would combine with the

7

cylindrical light rooms to create a double wall, a layering of surfaces between the city outside and the inner world of the sanctuary. The light that reached the sanctuary through the unglazed apertures of the cylindrical light chambers would bring no views, and was introduced equally from all sides, as if to indicate that solar orientation is somehow irrelevant to what goes on within, resulting in a space detached from its surroundings, floating in a sea of light (p. 403; i).

This sense of distance and suspension in light within the sanctuary would have been increased when we perceived that the ceiling of the sanctuary is remarkably ambiguous in terms of how it is structured, for the smooth-surfaced ceiling has no beams or other visible structure. Together, the ceiling and roof create an elliptical section, the ceiling forming a convex curve down into the sanctuary space as the roof forms a convex curve above (p. 403; j). This elliptical curving surface occurs in an oval-shaped portion of the ceiling which just touches the inner faces of the eight cylindrical light towers, and the ceiling and roof are flat all around the outer edges of the sanctuary (p. 402; h). While this elliptical roof section is clearly related to Le Corbusier's Ronchamp Chapel (also visited by Kahn on that 1959 trip), other precursors come to mind, particularly late Baroque churches, in their contrapuntal use of concave and convex curves, elliptical and cylindrical forms, and in their deployment of double-skin layered walls and sunlight-reflecting chambers. Finally, and perhaps most intriguingly, the structural ambiguity of the main space is remarkably like the Meeting Houses of the North American Shaker

8

communities of the eighteenth and nineteenth centuries, which often have large smooth ceilings with no beams or other visible means of support.

To clarify their sole purpose as light sources, Kahn made the cylindrical towers independent of the rest of the structure, and supported the roof on the sections of flat wall between the cylinders. Kahn indicates this independence of the cylindrical towers by providing a thin vertical slot between the outer surface of the cylinder and the neighbouring flat walls, allowing us to perceive the convex outside form, the inside of which is filled with light, and its separation from the flat walls to either side (p. 403; k). In experience, the serenity of the sanctuary would have been complemented by the labyrinthine quality of the ambulatory, neither inside nor outside, where narrow passages lead to the perforated, cylindrical chambers, the

6. (Previous page) Computer reconstruction of the entry hall into the sanctuary, Mikveh Israel Synagogue, fourth and definitive scheme, 1962–3.
7. (Previous page) Computer reconstruction of the sanctuary, Mikveh Israel Synagogue, fourth and definitive scheme, 1962–3.
8. Computer reconstruction of view from within the cylindrical light tower and stair, looking towards the sanctuary, Mikveh Israel Synagogue, fourth and definitive scheme, 1962–3.

arches of which curve both downwards and upwards, flooded with ever-changing sunlight and shadow patterns.

These habitable, light-filled hollow, shell-like concrete cylinders and the undulating walls and ceiling of the sanctuary were the closest Kahn ever came to achieving a modern reinterpretation of his beloved Roman ruins. We are again reminded of Frank Brown's 1961 descriptions of Roman buildings, similar to what Kahn would have heard as they walked together through Rome in 1950:

> The appropriate figure of each spatial concavity was directly reflected in the curved or straight contours of the exterior'; '... the ellipse. The unprecedented design of multifocal bowl and evasively curving shell defied clear definition from a particular viewpoint'; '... toward complete enclosure of space by curved surfaces ... The spaces they achieved by these means, though variform, were serenely bubble-like in volume and equilibrium. They were so proportioned to clasp the activity they enveloped in a calmly finite encirclement ... Space, above and at either hand, closed equidistantly about man at the center ... Light from high, in or under vaults, articulated volume supplely by brilliance and sharp shadow or by the shimmer of reflections and veils of shade.[10]

In 1972, an entirely new brief was presented to Kahn for the Mikveh Israel, essentially reversing all the priorities set by the original committee and embodied in Kahn's design. The new brief required the combination of all the sacred rituals and social functions into one chamber, which was also to house an expanded museum programme – effectively meaning, for Kahn, that 'the synagogue will not be built'.[11] Kahn struggled valiantly to make a sacred place out of these new programmatic requirements, and his designs are quite ingenious (p. 401; e), yet in the end it was a futile effort, for Kahn believed that the fundamental nature of the institution was no longer being honoured. The failure to realize the Mikveh Israel Synagogue project, upon which he worked for almost a dozen years, was one of the greatest disappointments of Kahn's entire career.[12]

Mikveh Israel Synagogue

Concept development

Kahn developed four major schemes for the Mikveh Israel Synagogue (plans for all four stages, and a fifth that followed ten years later, are shown here). Each scheme articulated his conception of different programme activities being housed in separate, independent structures, together forming an institutional campus within the city. While each volume presented a facade to the city, all were to be entered from a shared central court. To create an appropriate distance from the activity of the adjacent street, Kahn proposed enveloping the synagogue in a thick double wall, placing a series of cylindrical light towers around the perimeter of the plan that closely resembled the medieval walled town of Carcassonne. Sunlight would enter from outside, bouncing off the inside of these curved walls, and then enter the sanctuary, giving the sense that the worshippers within were literally suspended in light. Kahn designed the roof structure so that it thickened at the centre, forming in the sanctuary an elliptical, convex, downward-sloping ceiling intended to catch the light, which showed the continued influence on Kahn of Le Corbusier's Ronchamp Chapel, 1950–54. The development of the light towers, hollow roof and ceiling structures that enclose the sanctuary is detailed overleaf on pages 402–3.

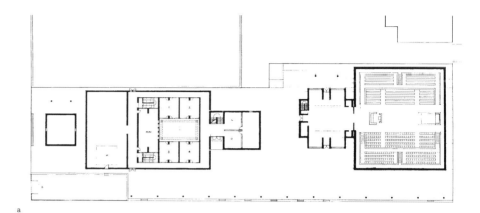

a

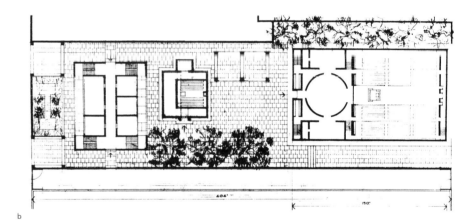

b

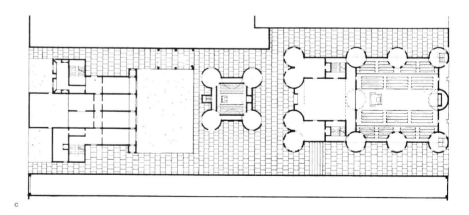

c

a. Plan of the Mikveh Israel Synagogue, first scheme, March 1962 (north at top); the daily chapel is on the second floor, directly over the square volume at the centre of the site.
b. Plan of the second scheme, June 1962 (north at top); the daily chapel is set at ground level, slightly west of the centre of the site, axially aligned with the main sanctuary to the east.
c. Plan of the third scheme, August 1962 (north at top). In this scheme Kahn first introduces cylindrical light chambers at the periphery of the two main spaces.

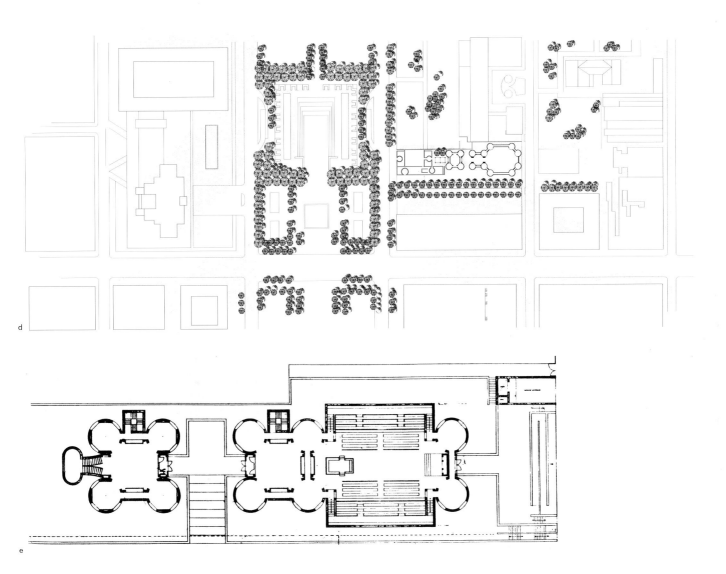

d

e

d. Site plan of the fourth and definitive scheme showing
Independence Mall, left, the Friends Meeting House,
right, and Christ's Church Walk, below (north at top);
redrawn under author's supervision.
e. Plan of the fifth scheme, 1972. Ten years after the
fourth scheme, a new building committee presented
Kahn with a new brief – a more secular interpretation
of the programme. Due to this radical change in the
nature of the building, Kahn felt this scheme lacked
the conviction of earlier schemes.

FIFTH STREET ELEVATION

INDEPENDENCE MALL URBAN RENEWAL AREA-UNIT 3, PARCEL 14-DEVELOPER CONGREGATION MIKVEH ISRAEL EXHIBIT **E**

f

CHRIST CHURCH MALL ELEVATION

INDEPENDENCE MALL URBAN RENEWAL AREA UNIT 3 PARCEL 14 DEVELOPER CONGREGATION MIKVEH ISRAEL EXHIBIT **D**

g

NOTE:
SHADED AREA INDICATES FLAT
PORTION OF CEILING WITHIN THE
SANCTUARY

LIGHTING LAYOUT
MIKVEH
21 JULY 65

h

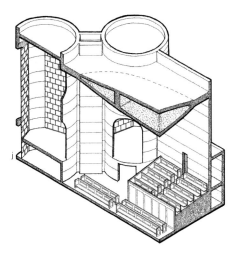

f & g. Elevation studies, Mikveh Israel Synagogue, fourth and definitive scheme, 1962–3; the cast-in-place concrete structure is clad in brick.

h. Lighting layout for the sanctuary, fourth and definitive scheme, showing the elliptical downward-curving ceiling; the flat areas around the edges are shaded.

i. Perspective sketch of the sanctuary interior, fourth and definitive scheme; drawing by Kahn.

j. Cut-away axonometric section showing the elliptical downward-curving ceiling and upward-curving roof structure of the sanctuary, fourth and definitive scheme; drawn under author's supervision.

k. Perspective sketch of the sanctuary, fourth and definitive scheme; drawing by Kahn. Note the vertical slots of light between the flat and curved wall sections.

Memorial to the Six Million Jewish Martyrs
New York City
1966–72
Unbuilt

Kahn first became involved in the Committee for the Six Million, the umbrella organization that inherited the twenty-year effort to build a Holocaust memorial in New York City, in 1966, and the following year, based on the recommendation of Philip Johnson, Kahn was offered the commission to design the Memorial.[13] The site, originally in Riverside Park, was now to be in Battery Park, at the southern end of Manhattan Island (p. 410; a), with a spectacular view of the Statue of Liberty and Ellis Island, which, along with Fort Clinton, directly to the north of the site, had served as the primary arrival and processing centres for immigrants coming to the United States.

From the very beginning, Kahn believed the Memorial should be built of glass, a decision, as Susan Solomon has noted, that 'instantly divorced his work from previous Holocaust memorials, which had been designed for execution in stone, metal, or concrete'.[14]

As Kahn related in a written press release, the committee 'decided that the Artist of the Memorial should express its meaning without pictorial representation', and Kahn intended to employ glass as the primary material for its luminous quality – its ability both to transmit light and cast sun-filled shadows.[15] He added that the views from the site of 'Ellis Island, Castle Garden, the Statue of Liberty – did much to inspire the use of glass, the sense of dematerialization to allow all of these symbolic structures, and all the life around, to enter the Monument'.[16]

Kahn once again started with the square. In this instance, the plan would remain a square and the Memorial formed of square structures throughout the project. Kahn's early studies all involved square glass pylons or piers, arranged on a raised plinth, and among his sketches are plans for four piers (2 x 2), nine piers (3 x 3) and sixteen piers (4 x 4), as well as various plans where one larger pier at the centre is surrounded and enclosed by various wall-like pier clusters (p. 410; b). Kahn's first drafted plan, similar to the 'garden' of piers he had proposed for the Salk Institute Meeting House, is composed of thirteen piers, four L-shaped clusters of three tall narrow piers at each corner, framing the larger central pier.

Kahn initially intended that the piers be solid glass castings. In September 1967, during the period when he was evolving his first designs, he visited the Corning glass factory in northern New York to learn more about the manufacture of the piers, and to ascertain whether Corning could supply the glass elements for the Memorial.[17] Kahn discovered that the annealing time required for proper heating and cooling of the cast glass in monolithic blocks of the size he was contemplating would be far too long to be feasible, and he decided to employ cast glass units, similar to masonry. Kahn's sketchbook contains notes on the various colours ('lead – yellow, iron – green') imparted by the glass mixture (he notes a preference for a 'pale straw' colour); the maximum sizing of the cast glass blocks ('6 inches x 6 inches x 6 feet' [15 x 15 centimetres x 1.8 metres]); and the best methods for grinding and finishing the surfaces ('not optical precision; ground with rouge or pumice on a flat sand bed, to prevent point loading') (p. 411; e).[18] After returning from this visit, Kahn stated his intention 'to create the appropriate combination of glass science and art to give those who enter the Monument a sense of containment, yet allow the sense of play of light around it'.[19]

In November 1967, Kahn presented his first and purest design for the Memorial (p. 410; c). The plan consisted of nine glass piers, each 12 feet (3.7 metres) square and 15 feet (4.6 metres) tall, arranged on a 60 foot (18 metre) square plinth in three rows of three, with the space between the piers equal to their dimension (12 feet), solid edges formed by thick, low walls, and entered on the diagonal up stairs at the four corners. As Kahn noted, the Memorial, though bi-axially symmetrical, was not entered on its central axes: 'The Monument was conceived of light created by nine piers arranged in a square without ritualistic direction'.[20] This closely parallels Kahn's exactly contemporary description of the Pantheon as 'a non-directional space, where only inspired worship can take place. Ordained ritual would have no place.'

9. Perspective sketch of the Memorial to the Six Million Jewish Martyrs, final scheme, spring 1968; drawing by Louis Kahn.

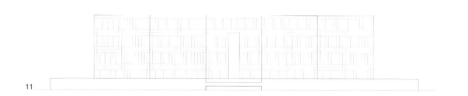

11

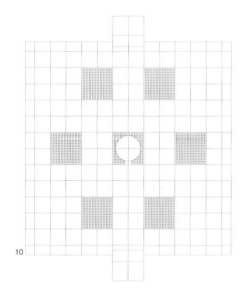

10

Kahn goes on to say of the Pantheon: 'The light is so strong as to feel its cut',[21] and one is struck by the thought that Kahn conceived of the cast glass as frozen or solidified light, cut and shaped into masonry blocks. It would be several years until, inspired by the artist Barnett Newman's description of 'divine light flaming into matter'[22] and by its source in Dante's *Paradiso*, where Beatrice tells how matter is made out of light,[23] Kahn would fully articulate his late conception of the relationship between light and material: 'This prevailing luminous source can be visualized as becoming a wild dance of flame which settles and spends itself into a material. Material, I believe, is spent light.'[24]

This first scheme was not approved, and in fact caused a major argument among the members of the Committee due to its unintended numerical symbolism. The number nine is equated, by Talmudic scholars, with the nine months of childbirth, a joyful event, and was thus seen as inappropriate to a Holocaust memorial. While Kahn had avoided any representation in his first design, he now acceded to what he termed 'the prevailing desire to give the Monument a sense of the ritualistic',[25] and changed from the geometrically perfect nine to seven piers, six piers around the centre to represent the six million lost, and one pier at the centre as a chapel. The central pier, or chapel, 'is to be inscribed. The six piers around the centre, of equal dimensions, are not inscribed. The one then, the chapel, speaks; the other six are silent.'[26] This definitive plan is again based upon a five-by-five bay grid, with the seven piers set in a 2-3-2 pattern, north to south, and a 1-2-1-2-1 pattern, east to west. The six cubic piers were to be solid glass, with the seventh glass pier, or chapel, provided with a small interior space, which Kahn initially proposed as square, a rotated square, and finally as a circle, creating a cylindrical room, with a conical-shaped ceiling under the flat roof.

Kahn describes his definitive design, developed in the spring of 1968:
The six and one stand on a granite base, sixty-six feet by sixty-six feet square, high enough to sit on the edge. Each glass pier is ten feet by ten feet square and eleven feet high. The space separating each pier is equal to the dimension of the pier itself. The piers are constructed

with solid blocks of glass placed one over the other without the use of mortar, reminiscent of how the Greeks laid their solid marble blocks in their temples.[27]

Kahn's references in this description, to both geometry and construction, are quite precise: the dimensions of the plinth, 66 feet (20 metres) square, are an exact match for the outer dimensions of Wright's Unity Temple; and the small protruding cylindrical pins and mating holes used to stabilize and lock together the mortar-less glass block masonry units are identical to those employed by the ancient Greeks in the construction of their marble temples.

'The top of each pier is sealed with thin layers of lead set into specially moulded joints', Kahn noted, going on to describe the effect of the woven bonding pattern of slab-like, cast glass blocks, which were to be laid so as to create an interlocking set of walls within each cubic pier, sufficient to

10. Plan of the Memorial to the Six Million Jewish Martyrs showing seven piers with central entries, final scheme, spring 1968; redrawn under author's supervision.

11. North elevation (the south is identical), above, and east elevation (the west is identical), below, Memorial to the Six Million Jewish Martyrs, final scheme, spring 1968; redrawn under author's supervision.

12. Computer reconstruction of the Memorial to the Six Million Jewish Martyrs with New York harbour beyond, final scheme, spring 1968.

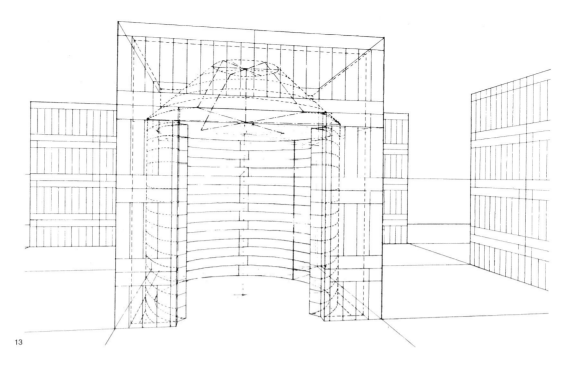

13

14

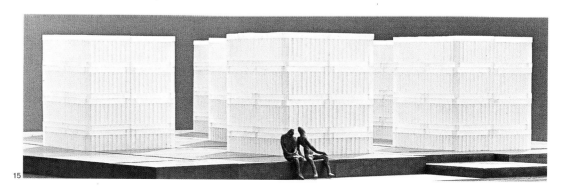

15

support the special layer of glass blocks at the top: 'The entire construction in depth will be evident as one looks through each pier and through the entire composition of piers' (p. 411; d).[28] The carefully crafted model Kahn had made of this design, and his numerous perspective studies, indicate that Kahn intended to exploit cast glass fully for 'its quality of material presence', where the non-optical polish would impart a non-reflecting quality to the matt surfaces,[29] and the thickness of the castings would create cloudy depths, all of which would transmit glowing and layered shadows of the internal woven pattern of the blocks – as much translucent as transparent, and providing the pale, coloured shadow only possible with glass; as Kahn described it: 'yet the sun could come through and leave a shadow yet filled with light'.[30]

As befitting the sober purpose of the Memorial, Kahn's design was perhaps his most sublime. The massive and yet ghostly translucence of the cast glass blocks and piers would have combined the dichotomous qualities of solid and fragile, heavy and light, depth and surface, anchored and ethereal, permanent and ephemeral, all made possible through Kahn's engagement of the nature of glass – at once the physically heaviest and visually lightest of building materials, allowing light to pass through, irrespective of thickness. And yet the Memorial would also have completely merged with its place and with nature, as Kahn described it: 'The Monument will get its mood from the endless changes of the light of day and of night, the seasons of the year, and the endless play of the weather, and even the sudden light of a flash of lightning. The drama of movement on the river will transmit its life to the Monument.'[31]

13. Perspective drawing of the Memorial to the Six Million Jewish Martyrs, final scheme, spring 1968; the hollow glass central chapel pier is surrounded by six solid piers.
14. Plexiglas model of the hollow glass central chapel pier with inscriptions, Memorial to the Six Million Jewish Martyrs, final scheme, spring 1968.
15. Plexiglas model of the Memorial to the Six Million Jewish Martyrs, final scheme, spring 1968.

Memorial to the Six Million Jewish Martyrs

Concept development

The Memorial is one of Kahn's most powerful designs due to his combination of primary geometries with cast glass – a material that has the capacity to be at once ethereal and massive, the whole filled with light. Kahn employed the square throughout, both for the overall plan of the plinth and for the form of the individual cast glass piers, as seen in his designs on these pages. His earliest design of November 1967 was his purest – nine glass piers, each 12 foot (3.7 metres) square and set 12 feet (3.7 metres) apart, a symmetrical design not to be entered on symmetrical axis, as Kahn said, 'without ritualistic direction' and similar to the Pantheon in Rome. Kahn's final design of spring 1968 consisted of seven piers, six of them solid, one for each million martyrs, and the seventh, central pier containing a cylindrical chapel-like space with inscriptions etched into its inner surface. Kahn's intention was that the piers would have non-reflective surfaces and that they would be as much translucent as transparent in their depths, an effect better represented by Kahn's own Plexiglas models than by recent digital reconstructions.

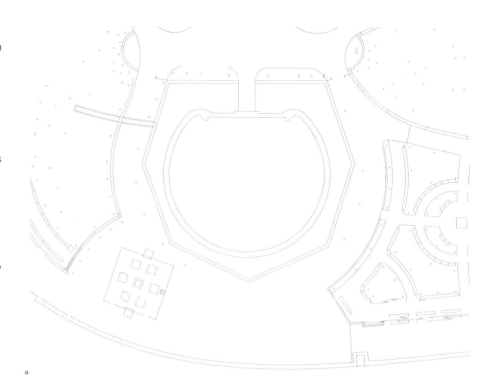

a

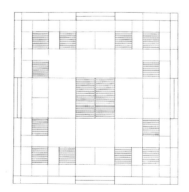

c

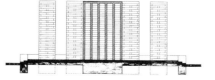

b

a. Site plan of the Memorial to the Six Million Jewish Martyrs, final scheme, spring 1968 (north is 45 degrees up and to left); redrawn under author's supervision. This plan shows the Memorial on the left at the edge of New York harbour, with the historic Fort Clinton in the centre.
b. Early elevation, plan and section of the Memorial, 1967.
c. Plan view of the model of the first scheme, November 1967, showing nine glass piers with corner entries.

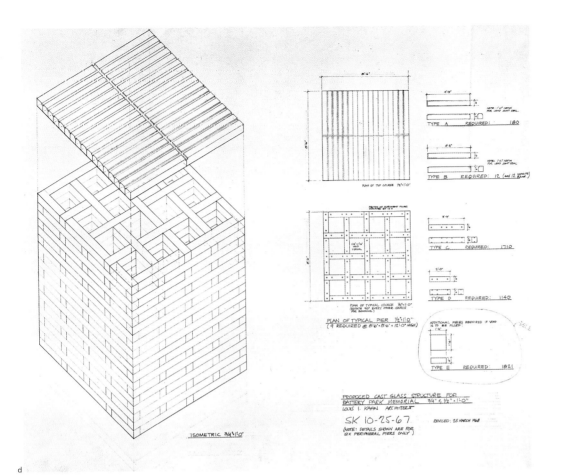

ISOMETRIC 3/4"=1'0"

PLAN OF TOP COURSE 3/8"=1'0"

TYPE A   REQUIRED: 180

TYPE B   REQUIRED: 12 (and 12 ...)

TYPE C   REQUIRED: 1710

TYPE D   REQUIRED: 1140

PLAN OF TYPICAL PIER   3/8"=1'0"
(9 REQUIRED @ 8'6"x 8'6" x 12'0" HIGH)

ADDITIONAL PIECES REQUIRED IF VOID IS TO BE FILLED

TYPE E   REQUIRED: 1821

PROPOSED CAST GLASS STRUCTURE FOR
BATTERY PARK MEMORIAL   3/4" & 1/2" = 1'-0"
LOUIS I. KAHN   ARCHITECT
SK 10-25-67   REVISED: 25 MARCH 1968
(NOTE: DETAILS SHOWN ARE FOR
SIX PERIPHERAL PIERS ONLY)

d. Isometric study, roof plan and plan of one
glass pier showing glass brick stacking,
25 October 1967.

e. Sketch plan of a glass pier, from Kahn's
sketchbook with notes made during a visit
to Corning Glass Company, September 1967.
On the same page, Kahn made notes on the
pale yellow colour and non-optical polish
finish he intended for the Memorial.

e

Hurva Synagogue
Jerusalem, Israel
1967–74
Unbuilt

The commission to design a new Hurva Synagogue for Jerusalem was in many ways for Kahn a dream come true, a chance to build a monument to join the ancient ruins which had so inspired him throughout his life. The Synagogue, called Hurva, 'ruin' in Hebrew, had occupied a prominent site on a hilltop to the west of the Temple Mount, with its Western Wall, upon which were located the Muslim Dome of the Rock Mosque and the Christian Church of the Holy Sepulchre, two of the most important religious monuments in the world. Originally built at the beginning of the eighteenth century and demolished shortly after, resulting in its name, the Hurva was

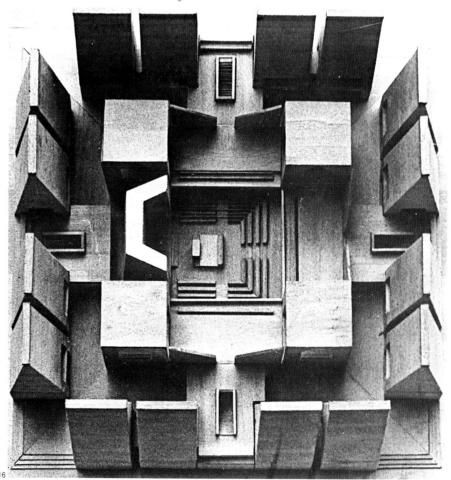

rebuilt in the nineteenth century, only to be destroyed again in 1948 during the war that led to the founding of the modern state of Israel. In 1967, the Israeli architect, Ram Karmi, was approached to build a new synagogue on the site of the previous Hurva, but he insisted that Kahn be offered the commission. Karmi's sister, Ada Karmi-Melamede, an architect who would later be a visiting professor at the University of Pennsylvania, travelled to Philadelphia with the property owner, Yaacov Solomon, to urge Kahn to accept the commission.[32] The Hurva Synagogue was now seen as a chance to place a great Jewish religious structure among the existing monuments, and the mayor of Jerusalem, Teddy Kollek, became in effect Kahn's client for this project.

Kahn developed his design for the Hurva Synagogue with uncharacteristic speed – he seemed quite certain, from the very start, what the building wanted to be. The plan both started as and remained a square in overall form, with a smaller square building set within it; as Kahn said, 'The new building should itself consist of two buildings – an outer one, and an inner one, giving the effect of a separate but related building.' The outer building, 'which would absorb the light and heat of the sun', was composed of sixteen enormous battered pylons, each 60 feet (18 metres) tall and 16 feet (4.9 metres) square in plan. Within, a 10 foot (3 metre) square niche or room, 'where candle services will be sung',[33] was to be built of massive blocks of Jerusalem stone, the warm, golden-coloured stone out of which the major historical monuments of the city were constructed. Entry occurred at the four open corners, up corner stairs and through the narrow spaces – initially only 4 feet (1.2 metres) wide, later enlarged to 7 feet (2.1 metres) – between the enormous pylons.

As Kahn described it, 'The inner building would be a single chamber, resting on four points', four hollow, square, room-sized piers which rise to 32 feet (9.7 metres) in height, then open to form four square, inverted pyramid, umbrella-like, thin shell roofs overhead, 50 feet (15 metres) tall, separated by narrow slots.[34] This inner building was to be built of reinforced concrete, providing shade and cool, so that 'the interior will be rather silver in colour'.[35] As Kent Larson has noted, Kahn carefully mixed and formed the concrete used in his buildings to give it the depth and colour of stone, imparting a 'patina of the ancient'.[36] These four upside-down pyramidal umbrella roof shells formed a rotated square overhead, and the plan itself is ordered and proportioned through a series of rotating squares.[37] From within, one would be able to see the sky and city through the spaces between the pylons, and in Kahn's words, 'the spaces between them will be such as to allow a sufficient amount of light to enter from the outer chamber, and completely surrounding the inner chamber, there will be an ambulatory from which people will also be able to witness a service taking place in the inner chamber. The construction of the building is like the large leaves of a tree, allowing light to filter into the interior'.[38]

In this design for the Hurva Synagogue Kahn synthesized an astonishing number of elements, both from his own work and from his favoured precedents. First must be noted the fact that, with its enormous battered pylons creating U-shaped facades protecting the separate and more open inner

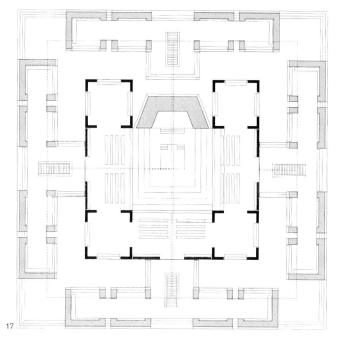
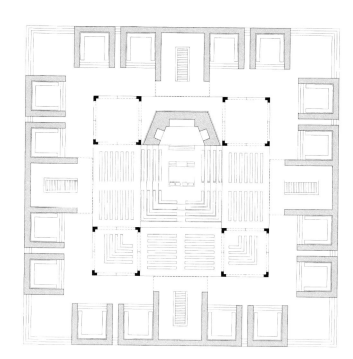

17

0   15m

0   50ft

17. Plans of the Hurva Synagogue, showing the chapel and mezzanine on the upper floor (left), and the entry and sanctuary on the ground floor (right), first and definitive scheme, 1967–9; redrawn under author's supervision.
18. Section of Hurva Synagogue, first and definitive scheme, 1967–9; redrawn under author's supervision. Solid black indicates concrete and cross-hatched grey indicates masonry.
19. Computer reconstruction of perspective section, Hurva Synagogue, first and definitive scheme, 1967–9.

building, the Hurva Synagogue project, proposed for one of the holiest sites in Jerusalem, is paradoxically and yet unequivocally related to Kahn's beloved Egyptian temples, documented in his powerful pastel sketches from 1951 of the temples at Edfu and Luxor (p. 422; b). The massive masonry outer walls receiving the sunlight; the tapered ceiling form; the small lines of light falling from above; and the 'non-directional space, where only inspired worship can take place', are undoubtedly related to the Pantheon, Kahn's favourite reference – one he made even more explicit in the third version of the Hurva Synagogue in 1973, where he opened a square oculus at the centre of the sanctuary roof. The Romanesque church at Périgueux, with its hollow, free-standing clusters of four piers supporting the roof vaults, drawn in Choisy's *Histoire* (p. 422; a), was also evidently related to Kahn's design. Wright's Unity Temple is again present in Kahn's thinking, not only in the general plan form of cruciform and square but also in precise dimensions, such as the Hurva Synagogue's 32 foot (9.5 metre) square central chamber and the 64 foot (19 metre) square of the sanctuary and balconies, both of which exactly match the inside edge dimensions of the equivalent spaces in Unity Temple.

During the design of the Hurva Synagogue Kahn also investigated a directly related precedent for this project, the ancient Temple of Solomon. In addition to requesting materials on the origins of the synagogue from the Jewish Theological Seminary in New York,[39] and revisiting his friend Henry Kamphoefner's book *Churches and Temples*,[40] Kahn very probably studied the speculative reconstruction of Solomon's Temple illustrated in his own copy of James Fergusson's *History of Architecture* of 1883 (p. 422; c). The upper level plan of this version of Solomon's Temple indicates that the most sacred, inner chamber was square in plan, with four large columns standing in the space, and that this was surrounded by a

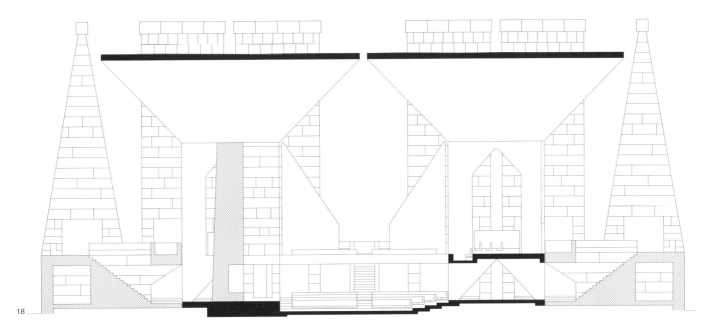

18

19

sequence of smaller square rooms, built within thick masonry walls and linked to form an ambulatory around the central space. [41]

From his own work, Kahn's larger concept of wrapping ruins around buildings as a way of reducing the sun's glare and heat, while at the same time creating a deeply shadowed realm within the building, is clearly evidenced in the Hurva Synagogue; Kahn called this concept 'a natural architecture of Jerusalem'. [42] More specifically, Kahn's early scheme for the First Unitarian Church, where four concrete umbrella roof structures were supported by four, four-column clusters, the whole surrounded by an outer thick masonry

shading wall split by thin vertical slots, is perhaps the most direct source for the Hurva Synagogue within Kahn's own work; it is intriguing to note that in 1961 Kahn said that the four-umbrella roof scheme 'was really a truer expression' of the original concept than what he actually built at Rochester.[43]

The inverted pyramidal forms of the concrete-shell roofs is yet another employment by Kahn of this fundamental Egyptian geometry, which Kahn invariably reinterpreted by placing it overhead, as in the Yale Art Gallery and the Jewish Community Center. When assembled to form the central sanctuary space, these folded shells are split by a line of light down the centre and apex of the space, in a manner clearly related to the Kimbell Art Museum, and its 'silvery light'. The dimensions of the central sanctuary space, 32 feet (9.5 metres) square and 50 feet (15 metres) tall, are identical to the contemporary design for the central entry hall of Exeter Library. Finally, the manner of the construction of the Hurva Synagogue – the masonry outer square building, formed as four independent volumes each composed of rectangular linked chambers, surrounding the top-lit square central concrete building – and the entry at the open corners between the masonry buildings are both directly derived from Kahn's Exeter Library.

Kahn's beautifully articulated and rendered section drawing and site plan, and the large clay site model (p. 422; d), all indicate the fundamental importance of the historic urban context. Jerusalem is a city which feels deeply rooted to its place, and this is reflected in the strongly topographic aspects of Kahn's section drawing, which begins at the far left by slicing through the centre of the Hurva Synagogue, and then following the fall of the land

20. Model of the Hurva Synagogue showing narrow corner entry between pylons, first and definitive scheme, 1967–9.
21. Model of the Hurva Synagogue with the central axis closed at ground level, the corner entries to the left and right, sixteen exterior masonry pylons and four interior concrete roof shells, first and definitive scheme, 1967–9.

to the east until it meets the Western Wall, above which Kahn anchors the right side with the faint profile of the Dome of the Rock. In the site plan, only the Western Wall and those spaces to its west, connecting to the Hurva, are rendered. The top of Temple Mount and the adjacent neighbourhoods around the Hurva are left without shadow, clearly indicating the importance to Kahn of the exterior spaces around the Western Wall, which he considered the true centre of the site, joining the Hurva to the Temple Mount. Kahn's extensive proposals for the area immediately around the Western Wall, not part of the Hurva site, reveal his simultaneous involvement in the deliberations of the Jerusalem Committee, a seventy-member group, including his friends Fuller, Johnson, Noguchi and Mumford, which was advising the city in matters of urban planning and preservation.[44]

Seen as one approached, the massive pairs of pylons would have been truly monumental, announcing what Mayor Kollek called a 'world synagogue'.[45] Connecting his project to its context through the way it was made, Kahn planned to emulate the enormous stonework of the ancient foundations of the city: 'I intend to use the same stone as the stones of the Western Wall, large, not small stones, rather as large as you can get, as monolithic looking as possible.'[46] Squeezing between these pylons at the corners, where the narrow 5 foot (1.5 metre) opening would require that we enter one at a time, we would come into the travertine-floored

ambulatory space, with the inner faces of the pylons marching off to either side. The masonry pylons are gently sloped outwards, and the concrete pier-rooms rise from the corners and open out into pyramidal roofs which angle sharply outwards at a steep 45 degree angle, coming within only 2 feet (0.6 metres) of the pylons. Within this astonishing ambulatory space, the sun would have played off these two massive structures, the pyramidal concrete roofs casting cool shadows, golden light bouncing off the masonry pylons onto the silvery-coloured concrete shells, while brilliant lines of sunlight and endlessly angled shadows would have played across all the surfaces. As Kahn said, 'The outside of the building belongs to the sun, the interior belongs to the shadows.'[47]

We would become aware of the almost black shadows of the small chapel-like rooms carved into each pylon at the ground floor, so dark within that we could see the light of a single candle: 'I sensed that the light of a candle plays an important part in Judaism. The pylons belong to the candle service and have niches facing the chamber.'[48] The central sanctuary space, entered by passing under a low shadowed seating area under the encircling balcony, is at once intimate, in its 32 foot (9.5 metre) square dimensions, and immense, in the manner in which it opens out in all directions and is crossed by a line of fiery light at its apex. While Kahn correctly characterized the central sanctuary as 'a very modest sized room, I think. It is designed so that four people or two hundred people may feel comfortable while praying there',[49] it is also given the light, massive enclosure and primary geometries of the Pantheon, a truly immeasurable space. Seating is provided on the north, east and south sides of the central sanctuary, and the ark is set into a monumental, freestanding wall, U-shaped in plan, to the west – 7 feet (2.1 metres) thick at the floor. This wall is the most massive of the entire building, and it slopes gently inward as it rises, terminating at the spring-line of the pyramidal roof shells.

Climbing the stairs at the centre of each side of the building, we would arrive at the upper, balcony level. Bridges span across to the balcony surrounding the sanctuary on three sides, and the pylon niches are opened to either side, allowing us to walk through and perceive the manner in which, at this upper level, their outer and inner walls are angled steeply inwards, matching the outer slope of the pylon, to meet at the centre (reminding us of the similar ceiling-walls of Mayan temples). In this upper

22. Section through Jerusalem with section through the centre of the Hurva Synagogue (left), the Western Wall (centre right) and Temple Mount (right); the Dome of the Rock can be seen in the distance, first and definitive scheme, 1967–9.

level promenade, we would move in and out of the hollow corner pier-rooms, with their triangle-topped openings, and across the spanning balconies and bridges, with views through the building and out to the city of Jerusalem from every point, the whole linked together in a complex movement sequence weaving in and out of the monumental volumes. Sunlight would have played within the unglazed, complexly layered spaces as among ancient ruins, and in this timeless but precisely grounded place, we could have described Kahn's work as he did his beloved ruins: 'The ancient building still vigorous in use has the light of eternity.'[50]

In the summer of 1969 Kahn revised his design for the Hurva Synagogue, creating an even more monumental place (p. 423; e & f).[51] The inner concrete structure was formed by four outward-curving shell walls, almost touching at the corners and split down their centres by 3 foot (0.9 metre) slots, covered by a solid flat roof, with only a tiny gap between the top of the curved walls and the roof (p. 423; g). Together the walls form a square room, its lower edge folded under and in to form a narrow balcony, and the whole lifted 10 feet (3 metres) off the ground floor, supported at the mid-points by pairs of massive piers, the corners cantilevered over 20 feet (6 metres). This awesome, dark, scale-less concrete volume, with the light mysteriously leaking in around the edges of the roof, the outward-curving surfaces, and the enormous cantilevered corners, marks a dramatic change in Kahn's approach – confirmed by his decision to remove both the ark and the bema from the central space. While this second design was fully developed, including a detailed model, the third design – with the Pantheon-like square oculus at the centre – dating from 1973, is documented only in two plans and a sketch section (p. 423; h).[52] At the time of Kahn's death the following year, Mayor Kollek had just written to Kahn of his eagerness to start the building of the Hurva.[53]

24

23. Computer reconstruction of the Hurva Synagogue showing a view between the pylons (left), and the sanctuary roofs and structure (right), first and definitive scheme, 1967–9.
24. Computer reconstruction of the ground floor sanctuary and the mezzanine level, with the pylons in the distance, Hurva Synagogue, first and definitive scheme, 1967–9.
25. Computer reconstruction of the upper balcony and chapel level, showing the stair entry, the sanctuary on the left and the chapels on the right, first and definitive scheme, 1967–9.

25

Hurva Synagogue

Concept development

In his first design for the Hurva Synagogue in Jerusalem, Kahn synthesized a number of his most fundamental precedents, including the battered walls of ancient Egyptian ruins, which he transformed into the sixteen stone pylons that surround and shade the sanctuary; the reconstructed plan of Solomon's Temple, with its thick double wall around the four-columned interior; the Romanesque churches such as Périgueux, where freestanding clusters of four piers support the arching roof vaults; and Wright's Johnson Wax Building, where the hollow columns open at the top, like umbrellas, to form the roof. Kahn also engaged design concepts from his own earlier projects, in particular the early scheme for the First Unitarian Church of August 1960, with its umbrella columns and slot of light around the edge, and its concept of a concrete building set within a masonry building. In Kahn's second design for the Hurva Synagogue of 1969 he placed a single, hollow, lifted concrete shell within the masonry pylons, and in the third scheme of 1973, he proposed a single central aperture in the roof, as in the Pantheon. These concept development pages relate to both the rich set of precedents that inspired Kahn's design and to the two later schemes.

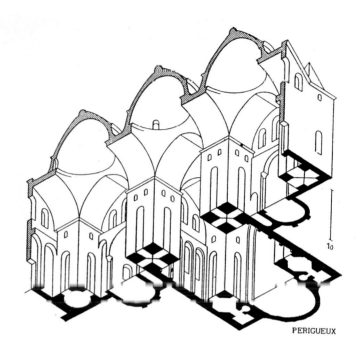

PERIGUEUX

a

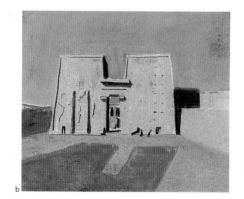

b

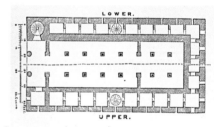

c

d

a. Auguste Choisy, up-view axonometric section of the Romanesque church at Périgueux, France, from Choisy's *Histoire de l'architecture*, 1899. Hollow square piers support the roof vaults.
b. Entry pylon, Temple of Edfu, Egypt, 1951; pastel by Louis Kahn. The pylons around Hurva Synagogue are reminiscent of this structure.
c. Speculative plan reconstruction of Solomon's Temple, Jerusalem, from James Fergusson, *History of Architecture*, 1883; Kahn used this book when he was a student and kept a copy in his library.
d. Clay site model of the Hurva Synagogue (left) showing Temple Mount and the Dome of the Rock (right), first and definitive scheme, 1967–9.

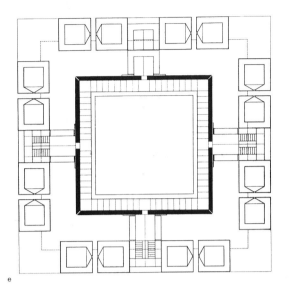

e

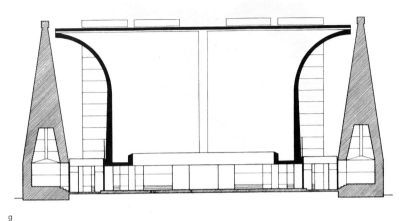

g

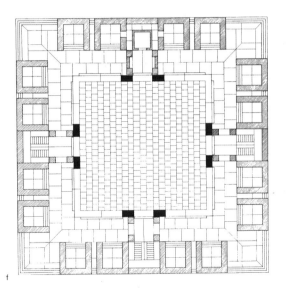

f

h

e. Upper mezzanine level plan, Hurva Synagogue, second scheme, 1969 (north to right).
f. Lower entry, chapel and sanctuary level plan, Hurva Synagogue, second scheme, 1969 (north to right).
g. Section of the second scheme, 1969. The cross-hatched grey indicates the masonry piers, solid black indicates the concrete shell.
h. Section (above) and section and plan studies (below), third scheme, 1973; drawing by Kahn.

In early 1968, at the same moment that Kahn was engaged in developing the first design for the Hurva Synagogue in Jerusalem, he was offered the commission to design a conference centre in Venice, Italy. The noted architectural historian and professor, Giuseppe Mazzariol, with the support of the Venetian architect, Carlo Scarpa, had recommended Kahn to the tourist agency of Venice.[54] Kahn was deeply honoured to be asked to work in Venice, where so many great architects throughout history had left their mark, and 'also because Le Corbusier has produced such an important design for the city'.[55] Le Corbusier's Venice Hospital project of 1964, proposed for a site on the edge of the city, was a complex weave of pinwheeling, rectangular volumes lifted above the lagoon on a forest of piers. Le Corbusier's design is in many respects quite close to Kahn's early Trenton Jewish Community Center design,[56] so it is somewhat surprising that Kahn's concept for the Palazzo dei Congressi was from the start almost the exact opposite of Le Corbusier's Hospital. Where Le Corbusier proposed a re-weaving of the edge of the urban fabric, employing numerous small-scale modular volumes, Kahn proposed a singular, massive, freestanding monument.

This difference resulted from the fact that Kahn conceived of the Palazzo dei Congressi as an institution of monumental significance – 'the sense of a congress which is to bring people together' – a place to celebrate meeting, which Kahn considered to be the greatest of all human actions.[57] Kahn's urban prototypes were the Greek theatre and the Italian piazza:

> I can see the congress hall as if it were a theater in the round – where people look at people ... My first idea, regardless of the shape of the site, was to make so many concentric circles with a nucleus in the middle. Because the site is so long and narrow, I simply sliced the theater in the round with two parallel cuts and it would still retain good visibility from everywhere ... Therefore the impression in the hall will be people seeing people. The curve of the meeting hall is slight in order to retain the sense that it is really a street-like piazza gently sloping. One could be reminded of [Il Campo] in Siena which was also created to give it a character of a civic theater.[58]

Kahn's 1951 drawings of the bowl-shaped hollow of Il Campo are among his most powerful (p. 430; b), and Kahn is here once again remarkably close to Aldo van Eyck, who in 1965 had diagrammed and described the way in which a concave space acts to bring people together in strikingly similar terms: 'People seated concentrically in a hollow gazing inwards towards the centre' (p. 431; c).[59]

Kahn proposed that the entire Palazzo dei Congressi be lifted up into the air on massive abutments at either end, ostensibly to minimize foundation bearing points in the water-saturated soils, with the congress hall suspended between in the form of a 400 foot (122 metre) long bridge: 'The whole structure, reinforced concrete with marble details, is conceived like a hanging bridge supported on the two ends by two columns on each end, where also the stairs and elevators reach the various levels' (p. 431; f).[60] The main hall was to seat 2,500 while the central theatre-in-the-round would seat 500. For the post-tensioned reinforced concrete floor slab of the congress hall Kahn employed a catenary curve, typical of the tension members of bridge structures, with a full-floor-deep compression beam above. In these attributes, Kahn's design for the Venice project is quite similar to his design for the top of the Kansas City high-rise tower (p. 431; g), where he had also suspended the structure from a catenary curve anchored to double piers at each corner.

Kahn conceived of the congress hall as a suspended urban plaza, where 'to each side of the hall there are two streets (fifteen feet wide) which lead to the seating place. These two streets are actually in the inside of the beams which carry the structure ... The side streets, which lead to the seats, are provided with niches where people can go away from the congress and discuss things separately.'[61] These streets also connect to a reception hall above: 'The reception hall on the [top] floor is also like a long plaza which is crowned with three domes (p. 432; h). The domes are made of rings of stainless steel and of solid glass, the exterior being covered with lead just as those of St. Mark ... [Above is the roof terrace] where the sky is the ceiling ... The parapet which encloses the roof is open to the view of Venice and the lagoon through three crescent openings.'[62] Kahn's design is solid at the top and open at the bottom, similar to both Le Corbusier's Hospital and the Doge's Palace, the facade of which Kahn

26. Clay site model of Venice, with Kahn's Palazzo dei Congressi sited in the Giardini Pubblici, right (one longer bar and two parallel shorter bars) and Le Corbusier's proposed Hospital of 1964, upper left (large cluster of forms adjacent to the road and railway bridges).

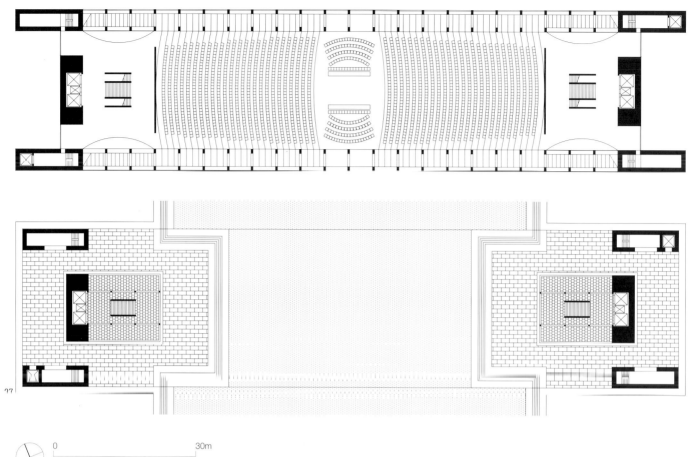

0   30m
0   100ft

27. Plans of the Palazzo dei Congressi, showing the congress hall level (above) and the ground level (below), second and definitive scheme, Arsenale site, 1972; redrawn under author's supervision.
28. Elevation (above) and longitudinal section (below), Palazzo dei Congressi, second and definitive scheme, Arsenale site, 1972. The building was to be suspended over the Canale delle Galeazze, on the western side of the Arsenale lagoon; redrawn under author's supervision.

sketched and analysed in his first drawings for the Palazzo dei Congressi.[63] By lifting the occupants up into the sky, Kahn also gives them a view of the horizon, and in this Kahn is again close to Van Eyck, who held that the centrally directed hollow is complemented by the outwardly directed view of the horizon, recognizing 'that man is both centre-bound and horizon-bound' (p. 431; c).[64]

The first site Kahn was asked to engage was the Giardini Pubblici, where the Biennale art festival is held, located in the Castello quarter at the eastern edge of the city (p. 433; j). In this site, the primary reason for lifting the structure off the ground was not to span open water but to save the large trees, precious and rare in the city of Venice.[65] This was also the reason for the narrow dimension of the building as a whole, 460 feet (140 metres) long, 100 feet (30 metres) wide, and 78 feet (24 metres) high. On this site, Kahn was also asked to propose artists' workshops and an entrance structure. Kahn's first plan (p. 433; k) places the Palazzo dei Congressi along the back edge of the Giardini Pubblici, aligned with an existing pedestrian boulevard, with a square entry structure positioned along the lagoon promenade, and the large artists' workshop structure at the rear of the site. The Biennale building, as the artists' structure was called, consisted of two three-storey volumes housing workshops, galleries and studios, each 60 by 200 feet (18 by 60 metres), facing each other across a central, full-height, top-lit 'square', as Kahn called it, which was 80 feet (24.5 metres) wide, 200 feet (60 metres) long and 50 feet (15 metres) tall. The central space could be opened at both ends, towards

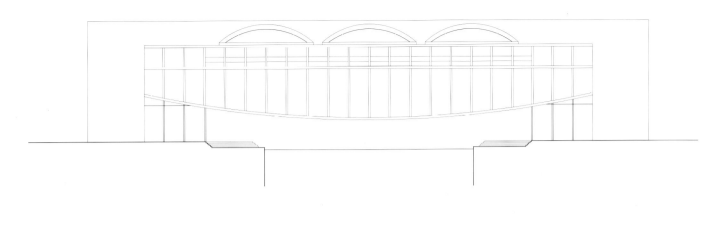

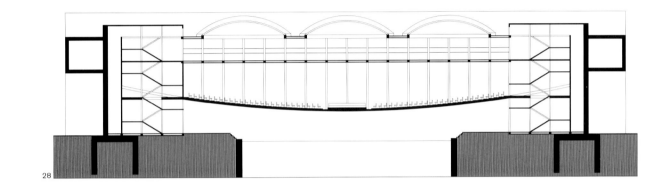

28

the gardens to the south-west and towards the end of a canal to the north-east, by huge sliding doors, 40 feet (12 metres) wide and 50 feet (15 metres) tall. At the four corners are located the stairs and mechanical and other services, and the whole design is quite similar to Wright's Larkin Building.

In a major public presentation made by Kahn in the Doge's Palace on 30 January 1969, and attended by more than 500 people, including many architects and students, the first design for the Palazzo dei Congressi was enthusiastically received. It was during this visit that Kahn visited and recorded his thoughts on the lead-clad roofs of the Doge's Palace, an event that confirmed his design for the roofs of the Kimbell Art Museum. It was also during this trip that Kahn became close friends with the Italian architect, Carlo Scarpa. Kahn and Scarpa discovered a mutual interest in the work of Frank Lloyd Wright, as may been seen in the photographs (p. 430; a) which show them together studying and discussing a copy of the 1965 reprint of the beautiful 1925 publication of Wright's work by the Dutch architect, Hendrik Wijdeveld, in his magazine *Wendingen*.[66] The last thing that Kahn wrote before his death, according to his wife Esther, was a foreword for a book on Scarpa's work, wherein Kahn referred to many concepts dear to his own heart, including 'the wholeness of inseparable elements' where 'the joint inspires ornament, its celebration. The detail is the adoration of Nature.'[67]

In September 1969 the Giardini Pubblici site failed to gain approval by the city council, and the project was put on hold. Three years later the tourist

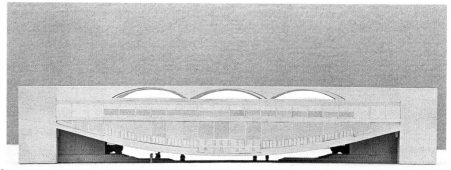

29

30

agency asked Kahn to design the Palazzo dei Congressi on a site in the city-owned Arsenale (p. 431; d & e), the ancient shipbuilding complex near the Giardini Pubblici. In many ways this was a far more appropriate site, in terms of both the scale of its massive buildings – including covered piers and shipbuilding structures with watercourses down their centres – and the possibility for Kahn's structure to act as a true bridge, across the Canale delle Galeazze (p. 432; i), with arrival now in the traditional Venetian manner – by boat, from the canal. Kahn's final design for the Palazzo dei Congressi, hovering above the canal at the western end of the large arsenal lagoon, captured the essence of the city of Venice, built in the water; here Kahn proposed a building truly without precedent, one that would bring the monumental scale of the modern ocean liner into this medieval city.

Kahn's design for Venice is also important in that it marks a dramatic change in his manner of making facades. Where before Kahn had tended to withdraw the glazing deep within the masonry or concrete structure, here he pushed it out flush to the face of the building, where, combined with mill-finished stainless steel panels, it became part of the exterior skin.[68] While Kahn would first realize this system in the Yale Center for British Art, it comes as no surprise that this woven pattern of matt and reflective surfaces was first inspired by the layered, light-filled atmosphere of water-borne Venice. Whether sitting on the gently curving floor or strolling down the stepping side streets, under the flat ceiling of the congress hall in this piazza in the air we would have been suspended between the sky and water, floating like the levitating architecture around us, looking out at the haze-blurred horizon across the lagoon, and, through our experience, engaging the intimate and ancient relationship of Venice and the sea.

29. Model of elevation, Palazzo dei Congressi, first scheme, Giardini Pubblici site, 1969.
30. Structural plan diagram indicating the locations of post-tensioning cables, Palazzo dei Congressi, first scheme, Giardini Pubblici site, 1969.
31. (Opposite) Computer reconstruction showing the view down the side 'streets' of the main congress hall, with seating to the right, Palazzo dei Congressi, second and definitive scheme, Arsenale site, 1972.

Palazzo dei Congressi

Concept development

In this design, Kahn sought to embody the concept of gathering, a place of public assembly and debate, which he felt was pre-eminent among human institutions. As a primary precedent, Kahn referred to Il Campo in Siena, Italy, which, by way of its gently curving concave surface, creates a public space where people focus not on a single speaker, but on those gathered together. Kahn's design suspends a similarly gently curved concave floor above the water-saturated surface of Venice. On the roof, he proposed a series of hill-like domes upon which people could sit and look out across the rooftops of the city. Here, Kahn engaged the 'twin phenomena' diagrammed by Aldo van Eyck: concave surfaces gather people towards a centre, whereas convex surfaces encourage outward views. It was during the design of this commission that Kahn met the Venetian architect, Carlo Scarpa, who was perhaps alone among their generation in matching Kahn's sensitivity to the nature of materials. The sources of inspiration for Kahn's design, as well as his development of the structural concept and the final Arsenale site plan, are documented on these pages and on page 432; page 433 relates to the design for the first site, in the Giardini Pubblici.

a. Carlo Scarpa (left), Louis Kahn (centre) and Kahn's assistant, Carlos Vallhonrat, in Venice, January 1969; the book in front of them is Frank Lloyd Wright's *Wendingen* portfolio of 1925.
b. Il Campo in Siena, Italy, pastel by Louis Kahn, 1951. Note the concave public space.

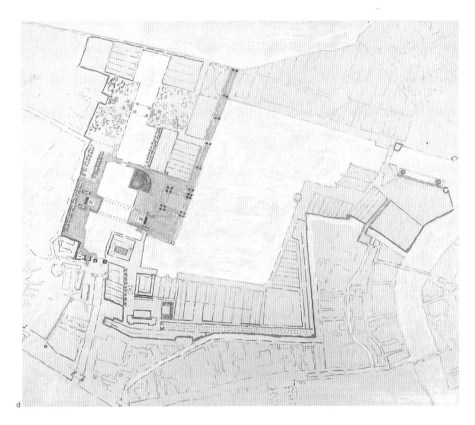

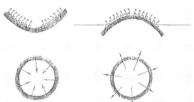

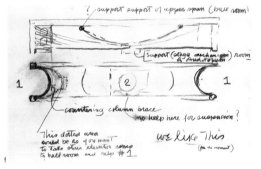

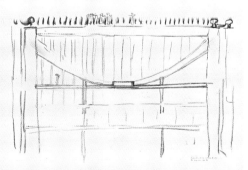

c

d

e

f

g

c. Aldo van Eyck, 'Twin phenomena' diagram, 1965.
This diagram shows how concave circular spaces
gather inwards (left), while convex circular spaces
open outwards (right).
d. Arsenale site plan, Palazzo dei Congressi, with
the congress hall bridging the Canale delle Galeazze
(centre left), second and definitive scheme, 1972
(north at top).
e. Arsenale site model with the Palazzo dei Congressi
on the right, 1972.
f. Suspended structure for main congress hall,
Palazzo dei Congressi; sketch by Kahn.
g. Sketch of the top of the Kansas City Office Tower,
Missouri, 1966–74, with a catenary suspended
structure system similar to that of the Palazzo dei
Congressi; drawing by Kahn. Note the people
shown on the roof.

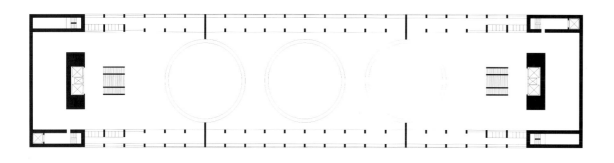

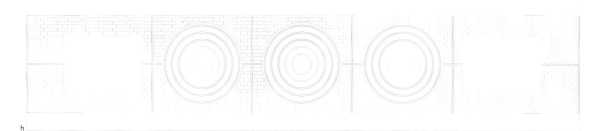

h

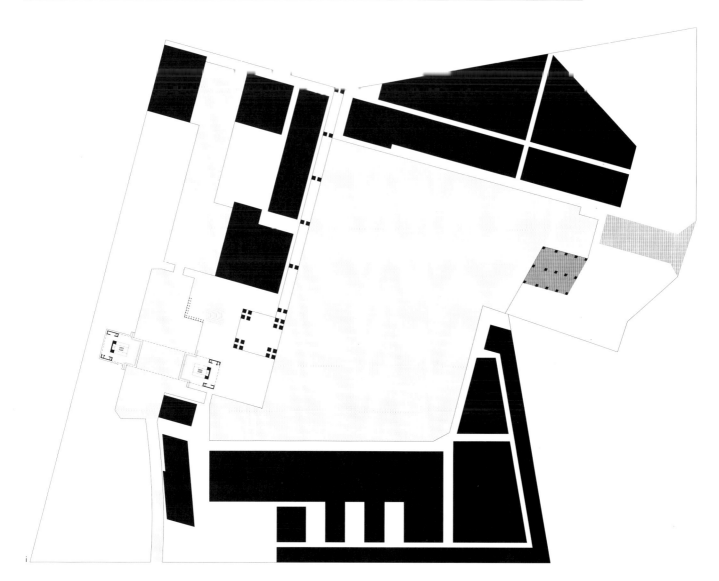

i

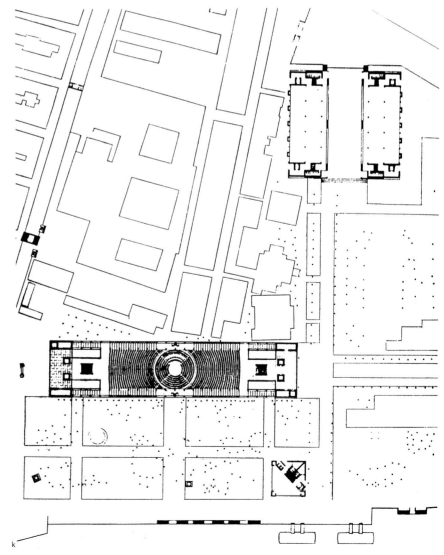

h. Floor plans of the Palazzo dei Congressi, second and definitive scheme, 1972; top reception hall floor with three domes, above, and the roof terrace, below; redrawn under author's supervision.

i. Arsenale site plan of the Palazzo dei Congressi, second and definitive scheme, 1972 (north at top); redrawn under author's supervision. The main congress hall is on the left, the proposed ampitheatre above, north of the Palazzo, and the arcaded walkway at the edge of the Arsenale lagoon in the centre.

j. Giardini Pubblici site model of the Palazzo dei Congressi, first scheme, 1969 (north at top); this shows the congress hall in the foreground and the artists' workshops behind on the left.

k. Giardini Pubblici site plan of the Palazzo dei Congressi, first scheme, 1969 (north at top); the artists' workshops are shown top right, the main congress hall, lower left, and the entry and lagoon below.

F. D. Roosevelt Memorial
New York City
1973–4
Unbuilt

In early 1973 Kahn was commissioned by the New York State Urban Development Corporation to design a memorial to Franklin Delano Roosevelt, proposed for the arrowhead-shaped southern tip of Roosevelt Island in the East River of New York City. For Kahn, who had been deeply involved in New Deal housing programmes, the commission was a particularly important one; as his client noted, Kahn 'loved Roosevelt and knew much more about him than most of us'.[69] Kahn conceived of the memorial in the most fundamental terms: 'I had this thought that a memorial should be a room and a garden ... The garden is somehow a personal nature, a personal kind of control of nature, a gathering of nature. And the room was the beginning of architecture.'[70] All of Kahn's designs for the Memorial involved an open-air landscape room, projecting out into the river, defined by massive, battered river walls to either side, a densely planted grove of trees tapering to a smaller stone room at the very end of the island, where one would find a statue of Roosevelt.

Each of Kahn's designs started with the square plan for the room at the southern end, approached from the north through a series of funnel-shaped gardens formed by lines of closely spaced trees on the east and west (p. 438; b). Kahn's first design proposed a 96 foot (29 metre) square, 60 feet (18 metres) in height, with a 60 foot (18 metres) diameter cylindrical room set within, open to the sky and lit from above (p. 439; c).[71] The parallels in this proportioning to the Pantheon are clear, and Kahn's designs all share that Roman precedent's vertical orientation, non-directional ritual and closure to horizontal views. Kahn's second design involved a circular hollow room, covered by a continuous barrel vault and forming a 40 foot (12 metre) diameter sunken central space, open to the sky, surrounded by the raised loggia, outside of which was an open plaza with views all around. Kahn's third design proposed two parallel thin-shell concrete barrel vaults, open to the inside and closed to the outside, set on the east and west sides of the square island to form a 56 foot (17 metre) square room open to the sky, with the views to east and west closed, while views to the south are framed and left open (p. 438; a).

Kahn's final design evolved in two phases, the first during the summer of 1973 and the second during the spring of 1974. The first of the two was in many ways the more interesting, proposing a 72 foot (22 metre) square island, built of 6 foot (1.8 metre) thick slabs of stone, separated from the arrowhead-shaped gardens and the rest of Roosevelt Island by a 6 foot (1.8 metre) wide canal, which was crossed by the statue base and narrow pedestrian bridges to either side (p. 439; d). The 60 foot (18 metre) square room, defined by L-shaped, 6 foot (1.8 metre) thick, 12 foot (3.7 metre) tall stone walls to east and west, contained only the statue and four 6 foot (1.8 metre) square, 12 foot (3.7 metre) tall columns to either side, representing the 'four freedoms' Roosevelt had defined: freedom of speech and worship, freedom from want and fear. These columns are closely related to Kahn's design for what he called the 'garden' at the entrance to the Salk Institute Meeting House, and, like them, relates to his definition of structure and light in the rhythm of columns and spaces between in the Greek temple, 'light, no-light, light, no-light'. In addition, the bounding walls to the east and west were opened with narrow slits that were precisely aligned 'to admit sunlight at dawn on the anniversary of Roosevelt's birth and at sundown on the anniversary of his death'.[72] This direct connection to the solar position may not only be related to such ancient monuments as Stonehenge, but also to Kahn's conception of the beginning of architecture occurring in the parting of the walls to admit light.

Kahn's last design for the Roosevelt Memorial, developed shortly before his death, is one of his most subtle yet most sublime conceptions (p. 439; e). At the southern edge of Roosevelt Island the natural shoreline is cut in, forming a broad bridge-like terrace with five large trees, which blocks the centre access, and we can only enter the Memorial along the right or left edges. Having arrived on the arrowhead-shaped island of the Memorial, we are again faced with a choice. The more indirect but easier route involves following the shore-walk atop the battered river walls on east or west, which brings us up the gentle incline to the entrance to the second garden. The more direct but more difficult route to the Memorial involves returning to the island's central

32. Model of the F. D. Roosevelt Memorial, final scheme, second phase, spring 1974; view into the room with the seated statue at the end of the approach garden.

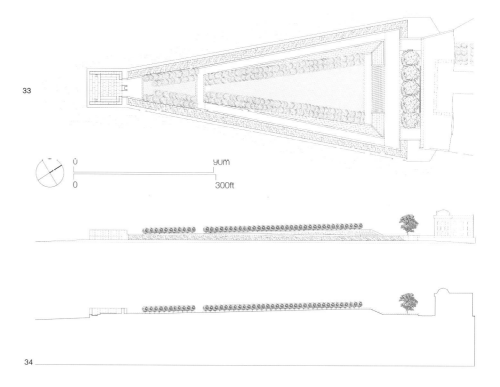

33

34

axis, mounting a wide grand stair to the top of the first, gently sloped, funnel-shaped garden, defined by double lines of densely spaced trees to east and west. From this narrow terrace at the top of the garden we would be able to see the first statue of Roosevelt, which faces to the north, and here Kahn provides his characteristic place for those who are not yet ready to enter.

The funnel-shaped gardens of the Memorial, with their forced perspective angles formed by the converging lines of trees, would have made the distance to the Memorial appear even greater, and the size of the Memorial appear even more massive. Designed by Kahn with the assistance of Harriet Pattison, the gardens exemplify Kahn's belief that the garden could possess the same architectural power as the room. This is illustrated in Kahn's story about the English landscape architect, Gertrude Jekyll, who designed the gardens for Edwin Lutyens's buildings: 'Explaining sensitivity in the making of her gardens, she said she was ascending a stairway one morning in one of them. A little boy whom she knew was running down the stairway as she was coming up, and she said, "Oh, Johnny, you're up so early." But he replied, "Aw, Miss Jekyll, I'm supposed to be invisible."'[73] For Kahn, the room and the garden were inspiring spaces for both experience and imagination, and this is nowhere more true than in the Roosevelt Memorial design.

To reach the Memorial room, we would descend gradually through this 350 foot (107 metre) long garden to the point the trees come together, about three-quarters of the way down the island, where we would enter the narrow plaza connecting the two waterside approaches and the two gardens. All ways now lead across this second, smaller, funnel-shaped 115 foot (35 metre) long garden, also defined by two tightly spaced rows of trees on either side,

35

which come together at the southern end to frame our view of the statue. We now enter the paved, wedge-shaped, bridge-like forecourt, 50 feet (15 metres) long, into which at the southern end is placed the plinth on which is the lifesize standing statue of Roosevelt. It is in this forecourt that we are given our first – and last – view of the midtown New York skyline to the west, previously blocked by the trees of the gardens, and to be again blocked by the walls of the Memorial room. We must move around this statue to either left or right, and through the 12 foot (3.7 metre) wide openings into the room of the Memorial.

We now enter Kahn's most archaic space, which he related to architecture before the Greeks.[74] A 60 foot (18 metre) square room, closed on the east and west sides by 12 foot (3.7 metre) tall, 6 foot (1.8 metre) thick solid granite walls and paved in 6 by 6 foot (1.8 by 1.8 metre) slabs of granite. The room opens at the south end, to the downriver view of bridges and the UN building, while the closer midtown skyscrapers to the east and busy piers of Queens to the west are blocked from view by the 12 foot (3.7 metre) tall walls. The floor runs right out to the edge ahead, merging with the horizontal surface of the river, and is stepped down to provide seats and a protective raised edge at the southern end of the room. To left and right, 6 foot (1.8 metre) wide stone benches are set into the 60 foot (18 metre) room to form a 36 foot (11 metre) square central space, where our focus is to the view downriver or to the seated statue of Roosevelt on the opposite side of the wall around which we entered. In experience, the Memorial would have been at once monumental, in the way it forms and sculpts the end of the island itself, in the way it is constructed from massive granite blocks, and in the way it is proportioned and axially organized; and yet at the same time it would have been intimate, in our quiet relation with the seated statue, in the meeting of individuals that takes place in the statue's room and in our paradoxical sense of being alone in the midst of the city.

After Kahn's death in 1974, his Roosevelt Memorial design, like most of his unrealized projects, was abandoned. Recent events, however, hold out some hope that perhaps this extraordinary design of Kahn's may yet be built.[75]

33. Plan of the F. D. Roosevelt Memorial, final scheme, second phase, spring 1974; redrawn under author's supervision.
34. Elevation (above) and longitudinal section (below) of the F. D. Roosevelt Memorial, final scheme, second phase, spring 1974; redrawn under author's supervision.
35. Perspective drawing of the F.D. Roosevelt Memorial, final scheme, first phase, summer 1973, with two sets of four columns in the room and the Manhattan skyline beyond.

F. D. Roosevelt Memorial

Concept development

Marking the height of Kahn's engagement of landscape in his designs, the Roosevelt Memorial was, as Kahn said, 'a room and a garden', to be placed at the southern end of Roosevelt Island. For Kahn, the garden was a gathering of nature, and the room was the beginning of architecture. All his designs for the memorial were intended to culminate in a profound and intimate experience, where one was alone with a statue of Roosevelt. Sited parallel to the edge of downtown Manhattan, with the United Nations buildings visible across the water, his designs all proposed a tree-walled formal and axial garden, which gently narrowed and sloped down to the room, a separate stone structure projected out into the river. This room was initially conceived as a steel cylinder, and later as a stone square, and in the final design this unroofed room was formed by massive 12 foot (3.7 metre) tall walls, focusing the visitor's attention on the statue of Roosevelt, the sky above and the river ahead. The sketches, plan and model, shown here, reveal the consistent qualities of Kahn's design through its various stages.

a

a. Franklin Roosevelt, Jr. (left), Louis Kahn (centre), and Averell Harriman at the presentation of the F. D. Roosevelt Memorial in 1973; Kahn's model of the third scheme is in the foreground.
b. Early perspective sketch, Roosevelt Memorial; drawing by Kahn. The room is on the left at the end of Roosevelt Island, the garden on the right and the plaza in the centre with its view of the skyline beyond.
c. Early sketch, plan and section, Roosevelt Memorial; drawing by Kahn.
d. Plan of the Roosevelt Memorial, final scheme, first phase, summer 1973.
e. Model of the final scheme, second phase, spring 1974. Note the two statues of Franklin Delano Roosevelt, one facing into the room, one facing the approach.

b

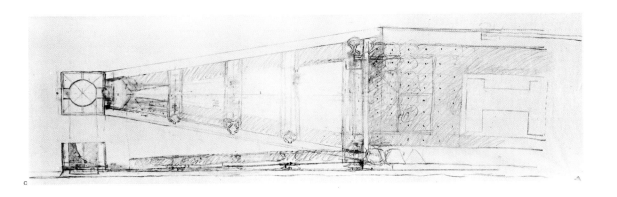

c

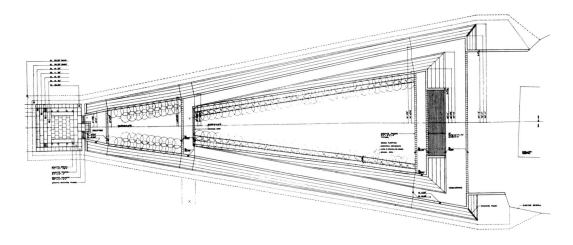

d

e

36

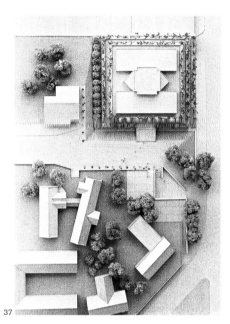

37

36. Model of the Graduate Theological Union
Library, Berkeley, California, 1971–4, viewed from
the north-west.
37. Plan view of the site model, Graduate
Theological Union Library (north down).
38. North-south section of the Graduate Theological
Union Library, looking east.
39. Graduate Theological Union Library, 1971–4; as
realized by Joseph Esherick and Richard Peters after
Kahn's death, 1977–87.
40. Detail of Graduate Theological Union Library
exterior, as realized by Esherick and Peters after
Kahn's death.
41. Upper level floor plan, Graduate Theological
Union Library (north to left).

Waiting for the right circumstances

As an unbuilt project realized by others after Kahn's death, the design for
the Graduate Theological Union Library in Berkeley, California of 1971–4
seems an appropriate project with which to bring this narrative to a
close.[76] The Graduate Theological Union, a collaboration of ten seminaries,
Protestant, Catholic and Jewish, associated with the University of California at
Berkeley, proposed to merge their collections to create one of the largest
libraries of religion in the world. The search committee visited libraries by a
number of leading architects, including Alvar Aalto, and finally selected Kahn
in the summer of 1971. The site was a south-facing hillside, north of the
university campus, flanked on the west by an existing road lined with tall palm
trees, part of the landscaping for the Hearst family country estate, which had
originally been proposed for the hilltop later occupied by the ten seminaries.[77]

Kahn's design for the Graduate Theological Union Library synthesized his
two library models, the pyramidal mass of the Washington University Library
and the cubic and cruciform plan of Exeter Library. While Kahn's early studies
include sketches of Aalto's Benedictine Seminary Library in Oregon, and
James Stirling's Cambridge University History Library,[78] both of which are
asymmetrical buildings, Kahn's approach to the Berkeley Library was from the
start based upon the square plan, strictly orientated to the cardinal directions
and internally focused. Kahn's design proposed a stepped pyramidal massing,
with the reading carrels ringing the exterior edges and opening on to terraces
densely planted with trees, the first time Kahn employed landscape elements
rather than architectural shells (built ruins) to shade the windows.[79]

The Library's pyramidal mass is ordered internally by an interpenetrating
cruciform, with the circulation and light wells in the four arms of the
cruciform, the book stacks placed in the dark inner corners, and four square
hollow piers carrying mechanical services framing a top-lit, vertical space at
the centre – this last similar to Wright's Unity Temple. At the top of the central
space, a full-floor-deep pair of concrete beams forms a giant X-shape, off
which clerestory light is bounced, as at Exeter Library. A circular opening at
the centre joins the top two floors, while two triangular openings, to east

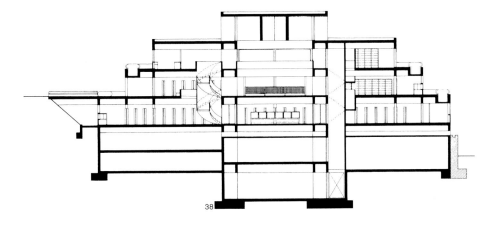

38

39

40

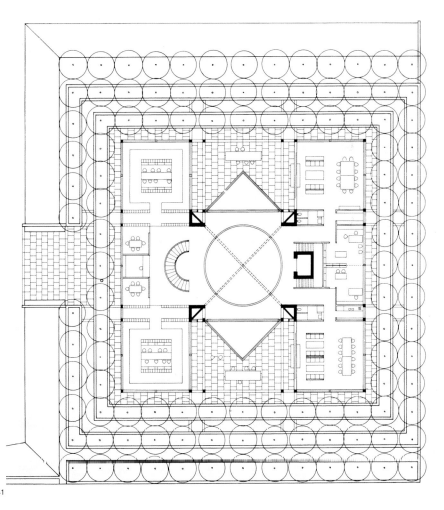

41

and west, connect all three floors, together bringing light to the deep
central section of the pyramid form. Though modified by the successor
architects due to changing circumstances,[80] the Berkeley Library remains
Kahn's only built offering to the ancient pyramids that so inspired
his architecture.

Conclusion: the voices of silence: tradition and history

The relation between Kahn's designs and the tradition of his discipline, as embodied in the history of architecture, has been at once the most influential aspect of his work and at the same time the most misunderstood and most often misrepresented. From the time of his initial statement of 1944 on monumentality, and the relation of modern architecture to history, Kahn was remarkably consistent – it was the intellectual context in which he worked which changed dramatically during the next thirty years. In 1944 Kahn had indicated that, while the forms of history could not be copied, the ordering principles that underlay them must be learned anew: 'Therefore the images we have before us of monumental structures of the past cannot live again with the same intensity and meaning. Their faithful duplication is unreconcilable. But we dare not discard the lessons these buildings teach for they have the common characteristics of greatness upon which the buildings of our future must, in one sense or another, rely.'[81] In this, his first major statement of principle, made when Kahn was forty-three years old, he is remarkably close to Frank Lloyd Wright's first national publication in 1908, when Wright, then forty-one years old, said of his work: 'At no point does it involve denial of the elemental law and order inherent in all great architecture; rather, it is a declaration of love for the spirit of that law and order, and a reverential recognition of the elements that made its ancient letter in its time vital and beautiful.'[82]

Kahn believed that history was neither a source of eclectic images nor a predetermining classical precedent, but rather that it constituted offerings from the past to the spirit of architecture, sources of inspiration and ordering principles to be engaged through the architect's intuitive insights into the nature of the institution to be realized in our time. In this understanding of the tradition of the discipline, Kahn distanced himself both from many in his own generation of modernists, who ignored the lessons of history, and from many in the younger generation of historicist post-modernists, who superficially employed historical forms without any interest in ordering principles. In 1944, at the beginning of the period dominated by the International Style, Kahn had stated that the discipline must engage its history: 'The influence of the Roman vault, the dome, the arch, has etched itself in deep furrows across the pages of architectural history. Through Romanesque, Gothic, Renaissance, and today, its basic forms and structural ideas have been felt. They will continue to reappear but with the added powers made possible by our technology and engineering skill'.[83] Then in 1959, in again calling for the engagement of history, Kahn also warned against superficial formal historicism: 'Modern space is really not different from Renaissance space. In many ways it is not. We still want domes, we still want walls, we still want arches, arcades, and loggias of all kinds. We want all these things, and with that belief, need them. But they are not the same in character because a space today demands different things' – which Kahn defined as modern materials, acoustic control, temperature and humidity regulation, natural lighting, and the concept of 'servant' and 'served' spaces.[84]

Kahn defined tradition as being embodied in the actual buildings from the past: 'These testimonials to the past are important, they are tradition; but tradition is like the product of distillation, the essence of what remains. Tradition is only valid when it can be everywhere, here and now as well as in the past.'[85] For Kahn, tradition was not a habit of design but an inheritance providing insight into the very nature of man: 'Tradition is a sense of validity. It tells you the nature of man ... It is an expression of truth. It has nothing to do with habit.'[86] Kahn distinguished between the ever-changing 'traditions' of styles or design habits and the eternal 'Tradition' of architecture: 'It's what man makes ... that remains indestructible ... This led me to realize what may be Tradition... [it] is what gives you the powers of anticipation from which you know what will last when you create'.[87] In this Kahn was again close to Wright, who in 1914 wrote: 'I deliberately chose to break with traditions in order to be more true to Tradition than current conventions and ideals in architecture would permit.'[88]

Kahn admired Le Corbusier because he was 'one in whom the spirit of architecture has not lost its continuity from the past'.[89] In this understanding of the place of tradition within the contemporary discipline of architecture, Kahn drew the same conclusions as many other leading modern artists and thinkers. In 1919, the modern poet, T. S. Eliot, wrote: 'Tradition is a matter of much wider significance [than fashion or style]. It cannot be inherited, and if you want it you must obtain it by great labour ... the historical sense involved a perception, not only of the pastness of the past, but of its presence', adding that the poet must surrender 'himself wholly to the work to be done. And he is not likely to know what is to be done unless he lives in what is not merely the present, but the present moment of the past, unless he is conscious, not of what is dead, but of what is already living.'[90] The modern composer, Igor Stravinsky, said in 1940: 'A real tradition is not the relic of a past that is irretrievably lost; it is a living force that animates and informs the present ... everything which is not tradition is plagiarism ... Far from implying the repetition of what has been, tradition presupposes the reality of what endures ... Tradition thus assures the continuity of creation.'[91] In 1948, the modern philosopher, Ludwig Wittgenstein, wrote: 'Tradition is not something a man can learn; not a thread he can pick up when he feels like it; any more than a man can choose his own ancestors'; while the previous year he had written: 'One keeps forgetting to go right down to the foundations. One doesn't put the question marks *deep* enough down.'[92]

In 1935 the modern philosopher, Martin Heidegger, whose thought is in so many ways close to Kahn's, identified the concept that distinguished between history as formal image and tradition as the source of ordering principles: 'Are we in our existence historically at the origin? Do we know, which means do we give heed to, the essence of the origin? Or, in our relation to art, do we still merely make appeal to a cultivated acquaintance with the past?'[93] Kahn believed that history was the source of eternal principles, which, in order to be engaged, required that one return to the origin, to the beginning: 'I am always looking for a source, a beginning. I know it's in my character to

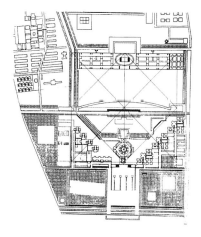

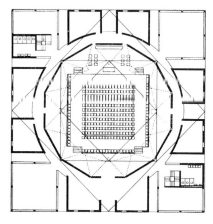

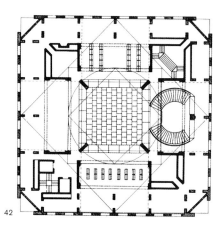

42

42 & 43. Diagrams by Florindo Fusaro illustrating Kahn's employment of rotated squares to generate plans. This page, from top: National Capital of Bangladesh, Dhaka; first scheme for the First Unitarian Church, Rochester, New York and Phillips Exeter Academy Library. Opposite page, from top: the Assembly Building, Bangladesh National Capital; the Assembly Building, Capital of West Pakistan, Islamabad; and Hurva Synagogue, Jerusalem.

want to discover beginnings. I like English history. I have volumes of it, but I never read anything but the first volume, and even in that, only the first three or four chapters. And of course my only real purpose is to read Volume Zero, you see, which has not yet been written.'[94] That which Kahn searched for at the beginning, he named 'the archaic', and in this, as in so many ways, his ideas are related to those of Plato; as George Steiner has noted, the ancient and modern search for origins begins with 'Plato's maxim – by no means self-evident – whereby in all things natural and human, the origin is the most excellent'.[95] Steiner has also noted that 'originality is antithetical to novelty. The etymology of the word alerts us. It tells of "inception", of a return, in substance and form, to beginnings. In exact relation to their originality, to their spiritual-formal force of innovation, aesthetic inventions are "archaic". They carry in them the pulse of the distant source.'[96]

In 1959, Kahn had stated: 'Preform is archaic form ... In the preform – in the beginning, in the first form – lies more power than in anything that follows',[97] and later he held that archaic Paestum was more beautiful than the Parthenon, though the Parthenon is considered the pinnacle of Greek art, stating that Paestum 'represents the beginning of architecture ... It is a beautiful time and we are still living in it.'[98] In this concept of beauty as having more to do with proximity to origins, Kahn is close to Goethe (it should be remembered that Kahn said he was 'raised on Goethe'), who in 1772 had said of architecture: 'Art is creative long before it is beautiful. And yet, such art is true and great, perhaps truer and greater than when it becomes beautiful.'[99] Kahn's statement of principle on the place of architectural history in design – 'What is has always been. What was has always been. What will be has always been'[100] – is closely related to the early modern poet Paul Valéry's 1921 statement on architecture: 'What is important for me above all else is to obtain from *that which is going to be*, that it should with all the vigour of its newness satisfy the reasonable requirements of *that which has been*',[101] suggesting that, while Kahn, by his own admission, rarely read anything, he was nevertheless a part of a living tradition, in both his work and his thought. This is evidenced by the following passage from Emmanuel Kant's *The Critique of Judgement* (1790), where he recalls 'the well-known inscription on the [Egyptian] Temple of Isis (Mother Nature): "I am all that is, and that was, and that shall be, and no mortal hath raised the veil from before my face."'[102]

Kahn's statement about his Beaux-Arts education in architecture is revealing, in that he recalls not the classical models or formal orders so much as the fact that 'the transcendent qualities were considered worthy'.[103] It is likely that Kahn's family not only raised him on Goethe and the German Romantic philosophers and poets,[104] but on the American Transcendentalists, most notably Ralph Waldo Emerson – yet another aspect shared with Wright. Emerson's *Essays* contain numerous parallels with Kahn's thoughts, including the importance of beginnings: 'The first questions are always to be asked';[105] and the fundamental search for the nature of man: 'The great genius returns to essential man.'[106] For Kahn, individual works of architecture must be measured against a timeless, ideal conception

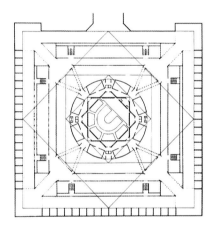

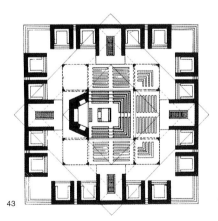

43

of architecture, based upon fundamental geometries and ordering principles: 'I never forgot such principles. From this I sensed the eternal qualities of architecture. In the beginning lies eternity';[107] while Emerson had said: 'I believe in Eternity. I can find ... the genius and creative principle of each and all eras in my own mind.'[108] Kahn, following Van Eyck, stated: 'The man of old had the same brilliance of mind that we assume we have only now';[109] and Emerson maintained: 'No greater men are now than ever were. A singular equality may be observed between the great men of the first and of the last ages.'[110] Kahn believed that 'history is that which reveals the nature of man',[111] and that the ancient building 'seems to want to tell you about the adventure of its making';[112] while Emerson held that 'The whole of history is in one man, it is all to be explained from individual experience.'[113] Finally, Kahn described the experience of visiting an ancient building: 'When you see the pyramids now, what you feel is silence';[114] while Emerson stated simply: 'The path of things is silent.'[115]

Kahn came to describe the presence of ancient architecture as 'silence', having developed this idea from the title of André Malraux's 1953 art history book, *The Voices of Silence*.[116] Kahn stated that, in his title, Malraux 'means only the feeling you get when you pass the pyramids, you feel that they want to tell you how they were made ... These are the voices of silence.'[117] Intriguingly, Paul Valéry had in 1891 used very similar words in describing the hypostyle hall of an Egyptian temple as 'the forest of silence', and noting the manner in which it exemplified 'the certitude that springs from ancient rhythms'.[118] Kahn believed that architecture could only be made by returning to these silent sources, which, by being the beginning, held the greatest meaning: 'Of all things, I honour beginnings ... that which made a thing become manifest for the first time is our great moment of creative happening'.[119]

Kahn believed in the history of his discipline, but not in the 'historicism' which held that progress mattered more than tradition, and that each age must invent its own forms – the notion of 'the spirit of the age' that led International Style practitioners to abandon disciplinary history.[120] Kahn's approach to history and archaic form is closer to what modern theologian and anthropologist, Mircea Eliade, has called 'the myth of the eternal return'. In his 1949 book of that title, Eliade wrote: 'for the man of the traditional and archaic societies, the models of his institutions ... are believed to have been "revealed" at the beginning of time, that, consequently, they are regarded as having a ... "transcendental" origin'. Eliade went on to assert: 'Every construction is an absolute beginning.'[121]

Kahn proposed a relation to primary sources altogether different from that employed in architectural education, either his own Beaux-Arts education or the educational pedagogies of the modernist academies. Kahn recognized that 'The origin of something is the source of its essence', as Heidegger had put it.[122] In this way, Kahn's understanding of the architect's relation to disciplinary history may be more closely related to theological education, where the first year is spent learning to read Greek and Hebrew so that we can make our own translations from the ancient primary sources, rather than being reliant upon the received translations or interpretations of others.[123] On the other hand, within schools of architecture, the 'scholarship' of architectural history most often acts to distance us from the subjects of our attention, rather than bringing them near.[124] In his direct engagement of historical monuments, Kahn is the exception to Heidegger's observation: 'Few are experienced enough in the difference between an object of scholarship and a matter thought.'[125]

Kahn believed that architecture must be defined by what is permanent and enduring, not by the constantly changing circumstantial requirements of the moment; as phrased by the modern poet, Rainer Maria Rilke: 'Though swiftly the world converts like cloud-shapes upheaval, everything perfect reverts to the primeval.'[126] For Kahn, the archaic was made architectural through engaging the most fundamental of geometries and eternal ordering principles: 'To me, when I see a plan I just see the plan as though it were a symphony, the realm of spaces in the construction and light. I sort of care less, you see, for the moment whether it works or not. Just so I know that the principles are respected which somehow are eternal about the plan.'[127] In 1909 Wright had defended his Larkin Building with strikingly similar reasoning, using words that could just as well be used to describe Kahn's work:

> There is a certain aesthetic joy in letting the thing alone which has for centuries been tortured, distorted and dickered with in the name of Art, letting its native dignity show forth once more ... the cube I find comforting; the sphere inspiring. In the opposition of circle and square I find motives for architectural themes ... combining these with the octagon I find sufficient materials for symphonic development ... There is quite room enough within these limitations for one artist to work, I am sure, and to accord well with the instinct for first principles.[128]

In 1961, as Kahn's work was first receiving international attention, the modern philosopher Paul Ricoeur noted: 'There is the paradox: how to become modern and to return to sources.'[129] One of the primary characteristics of Kahn's architecture, the result of his simultaneous search for archaic origins and engagement of modern social, cultural and constructional conditions, is the manner in which it is experienced as at once ancient and modern. Kahn's analysis of Barragán's house, 'Its material is traditional, its character eternal',[130] illuminates the qualities that made Kahn's architecture at once grounded in its time and place and yet transhistorical, belonging to no time. As Steiner wrote: 'The formally retrospective and technically conservative ... can generate utmost radicalism ... Every valid act of humane literacy, argument, and realized form is a past made present and a present charged with the recollections of the future.'[131]

Kahn believed that the archaic was of far greater significance than any contemporary architecture, which could in his mind only be an offering to the spirit of architecture embodied in the ancient monuments. In this belief Kahn was close to Heidegger, who in 1950 had written: 'But what if that which is early outdistanced everything late; if the very earliest far surpassed the very latest?'[132] Therefore Kahn was critical of those who sought to fix and define the modern movement as the dominant mode of architectural design, stating in 1960: 'Here the modern movement is only thirty years old, and we are already polishing and perfecting it. We should be in an archaic phase'.[133] At once modern and ancient, new and old, Kahn's work exemplifies the modern search for origins; as Wittgenstein had noted in 1941: 'You must say something new and yet it must all be old'.[134] And yet, in his work Kahn also continued an ancient tradition in the arts, exemplified by his ancestor, the composer Felix Mendelssohn's statement, when asked about the similarities between his music and that of Bach: 'Everything old and good remains new, even if that which is added is bound to be different from the old, because it emanates from new and different people.'[135]

44 Louis Kahn studying the masonry detailing of an ancient wall in Nepal, 1972; Kahn used his trips to sites as an opportunity to visit historic architecture around the world, as documented in his extensive collection of 35mm slides.

Conclusion

A man is always greater than his works because he can never fully express his aspirations. To express oneself in music or architecture, one must employ the measurable means of composition or design. The first line on paper is already a measure of what cannot be expressed fully. The first line on paper is less.[1] LOUIS KAHN

With Kahn, in death as in life, every event carries moral meaning. Having in the previous months made separate trips to Nepal, Israel, Bangladesh and Iran – all places where he had ongoing projects – in March 1974 Kahn flew to India, to give lectures and to inspect the Indian Institute of Management in Ahmedabad. Perhaps the last photograph taken of Kahn shows him talking and gesturing as he walks with his sponsor, Vikram Sarabhai, among the monumental classroom blocks and dormitories of the Indian Institute on Friday 15 March. Very late that night, Kahn boarded a flight for Bombay, from there flying to Kuwait, Rome, Paris and then to London. Missing his connection for New York, Kahn was forced to wait several hours at Heathrow Airport, where he met and had breakfast with his former Yale student, Stanley Tigerman. Kahn was 'exhausted, depressed', as Tigerman recalled, yet in a typical and touching example of Kahn's great heart, he asked Tigerman to tell Paul Rudolph, whom Kahn had not seen in many years, that he missed him. They also discussed a mutual Bengali friend who had left architecture for a political career, and Kahn said: 'I could never do anything but be an architect because that's all I know how to do.'[2]

Kahn finally arrived in New York, passing through customs at Kennedy Airport at 6.20 p.m. on Sunday, going from there to Pennsylvania Station in Manhattan to take a train. Anyone else would have caught a flight directly from Kennedy Airport to Philadelphia, but for Kahn, arrival in his city by train was an ethical imperative, a habit of the heart never to be broken. It is indeed a bitter irony that, with these additional few hours of self-imposed delay, Kahn never made it home. Louis Kahn died of a heart attack, in New York's Pennsylvania Station, at around 7.30 in the evening on Sunday 17 March 1974.

While most descriptions have focused on the undeniably sad circumstances surrounding Kahn's death,[3] his insistence on arriving in his beloved city of Philadelphia by train was an integral part of Kahn's

dedication to the discipline of architecture. The real sadness in this event comes from the fact that Kahn died in New York's Pennsylvania Station, rather than living to see the 30th Street Station in Philadelphia. The Pennsylvania Station in which Kahn died was not the great McKim, Mead and White Beaux-Arts structure, with its soaring vaults 150 feet (45 metres) above the street and its glass-roofed and glass-floored train room, where he had changed trains almost all his life, when teaching at Yale early in his career, when visiting his engineers and consultants, and when taking flights to his far-flung projects in his later years. No, that great building, so close in many ways to Kahn's ideals of the monumental public space, had been demolished in 1963 and turned into little more than a confusing underground subway stop. As Vincent Scully wrote in 1969, the original Pennsylvania Station

> was all public grandeur, embodying a quality rare in America ... A later generation was to deride its formal dependence upon the Baths of Caracalla. One is less sure than one used to be that such was a very relevant criticism at all. Much more memorable now that it is gone is the rhythmic clarity of the generous big spaces of the station and the majestic firmness with which the great piers and columns and the coffered vault defined them ... Through it one entered the city like a god. Perhaps it was really too much. One scuttles in now like a rat.[4]

In 1974, New York's Pennsylvania Station was no longer worthy of Kahn's delay, but his destination, the 30th Street Station in Philadelphia, remains to this day an appropriate gateway to a great city. A true monument, standing silent at the edge of the river, the geometric purity of its city-scaled spaces and enclosing masses complemented by the sharp-edged precision of its clean-cut square piers and coffering, the 30th Street Station was the place of arrival, the entry hall, for Kahn's Philadelphia. True to his principles in both his life and his work, Kahn died attempting to enact what he considered to be his ethical duty to the city and to architecture. If Kahn's obstinate dedication to his fundamental beliefs seems, like the original Pennsylvania Station, a bit 'too much', this is not so much a reflection on Kahn as on our own character as a society, and should serve as a 'sharp reminder of what we have lost'.[5]

Kahn's death at the age of seventy-three cut short a 'career' of only a little more than twenty years' duration. Yet, by any measure, Kahn's brief time as a 'building' architect places him among the greatest of all time. Kahn's importance to the development of Modern architecture in the second half of the twentieth century cannot be overestimated, while Kahn's significance for the future of architecture is only now beginning to be recognized. Yet Kahn must be measured not only against the architects of modern times but also against the great builders of the past whose works he so deeply respected. By always returning to the beginnings of things, Kahn approached architecture as if it had never existed before, asking the first questions of each use, material and space. Kahn's design process was focused on the ideal of perfection – unattainable, yet always sought – and as the result of this rigorous and lifelong questioning after the nature of things, Kahn's built 'answers' have a kind of certainty, a sense of eternity rare in our time.

For Kahn, the true purpose of architecture was the embodiment of institutions and the housing of the everyday rituals of experience, and in his search for fundamental ordering principles, Kahn established what we have here called a poetics of action in architecture. While Kahn unquestionably gave new meaning to the Modern precept of functional form, he also dramatically broadened the range of what should be considered a legitimate programme function, holding that the full palette of human experience must be re-engaged. Thus the central entry hall of the Exeter Library, the very heart and soul of the place, was not given in the architect's brief, but conceived by Kahn as an absolutely essential aspect of the experience of the Library. As Kahn said, he acted as the philosopher for his clients, interpreting and expanding their programme of uses in ways both culturally resonant and socially suggestive.

For Kahn, the act of construction was the only appropriate source for architectural form. In what Kahn held to be an ethical imperative, the materials of construction were to be honoured, always to be left exposed, the joints of their fabrication becoming the only ornament appropriate to modern building. Kahn understood that the materials and methods of construction were essential to both the process of design and the experience of space, and that the marks of a building's making should therefore be left exposed as a record of its creation. Kahn believed that the room was the beginning of architecture, and the modern idea that space could be continuous and undefined was anathema to him. For Kahn, each room deserved its own structure, light, material, and spatial definition – perceivable in the experience of those who inhabited it.

Kahn's work may be understood as redefining Modern architecture in two fundamental ways. First, by re-establishing the foundational significance of ancient monuments, the rituals they housed and the geometries that ordered them, for the design of contemporary institutions, Kahn's work was critical to the emergence of an experiential interpretation of architecture, based upon a poetics of action rather than functionally rationalized programmes. Second, by re-establishing the primacy of the art of construction in the design of contemporary buildings, Kahn was critical to the emergence of a 'tectonic' interpretation of architecture, based upon construction traditions and innovations rather than stylistic form. By the mid-century, Kahn was one of many who felt that Modern architecture had lost its direction and sense of purpose. Yet Kahn stands virtually alone in having opened a way out of this impasse, a way achieved by bringing Modern architecture back to its ethical foundations, by reconnecting construction to its archaic origin in revelation, and by returning space-making to its archaic origin in experience. In the end, Kahn's architecture is about inhabitation, and must be experienced; in its profound engagement of the immeasurable, Kahn's work admirably embodies Emerson's cautionary aphorism that in matters of the spirit, 'No answer in words can reply to a question of things.'[6]

1. (Previous page) Louis Kahn (right) and Vikram Sarabhai walking through the Indian Institute of Management, Ahmedabad, on Friday 15 March 1974. The classrooms (left) and the dormitories (right) are under construction. This is perhaps the last photograph taken of Kahn before his death two days later.

Selected writings
by Louis I Kahn

Monumentality (1944)

Gold is a beautiful material. It belongs to the sculptor.

Monumentality in architecture may be defined as a quality, a spiritual quality inherent in a structure which conveys the feeling of its eternity, that it cannot be added to or changed. We feel that quality in the Parthenon, the recognized architectural symbol of Greek civilization.

Some argue that we are living in an unbalanced state of relativity which cannot be expressed with a single intensity of purpose. It is for that reason, I feel, that many of our confrères do not believe we are psychologically constituted to convey a quality of monumentality to our buildings.

But have we yet given full architectural expression to such social monuments as the school, the community or culture center? What stimulus, what movement, what social or political phenomenon shall we yet experience? What event or philosophy shall give rise to a will to commemorate its imprint on our civilization? What effect would such forces have on our architecture?

Science has given to the architect its explorations into new combinations of materials capable of great resistance to the forces of gravity and wind.

Recent experimenters and philosophers of painting, sculpture and architecture have instilled new courage and spirit in the work of their fellow artists.

Monumentality is enigmatic. It cannot be intentionally created. Neither the finest material nor the most advanced technology need enter a work of monumental character for the same reason that the finest ink was not required to draw up the Magna Carta.

However, our architectural monuments indicate a striving for structural perfection which has contributed in great part to their impressiveness, clarity of form and logical scale.

Stimulated and guided by knowledge we shall go far to develop the forms indigenous to our new materials and methods. It is, therefore, the concern of this paper to touch briefly on the broader horizons which science and skill have revealed to the architect and engineer and sketch the faint outlines of possible structural concepts and expressions they suggest.

No architect can rebuild a cathedral of another epoch embodying the desires, the aspirations, the love and hate of the people whose heritage it became. Therefore the images we have before us of monumental structures of the past cannot live again with the same intensity and meaning. Their faithful duplication is unreconcilable. But we dare not discard the lessons these buildings teach for they have the common characteristics of greatness upon which the buildings of our future must, in one sense or another, rely.

In Greek architecture engineering concerned itself fundamentally with materials in compression. Each stone or part forming the structural members was made to bear with accuracy on each other to avoid tensile action stone is incapable of enduring.

The great cathedral builders regarded the members of the structural skeleton with the same love of perfection and search for clarity of purpose. Out of periods of inexperience and fear when they erected over-massive core-filled veneered walls, grew a courageous theory of a stone-over-stone vault skeleton producing a downward and outward thrust, which forces were conducted to a column or a wall provided with the added characteristic of the buttress which together took this combination of action. The buttress allowed lighter walls between the thrust points and these curtain walls were logically developed for the use of large glass windows. This structural concept, derived from earlier and cruder theories, gave birth to magnificent variations in the attempts to attain loftier heights and greater spans creating a spiritually emotional environment unsurpassed.

The influence of the Roman vault, the dome, the arch, has etched itself in deep furrows across the pages of architectural history. Through Romanesque, Gothic, Renaissance, and today, its basic forms and structural ideas have been felt. They will continue to reappear but with added powers made possible by our technology and engineering skill.

The engineer of the latter part of the nineteenth century developed from basic principles the formulas of the handbook. Demands of enormous building quantity and speed developed the handbook engineer who used its contents, more or less forgetting basic principles. Now we hear about continuity in structures, not a new word but recently an all important word in engineering which promises to relegate the handbook to the archives.

The I-beam is an engineering accomplishment deriving its shape from an analysis of the stresses involved in its use. It is designed so that the greater proportion of the area of cross section is concentrated as far as possible from the center of gravity. The shape adapted itself to ease of rolling and under test it was found that even the fillets, an aid in the rolling process, helped convey the stresses from one section to another in continuity.

Safety factors were adopted to cover possible inconsistencies in the composition of the material of manufacture. Large-scale machinery and equipment needed in its fabrication led to standardization.

The combination of safety factors (ignorance factor as one engineer termed it) and standardization narrowed the practice of engineering to the section of members from handbooks recommending sections much heavier than calculations would require and further limited the field of engineering expression stifling the creation of the more graceful forms which the stress diagrams indicated. For example, the common practice of using an I-beam as a cantilever has no relation to the stress diagram which shows that the required depth of material from the supporting end outward may decrease appreciably.

Joint construction in common practice treats every joint as a hinge which makes connections to columns and other members complex and ugly.

To attain greater strength with economy, a finer expression in the structural solution of the principle of concentrating the area of cross section away from the center of gravity is the tubular form since the greater the moment of inertia the greater the strength.

A bar of a certain area of cross section rolled into a tube of the same area of cross section (consequently of a larger diameter) would possess a strength enormously greater than the bar.

The tubular member is not new, but its wide use has been retarded by technological limitations in the construction of joints. Up until very recently welding has been outlawed by the building codes. In some cases, where it was permitted, it was required to make loading tests for every joint.

Structure designs must discard the present moment coefficients and evolve new calculations based on the effect of continuity in structures. The structural efficiency of rigid connection, in which the sheer value and the resisting moment is at least equal to the values of the supporting member, is obtained by the welding of such connections. The column becomes part of the beam and takes on added duties not usually calculated for columns.

The engineer and architect must then go back to basic principles, must keep abreast with and consult the scientist for new knowledge, redevelop his judgment of the behavior of structures, and acquire a new sense of form derived from design rather than piece together parts of convenient fabrication.

Riveted I-beam plate and angle construction is complex and graceless. Welding has opened the doors to vast accomplishments in pure engineering which allows forms of greater strength and efficiency to be used. The choice of structural forms are limitless even for given problems and therefore the aesthetic philosophy of the individual can be satisfied by his particular composition of plates, angles and tubular forms accomplishing the same answer to the challenge of the forces of gravity and wind.

The ribs, vaults, domes, buttresses come back again only to enclose space in a more generous, far simpler way and in the hands of our present masters of building in a more emotionally stirring way. From stone, the part has become smaller and cannot be seen by the naked eye. It is now the molecular composition of the metal observed and tested by the scientist through spectroscopy or by photoelastic recordings. His finding may go to the architect and engineer in the more elemental form of the formula, but by that means it shall have become an instrumental part of the builder's palette to be used without prejudice or fear. That is the modern way.

Gothic architecture relying on basically simple construction formulas derived from experience and the material available, could only go so far.

Beauvais cathedral, its builders trying to reach greater spans and height, collapsed.

The compressive stress of stone is measured in hundreds of pounds.

While not only the compressive, but also the bending and tensile stress of steel is measured in thousands of pounds.

Beauvais cathedral needed the steel we have. It needed the knowledge we have.

Glass would have revealed the sky and become a part of the enclosed space framed by an interplay of exposed tubular ribs, plates and columns of a stainless metal formed true and faired into a continuous flow of lines expressive of their stress patterns. Each member would have been welded to the next to create a continuous structural unity worthy of being exposed because its engineering gives no resistance to the laws of beauty having its own aesthetic life. The metal would have now been aged into a friendly material protected from deterioration by its intrinsic composition.

This generation is looking forward to its duty and benefit to build for the masses with its problems of housing and health.

It is aware of our outmoded cities.

It accepts the airship as a vital need.

Factories have adopted horizontal assembly and shifting population has required the transformation of large tracts of virgin territory at least temporarily for complete human living.

The building of a complete permanent town was attempted and almost built for the workers at Willow Run.

The nation has adopted the beginnings of social reform.

War production may become normal production on the same scale accepted as sound economics.

Still untried but pledged stand the noble principles of the Atlantic Charter.

In the days we look forward to must then the cathedral, the culture center, the legislative palace, world island – the seat of the congress of nations, the palace of labor and industry, the monuments to commemorate the achievements and aspirations of our time, be built to resemble Chartres, Crystal Palace, Palazzo Strozzi, or the Taj Mahal?

War engineering achievements in concrete, steel and wood are showing the signs of maturity appropriate to guide the minds entrusted with the conception of buildings of such high purpose. The giant major skeleton of the structure can assert its right to be seen. It need no longer be clothed for eye appeal. Marble and woods feel at ease in its presence. New wall products of transparent, translucent and opaque material with exciting textures and colour are suspended or otherwise fastened to the more delicate forms of the minor members. Slabs of paintings articulate the circulation in the vast sheltered space. Sculpture graces its interior.

Outstanding masters of building design indicated the direction an architect may take to unravel and translate into simple terms the complexity of modern requirements. They have restated the meaning of a wall, a post, a beam, a roof and a window and their interrelation in space. They had to be restated when we recall the conglomerations that style copying tortured these elements into.

Efforts towards a comprehensive architecture will help to develop these elements and refine their meaning. A wall dividing interior space is not the same wall dividing the outside from the interior. Masonry shall always function as retaining and garden walls. It may be used for exterior walls for its decorative qualities, but be supplemented by interior slabs designed to meet more directly the challenge of the elements.

Structural ingenuity may eliminate the interior post, but as long as it must exist its place is reserved and its independence respected in the planning of space.

Structural problems center about the roof. The permanence and beauty of its surfaces is a major problem confronting science. The surfacing of the domes, vaults and arches appearing as part of the exterior contours of the building may be an integral part of the structural design. Stainless metal, concrete or structural plastics, structural glass in light panes, or great reinforced glass castings may be the choice for domes and vaults, depending on the requirements, the climate and the desired effect. The surfacing of flat roofs should be given equally serious consideration whether it is planned for use or not.

The citizens of a metropolitan area of a city and their representatives have formulated a program for a culture center endorsed by the national educational center. The citizens' committee collaborated with the architect and his staff of engineers. Costs were not discussed. Time was not 'of the essence'. Its progress was the concern of many.

From above we see the noble outlines of the building. Much taller buildings some distance from the site do not impress us with the same feeling of receptiveness. Its site is a prominent elevation in the outlying countryside framed by dark forests defining the interior of broad strokes in land architecture.

On the ground the first reaction comes from the gigantic sculptural forms of the skeleton frame. This backbone of the architect's central idea successfully challenges the forces which during its design challenged to destroy it. To solve the more minute complexities of the entire organism, its creator had drawn his conclusions and made his decisions from the influences of many people and things around him.

The plan does not begin nor end with the space he has enveloped, but from the adjoining delicate ground sculpture it stretches beyond to the rolling contours and vegetation of the surrounding land and continues farther out to the distant hills.

The immediate ground sculpture disciplines his mind in shaping it into stronger geometric planes and cubes to satisfy his desire for terraces and pools, steps and approaches. The landscape designer countered or accentuated these planes with again geometric and tree forms interwoven with the lacy leaf pattern of the deciduous tree.

The plans reveal that the vast spans shelter smaller areas designed for specific use, which are derived from the whole by panels of glass, insulated slabs, and marble. These partitions are free of the structure and related only to the circulation pattern. The ground plan seems continuous. The great lobby is a part of the amphitheater which dips down to the stage. The light comes from above through an undulating series of prismatic glass domes.

Ahead, some distance from the entrance, is a great mural of brilliant color. As we approach it the forms clearly defined from a distance seem to divide into forms of their own, each with its own color power, clear and uncultured.

To one side is the community museum of sculpture, painting and crafts. It exhibits the work of the younger men and women attending the vocational and art academies. Here they are accepted because their talents can be judged by those who have themselves been instructed in the basic principles underlying the use of a material. The emotional adaptations are left for the exhibitor himself to evaluate by contact, comparison and experience.

Sculpture shows the tendency to define form and construction. Marble and stone is carved as of old. Castings in new alloys and plastics are favorite methods of obtaining permanency. Solids are interwoven with sheets and tubes of metal. The subject matter exhibited has no bounds. With the new materials and tools, chemical tints, and with manufacture at the artist's disposal, his work becomes alive with ideas. Metal sprays and texture guns, with fine adjustments have also become the instruments of the sculptor, painter and craftsman. One of the younger men had cast within a large, irregular cube of transparent plastic other forms and objects of brilliant colour. A sphere, planes at various angles, copper wire in free lines are seen through the plastic.

From these experiments in form the architect will eventually learn to choose appropriate embellishments for his structures. So far he has omitted them. His judgment leads him to free-standing forms in space.

Some of the younger artists are influenced by the works of an older sculptor who has developed a theory of scale in relation to space. He has argued that as the size of the structural work is increased the monolithic character of smaller work does not apply. He chose for large work a small consistent part or module of a definite shape, a cube, a prism, or a sphere which he used to construct block over block, with delicate adjustments to the effect of light and shadow, the overall form. His work seen from great distances retains a texturally vibrant quality produced by these numerous blocks and the action of the sun upon them.

Before we can feel the new spirit which must envelop the days to come we must prepare ourselves to use intelligently the knowledge derived from all sources. Nostalgic yearning for the ways of the past will find but few ineffectual supporters.

Steel, the lighter metals, concrete, glass, laminated woods, asbestos, rubber, and plastics, are emerging [as] the prime building materials of today. Riveting is being replaced by welding, reinforced concrete is emerging from infancy with prestressed reinforced concrete, vibration and controlled mixing, promising to aid in its ultimate refinement. Laminated wood is rapidly replacing lumber and is equally friendly to the eye, and plastics are so vast in their potentialities that already numerous journals and periodicals devoted solely to their many outlets are read with interest and hope. The untested characteristics of these materials are being analyzed, old formulas are being discarded. New alloys of steel, shatter-proof and thermal glass and synthetics of innumerable types, together with the material already mentioned, make up the new palette of the designer.

To what extent progress in building will be retarded by ownership patterns, dogmas, style consciousness, precedent, untested building materials, arbitrary standards, outmoded laws and regulations, untrained workmen and artless craftsmen, is speculation. But the findings of science and their application have taken large steps recently in the development of war materials which point to upset normally controlled progress and raise our hopes to the optimistic level.

Standardization, prefabrication, controlled experiments and tests, and specialization are not monsters to be avoided by the delicate sensitiveness of the artist. They are merely the modern means of controlling vast potentialities of materials for living, by chemistry, physics, engineering, production and assembly, which lead to the necessary knowledge the artist must have to expel fear in their use, broaden his creative instinct, give him new courage and thereby lead him to the adventures of unexplored places. His work will then be part of his age and will afford delight and service for his contemporaries.

I do not wish to imply that monumentality can be attained scientifically or that the work of the architect reaches its greatest service to humanity by his peculiar genius to guide a concept towards a monumentality. I merely defend, because I admire, the architect who possesses the will to grow with the many angles of our development. For such a man finds himself far ahead of his fellow workers.

Postscript by Robert McCarter

Louis Kahn's first major published essay engages a topic, monumentality, which was only just emerging in 1944, but would later become a major focus of the post-World War II debate on modernism in architecture and the arts. Kahn's approach was unique, for he argued that monumentality in architecture was not the product of size or material expense, but rather had to do with a spiritual quality that conveyed eternity, as well as the quality of craft employed in the making of a building. Kahn called for monumentality for contemporary social institutions, and the engagement of new modes and materials of construction to achieve similar spaces as those found in great historical monuments, but without any direct copying of historical forms.

'Monumentality', originally published in Paul Zucker (ed.), *New Architecture and City Planning: A Symposium* (New York: Philosophical Library, 1944), pp.77–78.

Order is
Design is form-making in order
Form emerges out of a system of construction
Growth is a construction
In order is creative force
In **design** is the means – where　　with what on when　　with how much
The nature of space reflects what it wants to be
　　　　　　　　Is the auditorium a Stradivarius
　　　　　　　　　　　or is it an ear
　　　　　　　　Is the auditorium a creative instrument
　　　　　　　　　　　　keyed to Bach or Bartók
　　　　　　　　　　　　played by the conductor
　　　　　　　　　　or is it a convention hall
In the nature of space is the spirit and the will to exist a certain way
　　　　　　　　Design must closely follow that will
　　　　　　　　Therefore a stripe painted horse is not a zebra.
　　　　　　　　Before a railroad station is a building
　　　　　　　　it wants to be a street
　　　　　　　　it grows out of the needs of street
　　　　　　　　　　out of the order of movement
　　　　　　　　A meeting of contours englazed.
Thru the nature – why
Thru the **order** – what
Thru **design** – how
A Form emerges from the structural elements inherent in the form.
　　　　　　　　A dome is not conceived when questions arise how to
　　　　　　　　build it.
　　　　　　　　　Nervi grows an arch
　　　　　　　　　Fuller grows a dome

Mozart's compositions are designs
      They are exercise of **order** – intuitive
      Design encourages more designs
      Designs derive their imagery from order
      Imagery is the memory – the Form
      Style is an adopted order
The same **order** created the elephant and created man
      They are different designs
      Begun from different aspirations
      Shaped from different circumstances

Order does not imply Beauty
      The same order created the dwarf and Adonis
Design is not making Beauty
      Beauty emerges from selection
            affinities
            integration
            love
Art is a form making life in order – psychic
Order is intangible
      It is a level of creative consciousness
      forever becoming higher in level
      The higher the order the more diversity in design

Order supports integration
From what the space wants to be the unfamiliar may be revealed
    to the architect.
From order he will derive creative force and power of self criticism
to give form to this unfamiliar.
Beauty will evolve

Postscript by Robert McCarter
The first of Louis Kahn's characteristic aphoristic statements, this text is the product of his teaching at Yale University, which began in 1947. While it was first published in *Perspecta 3: The Yale Architectural Journal*, the text was initially composed in Kahn's notebooks, the result of studio discussions with his students. Like most of Kahn's texts, it began as the spoken word. Here, Kahn first introduces what would become the key ideas of his design process, including that architectural form comes from construction; the nature of a space as something that 'wants to be'; the relation between 'order' (what we do) and 'design' (how we do it); and an extended argument against searching for beauty as an end in itself.

'Order Is', originally published in *Perspecta 3: The Yale Architectural Journal*, 1955, p.59.

A young architect came to ask a question. 'I dream of spaces full of wonder. Spaces that rise and envelop flowingly without beginning, without end, of a jointless material white and gold. When I place the first line on paper to capture the dream, the dream becomes less.'

This is a good question. I once learned that a good question is greater than the most brilliant answer.

This is a question of the unmeasurable and the measurable. Nature, physical nature, is measurable.

Feeling and dream has no measure, has no language, and everyone's dream is singular.

Everything that is made, however, obeys the laws of nature. The man is always greater than his works because he can never fully express his aspirations. For to express oneself in music or architecture is by the measurable means of composition or design. The first line on paper is already a measure of what cannot be expressed fully. The first line on paper is less.

'Then,' said the young architect, 'what should be the discipline, what should be the ritual that brings one closer to the psyche. For in this aura of no material and no language, I feel man truly is.'

Turn to Feeling and away from Thought. In Feeling is the Psyche. Thought is Feeling and presence of Order. Order, the maker of all existence, has No Existence Will. I choose the word Order instead of knowledge because personal knowledge is too little to express Thought abstractly. This Will is in the Psyche.

All that we desire to create has its beginning in feeling alone. This is true for the scientist. It is true for the artist. But I warned that to remain in Feeling away from Thought means to make nothing.

Said the young architect: 'To live and make nothing is intolerable. The dream has in it already the *will to be* and the desire to express this *will*. Thought is inseparable from Feeling. In what way then can Thought enter creation so that this psychic will can be more closely expressed? This is my next question.'

When personal feeling transcends into Religion (not a religion but the essence religion) and Thought leads to Philosophy, the mind opens to realizations. Realization of what may be the *existence will* of, let us say, particular architectural spaces. Realization is the merging of Thought and Feeling at the closest rapport of the mind with the Psyche, the source of *what a thing wants to be.*

It is the beginning of Form. Form encompasses a harmony of systems, a sense of Order and that which characterizes one existence from another. Form has no shape or dimension. For example, in the differentiation of a spoon from spoon, spoon characterizes a form having two inseparable parts, the handle and the bowl. A spoon implies a specific design made of silver or wood, big or little, shallow or deep. Form is 'what'. Design is 'how'. Form is impersonal. Design belongs to the designer. Design is a circumstantial act, how much money there is available, the site, the client, the extent of knowledge. Form has nothing to do with circumstantial conditions. In architecture, it characterizes a harmony of spaces good for a certain activity of man.

Reflect then on what characterizes abstractly House, a house, home. House is the abstract characteristic of spaces good to live in. House is the form, in the mind of wonder it should be there without shape or dimension. *A* house is a conditional interpretation of these spaces. This is design. In my opinion the greatness of the architect depends on his powers of realization of that which is House, rather than his design of *a* house which is a circumstantial act. Home is the house and the occupants. Home becomes different with each occupant.

The client for whom a house is designed states the areas he needs. The architect creates spaces out of those required areas. It may also be said that this house created for the particular family must have the character of being good for another. The design in this way reflects its trueness to Form.

I think of school as an environment of spaces where it is good to learn. Schools began with a man under a tree who did not know he was a teacher discussing his realization with a few who did not know they were students. The students reflected on what was exchanged and how good it was to be in the presence of this man. They aspired that their sons also listen to such a man. Soon spaces were erected and the first schools became. The establishment of school was inevitable because it was part of the desires of man. Our vast systems of education, now vested in Institutions, stem from these little schools but the spirit of their beginning is now forgotten. The rooms required by our institutions of learning are stereotypical and uninspiring. The Institute's required uniform classrooms, the locker-lined corridors and other so-called functional areas and devices, are certainly arranged in neat packages by the architect who follows closely the areas and budgetary limits as required by the school authorities. The schools are good to look at but are shallow in architecture because they do not reflect the spirit of the man under the tree. The entire system of schools that followed from the beginning would not have been possible if the beginning were not in harmony with the nature of man. It can also be said that the existence will of school was there even before the circumstances of the man under a tree.

That is why it is good for the mind to go back to the beginning because the beginning of any established activity of man is its most wonderful moment. For in it lies all its spirit and resourcefulness, from which we must constantly draw our inspirations of present needs. We can make our institutions great by giving them our sense of this inspiration in the architecture we offer them.

Reflect then on the meaning of school, *a* school, institution. The institution is the authority from whom we get their requirements of areas. A School or a specific design is what the institution expects of us. But School, the spirit school, the essence of the existence will, is what the architect should convey in his design. And I say he must, even if the design does not correspond to the budget. Thus the architect is distinguished from the mere designer. In school as a realm of spaces where it is good to learn, the lobby measured by the institute as so many square feet per student would become a generous Pantheon-like space where it is good to enter. The corridors would be transferred into classrooms belonging to the students themselves by making them much wider and provided with alcoves overlooking the gardens. They would become the places where boy meets girl, where the student discusses the work of the professor with his fellow student. By allowing classroom time to these spaces instead of passage time from class to class, it would become a meeting connection and not merely a corridor, which means a place of possibilities in self-learning. It becomes the classroom belonging to the students. The classrooms should evoke their use by their space variety and not follow the usual soldier-like dimensional similarity, because one of the most wonderful spirits of this man under the tree is his recognition of the singularity of every man. A teacher or a student is not the same when he is with a few in an intimate room with a fireplace as in a large high room with many others. And must the cafeteria be in the basement, even though its use in time is little? Is not the relaxing moment of the meal also a part of learning?

As I write alone in my office, I feel differently about the very same things that I talked about only a few days ago to many at Yale. Space has power and gives mode.

This, with the singularity of every person, suggests a variety of spaces with a variety of the ways of natural light and orientation to compass and garden. Such spaces lend themselves to ideas in the curriculum, to better connections between teacher and student, and to vitality in the development of the institution.

The realization of what particularizes the domain of spaces good for school would lead an institution of learning to challenge the architect to awareness of what School *wants to be* which is the same as saying what is the form, School.

In the same spirit I should like to talk about a Unitarian Church.

The very first day I talked before the congregation using a blackboard. From what I heard the minister speak about with men around I realized that the form aspect, the form realization of Unitarian activity was bound around that which is Question. Question eternal of why anything. I had to come to the realization of what existence will and what order of spaces were expressive of the Question.

I drew a diagram on the blackboard which I believe served as the Form drawing of the church and, of course, was not meant to be a suggested design.

I made a square center in which I placed a question mark. Let us say I meant it to be the sanctuary. This I encircled with an ambulatory for those who did not want to go into the sanctuary. Around the ambulatory I drew a corridor which belonged to an outer circle enclosing a space, *the school*. It was clear that School which gives rise to Question became the wall which surrounds Question. This was the form expression of the church, not the design.

This puts me in mind of the meaning of Chapel in a university.

Is it the mosaics, stained glass, water effects, and other known devices? Is it not the place of inspired ritual which could be expressed by a student who winked at chapel as he passed it after being given a sense of dedication to this work by a great teacher. He did not need to go in.

It may be expressed by a place which for the moment is left undescribed and has an ambulatory for the one who does not want to enter it. The ambulatory is surrounded by an arcade for the one who prefers not to go into the ambulatory. The arcade sits in the garden for the one who prefers not to enter the arcade. The garden has a wall and the student can be outside winking at it. The ritual is inspired and not set and is the basis of the form Chapel.

Back to the Unitarian Church. My first design solution which followed was a completely symmetrical square. The building provided for the schoolrooms around the periphery, the corners were punctuated by larger rooms. The space in the center of the square harbored the sanctuary and the ambulatory. This design closely resembled the diagram on the blackboard and everyone liked it until the particular interests of every committee member began to eat away at the rigid geometry. But the original premise still held of the school around the sanctuary.

It is the role of design to adjust to the circumstantial. At one stage of discussion with the members of the church committee a few insisted that the sanctuary be separated entirely from the school. I said fine, let's put it that way and I then put the auditorium in one place and connected it up with a very neat little connector to the school. Soon everyone realized that the coffee hour after the ceremony brought several related rooms next to the sanctuary, which when alone were too awkwardly self-satisfying and caused the duplication of these rooms in the separated school block. Also, the schoolrooms by separation lost their power to evoke their use for religious and intellectual purposes and, like a stream, they all came back around the sanctuary.

The final design does not correspond to the first design though the form held.

I want to talk about the difference between form and design, about realization, about the measurable and the unmeasurable aspects of our work and about the limits of our work.

Giotto was a great painter because he painted the skies black for the daytime and he painted birds that couldn't fly and dogs that couldn't run and he made men bigger than doorways because he was a painter. A painter has this prerogative. He doesn't have to answer to the problems of gravity, nor to the images as we know them in real life. As a painter he expresses a reaction to nature and he teaches us through his eyes and his reactions to the nature of man. A sculptor is one who modifies space with the objects expressive again of his reactions to nature. He does not create space. He modifies space. An architect creates space.

Architecture has limits.

When we touch the invisible walls of its limits then we know more about what is contained in them. A painter can paint square wheels on a cannon to express the futility of war. A sculptor can carve the same square wheels. But an architect must use round wheels. Though painting and sculpture play a beautiful role in the realm of architecture as architecture plays a beautiful role in the realms of painting and sculpture, one does not have the same discipline as the other.

One may say that architecture is the thoughtful making of spaces. It is, note, the filling of areas prescribed by the client. It is the creating of spaces that evoke a feeling of appropriate use.

To the musician a sheet of music is seeing from what he hears. A plan of a building should read like a harmony of spaces in light.

Even a space intended to be dark should have just enough light from some mysterious opening to tell us how dark it really is. Each space must be defined by its structure and the character of its natural light. Of course I am not speaking about minor areas which serve the major spaces. An architectural space must reveal the evidence of its making by the space itself. It cannot be a space when carved out of a greater structure meant for a greater space because the choice of a structure is synonymous with the light and that which gives image to that space. Artificial light is a single tiny static moment in light and is the light of night and never can equal the nuances of mood created by the time of day and the wonder of the seasons.

A great building, in my opinion, must begin with the unmeasurable, must go through measurable means when it is being designed and in the end must be unmeasurable. The design, the making of things, is a measurable act. In fact at that point, you are like physical nature itself because in physical nature everything is measurable, even that which is yet unmeasured, like the most distant stars which we can assume will be eventually measured.

But what is unmeasurable is the psychic spirit. The psyche is expressed by feeling and also thought and I believe will always be unmeasurable. I sense that the psychic Existence Will calls on nature to make what it wants to be. I think a rose wants to be a rose. Existence Will, *man*, becomes existence, through nature's law and evolution. The results are always less than the spirit of existence.

In the same way a building has to start in the unmeasurable aura and go through the measurable to be accomplished. It is the only way you can build, the only way you can get it into being is through the measurable. You must follow the laws but in the end when the building becomes part of living it evokes unmeasurable qualities. The design involving quantities of brick, method of construction, engineering is over, and the spirit of its existence takes over.

Take the beautiful tower made of bronze that was erected in New York. It is a bronze lady, incomparable in beauty, but you know she has corsets for fifteen stories because the wind bracing is not seen. That which makes it an object against the wind which can be beautifully expressed, just like nature expresses the difference between the moss and the reed. The base of this building should be wider than the top, and the columns which are on top dancing like fairies, and the columns below growing like mad, don't have the same dimensions because they are not the same thing. This story if told from realization of form would make a tower more expressive of the forces. Even if it begins in its first attempts in design to be ugly it would be led to beauty by the statement of form.

I am doing a building in Africa, which is very close to the equator. The glare is killing, everybody looks black against the sunlight. Light is a needed thing, but still an enemy. The relentless sun above, the siesta comes over you like thunder.

I saw many huts that the natives made.

There were no architects there.

I came back with multiple impressions of how clever was the man who solved the problems of sun, rain, and wind.

I came to the realization that every window should have a free wall to face. This wall receiving the light of day would have a bold opening to the sky. The glare is modified by the lighted wall and the view is not shut off. In this way the contrast made by separated patterns of glare which skylight grills close to the window make is avoided. Another realization came from the effectiveness of the use of breeze for insulation by the making of a loose sun roof independently supported and separated from the rain roof by a head room of six feet. These designs of the window and wall and of the sun and rain roofs would tell the man on the street the way of life in Angola.

I am designing a unique research laboratory in San Diego, California.

This is how the program started.

The director, a famous man, heard me speak in Pittsburgh. He came to Philadelphia to see the building I had designed for the University of Pennsylvania. We went out together on a rainy day. He said, 'How nice, a beautiful building. I didn't know a building that went up in the air could be nice. How many square feet do you have in this building?' I said, 'One hundred and nine thousand square feet'. He said, 'That's about what we need'.

That was the beginning of the program of areas. But there was something else he said which became the Key to the entire space environment. Namely that Medical Research does not belong entirely to medicine or the physical sciences. It belongs to Population. He meant that anyone with a mind in the humanities, in science, or in art could contribute to the mental environment of research leading to discoveries in science. Without the restriction of a dictatorial program it became a rewarding experience to participate in the projection of an evolving program of spaces without precedence. This is only possible because the director is a man of unique sense of environment as an inspiring thing, and he could sense the existence will and its realization in form which the spaces I provided had.

The simple beginning requirement of the laboratories and their services expanded to cloistered gardens and Studies over arcades and to spaces for meeting and relaxation interwoven with unnamed spaces for the glory of the fuller environment.

The laboratories may be characterized as the architecture of air cleanliness and area adjustability. The architecture of the oak table and the rug is that of the Studies.

The Medical Research Building at the University of Pennsylvania is conceived in recognition of the realizations that science laboratories are studios and that the air to breathe should be away from the air to throw away.

The normal plan of laboratories which places the work areas off one side of a public corridor and the other side provided with the stairs, elevators, animal quarters, ducts and other services. This corridor is the vehicle of the exhaust of dangerous air and also the supply of the air you breathe, all next to each other. The only distinction between one man's spaces of work from the other is the difference of the numbers on the doors.

I designed three studio towers for the University where a man may work in his bailiwick and each studio has its own escape *stairway sub tower* and *exhaust sub tower* for isotope air, germ-infected air and noxious gas.

A central building to which the three major towers cluster takes the place of the area for services which are on the other side of the normal corridor plan. This central building has nostrils for intake of fresh air away from *exhaust sub towers* of vitiated air.

This design, an outcome of the consideration of the unique use of its spaces and how they are served, characterizes what it is for.

One day I visited the site during the erection of the prefabricated frame of the building. The crane's 200-foot boom picked up 25-ton members and swung them into place like matchsticks moved by the hand. I resented the garishly painted crane, this monster which humiliated my building to be out of scale. I watched the crane go through its many movements all the time calculating how many more days this 'thing' was to dominate the site and building before a flattering photograph of the building could be made.

Now I am glad of this experience because it made me aware of the meaning of the crane in design, for it is merely the extension of the arm like a hammer. Now I began to think of members 100 tons in weight lifted by bigger cranes. The great members would be only the parts of a composite column with joints like sculpture in gold and porcelain and harboring rooms on various levels paved in marble.

These would be the stations of the great span and the entire enclosure would be sheathed with glass held in glass mullions with strands of stainless steel interwoven like threads assisting the glass and the mullions against the forces of wind.

Now the crane was a friend and the stimulus in the realization of a new form.

The institutions of cities can be made greater by the power of their architectural spaces. The meeting house in the village green has given way to the city hall which is no more the meeting place. But I sense an existence will for the arcaded city place where the fountains play, where again boy meets girl, where the city could entertain and put up our distinguished visitors, where the many societies which uphold our democratic ideals can meet in clusters of auditoria in the city place.

The motor car has completely upset the form of the city. I feel that the time has come to make the distinction between the Viaduct architecture of the car and the architecture of man's activities. The tendencies of designers to combine the two architectures in a simple design has confused the direction of planning and technology. The Viaduct architecture enters the city from outlying areas. At this point it must become more carefully made and even at great expense more strategically placed with respect to the center.

The Viaduct architecture includes the street which in the center of the city wants to be a building, a building with rooms below for city piping services to avoid interruption to traffic when services need repair.

The Viaduct architecture would encompass an entirely new concept of street movement which distinguished the stop-and-go staccato movement of the bus from the 'go' movement of the car. The area framing expressways are like rivers. These rivers need harbors. The interim streets are like canals which need docks. The harbors are the gigantic gateways expressing the *architecture of stopping*. The terminals of the Viaduct architecture, they are garages in the core, hotels, and department stores around the periphery and shopping centers on the street floor.

This strategic positioning around the city center would present a logical image of protection against the destruction of the city by the motor car. In a sense the problem of the car and city is war, and the planning for the new growth of cities is not a complacent act but an act of emergency.

The distinction between the two architectures, the architecture of the Viaduct and the architecture of the acts of man's activities, could bring about a logic of growth and a sound positioning of enterprise.

An architect from India gave an excellent talk at the University about the fine new work of Le Corbusier and about his own work. It impressed me, however, that these beautiful works he showed were still out of context and had no position. After his lecture I was asked to remark. Somehow I was moved to go to the blackboard where I drew in the center of the board a towering water tower, wide on top and narrow below. Like the rays of a star, I drew aqueducts radiating from the tower. This implied the coming of the trees and fertile land and a beginning of living. The buildings not yet there which would cluster around the aqueduct would have meaningful position and character.

The city would have form.

From all I have said I do not mean to imply a system of thought and work leading to realization from Form to Design.

Designs could just as well lead to realizations in Form.

This interplay is the constant excitement of Architecture.

Postscript by Robert McCarter
Transcribed from a lecture which Kahn gave for a *Voice of America* radio programme in November 1960, this text begins with the story of a young architect who asks Kahn a question, and proceeds in Kahn's typical dialogic manner. Kahn uses a series of institutional building types, such as the school, the church, the embassy, the medical research laboratory – all of which were actual projects in his office – and he focuses not on the particular, circumstantial aspects of these designs, but rather on their essential nature as architecture. Kahn introduces his key concepts of returning to beginnings, the measurable and the immeasurable, the idea of an inspired ritual, a space being defined by its structure and its light, and the deleterious effect of automobiles on the city.

Originally published as 'A Statement by Louis I. Kahn' in *Arts and Architecture* (February 1961) and retitled 'Form and Design' for *Architectural Design* (April 1961).

Let us go back in time to the building of the pyramids. Hear the din of industry in a cloud of dust marking their place. Now we see the pyramids in full presence. There prevails the feeling of Silence, in which is felt man's desire to express. This existed before the first stone was laid.

I find that when a building is being made, free of servitude, its spirit to be is high – no blade of grass can grow in its wake. When the building stands complete and in use, it seems to want to tell you about the adventure of its making. But all the parts locked in servitude make this a story of little interest. When its use is spent and it becomes a ruin, the wonder of its beginning appears again. It feels good to have itself entwined in foliage, once more high in spirit and free of servitude.

I sense Light as the giver of all presences, and material as spent Light. What is made by Light casts a shadow, and the shadow belongs to Light. I sense a Threshold: Light to Silence, Silence to Light – an ambiance of inspiration, in which the desire to be, to express crosses with the possible. The rock, the stream, the wind inspires. We see what is beautiful in the material first in wonder, then in knowing, which in turn is transformed into the expression of beauty that lies in the desire to express. Light to Silence, Silence to Light crosses in the sanctuary of art. Its treasury knows no favorite, knows no style. Truth and rule of commonness, law out of order are the offerings within.

Architecture has no presence but exists as the realization of a spirit. A work of architecture is made as an offering reflecting the nature of that spirit. One can also say that the realms of painting, sculpture, and literature exist in spirit, their natures revealed by works that are unfamiliar. In using the word 'unfamiliar', I recognize the singularity of every individual in attitude and talent. But the phenomena of individual realizations of a spirit are only new images of that same spirit. So it is in nature that the diversity of forms evolves from universal order.

Form is the recognition of an integrity of inseparable elements. This is true in both nature and art. In nature validity is nonconscious. Every grain of sand on the beach has a natural colour and shape, is of natural weight and in its

1. 'Silence to Light, The desire to express, The Threshold, The Inspirations, The Sanctuary of Art, The Treasury of the Shadows', drawing by Louis Kahn.

Silence to Light
Light to Silence

The desire to express crossing of a moment of the
The Threshold
The Inspirations
The Sanctuary of Art
The Treasury of The Shadows

natural position. It is part of the constant play of equilibria, governed solely by the laws of nature. What man makes must answer to the laws of nature, and is governed in his concepts by rules and choice. The one is measurable. The one is completely unmeasurable. What nature makes, it makes without man, and what man makes, nature cannot make without him.

Nature does not make a house. It cannot make a room. How marvelous that when I am in a room with another the mountains, trees, wind, and rain leave us for the mind, and the room becomes a world in itself. With only one other person one feels generative. The meeting becomes an event. The actor throws aside the lines of his performance. The residue from all his thoughts and experiences meets the other on equal terms. Even now, though I feel I am saying things differently from the way I have said them before, I have thought about them and the idea is therefore not essentially generative. The room, then, is a marvelous thing.

The one desires To be to express The one

Eternity is of two Brothers

to be to make The one light

Non Luminous The one light Luminous

2. 'Eternity is of two Brothers. The one desires to be to express. The one to be to make. The one light non luminous. The one light luminous', drawing by Louis Kahn.

Architecture deals primarily with the making of spaces to serve the institutions of man. In the aura of Silence and Light, the desire to be, to make, to express, recognizes the laws that confirm the possible. Strong, then, is the desire to know, heralding the beginning of the institutions of learning dedicated to discover how we were made. In man is the record of man. Man through his consciousness feels this record, which sparks his desire to learn what nature has given him and what choices he has made to protect himself and his desires in the odyssey of his emergence.

I believe that consciousness is in all life. It is in the rose, in the microbe, in the leaf. Their consciousness is not understandable to us. How much more would we comprehend if we were to uncover their secrets, for then a wider sense of commonness would enter expressions in art, giving the artist greater insight in presenting his offerings answering to the prevailance of order, the prevailance of commonness.

Dissension is out in the open. I do not feel that its roots come from need alone. Dissension stems from desire – desire for what is not yet made, not yet expressed. Need comes from the known. Supplying only what is lacking brings no lasting joy. Did the world need the Fifth Symphony before Beethoven wrote it? Did Beethoven need it? He desired it, and now the world needs it. Desire brings about the new need.

I look at the glancing light on the side of the mountain, which is such a meaningful light, bringing every tiny natural detail to the eye, and teaching us about material and choice in making a building. But do I get less delight out of seeing a brick wall with all its attempts at regularity, its delightful imperfections revealed in natural light? A wall is built in the hope that a light once observed may strike it again in a rare moment in time. How can anyone imagine a building of spaces not seen in natural light? Schools are being built with little or no natural light, supposedly to save on maintenance costs and to assure the teachers of their pupils' undivided attention. The most wonderful aspects of the indoors are the moods that light gives to space. The electric bulb fights the sun. Think of it.

I am reminded of Tolstoy, who deviated from faithlessness to faith without question. In his latter state he deplored the miracles, saying that Christ has radiance without them. They were holding a candle to the sun to see the sun better.

Structure is the maker of light. A column and a column bring light between them. It is darkness-light, darkness-light, darkness-light, darkness-light. In the column we realize a simple and beautiful rhythmic beauty evolved from the primitive wall and its openings. At first, walls were thick. They protected man. He felt the desire for freedom and the promise of the world outside. He made at first a rude opening. Then he explained to the unhappy wall that, in accepting an opening, the wall must now follow a higher order with arches and piers as new and worthy elements. These are the realizations in architecture of Light and Structure. The choice of a square room is also the choice of its light as distinguished from other shapes and their light. Even a room which must be dark needs at least a crack of light to know how dark it is. But architects in planning rooms today have forgotten their faith in natural light. Depending on the touch of a finger to a switch, they are satisfied with static light and forget the endlessly changing qualities of natural light, in which a room is a different room every second of the day.

I spoke of form as the realization of a nature. A shape is an expression of form. Form follows desire as a realization of a dream or a belief. Form tells of inseparable elements. Design is the struggle to develop these elements into shapes compatible with each other, reaching for a wholeness, for a name. Form in the mind of one is not the same as it is in the mind of another. The realization of a nature, form, and shape are not part of the process of design manipulation. In design there are wonderful realizations: the order of structure, the order of construction, the order of time, the order of spaces come into play.

As I see a sheet of music, I realize that the musician sees it to hear. To an architect, the plan is a sheet on which appears the order of the structure of spaces in their light.

The institutions of learning give the architect a program of requirements. These requirements are derived from previous plans which were designed to answer momentary needs. These needs are very far from the original spirit School. The architect must consider the program merely as a guide. The spirit School, in the sense of its conceived commonness, should be considered as though it is being realized for the first time.

Recently my class decided to speculate on the question: what is a university? We had no program. We thought of the nature of a university. Our minds were empty of knowing and full of adventure. One student gave emphasis to the central library as the place of the dedication of the mind. It was suggested also that the libraries of the different professions should be related to the main library by a conscious 'Architecture of Connection', since the university's most direct service to the community is the sanctioning of the professions. But we were distressed because we realized that the university is gradually falling into the sphere of the marketplace, competing with other schools for research money and inventing special degrees to attract students. Architecture, for instance, is being separated from urban design and city planning and thus shutting off students with broad natural talents in architecture, who refuse to accept such professional distinctions.

In the marketplace the professions tend to become businesses which suppress individual talent, whose leadership has always been followed. The architect can realize the spirit of his art and the emerging orders only when the problems before him are considered as part of a whole. Relegated to niches of specialization, he will become one of a team, designing parts and giving the world nothing but solutions of immediate needs. He will never be free or experienced enough to guide prevailing desires to inspirations. Although I feel that unique talent cannot be overthrown, it is hurt by being retarded. Talent has to be recognized early to do good work.

In considering the architecture of connection – library to library – my students developed their thoughts about the significant places to be found in the university. The garden became inseparable from the room, the court, the entrance place of invitation, the green, or the great court as the place of the happening.

Dissensions made us think of a place or a structure not yet named for the teacher, the student, and the directors. Like the stoa, it would not be partitioned, and its position on the campus would be on a great lawn with not a path crossing it. The division would be agreed upon later and the lawn modified by the use it evoked.

It was thought that a university has much to gain from the city, which in turn may consider the university as one of its most important institutions. But professional practice is in the marketplace, and the university in sanctioning the professions should be free of it. This brought to our minds the role of the city planner. We realized that there must be a place free of the university and free of the marketplace where both could meet. The visions of planners meet the political economy of the city. This separate place should be recognized as a new institution of man, equal to the institutions of government, of learning, and of health.

3. 'Spending to the emergence of material, The prevailing luminous, Groups to ignite a wild dance of flaming prevalence', drawing by Louis Kahn.

Spending to the emmergence of Material

The prevailing human wants

Groups to relate a wried desires

Of planning prevalance

The city is measured by its institutions, and its growth is felt in the works of its leaders who are sensitive to the desires of the people and who want to serve their desire for expression. The studies leading to the emergence of new institutions become the points of departure for planning. Movement plans and redevelopment schemes are merely corrective projects. The known institutions need new vitality, conscious recognition. As an example of current deterioration, think of City Hall, which evolved from the early meeting place on the village green. It is probably the most dishonored building in the city – a place associated with taxes, fees, courts, and jails, where nobody meets. Since the day of the meeting house, the interests of people have become greatly extended and diversified, but there is no place for us to air these interests. A place of auditoria, meeting rooms, and seminars would revive the spirit of representation and give every man a place which he feels is his own city house.

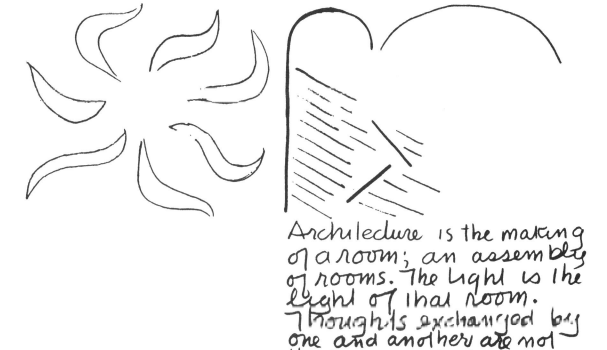

*Architecture is the making
of a room; an assembly
of rooms. The light is the
light of that room.
Thoughts exchanged by
one and another are not
the same in one room as
in another.*

*A street is a room; a community room by agreement.
Its character from intersection to intersection changes
and may be regarded as a number of rooms*

4

4. 'Architecture is the making of a room; an assembly of rooms. The light is the light of that room. Thoughts exchanged by one and another are not the same in one room as in another. A street is a room; a community room by agreement. Its character from intersection to intersection changes and may be regarded as a number of rooms', drawing by Louis Kahn.

Our inspirations assist us when we clear our senses of known solutions and methods. The realization of a yet unthought-of nature and the elements of its form can stimulate an entirely new point of view about everything. Today we talk about technology as though our minds will be surrendered to the machine. Surely the machine is merely a brain which we get, pot luck, from nature. But a mind capable of realization can inspire a new technology and humiliate the current one.

Teaching is a work. The beginning is dear to the teacher, for he senses what man is from what he accepts and is willing to support. The code of the teacher is often remote from another man's. Because of his desire to tell about his mind, he seeks words that are as close to his codes as possible without losing generativeness. I have used 'commonness' instead of 'spirit' for that very reason. Spirit is immediately assumed as understood. Commonness makes one think.

Art is the making of a life. When we hear the strains of a familiar musical masterpiece, it is as though a familiar person entered the room. But as you must see him again in order to believe his presence, so must the music be played again so you can remember all that touched you before.

In Mexico I met the architect Barragán. I was impressed by his work because of its closeness to nature. His garden is framed by a high private wall, the land and foliage remaining untouched as he found it. In it is a fountain made by a water source lightly playing over a jagged splinter and, drop for drop, falling in a great bowl of rhinoceros-gray-black stone filled to the brim. Each drop was like a slash of silver making rings of silver reaching for the edge and falling to the ground. The water in the black container was a choice from the path of water as a mountain stream in light, over rocks, and then in deep seclusion where its silver was revealed. He learned about water and selected what he loved most.

His house is not merely a house but house itself. Anyone could feel at home. Its material is traditional, its character eternal. We talked about traditions as though they were mounds of golden dust of man's nature, from which circumstances were distilled out. As man takes his path through experience, he learns about man. Learning falls as golden dust, which if touched gives the power of anticipation. The artist has this power and knows the world even before it began. He expresses himself in terms of psychological validities.

A student once asked, 'What is the intuitive sense?' Robert le Ricolais, mathematician, engineer, and scientist, answered, 'What made man venture to make the first thing? Surely it was not his knowledge but his sense of validity. But intuition must be fed. I might say that everything must begin with poetry.'

Postscript by Robert McCarter
Originally a lecture which Louis Kahn gave at the Guggenheim Museum in New York on 3 December 1968 and later delivered at the Eidgenössische Technische Hochschule in Zurich on 12 February 1969, this text starts by returning to the beginning of architecture – the time of the building of the pyramids. Kahn describes the life of a building, its construction, subsequent engagement in use, and finally its true revelation as a ruin. In this way Kahn introduces his key late concepts of 'Silence' and 'Light': Silence is man's desire to express; Light is that which gives presence to something made from that desire. Kahn goes on to say that material is spent Light, an idea he likely derived from his reading of Dante. As he addressed the audience, Kahn made four drawings with chalk on the blackboard, illustrating the nature of Light, and its relation to shadow and material.

'Architecture, Silence and Light', originally published in Arnold Toynbee et al., *On the Future of Art* (New York: Viking Press, 1970), sponsored by the Solomon R. Guggenheim Museum, pp.20 35.

I have some thoughts about the spirit of architecture. I have chosen to talk about the room, the street and human agreement.

The room is the beginning of architecture. It is the place of the mind. You in the room with its dimensions, its structure, its light respond to its character, its spiritual aura, recognizing that whatever the human proposes and makes becomes a life.

The structure of the room must be evident in the room itself. Structure, I believe, is the giver of light. A square room asks for its own light to read the square. It would expect the light either from above or from its four sides as windows or entrances.

Sensitive is the Pantheon. This nondirectional room dedicated to all religions has its light only from the oculus above, placed to invest the room with inspired ritual without favoritism. The entrance door is its only impurity. So powerful was this realization of appropriate space that even now the room seems to ask for its release to its original freedom.

Of the elements of a room, the window is the most marvelous. The great American poet Wallace Stevens prodded the architect, asking, 'What slice of the sun does your building have?' To paraphrase: What slice of the sun enters your room? What range of mood does the light offer from morning to night, from day to day, from season to season and all through the years?

Gratifying and unpredictable are the permissions that the architect has given to the chosen opening on which patches of sunlight play on the jamb and sill and that enter, move and disappear.

Stevens seems to tell us that the sun was not aware of its wonder until it struck the side of a building.

Enter your room and know how personal it is, how much you feel its life. In a small room with just another person, what you say may never have been said before. It is different when there is more than just another person. Then, in this little room, the singularity of each is so sensitive that the vectors do not resolve. The meeting becomes a performance instead of an event with everyone saying his lines, saying what has been said many times before.

Still, in a large room, the event is of commonalty. Rapport would take the place of thought. This room we are in now is big, without distinction. The walls are far away. Yet I know if I were to address myself to a chosen person, the walls of the room would come together and the room would become intimate. If I were now reading, the concern would be diction.

If this room were the Baptistry of Florence, its image would have inspired thoughts in the same way as person to person, architect to architect. So sensitive is a room.

The plan is a society of rooms. The rooms relate to each other to strengthen their own unique nature. The auditorium wants to be a violin. Its envelope is the violin case. The society of room is the place where it is good to learn, good to work, good to live.

Open before us is the architect's plan. Next to it is a sheet of music. The architect fleetingly reads his composition as a structure of elements and spaces in their light.

The musician reads with the same overallness. His composition is a structure of inseparable elements and spaces in sound. A great musical composition is of such entity that when played it conveys the feeling that all that was heard was assembled in a cloud over us. Nothing is gone, as though time and sound have become a single image.

The corridor has no position except as a private passage. In a school, the boy walks across a hall as in his own classroom where he is his own teacher, observing others as others do. The hall asks for equal position with the library.

The society of rooms is knit together with the elements of connection which have their own characteristics.

The stair is the same for the child, the adult, and the old. It is thought of as precise in its measures, particularly for the young boy who aspires to do the floors in no time flat, both up and down. It is good also to consider the stair landing as a place to sit near a window with possibly a shelf for a few books. The old man ascending with the young boy can stop here, showing his interest in a certain book, and avoid the explanations of infirmity. The landing wants to be a room.

A bay window can be the private room within a room. A closet with a window becomes a room ready to be rearranged. The lightless corridor, never a room, aspires to the hall overlooking the garden.

The library, the work court, the rooms of study, the place of meeting want to group themselves in a composition that evokes architecture. The libraries of all university schools sit well in a court entrance available to all its students as a place of invitation. The entrance courts and their libraries and the gardens and paths knitting them together form an architecture of connection. The book is an offering of the mind.

The work court of a school of architecture is an inner space encircled by workshops available to construct building experiments. The rooms of study and *ateletum* are of a variety of dimensions and spaces in their light, small for the intimate talk and work, and large for the making of full-size drawings and group work.

Rooms must suggest their use without name. To an architect, a school of architecture would be the most honored commission.

The street is a room of agreement. The street is dedicated by each house owner to the city in exchange for common services.

Dead-end streets in cities today still retain this room character. Through-streets, since the advent of the automobile, have entirely lost their room quality. I believe that city planning can start with realization of this loss by directing the drive to reinstate the street where people live, learn, shop, and work as the room out of commonalty.

Today, we can begin by planting trees on all existing residential streets, by redefining the order of movement which would give these streets back to more intimate use which would stimulate the feelings of well-being and inspire unique street expression.

The street is a community room.

The meeting house is a community room under a roof. It seems as though one came naturally out of the other.

A long street is a succession of rooms given their distinction, room for room, by their meeting of crossing streets. The intersecting street brings from afar its own developed nature which infiltrates any opening it meets. One block in a stream of blocks can be more preferred because of its particular life. One realizes the deadliness of uninterested movement through our streets which erases all delicacy of character and blots out its sensitive nature given to it of human agreement.

Human agreement is a sense of rapport, of commonness, of all bells ringing in unison – not needing to be understood by example but felt as an undeniable inner demand for a presence. It is an inspiration with the promise of the possible.

Dissension does not stem from need but from the mad outburst of frustration, from the hopelessness of the far awayness of human agreement. Desire, not need, the forerunner of the new need, out of the yet not said and the yet not made, seems to be the roots of hope in dissension.

How inspiring would be the time when the sense of human agreement is felt as the force which brings new images. Such images reflecting inspirations and put into being by inspired technology. Basing our challenges on present-day programming and existing technologies can only bring new facets of old work.

The city from a simple settlement became the place of the assembled institutions. The settlement was the first institution. The talents found their places. The carpenter directed building. The thoughtful man became the teacher, the strong one the leader.

When one thinks of simple beginnings which inspired our present institutions, it is evident that some drastic changes must be made which will inspire the re-creation of the meaning, *city*, as primarily an assembly of those places vested with the care to uphold the sense of a way of life.

Human agreement has always been and will always be. It does not belong to measurable qualities and is, therefore, eternal. The opportunities which present its nature depend on circumstances and on events from which human nature realizes itself.

A city is measured by the character of its institutions. The street is one of its first institutions. Today, these institutions are on trial. I believe it is so because they have lost the inspirations of their beginning. The institutions of learning must stem from the undeniable feeling in all of us of a desire to learn. I have often thought that this feeling came from the way we were made, that nature records in everything it makes how it was made. This record is also in man and it is this within us that urges us to seek its story involving the laws of the universe, the source of all material and means, and the psyche which is the source of all expression. Art.

The desire to learn made the first school room. It was of human agreement. The institution became the modus operandi. The agreement has the immediacy of rapport, the inspiring force which recognizes its commonalty and that it must be part of the human way of life supported by all people.

The institution will die when its inspirations are no longer felt and when it operates as a matter of course. Human agreement, however, once it presents itself as a realization is indestructible. For the same reason a man is unable to work below his level of comprehension. To explain inspiration, I like to believe that it is the moment of possibility when what to do meets the means of doing it.

City planning must begin to be cognizant of the strength and character of our present institutions and be sensitive to the pulse of human relationship which senses the new inspirations which would bring about new and meaningful institutions. Traffic systems, sociological speculations, new materials, new technologies are servants to the pulse of human rapport which promises revelations yet not felt but in the very core of human desires.

New spaces will come only from a new sense of human agreements – new agreements which will affirm a promise of life and will reveal new availabilities and point to human support for their establishment.

I realized in India and Pakistan that a great majority of the people are without ambition because there is no way in which they are able to elevate themselves beyond living from hand to mouth, and what is worse, talents have no outlets. To express is the reason for living. The institution of learning, of work, of health, of recreation should be made available to all people. All realms of expression will be opened. Each singularity will express in his way. Availabilities to all can be the source of a tremendous release of the values locked in us of the unmeasurable in living: the art of living.

One city can distinguish itself from the other by just the inspirational qualities that exist in sensing natural agreements as the only true source of new realizations. In that sense the spaces where it is good to learn, to work and to live may remain unexpressed if their nature is not redefined. It is not just enough to solve the problem. To imbue the spaces with new-found self-quality is a different question entirely. Solution is a 'how' design problem; the realization of 'what' precedes it.

Now a word about inspired technology. The wall enclosed us for a long time until the man behind it, feeling a new freedom, wanted to look out.

He hammered away to make an opening. The wall cried, 'I have protected you'. And the man said, 'I appreciate your faithfulness but I feel time has brought change'.

The wall was sad; the man realized something good. He visualized the opening as gracefully arched, glorifying the wall. The wall was pleased with its arch and carefully made jamb. The opening became part of the order of the wall.

The world with its many people, each one a singularity, each group of different experiences revealing the nature of the human in varied aspects, is full of the possibility of more richly sensing human agreement from which new architecture will come. The world cannot be expected to come from the exercise of present technology alone to find the realms of new expression. I believe that technology should be inspired. A good plan demands it.

A word about silence and light. A building being built is not yet in servitude. It is so anxious to be that no grass can grow under its feet, so high is the spirit of wanting to be. When it is in service and finished, the building wants to say, 'Look, I want to tell you about the way I was made'. Nobody listens. Everybody is busy going from room to room.

But when the building is a ruin and free of servitude, the spirit emerges telling of the marvel that a building was made.

When we think of great buildings of the past that had no precedent, we always refer to the Parthenon. We say that it is a building that grew out of the wall with opening. We can say that in the Parthenon light is the space between the columns – a rhythm of light, no-light, light, no-light which tells the tremendous story of light in architecture that came from the opening in a wall.

We are simply extending what happened long ago: the beginning may be considered the most marvelous – without precedent, yet its making was as sure as life.

Light is material life. The mountains, the streams, the atmosphere are spent light.

Material, nonconscious, moving to desire; desire to express, conscious, moving to light meet at an aura threshold where the will senses the possible. The first feeling was of beauty, the first sense was of harmony, of man undefinable, unmeasurable and measurable material, the maker of all things.

At the threshold, the crossing of silence and light, lies the sanctuary of art, the only language of man. It is the treasury of the shadows. Whatever is made of light casts a shadow. Our work is of shadow; it belongs to light.

When the astronauts went through space, the earth presented itself as a marvelous ball, blue and rose, in space. Since I followed it and saw it that way, all knowledge left me as being unimportant. Truly, knowledge is an incomplete book outside of us. You take from it to know something, but knowing cannot be imparted to the next man. Knowing is private. It gives singularity the means for self-expression.

I believe that the greatest work of man is that part which does not belong to him alone. If he discovers a principle, only his design way of interpreting belongs to him alone. The discovery of oxygen does not belong to the discoverer.

I invented a story about Mozart. Somebody dropped a dish in his kitchen, and it made a hell of a noise. The servants jumped, and Mozart said, 'Ah! Dissonance'. And immediately dissonance belonged to music, and the way Mozart wrote interpreting it belonged to him.

Architects must not accept the commercial divisions of their profession into urban design, city planning and architecture as though they were three different professions. The architect can turn from the smallest house to the greatest complex, or the city. Specializing ruins the essence of the revelation of the form with its inseparable parts realized only as an entity.

A word about beauty. Beauty is an all-prevailing sense of harmony, giving rise to wonder; from it, revelation. Poetry. Is it in beauty? Is it in wonder? Is it revelation?

It is in the beginning, in first thought, in the first sense of the means of expression.

A poet is in thought of beauty and existence. Yet a poem is only an offering, which to the poet is less.

A work of architecture is but an offering to the spirit architecture and its poetic beginning.

Postscript by Robert McCarter

Given as his lecture when he was awarded the American Institute of Architects Gold Medal in 1971, Louis Kahn here summarizes his late thinking on the integrated nature of architecture, from the room to the city. Starting with the simple room, and its light, as the beginning of all architecture, Kahn then expands his definition of architecture as a society of spaces to include both the street understood as a community room, and the city experienced as a gathering of institutions — as places made and maintained by human agreement. As is typical in Kahn's lectures throughout his life, his most powerful points are made with stories of human occupation of space, rather than with abstract arguments.

'The Room, the Street, and Human Agreement', originally published in *AIA Journal*, vol. 56, no. 3, September 1971, pp.33–34.

List of projects 1926–73

The following list identifies 230 designs by Louis I. Kahn (1901–74) including built and unbuilt commissions, planning studies and competition entries. Kahn's independent work as well as projects designed in his formal partnerships – Kahn & Kopelan (fl. c.1930–5; with Solis Daniel Kopelan, 1902–87), the Architectural Research Group (fl. 1932–4), Howe & Kahn (fl. 1941–2), Howe, Stonorov & Kahn (fl. 1941–2) and Stonorov & Kahn (fl. 1942–7) – are listed. When known, the names of associated or collaborating architects have been included with their respective projects. Several commissions included in the list were completed after Kahn's death by others, most notably David Wisdom & Associates (fl. 1974–83) and Pellecchia & Meyers (fl. 1973–9), who realized Kahn's intentions in Bangladesh and Nepal, and at the Yale Center for British Art. The list does not include work executed in the offices of John Molitor (1872–1928), William H. Lee (1884–1971), Paul P. Cret (1876–1945) and Zantzinger, Borie & Medary (fl. 1910–c.1932), where Kahn was employed in the years following his graduation from the University of Pennsylvania in 1924.

This list updates the list of Kahn's buildings and projects published in David B. Brownlee and David G. De Long's *Louis I. Kahn: In the Realm of Architecture* (New York: Rizzoli, 1991). The 1991 list was based upon an intense period of scholarly research into the drawings, papers, photographs and manuscripts in the Louis I. Kahn Collection held at the Architectural Archives of the University of Pennsylvania on permanent loan from the Pennsylvania Historical and Museum Commission since 1977. Over fifty researchers contributed to that effort including Julia Moore Converse, Director of the Architectural Archives and Curator of the Louis I. Kahn Collection, along with Neslihan Dostoglu, Peter Kohane, Peter S. Reed, Enrique Vivoni and professors David G. De Long and David B. Brownlee of the University of Pennsylvania. Research at the Athenaeum of Philadelphia (Magaziner and Lee collections), Columbia University's Avery Library (Howe Collection) and the University of Wyoming's American Heritage Center (Stonorov and Kastner collections), and an extensive survey of published sources was also conducted at that time.

Since 1991, previously unknown material has come to light, adding significantly to Kahn's documented works. Most notably, a donation of papers by Kahn's daughter, Sue Ann Kahn, to the Architectural Archives provided important insights into Kahn's work in the late 1920s and early 1930s, and especially his involvement with the Architectural Research Group. The publication of *Louis Kahn to Anne Tyng: The Rome Letters 1953–1954* (New York: Rizzoli, 1997) sheds new light on this significant moment in his life, identifies several previously unknown projects and refines the dating of several others. In all, over thirty designs, mostly dating from before 1950, have been discovered and added to the 1991 list.

William Whitaker, Chief Curator & Collections Manager
The Architectural Archives, University of Pennsylvania

Projects are listed in chronological order based on the earliest documented date found in the archival sources. All projects by Louis I. Kahn, with Kahn as principal architect, unless otherwise stated.

PJT = Project (all unbuilt or published projects)
IMP = Implemented (all built or completed projects or implemented planning studies)
DMD = Known to be demolished

1926

Palace of Fashion, Sesquicentennial International Exposition
South Broad Street and Pattison Avenue, Philadelphia, PA
George F. Pawling Construction Company (Kahn design consultant), DMD

Textile Industries Exhibit, Sesquicentennial International Exposition
Palace of Fashion, South Broad Street and Pattison Avenue, Philadelphia, PA
In association with Herman Polss, DMD

1930

Prototypical Service Station
Submitted to Shell Eastern Petroleum Products, Inc.
Kahn & Kopelan, PJT

1933

Model Slum Rehabilitation Project
Shown at the 'Better Homes Exhibition'
South Philadelphia, Philadelphia, PA
Architectural Research Group (Kahn designer), PJT

Stockholm City Planning Competition
Lower Norrmalm district, Stockholm, Sweden
Architectural Research Group, PJT

Slum Clearance Project Competition
Sponsored by the Phelps Stokes Fund
New York, NY
Architectural Research Group, PJT

Lenin Memorial Competition
Port of Leningrad, USSR
Architectural Research Group (Kahn designer), PJT

Indirect Slum Clearance Project
Submitted to the Philadelphia Housing Authority
Castor Avenue, Magee Avenue and Unruh Avenue, Philadelphia, PA
Architectural Research Group (Kahn designer) in association with Magaziner & Eberhard, PJT

Northeast Philadelphia Housing Corporation Housing Project
Submitted to the Public Works Administration
Algon Avenue, Faunce Street, Elgin Avenue, Frontenac Street and Cottman Avenue, Philadelphia, PA
Architectural Research Group (Kahn designer) in association with Magaziner & Eberhard, PJT

1934

Weisbrod and Hess (Interior Alterations)
Philadelphia, PA
Architectural Research Group, IMP

M. Buten Paint Store (Alterations)
6711 Germantown Avenue, Philadelphia, PA
In association with Hyman Cunin, DMD

1935

Saint Katherine's Village Housing Project
Between Frankford Avenue and Pennsylvania Railroad right-of-way at Liddonfield Station, Philadelphia, PA
In association with Magaziner & Eberhard, PJT

Unidentified Housing Project
Philadelphia, PA
Group 1, Allied Housing Architects of Philadelphia
In association with Clarence C. Zantzinger, Edmund R. Purves, John Graham, Jr, Edwin H. Silverman and Abraham Levy, PJT

Ahavath Israel Synagogue
Now Grace Temple, 6735–37 North 16th Street, Philadelphia, PA
1935–7, IMP

Jersey Homesteads
Housing, factory, school, stores, pumping station and sewage plant, Roosevelt, Monmouth County, NJ
Kahn assistant principal architect and co-designer with Alfred Kastner, both as employees of the Resettlement Administration, 1935–7 (Kahn's employment), houses and factory IMP, sewage plant and school built to Kastner designs IMP

1936

Medical Offices (Alterations)
For E. Cohen and N. Smolens
3114 Frankford Avenue, Philadelphia, PA
c.1936, IMP

Unidentified Housing Project
In association with Magaziner & Eberhard, PJT

Unidentified House
In association with Magaziner & Eberhard, c.1936, PJT

1937

Dental Offices (Alterations)
For Dr David K. Waldman
5203 Chester Avenue, Philadelphia, PA
IMP

Prefabricated House Studies
Sponsored by Samuel Fels
In association with Louis Magaziner and Henry Klumb, 1937–8, PJT

Horace Berk Memorial Hospital (Alterations and Additions)
Now Philadelphia Psychiatric Hospital, 1218–48 North 54th Street, Philadelphia, PA
1937–8, PJT

1938

Glenwood Low-cost Housing Project Competition
For the Philadelphia Housing Authority
Ridge Avenue, West Glenwood Avenue, Page Street and North 25th Street, Philadelphia, PA
Architectural Design Group #8 (George Howe principal architect, Kahn, Kenneth M. Day and others), PJT

Art Center, Wheaton College Competition
Sponsored by the Museum of Modern Art, New York and Architectural Forum
Norton, MA
In association with Oscar Stonorov and Rudolph Mock, PJT

U.S. Post Office and Court House Competition
Covington, KY
PJT

Old Swedes' (or Southwark) Housing Project
Housing and community building for the U.S. Housing Authority and the Philadelphia Housing Authority
Catherine Street, Swanson Street, Washington Avenue, 2nd Street, Christian Street and Front Street, Philadelphia, PA
In association with Kenneth M. Day, 1938–40, PJT

1939

Pennsylvania Hospital (or Kirkbride's) Housing Project
Housing and community building for the U.S. Housing Authority and the Philadelphia Housing Authority, Haverford Avenue, 42nd Street, Market Street and 46th Street, Philadelphia, PA
1939–40, PJT

Illustrations for United States Housing Authority Booklets
Housing Subsidies: How Much and Why?, Tax Exemption of Public Housing, The Housing Shortage, Public Housing and the Negro, Housing and Juvenile Delinquency, PJT (published)

Housing in the Rational City Plan
Panels for the exhibition 'Houses and Housing', organized by the United States Housing Authority
Museum of Modern Art, New York, NY
PJT

Philadelphia Psychiatric Hospital
Ford Road and Monument Avenue, Philadelphia, PA
PJT (commission reassigned to Thalheimer & Weitz)

1940

Apartment and Dental Offices (Alterations)
For A. Abraham
5105 Wayne Avenue, Philadelphia, PA
PJT

Van Pelt Court Apartments (Alterations)
For E. T. Pontz
231 South Van Pelt Street, Philadelphia, PA
IMP

Unidentified House (Interior Alterations)
2007 Delancey Street, Philadelphia, PA
PJT

Unidentified House (Interior Alterations)
2008 Chancellor Street, Philadelphia, PA
PJT

Battery Workers Union, Local 113 (Alterations)
Now Commandment Keepers of the House of God, 1903 West Allegheny Avenue, Philadelphia, PA
IMP

Sherman House and Office (Interior Alterations)
Philadelphia, PA
PJT

Mr and Mrs Jesse Oser House
628 Stetson Road, Elkins Park, PA
1940–2, IMP (subsequently altered)

1941

South Philadelphia Rehabilitation Project
Site bordered by Wharton, Front and Broad Streets
and Oregon Avenue, Philadelphia, PA
PJT

Pine Ford Acres
Housing, community building and maintenance
building for the Federal Works Agency and the
Federal Public Housing Authority
Middletown Borough, Dauphin County, PA
Howe & Kahn, 1941–3, IMP (housing DMD)

Pennypack Woods
Housing, community building and stores for the
Federal Works Agency and the Federal Public
Housing Authority
Crispin Street, Holme Avenue, Frankford Avenue
and Pennypack Street, Philadelphia, PA
Howe, Stonorov & Kahn, 1941–3, IMP

Mr and Mrs Louis Broudo House
Juniper Park Development, Elkins Park, PA
1941–2, PJT

Carver Court (or Foundry Street Housing)
Housing and community building for the
National Housing Agency and the Federal
Public Housing Authority
Caln Township (near Coatesville), PA
Howe, Stonorov & Kahn, 1941–3, IMP

M. Shapiro and Sons Prefabricated Houses
Newport News, VA
Stonorov & Kahn (Stonorov principal architect),
1941–2, PJT

1942

Stanton Road Dwellings
Housing and community building
Site bordered by Bruce Place, Stanton
Road, Alabama Avenue and 15th Street SE,
Washington, DC
Howe & Kahn, 1942–7, PJT

**Willow Run (or Bomber City),
Neighborhood III**
Housing and school for the Union of Automobile
Workers and Federal Public Housing Authority,
Washtenaw County (near Ypsilanti), MI
Stonorov & Kahn, 1942–3, PJT

Lincoln Highway Defense Housing
Housing and community building for the
National Housing Agency and the Federal
Public Housing Authority
Caln Road and Lincoln Highway, Caln Township
(near Coatesville), PA
Howe, Stonorov & Kahn, 1942–4, IMP

House for 194X
Sponsored by *Architectural Forum*
Stonorov & Kahn, PJT (not submitted)

Lily Ponds Housing
Housing and community building for the
United States of America, acting through
the Alley Dwelling Authority
Anacostia Avenue, Eastern Avenue and Kenilworth
Avenue NE, Washington, DC
Stonorov & Kahn, 1942–3, IMP (housing DMD)

Thermostore Refrigerator Unit
For Gimbels Department Store
Stonorov & Kahn (Stonorov principal architect)
1942–3, PJT (mock-up built)

1943

Hotel for 194X
Sponsored by *Architectural Forum*
Stonorov & Kahn, PJT (published)

**International Ladies Garment Workers Union
Health Center**
Now law offices, 2136 South 22nd Street,
Philadelphia, PA
Stonorov & Kahn, 1943–5, IMP

Model Neighborhood Rehabilitation Project
For publication in *Why City Planning is Your
Responsibility*, New York: Revere Copper and
Brass, 1943
Morris, 20th, McKean and 22nd Streets,
Philadelphia, PA
Stonorov & Kahn (Stonorov principal architect), PJT

Design For Postwar Living House Competition
Sponsored by California Arts and Architecture
Stonorov & Kahn, PJT

Model Neighborhood Rehabilitation Project
Sponsored by Architects' Workshop on City
Planning, Philadelphia Housing Association
and Citizens Council on City Planning
Moore Street, Howard Street, Water Street, Snyder
Avenue and Moyamensing Avenue, Philadelphia, PA
Stonorov & Kahn, PJT (model built and published
in *You and Your Neighborhood: A Primer for
Neighborhood Planning*, New York: Revere Copper
and Brass, 1944)

**Industrial Union of Marine and Shipbuilding
Workers of America, Local 1 (Alterations)**
2332–4 Broadway, Camden, NJ
Stonorov & Kahn (Stonorov principal architect),
1943–5, IMP

Phoenix Corporation Houses
Bridge Street, Phoenixville, PA
Stonorov & Kahn (Stonorov principal architect),
1943–4, PJT

1944

Philadelphia Moving Picture Operators' Union
Vine and 13th Streets, Philadelphia, PA
Stonorov & Kahn, PJT

Parasol House Construction System
For Knoll Associates Planning Unit
Stonorov & Kahn, PJT

Model Men's Shoe Store and Furniture Store
For Pittsburgh Plate Glass
Stonorov & Kahn, PJT (published)

**Dimitri Petrov House
(Alterations and Additions)**
713 North 25th Street, Philadelphia, PA
Stonorov & Kahn, 1944–8, PJT

National Jewish Welfare Board
Clubhouse furnishings
Washington, DC
Stonorov & Kahn (Stonorov principal architect), PJT

Paul W Darrow House
Adaptation of old power plant
Vare Estate, Fort Washington, PA
Stonorov & Kahn, 1944–6, PJT

Philadelphia Psychiatric Hospital (New Wing)
Ford and Monument Roads, Philadelphia, PA
Stonorov & Kahn in association with Isadore
Rosenfeld (hospital consultant), 1944–6, PJT

Borough Hall (Alterations)
Phoenixville, PA
Stonorov & Kahn (Stonorov principal architect), PJT

**Dr and Mrs Alexander Moskalik House
(Alterations)**
2018 Spruce Street, Philadelphia, PA
Stonorov & Kahn, 1944–5, IMP

**Offices, Radbill Oil Company
(Interior Alterations and Furnishings)**
1722–4 Chestnut Street (second floor),
Philadelphia, PA
Stonorov & Kahn, 1944–7, IMP

1945

Westminster Play Lot
Site bordered by Markoe Street, Westminster
Avenue and June Street, Philadelphia, PA
Stonorov & Kahn, c.1945, PJT

Unidentified House
Stonorov & Kahn, c.1945, PJT

**Edward and Tana Hoban Gallob House and
Studio (Alterations)**
2036 Rittenhouse Square, Philadelphia, PA
Stonorov & Kahn, 1945–7, PJT

**Gimbels Department Store
(Interior Alterations)**
Market and 8th Streets, Philadelphia, PA
Stonorov & Kahn (Stonorov principal architect),
1945–6, DMD

House for Cheerful Living Competition
Sponsored by Pittsburgh Plate Glass and
Pencil Points
Stonorov & Kahn, PJT

Business Neighborhood in 194X
Advertisement for Barrett Division, Allied
Chemical and Dye Corporation
Stonorov & Kahn, PJT (published)

Mr B. A. Bernard House (Additions)
195 Hare's Hill Road at Camp Council
Road, Kimberton, PA
Stonorov & Kahn, IMP

**Department of Neurology, Jefferson Medical
College (Interior Alterations)**
1025 Walnut Street, Philadelphia, PA
Stonorov & Kahn, 1945–6, IMP

**Mr and Mrs Samuel Radbill Residence
(Alterations)**
224 Bowman Avenue, Merion, PA
Stonorov & Kahn, 1945–6, IMP (partial)

**William H. Harman Corporation Prefabricated
Houses**
420 Pickering Road, Charlestown, Chester
County, PA, and Rosedale Avenue and
New Street, West Chester, PA
Stonorov & Kahn (Stonorov principal architect),
1945–7, IMP (some demolition)

**Drs Lea and Arthur Finkelstein House
(Alterations and Additions)**
645 Overhill Road, Ardmore, PA
Stonorov & Kahn, 1945–8, PJT

Solar House Prototype
For Libby-Owens-Ford Glass Company
Stonorov & Kahn, 1945–7, PJT (published)

Action for Cities
Panel for 'American Housing' exhibition
France
1945–6, IMP

Thom McAn Shoe Store (Alterations)
72 South 69th Street, Upper Darby, PA
Stonorov & Kahn, 1945–6, PJT

Two Dormitories, Camp Hofnung
Pipersville, Bucks County, PA
Stonorov & Kahn, 1945–7, IMP

Philadelphia Building at Camp Unity House
For the International Ladies Garment Workers Union
Forrest Lake, Bushkill Township, Northampton
County, PA
Stonorov & Kahn, 1945–7, IMP

1946

**Mr and Mrs Arthur V. Hooper House
(Alterations and Additions)**
5820 Pimlico Road, Baltimore, MD
Stonorov & Kahn, PJT

Container Corporation of America
Cafeteria, offices and paper stock depot
Nixon and Fountain Streets, Manayunk,
Philadelphia, PA
Stonorov & Kahn, PJT

**Memorial Playground,
Western Home for Children**
715 Christian Street, Philadelphia, PA
Stonorov & Kahn, 1946–7, DMD

Triangle Redevelopment Project
Site bordered by Benjamin Franklin Parkway,
Market Street and Schuylkill River, Philadelphia, PA
Associated City Planners (Kahn, Oscar Stonorov,
Robert Wheelwright, Markley Stevenson and
C. Harry Johnson), 1946–8, PJT

Greenbelt Co-op Shopping Center
For Greenbelt Consumer Services, Inc.
Greenbelt, MD
Ross and Walton architects (Kahn design consultant)
1946–8, IMP

1947

Coward Shoe Store
Now Lerner Woman, 1118 Chestnut Street,
Philadelphia, PA
Stonorov & Kahn (Stonorov principal architect),
1947–9, IMP (subsequently altered)

Dr and Mrs Philip Q. Roche House
2101 Harts Lane, Conshohocken,
Montgomery County, PA
Stonorov & Kahn, 1947–9, IMP

**X-Ray Department, Graduate
Hospital, University of Pennsylvania
(Interior Alterations)**
Lombard and 19th Streets, Philadelphia, PA
1947–8, IMP

Mr and Mrs Harry A. Ehle House
Mulberry Lane, Haverford, PA
In association with Abel Sorensen, 1947–8, PJT

**Jefferson National Expansion Memorial
Competition (first stage)**
St Louis, MO
PJT

Mr and Mrs Morton Weiss House
2935 Whitehall Road, East Norriton Township, PA
1947–50, IMP

Dr and Mrs Winslow T. Tompkins House
Lot 18, Apologen Road, Philadelphia, PA
1947–9, PJT

M. Buten Paint Store (Alterations)
Kaighns and Haddon Avenues, Camden, NJ
In association with George Von Uffel, Jr
1947–8, DMD

1948

Mr and Mrs Harry Kitnick House
Whitehall Road, East Norriton Township, PA
1948–9, PJT

**Mr and Mrs Joseph Rossman House
(Alterations)**
1714 Rittenhouse Square, Philadelphia, PA
1948–9, PJT

Jewish Community Center
Now Holcombe T. Green Jr Hall, Yale University,
1156 Chapel Street, New Haven, CT
Weinstein & Abramowitz architects (Kahn consultant
architect), 1948–54, IMP (subsequently altered)

**Bernard S. Pincus Occupational Therapy
Building, Philadelphia Psychiatric Hospital
(Additions)**
Ford Road, Philadelphia, PA
In association with Isadore Rosenfeld (hospital
consultant), 1948–51, IMP

**Samuel Radbill Building, Philadelphia
Psychiatric Hospital (Alterations and
Additions)**
Ford Road, Philadelphia, PA
In association with Isadore Rosenfeld (hospital
consultant), 1948–54, IMP (subsequently altered)

Mr and Mrs Samuel Genel House
201 Indian Creek Road, Wynnewood, PA
1948–51, IMP

1949

**Jewish Agency for Palestine
Emergency Housing**
Israel
PJT

**Dr and Mrs Jacob Sherman House
(Alterations)**
414 Sycamore Avenue, Merion, PA
1949–51, PJT

1950

**Mr and Mrs Nelson J. Leidner House
(Alterations and Additions to former
Oser House)**
626 Stetson Road, Elkins Park, PA
1950–1, IMP (additions DMD)

Ashton Best Corporation Garden Apartments
200 Montgomery Avenue, Ardmore, PA
PJT

**American Federation of Labor Health Center,
St Luke's Hospital (Alterations)**
Now Girard Medical Center, Franklin and
Thompson Streets, Philadelphia, PA
1950–1, DMD

Southwest Temple Redevelopment Area Plan
Columbia Avenue, 9th Street, Girard Avenue
and Broad Street, Philadelphia, PA
Architects Associated (Kahn with Kenneth M.
Day, Louis E. McAllister Sr, Douglas G. Braik
and Anne G. Tyng, consulting architects for
the Philadelphia City Planning Commission)
1950–2, IMP

East Poplar Redevelopment Area Plan
Girard Avenue, 5th Street, Spring Garden Avenue,
9th Street, Philadelphia, PA
Architects Associated (Kahn with Kenneth M.
Day, Louis E. McAllister Sr, Douglas G. Braik
and Anne G. Tyng, consulting architects for
the Philadelphia City Planning Commission)
1950–2, IMP

1951

University Redevelopment Area Plan
For the Philadelphia City Planning Commission,
the Philadelphia Redevelopment Authority, the
University of Pennsylvania and Drexel University
Philadelphia, PA
Architects Associated (Kahn with Kenneth M.
Day, Louis E. McAllister Sr, Douglas G. Braik
and Anne G. Tyng, consulting architects for
the Philadelphia City Planning Commission)
IMP (partial)

Row House Studies
Roosevelt Boulevard, Holme Avenue and Rhawn
Street, Philadelphia, PA
Architects Associated (Kahn with Kenneth M.
Day, Louis E. McAllister Sr, Douglas G. Braik
and Anne G. Tyng, consulting architects for
the Philadelphia City Planning Commission),
1951–3, PJT

Traffic Studies (submitted to the American
Institute of Architects, Philadelphia Chapter,
Committee on Municipal Improvements)
Philadelphia, PA
1951–3, PJT

Yale University Art Gallery and Design Center
1111 Chapel Street, New Haven, CT
Douglas Orr and Kahn associated architects,
1951–3, IMP (Design Center relocated c.1961)

**Manufacturing Building, Container
Corporation of America**
Longford Road, Oaks, Upper Pottsgrove
Township, PA
Kahn design architect, Howard Hill Carter
associated architect, 1951–2, IMP

Mr and Mrs H. Leonard Fruchter House
Ocean Drive, Stamford, CT
1951–4, PJT

Penn Center Studies
Philadelphia, PA
1951–8, PJT

Mill Creek Project
First-phase housing
46th and Aspen Streets, Philadelphia, PA
In association with Kenneth M. Day,
Douglas G. Braik and Louis E. McAllister,
1951–6, DMD (2003)

1952

Greenbelt Knoll
Housing development for Morris Milgram
Longford Road at Holme Avenue, Philadelphia, PA
Montgomery & Bishop Architects (Kahn design
consultant), 1952–7, IMP

Cinberg House (Alterations)
5112 North Broad Street, Philadelphia, PA
PJT

Offices, Zoob and Matz (Interior Alterations)
1600 Western Saving Fund Building,
Philadelphia, PA
IMP

City Tower Project
Philadelphia, PA
In association with Anne G. Tyng, 1952–7, PJT

1953

Apartment Redevelopment Project
New Haven, CT
PJT (published in *Perspecta 2)*

Riverview Competition
Housing for the elderly
State Road at Rhawn Street, Philadelphia, PA
PJT

Mr and Mrs Ralph Roberts House
Apalogen Road, Germantown, Philadelphia, PA
PJT

Wheaton Co-op Shopping Center
11111 Georgia Avenue, Wheaton, MD
John Hans Graham architect and Sweet & Schwartz
associated architects (Kahn consulting architect),
1953–4, IMP (without Kahn's recommendations)

1954

Jaffe House
Main Line (near Philadelphia), PA
PJT

Dr and Mrs Francis H Adler House
Davidson Road, Philadelphia, PA
1954–5, PJT

Mr and Mrs Weber De Vore House
Montgomery Avenue, Springfield Township,
Montgomery County, PA
1954–c.1955, PJT

**Adath Jeshurun Synagogue and School
Building**
6730 Old York Road, Philadelphia, PA
1954–5, PJT

**American Federation of Labor Medical
Services Building**
1328–34 Vine Street, Philadelphia, PA
1954–7, DMD (1973)

Jewish Community Center
Bath house, day camp and community building
999 Lower Ferry Road, Ewing Township (near
Trenton), NJ
John M. Hirsh and Stanley R. Dube supervising
architects, Kahn architect, Louis Kaplan associated
architect, 1954–9, bath house and day camp IMP

1955

Dr and Mrs Francis H. Adler House
Kitchen remodelling
7630 Huron Avenue, Philadelphia, PA
IMP

**Wharton Esherick Workshop (Alterations
and Additions)**
Horseshoe Trail, Paoli, PA
1955–6, IMP

Mr and Mrs Lawrence Morris House
Mount Kisco, NY
1955–8, PJT

1956

Washington University Library Competition
St Louis, MO
PJT

Enrico Fermi Memorial
Fort Dearborn, Chicago, IL
1956–7, PJT

Civic Center Studies
Philadelphia, PA
1956–7, PJT

Research Institute for Advanced Science (RIAS)
Baltimore, MD
1956–8, PJT

Mill Creek Project
Second-phase public housing and community centre
46th Street and Fairmount Avenue, Philadelphia, PA
1956–63, DMD (2003)

**Mr and Mrs Irving L. Shaw House
(Alterations and Additions)**
2129 Cypress Street, Philadelphia, PA
1956–9, IMP

Dissin House
Cheltenham Township, Montgomery County, PA
PJT

Dr and Mrs Bernard Shapiro House
417 Hidden River Road, Narberth, PA
1956–62, IMP (addition by Kahn in association with
Anne G. Tyng, 1973–5, IMP)

1957

Thermofax Sales Offices
153 North Broad Street, Philadelphia, PA
1957–9, PJT

Mr and Mrs Eugene Lewis House
2018 Rittenhouse Square, Philadelphia, PA
PJT

American Federation of Labor Medical Center
Red Cross Building, remodelling of hospital
and office building
253 North Broad Street, Philadelphia, PA
1957–9, PJT

Fred E. and Elaine Cox Clever House
417 Sherry Way, Cherry Hill, NJ
1957–62, IMP

Geisman House
Tulsa, OK
c.1957, PJT

**Alfred Newton Richards Medical Research
Building and Biology Building**
Now David Goddard Laboratories, University of
Pennsylvania, 3700 Hamilton Walk, Philadelphia, PA
1957–60 (phase I – Richards Building), IMP
1957–65 (phase II – Biology Building), IMP

**Biology Services Building (Alterations
and Additions)**
Now Florence and David Kaplan Memorial Wing
and Leidy Laboratories Room 201, University of
Pennsylvania, 415 University Avenue, Philadelphia, PA
1957–60, IMP (altered, second storey added)

1958

**Mount Saint Joseph Academy and Chestnut
Hill College**
Chestnut Hill, Philadelphia, PA
PJT

Offices, Zoob and Matz (Interior Alterations)
Western Saving Fund Building (14th floor),
Philadelphia, PA
IMP

Tribune Review Publishing Company Building
Cabin Hill Drive, Greensburg, PA
1958–62, IMP (subsequently altered)

1959

Mr and Mrs M. Morton Goldenberg House
Frazier Road, Rydal, PA
PJT

Mr Robert H. Fleisher House
8363 Fisher Road, Elkins Park, PA
PJT

Space Environment Studies
For General Electric Co., Missile and Space
Vehicle Department
(Kahn consultant architect), PJT

Awbury Arboretum Housing Development
For the International Ladies Garment Workers Union
Walnut Lane, Ardleigh Street and Tulpehocken
Street, Philadelphia, PA
1959–60, PJT

Margaret Esherick House
204 Sunrise Lane, Chestnut Hill, Philadelphia, PA
1959–61, IMP

US Consulate Chancellery and Residence
Luanda, Angola
1959–62, PJT

**William L. Tencate House (Alterations
and Additions)**
16–18 West Evergreen Avenue, Philadelphia, PA
1959, PJT

Salk Institute for Biological Studies
Laboratories, meeting house and housing
10010 North Torrey Pines Road, La Jolla, CA
1959–65, laboratories IMP

First Unitarian Church and School
220 South Winton Road, Rochester, NY
1959–62, IMP
School wing addition by Kahn, 1965–9, IMP

Fine Arts Center, School and Performing Arts Theater
Now Performing Arts Center, 303 East Main Street, Fort Wayne, IA
T. Richard Shoaff principal architect (Kahn architect)
1959, first contact, 1961–73, theatre and offices IMP

1960

Bristol Township Offices
2501 Oxford Valley Road, Levittown, PA
1960–1, PJT

General Motors Exhibit, 1964 World's Fair
Grand Central Parkway and Long Island Expressway, New York, NY
1960–1, PJT

Barge for the American Wind Symphony Orchestra
River Thames, England
1960–1, DMD

Market Street East Studies
For the Philadelphia City Planning Commission
Philadelphia, PA
1960–2, PJT

Chemistry Building, University of Virginia
Charlottesville, Virginia
Stainback and Scribner architects (Kahn design architect), 1960–3, PJT

Eleanor Donnelley Erdman Hall Dormitory, Bryn Mawr College
Morris and Gulph Roads, Bryn Mawr, PA
1960–5, IMP

Philadelphia College of Art
Now the University of the Arts, Broad and Pine Streets, Philadelphia, PA
1960–6, PJT

Franklin Delano Roosevelt Memorial Competition
West Potomac Park, Washington, DC
PJT

Dr and Mrs Norman Fisher House
197 East Mill Road, Hatboro, PA
1960–7, IMP

1961

Warehouses and office buildings, Carborundum Company
Mountain View, CA, Chicago, IL and Atlanta, GA
1961–2, PJT

Warehouse and office building, Carborundum Company
Niagara Falls, NY
IMP

Office of Louis I. Kahn, Architect (Interior Alterations)
1501 Walnut Street, Philadelphia, PA
1961–72, DMD

Plymouth Swim Club
Gallagher Road, Montgomery County, PA
PJT

Shapero Hall of Pharmacy, Wayne State University
Detroit, MI
1961–2, PJT

Gandhinagar, Capital of Gujarat State, India
Gandhinagar, India
1961–6, PJT

Levy Memorial Playground
Between West 102nd and West 105th Streets in Riverside Park, New York, NY
Isamu Noguchi sculptor (Kahn architect)
1961–6, PJT

Saint Andrew's Priory
Hidden Valley Road, Valyermo, CA
1961–7, PJT

Mikveh Israel Synagogue
Commerce Street, between 4th and 5th Streets, Philadelphia, PA
1961–72, PJT

1962

Lawrence Memorial Hall of Science Competition
Berkeley, CA
1962, PJT

Mrs C. Parker House (Alterations and Additions to Margaret Esherick House)
204 Sunrise Lane, Chestnut Hill, Philadelphia, PA
1962–4, PJT

Delaware Valley Mental Heath Foundation, Family and Patient Dwelling
833 Butler Avenue, Doylestown, PA
1962–71, PJT

Indian Institute of Management
Vikram Sarabhai Road, Ahmedabad, India
In association with Balkrishna Doshi and Anant Raje
1962–74, IMP

Sher-e-Bangla Nagar, Capital of Bangladesh
Dhaka, Bangladesh
Kahn architect, design and construction completed after Kahn's death by David Wisdom & Associates
1962–83, IMP

1963

Peabody Museum, Hall of Ocean Life, Yale University (Alterations and Additions)
New Haven, CT
1963–5, PJT

President's Estate, First Capital of Pakistan
Islamabad, Pakistan
1963–6, PJT

Interama Community B
Miami, FL
Kahn architect, Watson, Deutschman & Kruse associate architects, 1963–9, PJT

1964

Barge 'Point Counterpoint'
For the American Wind Symphony Orchestra
Pittsburgh, PA
1964–7, IMP

Mr and Mrs Louis I. Kahn Residence (Alterations and Additions)
921 Clinton Street, Philadelphia, PA
IMP

1965

Maryland Institute College of Art
Site bordered by Park Avenue, Howard Street and Dolphin Street, Baltimore, MD
1965–9, PJT

Marjorie Walter Goodhart Hall, Bryn Mawr College (Interior Alterations and Furnishings for Common Room)
Bryn Mawr, PA
IMP

The Dominican Motherhouse of Saint Catherine de Ricci
Providence Road, Media, PA
1965–9, PJT

Library and Dining Hall, Phillips Exeter Academy
Exeter, NH
1965–72, IMP

1966

Broadway United Church of Christ and Office Building
Broadway and Seventh Avenue, between 56th and 57th Streets, New York, NY
1966–8, PJT

Mr and Mrs Max L. Raab House
Site bordered by Waverly, Addison and 21st Streets, Philadelphia, PA
1966–8, PJT

Olivetti-Underwood Factory
Valley Road, Harrisburg, PA
1966–70, IMP (radically altered c.1997)

Mr and Mrs Philip M. Stern House
2710 Chain Bridge Road, Washington, DC
1966–70, PJT

Kimbell Art Museum
3333 Camp Bowie Boulevard, Fort Worth, TX
Kahn architect, Preston Geren associate architect, 1966–72, IMP

Memorial to the Six Million Jewish Martyrs
Battery Park, New York, NY
1966–72, PJT

Temple Beth-El Synagogue
220 South Bedford Road, Chappaqua, NY
1966–72, IMP

Kansas City Office Tower
Site 1, Walnut, 11th and Grand Streets, site 2, Main, Baltimore, 11th and 12th Streets, Kansas City, MI
1966–73, PJT

1967

Rittenhouse Square Housing
Philadelphia, PA
PJT

Hurva Synagogue
Jerusalem, Israel
1967–74, PJT

Hill Renewal and Redevelopment Project
Housing and school
New Haven, CT
1967–74, PJT

1968

Albie Booth Boys Club
Unlocated
PJT

Palazzo Dei Congressi
Site 1, Giardini Pubblici, Site 2, Arsenale,
Venice, Italy
1968–74, PJT

**DuPont–Columbia Journalism Award,
Columbia University**
1968–74, PJT

**Wolfson Center for Mechanical and
Transportation Engineering**
Mechanical and electrical buildings
Tel Aviv, Israel
Kahn architect, design and construction completed
after Kahn's death by J Mochly-I Eldar, Ltd.,
1968–77, mechanical engineering building IMP

1969

Raab Dual Movie Theater
2021–3 Sansom Street, Philadelphia, PA
1969–70, PJT

Art Center, Rice University
Houston, TX
1969–70, PJT

Inner Harbor, Project no. 1
For the Hammerman Corporation and
Gateway Developers
Pratt and Light Streets, Baltimore, MD
Kahn architect, Ballinger Company associate
architects, 1969–73, PJT

Yale Center for British Art
1080 Chapel Street, New Haven, CT
Kahn architect, design and construction completed
after Kahn's death by Pellecchia & Meyers,
1969–77, IMP

Art Library Study, Yale University
Chapel Street, New Haven, CT
PJT

1970

John F. Kennedy Hospital (Addition)
Philadelphia, PA
1970–1, PJT

**President's House, University of Pennsylvania
(Alterations and Additions)**
2216 Spruce Street, Philadelphia, PA
1970–1, IMP

**Family Planning Center and Maternal
Health Center**
Ram Sam Path, Kathmandu, Nepal
Kahn architect, design and construction completed
after Kahn's death by David Wisdom & Associates,
1970–5, IMP (partial)

1971

**Treehouse, Eagleville Hospital and
Rehabilitation Center**
Eagleville, PA
PJT

**Washington Square East Unit 2
Redevelopment**
Philadelphia, PA
c.1971, PJT

**International Bicentennial Exposition
Master Plan**
For the Philadelphia 1976 Bicentennial Corporation
Eastwick, Southwest Philadelphia, PA
Kahn, Bower & Fradley, Eshback, Glass, Kale &
Associates, Mitchell/Giurgola, Murphy Levy Wurman,
and Venturi & Rauch, 1971–3, PJT

Mr and Mrs Steven Korman House
6019 Sheaff Lane, Fort Washington, PA
1971–3, IMP

Mr and Mrs Harold A. Honickman House
Sheaff Lane, Fort Washington, PA
1971–4, PJT

Government House Hill Development
Housing and hotel
Jerusalem, Israel
1971–3, PJT

Graduate Theological Union Library
Now Flora Lamson Hewlett Library, Ridge Road
and Scenic Avenue, Berkeley, CA
Kahn, architect, design and construction completed
after Kahn's death by Esherick, Homsey, Dodge
& Davis and Peters, Clayberg & Caulfield, 1971–87,
IMP

1972

De Menil Foundation
Now Menil Collection, site bordered by Yupon, Sul
Ross, Mulberry and Branard Streets, Houston, TX
1972–4, PJT

Independence Mall Area Redevelopment
In conjunction with Bicentennial
Philadelphia, PA
1972–4, PJT

Pocono Arts Center
Luzerne County, PA
1972–4, PJT

1973

Rabat Project
Cultural and commercial complex
Bou-Regreg zone on the River Oued,
Rabat, Morocco
1973–4, PJT

Franklin Delano Roosevelt Memorial
For the New York State Urban Development
Corporation
Roosevelt Island, NY
1973–4, PJT

Abbasabad Development
Financial, commercial and residential areas
Tehran, Iran
In association with Kenzo Tange, 1973–4, PJT

Bishop Field Estate
Lenox, MA
Designed and built after Kahn's death, based
on Kahn's site plan, 1973–4, IMP

Ridgway Library (Alterations and Additions)
901–33 South Broad Street, Philadelphia, PA
c.1973, PJT

Notes
Bibliography
Index

Notes

Introduction

1. Louis Kahn, quoted in Alexandra Tyng, *Beginnings: Louis I. Kahn's Philosophy of Architecture* (New York: John Wiley & Sons, 1984), p.127.
2. See the Bibliography of this book; other than the brief 1975 study by Giurgola and Mehta, the only examination of the entire body of Kahn's work and thought is in the 1991 Brownlee and De Long, which, while it imparts important factual information, is fragmented among more than a dozen authors and is thereby of limited effectiveness as a comprehensive critical study.
3. Kenneth Frampton, 'Response', in David De Long, Helen Searing and Robert A. M. Stern (eds), *American Architecture: Innovation and Tradition* (New York: Rizzoli, 1986), p.135.
4. James Stirling to author, November 1990.
5. Louis Kahn, quoted in Richard Saul Wurman, *What Will Be Has Always Been: The Words of Louis I. Kahn* (New York: Rizzoli, 1986), p.260.
6. See also Vincent Scully, *Louis I. Kahn* (New York: George Braziller, 1962), p.43; Kahn was 'concerned primarily with interior space and its construction in terms of perceptible law'.
7. Ibid., p.43.

Chapter 1
Development of an architectural philosophy

1. Kahn, quoted in Wurman, op. cit., p.243.
2. This is the date shown on Kahn's passport of 1928, though Anne Tyng relates that Kahn told her he was actually born in 1902, and that an immigration official incorrectly documented his birth date as 1901 when he entered the United States in 1906. Anne Griswold Tyng, *Louis Kahn to Anne Tyng: The Rome Letters 1953–1954* (New York: Rizzoli, 1997), p.10, passport photo on p.14.
3. Ibid., pp.10–12.
4. William Huff, quoted in Joseph Burton, 'Notes from Volume Zero: Louis Kahn and the Language of God', *Perspecta* 20 (Cambridge, MA: MIT Press, 1983), p.75.
5. Anne Griswold Tyng, op. cit., p.14.
6. David Brownlee and David De Long, *Louis I. Kahn: In the Realm of Architecture* (New York: Rizzoli, 1991), p.20.
7. Ibid.
8. Anne Griswold Tyng, op. cit., p.14.
9. Louis Kahn, 'The Samuel S. Fleisher Art Memorial' (1974), in Alessandra Latour (ed.), *Louis I. Kahn: Writings, Lectures, Interviews* (New York: Rizzoli, 1991), p.344.
10. Louis Kahn, 'How'm I doing, Corbusier?' (1972), in Latour, *Louis I. Kahn: Writings*, op. cit., pp.298–9.
11. Kahn, 'The Samuel S. Fleisher Art Memorial' (1974), in Latour, *Louis I. Kahn: Writings*, op. cit., p.344.
12. Ibid., p.343.
13. When visiting Philadelphia in the mid-1980s to serve on juries at the University of Pennsylvania, I found myself riding in a taxi whose driver, upon discovering I was an architect, told me about Kahn, who had been his frequent client years before; Kahn asked the taxi driver's opinion on all the buildings they passed in their rides, and was very interested in the driver's views on architecture. Kahn's associate, David Polk, noted, 'Cab drivers would give [Kahn] ideas because he was always talking to cab drivers'; Polk interview in Alessandra Latour (ed.), *Louis I. Kahn: l'uomo, il maestro* (Rome: Edizioni Kappa, 1986), p.97.

14. Brownlee and De Long, op. cit., p.21.
15. Kenneth Frampton, 'Louis Kahn and the French Connection', *Oppositions* 22 (New York: IAUS/MIT Press, 1980), p.23. This article remains to this day the most insightful examination of these important influences on Kahn's development as an architect.
16. Paul Cret, 'The Architect as Collaborator of the Engineer' (1927), in Theo White (ed.), *Paul Philippe Cret: Architect and Teacher* (Philadelphia, PA: Art Alliance Press, 1973), p.26. Quoted in Frampton, 'Louis Kahn and the French Connection', op. cit., p.23.
17. Frampton, 'Louis Kahn and the French Connection', op. cit., p.27.
18. Why Choisy's *Histoire*, so important to the development of modern architecture, has never, since the last 1903 edition, been reprinted or republished in any form, abridged or otherwise, is simply beyond comprehension. This is all the more incredulous given that the book's illustrations and text are still both valid as history and influential on the thinking and practice of architects (through a very few of the drawings being reproduced in other books). Today, one must resort to searching the rare book sections of better university architecture libraries to find a single copy of what was the standard history text by which the first generation of modern architects was inspired.
19. Scully, *Louis I. Kahn*, op. cit., p.12.
20. Copies of the five volumes of Guadet's *Éléments*, the ten volumes of Viollet-le-Duc's *Dictionnaire*, Durand's *Recueil*, Choisy's *Histoire* and D'Espouy's *Fragments* remained in Kahn's library at his death; he had earlier brought his copy of Letarouilly's *Édifices* into the office, though it and a number of other books are no longer in Kahn's library held in the Louis I. Kahn Collection, University of Pennsylvania.
21. Brownlee and De Long, op. cit., p.21.
22. Le Corbusier, *Towards a New Architecture* (London: Architectural Press, 1927), pp.45, 173.
23. Frank Lloyd Wright, 'In the Cause of Architecture' (1928), in Frederick Gutheim (ed.), *In the Cause of Architecture* (New York: Architectural Record Books/ McGraw-Hill, 1975), pp.58–9.
24. Louis Kahn, 'Kahn on Beaux-Arts Training', in William Jordy (ed.), *Architectural Review* 155 (June 1974), p.332. Quoted in Brownlee and De Long, op. cit., p.22.
25. Scully, *Louis I. Kahn*, op. cit., pp.10–11.
26. Brownlee and De Long, op. cit., p.22.
27. Superbly documented in the beautiful book, Jan Hochstim, *The Paintings and Sketches of Louis I. Kahn* (New York: Rizzoli, 1991).
28. Anne Griswold Tyng, op. cit., p.10.
29. Brownlee and De Long, op. cit., p.23. Brownlee states that Kahn 'visited the archaic Greek temples at Paestum, but no sketches have been found from there, nor any sketches of the Roman antiquities'. Yet Hochstim published several sketches from those ancient sites; Hochstim, op. cit., pp.98, 99.
30. Scully, *Louis I. Kahn*, op. cit., p.13.
31. Brownlee and De Long, op. cit., p.24.
32. Ibid., p.21.
33. A strict translation of the title, 'Towards an Architecture', would have far better reflected Le Corbusier's fundamentalist intention.
34. Wright, 'In the Cause of Architecture' (1928), in Gutheim, op. cit., pp.153, 161.
35. Sarah W. Goldhagen, *Louis Kahn's Situated Modernism* (New Haven, CT: Yale University Press, 2001), pp.11, 12. While Goldhagen's recent study of Kahn offers a long overdue reminder of Kahn's fundamental commitment to community identity and human experience, her focus on the 're-conceptualization' of Kahn's work continues the tendency for architectural historians to ignore or downplay the fundamental importance of spatial experience – of the perceptual rather than the conceptual – in the reality of architecture.

36. George Howe, quoted in William Huff, 'Kahn and Yale', in Latour, *Louis I. Kahn: l'uomo, il maestro*, op. cit., p.343.
37. On Howe see Robert A. M. Stern, *George Howe: Toward a Modern American Architecture* (New Haven, CT: Yale University Press, 1975).
38. William Curtis, *Modern Architecture Since 1900*, 3rd edition (London: Phaidon Press, 1996), p.237.
39. Kahn, 'How'm I doing, Corbusier?' (1972), in Latour, *Louis I. Kahn: Writings*, op. cit., p.307.
40. Brownlee and De Long, op. cit., p.24.
41. This legendary back-handed compliment, repeated various times, was first made in 1954; Philip Johnson, *Writings* (New York: Oxford University Press, 1979), p.140.
42. Wright, 'In the Cause of Architecture' (1928), in Gutheim, op. cit., p.168.
43. Frank Lloyd Wright, 'Designing Unity Temple', in *An Autobiography* (New York: Horizon Press, 1943), pp.177–84; Louis Kahn, 'The room is the beginning of architecture' in 'An Architect Speaks His Mind' (1972), in Latour, *Louis I. Kahn: Writings*, op. cit., p.294.
44. Beautifully documented, along with the careers in housing of Stonorov and Kastner, in Piero Santostefano, *Le Mackley Houses di Kastner e Stonorov a Philadelphia* (Rome: Officina Edizioni, 1982).
45. Walt Whitman, 'Chanting the Square Deific', quoted by Wright in *The Architectural Forum*, vol.68, no.1 (January 1938), p.104. Full text in 'Leaves of Grass' (1855), in Walt Whitman, *Complete Prose and Collected Poetry* (New York: Library of America, 1982), p.559.
46. Kahn, quoted in Heinz Ronner and Sharad Jhaveri (eds), *Louis I. Kahn: Complete Works, 1935–1974*, 2nd edition (Basel: ETH/Birkhäuser, 1987), p.98.
47. Marcel Breuer's houses have been recently documented in Joachim Driller, *Breuer Houses* (London: Phaidon Press, 2000).
48. Brownlee and De Long, op. cit., p.29.
49. Louis Kahn, '"Standards" Versus Essential Space' (1942), in Latour, *Louis I. Kahn: Writings*, op. cit., p.15.
50. As noted in Brownlee and De Long, op. cit., p.31.
51. Ibid., p.33.
52. Ibid., p.36.
53. See in particular Sigfried Giedion, José Luis Sert and Fernand Léger, 'Nine Points on Monumentality' (1943), reprinted in *Harvard Architectural Review*, vol.4 (Cambridge, MA: MIT Press, 1984).
54. George Howe, 'Monuments, Memorials, and Modern Design', *Magazine of Art* 37 (October 1944), pp.202–7; quoted in Goldhagen, op. cit., p.27.
55. Paul Zucker (ed.), *New Architecture and City Planning: A Symposium* (New York: Philosophical Library, 1944); Louis Kahn, 'Monumentality' (1944), in Latour, *Louis I. Kahn: Writings*, op. cit., pp.18–27.
56. James Ackerman, *The Architecture of Michelangelo* (Harmondsworth: Penguin, 1961), p.290.
57. In a published studio discussion of 1953 between Louis Kahn, Philip Johnson, Vincent Scully, Pietro Belluschi and others, regarding Wright's Johnson Wax Research Tower of 1944 (the same year as Kahn's 'Monumentality' essay), Kahn stated, 'It is a built-up type of sculpture made of small pieces rather than of a single monolith.' Louis Kahn, 'On the Responsibility of the Architect' (1953), in Latour, *Louis I. Kahn: Writings*, op. cit., p.53.
58. Robert A. M. Stern, 'Yale 1950–1965', *Oppositions* 4 (New York: IAUS/Wittenborn, 1974), pp.36–7.
59. Walter Gropius offered Kahn a teaching position at Harvard in 1946; Brownlee and De Long, op. cit., p.44.
60. This great building, which would play an important part in Kahn's life, is documented in Steven Parissien, *Pennsylvania Station: McKim, Mead and White* (London: Phaidon Press, 1996). The building's destruction in 1963, one of the last crimes of 'urban renewal', sparked the historic preservation movement

and its resulting laws protecting landmark buildings.

61. Goldhagen, op. cit., p.46.

62. Paul Klee's notes and diagrammatic drawings for this course, published in two volumes as *The Thinking Eye* and *The Nature of Nature* (London: Lund Humphries, 1961 and 1973), remain perhaps the most innovative introduction to material and space from any of the disciplines of the Modern Movement. This work had a major influence on the thinking of architects in the second half of the twentieth century, yet it has been little studied.

63. For a full study of this astonishing school, see Mary Emma Harris, *The Arts at Black Mountain College* (Cambridge, MA: MIT Press, 1987).

64. Ibid., p.165.

65. Brownlee and De Long, op. cit., p.45.

66. Stern, 'Yale 1950–1965', op. cit., p.37.

67. I was delighted to find that my colleague Sarah Goldhagen had come to the same conclusions as I have on this matter, though by independent routes; she explores the influence on Kahn of Existentialism and abstract expressionist painting in depth; Goldhagen, op. cit., pp.45–54; see further comments on abstract expressionist painting in Chapter 2 of this book, and on Existentialism in Chapter 6 of this book.

68. Harris, op. cit., p.17.

69. Josef Albers' work is documented in Nicholas Fox Weber, *Josef Albers: A Retrospective* (New York: Guggenheim Museum, 1988).

70. Goldhagen, op. cit., p.52.

71. Josef Albers, 'The Educational Value of Manual Work and Handicraft in Relation to Architecture', in Zucker, op. cit., pp.688–94.

72. Harris, op. cit., p.17.

73. Fred Licht and Nicholas Fox Weber, *Josef Albers: Glass, Color, Light* (New York: Guggenheim Museum, 1994), p.148.

74. Anni Albers' work is documented in Nicholas Fox Weber and Pandora Tabatabai Asbaghi, *Anni Albers* (New York: Guggenheim Museum, 1999).

75. Anni Albers, 'Constructing Textiles', *Design* 47 (April 1946), p.22. Quoted in Harris, op. cit., p.24.

76. This comparison is confirmed by Anne Tyng's statement that, when she was studying for the architectural registration exam in 1948, 'Lou [Kahn] helped me on history, a subject that had not been emphasized at Harvard'. Anne Griswold Tyng, op. cit., p.39.

77. Avery Faulkner, a student at Yale, quoted in Stern, 'Yale 1950–1965', op. cit., p.38.

78. A general study of the period may be found in Spiro Kostof, 'The Shape of Time at Yale, Circa 1960', in G. Wright and J. Parks (eds), *The History of History in American Schools of Architecture 1865–1975* (New York: Temple Hoyne Buell Center for the Study of American Architecture/Princeton Architectural Press, 1990).

79. George Kubler, *The Shape of Time* (New Haven, CT: Yale University Press, 1962), pp.33, 55. See also his encyclopaedic *The Art and Architecture of Ancient America* (London: Penguin, 1962).

80. William MacDonald, *The Architecture of the Roman Empire* (New Haven: Yale University Press, 1965) and *Early Christian and Byzantine Architecture* (New York: George Braziller, 1962).

81. Frank Brown, *Roman Architecture* (New York: George Braziller, 1961).

82. Vincent Scully, *The Earth, the Temple, and the Gods* (New Haven, CT: Yale University Press, 1962).

83. Vincent Scully, *Frank Lloyd Wright* (New York: George Braziller, 1960).

84. The Hartford project by Wright, proposed for Hollywood, California, was composed of a series of concrete 'flying saucers' barely anchored to their mountain-top site, with extensive pools from which water, though a precious natural resource in this arid region, was to be constantly spilled into the canyon below, and is typical of what I have elsewhere called the 'disintegration' of Wright's work in the last decade of his life; Robert McCarter, *Frank Lloyd Wright* (London: Phaidon Press, 1997), pp.321–31.

85. Huff, op. cit., p.337. Henry Russell Hitchcock, *In the Nature of Materials: The Buildings of Frank Lloyd Wright, 1887–1941* (New York: Duell, Sloan and Pearce, 1942); Wright, *An Autobiography*, op. cit.

86. Stern, 'Yale 1950–1965', op. cit., p.36.

87. Kahn, quoted in Wurman, op. cit., unpaginated, copy of Kahn notebook page at the end of the book.

88. Huff, 'Kahn and Yale', in Latour, *Louis I. Kahn: l'uomo, il maestro*, op. cit., pp.331–3. Huff also points out that the student-hero of the novel, Rafferty Bloom, was based upon an actual student of Kahn's at Yale, Duncan Buel, whom Kahn later hired in his office, where he constantly referred to him as 'Rafferty'.

89. Edwin Gilbert, *Native Stone* (Garden City, NY: Doubleday, 1955), p.60.

90. Scully, *Louis I. Kahn*, op. cit., p.16.

91. Anne Griswold Tyng, op. cit., p.31.

92. Hochstim, op. cit., p.241.

93. Scully, *Louis I. Kahn*, op. cit., p.18.

94. The characterization of Brown was made by Jon Michael Schwarting to the author in 1983, based on his own time as a Rome Fellow with Brown.

95. Brown, op. cit., pp.9, 34, 38.

96. Spiro Daltas, one of the Fellows who was in residence at the Academy with Kahn during this time, told the author this story in 1984, when we were both living in Rome.

97. Kahn, quoted in 'The View from Janiculum Hill', *Colonnade* (University of Virginia, Spring 2001).

98. The week's delay in Cairo is noted in Hochstim, op. cit., p.241. Spiro Daltas, who was on this trip with Kahn, remembered that one day Kahn, dressed in his usual black wool suit in the ferocious desert sun, was so taken by the pyramids that he hardly noticed he was being carried away by a band of over-eager Bedouins offering camel rides, who had mistaken Kahn's cries of 'The light, look at the light!' to be agreement to a camel ride around the pyramids; author conversation with Daltas, 1984.

99. Vincent Scully, in Latour, *Louis I. Kahn: l'uomo, il maestro*, op. cit., p.147.

100. Kahn, quoted in Wurman, op. cit., p.243.

Chapter 2
Rediscovering an architecture of mass and structure

1. Louis Kahn, 'Order Is' (1955), in Latour, *Louis I. Kahn: Writings*, op. cit., p.59.

2. Buckminster Fuller, 'Designing a New Industry' (1946), in Joan Ockman (ed.), *Architecture Culture 1943–1968* (New York: Rizzoli, 1993), pp.86, 88.

3. Scully, interview in Latour, *Louis I. Kahn: l'uomo, il maestro*, op. cit., p.153.

4. Ancient Tuscan mason's saying, 'Peso non dorme mai'. Also translated as 'An arch never sleeps', in James Fergusson's two-volume *A History of Architecture in All Countries* (1883), p.5; this passage being marked in Kahn's copy in his library.

5. Patricia Cummings Loud, *The Art Museums of Louis I. Kahn* (Durham, NC: Duke University Press, 1989), pp.59, 55, 60.

6. Ibid., p.63.

7. See the proportional and geometrical analyses in Klaus-Peter Gast, *Louis I. Kahn: The Idea of Order* (Basel: Birkhäuser, 1998), p.27.

8. Loud, op. cit., pp.68, 69. Also Anne Griswold Tyng, op. cit., p.47.

9. David Anfam, *Abstract Expressionism* (London: Thames and Hudson, 1990), p.194; Goldhagen titled this characteristic of Kahn's work, paralleling abstract expressionist painting, 'the presentational aesthetic'; Goldhagen, op. cit., pp.49–55.

10. Louis Kahn interview, 'Order and Form: Yale Art Gallery and Design Center', *Yale Daily News* (6 November 1953); quoted in Goldhagen, op. cit., p.41.

11. Louis Kahn interview, 'The Architect Speaks', *Yale Daily News* (6 November 1953); quoted in Loud, op. cit., p.84.

12. Louis Kahn, 'This Business of Architecture' (1955), in Latour, *Louis I. Kahn: Writings*, op. cit., p.63.

13. Loud, op. cit., p.69.

14. Louis Kahn, 'Toward a Plan for Midtown Philadelphia' (1953), in Latour, *Louis I. Kahn: Writings*, op. cit., pp.45–6.

15. Emil Kaufmann, 'Three Revolutionary Architects, Boullee, Ledoux, and Lequeu', *Transactions of the American Philosophical Society* 42, Philadelphia, PA (October 1952). All of this material, and much more on other related architects, was soon after published in Kaufmann's book, *Architecture in the Age of Reason* (Cambridge, MA: Harvard University Press, 1955).

16. Marcello Angrisani, 'Louis Kahn e Storia', *Edilizia Moderna* 86, p.87.

17. Louis Kahn, interviewed by John Cook, in Wurman, op. cit., p.195.

18. Anne Griswold Tyng, op. cit.; structure sketch, 16 March 1954, p.113; 'enumerable' and 'external', p.77; 'classical', p.161; and 'I must build', p.140.

19. Goldhagen, op. cit., p.93. Also noted in Susan Solomon, *Louis I. Kahn's Trenton Jewish Community Center* (New York: Princeton Architectural Press, 2000), p.37.

20. Louis Kahn, 'A Synagogue: Adath Jeshurun of Philadelphia' (1955), in Latour, *Louis I. Kahn: Writings*, op. cit., p.62.

21. Paul Thiry, Richard Bennett and Henry Kamphoefner, *Churches and Temples* (New York: Reinhold Publishing Corporation, 1949), p.3J; quoted in Goldhagen, op. cit., p.94. Kamphoefner, the founding Dean of the School of Design at North Carolina State College and the founder of the influential Student Publication of the School of Design in 1951, which inspired Yale's *Perspecta* and other school publications started afterwards, is a figure whose importance to the post-World War II American architectural culture has not been adequately explored.

22. Mircea Eliade's writings began in the 1930s, and he explored this particular theme in such popular books as *Cosmos and History: The Myth of the Eternal Return* (New York: Princeton University Press, 1954; originally published in French, 1949); *Images et symboles* (Paris: Gallimard, 1952); and *The Sacred and the Profane* (New York: Harcourt Brace and Co., 1959; originally published in German, 1957).

23. Wright, *An Autobiography*, op. cit., pp.333, 239.

24. Here again we can detect the influence on Kahn of the artworks of Josef Albers. The Weber DeVore House plan is strikingly similar to Albers' paintings and particularly to the layered glass constructions of the 1920s and 1930s, which Albers brought with him to the US in 1933 but which were not exhibited until the 1956 show at Yale, referred to in Chapter 1 of this book; Nicholas Fox Weber, *Josef Albers: A Retrospective*, op. cit. Having learned that Kahn's father was a stained-glass craftsman, it is likely that Albers showed these works to his friend Kahn before this exhibition date.

25. Louis Kahn, quoted in Susan Braudy, 'The Architectural Metaphysic of Louis Kahn', *New York Times Magazine*, 15 November 1970, p.86.

26. Scully, *Louis I. Kahn*, op. cit., p.23. The comment about 'some contemporary criticism' is probably directed towards Bruno Zevi, whose book *Architecture as Space*, first published in Italian in 1948 and in English in 1957 (New York: Horizon Press), emphasizes experienced space over all other aspects of architecture.

27. Anne Tyng claims that it was she who 'came up with the proposal for four symmetrically arranged squares with hipped roofs' in one of her first days back from Rome (Anne Griswold Tyng, op. cit., p.192), yet the office drawings for the project show clearly that while the cruciform plan is in place in March 1955, the pyramidal hip forms were only arrived at as a solution for the roof sometime after June and possibly as late as October of that year. Goldhagen makes the same case for Tyng's authorship of the cruciform plan, quoting the junior designer on the project, Tim Vreeland (Goldhagen, op. cit., p.106). However, as I hope I make evident in the following paragraph, primary forms such as the cruciform, square, circle and pyramid used in the Bath House cannot be any one person's invention, and in any event Kahn had previously employed all of these primary geometries in his own work.
28. Susan Solomon published several examples of similar designs, including most notably the design by The Architects Collaborative (Gropius') office for a 'Prototype Elementary School', published in *Progressive Architecture* (October 1954), Solomon, op. cit., p.98.
29. Exhaustively documented in the exemplary and unequalled works of Otto Antonia Graf, such as *Die Einheit der Kunst, Otto Wagner 3* (Wien: Böhlau Verlag, 1990) and *Die Kunst des Quadrats, Zum Werk von Frank Lloyd Wright 2* (Vienna: Böhlau Verlag, 1983). Graf (literally) draws out the virtually identical geometries underlying architectural works from around the world and throughout time, showing our shared legacy of geometric space-making.
30. Scully, *Louis I. Kahn*, op. cit., p.25.
31. 'This was Kahn's first use of corner entrances', Solomon, op. cit., p.85.
32. Here again we may detect a relation to Frank Lloyd Wright's work, in this case both more recent and nearer – the lightweight, tent-like roof over heavy anchoring concrete walls of Wright's Beth Sholom Synagogue. While the tendency among critics is to focus on the rhetorical symbolism they see in Wright's forms during this late period (he would die in 1959 at the age of ninety-two), Wright's work was inevitably founded on a fundamental tectonic concept, something that would have held considerable appeal for Kahn.
33. *Archaeological Journal*, vol.5 (1846), p.22. Noted in Joseph Burton's catalogue of the collection at Kahn's home in 1978–1980, prior to its donation to the Louis I. Kahn Collection of the Architectural Archives, University of Pennsylvania.
34. See photo of 'roofless' opening day, 31 July 1955, in Solomon, op. cit., p.89.
35. Louis Kahn, 'Order in Architecture' (1957), in Latour, *Louis I. Kahn: Writings*, op. cit., p.72.
36. Rowe and Slutzky visited Kahn's office in December 1955; Brownlee and De Long, op. cit., p.59. Rowe and Slutzky, along with Bernhard Hoesli and John Hejduk, were at that time on faculty at the University of Texas, Austin, where Dean Harwell Hamilton Harris, a disciple of Frank Lloyd Wright, had brought them to teach the year before. This remarkable gathering of teachers by Harris had far-reaching influence on the education of several generations of architects at Texas, and is documented in Alexander Caragonne, *The Texas Rangers* (Cambridge, MA: MIT Press, 1995).
37. Rudolf Wittkower, *Architectural Principles in the Age of Humanism* (London: Alec Tiranti, 1952; first edition, 1949; second revised edition, 1952; third revised edition, 1962, 1971). It was most probably the 1952 edition that Rowe gave Kahn, and some in Kahn's office remember him owning another copy. No copies remain today in Kahn's personal library at the L. I. K. Collection, University of Pennsylvania, nor were any listed in Joseph Burton's catalogue of the library, op. cit.
38. Louis Kahn, notebook K12.22, 1955–62, quoted

in Brownlee and De Long, op. cit. pp.58 and 59; 'The Palladian Plan' reproduced in Wurman, op. cit., among the notebook pages at the end of the volume.
39. This rather sad story is told in detail by Solomon, op. cit., whose book is an exemplary study, showing sensitivity and insight into all the complex nuances of this commission and Kahn's often meandering design process.
40. August Komendant, *18 Years with the Architect Louis I. Kahn* (Englewood, NJ: Aloray, 1975), p.4.
41. In this rare case, I am in complete agreement with Michael Graves when he said, 'I think the Trenton Community Center should have been built because it was one of [Kahn's] best buildings. American critics have a very hard time with buildings that are not built and often do not understand their strength in a theoretical sense.' Michael Graves, interview in Latour, *Louis I. Kahn: l'uomo, il maestro*, op. cit., p.167.
42. This Greek site-planning is convincingly demonstrated in Kahn's colleague Vincent Scully's *The Earth, the Temples and the Gods*, op. cit.
43. Huff, 'Kahn and Yale', in Latour, *Louis I. Kahn: l'uomo, il maestro*, op. cit., p.343.
44. Jacqueline Robertson, quoted in Stern, 'Yale 1950–1965', op. cit., p.45.
45. Kahn, quoted in Wurman, op. cit., p.244.
46. Scully, *Louis I. Kahn*, op. cit., p.46.
47. Kahn, quoted in Huff, 'Kahn and Yale', in Latour, *Louis I. Kahn, l'uomo, il maestro*, op. cit., p.343.
48. Letter from Esther Kahn to Huff; quoted in Huff, 'Kahn and Yale', in Latour, *Louis I. Kahn, l'uomo, il maestro*, op. cit., p.365.
49. Brownlee and De Long, op. cit., p.46.
50. Ibid., p.62. Other sources have Kahn starting his teaching at the University of Pennsylvania as late as 1958, but I will defer to these 'local' experts, who were, at the time of their writing, at the source.
51. Albers was forced out at the age of sixty, and Yale's mandatory retirement age was sixty-eight; this last absurd policy was the reason for Howe's removal in 1955, and more recently, the travesty of Vincent Scully's forced retirement at the peak of his teaching effectiveness. Stern outlines this policy in reference to Howe, in Stern, 'Yale: 1950–1965', op. cit., p.42.
52. Louis Kahn, 'New Frontiers in Architecture' (1959), in Latour, *Louis I. Kahn: Writings*, op. cit. p.92.
53. Kahn, quoted in Ronner and Jhaveri, op. cit., p.109.
54. Ibid.
55. Komendant, op. cit., p.18. On the same page, Komendant is also the source for the rate of speed in the construction of the towers, 'up to three floors a week'.
56. Unfortunately, I am here referring to the experience that was possible before recent 'renovations', which have resulted in the installation of dropped ceiling panels in this entry porch, permanently hiding what Kahn intended as an important 'explanation' of the way the building works.
57. Komendant, op. cit., p.23.
58. Brownlee and De Long, op. cit., p.63.
59. Kahn, quoted in Braudy, op. cit.
60. Goldhagen admirably documents this aspect of the University of Pennsylvania; Goldhagen, op. cit., pp.120–22.
61. See Mimi and John Lobell, 'The Philadelphia School: An Architectural Philosophy' (1986), in Latour, *Louis I. Kahn, l'uomo, il maestro*, op. cit., pp.381–95.
62. For the only comprehensive introduction to Le Ricolais, see his colleague Peter McCleary's 'Robert Le Ricolais and the Search for the Indestructible Idea', *Lotus* 99 (Milan, 1998).
63. Kahn, quoted in Ronner and Jhaveri, op. cit., p.26.
64. Kahn, 'Toward a Plan for Midtown Philadelphia' (1953), in Latour, *Louis I. Kahn: Writings*, op. cit., p.28.
65. This combination of the square 'umbrella' roof,

supported by the central single column (inspired by Wright's Johnson Wax Building), and the alternating of their height, would re-emerge in Kahn's early designs for the Olivetti-Underwood factory, begun in 1966. It can also be found in almost exactly the same form in two built works in widely separated parts of the world: first in the design by Victor Lundy for the Warm Mineral Springs Motel in Venice, Florida, built in 1958; and second in Marco Zanuso's Brionvega Electronics Factory near Asolo, Italy, designed in 1963 and built in 1967. Suffice to say that the extent of Kahn's influence and legacy in modern architecture remains insufficiently known.
66. Louis Kahn, 'Space, Form, Use' (1956), in Latour, *Louis I. Kahn: Writings*, op. cit., pp.69–70.
67. Louis Kahn, 'Spaces, Order and Architecture' (1957), in Latour, *Louis I. Kahn: Writings*, op. cit., p.76.
68. This strong resemblance is also noted in Brownlee and De Long, op. cit., p.94.
69. Kahn, quoted in Wurman, op. cit., p.63.
70. Colin Rowe, *The Mathematics of the Ideal Villa and Other Essays* (Cambridge, MA: MIT Press, 1976). Both 'Neo-"Classicism"' essays were written in 1956–7, and first published in *Oppositions* 1 (1973).
71. Rowe, op. cit., pp.141–3.
72. Ibid., p.150.
73. Rowe, who was most probably at this time back in England, would have obtained the plans and model photos of this design from the 1957 *Architectural Review* publication (a British journal) and from Kahn directly – Kahn apparently included copies of drawings and photos in his correspondence with Rowe regarding the Jewish Community Center and other projects.
74. Rowe, op. cit., p.154.
75. Ibid., pp.154–5.
76. Kahn, 'Spaces, Order and Architecture' (1957), in Latour, *Louis I. Kahn: Writings*, op. cit., pp.75–9.
77. Louis Kahn, transcribed notes of studio discussion, University of Pennsylvania, 5 December 1960.

Chapter 3
Shaping an architecture of light and shadow

1. Nell E. Johnson (ed.), *Light is the Theme* (Fort Worth, TX: Kimbell Art Foundation, 1975), p.12.
2. Le Corbusier, *Towards a New Architecture* (London: Architectural Press, 1927), p.37.
3. Kahn, quoted in Wurman, op. cit., p.248.
4. Kahn, 'New Frontiers in Architecture' (1959), in Latour, *Louis I. Kahn: Writings*, op. cit., p.88.
5. Kahn, quoted in Wurman, op. cit., p.89.
6. Ibid., p.89.
7. Ibid., p.207.
8. Ibid., p.89.
9. Ibid., p.85.
10. Ibid., p.63.
11. Ibid., p.257.
12. Ibid., p.89.
13. Ibid., p.55.
14. Ibid., p.97.
15. Ibid., p.197.
16. Scully, *Louis I. Kahn*, op. cit., p.10.
17. Drawing number 505.23 among the Kahn personal sketches in the L. I. K. Collection shows large circular windows set over narrow slot-like openings below, a design that would be almost exactly built out by Carlo Scarpa in his last work, the Banca Popolare di Verona, of 1973–80; see also The Louis I. Kahn Archive, *Personal Drawings: The Completely Illustrated Catalogue of the Drawings in the Louis I. Kahn Collection*, 7 volumes (New York: Garland Press, 1987).
18. The same drawing also contains a sketch by Kahn of the section of Alvar Aalto's Viipuri Library of 1929, with its grid of circular skylights, suggesting

that perhaps Kahn at least briefly considered top-lighting for the Tribune Review project as well.

19. Louis Kahn, 'Louis I. Kahn' (1961), interview in Latour, *Louis I. Kahn: Writings*, op. cit., p.124.

20. Louis Kahn, 'Form and Design' (1961), in Latour, *Louis I. Kahn: Writings*, op. cit., pp.117–8.

21. Kahn, 'Louis I. Kahn' (1961), interview in Latour, *Louis I. Kahn: Writings*, op. cit., pp.122–3.

22. Ibid., p.123.

23. Ibid., p.126.

24. Ibid., p.122.

25. Ibid., p.123.

26. Ibid., p.126.

27. Ibid.

28. Here I must disagree with the computer rendered 'reconstruction' of the Angola project by Kent Larson, which suggests a strong pattern of bright spots of light from the roof exactly like that Kahn so strongly criticized as being 'a multiple pattern of glare'. The office drawings and the model make clear that a relatively small amount of light was all Kahn intended to penetrate the sunroof; Kent Larson, *Louis I. Kahn: Unbuilt Masterworks* (New York: Monacelli Press, 2000), pp.18–47.

29. Kahn, 'Louis I. Kahn' (1961), interview in Latour, *Louis I. Kahn: Writings*, op. cit., p.126.

30. This is well documented and described in Urs Buttiker, *Louis I. Kahn: Light and Space, Licht und Raum* (Basel: Birkhäuser, 1993), pp.98–103.

31. What they were probably not as aware of was the Wright family's deep involvement in the development of the Unitarian faith in the US, not to mention the rather astonishing fact that the Unitarian sect was founded by Wright's great-great-grandfather, Jenkins Jones, in 1726. See Meryle Secrest, *Frank Lloyd Wright* (New York: Alfred A. Knopf, 1992), pp.19–50; and also Robert McCarter, *Frank Lloyd Wright* (London: Phaidon Press, 1997), p.11.

32. Robert McCarter, *Unity Temple: Frank Lloyd Wright* (London: Phaidon Press, 1997), p.16.

33. Jean Paul Richter (ed.), *The Literary Works of Leonardo da Vinci*, 2 volumes (London: Sampson Low, Marston, Searle and Rivington, 1883); F. Peyer Im Hof, *Die Renaissance Architektur Italiens* (Leipzig: E. A. Seemann, 1870); Léon Palustre, *L'Architecture de la renaissance* (Paris: Librairies-imprimeries réunies, 1892); Francesco di Giorgio Martini, *Trattato di architettura, ingegneria e arte militare*, (c.1580; reprinted Milano: Il Polifilo, 1967).

34. It is not as clear to me as it is to Goldhagen that Kahn literally copied these plans from Richter or Wittkower (both op. cit.), but there can be little doubt that these plans were part of the 'living' tradition actively engaged by Kahn in designing this project; Goldhagen, op. cit., pp.146–7.

35. Letter from building committee to Kahn, 28 February 1960; quoted by Robin B. Williams in Brownlee and De Long, op. cit., p.452.

36. Kahn, 'Louis. I. Kahn' (1961), interview in Latour, *Louis I. Kahn: Writings*, op. cit, p.133, 134.

37. Ronner and Jhaveri, op. cit., p.118.

38. Notes by Kahn on a section drawing recently donated to the L. I. K. Collection (not yet catalogued, as of the date of this writing). While there is no date on the section, the matching plan is dated 9 August 1960. This design is not included among the five schemes documented in Ronner and Jhaveri, op. cit.; this is probably due to the fact that the key section drawing was (until 2001) held by the First Unitarian Church, and not in the L. I. K. Collection, used by Ronner and Jhaveri in making the 1987 revised second edition of their book.

39. Ronner and Jhaveri, op. cit., p.119.

40. Kahn's library contains a number of books on castles, including five volumes of *Archaeological Journal* (1846; the volumes on 'castles' are marked by Kahn); David MacGibbon and Thomas Ross, *The Castellated and Domestic Architecture of Scotland*, vol.1 (Edinburgh: 1887); four volumes of Thomas H. King, *Study Book of Medieval Architecture and Art*, (London: Henry Sotheran & Co., 1868); *España Castillos* (1960); six volumes of *The Antiquarian Itinerary* (1815; on 'monastic, castellated and domestic' architecture); and a variety of books on ancient British history.

41. Often cited by Kahn and others as his favourite example; see Brownlee and De Long, op. cit., p.107; and Scully, *Louis I. Kahn*, op. cit., figure 116.

42. Kahn, 'Louis I. Kahn' (1961), interview in Latour, *Louis I. Kahn: Writings*, op. cit., p.138.

43. Ibid., p.140.

44. Brownlee and De Long, op. cit.; date is on p.344; Anni Albers' involvement is on p.46.

45. Suggested in Goldhagen, op. cit., p.258. In Kahn's library are the three volumes of *In English Homes* by Charles Latham, 3rd edition (London: Country Life, 1909), and other books on the subject.

46. Kahn, 'Louis I. Kahn' (1961), interview in Latour, *Louis I. Kahn: Writings*, op. cit., p.136.

47. Brownlee and De Long, op. cit., p.330.

48. Louis Kahn, 'Talks with Students' (1964), in Latour, *Louis I. Kahn: Writings*, op. cit., p.163.

49. Kahn, from a letter to William Jordy, quoted in Ronner and Jhaveri, op. cit., p.133.

50. Brownlee and De Long, op. cit., pp.334–5.

51. This is based upon a comparison of the plans. The correlation between the plinth shapes is most striking on the sides of both plinths that are set high above the landscape. The east, south and west of the Acropolis corresponds quite closely to the south, west and north, respectively, of the Meeting House. It is also worth noting that during his trip of 1951, Kahn made more sketches of the plinth of the Acropolis than he did of the Parthenon and other buildings that sit at its top.

52. The often repeated story has this solution being 'discovered' when Tim Vreeland, a designer in Kahn's office, sketched a partial plan of Hadrian's Villa, on the Meeting House plinth, to which Kahn said, 'That's it!'; Scully, *Louis I. Kahn*, op. cit., p.37; Vreeland confirms in interviews, Brownlee and De Long, op. cit., p.443; but all miss the larger point. In any event, in a 1971 interview Kahn categorically denied that Hadrian's Villa was a source for the design of the Salk Meeting House, and takes Scully to task for not retracting the story before it appeared in Scully's 1962 book on Kahn, as Kahn had requested; quoted in Wurman, op. cit., p.117. Kahn ends this part of the interview by saying that being so misquoted is the worst that can happen to a man.

53. Scully, *Louis I. Kahn*, op. cit., p.37. For the plan itself, see Luigi Ficacci (ed.), *Giovanni Battista Piranesi: The Complete Etchings* (Cologne: Taschen, 2000), pp.394–432; the plan is on p.403.

54. An insufficiently recognized fact is that Nolli served as the chief assistant for Giovanni Battista Nolli in the creation of the latter's famous map of Rome of 1748. The Nolli map shows a 'figure-ground' of the public space in Rome of that date, with all streets, courtyards and public rooms (such as church interiors) outlined; public spaces are shown in white, while private space and structural walls are shown in hatched black. Within the map are located precise depictions of all the fragments of Roman ruins known at the time, shown in solid black. The map is based upon exhaustive measurements taken by Nolli and his assistant, Piranesi. Piranesi carefully placed all of these Roman ruins, which he and Nolli had documented into his own Campus Martius map, and then wove his imaginary inventions around them. Thus Piranesi's plan is at once absolutely accurate, in its depiction of known Roman ruins, and completely fantastical, in the buildings proposed in the spaces between.

55. L. I. K. Collection, Drawing numbers 540.120, 540.313, 540.136; see also The Louis I. Kahn Archive, *Personal Drawings*, vol.2, op. cit.

56. Louis Kahn, 'On Form and Design' (1961), in Latour, *Louis I. Kahn: Writings*, op. cit., p.108.

57. Louis Kahn, 'Talks with Students' (1964), in Latour, *Louis I. Kahn: Writings*, op. cit., p.164.

58. Ibid.

59. In this, the Meeting House is strikingly similar to the Institute for Advanced Studies in Princeton, New Jersey, where Einstein and many others from various sciences and humanities have for years taken their meals, used the library, and engaged in seminars together, and where many an 'unplanned meeting' in the dining hall has resulted in major scientific and artistic breakthroughs. For more on the theory of discovery in the arts and sciences, see Arthur Koestler, *The Act of Creation* (London: Pan, 1964).

60. This solution to the corner problem became an obsession both for Kahn and for his follower Romaldo Giurgola, whose great Parliament House, Canberra, Australia is a prime example.

61. Like many of Kahn's unbuilt works, the later revisions of the design often compromise the clarity and beauty of the first proposal. The most telling document as to Kahn's intention for the central court is his carefully drawn aerial perspective, identified as from Kahn's hand; Drawing number 540.20.1 in The Louis I. Kahn Archive, *Personal Drawings*, vol.2, op. cit., p.43.

62. This detail is very similar (though the stepping in section is reversed) to that at Wright's Guggenheim Museum, where the detail was also originally designed to let in both light and air.

63. Ronner and Jhaveri, op. cit., p.134.

64. The exterior of Kahn's final scheme for the Meeting House has been beautifully 'reconstructed' in Larson, op. cit., pp.48–77.

65. Kahn, 'On Form and Design' (1960), in Latour, op. cit., p.108.

66. This scheme is remarkably similar to the design for the Neurosciences Institute by Tod Williams and Billie Tsien, built across the road from the Salk Institute in 1995.

67. Contrary to what has been written in other studies, the linear water course was part of Kahn's initial conception, and arrived neither with Barragán's criticism – Joseph Rykwert, *Louis Kahn* (New York: Harry N. Abrams, 2001), p.76 – nor with the change from garden to stone plaza – Brownlee and De Long, op. cit., p.100.

68. Komendant, op. cit., p.45.

69. Louis Kahn, 'Remarks' (1965), in Latour, *Louis I. Kahn: Writings*, op. cit., p.206–7.

70. Komendant, op. cit., p.51.

71. Kahn, 'Remarks' (1965), in Latour, *Louis I. Kahn: Writings*, op. cit., p.207.

72. While there are a number of publications presenting the Salk Institute among other of Kahn's projects, it is the single subject of the excellent study by James Steele, *Salk Institute: Louis I. Kahn* (London: Phaidon Press, 1993).

73. Louis Kahn, 'Address' (1966), in Latour, *Louis I. Kahn: Writings*, op. cit., p.216.

74. These include several astonishing drawings of a type to my knowledge heretofore unknown in construction drawings: 'bird's eye' perspective views, looking directly down onto the studies, combined with cutaway sections.

75. Louis Kahn, 'I Love Beginnings' (1972), in Latour, *Louis I. Kahn: Writings*, op. cit., p.288.

76. Kahn, 'Address' (1966), in Latour, *Louis I. Kahn: Writings*, op. cit., p.214–15.

77. Brownlee and De Long, op. cit., p.333.

78. Ibid.

79. 'I could never draw it with gardens, I could never build a model where I put a garden in. But still my mind said garden, garden, garden.' Kahn, 'Address' (1966), in Latour, *Louis I. Kahn: Writings*, op. cit., p.215. This is not literally true, as there are both drawings and models of gardens in the court, yet they totally lack the same level of conviction and certainty otherwise typical of the design.

80. Ibid., p.209.

81. Louis Kahn, 'Silence' (1968), in Latour, *Louis I. Kahn: Writings*, op. cit., pp.232–3.

82. Unfortunately Kahn's meandering entry design was obliterated in the ill-advised addition constructed at the east end of the Salk Institute several years ago, which not only was built where the grove of trees originally stood but also creates an axial, symmetrical approach – exactly the opposite of what Kahn intended.

83. Kahn, quoted in Wurman, op. cit., unpaginated copy of a page from Kahn notebook, after p.306.

84. Scully, *Louis I. Kahn*, op. cit., pp.30–31.

85. Kahn, transcribed notes of studio discussions, University of Pennsylvania, 25 November 1960.

86. A typical example would be Brownlee and De Long, op. cit., p.94. In retrospect, Scully appears ever more prescient in this regard, as well as many others, in his 1962 book, op. cit.

87. Edgar Kaufmann (ed.), *Frank Lloyd Wright: An American Architecture* (New York: Horizon Press, 1955), p.84.

88. See Peter Smithson's later assessment of Kahn's contribution to Team 10, in 'Parallel Aims', *Architects' Journal* (London), vol.19, no.9 (4 March 1992), p.54.

89. This was distilled from Kenneth Frampton, *Modern Architecture: A Critical History*, 3rd edition (London: Thames and Hudson, 1992), pp.269–71.

90. Louis Kahn, 'New Frontiers in Architecture: CIAM in Otterlo, 1959', in Latour, *Louis I. Kahn: Writings*, op. cit., pp.90, 91, 94.

91. Alison Smithson (ed.), *Team 10 Primer* (Cambridge, MA: MIT Press, 1968).

92. Van Eyck's work and thought are best presented in the excellent Francis Strauven, *Aldo van Eyck: The Shape of Relativity* (Amsterdam: Architectura & Natura, 1998).

93. Van Eyck lecture, transcribed in Smithson, *Team 10 Primer*, op. cit., pp.20–22.

94. Louis Kahn, '1973: Brooklyn, New York', in Latour, *Louis I. Kahn: Writings*, op. cit., p.329.

95. Kahn (1971), quoted in Wurman, op. cit., p.113. This story so perfectly captured Van Eyck's approach to designing for the rituals of daily life that Van Eyck's principal disciple, Herman Hertzberger, would later quote this story of Kahn's in lectures on his, Hertzberger's own work.

96. Ibid., pp.113, 116. 'What will be' is again stated in Kahn's Pratt Institute lecture, Brooklyn, New York, 1973.

97. Dore Ashton, *Noguchi: East and West* (Berkeley, CA: University of California Press, 1993), pp.176–7, 192.

98. Kahn, quoted in Ana Maria Torres, *Isamu Noguchi: A Study of Space* (New York: Monacelli Press, 2000), p.136.

99. Isamu Noguchi, 'The Observatories of Maharajah Sawai Jai Singh II', *Perspecta* 6 (Cambridge, MA: MIT Press, 1960), pp.68–77.

100. Isamu Noguchi, in Torres, op. cit., p.136.

101. Kahn, 'Remarks' (1965), in Latour, *Louis I. Kahn: Writings*, op. cit., p.205.

Chapter 4
Inspired compositions in the poetics of action

1. Kahn, 'I Love Beginnings' (1972), in Latour, *Louis I. Kahn: Writings*, op. cit., p.291.

2. First enunciated in 1852 by Horatio Greenough, in Henry Tuckerman (ed.), *A Memorial of Horatio Greenough* (New York: G. P. Putnam & Co., 1853), pp.117–83. Later taken up by Louis Sullivan and, later still, transformed by Frank Lloyd Wright into 'form and function are one'.

3. Kahn, 'Spaces, Order and Architecture' (1957), in Latour, *Louis I. Kahn: Writings*, op. cit., p.76.

4. Kahn, quoted in Wurman, op. cit., p.91.

5. Kahn, 'On Philosophical Horizons' (1960), in Latour, *Louis I. Kahn: Writings*, op. cit., p.101.

6. Kahn, 'Form and Design' (1961), in Latour, *Louis I. Kahn: Writings*, op. cit., p.116.

7. Kahn, 'Spaces, Order and Architecture' (1957), in Latour, *Louis I. Kahn: Writings*, op. cit., p.75.

8. Kahn, when asked in an interview whether he agreed that form followed function, replied with a definitive 'No'. Quoted in Wurman, op. cit. p.203.

9. Kahn, quoted in Wurman, op. cit., p.62.

10. Kahn, 'On Philosophical Horizons' (1960), in Latour, *Louis I. Kahn: Writings*, op. cit., p.102.

11. Louis Kahn, 'Marin City Redevelopment' (1960), in Latour, *Louis I. Kahn: Writings*, op. cit., p.111.

12. Kahn, quoted in Wurman, op. cit., p.120.

13. Louis Kahn, 'A Statement' (1962), Latour, *Louis I. Kahn: Writings*, op. cit., p.152.

14. Kahn, 'Form and Design' (1961), in Latour, *Louis I. Kahn: Writings*, op. cit., p.114.

15. Kahn, 'Order Is' (1955), in Latour, *Louis I. Kahn: Writings*, op. cit., p.58.

16. Wurman, op. cit., p.109.

17. Ibid., p.202.

18. Kahn, 'An Architect Speaks His Mind' (1972), in Latour, *Louis I. Kahn: Writings*, op. cit., p.294.

19. Louis Kahn, 'The Room, the Street, and Human Agreement' (1971), in Latour, *Louis I. Kahn: Writings*, op. cit., p.265.

20. Kahn, 'I Love Beginnings' (1972), in Latour, *Louis I. Kahn: Writings*, op. cit., p.291.

21. Kahn, 'The Room, the Street, and Human Agreement' (1971), in Latour, *Louis I. Kahn: Writings*, op. cit., p.264.

22. Kahn, quoted in letter, Anne Griswold Tyng, op. cit., p.77.

23. Kahn, quoted in Wurman, op. cit., p.79.

24. Louis Kahn, 'Harmony Between Man and Architecture' (1974), in Latour, *Louis I. Kahn: Writings*, op. cit., p. 342.

25. Kahn, quoted in Wurman, op. cit., p.257.

26. Louis Kahn, 'Princeton 1961', Box 65, L. I. K. Collection; quoted in Goldhagen, op. cit., p.198.

27. Hannah Arendt, *The Human Condition* (Chicago: University of Chicago Press, 1958), pp.173, 49.

28. Brownlee and De Long, op. cit., p.353. One of Tyng's schemes, with seven square clusters of octagon cells set upon five circular plinths, is strikingly similar to Aldo van Eyck's 1984 ESTEC Complex in Noordwijk, The Netherlands.

29. Anne Griswold Tyng, op. cit., p.202; Tyng does not name Pattison. The relationship with Pattison and Nathaniel's birth are described in Brownlee and De Long, op. cit., p.80.

30. Kahn, 'A Statement' (1962), in Latour, *Louis I. Kahn: Writings*, op. cit., p.151.

31. Kahn, 'Remarks' (1965), in Latour, *Louis I. Kahn: Writings*, op. cit., pp.205–6.

32. Kahn, quoted in Wurman, op. cit., p.203.

33. Brownlee and De Long, op. cit., p.355.

34. Colin Rowe and Robert Slutzky, 'Transparency: Literal and Phenomenal, II' (1956), in *Perspecta* 13–14 (Yale University, 1971); Colin Rowe, *As I Was Saying* (Cambridge, MA: MIT Press, 1996), pp.73–106.

35. Kahn, 'A Statement' (1962), in Latour, *Louis I. Kahn: Writings*, op. cit., p.151.

36. Kahn, 'Remarks' (1965), in Latour, *Louis I. Kahn: Writings*, op. cit., pp.203–5.

37. Ronner and Jhaveri, op. cit., p.209.

38. Ibid., p.212.

39. Kahn tells the story of a visit to the Akbar Palace at Lahore, when, in order to demonstrate the reflectivity of mosaics by the light of a match, the guide closed the door of the room – and after only a moment in the closed room two people fainted for lack of air; as Kahn said, 'In that room, you felt that nothing was more interesting than air.'; Ronner and Jhaveri, op. cit., p.208.

40. See the exemplary geometrical and proportional analysis of the Indian Institute of Management in Klaus-Peter Gast, *Louis I. Kahn: The Idea of Order* (Basel: Birkhäuser, 1998), pp.113–84.

41. Kahn, 'Talks with Students' (1964), in Latour, *Louis I. Kahn: Writings*, op. cit., p.180.

42. Kahn, 'Remarks' (1965), in Latour, *Louis I. Kahn: Writings*, op. cit., p.204.

43. It is interesting to note that Kahn marked page 258 in his copy of Guadet's *Éléments et théorie de l'architecture* (1899), where there is a plan showing the semicircular fixed seating of the classrooms in the Sorbonne.

44. Kahn, 'Form and Design' (1961), in Latour, *Louis I. Kahn: Writings*, op. cit., p.114.

45. Kahn, 'Remarks' (1965), in Latour, *Louis I. Kahn: Writings*, op. cit., p.204.

46. Rykwert, op. cit., p.158.

47. After Kahn's death, Doshi initially designed the kitchen and dining hall to be placed to the south, adjacent to the dormitories, leaving the west end of the main building courtyard entirely open. The final executed designs were made by Anant Raje.

48. Kahn, 'Remarks' (1965), in Latour, *Louis I. Kahn: Writings*, op. cit., p.204.

49. Balkrishna Doshi, 'Louis Kahn in India', in 'Louis I. Kahn: Silence and Light', *Architecture and Urbanism 3* (Tokyo), vol.2, no.1 (special issue: January 1973), p.310.

50. Ronner and Jhaveri, op. cit., p.211.

51. Brownlee and De Long, op. cit., p.104, seem to imply that this was Kahn's first use of brick as load-bearing rather than non-load-bearing veneer.

52. Kahn, quoted in Wurman, op. cit., p.127.

53. Kahn, 'Address' (1966), in Latour, *Louis I. Kahn: Writings*, op. cit., p.218.

54. Ibid., p.220.

55. See the single-building study of this project, Florindo Fusaro, *Il Parlamento e la nuova capitale a Dacca di Louis I. Kahn* (Rome: Officina Edizioni, 1985).

56. There is, of course, a lot more to this sequence of events, and the colourful story of classic power politics is well told by Goldhagen, op. cit., pp.163–4.

57. Brownlee and De Long, op. cit., p.374.

58. Kahn, 'Remarks' (1965), in Latour, *Louis I. Kahn: Writings*, op. cit., pp.195–6; repeated in 'Louis I. Kahn' (1961), *Student Publication of the School of Design*, vol.14, no.3 (Raleigh, NC: North Carolina State University, 1964), p.5.

59. Kahn, 'Remarks' (1965), in Latour, *Louis I. Kahn: Writings*, op. cit., p.196.

60. The 5 foot (1.5 metre) diameter model for this triangulated cable space-truss structure now hangs in the Architectural Archives at the University of Pennsylvania; its date of 1960 is indicated on the model and confirmed by William Whitaker, Chief Curator and Collections Manager. For further information on Le Ricolais's structural designs, refer to McCleary, op. cit.

61. Kahn Office drawing dated 26 November 1963; L. I. K. Collection.

62. Telegram, Louis Kahn to Kafiluddin Ahmad, 22 January 1964, Box 117, L. I. K. Collection; quoted in Brownlee and De Long, op. cit., p.377.

63. Unfortunately, these light courts were covered with a grid of clear plastic skylights after Kahn's death. Whatever rain protection is provided by these skylights does not offset the cooling load increase caused by the trapping of hot air at the top of these courts, and the lack of ability to have them act as vertical stacks to promote through ventilation, as Kahn intended.

64. Kahn, 'Talks with Students' (1964), in Latour, *Louis I. Kahn: Writings*, op. cit., p.173.

65. Louis Kahn, Dhaka: May 1963 lecture; Pantheon:

June 1962 lecture. Noted in Goldhagen, op. cit., p.265, n.77.

66. In Kahn's library is Francesco di Giorgio Martini's book, *Trattato di architettura ingegneria e arte militare* – given to Kahn as a gift by the Olivetti Corporation in 1969, the same year that Kahn began to develop this final roof design – which includes drawings of the Hadrian's Villa ceiling by di Giorgio. For other connections, see Fusaro, op. cit., pp.84–5.

67. See *Student Publication of the School of Design*, vol.14, op. cit. On Félix Candela, see his 'Reinforced Concrete Shells', *Student Publication of the School of Design*, vol.9, no.2 (Raleigh, NC: North Carolina State University, 1960), pp.27–46. During this period, the School of Design in Raleigh was in fact the centre of advanced thinking on thin shell and various folded and parabolic structural forms, led by Kahn's friend Henry Kamphoefner, the Dean, and faculty members such as Félix Candela, Horacio Caminos, Eduardo Torroja, Mathew Nowicki and Eduardo Catalano.

68. Wittkower and Richter, both op. cit. Also documented in Fusaro, op. cit., pp.102–3.

69. Ronner and Jhaveri, op. cit., p.239.

70. Kahn, transcribed notes of studio discussions, University of Pennsylvania, 25 November 1960.

71. Brownlee and De Long, op. cit., pp.381–2. The secretariat was in fact never built.

72. Interview with Mark Rosario, a Bengali student in the Master of Architecture programme at the University of Florida, 2000. This is also reported in Goldhagen, op. cit., p.186.

73. I am not as convinced as is Goldhagen that this detail was dropped by Kahn above the third level because of labour difficulties; Goldhagen, op. cit., pp.190–1. I find it more likely that Kahn felt it was needed only close to the ground, where it could be seen by people – above 30 feet (9 metres), such delicate details become impossible to experience. It should be remembered that this kind of change in exterior material is common practice in high-rise construction.

74. Kahn had first proposed these cylindrical light towers within a rectangular sanctuary in his ultimately unrealized Mikveh Israel Synagogue, to be examined in Chapter 6 of this book. This type of 'double-wall' and light chamber effect is most characteristic of the church architecture of the Baroque era, particularly the northern German and Bohemian work of Balthasar Neumann and the Dientzenhofer family, as well as the Italians Francesco Borromini in Rome, and Guarino Guarini and Bernardo Vittone in Turin. In his library Kahn had several books which contained examples of these Baroque methods of using sunlight.

75. This mix of generous bounced light and small amounts of direct light are again typical of Baroque architecture, especially that of Borromini, Guarini and Vittone; see note above.

76. The masterplan by Doxiadis, called 'rather awful' by Joseph Rykwert (op. cit., p.205), appeared not to inspire Kahn or the other architects. Kahn had strong differences with Doxiadis on the matter of urban design, as was evident when, after a University of Pennsylvania lecture by Doxiadis on the Acropolis, Kahn became so incensed with Doxiadis's mathematical 'explanation' for the offset angles of the Greek buildings (rather than the visual connection to surrounding landscape and larger cosmic order that Kahn believed to underlie these Greek sites), that Kahn ran after his students to exhort them to ignore Doxiadis's 'totally false' urban theories.

77. In particular the plans, L. I. K. Collection number 675.58 in The Louis I. Kahn Archive, *Personal Drawings*, op. cit., and Ronner and Jhaveri, op. cit., p.266.

78. Kahn sketch numbers 675.173 and 675.174, in The Louis I. Kahn Archive, *Personal Drawings*, op. cit., p.229; and particularly the clay model IEP.21, in Ronner and Jhaveri, op. cit., p.269.

79. Brownlee and De Long, op. cit., p.387.

80. The first use of this collage technique is dated to 9 October 1966 in Brownlee and De Long (ibid.). However, from examination of Kahn's office drawings, it appears likely this technique had been employed prior to this date, perhaps on both the Salk Institute Meeting House and Dhaka National Capital projects.

81. The 32 foot (10 metre) dimension is noted on the office drawing dated 15 December 1968, and the hollow columns are shown on the office drawing dated 10 July 1968.

82. L. I. K. Collection, Kahn Office print set dated 22 April 1968, handwritten note reading 'brick construction'.

83. Brownlee and De Long, op. cit., p.388.

84. Wurman, op. cit., p.174.

85. Kahn, quoted in Colin St John Wilson, 'Building Ideas', *The Architects' Journal* (4 March 1992), p.21.

86. Kahn, quoted in Wurman, op. cit., p.46.

87. Kahn, quoted in Alexandra Tyng, op. cit., p.175.

88. In a letter summarizing their December 1955 discussion, Colin Rowe quoted Kahn: 'You deplored composition because it appeared to be no more than a manipulation of forms for the sake of effect. You wanted to grow a building.' Rowe to Kahn, 7 February 1956, L. I. K. Collection, Box 65; quoted in Peter Kohane, 'Louis I. Kahn and the Library', *Via 10. Ethics and Architecture* (New York: Rizzoli, 1990), p.102. During that discussion, it will be recalled, Rowe planted the seed of the 'bay or room system' of Palladio, which Kahn soon embraced and made his own.

89. Kahn, 'Address' (1966), in Latour, *Louis I. Kahn: Writings*, op. cit., p.213.

90. Kahn, quoted in Wurman, op. cit., p.79.

91. Ibid., p.178.

92. Kahn, 'Address' (1966), in Latour, *Louis I. Kahn: Writings*, op. cit., p.219.

Chapter 5
Precise experiments in the poetics of construction

1. Kahn, 'Remarks' (1965), in Latour, *Louis I. Kahn: Writings*, op. cit., p.206.

2. Kahn, 'On Form and Design' (1960), in Latour, *Louis I. Kahn: Writings*, op. cit., p.105.

3. Kahn, 'The Room, the Street, and Human Agreement' (1971), in Latour, *Louis I. Kahn: Writings*, op. cit., p.268.

4. Igor Stravinsky, *Poetics of Music* (Cambridge, MA: Harvard University Press, 1942), p.4.

5. Frank Lloyd Wright, *Ausgefuhrte Bauten und Entwurfe von Frank Lloyd Wright* (Berlin: Wasmuth, 1910; English edition, New York: Rizzoli, 1986), p.14.

6. Kahn, '1973: Brooklyn, New York', in Latour, *Louis I. Kahn: Writings*, op. cit., p.323.

7. Ibid., p.327.

8. Ronner and Jhaveri, op. cit., p.223.

9. 'Hostinato rigore, obstinate rigor – Leonardo's motto'. Paul Valéry, 'Introduction to the Method of Leonardo da Vinci' (1894), in James R. Lawler (ed.), *Paul Valéry: An Anthology* (Princeton, NJ: Princeton University Press, 1956), p.36.

10. Kahn, 'An Architect Speaks His Mind' (1972), in Latour, *Louis I. Kahn: Writings*, op. cit., p.295.

11. Kenneth Frampton, *Studies in Tectonic Culture* (Cambridge, MA: MIT Press, 1995), p.307. As Frampton points out, Scarpa, upon assuming the post of Dean at the architecture school in Venice, had Vico's *verum ipsum factum* inscribed above the entrance and on every diploma.

12. Louis Kahn, 'Foreword' (1974), in Latour, *Louis I. Kahn: Writings*, op. cit., p.332.

13. Frank Lloyd Wright, *The Future of Architecture* (New York: Horizon Press, 1953), p.62.

14. Valéry, 'Introduction to the Method of Leonardo da Vinci', op. cit., p.82.

15. Kahn, 'Talks with Students' (1964), in Latour, *Louis I. Kahn: Writings*, op. cit., p.182.

16. Kahn, 'I Love Beginnings' (1972), in Latour, *Louis I. Kahn: Writings*, op. cit. p.290.

17. Kahn, quoted in Wurman, op. cit., p.182.

18. Kahn, 'Space, Form, Use' (1956), in Latour, *Louis I. Kahn: Writings*, op. cit., p.69.

19. Ibid.

20. Plate 66, Paul Letarouilly, *Édifices de Rome Moderne*; originally published in 1840 (New York: Princeton Architectural Press, 1984). This source for Kahn's library carrels is also noted in Kohane, 'Louis I. Kahn and the Library', op. cit., p.114. It was Scully, as already noted in Chapter 1, to whom Kahn recalled his tracing from these books as a student; Scully, *Louis I. Kahn*, op. cit., p.12.

21. Kahn, 'Space, Form, Use' (1956), in Latour, *Louis I. Kahn: Writings*, op. cit., p.70.

22. Kahn, 'Spaces, Order and Architecture' (1957), in Latour, *Louis I. Kahn: Writings*, op. cit., p.76.

23. Ibid.

24. Kahn, quoted in Wurman, op. cit., p.182. This drawing by Boullée, 'Library Hall' (plate 149 in the 1955 Kaufmann, *Architecture in the Age of Reason*, op. cit.), was also included in the publication for which Kahn wrote an introduction in 1967; *Visionary Architects: Boullée, Ledoux, Lequeu* (Houston, TX: University of St. Thomas, 1968), plate 36, p.62.

25. Brownlee and De Long, op. cit., p.390.

26. Kahn, 'Talks with Students' (1964), in Latour, *Louis I. Kahn: Writings*, op. cit., p.183.

27. Kahn, quoted in Wurman, op. cit., p.181.

28. Ibid., p.178.

29. Bergen Branch, Free Public Library, Jersey City, New Jersey; plan published in David Gebhard, *Schindler* (London: Thames and Hudson, 1971); plate 24 in the 1997 reprint by William Stout Publishers, San Francisco. Gebhard notes the influence of Wright's Unity Temple on this project by Schindler, who at the time of its design was still in the employ of Wright.

30. Kahn Office Drawings, folder 710.001, L. I. K. Collection; see also The Louis I. Kahn Archive, *Personal Drawings*, op. cit., vol.4: numbers 710.37, 710.38, 710.40, 710.65, 710.75, 710.79, 710.96, 710.129, among others.

31. As described by Kenneth Frampton, letter to author, 24 August 2001.

32. Kahn, quoted by Vincent Scully, interview in Latour, *Louis I. Kahn: l'uomo, il maestro*, op. cit., p.153. Quoted in full in Chapter 2 of this book, see p.63.

33. Kahn, quoted in Wurman, op. cit., p.178.

34. A number of commentators have suggested that Kahn copied these wood insets from the local mill buildings in Exeter. While there are indeed similarities between the windows of Exeter Library and those of the nearby mills, both being double-height, flat-arched masonry openings, with wooden insets – carrels in Exeter Library and operable window sashes in the mills – it should be clear by now that Kahn's design process did not involve anything so simplistic as copying specific forms verbatim. Recently, Paul Goldberger made an even more ludicrous 'scholarly insight' (his term) when he claimed that Kahn copied the 45-degree corners of Exeter Library from the brick warehouses in the Northern Liberties neighbourhood of Philadelphia where Kahn lived as a child; 'The Sky Line: Many Mansions', *The New Yorker* (12 November 2001), p.131.

35. Kahn, quoted in Wurman, op. cit., p.181.

36. Ibid., p.178.

37. Louis Kahn, 'The Mind of Louis Kahn', *Architectural Forum* 137 (July–August 1972), p.77.

38. Kahn, 'Remarks' (1965), in Latour, *Louis I. Kahn: Writings*, op. cit., p.206.

39. Kahn, 'Talks with Students' (1964), in Latour, *Louis I. Kahn: Writings*, op. cit., p.181.

40. In fact, a number of publications continue mistakenly to show this penultimate plan for Exeter Library, which dates from the summer of 1967, rather than the final plan as built, which dates from the autumn of 1968; Toshio Nakamura (ed.), 'Louis I. Kahn: Conception and Meaning', *Architecture + Urbanism* (Tokyo; special issue: November 1983), p.164; 'Louis I. Kahn: Silence and Light', *Architecture + Urbanism 3*, vol.2, no.1 (Tokyo; special issue: January 1973), p.238; Buttiker, op. cit., p.136.

41. Kahn, quoted in Wurman, op. cit., p.181.

42. These inclined-top table-bookcases at the edge of overlooks into lower areas are to be found in the libraries of Alvar Aalto, the probable source for this detail.

43. Kahn, quoted in Wurman, op. cit., p.180.

44. Arendt, op. cit., p.52.

45. Kahn, quoted in Wurman, op. cit., p.179.

46. Ibid., p.180.

47. Kahn, 'The Mind of Louis Kahn', *Architectural Forum*, no. 137 (July–August 1972), p.77.

48. Kahn, quoted in Wurman, op. cit., p.178.

49. Rykwert, op. cit., p.176.

50. Brownlee and De Long, op. cit., p.346.

51. Ronner and Jhaveri, op. cit., p.205.

52. Kahn Office drawing dated 29 September 1968, L. I. K. Collection.

53. Kahn Office drawing dated 5 November 1968, L. I. K. Collection.

54. Brownlee and De Long, op. cit., p.350.

55. Ibid.

56. The University of Virginia building was left out, inexplicably, from Ronner and Jhaveri's first edition of *Louis I. Kahn: Complete Works, 1935–1974* (1977).

57. As originally designed and built by Jefferson; an ill-advised later addition by McKim Mead and White closed the south end of the Lawn, destroying the open vista that Jefferson had intended to symbolize the American relation to the natural landscape.

58. The 'lineage' of these folded-plate structures is confirmed by the fact that one of Komendant's Salk Institute drawings for the concrete structures, shown staggered and only two storeys in height, was incorrectly identified and placed in the L. I. K. Collection, folder 635.002, for the University of Virginia Chemistry Building, where the beams were designed to stack vertically and to be three storeys in height. Kahn most probably pulled this drawing of the first Salk Institute scheme, of which, as he said, he 'felt the loss', and had his staff use it as a model for the University of Virginia Chemistry Building structure, leading to its being misfiled with the latter project.

59. Kahn Office drawing, 'Laboratory structural details', sheet 17 (15 March 1963), L. I. K. Collection.

60. Among the books are Michael Brawne, *Kimbell Art Museum: Louis I. Kahn* (London: Phaidon Press, 1992); Nell E. Johnson, *Light is the Theme: Louis I. Kahn and the Kimbell Art Museum* (Fort Worth, TX: Kimbell Art Foundation, 1975); Luca Bellinelli (ed.), *Louis I. Kahn: The Construction of the Kimbell Art Museum* (Milan: Skira, 1997); and Michael Benedikt, *Deconstructing the Kimbell* (New York: Lumen Books, 1991). Kahn's three museums are examined in the excellent Patricia Cummings Loud, *The Art Museums of Louis I. Kahn*, op. cit.

61. Loud, op. cit., p.101.

62. Kahn, 'New Frontiers in Architecture' (1959), in Latour, *Louis I. Kahn: Writings*, op., cit., pp.92–3.

63. Loud, op. cit., pp.105–6.

64. '… the desire to have natural light. Because it is the light the painter used to paint his painting', Kahn, 'How'm I Doing, Corbusier?' (1972), in Latour, *Louis I. Kahn: Writings*, op. cit., p.309. Also quoted in Wurman, op. cit., p.239.

65. Tadao Ando's Museum of Modern Art, designed for the south-west quadrant of the Will Rogers Park and which opened in December 2002, completes this impressive grouping of art museum buildings.

The 'campus' description comes from Brawne, op. cit., p.7.

66. For this scheme, as in the designs for the Salk Institute Meeting House, a plan quite similar to the Roman Diocletian's Palace at Split is to be found among the Kahn Office drawings, folder 730.003, L. I. K. Collection.

67. Loud, op. cit., p.124,

68. Peter McCleary finds this to be an indication that Kahn's intention that the way a room is made – its structure – should be evident in the experience of the room, was in some way not realized; McCleary, 'The Kimbell Art Museum: Between Building and Architecture', *Design Book Review* 11 (Winter 1987), p.51. Yet such overlapping definitions of structure and space are not uncommon, particularly in both modern architecture and Baroque churches, and this is an example of the disagreement between architects and engineers over the 'purity' of Kahn's structural ideas as opposed to his primary focus on the spatial experience of the occupant. Being able to perceive 'how a space is made' does not necessarily mean understanding the precise dynamics of its structural action – particularly with concrete structures, Kahn's favoured type, which hide their lines of force within their plastic mass.

69. L. I. K. Collection, number 730.148 in The Louis I. Kahn Archive, *Personal Drawings*, vol.5, op. cit.

70. Brownlee and De Long, op. cit., p.512. The text that Meyers showed Kahn was Fred Angerer's *Surface Structures in Buildings* (New York: Reinhold Publishing Corporation, 1961), p.43. This event is sometimes dated to 7 December 1967, the date on Meyer's first drawing of the cycloid geometry in the office files, yet Kahn described 'cycloid vaults' in his November 1967 lecture at the New England Conservatory of Music in Boston – quoted in Chapter 5 of this book on p.347; Loud, op. cit., p.117.

71. Frampton, *Studies in Tectonic Culture,* op. cit., p.243.

72. Kahn, 'Space and Inspirations' (1967), in Latour, *Louis I. Kahn: Writings*, op. cit., p.228.

73. Kahn, quoted from Kimbell dedication address (October 1972), in Wurman, op. cit., p.177.

74. See the careful proportional analysis in Gast, op. cit., p.97.

75. Komendant, op. cit., p.123.

76. Kahn, quoted in Wurman, op. cit., p.242.

77. This is mistakenly described as a segment of a circle in Brawne, op. cit., p.17. To be fair, I must note that, inexplicably, Kahn himself also incorrectly describes these slots as 'semicircular', Wurman, op. cit., p.238. In fact, they are parallel to the cycloid above, and are not formed by any segment of a circle.

78. Wurman, op. cit., p.238.

79. Kahn, 'I Love Beginnings' (1972), in Latour, *Louis I. Kahn: Writings*, op. cit., p.291.

80. Loud, op. cit., pp.147–8.

81. Kahn, quoted in Wurman, op. cit., p.112.

82. Doug Suisman, 'The Design of the Kimbell: Variations on a Sublime Archetype', *Design Book Review* 11 (Winter 1987), p.38. Suisman, who is based in Los Angeles, the land where the automobile is king, orientates his analysis to the tourist-architect, flying into the airport and driving to the Kimbell Museum, rather than the experience of those who live in the Fort Worth area. Kahn's antipathetic attitude towards the automobile has been established earlier.

83. A limited amount of light originally entered this space from the light courts and light wells of the curatorial and conservation areas at either end, but this has been closed off in recent years. Also in recent years, several superb modern paintings have often been hung in this hallway, so that attaining the lavatory door has become like running a gauntlet of masterworks; this was never Kahn's intention, as this hallway is not provided with natural lighting, and is more a reflection of the Kimbell Museum's burgeoning collection.

84. This is noted particularly by those whose job requires that they stay inside the museum most of the day; in discussions with the museum guards, dating back to 1975, I have been repeatedly told that they feel no need to look outside, for they are always aware of what the weather is like, as they have learned to read the weather in the colours and intensity of light on the vaults.

85. Loud, op. cit., p.157.

86. Ibid., p.105.

87. Kahn designed the landscape plan with Harriet Pattison, who, after serving an apprenticeship with Dan Kiley and receiving a landscape architecture degree from the University of Pennsylvania, was working in the office of the landscape architect of record, George Patton.

88. Frampton, *Studies in Tectonic Culture,* op. cit., p.246.

89. L. I. K. Collection, drawing numbers 785.14 and 785.16, in The Louis I. Kahn Archive, *Personal Drawings*, op. cit.

90. Rykwert, op. cit., p.136.

91. The Scarpa lettering is in drawing number 735.115, The Louis I. Kahn Archive, *Personal Drawings*, op. cit.; one of Kahn's sources for the Dhaka assembly roof was Francesco di Giorgio Martini, *Trattato di architettura, ingegneria e arte militare*, op. cit.

92. An even closer precedent is Wright's Lenkurt Electric Company project for San Mateo, California, of 1955 – an expanded version of the Johnson Wax Building, proposed to have a single-storey, double-square plan, a 32 foot (10 metre) grid of thin-shell concrete umbrella columns, with skylights between. I do not mention this possible precedent in the main text as it is unclear how widely publicized this unrealized project was at the time Kahn was designing the Olivetti project, whereas Kahn's first-hand knowledge of Johnson Wax is well established.

93. A number of the drawings are signed by Komendant, and in his book, op. cit., p.98, he refers to the skylights: 'Kahn did not like plastic [which was required to provide glare-free light]. Finally, [Kahn] had to accept it, and the design was completed in collaboration with an Italian architect.' Renzo Piano, who has gone on to become internationally recognized as one of the greatest architects of the last quarter of the twentieth century, has dozens of his distinctive, colour-coded drawings in the L. I. K. Collection for the Olivetti project; folders 735.005–735.010; also per William Whitaker, Chief Curator and Collections Manager.

94. Jules Prown, interview in Latour, *Louis I. Kahn: l'uomo, il maestro*, op. cit., p.135.

95. This project, on the site of the former Calvary Baptist Church, might well have been designed by Kahn if he had lived. There are a number of preliminary designs for it in the L. I. K. Collection. After a nearly thirty-year delay, the Art Library has been designed by Richard Meier for a different site.

96. Loud, op. cit., p.188. These gallery spaces are among the strangest spaces Kahn ever designed, yet he prepared exhaustive studies for them with interior perspectives, models and section drawings, so we can be certain that he felt them to be appropriate. Kahn was saved from himself by Prown's rejection of these first gallery designs.

97. William Jordy, 'Kahn at Yale', *Architectural Review* (July 1977), pp.39–40. Loud also notes this characterization by Jordy; Loud, op. cit., p.180.

98. Loud, op. cit., pp.193–6.

99. Kahn's construction drawing set dated 12 May 1972, revised 14 July 1972, shows the cylindrical stair not with the flat top, as built, but with the top cut off at a 45 degree angle. Despite the existence of a later set of drawings, dated 15 March 1973, showing the correct flat top for the cylindrical stair, the earlier, incorrect detail has inexplicably been copied in almost every book on Kahn. To cite only a few: Ronner and Jhaveri, op. cit.; *Architecture + Urbanism* (special issue: November 1983), op. cit.; Buttiker, op. cit.; Giurgola, op. cit.; in fact, the only book to date to publish the correct section is Klaus-Peter Gast, *Louis I. Kahn* (Basel: Birkhäuser, 1999).

100. Loud, op. cit., p.204.

101. Komendant, op. cit., pp.133–5.

102. Though never built, Kahn's design for the Kansas City Office Tower has exerted considerable influence, most notably in Gunnar Birkerts's Federal Reserve Bank of Minneapolis, Minnesota of 1973, where the catenary-curved suspension truss is employed, and in Norman Foster's Shanghai Bank, Hong Kong of 1986, where the concept of suspending the floors in sections is realized.

103. Komendant, op. cit., p.158. Stanley Tigerman, who had breakfast with Kahn at Heathrow Airport the day Kahn died, notes that Kahn was deeply depressed by the episode with the Kansas City project: 'I think that high-rise project he lost in Kansas City affected him tremendously, the one SOM plucked out of Lou's hand'. Wurman, op. cit., p.299.

104. Kahn's student project was first published in Scully, *Louis I. Kahn*, plate 7; and the resemblance to the Kathmandu project was also noted by Buttiker, op. cit., p.163.

105. Kahn, 'How'm I Doing, Corbusier?' (1972), in Latour, *Louis I. Kahn: Writings*, op. cit., p.308.

106. Louis Kahn, 'Architecture and the University' (1953), in Latour, *Louis I. Kahn: Writings*, op. cit., p.55.

107. G. Holmes Perkins, 'Louis Kahn: Teacher', in Latour, *Louis I. Kahn: l'uomo, il maestro*, op. cit., p.371.

108. Jacob Bakema, quoted in Wurman, op. cit., p.268.

109. Kahn, quoted in Wurman, op. cit., p.58.

110. Kahn, quoted in Romaldo Giurgola and Jaimini Mehta, *Louis I. Kahn* (Boulder, CO: Westview Press, 1975), p.247.

111. Louis Kahn, 'Architecture' (1972), in Latour, *Louis I. Kahn: Writings*, op. cit., p.272.

112. Scully, quoted in Latour, *Louis I. Kahn: l'uomo, il maestro*, op. cit., p.153.

113. Abba Tor, quoted in Latour, *Louis I. Kahn: l'uomo, il maestro*, op. cit., p.125.

114. G. Holmes Perkins, op. cit., p.371.

115. Alison and Peter Smithson, quoted in Wurman, op. cit., p.298.

116. Brownlee and De Long, op. cit., p.103.

117. Scully, quoted in Latour, *Louis I. Kahn: l'uomo, il maestro*, op. cit., p.149.

Chapter 6
Unbuilt offerings: in the spaces of eternity

1. Kahn, quoted in Alexandra Tyng, op. cit., p.108.

2. The depth and quality of Kahn's unbuilt works is reflected in the fact that six of them have recently been the subject of a full-length book, involving digital 'reconstructions'; Kent Larson, *Louis I. Kahn: Unbuilt Masterworks* (New York: Monacelli Press, 2000).

3. Kahn, quoted in John Lobell, *Between Silence and Light: Spirit in the Architecture of Louis I. Kahn* (Boston, MA: Shambhala Publications, 1979), p.84; also repeated, without quotation marks, in Giurgola and Mehta, op. cit., p.183.

4. Brownlee and De Long, op. cit., p.362.

5. Kahn, 'Remarks' (1965), in Latour, *Louis I. Kahn: Writings*, op. cit., p.202.

6. It has been suggested that this plan was derived by Kahn directly from the kabbalistic Tree of Life, or Tree of the Sephiroth; see Jeffery Kieffer, 'Louis I. Kahn and the Rituals of Architecture' (1981) and 'Criticism', in *Architecture + Urbanism* (April 1993);

Burton, op. cit., pp.80–3. However, Larson points out that the book in Kahn's library from which he supposedly copied this form in 1962, entitled *The Zohar*, was not in fact published until 1963; Larson, op. cit., p.93.

7. Kahn, 'Remarks' (1965), in Latour, *Louis I. Kahn: Writings*, op. cit., p.203.

8. L. I. K. Collection, Kahn Office drawings, folder 615.005 contains landscape drawings by Pattison, dated 1 May 1967. Pattison received her landscape architecture degree from the University of Pennsylvania that same spring, 1967.

9. Brownlee and De Long add Brunelleschi's Santo Spirito (c.1436) and the Aurelian Walls of Rome (3rd century A.D.) as additional possible precedents – with Kahn, all of history seems to open up; Brownlee and De Long, op. cit., p.80.

10. Brown, op. cit., pp.28, 29, 33. Larson also notes these parallels with the Brown book on Roman architecture; Larson, op. cit., pp.103–7.

11. Brownlee and De Long, op. cit., p.365.

12. As reported by Kahn's daughter, Sue Ann, to Larson, op. cit., p.81.

13. Brownlee and De Long, op. cit., p.400.

14. Solomon, quoted in Brownlee and De Long, op. cit., p.401.

15. Kahn, quoted in Ronner and Jhaveri, op. cit., p.336.

16. Ibid., p.338.

17. Brownlee and De Long, op. cit., p.401.

18. L. I. K. Collection, The Louis I. Kahn Archive, *Personal Drawings*, vol.4, op. cit.; numbers 690.9–10.

19. Kahn, quoted in Ronner and Jhaveri, op. cit., p.339.

20. Ibid., p.337.

21. Kahn, 'Space and Inspirations' (1967), in Latour, *Louis I. Kahn: Writings*, op. cit., p.227.

22. Passage marked in Kahn's personal copy of Thomas B. Hess, *Barnett Newman* (New York: Museum of Modern Art, 1971), p.73.

23. Dante, *The Divine Comedy*, 'Paradiso', Canto 29, lines 22–30; as paraphrased in George Steiner, *Grammars of Creation* (New Haven: Yale University Press, 2001), p.105; 'matter [is made] out of light (a strangely Einsteinian thought)'. Kahn owned an 1886 edition of Dante's *The Divine Comedy*; see Burton, op. cit., p.73.

24. Kahn, 'I Love Beginnings' (1972), in Latour, *Louis I. Kahn: Writings*, op. cit., p.286. Kahn first stated that 'light … is the maker of a material' in 1969, 'Silence and Light' (1969), in Latour, *Louis I. Kahn: Writings*, op. cit., p.235.

25. Kahn, quoted in Ronner and Jhaveri, op. cit., p.338.

26. Ibid.

27. Ibid.

28. Ibid.

29. Noted on Kahn's sketch 690.9–10, op. cit., see note 18. Here we must be cautious in accepting the digital reconstructions proposed by Larson, op. cit., pp.110–23, as being an entirely accurate representation of Kahn's intentions, for the surfaces are shown with a highly polished, 'optical' quality finish, quite different from the matt, almost sand-blasted quality that Kahn describes in his notes from the visit to Corning, and shows in his models and drawings. Larson also shows a green colour, where Kahn indicated a preference for a 'pale straw' colour in his notes.

30. Kahn, quoted in Ronner and Jhaveri, op. cit., p.336; Kahn's friend Carlo Scarpa would create similar light-filled shadows with the protruding cubic windows, with glass on five sides, in his Banca Popolare di Verona of 1973–80.

31. Kahn, quoted in Ronner and Jhaveri, op. cit., p.337.

32. Larson, op. cit., p.127; also confirmed in conversations, author and Ada Karmi-Melamede.

33. Kahn, quoted in Ronner and Jhaveri, op. cit., p.363.

34. The L. I. K. Collection office section drawing, dated July 1968, while often reproduced as if it were solid at the centre, shows upon close examination that Kahn intended a very narrow slot between the concrete umbrella roofs, as necessary for independent structural action; Larson's otherwise admirable digital 'reconstruction' of this design employs much larger slots between the roof shells, leading to excessive sunlight reaching the floor of the sanctuary; Larson, op. cit., pp.124–57.

35. Kahn, quoted in Ronner and Jhaveri, op. cit., p.363.

36. Larson, op. cit., p.167.

37. See Fusaro's exemplary geometric analyses of the rotated squares underlying the designs for Hurva, Dhaka, Exeter and the first Rochester scheme, in Fusaro, op. cit., p.75 and pp.444–5 of this book.

38. Kahn, quoted in Ronner and Jhaveri, op. cit., p.363.

39. Brownlee and De Long, op. cit., p.142; also Larson, op. cit., p.129; both reference a letter from Kahn to the seminary, dated 2 July 1968.

40. Thiry, Bennett and Kamphoefner, op. cit.

41. This source is noted in Brownlee and De Long, op. cit., p.142; and in Larson, op. cit., p.135.

42. Ronner and Jhaveri, op. cit., p.367.

43. Kahn, 'Louis I. Kahn' (1961), interview in Latour, *Louis I. Kahn: Writings*, op. cit., p.140.

44. Ronner and Jhaveri, op. cit., p.362.

45. Brownlee and De Long, op. cit., p.142.

46. Ronner and Jhaveri, op. cit., p.363.

47. Kahn, quoted in Wurman, op. cit., p.217.

48. Kahn, quoted in Ronner and Jhaveri, op. cit., p.365.

49. Ibid., p.364.

50. Alexandra Tyng, op. cit., p.166; from a 1964 letter from Louis Kahn to Harriet Pattison.

51. See the exemplary digital 'reconstruction' in Larson, op. cit., pp.158–77.

52. This third scheme, incorrectly labelled the second scheme in Ronner and Jhaveri, op. cit., p.365, was not nearly as developed as the first or even the second scheme, and therefore it is doubtful that it deserves the equal treatment accorded it in Larson, op. cit., pp.178–91.

53. Larson, op. cit., p.189; quoting letter to Kahn from Kollek, dated 1 March 1974, Box 39, L. I. K. Collection.

54. Giuseppe Mazzariol, 'Un progetto per Venezia', *Lotus* 6 (1969), p.17.

55. Kahn, quoted in Ronner and Jhaveri, op. cit., p.368.

56. Frampton raises the intriguing possibility that Le Corbusier's Venice Hospital design was in fact influenced by his assistant Shadrach Woods's design for the Berlin Free University of 1963, which was itself influenced by Kahn's Trenton Jewish Community Center and Philadelphia Planning studies, both of 1956. Kenneth Frampton, *Le Corbusier* (London: Thames and Hudson, 2001), p.224; on the same page Frampton also states of Le Corbusier: 'Except for Louis Kahn, there is perhaps no other architect of the twentieth century whose creative capacity increased rather than diminished during the final period of his activity.'

57. Kahn, quoted in Wurman, op. cit., p.218.

58. Kahn, quoted in Ronner and Jhaveri, op. cit., p.369.

59. Van Eyck's diagram and description, 'twin-phenomena', were published in Alison Smithson, op. cit., p.104.

60. Kahn, quoted in Ronner and Jhaveri, op. cit., p.370.

61. Ibid.

62. Ibid.

63. L. I. K. Collection, in The Louis I. Kahn Archive,

Personal Drawings, vol.6, op. cit., drawing number 780.1.

64. Alison Smithson, op. cit., p.104.

65. The young Mario Botta was hired by Kahn's associate, Carlos Vallhonrat, to assist him in measuring the trees of the Biennale site. This was Botta's only association with Kahn. Botta had applied to work for Le Corbusier, but had arrived at the rue de Sèvres studio shortly after Le Corbusier died; both from 1988 conversation of author with Le Corbusier partner José Oubrerie, who was also teaching at the University of Venice at the time. Botta's well-known claim to have 'worked for both Le Corbusier and Kahn' is a bit of a stretch on both counts.

66. H. Th. Wijdeveld (ed.), *The Life-Work of the American Architect Frank Lloyd Wright* (New York: Horizon Press, 1965); the photos of Scarpa and Kahn are in Latour, *Louis I. Kahn: Writings*, op. cit., pp.80 and 99.

67. Kahn, 'Foreword' (1974), in Latour, *Louis I. Kahn: Writings*, op. cit., p.332; Esther Kahn's recollection, 'The last thing [Kahn] wrote was the foreword for Scarpa's book', is quoted in Wurman, op. cit., p.280.

68. This is also noted in Larson, op. cit., p.221.

69. Theodore Liebman, director of design for the NYSUDC; quoted in Brownlee and De Long, op. cit., p.139; original quotation from Paul Goldberger, 'Design by Kahn Picked for Roosevelt Memorial Here', *The New York Times* (25 April 1974).

70. Kahn, '1973: Brooklyn, New York', in Latour, *Louis I. Kahn: Writings*, op. cit., p.321.

71. One of these designs indicates that the inner thin-walled cylinder would be split along the north-south axis, reminding one of the recent tightly curved steel wall sculptures of Richard Serra; numbers 885.1, 885. 2, in The Louis I. Kahn Archive, *Personal Drawings*, vol.7, op. cit.

72. Brownlee and De Long, op. cit., p.139; referenced in Laurie Johnston, 'Plans for Memorial at Roosevelt Island Announced at Dedication Ceremony at Site', *The New York Times* (25 September 1973).

73. Kahn, 'I Love Beginnings' (1972), in Latour, *Louis I. Kahn: Writings*, op. cit., p.292.

74. Brownlee and De Long, op. cit., p.139.

75. The office of Romaldo Giurgola was commissioned in the 1980s to pursue completion of this memorial, employing Kahn's final design. While some work has been accomplished, fundraising still needs to be done, and the much-changed conditions on Roosevelt Island must be taken into account; at the time of Kahn's design, the urban redesign of the island had just begun, under the direction of Philip Johnson, and the south end of the island, where Kahn's memorial was sited, was abandoned and derelict. Today, the entire island has been intensively redeveloped, and many of the generous public spaces originally planned have been turned over to private developers, making the public approach to the southern end of the island much less open.

76. This important design of Kahn's is not even mentioned in Brownlee and De Long, op. cit.

77. Not having anticipated the rapidity of the Bay Area's urban growth, the Hearst family had assumed that Berkeley would remain sufficiently rural and distant to serve as the location of their 'country' estate. When the actual extent of East Bay urban growth became clear, the Hearst family abandoned the Berkeley site, leaving extensive terracing, plantings and fountains already completed, and located their country estate at San Simeon, where Julia Morgan designed the large house called Hearst Castle.

78. L. I. K. Collection, Office drawings folder 065.003.

79. This 'green filter', unique in Kahn's work, is noted in Buttiker, op. cit., p.165; Kohane traces it to Boullée's Cenotaph for Newton and to Durand's reconstructions of the Roman mausolea of Hadrian and Augustus, which also incorporated stepped

terraces of trees; Kohane, 'Louis I. Kahn and the Library', op. cit., p.128.

80. When given the Graduate Theological Union (GTU) Library commission after Kahn's death, Berkeley architects Joseph Esherick (Esherick, Homsey, Dodge and Davis) and Richard Peters (Peters, Clayberg and Caulfield) explored a series of alternatives before coming to the conclusion that Kahn's design was indeed the best. While changing circumstances required considerable modifications to Kahn's plan, particularly on the interior, the GTU Library, designed and constructed from 1977–87, still stands as Kahn's last built work. The author's father, Dr Neely McCarter, served as president of the Pacific School of Religion, one of the ten constituent units of the GTU, from 1979 to 1991, and so the author has more than a passing interest in this final project of Kahn's.

81. Louis Kahn, 'Monumentality' (1944), in Latour, *Louis I. Kahn: Writings*, op. cit., p.19.

82. Wright, 'In the Cause of Architecture' (1914), in Gutheim, op. cit., p.53.

83. Kahn, 'Monumentality' (1944), in Latour, *Louis I. Kahn: Writings*, op. cit., p.19.

84. Kahn, 'New Frontiers in Architecture' (1959), in Latour, *Louis I. Kahn: Writings*, op. cit., p.90.

85. Kahn, 'Harmony Between Man and Architecture' (1974), in Latour, *Louis I. Kahn: Writings*, op. cit., p.339.

86. Kahn, quoted in Wurman, op. cit., p.94.

87. Kahn, 'Space and Inspirations' (1967), in Latour, *Louis I. Kahn: Writings*, op. cit., pp.229–30.

88. Wright, 'In the Cause of Architecture' (1914), in Gutheim, op. cit., p.123.

89. Kahn, quoted in Ronner and Jhaveri, op. cit., p.368.

90. T. S. Eliot, 'Tradition and the Individual Talent' (1919), in F. Kermode (ed.), *Selected Prose of T. S. Eliot* (New York: Harcourt Brace Jovanovich, 1975), pp.38 and 44.

91. Stravinsky, *Poetics of Music*, op. cit., p.57.

92. Ludwig Wittgenstein, *Culture and Value* (Chicago: University of Chicago Press, 1980), pp.76 and 60.

93. Martin Heidegger, 'The Origin of the Work of Art' (1935), in D. F. Krell (ed.), *Basic Writings* (New York: Harper and Row, 1977), p.187.

94. Kahn, 'I Love Beginnings' (1972), in Latour, *Louis I. Kahn: Writings*, op. cit., p.286.

95. George Steiner, *Grammars of Creation*, op. cit., p.2.

96. George Steiner, *Real Presences* (Chicago: Chicago University Press, 1989), pp.27–8.

97. Kahn, 'New Frontiers in Architecture' (1959), in Latour, *Louis I. Kahn: Writings*, op. cit., p.91.

98. Kahn, quoted in Wurman, op. cit., p.91.

99. Johann Wolfgang von Goethe, 'On German Architecture' (1772), in John Geary (ed.), *Goethe: Essays on Art and Literature*, vol.3 (Princeton, NJ: Princeton University Press, 1986), p.8.

100. Kahn, quoted in Wurman, op. cit., p.116.

101. Paul Valéry, 'Eupalinos, Or the Architect' (1921), in Jackson Mathews (ed.), *Collected Works of Paul Valéry, Volume 4: Dialogues* (Princeton, NJ: Princeton University Press, 1956), p.88; Valéry emphasis.

102. Emmanuel Kant, *The Critique of Judgement* (1790), trans. J. C. Meredith (Oxford: Clarendon Press, 1928), p.179. Quoted in Richard Hill, *Designs and Their Consequences* (New Haven, CT: Yale University Press, 1999), p.217.

103. Kahn, quoted in Wurman, op. cit., p.121.

104. As noted in Chapter 1; Burton, 'Notes from Volume Zero', op. cit.

105. Ralph Waldo Emerson, 'Intellect', in Joel Porte (ed.), *Ralph Waldo Emerson: Essays and Lectures* (New York: Library of America, 1983), p.417.

106. Emerson, 'Self-Reliance', in Porte, op. cit., p.280.

107. Kahn, quoted in Robert Hughes, 'Brick is Stingy, Concrete is Generous', *Horizon*, vol. XVI, no.4 (Fall 1974), p.33.

108. Emerson, 'History', in Porte, op. cit., p.240.

109. Kahn, '1973: Brooklyn, New York', in Latour, *Louis I. Kahn: Writings*, op. cit., p.329.

110. Emerson, 'Self-Reliance', in Porte, op. cit., p.280.

111. Kahn, quoted in Wurman, op. cit., p.116.

112. Louis Kahn, 'Architecture: Silence and Light' (1970), in Latour, *Louis I. Kahn: Writings*, op. cit., p.248.

113. Emerson, 'History', in Porte, op. cit., p.237.

114. Kahn, quoted in Wurman, op. cit., p.57.

115. Emerson, 'The Poet', in Porte, op. cit., p.459.

116. André Malraux, *The Voices of Silence* (New York: Doubleday & Co., 1953).

117. Kahn, 'How'm I doing, Corbusier?' (1972), in Latour, *Louis I. Kahn: Writings*, op. cit., pp.308–9.

118. Valéry, 'Paradox on the Architect', in Mathews, op. cit., p.187.

119. Kahn, '1973: Brooklyn, New York', in Latour, *Louis I. Kahn: Writings*, op. cit., p.329.

120. This is defined, and given its most incisive critique, in Karl Popper, *The Poverty of Historicism* (London: Routledge & Kegan Paul, 1957); one of Colin Rowe's favourite books.

121. Eliade, *The Myth of the Eternal Return*, op. cit., pp.xiv and 76.

122. Heidegger, 'The Origin of the Work of Art', op. cit., p.149.

123. Having grown up on seminary campuses, the author has always been struck by the poetic yet eminently rational logic of this theological pedagogy, and wondered why such a return to origins has never been part of architectural education.

124. It is Scully who made this rather startling admission; 'Introduction', in C. Bolon, R. Nelson and L. Seidel (eds), *The Nature of Frank Lloyd Wright* (Chicago: University of Chicago Press, 1988), p.xiii.

125. Martin Heidegger, 'The Thinker as Poet', in *Poetry Language Thought*, trans. Albert Hofstadter (New York: Harper and Row, 1971), p.5.

126. Rainer Maria Rilke, 'Sonnets to Orpheus', part 1, 19 (1922); this translation by Albert Hofstadter, in Martin Heidegger, *Poetry Language Thought*, op. cit., p.97.

127. Kahn, quoted in Wurman, op. cit., p.54.

128. Wright, quoted in Jack Quinan, *Frank Lloyd Wright's Larkin Building: Myth and Fact* (Cambridge, MA: MIT Press, 1987), p.167; William Curtis also noted the appropriate fit of this Wright statement to Kahn's work; 'Louis I. Kahn', *A&V: Monografías de Arquitectura y Vivienda* (February 2001), p.103.

129. Paul Ricoeur, 'Universal Civilization and National Cultures' (1961), *History and Truth* (Evanston, IL: Northwestern University Press, 1965), p.277.

130. Kahn, 'Architecture: Silence and Light' (1970), in Latour, *Louis I. Kahn: Writings*, op. cit., p.257.

131. Steiner, *Grammars of Creation*, op. cit., p.258.

132. Martin Heidegger, *Early Greek Thinking* (1950) (New York: Harper and Row, 1975), p.18.

133. Kahn, quoted in William Jordy, 'The Formal Image: USA', *Architectural Review* 127 (March 1960), p.160. Quoted in Goldhagen, op. cit., p.188.

134. Wittgenstein, *Culture and Value*, op. cit., p.40.

135. Mendelssohn, quoted by Ralf Wehner; notes for the recording of Mendelssohn, *Paulus*, Oratorio, opus 36; Harmonia Mundi, HMC 901584.85, 1996.

Conclusion

1. Kahn, quoted in Wurman, op. cit., p.260.

2. Kahn, quoted by Tigerman, interviewed in Wurman, op. cit., p.299.

3. Brownlee and De Long, op. cit., p.141.

4. Vincent Scully, *American Architecture and Urbanism* (New York: Praeger, 1969), pp.142–3.

5. Frampton, 'Response', op. cit.

6. Emerson, 'The Over-Soul', in Porte, op. cit., p.394.

Select Bibliography
Edited by Robert McCarter

Angrisani, Marcello *Lo spazio interno architettonico da Frank Lloyd Wright a Louis I. Kahn* (Naples: L'Arte Tipografica, 1963)

Angrisani, Marcello 'Louis I. Kahn e la storia', *L'Edilizia Moderna* 86 (1965)

Auer, Gerhard 'Licht und Ordnung: über die Lichtentwürfe Frank Lloyd Wrights und Louis Kahns', *Architekt* (September 1990)

Aymonino, Aldo *Funzione e simbolo nell'Architettura di Louis I. Kahn* (Rome: CLEAN Edizioni, 1991)

Bellinelli, Luca (ed.), *Louis I. Kahn: The Construction of the Kimbell Art Museum*, Cataloghi dell'Accademia di Architettura dell'Università della Svizzera italiana, (Milan: Skira, 1997)

Benedikt, Michael *Deconstructing the Kimbell* (New York: Lumen Books, 1991)

Blake, Peter (ed.), 'The Mind of Louis Kahn', *Architectural Forum* 137, no.1 (July–August 1972)

Bottero, Maria 'Louis Kahn e l'incontro fra morfologia organica e razionale', *Zodiac* 17 (1967)

Brawne, Michael *Kimbell Art Museum: Louis I. Kahn* (London: Phaidon Press, 1992)

Brown, Jack Perry (ed.), *Louis I. Kahn: A Bibliography* (New York: Garland Press, 1987)

Brownlee, David and David De Long *Louis I. Kahn: In the Realm of Architecture* (New York: Rizzoli, 1991)

Burton, Joseph 'Notes from Volume Zero: Louis Kahn and the Language of God', *Perspecta: The Yale Architectural Journal* 20 (Cambridge, MA: MIT Press, 1983)

Burton, Joseph 'The Aesthetic Education of Louis I. Kahn, 1912–1924', *Perspecta: The Yale Architectural Journal* 28 (Cambridge, MA: MIT Press, 1997)

Buttiker, Urs *Louis I. Kahn: Light and Space, Licht und Raum* (Basel: Birkhäuser, 1993)

Chang, Ching-Yu (ed.), 'Louis I. Kahn: Silence and Light', *Architecture + Urbanism* 3, 2 volumes, no.1, special issue (January 1973)

Coombs, Robert 'Light and Silence: The Religious Architecture of Louis Kahn', *Architectural Association Quarterly*, vol.13, no.1 (October 1981)

Curtis, William 'Authenticity, Abstraction, and the Ancient Sense: Le Corbusier's and Louis Kahn's Ideas of Parliament', *Perspecta: The Yale Architectural Journal* 20 (Cambridge, MA: MIT Press, 1983)

Davies, Peter (ed.), 'The Span of Kahn', *Architectural Review* 155 (June 1974)

Devillers, Christian 'L'Indian Institute of Management ad Ahmedabad 1962–1974 di Louis I. Kahn', *Casabella* 54 (September 1990)

Doshi, Balkrishna V. *Le Corbusier and Louis I. Kahn: The Acrobat and The Yogi of Architecture* (Ahmedabad: Vastu Shilpa Foundation, 1993)

Fernández-Galiano, Luis (ed.), 'Louis I. Kahn', *A+V: Monografias de Arquitectura y Vivienda* (November–December 1993; 2nd edn, February 2001)

Frampton, Kenneth 'Louis Kahn and the French Connection', *Oppositions* 22 (New York: IAUS/MIT Press, 1980)

Frampton, Kenneth 'Louis Kahn', special issue, *Arquitecturas Bis* (1982)

Frampton, Kenneth 'Louis Kahn: Modernization and the New Monumentality', *Studies in Tectonic Culture* (Cambridge, MA: MIT Press, 1995)

Fumo, Marina and Gigliola Ausiello *Louis I. Kahn: Architettura e Tecnica* (Naples: CLEAN Edizioni, 1996)

Fusaro, Florindo *Il Parlamento e la nuova capitale a Dacca di Louis I. Kahn* (Rome: Officina Edizioni, 1985)

Futagawa, Yukio (ed.), 'Louis I. Kahn: Richards Medical Research Building, Pennsylvania, 1961';

'Salk Institute for Biological Studies, California, 1965', *Global Architecture*, no.5 (Tokyo: ADA Edita, 1971)

Futagawa, Yukio (ed.), 'Louis I. Kahn: Yale University Art Gallery, New Haven, Connecticut, 1951–53', 'Kimbell Art Museum, Fort Worth, Texas, 1966–72', *Global Architecture*, no.38 (Tokyo: ADA Edita, 1976)

Futagawa, Yukio (ed.), 'Louis I. Kahn: Indian Institute of Management, Ahmedabad, 1963'; 'Exeter Library, Phillips Exeter Academy, Exeter, New Hampshire, 1972', *Global Architecture*, no.35 (Tokyo: ADA Edita, 1976)

Futagawa, Yukio (ed.), 'Louis I. Kahn: National Capital of Bangladesh, Dhaka, 1962–83', *Global Architecture*, no.72 (Tokyo: ADA Edita, 1994)

Futagawa, Yukio (ed.), 'Louis I. Kahn: Margaret Esherick House, Chestnut Hill, Pennsylvania, 1959–61'; 'Norman Fisher House, Hatboro, Pennsylvania, 1960–67', *Global Architecture*, no.76 (Tokyo: ADA Edita, 1996)

Gast, Klaus-Peter *Louis I. Kahn: The Idea of Order* (Basel: Birkhäuser, 1998)

Gast, Klaus-Peter *Louis I. Kahn* (Basel: Birkhäuser, 1999)

Gattamorta, Gioia, Luca Rivalta and Andrea Savio *Louis I. Kahn: itinerari* (Rome: Officina Edizioni, 1996)

Gilbert, Edwin *Native Stone* (Garden City, NY: Doubleday & Co., 1955)

Giurgola, Romaldo and Jaimini Mehta *Louis I. Kahn* (Boulder, CO: Westview Press, 1975)

Giurgola, Romaldo *Louis I. Kahn* (Zürich: Artemis, 1979)

Goldhagen, Sarah W. *Louis Kahn's Situated Modernism* (New Haven, CT: Yale University Press, 2001)

Goller, Bea and Xavier Costa *Kahn Libraries* (Barcelona: Gili, 1989)

Graham, Lanier (ed.), *Louis I. Kahn* (New York: Museum of Modern Art, 1966)

Greenberg, Stephen (ed.), 'Kahn', *Architects' Journal* (London), vol.19, no.9, special issue (4 March 1992)

Gregotti, Vittorio (ed.), 'Louis I. Kahn 1901–1974', *Rassegna* 21, no.1, special issue (March 1985)

Haraguchi, Hideaki *Ruisu kan no kukan kosei: akusome de yomu nijisseiki no kenchikukatachi* (Tokyo: Shokokusha, 1998)

Hitchcock, Henry-Russell 'Notes of a Traveler: Wright and Kahn', *Zodiac* 6 (1960)

Hochstim, Jan *The Paintings and Sketches of Louis I. Kahn* (New York: Rizzoli, 1991)

Holman, William (ed.), *The Travel Sketches of Louis I. Kahn* (Philadelphia, PA: Pennsylvania Academy of Fine Arts, 1978)

Hubert, Bruno *Le Yale Center for British Art* (Marseilles: Éditions Parenthèses, 1991)

Huff, William 'Louis Kahn: Sorted Recollections and Lapses in Familiarities', *Little Journal: The Western New York Chapter of the Society of Architectural Historians*, vol.5, no.1 (September 1981)

Huff, William 'Kahn and Yale', *Journal of Architectural Education* vol.35, no.3 (ACSA, Spring 1982)

Johnson, Eugene and Michael Lewis (eds), *Drawn from the Source: The Travel Sketches of Louis I. Kahn* (Cambridge, MA: MIT Press/Williams College Museum of Art, 1996)

Johnson, Nell E. (ed.), *Light is the Theme: Louis I. Kahn and the Kimbell Art Museum* (Fort Worth, TX: Kimbell Art Foundation, 1975)

Jordy, William 'Kahn on Beaux-Arts Training', *Architectural Review* 155 (June 1974)

Jordy, William 'Kahn at Yale', *Architectural Review* (July 1977)

Juarez, Antonio *El universo imaginario de Louis I. Kahn* (Barcelona: Fundación Caja de Aquitectos, 2006)

Kahn, Louis 'Order and Form: Yale Art Gallery and Design Center' and 'The Architect Speaks', *Yale Daily News* (6 November 1953)

Kahn, Louis 'Louis I. Kahn', *Student Publication of the School of Design*, vol.14, no.3 (Raleigh, NC: North Carolina State University, 1964)

Kahn, Louis Introduction, *Visionary Architects: Boullée, Ledoux, Lequeu* (Houston, TX: University of St. Thomas, 1968)

Kahn Archive, The Louis I. (ed.), *Personal Drawings: The Completely Illustrated Catalogue of the Drawings in the Louis I. Kahn Collection, University of Pennsylvania and Pennsylvania Historical Society and Museum Commission*, 7 volumes (New York: Garland Press, 1987)

Kahn, Louis *Louis I. Kahn: Conversations with Students, Architecture at Rice University* (New York: Princeton Architectural Press, 1998)

Kieran, Kevin and Larry Bowne 'Building Character: Modern Construction Beyond Determinism in the Work of Frank Lloyd Wright and Louis Kahn', *9H: On Continuity*, no.9 (1995)

Kohane, Peter 'Louis I. Kahn and the Library: genesis and expression of Form', *Via 10. Ethics in Architecture* (New York: Rizzoli, 1990)

Komendant, August *18 Years with the Architect Louis I. Kahn* (Englewood, NJ: Aloray, 1975)

Kostof, Spiro 'The Shape of Time at Yale, Circa 1960', in G. Wright and J. Parks (eds), *The History of History in American Schools of Architecture 1865–1975* (New York: Temple Hoyne Buell Center for the Study of American Architecture/Princeton Architectural Press, 1990)

Kudo, Kunio *Watakushi no Ruisu kan* (Tokyo: Kajima Shuppankai, 1975)

Kudo, Kunio *Ruisu kan ron: kenchiku no jitsuzon to hoho* (Tokyo: Shokokusha, 1980)

Kultermann, Udo 'The hollow column and the family of human institutions', *Architectura: Zeitschrift für Geschichte der Baukunst* 22 (1992)

Larson, Kent *Louis I. Kahn: Unbuilt Masterworks* (New York: Monacelli Press, 2000)

Latour, Alessandra (ed.), *Louis I. Kahn: l'uomo, il maestro* (Rome: Edizioni Kappa, 1986)

Latour, Alessandra (ed.), *Louis I. Kahn: Writings, Lectures, Interviews* (New York: Rizzoli, 1991)

Leslie, Thomas *Louis I. Kahn: Building Art, Building Science* (New York: George Braziller, 2005)

Lobell, John *Between Silence and Light: Spirit in the Architecture of Louis I. Kahn* (Boston, MA: Shambhala Publications, 1979)

Loud, Patricia Cummings *The Art Museums of Louis I. Kahn* (Durham, NC: Duke University Press, 1989)

Maeda, Tadanao *Ruisu kan kenchiku ronshu* (Tokyo: Kajima Shuppankai, 1992)

Maeda, Tadanao *Ruisu kan kenkyu: kenchiku e no odusseia* (Tokyo: Kajima Shuppankai, 1994)

Maniaque, Caroline 'Essays on Residential Masterpieces: Louis I. Kahn', *Global Architecture: Houses*, no.44 (Tokyo: ADA Edita, 1994)

Masheck, Joseph 'Kahn: The Anxious Classicist', *Building-Art: Modern Architecture Under Cultural Construction* (Cambridge: Cambridge University Press, 1993)

Matsukuma, Hiroshi *Ruisu kan: kochiku eno ishi* (Tokyo: Maruzen, 1997)

Mazzariol, Giuseppe 'Un progetto per Venezia', *Lotus* 6 (1969)

McCleary, Peter 'The Kimbell Art Museum: Between Building and Architecture', *Design Book Review* 11 (Winter 1987)

Nakamura, Toshio (ed.), 'Louis I. Kahn', *Architecture + Urbanism*, special issue (1975)

Nakamura, Toshio (ed.), 'Louis I. Kahn: Conception and Meaning', *Architecture + Urbanism*, special issue (November 1983)

Norberg-Schulz, Christian 'Kahn, Heidegger, and the Language of Architecture', *Oppositions*

18 (Cambridge, MA: MIT Press, 1979)

Norberg-Schulz, Christian *Louis I. Kahn: idea e immagine* (Rome: Officina Edizioni, 1980)

Nordenson, Guy, 'The lineage of structure and the Kimbell Art Museum', *Lotus* 98 (1998)

Prown, Jules David *The Architecture of the Yale Center for British Art* (New Haven, CT: Yale University Press, 1977)

Robinson, Duncan and David Finn *Yale Center for British Art: A Tribute to the Genius of Louis I. Kahn* (New Haven, CT: Yale University Press, 1997)

Roca, Miguel Angel *Louis Kahn, arquetipos y modernidad* (Buenos Aires: Ediciones Summa, 1984)

Ronner, Heinz and Sharad Jhaveri (eds), *Louis I. Kahn: Complete Works, 1935–1974*, 2nd edn (Basel: ETH/Birkhäuser, 1987)

Rowe, Colin 'Neo-"Classicism" and Modern Architecture, II', *The Mathematics of the Ideal Villa and Other Essays* (Cambridge, MA: MIT Press, 1976)

Rykwert, Joseph *Louis Kahn* (New York: Harry N. Abrams, 2001)

Sabini, Maurizio (ed.), *Louis I. Kahn* (Barcelona: Ediciones del Serbal, 1994)

Savio, Andrea *Louis I. Kahn: Salk Institute* (Florence: Alinea, 1989)

Scully, Vincent 'The Heritage of Wright', *Zodiac* 8 (1961)

Scully, Vincent 'Wright, International Style and Kahn', *Arts* (March 1962)

Scully, Vincent *Louis I. Kahn* (New York: George Braziller, 1962)

Sekler, Eduard 'Formalism and the Polemical Use of History: Thoughts on the recent rediscovery of revolutionary classicism', *Harvard Architecture Review*, no.1 (Cambridge, MA: MIT Press, 1980)

Smith, Charles R. *Paul Rudolph and Louis Kahn: A Bibliography* (Metuchen, NJ: Scarecrow Press, 1987)

Smithson, Alison (ed.), *Team 10 Primer* (Cambridge, MA: MIT Press, 1968)

Smithson, Alison and Peter 'Louis Kahn', *Architect's Yearbook* 9 (1960)

Solomon, Susan *Louis I. Kahn's Trenton Jewish Community Center* (New York: Princeton Architectural Press, 2000)

Spiker, David and Kirk Train 'The Yale Center for British Art', *Perspecta: The Yale Architectural Journal* 16 (Cambridge, MA: MIT Press, 1980)

Stark, Ulrike *Architekten. Louis Kahn* (Stuttgart: IRB Verlag, 1998)

Steele, James *Salk Institute: Louis I. Kahn* (London: Phaidon Press, 1993)

Stern, Robert A. M. 'Yale 1950–1965', *Oppositions* 4 (New York: IAUS/Witterborn, 1974)

Stoller, Ezra *The Salk Institute* (New York: Princeton Architectural Press, 1999)

Suisman, Doug 'The Design of the Kimbell: Variations on a Sublime Archetype', *Design Book Review* 11 (Winter 1987)

Tentori, Francesco 'Ordine e forma nell'opera di Louis I. Kahn', *Casabella* 241 (1960)

Tentori, Francesco 'Il passato come un amico', *Casabella* 275 (1963)

Twombly, Robert *Louis Kahn: Essential Texts* (New York: W. W. Norton, 2003)

Tyng, Alexandra *Beginnings: Louis I. Kahn's Philosophy of Architecture* (New York: John Wiley & Sons, 1984)

Tyng, Anne Griswold *Louis Kahn to Anne Tyng: The Rome Letters 1953–1954* (New York: Rizzoli, 1997)

Uberti, Ludovico Degli *Le Corbusier e Louis Kahn in India e Bangladesh: gli edifici e la città* (Rome: Palombi Fratelli, 1997)

Unspecified author 'Hommage à Louis Kahn (1901–1974)', special issue, *Werk* 7 (1974)

Unspecified author 'Louis I. Kahn: Oeuvres 1963–69', *L'architecture d'aujourd'hui* 40, no.142,

special issue (February–March 1969)

Unspecified author 'Louis I. Kahn: Royal Gold Medallist', *RIBA Journal* 79 (August 1972)

Unspecified author 'Louis I. Kahn', special issue, *Design Book Review* 21 (Summer 1991)

Unspecified author 'The Philadelphia School', *Progressive Architecture* 42 (April 1961)

Watari, Koichi *Play Mountain: Isamu Noguchi + Louis I. Kahn* (Tokyo: Watari Museum, 1996)

Wickersham, Jay 'The Making of Exeter Library', *Harvard Architecture Review*, no.7 (New York: Rizzoli, 1989)

Wiggins, Glenn *Louis I. Kahn: The Library at Phillips Exeter Academy* (New York: Van Nostrand Reinhold, 1997)

Wurman, Richard Saul and Eugene Feldman (eds), *The Notebooks and Drawings of Louis I. Kahn* (Cambridge, MA: MIT Press, 1973)

Wurman, Richard Saul *What Will Be Has Always Been: The Words of Louis I. Kahn* (New York: Rizzoli, 1986)

Index

Entries in **bold** type are buildings and projects by Louis I. Kahn.

Author's Acknowledgements

I cannot remember a time, in either my academic studies or professional practice as an architect, that I have not looked to Louis Kahn and Frank Lloyd Wright as the principal disciplinary exemplars to whom I related my own design work. In this study I have endeavoured to indicate that the traditional relationship between the contemporary architect and disciplinary history – the tradition of practice – was one of Louis Kahn's most important attributes as an architect, and the primary reason he remains of such fundamental importance to the future of architecture. As George Steiner has noted, constructive criticism of any art is the result of a powerful, transformative experience that we ourselves have undergone, the quality and beauty of which we seek to communicate to others, hoping they will feel compelled to undergo the same experience: 'In this attempt at persuasion originate the truest insights criticism can afford.'

As a primary acknowledgement, I must note that I began my analytical studies of Louis Kahn as the result of the most probably unintentional prompting of my teacher, colleague and friend Kenneth Frampton, who in a 1983 symposium, stated: 'One of the greatest paradoxes of the current debate as to the appropriate form for post-modern culture is the prevailing consensus that two of the most seminal figures of twentieth-century American architecture are somehow to be set aside and left out of any serious re-evaluation of our present predicament. I have in mind Frank Lloyd Wright and Louis Kahn.' I took this assertion as a directive, and have spent a significant portion of my time since that date engaged in an extended study of the works of Wright and Kahn. In 1990, my efforts with respect to Kahn were given a further prompting when the late British architect James Stirling, after giving a lecture at Columbia University, and noting both the photographs of Kahn's buildings in my office and the absence of Kahn's influence in the design studios, asked of the students: 'Why doesn't anyone study Kahn?'

This publication completes a cycle I conceived in 1990, to write monographic studies on Frank Lloyd Wright and Louis Kahn – the two great American architects whose work truly belongs to the world history of architecture – that would emphasize the primary (but all too often ignored) focus of their efforts: the experience of interior space. While in my mind this goal was of necessity always understood to be set a considerable time in the future, due to my responsibilities as academic leader, teacher and practitioner, I am indeed most grateful to Phaidon Press, and in particular Richard Schlagman and Amanda Renshaw, for encouraging me to complete this double disciplinary duty years ahead of my imaginary schedule. In this I am indebted to Vivian Constantinopoulos, with whom I worked on a number of books, including the beginnings of this one, from 1993 to 2001; to Iona Baird, with whom I worked from 2001 to 2003; and to Victoria Clarke, who expertly shepherded this book through to publication from 2003 to 2005.

All of the materials from Kahn's office, including his personal sketches and notebooks, office drawings, correspondence, project files, personal library, models, etc., are held in the Louis I. Kahn Collection, owned by the Pennsylvania Historical and Museum Commission, and on permanent loan to the University of Pennsylvania Architectural Archives; the Collection is housed in the original University Library building by Frank Furness, the same building in which Louis Kahn taught studio. The Director of the Architectural Archives, Julia Moore Converse, and the Collections Manager, William Whitaker, were of immeasurable assistance in my research, particularly during my several weeks spent in the Archives themselves in fall 2000 and 2001.

Without Bill Whitaker's meticulous scholarship, inexhaustible good humour and astonishing memory for detail I would not have been able to accomplish the first-hand inspection of Kahn's design drawings so essential to completing this book.

The new drawings and models prepared for this publication were made by sixty-five students in the University of Florida's School of Architecture, who enrolled in two of my graduate design studios which employed unbuilt works by Kahn as sites in 1992 and 1994, and my two graduate seminars which examined Kahn's drawings for built and unbuilt works in 2000 and 2001. Jason Towers had the additional responsibility of preparing the drawings for publication.

I am most grateful to my fellow faculty members and to my students in the School of Architecture at the University of Florida, all of whom put up with a sometimes distracted school director and teacher during the fourteen-year period I was working on this and other texts. I owe special thanks to Wayne Drummond, who as my Dean from 1991 to 1999 supported me in my atypical level of scholarly and professional activity, and who encouraged me always to continue to teach – in the end, my true calling in the university. More recently, without the sabbatical year provided by the University of Florida in 2001–2, and the travel and research support provided by the School of Architecture, this book could never have been completed. Also at the University of Florida, Fine Arts and Architecture Librarian Ann Lindell, and her predecessor Edward Teague, provided information essential to assembling the Bibliography. Without the dedication, efficiency, kindness and generosity of Mary Kramer, Office Manager for the School of Architecture, I would not have been able to function over the last eight years, either as School Director or faculty member. And without the support and encouragement of my wife and partner in architecture Susan, and my daughter Kate, this and my other 'overtime' writing efforts would never have even got started.

Finally, this book is dedicated to the memory of John Phillip Reuer, my teacher, mentor, colleague and friend, who, in his 'History of Design' course at the School of Design, North Carolina State University, showed me the first image I ever saw of a building by Louis Kahn in spring 1974 – the spring Kahn passed away. In early 2002, as I was completing the manuscript for this book, John passed away, and this uncanny parallel of beginnings and endings will surely remain what Kahn might have called one of the truly immeasurable events of my life.

Note to the Reader

For ease of reference, US floor plan nomenclature has been used in the main text and captions (i.e. basement, ground, second, third floors, and so on).

The Louis Kahn plans, original sketches, drawings and models in this book are all drawn or built by Kahn or Kahn's office, unless otherwise stated in the captions or listed in the credits below.

Credits

Text

The selected writings by Louis I. Kahn on pages 455–461 and 464–485 are reprinted with the permission of the Louis I. Kahn Collection, University of Pennsylvania and the Pennsylvania Historical and Museum Commission. 'Order Is' on pages 462–3 is reprinted with the permission of *Perspecta: The Yale Architectural Journal*.

New Drawings, Models and Computer Reconstructions

Primary drawing assistant: Jason Towers

Adler House
Drawings: Hector Hernandez

Bangladesh National Capital
Site plan, drawing: Justin Moore
Assembly building, drawings: Jason O'Brien
Hostels, dining hall, drawings: Li Wang

Dominican Motherhouse
Drawings: Katie Carroll, Daisa Ruiz
Model: Patrick Ballasch, Lauren Kay, Lourdes Santiago

Erdman Hall Dormitory, Bryn Mawr College
Drawings: Dervla Reilly, Jason Towers

F.D. Roosevelt Memorial
Drawings: Doug DeGanes

First Unitarian Church and School
Drawings: Gary Badge

Fleisher House
Drawings: Jill Namoff

Fort Wayne Performing Arts Theater
Drawings: Michael Kleinschmidt

Frank Lloyd Wright Buildings
Herbert Jacobs House, drawing: John Brandies
Darwin Martin House, drawing: Max Strang
Unity Temple, drawing: Karen Sharp

Hurva Synagogue
Building, drawings: Rick Dunn
Site plan, drawings: Duy Ho
Model: Columbia University students in course taught by Kenneth Frampton
Computer reconstructions: Kent Larson

Indian Institute of Management
Site plan and main building, drawings: Warren Barry
Dormitories, drawings: Jason Pelletier
Faculty housing, drawings: Lucas London

Interama Inter-American Community
Drawings: Jason Towers

Jewish Community Center, Trenton and Bath House
Site model: Manuel Arias, Alejandro Pereza, Gregory Wehling
Jewish Community Center final scheme, drawings: Amy Chin
Bath House, drawings: Johannes Welch

Kimbell Art Museum
Drawings: Michael Kleinschmidt

Library and Dining Hall, Phillips Exeter Academy
Drawings: Lee Peters

Memorial to Six Million Jewish Martyrs
Drawings: Chris Johns, Jason Towers
Computer reconstructions: Kent Larson

Mikveh Israel Synagogue
Drawings: Warren Barry, John McInnis
Computer reconstructions: Kent Larson

Morris House
Drawings: Jason Towers

Palazzo dei Congressi
Drawings: Jason Pelletier
Computer reconstructions: Kent Larson

Salk Institute for Biological Studies
Laboratories, drawings: Joe Kelly, Joyce Lee
Meeting House, drawings: Matt Wheeler
Meeting House, site model: Michael Calvino, David Fischer, Erik Kasper
Meeting House, building model: Trent Baughn, Eric Blumberg, Vanessa Haynes, Juan Linares, Diana Littlewood, Eddie Mastalerz, Pamela Nixon, Kiernan Quinn, Michael Reuf, Davy van Loon
Meeting House, computer reconstructions: Kent Larson

Tribune Review Publishing Company Building
Drawings: Michael Kleinschmidt

University of Pennsylvania Medical Research Towers
Drawings: Nayhal Adhyaru, Carolee Eyles

US Consulate Chancellery and Residence, Angola
Drawings: Jill Namoff, David Register
Computer reconstructions: Kent Larson

Yale Art Gallery
Drawings: Adriana Portela

Yale Center for British Art
Drawings: Jason Pelletier
Model: Columbia University students in course taught by Kenneth Frampton

Pictures

Aga Khan Trust For Culture, Geneva: 276; © Peter Aprahamian: 134, 188, 189, 194–209; Courtesy The Architectural Archives, University of Pennsylvania: 23b, 24, 25, 28, 57, 296t, 450–1; The Architectural Archives, University of Pennsylvania/Photo: Eileen Christelow: 8–9; The Architectural Archives, University of Pennsylvania/Gift of The First Unitarian Church, Rochester, New York. 178l; The Architectural Archives, University of Pennsylvania/Drawing by Florindo Fusaro: 283tl; The Architectural Archives, University of Pennsylvania/Anne Griswold Tyng Collection: 12, 52, 80t, 226; The Architectural Archives, University of Pennsylvania/August Komendant Collection: 125l; The Architectural Archives, University of Pennsylvania/Robert Le Ricolais Collection: 284t; The Architectural Archives, University of Pennsylvania/Marshall D. Meyers Collection: 122r, 130bl, 181t; The Architectural Archives, University of Pennsylvania/Photo: George Pohl: 128c, 214cr, 214b, 215l, 283tr, 283bl, 283br, 286t, 295tl, 296b, 380t, 380c, 385tr, 408c, 408b, 410br, 412, 416, 417, 422b, 428t, 433t, 434, 439b, 440; The Architectural Archives, University of Pennsylvania/Photo: Martin E. Rich: 110; The Architectural Archives, University of Pennsylvania/Gift of Henry Wilcots: 447; The Architectural Archives, University of Pennsylvania/Photo: James Williamson: 387; The Architectural Archives, University of Pennsylvania/Gift of Richard Saul Wurman: 128t, 129t, 178bl, 216, 298, 430t; Athenaeum of Philadelphia/Philadelphia Museum: 17; © Bettman/Corbis: 29; © Urs Buttiker: 30, 74, 75, 95, 98, 101, 102, 120, 121, 146, 147, 160, 162, 163, 168, 171, 172, 173, 174t, 229, 230, 231, 244, 245, 247, 248, 250, 253, 268, 275, 280–1, 297t, 300, 308, 310, 318, 319, 320, 331bl, 331br, 332, 333, 334, 335, 366l, 367tr, 372, 374r, 375, 385b, 441tl, 441bl; Collection Mr and Mrs James H. Clark Jr, Dallas: 47; Photograph by Peter Cook: 22; © Howard Davis/Great Buildings.com: 311, 360l; © John Ebstel/Courtesy Keith de Lellis Gallery, New York: 51, 53br, 54, 62, 86b, 90–91, 94, 96–7, 142, 143, 144–5, 392; Aldo van Eyck: 219t, 431tl; © David Finn: 374l, 378, 379; Courtesy Kenneth Frampton: 380b; © J. Paul Getty Trust. Used with permission. Julius Shulman Photography Archive, Research Library at the Getty Research Institute: 114, 115, 118; © Jeff Goldberg/Esto: 377; John Hewitt: 184; Index/Pizzi: 215tr; S. C. Johnson Wax: 217; Louis I. Kahn Collection, University of Pennsylvania and the Pennsylvania Historical and Museum Commission: 31, 32r, 33t, 34, 35, 36, 38, 39, 40, 41, 44, 45, 53tr, 55, 56, 64, 71, 78b, 79, 80b, 81, 82b, 84t, 85, 86t, 87, 88, 104, 105tl, 105bl, 105br, 106t, 107, 108tl, 108b, 109, 119, 122l, 127t, 128bl, 128br, 129b, 130tr, 131, 132t, 138, 148t, 149c, 149b, 150, 156, 158t, 158cl, 158b, 159t, 159c, 161, 164, 176, 177t, 179, 181b, 182, 190, 191, 211t, 211br, 212tr, 213bl, 214t, 214cl, 215cr, 215b, 219b, 233t, 233b, 234b, 235, 236, 254, 255b, 256c, 256b, 257c, 258, 261, 278, 279, 282bl, 282br, 284c, 284b, 285tl, 285tr, 285c, 286b, 287c, 287b, 288, 294, 295tr, 295bl, 295br, 302, 303, 304, 322t, 323cr, 323b, 326, 336, 337t, 338, 339, 340, 363t, 363bl, 364, 366r, 367tl, 367cl, 368, 381, 382, 383, 384r, 385l, 400, 401b, 402, 403tr, 403br, 404, 408t, 410bl, 411, 418, 423, 424, 428b, 431tr, 431cl, 431cr, 431b, 433b, 437, 438, 439t, 439c, 441tr, 441br, 473, 474, 477, 478; Louis I. Kahn Collection, University of Pennsylvania and the Pennsylvania Historical and Museum Commission/Photo: Robert Damora: 82t; Louis I. Kahn Collection, University of Pennsylvania and the Pennsylvania Historical and Museum Commission/Photo: Lionel Freedman: 60, 72, 73, 76–7; Louis I. Kahn Collection, University of Pennsylvania and the Pennsylvania Historical and Museum Commission/Diagram by Florindo Fusaro: 444, 445; Louis I. Kahn Collection, University of Pennsylvania and the Pennsylvania Historical and Museum Commission/Photo: Robert Lautman: 390–1; Louis I. Kahn Collection, University of Pennsylvania and the Pennsylvania Historical and Museum Commission/© The Museum of Modern Art, NY: 124t, 125r, 126, 127b, 178br, 213t, 256t, 282l, 384l; Louis I. Kahn Collection, University of Pennsylvania and the Pennsylvania Historical and Museum Commission/Photo: Mildred Schmertz: 123; Louis I. Kahn Collection, University of Pennsylvania and the Pennsylvania Historical and Museum Commission/Photo: Minor White: 175;

Courtesy Nathaniel Kahn: 430b; Collection of Sue Ann Kahn: 26l, 58, 59, 136; Collection of Sue Ann Kahn/Courtesy Jan Hochstim: 10; Kimbell Art Museum/Photo: Michael Bodycomb: 346, 348, 350, 351, 355, 357, 360r, 361; Kimbell Art Museum/Photo: Steven Watson: 358–9; Kimbell Art Museum/Photo: Bob Wharton: 352, 362; © Balthazar Korab Ltd: 84b, 330, 331tl, 347; © Kent Larson/Massachusetts Institute of Technology: 154, 155, 186, 187, 388, 395, 396–7, 398, 407, 415b, 420, 421, 429; Courtesy Álvaro Malo/University of Arizona: 222; Courtesy Robert McCarter: 23t, 32l, 68, 69, 78t, 92, 93, 105tr, 108tr, 116, 117, 130tl, 132b, 140, 141, 148b, 149t, 152, 153, 157, 158cr, 159b, 166, 167, 180, 185, 192, 193, 212tl, 213br, 228, 238, 239, 257b, 260, 287t, 290, 291, 292, 307, 312, 313, 322b, 323t, 324–5, 328, 329, 337bl, 337br, 342, 343, 363br, 365, 370, 371, 394, 401t, 403l, 406, 410t, 414, 415t, 426, 427, 432, 436; © Norman McGrath: 373; © Grant Mudford, Los Angeles, CA, USA: 53l, 314, 315; © 2005, Digital image, The Museum of Modern Art, NY/Scala, Florence: 112; Nationalbibliothek, Wien: 285b; Tim Nightswander: 49; © Orch: 4, 240–1, 242, 243, 246, 249, 264–5, 266, 267, 269, 272–3, 277; The Pennsylvania Academy of Fine Arts/Gift of Mrs Louis I. Kahn/Courtesy Jan Hochstim: 26r; The Pennsylvania Academy of Fine Arts, Philadelphia Archives/Photo: Rick Echelmeyer: 15; Philadelphia Museum of Art/Gift of Louis I. Kahn: 225; Private Collection/Courtesy Jan Hochstim: 48, 211bl, 422cl; Joan Ruggles Photography: 13; © Roberto Schezen/Esto: 66, 67, 170, 174c, 174b, 232, 233r, 251, 252, 263, 271, 274, 297b, 317, 321, 376; © Ezra Stoller/Esto: 344–5, 367b; © View/Peter Cook: 220; Courtesy The Frank Lloyd Wright Archives: 124b; © The Frank Lloyd Wright Foundation: 33b.

Phaidon Press Limited
Regent's Wharf
All Saints Street
London N1 9PA

Phaidon Press Inc.
180 Varick Street
New York, NY 10014

www.phaidon.com

First published 2005
Reprinted 2007
Reprinted in paperback 2009
© 2005 Phaidon Press Limited

ISBN 978 0 7148 4971 3

A CIP catalogue record for this book
is available from the British Library.

Designed by Nick Bell design and
John Dowling, Dowling Design
Printed in China

To the memory of
John Phillip Reuer 1931–2002